D1369291

Understanding Child Development

Fourth Edition

Understanding Child Development

FOR ADULTS WHO WORK WITH YOUNG CHILDREN

Fourth Edition

ROSALIND CHARLESWORTH
WEBER STATE UNIVERSITY

Delmar Publishers
An International Thomson Publishing Company

Albany • Bonn • Boston • Cincinnati • Detroit • London • Madrid • Melbourne
Mexico City • New York • Pacific Grove • Paris • San Francisco • Singapore • Tokyo
Toronto • Washington

NOTICE TO THE READER

Cover design courtesy of John MacDonald

Delmar Staff

Senior Editor:	Jay S. Whitney
Associate Editor:	Erin O'Connor Traylor
Production Coordinator:	Sandra Woods
Art and Design Coordinator:	Timothy J. Conners

COPYRIGHT © 1996
By Delmar Publishers
a division of International Thomson Publishing Inc.
The ITP logo is a trademark under license

Printed in the United States of America

For more information contact:

Delmar Publishers
3 Columbia Circle
Box 15015
Albany, New York 12203-5015

International Thomson Editores
Campos Eliseos 385, Piso 7
Col Polanco
11560 Mexico D F Mexico

International Thomson Publishing Europe
Berkshire House 168-173
High Holborn
London WC1V7AA
England

International Thomson Publishing GmbH
Königswinterer Strasse 418
53227 Bonn
Germany

Thomas Nelson Australia
102 Dodds Street
South Melbourne, 3205
Victoria, Australia

International Thomson Publishing Asia
221 Henderson Road
#05-10 Henderson Building
Singapore 0315

Nelson Canada
1120 Birchmount Road
Scarborough, Ontario
Canada M1K5G4

International Thomson Publishing - Japan
Hirakawacho Kyowa Building, 3F
2-2-1 Hirakawacho
Chiyoda-ku, Tokyo 102
Japan

2 3 4 5 6 7 8 9 10 XXX 01 00 99 98 97 96

Library of Congress Cataloging-in-Publication Data

Charlesworth, Rosalind.
   Understanding child development : for adults who work with young
children / Rosalind Charlesworth.—4th ed.
     p. cm.
   Includes bibliographical references and index.
   ISBN 0-8273-7332-5
   1. Child development.   I. Title.
HQ767.9.C436   1995
305.23′1—dc20   95-16990
                                   CIP

Contents

▼

SECTION VI COGNITIVE GROWTH AND DEVELOPMENT FROM PRESCHOOL TO PRIMARY

SECTION VII AFFECTIVE GROWTH AND DEVELOPMENT FROM PRESCHOOL TO PRIMARY

SECTION VIII THE PRIMARY CHILD: MAKING THE TRANSITION FROM PRESCHOOL TO PRIMARY

SECTION IX SPECIAL AREAS OF DEVELOPMENT

SECTION X THE WHOLE CHILD

Preface

Understanding Child Development is designed for teachers in training and teachers in service whose major interest is the prekindergarten, kindergarten, and primary child. It is also a valuable tool for social service workers, special educators, parents, home visitors, and others who require a practical understanding of the young child. For students, it introduces the uniqueness of the young child as distinguished from the older child and shows how to work with young children in a way that corresponds with the child's developmental level. For teachers in service, the text offers an opportunity to evaluate their views of the young child and compare them with the views presented in the text. For all adults who work with young children, the book presents a picture of the child in the context of family, school, culture, and language.

The young child and the means for studying his or her growth and development are introduced first in the text. Next, the child from conception to birth is described followed by infant and toddler development. The period from preschool to primary follows with indepth descriptions of physical and motor growth and development, ways of learning, and cognitive and affective growth and development. The next section describes the growth and development of the primary child and continuity in learning from preschool to primary. Throughout, the adult role in growth and development is stressed. Both teachers and families have critical roles. Social and cultural factors that influence the child's development are described.

Play, technology, and special needs and disabilities are discussed as areas of concern in the life of the young child. Finally, the whole child is considered along with the role of the adult who works with young children in the development of public policy that supports child development and the family.

The text contains many examples. The unit approach begins with behavioral objectives and presents the material in a logical progression. The suggested activities offer practical learning applications that enhance individual experiences and add to the excitement in the classroom when shared with other students.

Work with young children is a challenging activity today. Those who work with young children agree that development and education are inseparable at this age. In this text, developmental concepts are placed in a practical perspective. Theory, research, and practice are mixed in a no-nonsense fashion that applies to everyday interaction with young children.

What's new in the fourth edition?

- Flash for Windows™ is a new computerized study guide diskette included in the back of each text. Now mastering the material is made easy with electronic flashcards of all key words in child development, activities and answers.

-             icon appears at each paragraph where a unit objective is discussed. This useful icon cross references the unit objectives to the text for easy identification.
- KEYTERMS appear in a list at the bottom of pages where first introduced. Students use this as a helpful study tool while reading or reviewing for exams.
- All key terms are defined in a new alphabetical glossary that appears in the back of the text.
- New full-color insert illustrates key theorists in early education as well as prebirth development.
- New color highlights for all pedagogical elements in a visually attractive design.
- New updated reference section includes all current research in the back of the text.

Dr. Rosalind Charlesworth is a professor in the Department of Child and Family Studies in the College of Education at Weber State University in Ogden, Utah, where she teaches Child Development and Early Childhood Education courses. She has also taught developmental courses to students in home economics, education, and behavioral sciences. Her career history includes experience in teaching young children in laboratory, public school, and day-care settings and in research in social and cognitive development, developmentally appropriate practices, and teachers' beliefs and practices. Originally, this text grew out of several years of experience in teaching child development courses for adults who planned to work with preschool children. It has expanded with further experience teaching both preservice and graduate-level students who work with young children, from birth through age eight.

The author wishes to express her appreciation to the following individuals and early childhood education and development centers:

The following students at Bowling Green State University in Ohio, the University of Houston at Clear Lake City, and Louisiana State University at Baton Rouge, who provided many examples from their projects and contributions to class discussion: Donna Jolly, Zheng Zhang He, Stacie Ducote, Rhonda Balzamo, Deneé Babin, Lisa Kirk, Pattie Guidry, Gay Koenig, Jill Ochlenschlager, Jill Evans, Donna Wendt, Tammy Overmeyer, Jill Flaugher, Kathleen Roberts, Sue Heestand, Beth Leatherman, Elizabeth M. Schumm, Nancy Miller, K. Weber, Adrienne Rossoni, Susan Rollins, Carol Roach, Kristine Reed, Kathy Kayle, Bede Hurley, Linda Boone, Ruthie Johnson, and Carolyn Nattress.

Those Louisiana teachers whose students provided writing and/or drawing samples: Joan Benedict, Cleator Moore, Robyn Planchard, and Lois Rector.

And last, but not least, to my daughter Kate for her tolerance and understanding through four editions of this book.

To the many users of the text; especially the reviewers who offered numerous valuable suggestions:

Nancy Baptiste
New Mexico State University
Las Cruces, NM

Dr. Clarissa Leister
East Tennessee State University
Johnson City, TN

Erie Tejada
University of Texas-Brownsville
Brownsville, TX

The staff at Delmar Publishers

DEDICATION

To Edith M. Dowley, Ruth Updegraff, Shirley G. Moore, Willard W. Hartup, and Ada D. Stephens, who nurtured my professional development, and to my daughter Kate, who has provided a rich source of developmental information and inspiration.

Section I

The Young Child

Our children are our hope for the future and our responsibility for the present. Knowledge of their growth and development will aid adults who work with them to provide the most supportive environments possible.

Our country is a potpourri of many cultural and ethnic groups. These groups provide children with an environment of rich diversity and complexity in which to develop. As you proceed through the text, you will meet children, parents, and teachers from many different cultural backgrounds such as Native American, European and African heritage. Others descend from Asian immigrants or our more recent twentieth century immigrants. The challenge for those who work with young children is to provide each child with the best developmental opportunities.

Many changes have occurred in our population of young people since the field of child study first became a major focus in the early twentieth century. For example, the numbers of what are termed **high-risk** children have increased dramatically. High-risk children are children who are at risk for school failure and possibly even for survival due to various environmental, mental, physical, and/or emotional problems. Some of these problems have hereditary causes, but many have environmental

beginnings that can be addressed. These children need to be helped as early as possible to meet the challenges of child development. All who work with young children, such as parents, teachers, doctors, nurses, psychologists, speech therapists, physical therapists, etc. need to collaborate whenever possible.

Several factors have increased our high-risk population. One factor is the progress of medical advances. For example, many infants who in earlier times would not have survived the prenatal period are supported through prenatal and consequent postnatal difficulties today. Changes in our culture, such as the dramatic increase in the number of teenage pregnancies and increased use of abusive substances (e.g., alcohol, drugs, tobacco), have added further to the numbers of our young children who are at risk. Other children are at risk because they come from non-English speaking families; they need help making the transition. A serious problem that carries many risks is that millions of our young children live in a poverty environment. Of the over 30 million poor in our country, about 6,000,000 are children under six.

In this first section, you will be introduced to the theories that guide child study and the methods used to learn about children. You will be offered an overview of early child development.

Unit

1

Developmental and Learning Theories

OBJECTIVES

After studying this unit, the student should be able to:

- Define the term *theory* and identify developmental and learning theories, including the normative views.

- Recognize definitions of cognitive, affective, physical, motor developmental and learning areas.

- Name ten important theorist/researchers.

- Identify some practical applications of theory.

- Describe cautions that should be used when applying theory to the lower socioeconomic level and/or minority group child.

The study of children has been a subject of great interest during the twentieth century. Scholars have gathered information about and from children and have used this information to formulate ideas about how children grow and develop. Most scholars are researchers who mainly gather information. Some scholars are researchers and theorists. Theorist/researchers go beyond their data to develop broad ideas that attempt to explain how children learn and grow. These ideas are called theories. A theory is designed to show one plan or set of rules that explains, describes, or predicts what happens and what will happen when children grow and learn. Several popular theories are described in this unit.

TYPES OF THEORIES

Some theorists focus on growth, some on how learning takes place, and some on both. The term growth usually refers to a sequence of changes or stages that takes place over time on the way to becoming an adult and is controlled, for the most part, by an inherited timetable. For example, the child's head reaches full growth before his trunk. Learning refers to behavioral changes that come about due to influences from the environment. The child in the United States might learn English or Spanish as a first language, while the child in Germany learns German. Developmental theories usually explain

---

KEYTERMSKEYTERMSKEYTERMSKEYTERMSKEYTERMSKEYTERMSKEY

theories	Learning
growth	Developmental theories

changes in the child due to interaction between growth and learning. Each child develops in a manner similar to every other child. For example, infants explore objects by sight, taste, touch, sound, and smell before they learn that these objects still exist when out of sight. Theories emphasizing change that originates in the environment through learning are called behaviorist theories. For example, if children hear language, imitate it, and are rewarded for making sounds, they will learn to talk. Behaviorist theories explain how the child learns regardless of his age or stage. Some learning-oriented theories explain what is happening in the mind. Others look only at behavior that can be seen.

The maturational or normative view is another way of looking at development. Norms tell us what most children do at a certain age. The normative/maturational view stresses certain norms, such as the time when most children can sit up, crawl, walk, talk, count to ten, or play cooperatively with other children. Other norms tell us the average size, shape, weight, or height of a child at a specific age. Further, norms can suggest typical behavior characteristics, such as the fact that toddlers are naturally negative because they try so hard to be independent. Theories and norms are related in that theories may try to explain why norms occur as they do.

Theories can differ regarding the specific part of growth and learning they try to explain and describe. For purposes of study, child growth is usually divided into four areas: cognitive, affective, physical, and motor.

Cognitive growth centers on the mind and how the mind works as the child grows and learns.

Jenny, age fourteen months, points to her pet cat and says, "Ki Ki." Jenny is learning to speak and has learned the concept *cat* ("Ki Ki").

Pete, age three, wants a cup. He tries but can't reach. He pulls the kitchen stool over, climbs up and gets the cup. Pete has solved a problem.

Lai, age five, is given a plate of cookies and told to give the same number of cookies to each child in her class. She goes from one child to another, giving each child one cookie at a time. Lai understands that by using the idea of one-to-one correspondence you can divide a group of things into groups of equal size.

Bill, age six, takes three red blocks and four blue blocks and combines them into one group. Then he picks up his pencil and on a sheet of paper he writes $3 + 4 = 7$. Bill is making the connection between concrete objects and abstract symbols.

Affective growth centers on the self-concept and the development of social, emotional, and personality characteristics (Figure 1–1).

Mrs. Smith holds Tony, age one month, in her arms, rocking him and softly singing a lullaby. Mrs. Smith is helping Tony experience the attachment necessary as the basis for later independence.

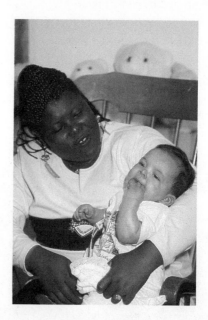

Figure 1-1 Emotional support from a warm, concerned adult helps the child develop in the affective domain.

KEYTERMSKEYTERMSKEYTERMSKEYTERMSKEYTERMSKEY

| behaviorist theories | normative/maturational view | Affective growth |
| Norms | Cognitive growth | |

John, age four, almost always smiles and looks happy. Other children like him and want to play with him. He is always kind to other children and tries to find a place for them in his play activities. John has a positive self-concept and has developed well in the affective area.

Patty, age five, takes whatever she wants and hits children who try to defend their property. She has not yet acquired the skills to interact positively with others.

Thuy, age six, would like to have a candy bar before dinner. However, her mother has told her she will have to wait until after dinner. Just thinking about taking a candy bar makes her feel guilty. At six Thuy has developed a conscience that tells her not to disobey her mother.

Physical growth has to do with development of the body and its parts (Figure 1–2).

John, age four, weighs 36.6 lb (16.6 kg) and is 3.4 ft (104 cm) tall. This is average for his age.

Kerry, age two-and-a-half, weighs 35.5 lb (16.1 kg) and her height is 2.95 ft (90 cm). She is below average in height and above in weight. She appears short and chubby.

Derrick, at age seven, is well proportioned. His legs have outgrown their toddler stubbiness.

Motor development refers to the development of skill in the use of the body and its parts (Figure 1–3).

Pete, age three, does well at lunch. He eats his soup with a spoon and spills very little and easily pours milk from a pitcher.

Patty, almost age five, hasn't yet learned to skip, can hop on one foot only three times without losing her balance, and can't walk a straight line.

Derrick (age seven) and several of his classmates have joined an after school soccer team. Derrick can now coordinate his body and his mind and is ready to engage in team sports with rules.

Childhood development theories explain basic processes that determine how and what children learn. Some theorists feel people learn in much the same way, whatever their age. Others feel learning is done in a different way as the person progresses through different stages. It is important for teachers of young children to be familiar with a variety of theoretical approaches to understand, explain, and respond to young children's behavior.

Figure 1–2 **The preschool child has reached a stage of physical/motor development in which he can participate and enjoy complex activities such as playing catch.**

Figure 1–3 **The kindergartner is nearing the time when motor control is such that skills can be used to play simple group games such as bounce the ball with a parachute.**

KEYTERMSKEYTERMSKEYTERMSKEYTERMSKEYTERMSKEY

Physical growth   Motor development

Some theorists whose ideas have been very influential are Jean Piaget, Lev Vygotsky, Sigmund Freud, Erik Erikson, B. F. Skinner, Robert R. Sears, Albert Bandura, Carl Rogers, and Abraham Maslow. The normative/maturational view of Arnold Gesell has added a great deal to our knowledge of child development also. Figure 1–4 outlines the areas that these men attempt to explain through theory development and research.

Tries to Explain Changes in:	Type of Theory	
	Developmental: Growth and Learning Interact	Behaviorist: Learning is the Main Determiner of Behavior
Cognitive Area –language –concepts –problem solving –intellectual needs	Cognitive-Developmental (Jean Piaget; Lev Vygotsky) Normative/Maturational (Arnold Gesell) Self-Actualization (Abraham Maslow) Example: A supportive adult and a rich environment with freedom for exploration will allow for learning and intellectual growth.	Behaviorist (B. F. Skinner) Examples: Learning to speak. Learning red, blue, and yellow are colors. Social Cognitive Theory (Albert Bandura) Example: The child observes the language users of his culture and imitates what he sees and hears.
Affective Area –aggression –dependency –cooperation –fears –self-concept –affective needs –motivation	Psychosexual (Sigmund Freud) Psychosocial (Erik Erikson) Self-Concept (Carl Rogers) Self-Actualization (Abraham Maslow) Examples: Through play the young child learns the benefits of cooperation. Dependency must develop first in order for the child to become independent later.	Behaviorist (B. F. Skinner; Robert R. Sears) Examples: Learning to hug and not to hit. Learning to help others. Social Cognitive Theory (Albert Bandura) Example: The child observes another child being praised for helping set the table. The child imitates what he has seen and heard.
Physical and Motor Areas –body size and growth rate –motor skills (creeping, walking, grasping, etc.)	Normative/Maturational (Arnold Gesell) Example: The head and thus the brain has the fastest growth rate during early childhood, therefore neurological growth is rapid and determines cognitive and motor growth.	Behaviorist (B. F. Skinner) Examples: Complex skills, such as riding a bicycle or skating, and physically related behavior, such as eating nutritious food. Social Cognitive Theory (Albert Bandura) Example: The child is told to watch while the coach kicks the soccer ball and then is asked to try to kick it the same way.

Figure 1–4   Theories of child development and learning. On the left side are the three major areas of development. The headings across the top indicate the two types of theories: developmental and behaviorist.

Each theorist is interested mainly in one area of development and/or learning. Skinner is the exception. His theory offers an explanation for any learned behavior, whether cognitive, affective, physical, or motor. Sears and Bandura are known for their work on social learning, Piaget for his work on the development of logical thought, Vygotsky for his contributions to our view of how children learn to think and speak and the importance of adult and peer social interaction to the young child's learning, and Freud and Erikson for their theories of social and personality development. Rogers focuses on the development and organization of the self-concept; Maslow on the hierarchical nature of human needs; and Gesell on the development of norms of growth and development and their practical applications for child rearing and teaching.

Several of these theorist/researchers view growth and learning as proceeding in an orderly fashion from birth to adulthood. Figure 1–5 shows the stages associated with these theorists. The masses of data gathered by Gesell indicate that physical and motor growth develop at a continuous, rapid rate that levels off at about six years of age. According to Piaget, the young child proceeds through two periods of cognitive development from birth to about age seven. In the affective area Sears, Freud, and Erikson each look at different aspects of development. Sears focuses on needs and motivation. He considers needs such as dependency, aggression, and sex role identification. Parallel with Piaget, Sears has identified two stages that children pass through during early childhood. Erikson was one of Freud's students. Therefore, it is not surprising that the structure of their early childhood stages into three steps is the same. However, while Freud's stages focus on the child's psychosexual interests, Erikson's focus on the psychosocial side. Vygotsky believed that child development proceeds through a series of five stages. He focused on the social aspects of learning; that is, the role of adults and older children in supporting cognitive development.

Maslow and Rogers are neither strictly learning nor strictly developmental theorists. Their ideas focus on the process of achieving a positive self-concept. Love from parents and positive interaction with peers help the child move towards adult self-actualization. The self-actualized adult is one whose basic needs for survival, security, belonging, and esteem are fulfilled. The adult is then able to fulfill intellectual and aesthetic needs and become a fully functioning person.

THEORY APPLICATION

To clarify the ideas of these important theorists, a brief example of an application of each theory follows.

Application 1: Piaget

A teacher of young children wants to know if preschool children really need to role play. From reading Piaget, the teacher finds that Piaget feels dramatic play is essential to cognitive development. Through pretending to be someone else and through the use of objects for purposes other than their original intent (such as sand used to make a pie), children have their first symbolic experiences. These experiences are the basis for the more abstract symbol learning children do when they learn to use letters, numbers, and words as symbols (Figure 1–6).

Application 2: Vygotsky

A childcare provider wonders why it is important to provide support for children's language development through activities such as conversation and storybook sharing. At a professional meeting she attends a session where she learns about **scaffolding**. This is a process through which an adult supports the child's language development reinforcing the child's efforts at verbal expression. Scaffolding can be used during storybook sharing when the adult extends the experience by asking the child questions. The process continues by encouraging the child to ask questions and relating the story to the child's personal experiences.

KEYTERMSKEYTERMSKEYTERMSKEYTERMSKEYTERMSKEYTERMSKEY

scaffolding

Age	Physical Motor	Affective			Cognitive	
	(Gesell)	Needs/Motivation (R. R. Sears)	Social/Personality (Erikson)	Personality (Freud)	(Piaget)	(Vygotsky)
Birth 16 mo	The body develops rapidly from head to toe (lifts head, then shoulders, then sits up) and from the center out (reaches, then grasps).	**Phase I: Early Learning Based on Innate Needs** Food, comfort, personal contact.	**Crisis I: Trust versus Mistrust** The relationship with the caretaker during feeding is central.	**Oral Stage:** The mouth is the source of pleasure; feeding and teething are central.	**The Sensori-motor Period** The child's sensory (hearing, tasting, touching, seeing, smelling) and motor skills develop and are the means for learning.	**Infancy** (2 mos–1 yr) **Early Childhood** (1–3 yr)
18 mo to 2 yr		**Phase II: Secondary Behavioral Systems Based on Family-Centered Learning** Dependency, aggression, sex role learning	**Crisis II: Autonomy versus Shame and Doubt** The child strives for independence.	**Anal Stage:** Bowel movements are the source of pleasure. Toilet training is critical area.	**The Preoperational Period** Language and cognitive development are rapid as learning takes place through imitation, play, and other self-initiated activities.	
3 yr 6 yr	By age six, the rate of development levels off.		**Crisis III: Initiative versus Guilt** The child plans and carries out activities and learns society's boundaries.	**Phallic Stage:** Sex role identification and conscience development are critical.		**Preschool Age** (3–7 yr)
7 to 13 yr	Child can engage in activities requiring more physical strength and coordination.	**Phase III: Secondary Motivational Systems Based On Extra-familial Learning** Independence balances dependence. Learn to resist aggression.	**Crisis IV: Industry versus Inferiority** Need to be productive and successful. Failure results in feeling inferior.	**Latency Stage** Child consolidates previous stages' developments.	**Concrete Operations** Abstract symbols and ideas can be applied to concrete experiences.	**School Age** (7–13 yr)

Figure 1–5   Stages of development from birth to age thirteen

Figure 1–6 **Primary-level students enjoy working together on long-term, complex projects.**

Application 3: Erikson

A preschool teacher wonders how much freedom four- and five-year-olds need to work on their own. From Erikson, the teacher finds the child must learn to take initiative when appropriate but at the same time, learn the rules for the kinds of behaviors that are not allowed. The teacher realizes a delicate balance must be found between being too permissive and too restrictive.

Application 4: Freud

Mrs. Ramirez, a day-care mother, is concerned that two-year-old Tasha is not responding to toilet training. Mrs. Ramirez talks to a Freudian-trained psychologist at the Health Center. The psychologist explains to Mrs. Ramirez that toileting is a very significant activity for a child Tasha's age and should be handled gently and patiently.

Application 5: Maslow

Mr. Ogden, a kindergarten teacher, is concerned that the breakfast program at his school may not be funded next year. A good breakfast, he feels, is necessary not only for health reasons but also to give the child the security of knowing his basic needs will be met in a predictable fashion. The child who is concerned about where her next meal is coming from will not be able to concentrate on the social and cognitive needs that her school program is designed to fulfill.

Application 6: Rogers

The local early childhood education professional group is contacting state legislators to gain their support to lower the adult/infant ratio in child-care centers in the state. This group of educators supports its stand with the ideas of several experts, including Carl Rogers. According to Rogers, children must be loved and feel secure to grow into loving adults. This love and security comes through their relationships with their caregivers. Infants, especially, need a great deal of individual attention, and a low adult/infant ratio helps fulfill this need.

Application 7: Skinner

A day-care provider is worried about a very aggressive child she has in her home each day. She seeks help from a psychologist who suggests a Skinnerian approach. The day-care mother observes the child carefully each day for a week. She keeps a count of each time the child hurts another child or breaks a toy. She also notes each incident in which he does something that is not aggressive. The next week, she makes a point of giving him attention whenever he does anything positive and ignores his bad behavior unless he is hurting someone, in which case he is sent to a "time out" chair until he cools down. After three weeks, she again counts incidents of his aggressive behaviors and his positive behaviors. She finds that the positive behaviors have increased and the negative behaviors have decreased.

Application 8: Sears

A day-care director thinks that preschool children should be given plenty of TLC (tender loving care). Some of the teachers at the center disagree; they feel preschoolers should be more independent. The director consults someone who is familiar with the work of Robert R. Sears. His research indicates that the preschooler is still dependent on adults for physical and verbal attention. This dependence is important as a basis for later independence. It is not until school age that there is a sharp shift in dependency needs.

Application 9: Bandura

A parent is concerned about her child's use of unacceptable language. She speaks with his teacher, who probes to find out where he might have heard and then imitated such language. The mother realizes that her father, who lives with the family, checkers his speech with a great deal of profanity. Her son spends a lot of time with his grandfather and has observed and imitated his vocabulary.

Application 10: Gesell

A mother is concerned about her three-and-a-half-year-old daughter's behavior. Her daughter's teacher reads to her from a book by Gesell and his coworkers:

> Something unexpected and confusing seems to happen to the smooth, conforming three-year-old as he turns three-and-a-half. Where did all this turbulence and trouble come from? Why is there such opposition, so much refusal to obey or even to try? (Gesell et al., 1974, p. 191)

The mother reads on and is relieved to find her child is a normal, if negative, three-and-a-half-year-old girl.

It is essential that adults who work with young children have a sound, underlying theoretical basis to support their actions (Glascott, 1994). Throughout this book, theory is applied to practice. However, caution is also taken to clarify some of the limitations of taking any theory too literally. Theory should always be considered within the child's sociological context of family, community, culture, and language.

CAUTIONS REGARDING THEORY

Since the publication of the **National Association for the Education of Young Children (NAEYC) developmentally appropriate practices**

(DAPs) (Bredekamp, 1987), there has been increasing attention to the appropriateness of applying developmental theory to early education and development of children from diverse cultures and children with diverse capabilities. DAPs are instructional practices that are both age and individually appropriate as defined by NAEYC (Bredekamp, 1987). It is believed by a number of professionals in the early childhood field that since the most popular theories were created by European-oriented theorist/researchers they may not apply to children from diverse cultures with diverse capabilities. The theories focus narrowly on one cultural group (New & Mallory, 1994). It is the view of this author that child development theory does have broad-based applications. However, child development and behavior certainly should be viewed for the individual child within his cultural context as suggested by a variety of professionals in the field (see Mallory & New, 1994; Serpell, 1994). For this reason, sociocultural views of behavior and development are woven in throughout this text. To understand any individual child's development, adults who work with young children may need to select and combine various theories.

SUMMARY

Both developmental- and behavior-oriented theories attempt to explain what happens as children grow and learn mentally, socially, physically, and motorically. The normative/maturational view gives descriptive information regarding what the "average" child does in all these areas. Each type of approach to explaining early development can be applied to everyday work with children. More details regarding the views of these theorist/researchers and their application to everyday practice are included in the units to come. Ideally, child development and early childhood education should work hand in hand as one (Elkind, 1993, 1981). This text is designed to demonstrate how this goal can be achieved.

KEYTERMSKEYTERMSKEYTERMSKEYTERMSKEYTERMSKEY

National Association for the Education of Young Children (NAEYC)

developmentally appropriate practices (DAPS)

FOR FURTHER READING

Beilin, H., & Pufall, P. B. (Eds.) (1992). *Piaget's theory: Prospects and possibilities*. Hillsdale, NJ: Erlbaum.

Demetriou, C., Shayer, M., & Efklides, A. (Eds.) (1993). *Neo-Piagetian theories of cognitive development*. New York: Routledge.

Miller, P. H. (1989). *Theories of developmental psychology, 2nd ed.* New York: W. H. Freeman.

Moll, L. C. (Ed.). (1990). *Vygotsky and Education*. New York: Cambridge University Press.

Newman, F., & Holzman, L. (1993). *Lev Vygotsky: Revolutionary scientist*. New York: Routledge.

Rogers, C. (1983). *Freedom to learn for the 80's*. Columbus, OH: Charles E. Merrill.

Smith, L. (Ed.) (1992). *Jean Piaget: Critical assessments*. New York: Routledge.

Van Der Veer, R., & Valsiner, J. (1993). *Understanding Vygotsky: The life and work of Lev Vygotsky, a quest for synthesis*. Cambridge, MA: Blackwell.

Van Der Veer, R., & Valsiner, J. (1993). *The Vygotsky reader*. Cambridge, MA: Blackwell.

Vasta, R. (Ed.) (1992). *Six theories of child development*. London and Philadelphia: Jessica Kingsley Publishers.

SUGGESTED ACTIVITIES

1. Go to the library. Find an article in a journal, such as *Young Children*, *Dimensions*, or *Childhood Education*, that describes a way to apply the theories of Piaget, Skinner, or Gesell to your work with young children. Discuss the article and share your evaluation of the article with the class.

2. Go to a curriculum resource center and interview the director. Ask the director if there are any theory-based materials at the center. If so, examine them. Share a list of the materials and an evaluation of them with a small group of fellow students.

3. Interview three teachers of young children. Find out if they make any applications of the theories of Piaget, Vygotsky, Skinner, Freud, Erikson, Sears, Bandura, Gesell, Maslow, or Rogers. Ask for responses to the following questions.

   a. How are you influenced by Piaget, Vygotsky, Skinner, Sears, Bandura, Erikson, Gesell, Freud, Maslow, or Rogers?

   b. Describe a specific application of one of the theories.

   c. Tell me about what you do. Which activities do you believe are most important for your students? How important is it for children to have opportunities for exploration and for play?

   Compare your results with those of other students in the class. Determine which areas are emphasized most strongly.

REVIEW

A. Explain what a theory is.

B. Name one or more theorist/researchers who is associated with each of the following areas:

   1. cognitive development
   2. normative development
   3. affective development
   4. all areas of learned behavior
   5. affective learning

C. Match the names in Column I with the application descriptions in Column II.

Column I

1. Sears
2. Gesell
3. Rogers
4. Maslow
5. Piaget
6. Skinner
7. Erikson
8. Freud
9. Bandura
10. Vygotsky

Column II

a. Johnny is playing nicely. His teacher compliments him.

b. Mary is pretending to make a pie from wet sand.

c. Mr. Jones tells the children they can plan and carry out an activity of their choice today.

d. Bill and Kate's father shares a storybook with them. He encourages them to ask questions and to relate the story to their own experiences.

e. Jenny bumps her knee. Ms. Smith kisses the sore knee to make it well.

f. "How old are children usually when they begin to walk?"

g. Five-year-old Theresa is very concerned about being female.

h. Chan is a loved and secure four-year-old who is very loving toward other children.

i. Every evening Liu Pei watches her mother fix dinner. One day she asks if she can help. Her mother is surprised to see how much Liu Pei has learned from her observations.

j. Jason Goodbird is identified by his teachers as a child who gets the most out of the activities at preschool. They note that he comes from a secure and loving home environment.

D. Explain why we must be cautious when using developmental theories.

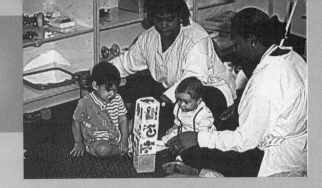

Studying the Young Child

OBJECTIVES

After studying this unit, the student should be able to:

■ Explain important historical factors in child study.

■ Identify these methods of child study: the diary, observation, and the interview.

■ List examples of current child study research questions.

■ Explain how teachers can be researchers.

dults who work with young children have become more aware in recent years of the need to know how young children develop. Adults now realize that knowledge of child development is necessary to understand, interact with, and plan for children. This has not always been the case. In fact, only during this century did the study of how children grow and learn develop into an area that stands on its own merit. Before the twentieth century, most adults did not feel there was anything special to be known about young children.

A BRIEF HISTORY OF CHILD STUDY

Child development researchers study a host of questions and problems to find answers that will help those who work with young children. Examples of concerns relevant to child study in the twentieth century include: the effects of childcare experience on young children's development, the effects of formal early education on children and their families, the influence of technology on the child's behavior and development, the characteristics of infants, literacy de-velopment, and the role of the father in the lives of young children.

Prior to this century, there was interest in child growth and development but little research. People proposed ideas about how the child grows and learns. They did little, if anything, though, to check if their ideas were supported in the real world of children and the adults with whom they interact.

Some questions that have been asked for centuries include the following.

- What do children already know when they are born, and what do they learn?
- What capacity do children have for learning?
- Are children born "good" or born "bad"?
- Is childhood a stage in and of itself, or are children miniature adults?
- Should children be free to learn and grow on their own, or should adults use control through habit training and drill?
- Are children property, or do they have their own rights?

In the late 1800s, **baby biographies** began to appear. These were the first kinds of recorded child research. Parents kept diary records of interesting things their child did each day. These diaries inspired much of the early child research. As the twentieth century approached, G. Stanley Hall did the first organized research on a large group of children. He asked parents all over the United States to fill out questionnaires about their children. This was the beginning of child development as a field of study as we know it today.

As we study young children, we have a desire to learn everything. David G. Smith reminds us that we really cannot define what a child is. We have to look at each child in relation to others such as parents, teachers, and peers. Each one who has contact with a child has a personal picture of that child. Even when these pictures are assembled into one, we still do not have all the pieces. As we consider child research and its applications, we need to be cautious and keep in mind that although it tries to explain all, it really cannot. Smith (p. 4) reminds us that "because the aim of Child Psychology's effort is to understand the child more completely, to contain him, and to control him, it misses the point. Children are always beyond our understanding because they are beyond us." Keeping this caution in mind, we can benefit from the bits and pieces of understanding that we can glean from research in child development.

While we will never know all there is to know about any child, keep in mind that we want to know as much as we can. To accomplish this, Bronfenbrenner (1992, 1989, 1979) has developed an **ecological research model**. Bronfenbrenner stresses the importance of viewing the children in all their roles in all the areas of their environment. Children must be studied within their **microsystem**, which includes their relationship to home, school, neighborhood, peer group, and church. Of equal importance are three other ecological systems that impact children's lives. Surrounding the microsystem is the **mesosystem**. The mesosystem includes the interactions and relationships between and among home, school,

church, peer group, and neighborhood. Moving farther out into the world, additional influences come from the **exosystem**, which includes influences such as the local school board, local government, parents' work place, mass media, and local industry. Beyond this system is the **macrosystem**, which encompasses the dominant beliefs and ideologies of the culture.

Within any microsystem component such as the classroom "the structure and content of the setting, and the forms of developmental process that can take place within it, are to a large extent defined and delimited by the culture, subculture, or other macrosystem structure in which the microsystem is embedded" (Bronfenbrenner, 1989). As you look at children on a daily basis in the classroom, it is essential to consider these other outside factors as they influence children's behavior.

There is relatively little developmental research on diverse populations in our country and in other countries published in our most prominent English-language journals (New, 1994). Therefore, we must be cautious in applying research results found in studies of one culture to children in a different culture. Cultural context is critical in the study of children (New, 1994). It is vital that adults who work with young children and their families study each child and family within their unique cultural context.

METHODS OF CHILD STUDY

Each adult who works with young children needs to study those children in much the same way a researcher does. Adults need to know as much as possible about each child to plan appropriate learning environments. It is important that what is learned from a child development course is checked against and applied to children whom the adult knows. From the study of the children in their care, adults can obtain valuable information to use in planning for the children and their families. A rich collection of specific information can be obtained to share with parents during conferences.

KEYTERMSKEYTERMSKEYTERMSKEYTERMSKEYTERMSKEYTERMSKEY

| baby biographies | microsystem | exosystem |
| ecological research model | mesosystem | macrosystem |

Child-study methods fall into two main categories: experimental and naturalistic (Pellegrini, 1991). The experimental approach sets up environments designed to control and elicit specific types of behavior. Experiments are designed to look at specific cause and effect relationships. The naturalistic approach looks at children in their everyday environments. Naturalistic studies look at what children do under normal everyday circumstances. Currently naturalistic methods are gaining in popularity. Various types of descriptive studies of children going about their everyday activities are increasing in number. Descriptive types of studies offer a broader and more in-depth picture of what is happening in the child's life. For this type of study, the researcher takes on a role like that of the anthropologist visiting a new and unknown culture. The researcher takes detailed notes, may make audio and videotapes, and may interview those persons under study. The researcher may stay in the background or become an active participant within the classroom. This type of descriptive information can supplement information from more structured observations in either naturalistic or laboratory settings. This view of research affords increasing opportunities for teachers to be researchers in their own classrooms.

Several of the many methods that have been used in childhood research can be used by teachers, parents, and others who work with young children. These include the diary method, individual interviews with caretakers and/or children, and naturalistic observations. **Portfolio** systems are being developed as guides for organizing the information collected by the teacher and the student (Gelfer & Perkins, 1992; Grace & Shores, 1992). Portfolio systems also provide an ongoing record of the child that can be used to assist in making smooth transitions to new classrooms and new programs. During the course of your study of child development, numerous activities will be suggested that offer you the opportunity to try out these techniques. Taking advantage of as many of these opportunities as possible will prove beneficial later in your career. The following are examples of these methods.

Diary Method

APRIL 28: At 13 months, Candy walks well without holding on. She can't run or anything like that, but she can turn around in the middle of the room, stoop over and pick something off the floor, and only when she has to get somewhere in a very great hurry does she now drop to her hands and knees. (Peterson, 1974, p. 24)

Parent Interview

Interviewer: We'd like to get some idea of how Billy acts when he's naughty. When he has deliberately done something he knows you don't want him to do, when your back is turned, how does he act?
Mother: Well, right now he is lying. If he is caught, he will lie his way out, which is very disturbing to me. If there is anything I can't stand, it's lying. I just want him to face the fact he's been naughty, and I will be much kinder with him; but sometimes if he's very bad, I just put him up in his room, which has a terrible effect on him. Sometimes I just give him a good scolding, and sometimes I fall back on the old dodge of telling him when his father gets home he will deal with him, which I know is wrong, but I just don't know how to handle him. I'll admit he is a problem. (Sears et al., 1957, p. 379)

Interview with a Child

Interviewer: What makes the clouds move along?
Child: God does.
Interviewer: How?
Child: He pushes them . . . (the clouds) stay (in the air) because God wants them to stay. (Piaget, 1966, p. 63)

Naturalistic Observation

Nora is 18 months old: Nora crawls under the kitchen table and sits near the family cat. She pulls up the cat's tail and brushes her stomach with the tail. The cat meows and moves away. Nora hits the cat and says,

"Don't." Nora again picks up the end of the cat's tail but the cat pulls away. Nora pulls again and the cat pulls away again, bristling up in annoyance. She watches intently as the cat's tail flicks back and forth. She laughs and moves her hand back and forth, almost in rhythm with the cat's tail. Nora clicks her tongue and calls "kitty, kitty," babbling to the cat. She strokes the cat and drinks from her bottle. (Carew et al., 1976, p. 247)

From the diary record we learn what a parent or other adult feels is important enough to write down. The information is thus very selective. However, an adult who understands and applies a thorough knowledge of child development to making selections can learn a great deal about what is happening with children as individuals and as a group. A teacher does not have time to write a detailed diary entry on each child every day but can write descriptions of individual incidents or anecdotes that seem of special importance (Bentzen, 1993; Nicolson & Shipstead, 1994).

Parent and child interviews are used to obtain information that is specific to something the interviewer would like to know. The parent interview information depends on the accuracy of the parent's memory of past events and the parent's opinion of the child's behavior. It can be quite subjective, but it is still very important and can yield information that would otherwise not be available (Figure 2–1). Child interviewing is critical to the process of teaching (Figure 2–2). Informal questioning (described more in later units) is a necessary means for finding out what young children know and how they think. Observation and interviewing are two of the teacher's most important tools.

In the example given, the naturalistic observation was done by an outside person and describes what the child did in a factual way and in great detail (Figure 2–3). The reader is left to decide what is important about the incident. This type of record is usually referred to as a **running record** or a **specimen record** (Bentzen, 1993; Nicolson & Shipstead, 1994). It is time consuming to gather information in this manner, but the yield can be very revealing. Developmental and educational researchers are turn-

Figure 2–1 **From an interview with parents, information is obtained on the parent's current child-rearing attitudes and current and past child-rearing methods.**

ing more and more to naturalistic observations and interviews to gather information on children and teachers (New, 1994; McLean, 1993). Naturalistic observation can be done in a more structured and less time-consuming fashion using some predetermined categories or a checklist of behaviors (Bentzen, 1993; Nicolson & Shipstead, 1994).

Besides naturally occurring settings, such as the home, school, or playground, observations can also take place in laboratory settings. Laboratory settings are environments specially structured to elicit a cer-

Figure 2–2 **Specific facts can be learned during a one-to-one child interview.**

KEYTERMSKEYTERMSKEYTERMSKEYTERMSKEYTERMSKEY

running record   specimen record

Figure 2–3   Naturalistic observation is used to find out what children do during their normal daily activities.

tain type of behavior. For example, we may want to know how children behave with certain kinds of materials or people (such as peers or strange adults). By setting up the environment in a special way, there is more assurance that the type of information desired will be obtained.

It is essential for adults who work with young children and who gather data from young children to be skilled observers. For example, with the increasing diversity of our school population, teachers need to research each of their students to plan for them in a culturally relevant way. New (1994) suggests three roles teachers can take. First, using photographs, videotapes, audio tapes, children's work samples, anecdotal records, and other observation data, teachers can document children's daily activities. Secondly, teachers can experiment with a variety of teaching strategies and materials seeking practices that promote motivation and learning for their students. Thirdly, teachers can take on the role of anthropologists as they study the culture of each of their students.

Some popular child development research areas have been infant attachment, infant childcare, emotional development (especially children's reactions to violence), the relationships between parent discipline styles and children's school behavior, inclusion of children with disabilities in mainstream classrooms, literacy development, developmentally appropriate instructional practices, and, increasingly, research on diverse populations of children and their families. In early childhood education there has been an expanded use of methodology involving collaboration between researchers and teachers, and teachers as researchers of their own practice.

TEACHER RESEARCHERS

A **teacher researcher** is a classroom teacher who does a carefully planned and documented study of activities designed to solve a classroom instructional problem or introduce a new teaching practice. The study usually is done in collaboration with university personnel.

The role of teachers as researchers is becoming increasingly important (New, 1994). Teachers are gathering information about their students, their students' families, their students' communities, and about themselves. Teachers are becoming more reflective about their own practice and writing their own stories (McLean, 1993). Case studies, oral histories, and other narratives documenting teachers' life experiences are rapidly appearing in print. Teachers' stories provide in-depth information upon which others can reflect. These stories provide in-depth whole pictures in contrast to the more specific, but less colorful, information that has conventionally been the result of research on larger groups of subjects.

Whether engaged in formal or informal projects, adults who work with young children can and should be researchers who systematically collect information about children and their ecological systems in order to answer questions that will make their work more effective.

SUMMARY

The study of child development is a fairly young area of research. It continues to grow rapidly and the methods of child study (diary, interviews, and natu-

teacher researcher

ralistic observation) can be used by teachers and other adults who work with young children to find out about children, their families, and their environments. There are still (and will continue to be) many unanswered questions regarding how children grow and learn. Meanwhile, adults who work with young children can make the most of what is known and can contribute new knowledge from their own experiences. Child development research has looked into many areas of behavior and development. As you proceed through this text, you will become more familiar with these areas.

FOR FURTHER READING

Beaty, J. J. (1994). *Observing development of the young child, 3rd ed.* Columbus, OH: Charles E. Merrill.

Bentzen, W. R. (1993). *Seeing young children: A guide to observing and recording behavior, 2nd ed.* Albany, NY: Delmar Publishers.

Cohen, D. H., Stern, V., & Balaban, N. (1983). *Observing and recording the behavior of young children, 3rd ed.* New York: Teachers College Press.

Fisher, C. B. (1993). Integrating science and ethics in research with high-risk children and youth. *SRCD Social Policy Report, 7* (4).

Grace, C., & Shores, E. F. (1992). *The portfolio and its use.* Little Rock, AR: Southern Early Childhood Association.

Greenfield, P. M., & Cocking, R. R. (Eds.) (1994). *Cross-cultural roots of minority child development.* Hillsdale, NJ: Erlbaum.

McAfee, O. D., & Leong, D. U. (1994). *Assessing and guiding young children's development and learning.* Des Moines, IA: Longwood Division of Allyn & Bacon.

Nicolson, S., & Shipstead, S. G. (1994). *Through the looking glass: Observations in the early childhood classroom.* New York: Merrill/Macmillan.

Pellegrini, A. D. (1991). *Applied child study: A developmental approach.* Hillsdale, NJ: Erlbaum.

Spodek, B. (Ed.) (1993). *Handbook of research on the education of young children.* New York: Macmillan.

SUGGESTED ACTIVITIES

1. Ask the parents of a young child to keep a diary of their child's behavior and activities for one day. Compare the diary with those obtained by other class members. Note the amount of detail and the kinds of things that each set of parents seems to find important.

2. Observe the child whose diary record was obtained. Try to observe for at least one hour. Write down as many details as possible. Compare the information obtained through observation with that obtained through the diary method.

3. Individually or with a small group of classmates, develop ten to twenty questions to ask parents about their children. Interview the parent (or several parents) using the questions devised. What was learned that could not have been obtained from the diary record or from naturalistic observation?

4. Interview a child between the ages of three and eight. Devise some questions of your own or use those below.
   a. "Tell me your name." (Assessing self concept and language—does the child use a complete sentence?)
   b. If the child is five or under, show him or her an assortment of objects of various colors. "Show me the red (blue, yellow) things." (Assessing color concepts.)
   c. Place a pile of pennies or other objects in front of the child (15 objects for children 15 months to age four; 25 for age five; 100 for age six and older). "Count these pennies. Count as many as you can." (Assessing math concept, rational counting.)

d. "Tell me, what does a dog (airplane, stove, car) do?" (Assessing oral language—does the child use action words, such as bark, fly, cook, or goes fast? Do the responses reflect experience with these things?)

e. Provide a blank sheet of paper and a black felt-tip pen. "Here is some paper and a pen. Write your name." If the child writes his name or something close to it, "Write some more, anything you can." If he hesitates, "You can draw also." (Assessing knowledge of written language—can the child use written or pictorial symbols?)

f. "Where do dreams come from?" (Younger children will usually answer that they come from outside of their bodies somewhere.)

g. "Tell me something that makes you happy (sad)." (Assessing child's ability to associate feelings with particular events and to express these feelings.)

5. Interview a child between the ages of one and two. If at the child's home, have the child's mother select ten favorite toys or other objects (such as a glass, spoon, towel) with which the child is very familiar. If the child is in a day-care center, ask the teacher to select and/or suggest items. Put the item on a rug or blanket on the floor. Ask the child to bring over each item and then return it to the pile. For example, say, "Bring me the ball" (emphasizing ball). He brings the ball. "Thank you. Now put the ball back on the rug." Next, ask the child to show you the parts of his body. That is, ask, "Show me (or point to) your nose" ("your eyes," "your feet," etc.). What did you learn about the child? Compare the results with those of classmates who did the same activity.

6. Read a research article. Write a short report including the following:
   a. Bibliographic information: author(s), title, name of periodical, volume number, date published, page numbers
   b. A short summary of the article: the purpose of the study; the age, sex, socio-economic level, and ethnic group of the children studied; the method(s) used; the results and conclusions
   c. A reaction which states your opinion of the value of the study and its possible practical application

REVIEW

A. Read each of the following examples carefully. Note which are examples of the (1) diary method, (2) naturalistic observation method, (3) parent interview method, (4) child interview method, or (5) laboratory observation method.

a. Adult A: Tell me about John's infancy. Did you always pick him up when he cried or did you wait a while?
   Adult B: I always picked him up right away. I found he usually didn't cry unless he wanted something.

b. Bobby said his first word today. He jumped out of the car when we arrived home from the store. He turned and pointed at our car and said, "Car!" What a big day for us.

c. Adult: Where do dreams come from?
   Child: They fly in the window when I am asleep.

d. Adult A: How do you feel about punishments and rewards?
   Adult B: For punishment, I usually have Mary take time out and sit on a little chair until she cools off. Once in a while she loses a privilege like dessert or going to her friend's house. Fortunately, she loves praise. I find if I give her a lot of attention for all the good things she does, I seldom have to punish her.

e. Maria looked at the vase of flowers on the table and then at her mother. She was on her hands and knees. Her right hand slowly left the floor and moved in the direction of the flowers. "No, No!" said her mother firmly as she got up and went over to her. She handed Maria a toy horse saying, "Play with this." Maria turned and smiled. She took the horse and immediately put it in her mouth and rubbed it against her gums.

f. Tony went for his first checkup today. The doctor was very pleased. He weighs 12 pounds and is 23 inches long. He can now have rice, oatmeal, pears, peaches, and applesauce. We tried applesauce for lunch and he loved it.

g. Isabel and Derrick were playing with blocks and cars. Derrick smiled a big broad smile as he sat back on his heels and looked at the structure they were working on. "We made a big parking garage. Just like the one downtown!" He looked at Isabel and suggested, "Let's park all the cars inside, O.K.?" Isabel silently began collecting cars and passing them over to Derrick.

h. Mrs. Tanaka was interested in finding out what her three-year-olds said to each other when they played at the sandtable. She set the sandtable up in a corner of the room where the children could play in private but she could observe unobtrusively. She got this idea from one of the research methods she learned about in her child development course.

B. Match the method of child study in Column I to the type of information obtained in Column II.

Column I	**Column II**
1. diary	a. parent's memory of past events
2. naturalistic observation	b. specific information from the child
	c. a situation set up specially to observe a particular type of behavior
3. parent interview	d. a detailed description of behavior in a normal setting
4. child interview	e. what the parent or other adult feels is important
5. laboratory observation	

C. Explain how a teacher might also be a researcher.

A Brief Look at the Young Child

OBJECTIVES

After studying this unit, the student should be able to:

- List settings in which professionals work with young children.

- Recognize typical infants, toddlers, three-, four-, and five-year-olds, and six- through eight-year-olds.

- Discuss the similarities and differences among infants, toddlers, three-, four-, and five-year-olds, and six-through eight-year-olds.

- Identify and describe examples of the five "*P's*," four "*R's*," and "TLC."

Who is the young child? According to the National Association for the Education of Young Children, children from birth through eight years of age are considered to be **young children** (Bredekamp, 1987). They are usually grouped into rough age categories:

Infants:	birth to one
Toddlers:	one year to three years
Preschoolers:	three years to five years
Kindergartners:	five years to six years
Primary:	six years through eight years

The young child is a small person who is complex and at times puzzling. In this unit an overview is presented that lays the groundwork for the more detailed units to follow. In this unit the young child is introduced.

What does the young child do? The newborn is interested in personal comfort: being warm, being well fed, and having a dry diaper. Very quickly he learns to expect attention and cuddling from the caring others in his environment. Soon the infant becomes aware of his own body and of things in the environment that he can control. By age one the infant can move about, and from age one to three he is most interested in moving about and exploring everything. By the time the child is a preschooler, paint, clay, balls, games, dolls, trucks, and books all serve as raw material for the young child's play. By age three the child accomplishes many routine tasks such as eating, sleeping, bathing, toileting, and dressing. Young boys and girls can walk, run, climb, yell, speak conversationally, and whisper. They can express their feelings clearly—happiness, sadness, contentment, anger, and irritability.

KEYTERMSKEYTERMSKEYTERMSKEYTERMSKEYTERMSKEY

young children

Three- and four-year-olds are usually referred to as **preschoolers**, meaning they have not yet entered elementary school, although many fives have not yet entered kindergarten and are really still preschoolers. Fives are usually labeled as **kindergartners** even though kindergartners may be four, five, or six, depending on their birthdates and when they are allowed to enter school. Ages six through eight or grades first through third is the **primary period**. As you study the growth and development of young children you will see that these age labels are rather arbitrary and do not necessarily tell us where a child is developmentally. Therefore, consider the following descriptions as examples but do not expect every child to be exactly like the ones described.

Infants are, as already mentioned, very dependent. Between one and three the young child moves towards increased independence. Preschoolers are ready to "strike out on their own" beyond the safe confines of home and parents. Of course, many children have spent extended periods away from home before age three—in a day-care home, at a relative's home, or in a center-based infant and/or toddler playgroup or full-day, day-care group. By three, however, children have skills that enable them to function well without the almost constant adult attention needed in the infant and toddler years.

For the adult who works with young children in full-time day care, part-time preschool programs, medical settings, social service centers, or at home, questions constantly arise regarding these small people and what to do with them. This unit develops an initial picture of young children through descriptions of their characteristics and by presenting essentials of the adult's role in working with young children.

VIEWS OF YOUNG CHILDREN

Many authors have developed general descriptions of the young child. The descriptions that follow are of the newborn, infant, toddler, three-, four-, five-year-old and six- through eight-year-old.

The Newborn

The new baby is utterly dependent on the adults around him. . . . He is conscious of changes in temperature, of being lifted and handled, of some sounds, of bright lights and of the closeness of another human body. . . . He cannot do anything himself except breathe, suck and cry for help. (Lee, 1977, p. 5)

These first months are inclined to be somewhat stormy, but the weather will seem much less erratic and will take on much more meaning if the child's behavior is regarded not as erratic but as an expression of his organic needs and interests. . . . Crying is essentially language, even though at times it appears to be indulged in for purposes of sheer self-activity. (Gesell, Ilg, Ames, & Rodell, 1974, pp. 75–76)

The Infant

By the end of a month the baby has settled into a routine of life. . . . The baby at three months is alert, interested in life and delighted to be with other people, Figure 3–1. He smiles and uses his voice in many ways other than crying. His bodily movements are much more controlled . . . He lies awake for longer periods both when put down and after waking up. . . . The baby at six months is growing up fast. He has more than doubled his weight at birth and has grown about five inches longer. . . . The word that springs most easily to mind when we think of the baby at nine months is 'mobile'. . . . At a year old the baby is a lively member of the family, friendly and confident. (Lee, 1977, pp. 7–10)

At 16 weeks . . . His fingers finger his fingers! Thus he himself touches and is touched simultaneously. This double touch is a lesson in self-discovery. He comes to appreciate what his fingers are; and that objects are something different. . . . At 40 weeks . . . He has a new capacity for imitation. Accordingly he "learns" new nursery tricks like pat-a-cake and bye-bye. . . . (At age one) He likes to play with several small objects rather than a solitary one. He picks them up one by one, drops them, picks them up again, one by one. (Gesell et al., 1974, pp. 99, 115, 123)

KEYTERMSKEYTERMSKEYTERMSKEYTERMSKEYTERMSKEYTERMSKEY

| preschoolers | kindergartners | primary period |

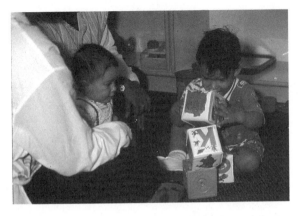

Figure 3–1 The infant is engrossed in the activity in the environment.

The Toddler

This (the second year) is a year of exploration and discovery on two fronts—the physical world and the world of language and speech. . . . He spends most of his time relentlessly exploring, discovering, experimenting with everything he can find. He may scream or squeal with rage when he cannot manage something he wants to do such as put on a shoe or push blocks through the bars of his playpen. . . . By the time he is halfway through his second year he is fairly steady on his feet and becomes more independent in his excursions about the house. . . . (During the second year) he is loving and responsive but increasingly shows that he has a will of his own and tries very hard to be independent. (Lee, 1977, p. 12)

He (18-month-old) lugs, tugs, dumps, pushes, pulls, pounds. When he seizes a teddy bear he clasps it grossly to his chest. He is also something of a furniture mover. Gross motor activity takes the lead over fine motor . . . the two-year-old is under a . . . compulsion to exercise his vocal abilities, to repeat words, to name things, to suit words to action and action to words. (Gesell et al., 1974, pp. 141–142, 156)

The Three-Year-Old

Three—at least for the first half year—is a sociable and agreeable child (Figure 3–2). This is a charming and generally loveable age. Nursery school teachers are unanimous in their praise of three-year-old behaviors. (Growing Child, 1973)

Enjoy the sociable and agreeable Three while you can—toward the end of this year this now delightful child may turn bossy and demanding as, his initial social needs met, the child becomes preoccupied with seeing that things be done *his* way, that *his* routines be followed. (Growing Child, 1973)

The three-year-old is a happy and companionable child, who needs opportunities for independence, play with many different materials, time to be with other children, a great deal of conversation and story-telling, and the support and example of affectionate, reliable adults. (Lee, 1977, p. 20)

The Four-Year-Old

Four has a lively mind . . . [Four is] assertive (Figure 3–3). Indeed, Four tends to go out of bounds both with muscles and with mind. And why should he not? If he remained a delightful, docile Three, he would not grow up. So he surges ahead with a burst of movement and of imagination. (Gesell, Ilg, Ames, & Rodell, 1974, p. 200)

Figure 3–2 The three-year-old is often a cheery companion.

Figure 3–3   Four-year-olds like the companionship of other children and are more independent of adults than are three-year-olds.

In the nursery school or playgroup the four-year-old children do not seek the active companionship of the teachers and assistants in their play. They ask for the material they need, or sometimes for advice; they go to an adult for help when they are hurt; they like to have an adult's approval of something they have made or painted; they cheerfully respond to most adult requests and reminders; and they sometimes need adults to arbitrate in disputes. (Lee, 1977, p. 21)

The Five-Year-Old

Most five-year-olds are confident and friendly. They expect to be liked and valued and they are ready to go out to meet new experiences. They are eager to learn and please the adults. They talk readily and ask a great many questions, particularly 'why?', and they show a surprising amount of persistence when they want to master some new skill. (Lee, 1977, p. 23) See Figure 3–4.

Children of this age like and trust grown-ups and although they like to be independent they do in fact depend a great deal on adults for organization, help and advice and as arbiters in the wrangles that inevitably spring up among a group of rivals. Parents and teachers are responsible for the planning and organization of home and classroom within which the children are active, but ideas often expand from the play and work of the children themselves. (Lee, 1977, p. 24)

Figure 3–4   Kindergartners are more independent than preschoolers.

The Six- Through Eight-Year-Old

By their sixth birthday children are friendly, trusting and cooperative toward adults, intensely interested and curious about the world, lively and energetic. . . . His muscular control is improving and he likes to run on tiptoe, skip and dance to music. He is competent with pencils and paintbrushes, can dress himself even though he is rather slow about it . . . Six-year-olds have an interest in reality. They ask constantly, 'Is it true?'. Their fantasy play has strong elements of real life in it, copying adult behaviour for the most part, . . . (Lee, 1977, pp. 26–27)

The children [in the primary years] seem to be in a stage of developmental integration. [They] can take care of their own personal needs. . . . They observe family rules about mealtimes, television, and needs for privacy. They can also be trusted to run errands and carry out simple responsibilities at home and at school. In other words, these children are in control of themselves and their immediate world (Allen & Marotz, 1994, p. 116) . . . they enjoy being challenged and completing tasks. They also like to make recognizable products and to join in organized activities. (Allen & Marotz, 1994, p. 118) See Figure 3–5.

Figure 3–5 **This primary-age child can do long-term projects that require good fine motor coordination, such as cutting out small pieces of paper and gluing them into a representational form for this collage.**

In these brief descriptions of child growth from birth to six, an increase in independence and self-confidence is evident. At the same time, there seems to be a cycle marked by calmness at three to increased activity at four to calmness again as the child reaches five. The adult who works with young children must be aware that these changes are normal.

THE ADULT ROLE

Ira Gordon (1976) suggested several factors common to the roles of parent and teacher as reflected in our knowledge of child development. Gordon stated that parenting and teaching involve many common elements, which he referred to as the **five P's, four R's**, and TLC.

The five *P's* are (1) provides the learning environment, (2) predictability, (3) ping-pong, (4) persistence, and (5) professor. The adult provides the environment. That is, the adult organizes it and determines what kind and how much stimulation there will be. The adult organizes both space and time. The adult also organizes the people involved and where they will be in relation to the children. Predictability concerns the child's need to know what is going to happen next. Children need to be able to predict events in time sequence and also to predict adult responses to their actions. Ping-pong is the back and forth, give and take of social interaction. The adult needs to respond appropriately to each child.

Persistence is the characteristic that pushes children to stay with a problem or an activity until they are finished. The adult must allow the child time with no interruptions so that he can complete tasks. Gordon feels that these first four *P's* are positive. The fifth, professor, is negative. Professor is just "talking followed by talking followed by talking, without paying any attention whatsoever to whether anybody is tuned in, responding or attending" (Gordon, 1976, p. 178). Adults often do too much talking and not enough listening and observing.

The four *R's* are responsiveness, reasoning, rationality, and reading (Gordon, 1976). Adults must be responsive to the child. They must learn to read the child's signals and respond with help and attention. Adults should try to act in accordance with the child's rhythms. They must note the best times for various activities as they fit the child. Adults also must be aware of not setting traps. That is, they must take preventative measures to avoid setting up situations that will lead to trouble. Reasoning and rationality go hand in hand. They involve giving the child reasons and explanations when necessary. Reading to children is a key experience that can build a good adult-child relationship. Story time is a special, close, warm time. It is also a time when the child can learn the excitement and value of books and acquire basic concepts and language skills (Figure 3–6).

TLC, of course, is tender loving care, or warmth. As developmental research regarding the adult and child relationship is reviewed, warmth always appears as an important positive factor. A child can never receive too much love. Love must take its place with the five *P's* and the four *R's*.

KEYTERMSKEYTERMSKEYTERMSKEYTERMSKEYTERMSKEY

five P's   four R's

Figure 3–6   **Reading enriches both mental and emotional development.**

SUMMARY

This text describes growth and development from the prenatal period through the eighth year of life. The study of child development helps adults understand the general ages and stages of young children. However, it is through our interactions with young children that we come to know and understand them. There are a number of important things the adult can do when working with the young child to enhance that child's development. These things are described throughout the text.

FOR FURTHER READING

The following books by Beverly Cleary give some charming insights into the thoughts, actions, and feelings of young children.

Cleary, B. (1955). *Beezus and Ramona.* New York: Morrow.
Cleary, B. (1968). *Ramona the pest.* New York: Morrow.
Cleary, B. (1975). *Ramona the brave.* New York: Scholastic Book Service.

OTHER SUGGESTED READING

Elkind, D. (1993). *Images of the young child.* Washington, DC: National Association for the Education of Young Children.
Paley, V. G. (1984). *Boys and girls: Superheroes in the doll corner.* Chicago: University of Chicago Press.
Paley, V. G. (1981). *Wally's stories: Conversations in the kindergarten.* Cambridge: Harvard University Press.
Williams, L. R., & Fromberg, D. P. (Eds.) (1993). *Encyclopedia of early childhood education.* New York: Garland.

SUGGESTED ACTIVITIES

1. Start a child development journal. A journal is a record of daily actions and reactions. In this case, it is a record of your activities and reactions regarding children and your role with them. Use a spiral notebook for the journal. Each day as you read, attend class, observe, and interact with young children, store your reactions in your memory. Each evening, take out the journal, write the day's date, and record whatever you feel is important. Start by recording your present feelings about children. As a start, think about your past experience as a child and with other children and write down whatever seems important. As you go through the course, record any changes or confirmations that occur because of your new experiences. A journal entry might appear as follows.

Date   Entry

1/23/95   Today I observed at the Child Development Center. Johnny, who I find very irritating due to his constant whining, was lying on the floor screaming and kicking. I had a chance to speak with one of the teachers later and found out that Johnny's parents have just separated after a long period of fighting and bickering. No wonder Johnny is such a sad person. I can see now where you need to know the whole picture to make an accurate judgment about a child. Johnny's situation makes me feel very sad. A happy note!: Terry moved away from the blocks today and painted a picture. In class we talked about the value of play for young children—I'll never again feel that play is a waste of time. I'm really beginning to see its value.

2. Go to a child development center. Observe an infant, a toddler, a three-year-old, a four-year-old, and a five-year-old. Spend twenty minutes watching each child. Compare their behavior with the general descriptions in this unit. Were these children the same or different from what you expected from your reading in the text? In what ways? List questions regarding the comparison and/or additional things you would like to know about the specific children observed and about child development. Share the experiences in class.

3. Go to an elementary school. Observe children in kindergarten through third grade. Spend 20–30 minutes at each grade level. Compare the behaviors you observe with the descriptions in this unit. Were these children the same or different from what you expected from your reading in the text? In what ways? List questions regarding the comparisons and/or additional things you would like to know about the children you observed and about child development. Share your experiences in class.

4. Observe two or three children for one hour at school and for one hour at home. Write a description of each interaction the child has with an adult. Compare similarities and differences between the child's home and school behavior. Compare similarities and differences between the behavior of the adults at home and at school. If differences were observed, speculate on the reasons for those differences. Share your experience in class.

5. Interview a teacher of young children. Ask the person to talk about characteristics of the typical infant, toddler, three-, four-, five-year-olds and six- to eight-year-olds. Ask the teacher if there is any preference as to which age she or he would rather teach. Compare these pictures of "typical" young children with those in the book. Discuss your findings with the other students in class.

6. Interview two of the following: a nurse, a pediatrician, a social worker, a dentist, a camp director, a psychologist, or another professional who works with young children in a nonteaching role. What differences do they see in infants, toddlers, three-, four-, and five-year-olds and six- to eight-year-olds? What kinds of special techniques, if any, do they use with young children that are different from those they use with older children and adults? What do they find most rewarding and most frustrating about working with young children?

REVIEW

A. List five settings in which adults work in a professional capacity with young children.

B. Decide whether each of the following incidents involves an infant, a toddler, a three-year-old, a four-year-old, a five-year-old, or a six- through eight-year-old child.

  1. Tom and Larry are playing nicely together with blocks. They have built a large fort. Suddenly Bill comes along and tries to knock it down. "Mr. Jones! Mr. Jones! Help! We need you!" shouts Tom.

  2. Five children are cuddled up against one teacher as she reads them a story. Each seems to need a part of her lap.

  3. The dentist announces he is ready to see Mary. She enters the office with confidence and a cheery smile. "Climb up in this big chair, Mary." Mary climbs up agilely and confidently.

4. Mrs. Cohen is concerned. What *was* a sweet and agreeable child just a short time ago is now hard to get along with. He is bossy and rude and always testing limits. Mr. Jones assures her this type of behavior swing is normal at this age.

5. Bill and Derrick are putting Legos® airplanes together. They are in deep concentration, discussing where each of the small parts belongs and sharing information they have read about different kinds of aircraft. They are both saving up their allowance to buy a model space shuttle building kit.

6. Billy is racing around the house laughing and yelling. Mrs. Garcia, his day-care mother, feels he is taunting her and trying to show his superiority.

7. As spring approaches, Mr. Woods suddenly finds the children in his group are becoming more creative and thinking of more projects on their own. He finds he needs to provide more materials and activities to fit their ideas than he had to do in the past.

8. Mrs. Hopkins finds Kate has pulled herself to her feet and is cruising around the livingroom holding on to each piece of furniture as she goes.

C. Considering the descriptions of typical young children and any observations you have done, do you feel children of any particular age have more likenesses than differences? That is, can we really say there is a "typical" child at any age?

D. Match the terms in Column I with the incidents in Column II.

Column I	Column II
1. provision of the learning environment	a. Joe: What is this? Mrs. G: It's a guinea pig. You can hold it if you like. Joe: I'll just touch it. (He touches the head gently with one finger.) He's smooth. Mrs. G. smiles.
2. predictability	b. "After lunch we have playtime and then a nap."
3. ping-pong	c. "Tanya, you must behave yourself and use those paints the right way. We can't afford to waste paint. . ." Tanya looks uncomfortable and her gaze is wandering about the room.
4. persistence	d. Mrs. Garcia has taken great care to set up her home to fit the needs of the four pre-school children who spend each day with her. Her dining room has been converted to a playroom. There are dress-up clothes, large blocks made from cartons covered with Contac® paper, a set of Legos®, Tinker Toys®, homemade puzzles and games, stuffed animals and dolls which belonged to her now-grown children, and, in a small cage on a low table, a black and white guinea pig.
5. professor	e. Billy has been building with Legos® for half an hour. Mrs. G. tells him it will soon be time for lunch but he may save his creation to play with later if he wishes.

E. Give a specific example for each of the four *R's* and TLC.

Prenatal and Infancy Periods

We have become increasingly interested in conception and prenatal development. Researchers have been looking into many questions in this area. For example, conception has been looked at closely to solve problems of infertility. The effects of various substances and experiences during the prenatal period are the focus of inquiry. Nutrition is one of the most critical aspects of prenatal maternal health care. Relative to the richness and advanced knowledge available in our country, our rates of infant mortality, low birth weight, and premature births is quite high. A major contributing factor is the relative lack of attention given to prenatal medical care for pregnant women who are living near or at the poverty level. The effects of various methods of delivery on mother and newborn have also been the focus of some attention.

As we interact with infants, we find ourselves curious regarding what they understand and how they understand what is happening in their environment. We frequently communicate with them through speech and gesture as if we were carrying on a two-way spoken conversation while they respond with expressions and movements that communicate their interest in what we say and do.

In this section, we will look at the beginnings of life: at conception, prenatal development, and the influence of heredity and environment on the developing child. Next, we'll look at the development of the typical newborn and the infant, and finally at social and cultural factors that may affect development.

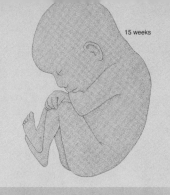

15 weeks

Conception and Prenatal Development

OBJECTIVES

After studying this unit, the student should be able to:

■ Describe the sequence of events that results in fertilization and conception.

■ Recognize the three stages of prenatal development.

■ Recognize the functions of the placenta, umbilical cord, and amniotic fluid.

■ Describe the highlights of fetal development.

■ Recognize the sensitivities of the fetus.

■ List and discuss environmental factors that can affect the developing fetus.

■ Discuss the problems associated with teenage pregnancies.

As you read this text, you will meet a number of young children at different ages and stages of development. In this unit we will explore life before birth beginning with the joining of the sperm and the egg at conception and following development through the prenatal (prebirth) period. We'll also look at some of the environmental factors that can affect the developing child prior to birth. Finally, the responsibilities of adults in caring for the prenatal infant will be discussed.

CONCEPTION

About every 28 days, at the midpoint of the menstrual cycle, a female egg cell or **ovum** housed in a fluid-filled sac called a **follicle** leaves one of the female's ovaries and journeys into the abdominal cavity and then into a fallopian tube. It is the largest cell in the human body (Figure 4–1). Once it reaches the fallopian tube, there is a period of between 10 and 24 hours in which it can be fertilized by a sperm from a male (Berk, 1994).

The male system produces many thousands of sperm. During sexual intercourse, when orgasm is reached, the male ejaculates a liquid called **semen**, which may contain over 300 million **sperm**. These sperm are only 1/600 inch long and are shaped like tadpoles. Their life span is only 24 to 48 hours. Sperm have a long route to travel to reach the ovum in a rel-

KEYTERMSKEYTERMSKEYTERMSKEYTERMSKEYTERMSKEY

ovum	semen
follicle	sperm

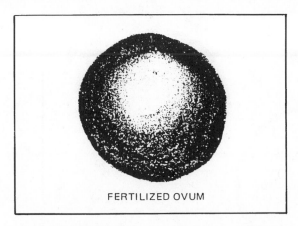

FERTILIZED OVUM

Figure 4–1 **The ovum, the female egg, is the largest cell in the human body. (From Anderson,** *Basic Maternal-Newborn Nursing*, **by Delmar Publishers)**

atively short time. They must race from the vagina, through the cervix, into the uterus, and then up the fallopian tube, which may or may not have an egg ready for fertilization. All sperm are not equally strong or equally fast. From the millions of sperm that are initially released, usually about 300 to 500 reach the egg. If one sperm makes it through the outer membrane into the egg, a chemical reaction takes place that prohibits any more sperm from gaining entrance (Berk, 1994). The moment when **fertilization** takes place is referred to as **conception**. Child development begins with the ovum and sperm uniting into one cell called the **zygote** (Figure 4–2).

When does human life begin? Much national concern continues to focus on the legal and moral status of **abortion**, the termination of the life of an unborn child. The question of when human life actually begins has been the subject of much discussion (Sagan & Druyan, 1990).

Historically, up until the late nineteenth century, abortion during the early weeks of pregnancy was permissible and the woman had the right to choose. By 1900, abortion was banned in every state during all of pregnancy except to save a woman's life (Sagan

& Druyan, 1990). Advances in medicine seemed to have influenced this change. More knowledgeable and better trained physicians focused on the welfare of the fetus rather than the health of the mother. Only physicians could make the decision to abort. It wasn't until the 1970s that the court case **Rowe v. Wade** legalized abortion. As we reach the close of the twentieth century, the moral and legal issues are again the focus of much attention and much heated argument.

THE PERIODS OF PRENATAL DEVELOPMENT

The period of pregnancy is referred to as the **gestational period**. It usually lasts about $9^{1}/_{2}$ calendar months (Berk, 1994). The gestation period proceeds in three stages: the zygote (conception to 2 weeks), the **embryo** (3 to 8 weeks) and the **fetus** (9 weeks until birth) (Figure 4–3).

The Zygote

The first stage begins when the sperm and ovum unite into one cell, which floats freely down the fallopian tube. This stage lasts for about 2 weeks. During this period, the cell division takes place very rapidly, with one cell dividing into billions. By about day six, the cell arrives in the uterus, where it begins to implant or attach to the wall of the uterus so it can obtain nutrients. The **placenta** (the covering that protects the developing infant and serves as a medium of exchange for food and oxygen) and the **umbilical cord**, which connects the developing child to the mother and is his lifeline, are beginning to develop (Annis, 1978) (Figure 4–4).

The Embryo

The second stage begins when the zygote is implanted in the uterine wall and continues until about the eighth week. This is a critical stage because it is during this stage that 95 percent of the body parts ap-

KEYTERMSKEYTERMSKEYTERMSKEYTERMSKEYTERMSKEYTERMSKEY

fertilization	Rowe v. Wade	placenta
conception	gestational period	umbilical cord
zygote	embryo	
abortion	fetus	

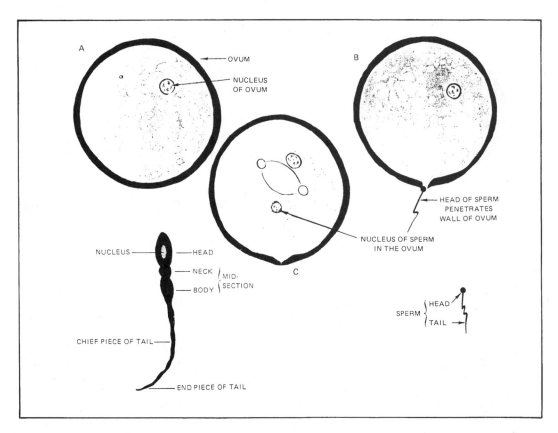

Figure 4.2   **The tadpolelike male sperm are small in comparison to the ovum and have a life span of 24 to 48 hours. (From Anderson, *Basic Maternal-Newborn Nursing*, by Delmar Publishers)**

pear (Annis, 1978). By the end of this stage, the developing embryo begins to resemble a miniature person (Figure 4–5). It is during this stage that the prenatal child is most vulnerable to damage by drugs, alcohol, disease, infection, radiation, and poor nutrition (Berk, 1994). The woman who contracts German measles, who uses cocaine, or is poorly nourished places her child at high risk. For example, if a woman contracts German measles during her pregnancy, her child stands a risk of being born deaf, blind, or with heart disease.

The development of the placenta takes place during the embryo stage. The placenta is the vehicle through which the fetus receives nutrients and oxygen and disposes of waste. The umbilical cord connects the fetus and the placenta. The uterus is lined by a sac called the **amnion**, which contains **amniotic fluid**. The fluid serves several purposes. It protects the fetus from injury and provides room for movement and growth. The amniotic fluid maintains an environment of even temperature and provides oral fluid. The fluid also collects waste products (Berk, 1994).

The Fetus

The fetal period begins at about nine weeks and extends until birth. As mentioned earlier, the child now begins to look like a human being. All the organs that began development during the embryonic

amnion   amniotic fluid

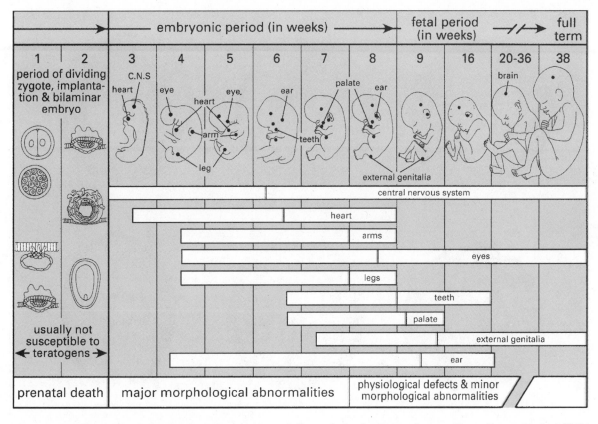

Figure 4–3   The prenatal developmental sequence and the periods of greatest danger. (From Berns, *Topical Child Development*, by Delmar Publishers)

stage will grow and develop rapidly during the fetal stage. The head becomes more proportional to the rest of the body and the limbs are more clearly differentiated. By the fourth month, the placenta is fully operational. A few of the highlights of fetal development (Berk, 1994) include:

- By the twelfth week, male and female external genitalia are visible.
- By the twenty-first week, the fetus could survive outside of the uterus.
- By the twenty-fourth week, the fetus has eyelashes and eyebrows and the eyelids are open.
- Toenails and fingernails are formed by 40 weeks of gestational age.
- About 1 or 2 weeks before delivery for the first child and at the time of delivery for subsequent

babies, the baby drops down into the pelvis and is ready for birth.

Fetal Sensory Capacity and Learning

Dr. Arnold Gesell (Ames, 1989) had a long-time interest in fetal behavior. He believed that the fetus developed in a fixed sequence in the same manner as the growing child. He documented many movements, such as a clapping motion and a grasping reflex, that would appear after birth. The sensory and learning capacities of the fetus are of great interest to those who study prenatal development.

Modern equipment and techniques have enlightened us as to the sensory capacities of the fetus (Cole & Cole, 1989). By 4 months gestation age, the

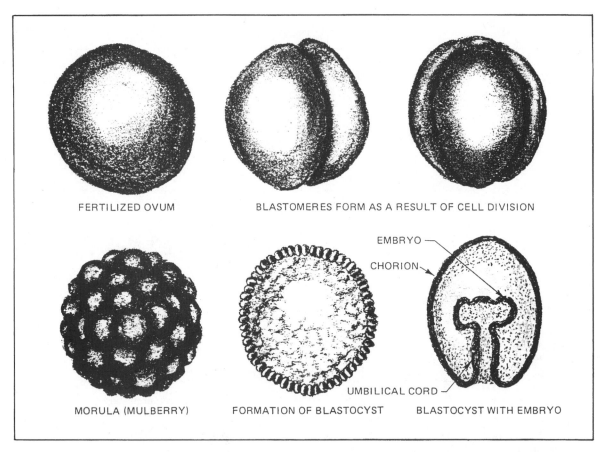

FERTILIZED OVUM

BLASTOMERES FORM AS A RESULT OF CELL DIVISION

EMBRYO

CHORION

MORULA (MULBERRY)

FORMATION OF BLASTOCYST

UMBILICAL CORD

BLASTOCYST WITH EMBRYO

Figure 4–4   From fertilization to implantation, the zygote goes through several stages of development from one cell to many cells and to development of an embryo. (From Anderson, *Basic Maternal-Newborn Nursing*, by Delmar Publishers)

fetus can sense changes in the mother's position as it floats in the amniotic fluid. There is some evidence that by the seventh month the infant may have some rudimentary visual perception that enables him to see light that penetrates the mother's skin. Tiny microphones have been placed in the uterus and revealed that the uterus is fairly noisy. There is the sound of air passing through the mother's stomach and the sound of her heartbeat. Distinctive noises from outside will cause fetal movement. This may be partly due to fluid vibration, but there is evidence that the auditory system is also involved. Research indicates that some learning takes place in the uterus. For example, newborn infants respond positively to an audiotaped heartbeat played just as it would sound in the womb.

ENVIRONMENTAL EFFECTS DURING PRENATAL DEVELOPMENT

As shown in Figure 4–6, there are several types of prenatal environmental influences that can affect the fetus. These can be classified as nutritional; maternal characteristics, experiences, and personal habits; and drugs and disease (Annis, 1978).

Nutrition

Improper prenatal nutrition is one of the greatest dangers to the fetus. Annis (1978) lists a number of factors associated with prenatal maternal malnutrition. These complications include "stillbirths, low-

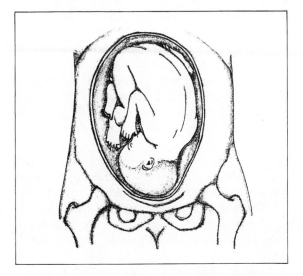

Figure 4–5 **At the beginning of the fetal period, the fetus is now recognizable as a human being. (From Caldwell & Hegner, *Nursing Assistant* 5th ed., by Delmar Publishers)**

birth-weight babies (babies weighing under 5½ pounds or 2,500 grams after a normal period of prenatal development), short-gestation-period babies, and neonatal deaths, as well as many difficulties appearing in the offspring after birth, such as mental deficiency, rickets, cerebral palsy, epilepsy, speech defects, general physical weakness, and susceptibility to illness and disease" (Annis, 1978, p. 63). Not only does a woman need to eat a healthy diet during pregnancy, but she should begin pregnancy in a good nutritional state. If the pregnant woman is not in good nutritional health, nutritional improvement during pregnancy does have a positive effect. For example, Joos et al. (1983) found that supplying a nutritional supplement to pregnant undernourished women had a positive effect on the motor development of their infants. The effect was small probably because there was no postnatal supplement. Nutritional deficiencies continue to be a major worldwide health problem that place women's successful reproductive capacity at risk (Infants and children at risk, 1992).

Environmental Influence	Results for Child
Poor Nutrition	Stillbirth, neonatal death, low birth weight, short gestation Mental deficiency, rickets, cerebral palsy, epilepsy, speech defects, general physical weakness
Maternal Characteristics o Emotional state o Physical size o Age o Rh incompatibility o Low blood oxygen level	Crankiness Difficult delivery Retardation Stillbirth Nervous system damage
Maternal Experience and Personal Habits o X-ray o Smoking o Alcohol o Caffeine	Tissue damage; retardation Low birth weight; death Slow growth; retardation Miscarriage
Drugs and Disease o Drugs o Disease	Limb malformation; addiction; delivery complications Generally retarded growth, possible neurological damage

Figure 4–6   Negative prenatal environmental influences

Maternal Characteristics and Experiences

Maternal characteristics, such as a mother's emotional state, age, physical size, possible Rh incompatibility with the fetus, low blood oxygen level in the bloodstream, and state of fatigue, can effect the fetus. Personal habits that include the use of alcohol, drugs, tobacco, and coffee also may be harmful (Annis, 1978). A long period of emotional upset on the part of the mother can have a negative effect on the fetus. There is a relationship between tense, anxious pregnancies and the delivery of cranky infants.

The mother between the ages of twenty and thirty has the best chance of having a normal, healthy child. Young, teenaged mothers may have relatively poor eating habits and thus may not be in a good nutritional condition for nurturing a developing infant. Among the large numbers of unwed mothers, there is a large proportion of teenagers. These young, unwed mothers and mothers from impoverished environments are more likely to have infants who are at high risk due to poor maternal nutrition. In addition, the adolescent girl's body is not yet fully mature and ready for childbearing. This adds another factor that results in the infants of teenagers being much more likely to be born at risk than those of fully mature women. These teens' infants are more likely than those of adults to be subject to low birth weight, mental retardation, birth defects, or possibly death before infancy is completed (Stevens, 1980). The reproductive system of the mother older than thirty may be on the decline. The possibility of having a Down's syndrome child is much higher for the older mother who is experiencing her first pregnancy. The mother's size also may be an influence on the pregnancy. Short, small women generally have more difficult pregnancies. Infants of overweight mothers are also more at risk.

When blood types of mother and father are incompatible, denoting the presence of an **Rh factor**, the infant may develop severe anemia, which can result in stillbirth, brain damage, or birth too early for survival. The prenatal infant must have an adequate supply of oxygen in her blood. **Anoxia** is the state in which the oxygen supply in the blood dips below the safe level. In this case, the nervous system and the brain are likely to receive damage resulting in cerebral palsy, epilepsy, mental deficiency, and possibly behavior problems such as hyperactivity and learning difficulties. Anoxia is most likely to occur during the birth process, when the child is most in need of an adequate oxygen supply. Anoxia may also be related to maternal fatigue. Radiation, such as X-rays, is another danger to the developing fetus. Both mental and physical retardation due to tissue damage can result. Death may result from large doses of radiation.

Personal habits of the mother are another important factor to consider. Cigarette smoking is associated with low birth weight, spontaneous abortion, stillbirths, and neonatal death. Smoking may slow the fetal heart rate and affect the circulatory system of the fetus. Some research has indicated that if smoking is light or stopped by the fourth month, the baby will not be damaged. Overall, however, pregnant women are wise not to smoke at all. Alcohol, especially in large amounts, presents another danger to the prenatal child. Children of alcoholic mothers show slow physical growth and generally retarded development. Small amounts of alcohol also increase the risk to the infant. Even moderate drinking (2 ounces per day) may be dangerous. Streissguth, Barr, and Martin (1983) obtained pregnant women's self-reports on alcohol use during the fifth month of pregnancy. Alcohol use showed a positive relationship with less alert behavior from their newborns. Caffeine, found in coffee, tea, and cola drinks, is thought to have possible negative effects on the amniotic fluid, which might be associated with a greater chance of miscarriage. As a general rule, any woman who is or suspects she is pregnant is wise not to smoke or drink alcoholic beverages, coffee, tea, cola, and any other beverages that contain caffeine.

The increasing number of adolescent pregnancies brings with it an increasing number of infants who may suffer the effects of prenatal maternal experiences and habits (Honig, 1984). More teenage girls are smoking. Smoking is habitual among 15

KEYTERMSKEYTERMSKEYTERMSKEYTERMSKEYTERMSKEY

Rh factor	Anoxia

percent of girls between 12 and 18 years of age. The younger a smoker starts, the heavier smoker they tend to be. Therefore, the chances that the teen mother will be weak and unhealthy puts her infant at even greater risk. Alcohol use has also increased in frequency and amount among adolescents. Pregnant teenagers are very likely to suffer undue stress due to fear regarding their situation, abandonment by the baby's father, or negative response from parents (Honig, 1984).

Drugs and Disease

Drugs and disease are sometimes damaging to fetal development. The effect can be particularly severe during the first 3 months—the time when the woman is least likely to be aware that she is pregnant. No drug should be taken by a pregnant woman except under a doctor's prescription. One of the most disastrous drug episodes concerned the use of thalidomide by pregnant women in Europe in the early 1960s. This drug, taken for the relief of morning sickness, caused retarded limb development when taken during the embryonic period. Children were born without arms and legs or with undeveloped arms and legs similar to those of an embryo. Limb malformations have also been related to the ingestion of hormones, such as those in birth control pills, by pregnant women. Tranquilizers and even aspirin have been shown not to be safe. Drugs taken during and before delivery should be kept at a minimum, as they may also have negative effects on the infant.

Drug addiction presents another danger to the pregnant woman. Cocaine appears to be first on the list of illegal drugs used by women of child-bearing age. Although it is widely believed that these cocaine-exposed infants are severely damaged, research indicates that most of these infants are not significantly impaired. However, in the long run they may evidence problems that will require many special services. Probably the most essential element in ensuring cocaine-exposed infants a healthy life is treatment of their mothers to overcome their addiction so they can create a healthy home environment (Hawley &

Disney, 1992). Heroin-addicted mothers appear to have delivery complications. The children of addicts are sometimes born exhibiting behavior similar to that of a person withdrawing from heroin. Cocaine and crack addiction among pregnant women has resulted in the birth of addicted and damaged infants. A 1988 study in thirty-six hospitals identified that 11 percent (375,000) of infants born were affected by substance abuse (Weston, Ivins, Zuckerman, Jones, & Lopez, 1989). The drugs affect not only the fetus directly but also the fetal environment and the mother. For example, marijuana retards the development of the placenta, which results in reduced blood flow to the fetus.

Drugs affect the mother's central nervous system, placing the fetus at additional risk. In their review of research Weston et al. (1989) describe a variety of possible drug effects (Weston et al., 1989). The drug may be addictive to the infant, but after withdrawal the infant may develop fairly normally. More likely the drug may also be toxic. That is, it may directly affect the fetus in many ways, which will retard or modify infant development. The endocrine or central nervous systems may be damaged. Resulting abnormalities might be reductions in pain threshold, loss of ability for self-control, attention, interpersonal relationships, and bonding with other humans. The genital/urinary system and the cardiovascular systems can be damaged. Other dangers include the effects from maternal seizures, which may result in death; mental problems such as delusions and paranoia, which might lead to suicide; aggressive behavior, which might result in injury; or impaired motor coordination, which may result in an accident. Many doctors advise the safest approach is not to take any drug during pregnancy unless there is a specific medical need for it.

Another danger to the developing infant during the prenatal period is fetal alcohol syndrome (FAS). Each year fifty thousand babies are born to mothers who drink alcohol during pregnancy. It has been estimated that FAS is responsible for 20 percent of all cases of mental retardation (Hymes, 1990).

Chemicals may find their way into the environment and endanger infants. The toxin PCB (poly-

thalidomide   fetal alcohol syndrome (FAS)

chlorinated biphenyl) has been found in some of our food and water supplies and has been ingested by pregnant women. Jacobson et al. (1985) studied one hundred twenty-three mothers and their newborns who had been exposed to PCBs. The mothers had eaten PCB-contaminated fish. When tested at age 7 months the infants were found to have deficits in visual recognition memory.

As discussed earlier in the unit, diseases may be damaging. German measles can seriously damage the fetus. The effect of chickenpox, mumps, measles, and hepatitis is less well documented. The common cold does not seem to have an effect on the fetus but influenza (flu) does seem to. Syphilis, gonorrhea, diabetes, iron deficiency anemia, and sickle-cell anemia all present dangers to the unborn child. The total number of children affected by these diseases and disorders is small, but nevertheless, it is important that pregnant women be under a doctor's care and avoid these dangers if at all possible.

Another threat to prenatal development is **acquired immune deficiency syndrome (AIDS)** (*The AmFAR Report*, 1993). AIDS is a communicable disease caused by a virus that attacks the immune system. The AIDS victim is left without the normal bodily disease-fighting mechanisms and is thus susceptible to death from diseases that ordinarily would not be life-threatening. The disease is carried in the person's blood. It may be transmitted to sexual partners, those who share drug needles, through blood transfusions, and to unborn children through transfer of blood from pregnant woman to unborn child (Skeen & Hodson, 1987). About 80 percent of human immunodeficiency virus (HIV)-infected children under thirteen have a parent with AIDS or AIDS-related complex or a parent who is at risk for AIDS (Weston et al., 1989). Since teens are most likely to be indiscriminantly sexually active and to share drug needles, AIDS is a clear and present danger to their unborn infants.

Rinkel (1992) points out some myths about the effects of prenatal drug exposure on infants and young children. She points out that we do not have research that tells us the long-term consequences in spite of the sensational reports that have appeared in the media. For example, legal substances such as alcohol and tobacco are used by far more pregnant women than illegal substances are and have proven negative effects on prenatal and postnatal development. Further, the stereotype of the inner-city African-American female drug user is far from reality. Drug use is just as prevalent among middle-class and rural women. As already mentioned, there is no documented behavior profile for fetal-drug-exposed preschoolers and school-age children. Rinkel expresses concern that many behavior patterns are being blamed on drugs that may have other causal links. Finally, it is not yet known whether these children need any different educational program than other high-risk students. There is still a great deal to be learned regarding the long-term effects of fetal drug exposure.

ROLE AND RESPONSIBILITIES OF THE ADULT

The steps suggested by Apgar and Beck map out the roles and responsibilities of adults relative to our unborn children. First, planning ahead is important. **Genetic counseling** can be considered before pregnancy. Next, a woman contemplating pregnancy should have a complete physical checkup. During the checkup, the many factors that might endanger an unborn child should be discussed to be sure she understands their importance. During pregnancy, the woman should have regular medical checkups. Parents can attend childbirth education classes so they know what to expect during labor and delivery. Brazelton (1992) recommends that at 7 months the parents should become acquainted with their **pediatrician**, the physician who will care for their child after birth. He believes that if the parents wait longer they will be more concerned with delivery and won't take the time to get acquainted with their child's future doctor. He especially encourages fathers to come in, even if it is only for 10 minutes. He has found that even a short visit seems to make the fathers more interested in coming in with the child for future well-baby checkups.

KEYTERMSKEYTERMSKEYTERMSKEYTERMSKEYTERMSKEYTERMSKEY

acquired immune deficiency syndrome (AIDS)	Genetic counseling pediatrician

Expectant mothers should have access to the services of a **perinatologist**, a physician who specializes in the care of women who are at high risk during pregnancy. High-risk factors would include age of mother, diabetes, high blood pressure, lupus, sickle-cell anemia, or a previous history of birth problems such as multiple births, miscarriages, stillbirths, or physical deformities (BR Second City, 1990). Unfortunately, poor and unwed mothers usually do not have access to this type of prenatal medical care. In 1988 one in every four births was to an unwed mother (Unwed mothers, 1990). The trend has continued into the nineties.

Is there an answer to this problem? Universal access to prenatal care has been proposed (Raspberry, 1989, October 20). Many cities have opened free prenatal clinics for teens but they are sometimes underfunded and understaffed. Often the young pregnant woman cannot get an appointment or does not see the need for one until she is well along in her pregnancy. Some successful experimental programs have been tried in which neighborhood mothers have been trained as counselors for teen pregnant girls. This method can cut the teen pregnancy repeat rate in half (Raspberry, 1989, October 20).

Another attack on the problem is to develop special programs in the high school to serve the needs of pregnant and parent teens for life skills such as child care, job interview techniques, and high school completion. An example of such a program is GRADS (Graduation, Reality, and Dual-Role Skills) in Canton, Ohio (Schenck, 1990). Teens receive life-skills training, information on AIDS and nutrition, and help with personal problems. The teacher of the course not only works with the teens but also with their families and with community agencies. The program also includes the training of Mentor Mothers, women from the community who are assigned as positive role models and counselors for the teens.

A model prevention program in family life education was developed in Bowling Green, Kentucky (Theriot & Bruce, 1988). This program, the "Teen Pregnancy Awareness Project," was instituted for 6th-, 7th-, and 8th-graders. The program was based on a curriculum recommended by The Children's Defense Fund. The curriculum stresses abstinence and improvement of self-esteem. Parental consent is required for participation, and parental involvement is built into the program.

The adult who works with the young child must be alert to past influences that may affect the way a child acts today. When Billy is exceptionally active and is disorderly, his behavior may not be under his control. A look at the past may reveal mild anoxia occurred during delivery. The adult will then realize that Billy needs more than the usual amount of help to develop self-control. A good medical history should always be a part of a school intake application. With the increase in AIDS-infected and substance-addicted infants, we face a future with students who have problems we have never faced before and we have yet to develop methods of working with them.

SUMMARY

The prenatal period, which extends from conception to birth, is a time of phenomenal development but also a time when there are many potential threats to normal healthy growth.

The gestation (prenatal period) is divided into three stages. The first stage, the zygote, lasts about 2 weeks. The second stage, the embryo, begins when the zygote is firmly implanted in the uterine wall and lasts until about the eighth week after conception. The third stage is the fetal period, which begins at about 9 weeks and extends until birth.

The fetal environment can be threatened by many outside factors which can intrude and damage the developing child. Since the developing infant receives all nutrients and oxygen from the mother's system the mother's health is critical. Her health is affected by her nutritional status, use of alcohol, drugs, or tobacco, and her contact with communicable diseases. These factors can directly affect the baby and can have a negative effect on growth and development. Pregnant teens who are unwed and/or from lower socio-economic levels are especially at risk.

KEYTERMSKEYTERMSKEYTERMSKEYTERMSKEYTERMSKEYTERMSKEY

perinatologist

FOR FURTHER READING

Brackbill, Y., McManus, K., & Woodward, L. (1985). *Medication in maternity*. Ann Arbor, MI: University of Michigan Press.

Brazelton, T. B. (1992). *Touchpoints: The essential reference*. Reading, MA: Addison-Wesley.

Bremner, J. G. (1994). *Infancy*, (2nd Ed.). Cambridge, MA: Blackwell.

Child Development. (1983). *54*(5), whole issue on biological risk.

Freeman, E. W., & Rickels, K. (1993). *Early childbearing: Perspectives of black adolescents on pregnancy, abortion, and childbearing*. Thousand Oaks, CA: Sage.

Larner, M., Halpern, R., & Harkavy, O. (1992). *Fair start for children: Lessons from seven demonstration projects*. New Haven and London: Yale University Press.

McAnarney, E. R. (Ed.). (1983). *Premature adolescent pregnancy and parenthood*. Orlando, FL: Gruen.

Rosenblith, J. F. (1992). *In the beginning: Development from conception to age two* (2nd Ed.). Thousand Oaks, CA: Sage.

Smotherman, W. P. & Robinson, S. R. (1988). *Behavior of the fetus*. Caldwell, NJ: Telford Press.

Southern Early Childhood Association. (1991). *Prenatal cocaine exposure: The South looks for answers*. Little Rock, AR: Author.

State of America's Children Yearbook. (1994). Washington, DC: Children's Defense Fund.

Zollar, A. C. (1990). *Adolescent pregnancy and parenthood: An annotated guide*. New York: Garland.

SUGGESTED ACTIVITIES

1. Find out how knowledgeable your friends are regarding conception and prenatal development. Ask the following questions:
   a. How does conception take place?
   b. After conception, how long is the gestation period?
   c. What is a zygote? embryo? fetus?
   d. What are the purposes of the umbilical cord? the placenta? the amniotic fluid?

2. Organize a debate on the following statements:

   Women should have the choice regarding what happens to their bodies. Each woman should have the right to decide if an abortion is warranted or not.

   Select two teams: one in favor of the statements and one against. Give each team a week to research and prepare an argument for or against the statements. One member of each team should be the captain and organize the team arguments. Have the debate in class. Let each team member speak for 3 minutes, alternating sides. Then have the captains each give a 3-minute summary. Finally, have the class members vote on which side presented the most valid case.

3. Ask five friends to list as many factors as they can think of that may enhance or endanger prenatal development. Compare their lists with the items described in the book. How many did each list? Do you feel well informed or need more information? Give them a list of the dangers described in the book. What are their reactions?

4. Investigate programs in your community for teen parents and teen pregnancy prevention. Design a prevention model that you feel would promote fewer teen pregnancies and also would provide prenatal care for those teens who do become pregnant.

5. Make an entry in your journal.

Child Development Theorists

Among the influential
people in child
development are,
clockwise from top,
Jean-Jacques Rousseau,
Johann Pestalozzi,
Freidrich Froebel,
Maria Montessori,
Sigmund Freud,
Erik Erikson,
Jean Piaget,
B. F. Skinner,
and (center) Lev Vygotsky

Prebirth

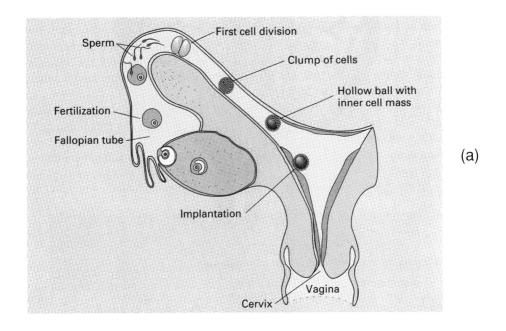

(a)

(a) Fertilization occurs in the upper third part of the fallopian tube. By the time the fertilized ovum reaches the uterus, it has divided many times and now each layer of the cell mass will become a specialized part of the embryo. (b) Development of fetal membranes. (c) Development of twins.

(b)

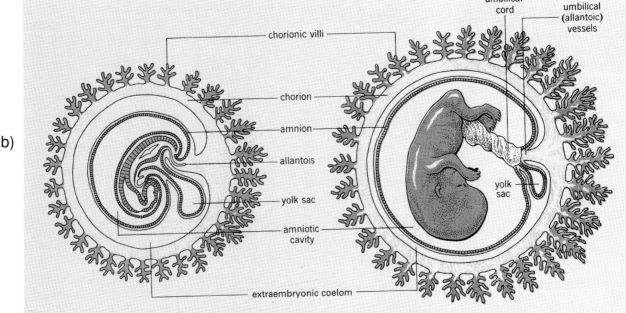

Development

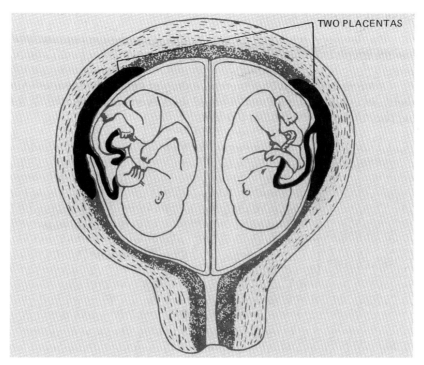

Fraternal twins: two sacs - two placentas

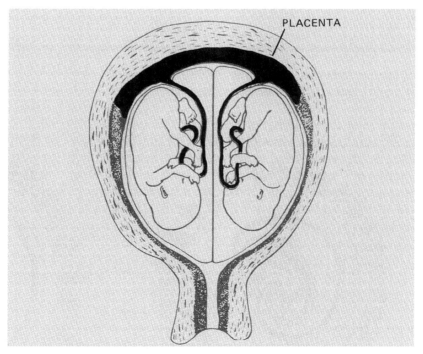

Identical twins: two sacs - one placenta

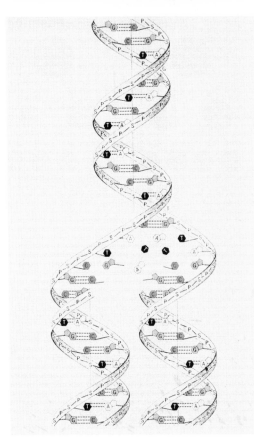

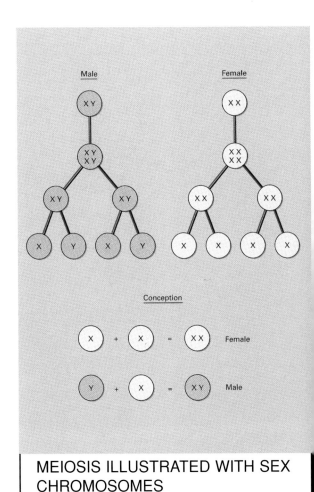

Male

Female

Conception

X + X = X X   Female

Y + X = X Y   Male

MEIOSIS ILLUSTRATED WITH SEX CHROMOSOMES

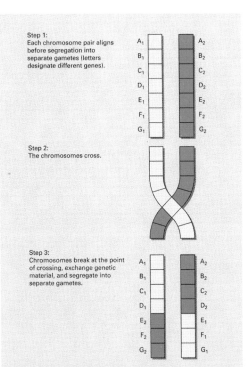

Step 1:
Each chromosome pair aligns before segregation into separate gametes (letters designate different genes).

Step 2:
The chromosomes cross.

Step 3:
Chromosomes break at the point of crossing, exchange genetic material, and segregate into separate gametes.

HOW CHROMOSOMES CROSS OVER

REVIEW

A. Put the following events in the correct sequence by listing the numbers in their appropriate order on the right side of the page.
1. The male ejaculates semen.
2. The ovum reaches the fallopian tube.
3. The menstrual cycle reaches its midpoint.
4. A sperm enters the membrane of the ovum.
5. The ovum, in the fluid-filled follicle, leaves the ovary and heads for the fallopian tube.
6. The sperm race toward the waiting ovum.

B. Match the prenatal stages in Column I with the descriptions in Column II.

Column I	**Column II**
1. germinal stage	a. third stage of prenatal development, from about 2 to 9 months
2. embryonic stage	b. first stage, which lasts until 10 days to 2 weeks after conception (zygote)
3. fetal stage	c. a very critical stage during which defects are most likely to develop

C. Match the functions in Column II with the terms in Column I.

Column I	**Column II**
1. placenta	a. connects the fetus and the placenta
2. umbilical cord	b. this substance protects the fetus from injury and provides for movement and growth
3. amniotic fluid	c. vehicle for receiving nutrients and oxygen

D. List four highlights of fetal development.

E. Select the statements that are true.
1. The fetus is sensitive to light.
2. The uterus provides the fetus with a quiet environment.
3. The fetus has no sense of the mother's movement when suspended in the fluid amniotic environment.
4. The fetus responds to outside noises.
5. No learning takes place in the uterus.

F. Discuss the environmental dangers to the prenatal child and how the child might be protected.

G. Why should we be especially concerned about the increasing number of pregnant teenagers?

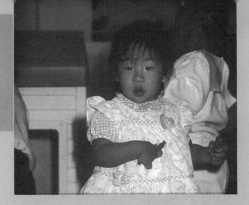

Heredity, Environment, and Development

OBJECTIVES

After studying this unit, the student should be able to:

■ Explain why it is important for the adult who works with young children to know the children's histories.

■ Explain what is meant by the *nature-nurture controversy.*

■ Understand the interactionist point of view of heredity and environment.

■ Provide examples of how the study of adoptees and twins can assist in our understanding of the heredity/environment relationship.

■ Identify hereditary predispositions and environmental dangers that may hinder children's optimal development.

■ Define the terms *gene* and *chromosome.*

■ Recognize when the genetic counselor's services may be needed.

Both hereditary and environmental factors influence the course of child development. **Hereditary** factors are determined at conception. **Environmental** factors begin to play a role as soon as conception occurs. The adult who works with young children needs to understand the development of the child from the time of conception. With this knowledge, adults can gauge where children are in their development. When speaking with parents, the adult can also ask questions that will provide information on critical background factors that have influenced the child's development prior to the time the child comes under the adult's care. This information can be used to evaluate and interpret the child's current behavior.

KEYTERMSKEYTERMSKEYTERMSKEYTERMSKEYTERMSKEY

Hereditary   Environmental

THE MOMENT OF CONCEPTION: HEREDITY

At the moment the sperm enters the ovum and the child begins to form, characteristics from both the mother's and the father's sides of the family are merged into one or more new individuals. In the case of multiple births, **monozygotic (MZ) siblings** develop from one egg that has divided into two or more parts after fertilization so the same hereditary characteristics are present in each. **Dizygotic (DZ) siblings** develop from separate eggs fertilized at the same time. Characteristics such as skin, hair, and eye color, potential physical size and proportions, and even potential temperament and cognitive characteristics are set in place. Once the instant of conception has passed, environment begins to exert a strong influence on what children will be like as they grow and learn. As in the past, concern and curiosity continues regarding the relative influence of heredity and environment. This **nature versus nurture** controversy has gone on for many years (Wolfe, 1972, 1977) and continues today (Baumrind, 1993; Jackson, 1993; Scarr, 1993).

Although considered a **maturationist** (one who feels growth patterns are fixed), Arnold Gesell recognized that growth has a certain amount of plasticity (Ames, 1989). He believed growth follows fixed laws; that is, heredity has the edge, but within limitations he recognized that there is room for adaptation. He believed that environment plays a screening or selective role among competing possibilities for behavior. "Environmental factors support, inflect and modify, but do not generate the progressions of development" (as quoted in Ames, 1989). The general sequence of development is fixed, but environment plays a role in exactly how that sequence is played out.

Other developmental psychologists suggest that rather than taking sides on the nature versus nurture issue, an **interactionist** point of view could be more productive (Horowitz, 1989). This interactionist position views the organism (the human child) as entering the environment with a variety of potential behaviors that may or may not develop depending on the process of development and the opportunities presented in the environment. It is neither the genetic factors in the organism nor the environment that controls development but the process of development itself that is the critical and controlling factor. What happens prenatally has an important role in the determination of the probability that any particular set of behaviors will emerge rather than another set of behaviors. Horowitz (1989) points out that there are, of course, some universals in all human development. That is, there are regularities in the development of all normal human beings. Differences appear in just how these regularities appear in a particular individual. For example, language is a universal but its exact construction depends on experiences in the social and cultural context as they relate to individual differences. The environment may facilitate or not facilitate development. The organism may be vulnerable to outside forces or protected from outside forces. The organism may reach the optimal developmental outcome or only the minimal. The organism may be impaired or unimpaired. Development has many dimensions. As we look at a particular child or at research on numbers of children, we need to look at all the evidence and not naively accept simple cause and effect or simple heredity/environment answers to our questions about development. With this in mind, we can look at some of the ways heredity and environment have been studied.

AFTER CONCEPTION: ENVIRONMENT AND HEREDITY

As already mentioned scientists continue to be intrigued by the complexities of heredity and environment. While in the past researchers focused on the determination of just how much each factor contributes to human behavior, today the process of interaction between the two is seen as the direction in which to go. Even children with identical heredity, the monozygotic (single-egg) twins, start out in dif-

monozygotic (MZ) siblings

Dizygotic (DZ) siblings

nature versus nurture

maturationist

interactionist

ferent surroundings during the prenatal period relative to their positioning in the womb and the relationship this may have to their prenatal development (Wolfe, 1977). The twin process of prenatal development may be different due to a variety of factors. For example, they each wait for birth in a different area of the uterus with their umbilical cords attached to different parts of the placenta. They each have their own circulatory system and may receive different amounts of nutrients from their mother. The twin who is born first may have a more difficult time getting out into the world because the birth canal is tighter. The second twin may suffer from a short supply of oxygen while he waits for the first twin. Even identical twins, starting with the same hereditary background from the moment of conception, live in different environments (Figure 5–1). Peter Wolfe concludes:

> From the moment of conception to the moment of birth, heredity and environment contribute to development as inseparable factors. Although the distinction between heredity and environment may be useful for some technical discussions, it is an artificial abstraction that has no direct reference to actual developmental processes. (Wolfe, 1972/1977, p. 15)

A phenomenon referred to as the "vanishing twins" has been identified as a possible cause of some birth defects (Vanishing twins, 1993). One twin dies in the womb and damages the surviving twin. The twin that dies may produce a blood clot, which impedes the development of the survivor. Cases have also been identified in which identical twins have some significant genetic differences; for example, one is a gymnast and the other has muscular dystrophy. It may be that it is the differences in the genetic makeup of groups of cells that causes the egg to split.

Currently there is increased contact and cooperative research between developmental psychologists and **behavioral geneticists** (Plomin, 1983). "Developmental behavioral genetics is the study of genetic [hereditary] and environmental influences on individual differences in behavioral development" (Plomin, 1983, p. 526). Developmental behavioral geneticists

Figure 5–1 **Identical twins have the same heredity, but the environment offers opportunities for them to be different in many ways.**

are concerned with heredity and environment as a two-way interaction and influence. That is, they look for the influence of heredity on environment as well as environment on heredity. They view genes as active, not static. They are particularly interested in individual differences in children and how the environment can accommodate these differences, rather than trying to change the child to fit the environment.

The Colorado Adoption Project (CAP) (Plomin, DeFries, & Fulker, 1988) is a major longitudinal study of 245 adoptive and 245 nonadoptive families. CAP began in 1974. The children have been studied in their homes at 1, 2, 3, and 4 years of age. The biological and adoptive parents of the adopted children and the nonadoptive parents have been studied also to get at the relationships among genetic and environmental factors and development. In studying the adoptive and nonadoptive home environments and parent-child interactions, it was found that the environment was influenced by genetic characteristics of the children relative to toys selected and to the way the parents interacted with the children. Genetic influence was found to be strongest for **intelligence quotient (IQ)** and language development and relative to parental warmth and the child's degree of "easiness."

Several important principles have come out of the CAP studies (Plomin et al., 1988). From the infant studies it was concluded that the origins of individual differences in infancy include heredity and variations in family environment. The relative extent of genetic and environmental influence varies for different characteristics (p. 314). One other principle was added from the results of the early childhood studies: Individual differences among children are substantial and reliable.

> Throughout infancy and early childhood, the range of individual differences is impressive, which calls into question the usefulness of average descriptions of children's development at a particular age. Stanford-Binet IQ scores within the CAP vary from 84 to 139 after the lowest and highest IQ's are eliminated. (p. 314)

Some other ranges included, for example, at age two, some children scored eight times higher on a measure of communicative competence than others. By three, some scored eleven times higher than others. Behavior problem scores ranged from 2 to 60. The authors emphasize that it is imperative to look beyond averages to individual differences when working with young children.

IQ seems to be most influenced by the time an adopted child spends in the adoptive home. That is, correlations between adopted child IQ and adoptive parent IQ became stronger from infancy to early childhood. Temperament, on the other hand, doesn't seem to be affected by a shared environment. The overall conclusions of the CAP study are that genetic factors aren't passively acted upon by the environment, but that the genetic factors affect the environment as much as the environment may influence development of the genetic components of the child.

The study of twins was another of Arnold Gesell's interests (Ames, 1989). In his co-twin control experiments he looked at whether special training in an emerging behavior would put one identical twin ahead of the other. In this case, one identical twin was trained in stair-climbing and cube block building behavior. When the untrained twin was finally given the opportunity to climb stairs, she did better than the trained twin. When the cubes were introduced to the untrained twin, she did just as well as the trained twin. In this case nature was in control—early training provided no advantage in the long term. These studies can provide some food for thought for those who believe in putting academic pressure on young children before they are maturationally ready.

More recent twin studies have also supported the power of heredity. Scarr and McCartney (1983) suggest a model that promotes the idea that heredity exerts more control on behavior and development than was previously thought. They see heredity as the stronger factor in producing individual differences. They suggest that nature and nurture work together directed by genetic factors. Genes direct the child's experience but the environment must provide the experiences necessary for development to occur. Scarr and McCartney support this view with the results found from the study of adopted twins raised in different families. Three factors can be accounted for by their model: (1) identical twins reared apart are more similar than nonidentical twins reared apart; (2) biological siblings are more similar than are adopted siblings in the same family; and (3) identical twins reared in different homes have many unexpected similarities. This point of view suggests that in providing experiences for children we need to consider the personality and the social and intellectual characteristics they bring with them as well as what we as adults feel we should provide. That is, as Plomin suggests, consideration must be given to accommodating the environment to the child rather than always trying to accommodate the child to the environment.

GENETICS

Genetics is the study of the factors involved in the transmission of hereditary characteristics in living organisms. Through genetic studies, scientists are able to predict the passing of a trait from one generation to the next. For example, if a blue-eyed man and a brown-eyed woman marry, a geneticist can predict how many blue-eyed and brown-eyed grandchildren they are likely to have (Wolfe, 1972, 1977). Geneticists can also predict the chance of a couple having a child with certain diseases such as phenylketonuria (PKU—an inability of the system to use protein properly), and hemophilia (a disposition to bleed heavily and easily). Tests can be done before conception to find out if a couple's child might carry negative traits such as these. Tests also can be done after conception to determine the presence of these factors and others. The sex of the child can also be determined. Cole and Cole (1989) give examples of diseases or conditions that can be identified during the prenatal period:

- Down's syndrome (mental and physical retardation occurs)
- Huntington's chorea (during middle age the central nervous system and body deteriorate)
- Klinefelter's syndrome (males do not develop sexual maturity at adolescence)
- Muscular dystrophy (muscles weaken and waste away)
- Phenylketonuria (PKU)—cannot digest protein in the normal way)
- Sickle-cell anemia (red blood cells are abnormal)

The study of genetics dates back to 1886 when Gregor Mendel discovered genes (Young, 1981). The **gene** is the biological unit of heredity. Genes are in specific locations on each chromosome. **Chromosomes** are the major units that control heredity. In each gene genetic information is contained within a substance called **DNA**. A scientist named Kary Mullis (Dwyer, 1993) has devised a method to actually reproduce a gene or DNA fragment. A section of DNA can be forced to copy itself. Many biological laboratories are now applying Mullis's procedure in research designed to better understand genetics.

The set of genes that the individual receives at conception that makes him unique; it is referred to as the **genotype**. The individual's external appearance is referred to as the **phenotype** and is determined by both environmental and genotypical factors. Humans have forty-six chromosomes in twenty-three pairs. All the pairs but one have matched members. This twenty-third pair determines sex: females are X and X and males are X and Y. The transmittal of these genes determines whether the individual will be male or female. Females inherit an X chromosome from both mother and father. Males inherit an X chromosome from their mother and a Y from their father. Some traits such as height, hair and eye color, and fingerprint patterns are determined by several pairs of genes in combination.

Sometimes genes appear in an unusual pattern that creates an abnormality. For example, some girls have been discovered to have an extra X (Rovet & Netley, 1983). These girls have intellectual deficits that probably are genetically determined.

Genetic research is a continuous process and new discoveries are made each year. A technique has been discovered whereby cystic fibrosis, a disease in which the lack of an enzyme causes mucous obstruction in the lungs and digestive system, can now be diagnosed in a human egg before conception. Researchers have hopes of applying this technique to the discovery of other genetic diseases. They believe this type of preconception diagnosis will make abortion unnecessary if the warning is heeded; birth control methods can be used to avoid fertilization of the egg (Egg Diagnosis, August 4, 1990). In another breakthrough, scientists believe they have identified the gene that determines the sex of the child. It is hoped that this breakthrough might open the way to finding new ways to treat infertility and problems of sexual development (Scientists track down sex-determining gene, July 19, 1990).

GENETIC COUNSELING

The profession of genetic counseling emerged to help parents and prospective parents deal with the problems of heredity ("The Genetic Counselor," 1977). The genetic counselor can help parents make major decisions regarding childbearing. Consider

KEYTERMSKEYTERMSKEYTERMSKEYTERMSKEYTERMSKEY		
gene	DNA	phenotype
Chromosomes	genotype	

one couple thinking of having a child. They know that hemophilia is a trait in the wife's family. The genetic counselor can advise them of their chance of having a child with this disease. The couple can then choose whether or not to try to have a child. Assume a woman wants to have prenatal information regarding the possibility of a genetic defect. She can decide to have genetic screening. She can choose from among several methods of getting prenatal information (Berk, 1994). **Amniocentesis** is a frequently used method. At about 16 to 17 weeks into the pregnancy, the amniotic fluid is sampled. The amniotic fluid can reveal the sex of the child and up to seventy possible birth defects. This procedure has become common for pregnant women who are curious about the sex of the child and/or are concerned about possible birth defects. A more recently discovered method is **chorionic villus sampling (CVS)**. Using this method, a fetoscope, guided by ultrasound is inserted through the cervix into the uterus. Cells are cut from the chorionic villi. The chorionic villi are membranous cellular projections that anchor the embryo to the uterus. At about 10 weeks they disappear. The advantage of this procedure is that it can be done earlier than amniocentesis (during the eighth week of pregnancy) when abortion is safer. However, the risk of spontaneous abortion is twice as high (2 percent). A third frequently used method of gaining information prenatally is **ultrasound** or **sonography**. High-frequency sounds that cannot be heard by the human ear are transmitted through the mother's abdomen to the uterus. They are then reflected back from the fetus as echoes that are turned into electrical impulses. These signals display the fetus image on a television monitor. This procedure can confirm the pregnancy, determine multiple pregnancies, detect some abnormalities in development, and assist with diagnostic procedures such as amniocentesis or intrauterine fetal treatment.

"One family in ten has a child born with a *serious, identifiable genetic disease*" ("The Genetic Counselor," 1977, p. M15). If an engaged couple knows or suspects there may be diseases such as he-

Figure 5–2   **The genetic counselor helps the engaged couple search their family histories for any potential hereditary problems that might affect their future children.**

mophilia, cystic fibrosis, sickle-cell anemia, Down's syndrome, fragile X syndrome or Tay-Sachs disease in their family genetic makeup, they can seek genetic counseling before marriage (Figure 5–2). The counselor questions the couple regarding their family history and gives them as many facts as are available about their special concern. The counselor then tries to help them make the best decision concerning whether or not to try to conceive a child. Counselors also help couples who already have a child with a genetic defect to decide whether or not to have another child. Further, they can help the already expectant parents decide whether to go ahead with the pregnancy to full term or abort the already conceived fetus. It is always the parents' decision, however.

Richard Restak (1975) warned that there are dangers in knowing too much about genetics. Decision making in genetics is a very serious matter. At first sight, it might seem wonderful to be able to reduce the number of defective babies born. However, there are some ethical and moral issues involved. In a situation in which conception has occurred, there is the question of abortion. In a situation in which there is early warning before conception, there is a question of whether to proceed with steril-

KEYTERMSKEYTERMSKEYTERMSKEYTERMSKEYTERMSKEYTERMSKEY

Amniocentesis	ultrasound	sonography
chorionic villus sampling (CVS)		

ization to do away with the risk of conceiving a defective child. A decision regarding aborting a fetus, even though a defective child would be produced, or to consider not ever having a child can be very painful. Whatever the decision, it is not an easy one. When seeking genetic counseling, it is important to find the most well-trained and well-qualified counselor available who will explain with care the dangers of knowing too much and the kinds of consequences that may result from certain decisions.

The consumer of genetic testing and genetic counseling needs to beware (*The telltale gene*, 1990). Many obstetricians do not give adequate counseling after performing genetic tests. Many women are not told why they have had the test or what the results mean. Consumers of genetic services need to be encouraged to seek out the answers to their questions.

ENVIRONMENTAL DANGERS

Strong hereditary predispositions are weakened by some of the social and economic hazards that befall the teen parent, both married and unmarried. In this unit we will extend that topic to look further at teen parents, the effects of substance abuse, and the effects of AIDS on the infant.

Teen Parents

A recent headline read that 24 percent of infants are born to unmarried mothers. For African/American infants, the rate is even higher, six out of ten or 60 percent. However, marriage does not ensure a secure economic situation for teens. Married teens have a higher infant mortality rate than unmarried teens. Having left the haven of the household they may have even less support than at home. Most teen parents are in a situation in which they have little, if any, prenatal or postnatal care for themselves and their child.

To provide health care for adolescents, school-based health clinics are increasing in number (Health clinics in schools, 1990). The clinics provide medical care such as needed for colds or other minor ail-

ments, physical examinations, and required immunizations. They may also provide mental health care.

The problem of teen pregnancy is so serious in the Southeast states that the Carnegie Corporation funded the Southern Strategic Planning Group On Adolescent Pregnancy Prevention (Group maps strategy to break teen pregnancy cycle, May 30, 1989). The group generated a number of recommendations:

- Implement better coordination of federal, state, and local programs.
- Provide comprehensive health-care opportunities for children and adolescents, especially those living at or below federal poverty levels.
- Provide more early childhood education programs in a school setting for all four- and five-year-olds. They can begin to develop socialization, communication, decision-making, goal-setting and social-resistance skills.
- Better educate males regarding their roles and responsibilities.
- Create incentives for teens to stay in school.
- Link job training and welfare reform to assist teens.
- Include effective parenting skills in a family-life education curriculum.

Substance Abuse

Another frightening headline read "Babies abandoned by crack cocaine addicts crowding hospitals" (July 2, 1989). Substance-abusing women of all ages are having babies. Many of these babies are being abandoned. Although many of the babies appear healthy, as we learned in Unit 4, they may suffer life-long problems due to the damage from the crack cocaine that entered their systems during their prenatal period. It is not unusual for these infants also to be AIDS carriers. Placing the babies in foster homes provides hope but is a slow process due to the amount of paperwork to be completed.

Attachment, the emotional bond between parent and child, has been the focus of much study. (See Unit 8.) Rodning, Beckwith, and Howard (1989) looked at attachment organization and play organization in pre-natally drug-exposed toddlers. The drug-exposed tod-dlers' performance in attachment and play situations was compared with that of toddlers who were prema-ture at birth. Both groups lived at the poverty level. In both groups the mothers had no or inadequate prena-tal care. The drug-exposed toddlers were found to be developmentally behind in their performance in each play situation and negative in their attachments to their caregivers. The most insecurely attached tod-dlers were the ones living with their biological moth-ers who continued to abuse drugs. The greatest deficits appeared in spontaneous play. The drug-exposed toddlers were less able to play sponta-neously, engage in representative play, and were less organized in their play, had less variety, and did not follow through with a complete activity. While they performed more adequately in adult-structured tasks, they could not organize their own activities at a nor-mal toddler level. Their facial expressions were bland, showing neither pleasure nor distress.

In Oakland, California, the CARE (Chemical Addiction Recovery Efforts) Clinic, part of the Center for the Vulnerable Child at Children's Hospital is attempting to offer services for the drug-exposed infants and their families in order to try to keep the infants with their biological parents (Tittle & Claire, 1989). The clinic offers medical services, parenting education, psychological support groups and individual counseling, and social events. So far this model is working successfully.

AIDS Exposure

With the increase in prenatal AIDS exposure, postnatal or pediatric AIDS (AIDS contracted by children under thirteen) has become a problem of epidemic proportions. Dokecki, Baumeister, and Kupstas (1989) reviewed the various aspects of the situation. The rate of increase has doubled every year since 1982. These children have significant develop-mental delay in cognitive and motor areas. With no cure and no vaccine, prevention needs as much at-tention as we can provide. Teenagers are especially vulnerable and need to be educated regarding steps they can take to avoid AIDS, namely to abstain from sex and avoid sharing drug needles. In addition, they can avoid drugs and alcohol altogether, since these substances lower resistance and cloud decision mak-ing. Of course, this advice applies to adults as well as teens. AIDS can be transmitted at any age.

SUMMARY

At the moment of conception, hereditary factors from the mother and the father merge into a new in-dividual. Both heredity and environment are influ-enced by the process of development. While some characteristics such as eye and hair color are basi-cally set, others may develop along different paths depending on the interaction of heredity and environ-ment as the developmental process occurs. The con-ventional way to study this interaction is through comparing adoptive with nonadoptive families, or comparing twins who live with their natural parents with twins who have been adopted.

Genetics is the study of the transmission of hereditary characteristics to living organisms. Progress in genetic study is increasing the capability to identify genetic predisposition to abnormalities or to disease before or shortly after conception.

Genetic counselors use the information gained from genetic testing to assist couples in making deci-sions regarding attempts to conceive a child or carry a defective child to full term. Even the strongest and most promising hereditary predispositions can be weakened by damaging prenatal and postnatal envi-ronmental factors. These factors can be brought on by a parent who is too young or poorly nourished, has received little or no prenatal care, practices sub-stance abuse, or prenatally acquires a disease such as AIDS.

FOR FURTHER READING

Child Development. (1983). *54* (2), special section on behavioral genetics.

Child Development. (1983). *54* (5), whole issue on biological risk.

Gunnar, M. R., & Thelen, E. (Eds.). (1989). *Systems and development: The Minnesota symposium on child psychology, Vol. 22*. Hillsdale, NJ: Erlbaum.

Larner, M., & Harkavy, O. (1992). *Fair start for children: Lessons learned from seven demonstration projects*. New Haven and London: Yale University Press.

Nightingale, E. O., & Goodman, M. (1990). *Before birth: Prenatal testing for genetic disease*. Cambridge, MA: Harvard University Press.

Plomin, R. (1994). *Genetics and experience*. Thousand Oaks, CA: Sage.

Plomin, R. (1990). *Nature and nurture: An introduction to human behavioral genetics*. Pacific Grove, CA: Brooks/Cole.

Plomin, R., Emde, R. N., Braungart, J. M., Campos, J., Corley, R., Fulker, D. W., Kagan, J., Reznick, J. S., Robinson, J., Zahn-Waxler, C., & DeFries, J. C. (1993). Genetic change and continuity from fourteen to twenty months: The MacArthur Longitudinal Twin Study. *Child Development, 64* (5), 1354–1376.

Plomin, R., & McClearn, G. E. (Eds.). (1994). *Nature, nurture, and psychology*. Hyattsville, MD: American Psychological Association.

Riese, M. L. (1990). Neonatal temperament in monozygotic and dizygotic twin pairs. *Child Development, 61*, 1230–1237.

Rosenblith, J. F. (1992). *In the beginning: Development from conception to age two*, (2nd Ed.). Thousand Oaks, CA: Sage.

SUGGESTED ACTIVITIES

1. Interview a genetic counselor. Find out whether more couples visit prior to marriage, after marriage but before conceiving, or after conception. Ask if many single women seek advice. Under what circumstances does the counselor feel abortion is warranted? Share the results with the class.

2. Find a research study in one of the areas of potential prenatal danger such as nutrition, maternal characteristics, maternal experiences, drugs, or disease, or a research study that describes research on twins as compared with nontwins. Write a report including:
   a. title
   b. author(s)
   c. journal, date, pages
   d. a short summary
   e. an evaluation of the study and its implications.
   f. a discussion of whether the study supports what is stated in the text
   g. a discussion of what you learned that helps you understand the area better

3. With another classmate, prepare a debate: "Heredity or Environment—Which Has More Influence on Development?" Each person takes one side. Each prepares a 5-minute speech in support of one side. Then attack each other's arguments. Have the class vote for a winner of the debate.

4. Make an entry in your journal.

REVIEW

A. Explain what is meant by the following: The adult who works with young children must be aware of each child's prior medical history.

B. Indicate which of the following characteristics is determined more strongly by heredity than environment, if the environment is a healthy one.
1. physical size
2. eye color
3. hair color
4. disposition (happy or cranky)
5. skin color

C. Explain how heredity and environment might relate to the developmental process for the children in the following situations.
1. Jenny and Joanie are identical twins. Jenny is delivered first. Jenny is always referred to as "the older girl." At age three, Joanie is much more active and difficult to control than Jenny. Joanie is also more babyish and less independent than Jenny.
2. Brad's father is a professional football player; his mother, a dancer. Both parents are very concerned about good nutrition and getting plenty of physical activity.
3. Mary's mother and father are both average in size and build. They are struggling to make ends meet and have little money for nutritious foods such as fresh fruits and vegetables and whole grain breads and cereals. They also tend to waste much of their meager food budget on junk foods such as candy and potato chips.
4. Donnie's mother was a drug and alcohol abuser before and during her pregnancy. She shared drug needles with numerous friends.

D. Define the terms *gene, chromosome,* and *DNA*. Explain how they are related.

E. Write the number of each case that requires a genetic counselor.
1. A pregnant woman is over 40 years of age.
2. An engaged man has an uncle who had cystic fibrosis.
3. A newborn is found to be deaf.
4. A couple is curious as to whether their future children are more likely to have green eyes and red hair like the father or brown eyes and black hair like the mother.
5. A child is born with underdeveloped legs.

Unit 6

The First Two Weeks of Life

OBJECTIVES

After studying this unit, the student should be able to:

■ State the environmental changes that take place at birth for the newborn.

■ Recognize the attributes of the Leboyer method of delivery and state its advantages.

■ Identify the important aspects of the neonatal period.

■ Describe how to assist the parents of premature infants to overcome the initial difficulties of parenting and provide needed developmentally supportive interactions.

■ Discuss the responsibilities to the neonate and the neonate's parents of the adult who works with the young child.

Carol and Frank are very excited about the birth of their first child (Spezzano & Waterman, 1977). Frank is with Carol during labor and delivery. Carol has minimal medication. She and Frank have taken a parent preparation course in which Carol learned deep breathing exercises for relaxation. Their baby, Roger, weighs seven pounds and is healthy.

As soon as he saw his son, Frank began to laugh and cry and hug Carol vigorously. She could not get her hands on the baby fast enough. When he was given to her, Carol put Roger against her body in such a way that she could look in his eyes. Then she began cooing and talking to him. [Frank has] feelings of awe and protectiveness. (Spezzano & Waterman, 1977, p. 116)

Thus, a life begins and parents and child form their first bond.

The parents have already developed expectations regarding their baby. The mother's competence as a caregiver is confirmed each time the baby responds to her. For example, the baby responds with cuddling when held or turns his or her head at the sound of the mother's voice (Brazelton & Cramer, 1990). These positive responses from the infant tell mother that she is "doing the right thing" (Brazelton & Cramer, 1990, p. 46).

52

The first 2 weeks of life are exciting and critical for the developing child having entered the world through the process of birth. Once born, this tiny person is referred to as a **newborn**. For the first 2 weeks, the term **neonate** is used; the 2-week period is called the **neonatal period**. During these first 2 weeks, neonates must be watched closely to be sure they have a good start in life.

BIRTH

Does the child have a pleasant experience entering the world? If not, how can it be improved? First, consider the great change that takes place from prenatal to postnatal life. The child's environment changes from the uterus and its surrounding amniotic fluid to air. The temperature changes from a relatively constant one to one that changes often. This small being moves from a state of minimal stimulation to one in which all the senses are stimulated. For nutrition, there is a change from a dependence on nutrients from mother's blood to a dependence on food from outside and on the functioning of the neonate's own digestive system. Oxygen no longer passes from mother's blood through the placenta to the unborn. The neonate's lungs must now operate and send oxygen to the blood. Waste materials no longer pass into the mother's bloodstream through the placenta; the neonate's own elimination system must take on this job. The neonate's own skin, kidneys, lungs, and intestinal system must start to work. Without doubt, the change from prenatal to postnatal life is a big one. The question that must be dealt with is how to make the process of birth and the move into postnatal life as comfortable as possible for the child and the parents (Figure 6–1).

Not every birth scene has been as warm and exciting as Roger's birth. In the past there was criticism that certain common methods of delivery and postde-

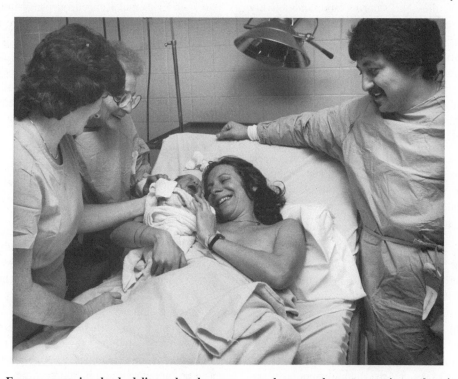

Figure 6–1   For everyone involved, delivery has become a much more pleasant experience than it used to be. (Courtesy of Mimi Cotter/International Stock Photography)

KEYTERMSKEYTERMSKEYTERMSKEYTERMSKEYTERMSKEY

| newborn | neonate | neonatal period |

livery treatment were much too hard on both child and parents (Newton, 1975). Negative factors included separating the mother from her family during labor and childbirth, confining the normal laboring woman to bed, stimulating labor with chemicals, routine use of forceps for delivery, and separating the mother from her newborn infant. Others include delaying the first breast feeding, restricting infants to 4-hour feeding schedules and withholding night feedings, and limiting visits by the baby's sisters and brothers. Unfortunately, many of these unsafe practices are still used according to the results of a large-scale worldwide study done by Dr. Murray Enkin and his colleagues in a pregnancy project located at Oxford University in England (Ubell, 1993). For example, many obstetricians still don't provide pregnant women with needed social and psychological support. In many hospitals infants are still separated from their mothers immediately following delivery. Mothers are forced to lie on their backs during labor and delivery when standing or lying on their sides may be more comfortable. Forceps are used with difficult deliveries when a suction cup method is easier and safer, and more Cesarian deliveries are made than are necessary.

We have seen the picture of mother, father, and doctor smiling happily as they view the newborn baby. Leboyer (1976, pp. 10–12) describes this scene:

> A small creature has just been born. The father and mother gaze at it with delight. The young practitioner shares their joy. One dazzling smile lights up all their faces. They radiate happiness. All of them, that is, except the child.

Leboyer (1976, p. 12) describes the child's expression as "The mask of agony, of horror." He feels the infant is upset by the birth lights, the noise, and the rough handling he receives just after emerging from the womb. Leboyer devised a method of delivery in which participants try to make the change from the womb to the outside world as relaxed and happy and with as little environmental change as possible. The lights are dim, the baby is placed on the mother's stomach so he is in contact with her body and the rhythm of her heartbeat. The umbilical cord remains attached until the baby has

had some time to get used to his new surroundings. The child is gently massaged to soothe and calm him.

Although the pure Leboyer method has not become popular in the United States, Leboyer's ideas have prompted medical personnel to modify the atmosphere of the delivery environment. In the seventies home birth became popular. However, the dangers of delivering with no medical monitoring were perceived to both outweigh the advantages of women having more control over the birth process and the lower cost. As an alternative that offered a homelike atmosphere with medical safeguards, birthing centers opened around the country. Birthing center deliveries have become quite popular (Jones, 1990). At the birthing center, the doctor coaches the mother through the birthing process. The father bathes his wife and his newborn baby. Two hours after the delivery, the family goes home. Birthing centers have become so popular that even hospitals are now including birthing centers as an option for parents. The work of Klaus and Kennell on parent-infant bonding has also influenced the trend toward increased humanization of infant delivery methods and the improvement of the delivery room atmosphere (Goldberg, 1983).

There are also a number of other options in delivery that are available to expectant mothers (Yarro, 1977). Cesarian section has been used for potentially difficult births. The baby is removed from the uterus surgically. Lamaze preparation for childbirth is very popular. The parents take a 6-week course that introduces them to the details of labor and delivery. The mother learns how to control and relax her muscles and what kind of physical exercise is appropriate. The father learns how to assist her during labor and delivery. There has been a movement toward natural childbirth, which is birth without the aid of drugs for pain reduction. Many hospitals allow brothers and sisters to visit the mother in her room and view their new brother or sister in the hospital nursery. Rooms are being set up in some hospitals where the whole family can participate in the delivery. Some doctors even train fathers to deliver their own children with supervision (Steinman, 1979). More hospitals are also providing rooming in, a procedure whereby baby stays in the same room with mother.

KEYTERMSKEYTERMSKEYTERMSKEYTERMSKEYTERMSKEY

Cesarian section   **natural childbirth**

THE NEONATE

As already described, the newborn goes through many changes in environment and bodily functions within a very short time. Once born, the child must be watched carefully, especially during the first 5 minutes. It is essential that the newborn's vital signs be monitored. The usual means for monitoring the vital signs is by use of the **Apgar Scale** (Apgar & Beck, 1973; Apgar, 1953). With this scale, the obstetric team checks to be sure the infant is ready for life outside the uterus. Heart rate, respiratory effort, muscle tone, color, and reflexes are checked at 1 minute and at 5 minutes after delivery (Figure 6–2). A score of four or less out of a possible ten indicates the newborn needs immediate help. Most infants have scores of seven or above.

There are several factors concerning the newborn's emotional state that are of importance during the first 2 weeks. These factors are bonding, responsiveness and sensitivity, and temperament. **Bonding** is the process whereby parents and child determine they are special to each other. When the concept of bonding was first introduced by Klaus and Kennell in the seventies, it was thought there was a critical period immediately after birth during which bonding had to take place. For example, Carol, Frank, and Roger as described in the beginning of this chapter would be forming such a bond. It was felt the initial shared glance formed the basis of the bond (Spezzano & Waterman, 1977). More recently, this point of view has been modified (Goldberg, 1983; Palkovitz, 1985).

From her 1983 research review, Goldberg concluded that the popularization of Klaus and Kennell's findings (1982) had both positive and negative effects on the beliefs of both medical personnel and the public. On the positive side delivery became much more humane especially with fathers being encouraged to participate. The evidence suggests there are many positive effects on the family from having the father present during delivery and providing for early parent-child contacts. However, if for some reason (such as Cesarian delivery or a

Sign	Apgar Score		
	0	1	2
Pulse (heart rate)	Absent	Slow (less than 100)	Rapid (over 100)
Appearance (skin color)	Body is blue	Body pink, arms and legs blue	Entirely pink
Activity (muscle tone)	Flaccid, limp, motionless	Some movement of arms and legs but weak and inactive	Strong, active overall body motions
Reflexes (Grimace when slapped on the feet)	No response	Grimace or slight cry	Vigorous crying
Respiration (breathing)	Absent (no respiration)	Slow, irregular breathing	Effort to breathe is strong with vigorous crying

Figure 6–2   The Apgar Scale is used to check the readiness of the newborn to join the world. Each vital sign is rated from zero to two with the highest possible total score being ten.

KEYTERMSKEYTERMSKEYTERMSKEYTERMSKEYTERMSKEYTERMSKEY

Apgar Scale   Bonding

premature birth) this contact is not immediately possible, it will not mean there is irreparable damage to the parent-child relationship. Parents have been made to feel unnecessarily guilty and upset over missing an immediate contact experience. Klaus and Kennell changed their definition of the term *bonding* to refer to the long-term development of relationships rather than to just the immediate postdelivery relationship (Goldberg, 1983). Unfortunately, the term *bonding*, defined as the development of an immediate postdelivery connection between mother and child continued in the popular press (Wheeler, 1993). Dr. Diane Eyer, who has written a book on the scientific fictional nature of bonding, suggests the term has been so extended into a description of any close relationship that it should be done away with as a term in developmental psychology (as cited in Wheeler, 1993).

Premature Infants

At one time it was believed that the child born prior to the completion of the 40-week gestation period, the **premature infant**, would develop according to the fixed laws of development even though out of the uterine environment. Gesell (Ames, 1990) believed you could arrive at the child's accurate developmental age by subtracting the period of prematurity from chronological age. Today most medical experts believe the child needs the full 40 weeks in the womb and that being born too soon is associated with some high-risk factors. Duffy, Als, and McAnulty (1990) compared healthy preterm and full-term infants at 42 weeks postconception. They found some significant differences between the two groups in several developmental areas. The preterm (premature) infants showed more stress in making the transition from sleep to wakeful behavior. They also evidenced some motor and neurological difficulties. Some of the differences may be due to medical complications that usually accompany premature delivery while others may be due to the early change of environment. Fortunately, we continue to learn more

about helping premature infants to develop to the fullest extent possible.

Preterm neonates who received tactile stimulation while in the neonatal intensive care unit have benefitted significantly (Kilgo, Holder-Brown, Johnson, & Cook, 1988). The tactile stimulation consisted of both stroking and motor movement exercises. Touch is an extremely powerful stimulant (Ackerman, 1990). Besides massaging, doctors have discovered that putting premature infants on small, gently swaying waterbeds makes them less irritable, enables them to sleep better, and makes them more alert and responsive.

Researchers at Stanford University found that educational, medical, and family support for premature infants not only improves general development, but also increases IQ scores and decreases the frequency of behavior problems when premature infants who have had all these services are compared with premature infants who have had medical attention only (Preemie's IQ, 1990). The support children were enrolled in a center-based developmental preschool program from age one to age three. Twice each month parents attended meetings in which child-rearing information and social support were provided. The researchers predict these children will be much less likely than the comparison group of premature infants to have learning difficulties and special education placement during their elementary school years.

A new form of drug assistance for very premature infants born between the twenty-fourth and thirty-second weeks of gestation has shown impressive results (Kantrowitz with Crandall, 1990). **Exosurf®** is a drug that helps babies form surfactant, a substance usually produced in the lungs by the time the fetus is 32 weeks into gestation. This substance coats the inner lining of the lungs and keeps the airspaces from collapsing. Surfactant is necessary for the baby to breathe. Premature infants frequently are born before enough surfactant has developed with the result that they have serious and sometimes fatal breathing problems. Therefore,

KEYTERMSKEYTERMSKEYTERMSKEYTERMSKEYTERMSKEY

premature infant   Exosurf®

Exosurf is a boon to infants born with lack of surfactant in the lungs.

Support for the parents of premature infants is essential. Brazelton and Cramer (1990) describe the feelings of the parents of a premature daughter. Clarissa was delivered at 27 weeks gestation. She was severely distressed. At one minute her Apgar score was 5 and at five minutes it was 7. She had severe medical complications that required surgery and antibiotics. The parents visited her regularly during her time in neonatal intensive care. They were a part of Clarissa's therapy and were involved when the **Neonatal Behavior Assessment Scale (NBAS)** was administered. (See page 59 for a description of the NBAS.) By having a close-working relationship with the medical team, they were better able to handle Clarissa's developmental problems. In addition, they were able to recognize her behavioral progress and the significance of the smallest developmental increments. They also learned to accept Clarissa as a challenge and to accept her fussiness and moodiness as normal premature behavior. They could then view her as a challenge rather than a burden. Because premature infants tend to be fussy, irritable, more exhausting and less fun for their parents than full-term babies, they may not get the tactile and social stimulation they so desperately need. On the other hand, babies who are premature or otherwise stressed during the delivery may be oversensitive to every stimulus in the environment and can be calmed by being placed in a low-stimulation setting (Brazelton, 1992).

A support group for parents can be essential to family stability. An example of such a group is affiliated with Woman's Hospital in Baton Rouge, Louisiana. Parents of any infant who spends time in a neonatal intensive care unit may join. The organization is called Neonatal Intensive Care Unit (NICU) Parents. Meetings focus on both child-rearing and family problems. A newsletter establishes communication providing many kinds of information such as requests for donations for a premature infants clothing exchange, community services available for parents and children, and what to look for in child care.

Infant Sensitivity

Infant sensitivity and responsiveness should not be underestimated. Infants are not, as some once thought, "lumps of clay to be molded by their environment—for better or for worse" (Brazelton, 1976). Babies are powerful influences on their environments. Adults who understand this quality in the infant can use it to advantage in developing a relationship. The neonate has many built-in strengths. At birth, the infant responds to voices, looks at human faces, shows a preference for milk smells, and distinguishes the taste of breast milk from cow's milk. Newborns are very sensitive to their environment. Parents can be shown how sensitive and responsive their newborn is, thereby viewing the child as a person to whom they can relate. This knowledge ties them more closely to their young child. Parents can learn to note and react to responses, as shown in the following examples.

> Mother shakes a rattle softly by neonate's ear. Neonate jerks as if startled and turns his head toward the sound.
>
> Dad uncovers neonate. Neonate responds by moving arms and legs about.
>
> As mother undresses neonate, she notes that he responds with resistance to the restriction of his body.
>
> When held in the arms in a cradle or shoulder position, neonate responds by cuddling.
>
> Dad enjoys playing games with neonate. Dad likes to call to him from out of his line of vision and see how he responds by turning toward his father's voice.

Thus, a reciprocal exchange is well under way within the first 2 weeks of life.

The adult's interpretation of the newborn's cries may be very critical in determining several aspects of the adult/child relationship. Zeskind and Marshall (1988) found that mothers are sensitive to the pitch of the cries of newborn infants. Mothers rated infant cries on a seven point scale: urgent/not urgent, distressing/not distressing, arousing/soothing, and sick/healthy. All

KEYTERMSKEYTERMSKEYTERMSKEYTERMSKEYTERMSKEY

Neonatal Behavior Assessment Scale
  (NBAS)

the cries were responses to the same pain-causing stimulus. The only differences were in the intensity of each infant's response. The variability of the individual cry seemed to be the best indicator of its seriousness. Infants with more variability in their cries may receive more attention. They may also receive more positive attention and stimulation if the cry is low pitched. More negative attention might be received if the parent finds the cry irritating and stressful. An irritating cry would also have a better chance of being ignored and thus deprive the baby of essential stimulation.

A growing body of neonate research is documenting just how sensitive neonates are to the world around them. Brazelton and Cramer (1990) describe the five senses as they function in the newborn child. Newborns are definitely capable of being visually alert. When babies are picked up and rocked, their eyes open and they look ready for interaction. The ability to see in the delivery room may be an important factor in the bonding process. The eye-to-eye contact with the newborn reinforces attachment. Even newborns are fascinated by the human face and show a preference for a real face versus a drawn face. Newborns try to keep interesting objects in view and display tracking behavior when the objects move.

The capability of newborns to hear is also apparent at birth. They show a preference for female voices. They find auditory stimuli interesting and will look alert and turn toward a soft rattle or human voice. Right after birth infants will synchronize their movements to their mothers' voices. Newborns are attracted to sweet smells such as milk or sugar solutions and turn away from unpleasant odors such as vinegar and alcohol. They even seem to be able to distinguish the odor of their own mother's milk from other mother's milk and from formula. Babies will resist salt water, whereas they will suck faster for sugar water. As already mentioned newborns are sensitive to touch. This is an important means of communication between infant and caregiver. Slow patting is soothing whereas fast patting is alerting for the baby. Before birth the infant establishes hand-to-mouth sensitivity. Contact between hand and mouth

seems to serve the purposes of self-comfort, control over motor activity, and self-stimulation. The senses are all at work for the newborn.

Infant Temperament

The quality of the relationship between the adult and infant is influenced by the child's **temperament**. Children are born with distinctive personal characteristics that seem to stay with them as they grow (Flaste, 1976). Some children are "difficult"; some are "easy." Some are active and some are passive. Neonatal activity level is positively related to activity level at later ages (Korner et al., 1985). That is, when observed during normal activity between the ages of four and eight, children who were the most active as neonates tend to still be the most active. Whether this is due to biological factors (heredity) or environmental factors (such as parent expectation) is still open to question.

The child who is a quiet, slow reactor may not get as many positive responses from adults as the child who is outgoing and quick. The "difficult" infant is more likely to grow up with emotional problems because he elicits negative responses from others. Adults need to recognize that each child is born with different characteristics and should be treated as an individual, as shown in the following examples.

Katie is a laughing, easygoing baby. She is alert and very responsive to adults. She gets a lot of adult attention. Her mother can hardly stand to stay away from her when she's awake.

Mary is quiet and docile. Adults have to work hard at relating to her. Her mother takes advantage of her passiveness and spends little time in play activities with her.

Gary is active and alert. At one week his eyes dart about and his limbs always seem to be moving. His quiet, shy mother is already overwhelmed by his energy: "I can hardly change his diaper, he's so wiggly."

One mother interacts with her child, another ignores her, and the third tries, but is frustrated.

KEYTERMSKEYTERMSKEYTERMSKEYTERMSKEYTERMSKEY

temperament

Figure 6–3   Early attachment forms the basis for a healthy, enjoyable relationship between parent and child.

Neonates are complex individuals. They are born with their own personality characteristics. They are sensitive to their environment and ready to interact and form a bond with the adults they meet. The adult's responsibility is to get to know the newborn and be ready for the give and take of a close, rewarding relationship (Figure 6–3). With some adult/child pairs, attachment is immediate. For others, love grows more slowly.

Neonatal Assessment

Assessment of the newborn's behavior can serve to help caregivers understand the baby and can assist in assessing any damage due to prenatal environmental problems such as discussed in Unit 4. It has already been noted that premature birth is related to developmental difficulties. Low Apgar scores may also indicate future problems. Brazelton and Cramer (1990) believe that a thorough behavioral assessment is most useful for predicting future development. For this purpose Brazelton and his colleagues designed the Neonatal Behavioral Assessment Scale (NBAS).

The NBAS is designed as a dynamic assessment of interactive behavior. The assessment incorporates the same types of stimuli parents use such as touch, rocking, voice, facial movement, bright colors, bright light, and temperature change. The NBAS responses indicate the degree of control the newborn has over his sensory capacities. It is very useful for helping

parents understand their baby and for identifying infants whose behavior may be difficult for parents to handle. Through understanding the difficulties their infant is having, parents can be helped not to feel discouraged and frustrated when the baby does not react as expected. Hypersensitive and disorganized babies are hard to understand and to cope with. They overreact to stimuli and change quickly from sleep to crying and back to sleep without affording the parents time for fun and play.

PROFESSIONAL RESPONSIBILITIES: THE NEONATE AND THE PARENT

Some parents need help in learning how to relate to their new baby. The adult who works with young children has the responsibility of helping parents learn about child development and how to apply this knowledge to interact with and understand their child from birth. The adult who works with young children also has the responsibility of helping parents and children get other professional help if needed. When a child is expected, you can help parents who need it get training in how to relate to children from birth. Parents need to understand the neonate is a complex, active person who can benefit from active involvement with people and the environment.

In his presidential address to the Society for Research in Child Development in April 1989, T. Berry Brazelton (1990) emphasized our increasing problems with damaged infants. In Boston 25 percent of the newborns were addictive at birth. With their damaged nervous systems they did not respond positively to caregiver overtures. Caregivers must understand that damaged infants may be difficult to work with and demand a great deal of patience. Brazelton's goal is to develop both a preventative and an intervention model for attacking this problem.

Federal legislation (discussed in Unit 35) mandates that each state develop a plan for providing continuous services for at-risk infants and toddlers and their families from birth through school age. However, a problem has arisen as to which agencies are obliged to deliver which particular services at each level. For example, Cardinal and Shum (1993) surveyed the neonatal intensive care units (NICU) in California to discover the types of services being provided to high-risk infants. They found there was good support while the infant was in the NICU, some support for the transition from NICU to home, and very little support and follow-up after the infant was home. Surveying the research on the effectiveness of existing NICU interventions, O'Brien and Dale (1994) found very few studies had been done. The few available studies indicated that the programs focused on the infants with little, or no, support to the families.

Cynthia T. Garcia Coll (1990) points out that minority infants from lower socioeconomic levels are especially at risk. They are more likely to have the disadvantages associated with being economically deprived, having younger mothers, living in single-parent households, and lacking adequate prenatal care. On the other hand, they may have the advantages of greater extended family support networks. These infants are more likely to be premature, low birth weight, and vulnerable to poor health status. Overall a larger percentage of minority newborns born into socioeconomically deprived families fall in the high-risk category. On the other hand, there are cultural differences in infants' responses to these dangers to development. Coll suggests the importance of discovering culturally sensitive intervention and prevention strategies. That is, strategies should be compatible with the customs and values of the culture.

SUMMARY

The first 2 weeks are an important period in a child's life. Birth is a time of extreme environmental change for the child. In recent years, efforts have been made to make this a less traumatic event than it was in the past. Fathers are more involved in the process of birth, and both parents are allowed more contact with the infant immediately following birth. Neonatal research has demonstrated that even during the first 2 weeks the baby is alert, aware, and sensitive to the environment. Providing a stimulating, warm environment can enhance the development of the child from the time he first enters the outside world.

Premature neonates are at high risk relative to several factors. There may be some risky medical procedures involved in the delivery that will affect their future development, and they have missed some of the developmental milestones that take place during the normal gestation period. A high percentage of them are the offspring of teenagers from low socioeconomic levels. Further, premature infants tend to be irritable and difficult to parent, leaving them open to more negative attention and more likely to be ignored so they do not receive the positive stimulation from others that all infants require to thrive. More family support is needed to assist parents through the difficulties they may encounter in caring for a premature infant.

FOR FURTHER READING

Berman, P. & Pedersen, F. A. (Eds.). (1987). *Men's transition to parenthood: Longitudinal studies of early family experience*. Hillsdale, NJ: Erlbaum.

Blass, E. M., & Ciaramitaro, V. (1994). A new look at some old mechanisms in human newborns. *Monograph of the Society for Research in Child Development, 59* (1, Serial No. 239).

Brazelton, T. B. (1992). *Touchpoints*. Reading, MA: Addison-Wesley.

Ensher, G. L. & Clark, D. A. (1986). *Newborns at risk: Medical care and psychoeducational intervention*. Rockville, MD: Aspen.

Karen, R. (1994). *Becoming attached*. New York: Warner Books.

Klaus, M. H. & Kennell, J. (1982). *Parent-infant bonding* (2nd Ed.). Saint Louis, MO: Mosby.

Klaus, M. H. & Robertson, M. O. (Eds.). (1982). *Birth, interaction and attachment*. Piscataway, NJ: Johnson and Johnson Child Development.

Larner, H., Halpern, R., & Harkavy, O. (1992). *Fair start for children: Lessons learned from seven demonstration projects.* New Haven & London: Yale University Press.

Rosenblith, J. F. (1992). *In the beginning: Development from conception to age two*, (2nd Ed.). Thousand Oaks, CA: Sage.

Weiss, M. J. & Zelazo, P. R. (Eds.). (1990). *Newborn attention.* Norwood, NJ: Ablex.

Widerstrom, A. H., Mowder, B. A., & Sandall, S. (1991). *At-risk and handicapped newborns and infants: Development, assessment, and intervention.* Des Moines, IA: Longwood Division of Allyn & Bacon.

Wilson, A. L., & Neidich, G. (1991). Infant mortality and public policy. *SRCD Social Policy Report, V* (2).

SUGGESTED ACTIVITIES

1. Develop a set of interview questions focusing on the various methods of infant delivery. Interview any two of the following regarding their opinions on delivery environment and procedures: a) an obstetrician; b) an obstetric nurse; c) a pediatrician; d) a pediatric nurse; e) an M.D. who has a family practice; f) a nurse practitioner; g) a midwife. Evaluate the responses relevant to text and class discussion.

2. Visit a hospital maternity ward. Locate the visitors' viewing window for the infant nursery. Observe a newborn who is less than 4 hours old. Observe another newborn who is 2 days old. Note the following as you observe each newborn.
   a. Each newborn's appearance
   b. Each newborn's movements
   c. Compare the appearance and movements of the two infants. What differences do you observe?
   d. Body proportions: compare with adult proportions
   e. Does either seem to respond to light, sound, or touch?

3. Interview six expectant mothers and fathers. Find out what kinds of plans they have for delivery.
   a. Are they taking a childbirth preparation class? If so, what are they learning? How do they feel about the class?
   b. What type of delivery is planned?
   c. What role does each see for himself and herself during the first 2 weeks?
   d. How sensitive do they think their newborn will be to sights, sounds, smells, taste, and touch?
   e. Compare and contrast their answers.

4. Interview the married mother of a neonate. Ask questions such as the following:
   a. How did you and your husband feel when you found out you were pregnant?
   b. How did your life change?
   c. When did you first start regular prenatal care? How often did you see your doctor?
   d. How did the first 3 months go? Were there any problems?
   e. How were the second 3 months? When did you first feel the baby kick?
   f. How were the last 3 months?
   g. Was your husband there? What did he say and do? When you first saw the baby, how did you feel? What did the baby look like?
   h. What decision did you make regarding the place of birth? If not in a hospital, describe the setting.
   i. How was your stay in the hospital? What was it like?
   j. Did the baby adjust easily to feeding? How active was he?
   k. Since you came home, have you gotten settled into a schedule?
   l. How have you and your husband had to change your lives?
   m. How do you feel?
   n. What role does your husband take in infant care?

Write an evaluation and summary of your interview.

5. Interview a single teen mother of a neonate using the questions from Activity 4 above with the following modifications. For items a, l, and n use these substitute questions:
   a. How did you and the baby's father feel when you found out you were pregnant?
   l. How have you and the baby's father had to change your lives?
   n. What role/responsibilities does the baby's father take in infant care and support?

6. Make an entry in your journal.

REVIEW

A. Complete each statement with the environmental change that takes place at birth.
   1. The environment changes from amniotic fluid to _____ .
   2. _____ goes from being constant to changing.
   3. There is a change from minimal stimulation to one in which all the _____ are stimulated.
   4. Nutrition changes from dependence on _____ to _____ and _____ .
   5. Oxygen no longer comes from _____ but must be processed by the neonate's _____ .
   6. Elimination is no longer through the placenta to the mother's bloodstream, but the baby's _____ must start work.

B. Write the number of each statement that describes the Leboyer method of delivery and treatment of the newborn.
   1. Forceps are used for delivery.
   2. The lights are dim.
   3. The baby is placed on the mother's stomach.
   4. The baby is taken away after the mother has a quick look.
   5. The infant is gently massaged.
   6. The lights are bright so everyone can see.

C. Give your opinion of conventional hospital delivery versus home and birthing center delivery.

D. Match the definitions and descriptions in Column I with the items in Column II.

Column I	**Column II**
1. Parent and newborn gaze into each other's eyes—each begins to learn the other is special.	a. NBAS
2. At birth, some babies are happy and calm; others cranky and overactive.	b. bonding
3. The first 2 weeks of life.	c. premature infant
4. Used to check on the newborn's readiness to enter the world.	d. neonatal period
5. Newborn responds to voices, faces, tastes, and smells.	e. Apgar Scale
6. A scale used to obtain a dynamic assessment of newborn interactive behavior.	f. surfactant
7. A substance that coats the inner lining of the lung and keeps the air spaces from collapsing.	g. newborn sensitivity
8. An infant born before the completion of the full gestation period.	h. infant temperament

E. A preschool teacher finds out Tony's mother is expecting another child. Tony and his mother have a cold, strained relationship. The teacher is afraid the mother will have a poor relationship with the next child. What could she do?

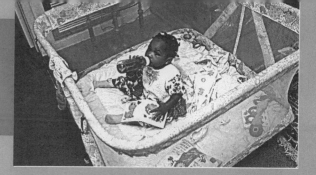

Infancy: Theoretical Views and General Characteristics

OBJECTIVES

After studying this unit, the student should be able to:

- Recognize the theories of Erikson, Freud, Piaget, Vygotsky, Skinner, Sears, Bandura, Rogers, and Maslow and the point of view of Gesell regarding infants.

- Cite examples of infant sensory competence.

- Discuss why the sensory competencies of some infants may not be as well developed as those of others.

Kate is a baby.

1. She can smile.
2. She can frown.
3. She can see.
4. She can cry.
5. She can touch.
6. She can clap.

A first-grade child wrote this description when Kate, age five months, visited her class. Even a six-year-old can see that a five-month-old is active and alert. While the description was accurate in showing that Kate had many abilities, Kate was also totally dependent on the people in her environment to fulfill all her needs. Mother, father, brother, sister, and any other people who care for her are of great importance (Figure 7–1). What happens to her during infancy

will be reflected in her behavior as a preschooler, and even as an adult.

THE THEORISTS LOOK AT THE INFANT

Each of the theorists who were introduced in Unit 1 has his own view of the infant. The views of Erikson, Freud, Sears, Bandura, Maslow, Rogers, Piaget, Vygotsky, and Gesell vary; each looks at the infant in a different way.

For Erik Erikson, the child passes through various crisis stages while developing (Maier, 1978). The crisis to be resolved during infancy is one between basic **trust** and mistrust. The child must develop trust and with this, the basic feeling of hope that keeps human beings going in spite of the many disappointments they may meet in life. Trust develops through

KEYTERMSKEYTERMSKEYTERMSKEYTERMSKEYTERMSKEYTERMSKEY

trust

Figure 7–1 **Infants are fascinated with other children as well as adults.**

the relationship with the mother during the feeding experience and other activities in which the mother meets the infant's basic needs. Infants learn that they can trust mother to satisfy their most basic needs. This trust of mother can then transfer to the infant's world and society as a whole. Warmth and love, along with the necessary food, result in healthy affective development for the infant. If trust does not develop, the child will become fearful, suspicious, and mistrustful.

Freud's basic belief was that early experience had specific effects on later behavior (Mead, 1976). During infancy, the mouth and its functions are very important. Both nutritive and nonnutritive sucking experiences affect the shaping of the child's personality. Also critical during this period are close relationships with other human beings. While cuddled in a caregiver's arms, a child is fed and develops feelings of love, warmth, and dependence. Freud felt that if these experiences were not positive the child can become anxious and develop a dependent, passive, helpless personality. Freud brought to child rearing the idea that infants and young children should live a pleasant, nonfrustrating life in order to grow up mentally healthy (Lomax, 1978).

Robert R. Sears and his colleagues (Sears, Maccoby, & Levin, 1957) were interested in the methods of infant care that mothers choose and the effect of the methods on their children's behavior. The infant is seen starting out with a few inborn patterns of motion such as sucking and swallowing and arm

and leg movements. Infants need these to survive, but they must soon learn new motions. They learn these things through child-rearing experiences. Sears also saw the feeding experience as the center for learning for the infant. The infant learns to need other things, such as affection in the form of hugs, kisses, and smiles, which the infant discovers are a part of receiving food. Sears also viewed the mother/child relationship as central to infant learning.

Remember that Bandura's social cognitive theory is not a stage-governed or developmental theory but suggests how at any age children abstract and integrate what they find out through their social experiences (Perry, 1989). Bandura's theory does recognize that with age the environmental influences change and the child's skills in dealing with the environment change. As the infant encounters his first social experiences, he begins to build mental pictures based on these experiences. Vicarious or observational experiences would be especially important for the infant. Imitation begins in the neonatal period. For example, Meltzoff and Moore (1983) found that neonates can imitate adult facial expressions. Infants learn the rules of behavior through observing the responses and behaviors of others. An infant learns quickly that crying can bring relief for his physical discomfort. He observes that he can control others through his actions and thus begins to build a view of himself as a competent individual. Social cognitive theory does not view the child as a passive receiver of knowledge but as having an active role in constructing knowledge as he figures out what his impressions from the environment mean (Perry, 1989).

Rogers and Maslow (Mead, 1976) emphasize the importance of parents accepting themselves and others. The parents' feelings of acceptance toward their child are critical during infancy. Parents also need to accept that it is normal to sometimes have negative feelings toward their child. That is, no parent is the perfect, loving parent all the time. Trying to deny negative feelings leads to tension and hostility and can mask positive feelings. It is also important from the beginning for parents and other caregivers to learn to read messages from children regarding their needs and to respond appropriately. The experiences that promote a positive self-concept begin at birth.

In Piaget's view (Maier, 1978), the infant is in the first stage or period of cognitive development. This stage, called the **sensorimotor period**, lasts until age two. This is the period of initial learning. During this stage, children learn to use their senses—touch, taste, sight, sound, and smell—as a means to find out new things. Children also learn and grow through their motor activity. They learn about the world as they grasp, crawl, creep, stand, and walk. As they move farther and faster, they are able to learn more through their senses. When infants find something new, they look at it, hold it, smell it, and then put it in their mouths to taste, bite, and feel (Figure 7–2). For Piaget, the adult is important since it is the adult who provides the environment; but infants do have some control over what they learn as they perform their sensory and motor actions.

Vygotsky viewed child development as a series of stages (Van Der Veer, 1986). Each stage is a period of stability that begins and ends with a crisis in development. Developmental change occurs rapidly during each crisis period and may result in educational problems because something new is developing. For Vygotsky, birth begins one of these crisis periods, which lasts for about 2 months. Vygotsky recognized the changes from the uterine to the outside environment described in Unit 6 as being traumatic. This crisis, or transitional period is the time when the first mental processes develop. Primitive mental activity takes place during these first weeks. When the child first smiles at the sound of the human voice, real reciprocal social interaction between child and adult begins. For Vygotsky, infancy extends from 2 months until age one. During infancy, the child is totally dependent on social interaction with others for everything and develops a specific need for this interaction. The child doesn't view himself as separate from the adult; he is one part of an affective bonding. At around 12 months, a new crisis develops as the child begins to walk, language appears, and affective reactions change. Vygotsky was ahead of his time in his emphasis on

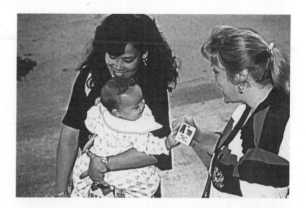

Figure 7–2   **Infants are fascinated by common objects and materials; in this case, an identification badge.**

the value and necessity of social interaction during the first year (Van Der Veer, 1986).

For Arnold Gesell, behavior is seen as subject to predictable change with age and maturation (Gesell et al., 1974). Children can do only what their neurological development allows them to do. That is, as the mind develops, the child can do more things, since the mind controls actions. Through the study of many young children, Gesell and his colleagues developed norms in the cognitive, affective, physical, and motor areas that tell us what the average child at each age is likely to be able to do. The adult can consult these norms to know what to expect of a child at a specific age. There is a wide variation, of course, at each age. That is, some three-year-olds may be more like two-year-olds, while others are more like four-year-olds. Therefore, norms must be applied with caution when considering an individual child.

To Gesell, because the infant has a natural interest in everything, there is no need for any special stimulation for the infant beyond what is normally available in the home:

> So far as we know, enriching the child's environment and providing him with the fullest opportunities possible permits him to express himself at his very best, but it does not make him "better" or smarter or speedier than he was born to be. (Gesell et al., 1974, p. 15)

KEYTERMSKEYTERMSKEYTERMSKEYTERMSKEYTERMSKEY

sensorimotor period

Potential is determined by heredity, but how it is used is determined by the environment. The child has unique qualities at each age. For example:

> *Sixteen Weeks.* Most . . . now are expansive and expressive. There is a delightful symmetry of posture, an interest in both objects and people. The baby smiles spontaneously. He is beginning to explore, both by grasping objects as he lies supine and by looking at them as he sits propped up. (Gesell et al., 1974, p. 41)

The theorists discussed thus far look at development (the interacting of both growth and learning) as central in the child's life. Skinner (1979) gears his view of the child to learning specific behaviors in the best possible environment. His view of infant learning is reflected in the approach he used with his younger daughter. For his second daughter, Skinner decided that to simplify the care of the baby, he would build a perfect infant environment. He built what he called a **baby tender** (later called an air crib). It was a crib-sized space, enclosed like a small room, with a glass picture window on one side. Air vents were located at the bottom. The air was filtered, warmed, and moistened before it entered the crib. The infant wore only diapers and could thus move at will. No tight clothes, quilts, or covers kept her from moving freely. Deborah grew up strong and healthy in her special crib. For Skinner, "The problem is two-fold: to discover the optimal conditions for the child and to induce the mother to arrange these conditions" (Skinner, 1979, p. 31). Skinner found that some important learning took place in this environment that would not have normally occurred. For example, when wet, the diaper cooled immediately and was very uncomfortable. He felt that Deborah learned early to hold her urine to avoid discomfort. For Skinner, then, the right environment is the key to healthy development.

The infant is seen by these theorists as a person who actively seeks to learn about the world through the senses and motor activity. The infant's relationship with caregivers and the quality of the surrounding environment are of the utmost importance in the degree to which the individual's potential is developed. During infancy, the child moves from dependence mainly on the senses to a combination of sensory and motor learning. This develops as children gradually move from a lying position to a sitting position and from being confined to one place (unless moved by another) to moving their own bodies. When children can sit, they can grasp objects with both hands. This opens new activities involving larger objects and coordination of two objects. For example, a favorite activity for the child who is sitting up involves putting small objects into larger objects or containers and then taking or pouring them out again (Figure 7–3). When children can move on their own, a new world opens up. They explore with excitement every nook and cranny available to them.

THE COMPETENT INFANT

Infants are sensitive individuals ready and eager to interact with their environment. Research on infant competency has documented that infants are aware of much of what is going on in their environments and are ready to learn and interact (Caulfield, 1994; Honig, 1981b). T. G. R. Bower (1977) summarized some of the competencies of the infant. Whereas the

Figure 7–3 Older infants enjoy putting smaller objects in large objects such as fitting these nesting barrels into each other.

KEYTERMSKEYTERMSKEYTERMSKEYTERMSKEYTERMSKEYTERMSKEY

baby tender

very young infant lacks control of body parts for motor activity, perceptual abilities serve for much early learning. Perception refers to the ways we know about what goes on outside our bodies. We perceive through six systems: touch, taste, smell, hearing, and sight are the five of which we are most aware. The sixth is proprioception. This sense tells us where the parts of our body are in relation to the whole. Babies do not perceive the world exactly as adults do because all their sense receptors (such as eyes, ears, and nose) have more development to achieve. How do we know a baby is sensitive? Consider these examples of newborn behavior.

- Dad gently tickles infant's right leg. Infant moves his left foot toward the right leg as if to get rid of whatever is on his right leg.

- Infant is offered a choice of sugar water or milk. He chooses the sugar water.

- The smell of burning toast wafts over to baby. He turns his head to the other side.

- Big sister drops a toy on the hardwood floor of the bedroom. Baby's eyes shift in the direction of the sound.

- Mom jokingly holds a ball in her hand and moves it directly toward baby, saying, "Gonna get you, gonna get you." Baby moves her head back as if to defend herself.

- A bright plastic object hangs from a rod across baby's crib. Baby reaches out for the object time after time. Most of the time, he is close. Sometimes he touches the object.

These examples show that babies have many competencies that enable them to relate to objects. They are sensitive to touch, taste, smell, sound, and danger. They also can coordinate eye and hand movement and use their senses to relate to people. Note the following example.

Mother is holding baby in her arms. They look directly at each other. Mother opens her mouth; baby opens his. Mother blinks her eyes; baby blinks his.

This baby seems to sense his body parts match mother's and can do the same things hers can. Infants learn by 2 weeks of age to coordinate their perceptions of others.

Mother speaks directly to baby (2 weeks old). He watches intently. Mrs. Jones, a stranger, talks to baby directly. His attention does not stay with Mrs. Jones. His gaze shifts away from her and back again.

This infant can perceive the difference between his mother and a strange woman.

Research on infant perception is extensive. Visual perception has been looked at more often than auditory (Horowitz, 1984). Memory for visual information seems to be present at birth and capacity develops rapidly. Critical factors for infants seem to be contour density and spatial frequency information. A great deal of research has been done on perception of the human face. Infants as young as 2 months can discriminate facial features and at 3 months many infants can discriminate the faces of strangers from familiar faces. Perception of motion cues has also been of interest. This factor is important in looking at rhythmicity, reciprocity, and synchrony in infant-parent interactions. (These factors are discussed later in the text.) Infants seem to be very receptive to human voice cues. That is, infants can perceive the messages relayed by different tones and degrees of loudness. The following are some examples of studies of infant sensory development.

Nelson and Horowitz (1983) looked at infants' responses to facial motion. They found that infants as young as 2 months of age can discriminate changes in facial features. These researchers did not find that facial motion in and of itself helped infants recognize faces. However, stopping movement seemed to aid recognition while starting movement gained attention. Yonas, Pettersen, and Granrud (1982) found that by 7 months of age infants were using the known size of objects (in this case the human head) as a gauge of the distance of an object. At this point, infants can use size to decide whether or not an object is close enough to grasp.

KEYTERMSKEYTERMSKEYTERMSKEYTERMSKEYTERMSKEY

Perception   proprioception

As the baby's brain and the nervous system develop, he becomes more sensitive and can begin to coordinate perceptions with motor activity. Reaching and grasping are early examples of coordinated activity.

- Three-month-old John tries to reach for an object but often misses.

- Six-month-old Missy reaches easily and has no problem getting her hand to the right place.

Infants develop patterns of social referencing or looking for cues or signals from adults that will help them decide what to do next. Hirshberg and Svejda (1990) compared 12-month-old infants signaling to mothers and to fathers. Parent reaction to the infant's approach to toys was varied: neutral, happy and positive ("Oh, look!"), or fearful and negative ("Oh, no!"). Overall, the infants did not show a preference for seeking cues more frequently from mothers or from fathers. They did, however, seek out their mothers rather than their fathers if they felt distressed. The affective type of parent reaction (neutral, positive, or negative) had no significant effect on the infants' responses.

Infants can discriminate emotional states presented vocally and visually. Caron, Caron, and MacLean (1988) had infants listen to and view videotapes of women reading passages in sad as compared with happy, or happy as compared with angry voices and facial expressions. Infants also viewed expressions without voice. These researchers found that by 5 months of age, infants could distinguish the voice/facial emotional expressions. Voice appears to provide more useful cues for discrimination before facial expression for young infants.

All infants do not develop their perceptual competencies to the same degree. There are a number of factors that might account for this. For example, preterm infants may be developmentally delayed in their sensory growth. Rose (1983) studied visual recognition memory of full-term and preterm infants. Full-term infants needed less time to become familiar with three-dimensional shapes in order to be able to recognize each familiar shape when it was presented with an unfamiliar shape. Rose suggests that adults must recognize this need for preterm infants to have longer time periods in which to become familiar with the environment and process information. In a subsequent study (Rose, Feldman, McCarton, & Wolfson, 1988) Rose and her colleagues looked at information processing comparing preterm and full-term infants who were 7 months old with age corrected for time of expected delivery. (The preterms, on the average were 8 1/2 weeks older than the full-term infants.) The preterm infants demonstrated deficits in visual recognition memory. The deficits were strongly associated with RDS (respiratory distress syndrome) or breathing difficulty at the time of delivery.

Other factors, such as adequacy of health care and nutrition, level of mother's education, and parenting skills, may affect the child's level of sensory competence (Sameroff & Seifer, 1983). The child's physical appearance may also influence adults' assessment of the child's competence. For example, Stephan and Langlois (1984) found that Anglo, African-American, and Mexican-American adults perceived more attractive infants as more competent. It is possible that more attractive infants receive more attention, thus more stimulation, and develop their perceptual competencies to a greater extent than less attractive infants. The mother's feelings about her own competence are also related to the infant's level of performance (Heinicke et al., 1983). Heinicke et al., (1983) found that mothers who felt confident about themselves had more competent infants. All these factors support the necessity for adults who work with infants to be knowledgeable about child development so they can provide developmental information and psychological support to parents.

For perceptual growth to take place as it should, the senses must have exercise (Figure 7–4). That is, children must have practice in perceiving: tasting, touching, hearing, smelling, and seeing. The infant is born with many perceptual competencies, but for these competencies to develop as they should, the infant must have experiences with many types of stimuli.

THE INFANT'S BASIC NEEDS

For infants to develop fully, the environment must support their basic needs (Honig, 1981b;

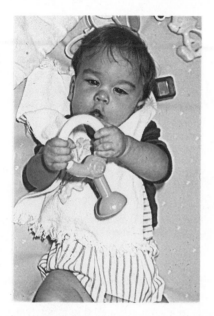

Figure 7–4   An infant uses her emerging perceptual competencies.

Horowitz, 1982). To thrive, infants need proper nutrition, responsive caregivers with whom social attachments can be developed, and a stimulating environment that encourages them to use all of their senses (Caulfield, 1994).

SUMMARY

Infants are complex individuals who develop at a rapid rate. Theorists agree that warm, loving, responsive adults are essential to ensure optimum development at this stage. Children are born with the basic competencies needed to put their senses to work in order to learn about the world. Infant research indicates that the effects of many different environmental variables can promote or diminish infant competency.

FOR FURTHER READING

Allen, K. E. & Marotz, L. (1994). *Developmental profiles: Prebirth to eight*, (2nd Ed.). Albany, NY: Delmar.

Brazelton, T. B. (1992). *Touchpoints: Your child's emotional and behavioral development.* Reading, MA: Addison-Wesley.

Bremner, G. (1989). *Infancy.* Cambridge, MA: Basil Blackwell.

Rosenblith, J. F. (1992). *In the beginning: Development from conception to age two.* Thousand Oaks, CA: Sage.

Rovee-Collier, C. & Lipsitt, L. (Eds.). (Yearly). *Advances in infancy research.* Norwood, NJ: Ablex.

Slater, A. M. & Bremner, J. G. (Eds.). (1989). *Infant development.* Hillsdale, NJ: Erlbaum.

Weiss, M. J., & Zelazo, P. R. (Eds.). (1991). *Newborn attention: Biological constraints and the influence of experience.* Norwood, NJ: Ablex.

White, B. L. (1988). *Educating the infant and toddler.* Lexington, MA: Heath.

Widerstrom, A. H., Mowder, B., & Sandall, S. (1991). *At-risk and handicapped newborns and infants: Development, assessment, and intervention.* Des Moines, IA: Longwood Division of Allyn and Bacon.

Wilson, L. C. (1995). *Infants and toddlers: Curriculum and teaching*, (3rd. Ed.). Albany, NY: Delmar.

SUGGESTED ACTIVITIES

1. Arrange to care for an infant for 20 to 30 minutes. This can be at a friend's or relative's house, in a family childcare home, or in an infant-care center. Record what you do, what the infant does, and your reactions to the infant. Discuss this experience with a small group in class.

2. Describe any experiences you've had with infants. How did you feel about these babies? Is there any one of them who is (was) a favorite? Why? Any one infant you find (found) difficult with whom to relate? Compare your experiences and reactions with those of other class members.

3. Make an entry in your journal.

REVIEW

A. Match each theorist in Column I with the definitions of theories or behavior in Column II.

Column I	Column II
1. Erikson	a. Parents need to be accepting of their children and themselves.
2. Bandura	b. The infant is in the sensorimotor period.
3. Piaget	c. The right environment is the key to healthy growth and learning.
4. Skinner	d. The child develops a sense of trust or mistrust through his experiences during feeding.
5. Sears	
6. Vygotsky	e. During infancy the child receives oral satisfaction while being cuddled by a caregiver.
7. Gesell	
8. Rogers and Maslow	f. During feeding, the child learns to need associated things, such as smiles.
9. Freud	g. The child can only do what his neurological development allows him to do.
	h. After a 2-month crisis period, the infant settles into a stable period, during which he develops his first reciprocal relationships with adults and has his first mental images.
	i. The infant builds mental pictures based on his social interactions. Observational learning helps him construct knowledge.

B. Name the sensory area in which the infant in each example demonstrates competency.
   1. Aunt Mary is wearing a very strong perfume. Infant turns his head toward her as she stands next to his crib.
   2. Infant smiles and becomes active as mother peers into the crib.
   3. When offered a soft, furry toy and a hard, wooden toy, infant feels both and then chooses the soft, furry toy.
   4. Four-year-old brother Johnny bangs on a toy drum. Infant's eyes move in Johnny's direction.

C. Name two early developing activities that coordinate motor activity and perception.

D. What are some reasons why certain infants may not fully develop their sensory competencies?

Unit 8

Infancy: Affective Development

OBJECTIVES

After studying this unit, the student should be able to:

- Identify the developmental stages of adult/infant interaction.
- Identify examples of infant/adult reciprocity.
- Explain the development of stranger anxiety.
- Describe the roles of fathers with infants.
- Explain the role of infant temperament in the adult/infant relationship.
- Understand the significance of the infant/mother reunion.
- Identify significant aspects of attachment behavior.
- Explain how infant and parent develop communication skills.
- List the primary emotions.
- Describe minority culture mother/infant interactions.

Washington, DC, psychiatrist Frances Cress Welsing feels a lack of "lap time" during childhood results in troubled children who turn to drug abuse and adolescent sex to try to fulfill dependency needs unfulfilled earlier in life (Raspberry, 1985). Children who grow up without warm, nurturing relationships are unable to offer this experience to their children and thus the cycle continues from one generation to the next. Adults who work with young children have the opportunity to model for parents the appropriate ways of interacting with children and explain to them the factors that are important in affective development. Infant **affective development** has been the focus of a great deal of research. Rhythm and reciprocity, attach-

KEYTERMSKEYTERMSKEYTERMSKEYTERMSKEYTERMSKEY

affective development

ment, interactions with adults and peers, temperament, the caregiver's role, and the infant as a controller of the behavior of others have all been studied.

AFFECTIVE BEHAVIOR: ATTACHMENT AND INTERACTION

Once an initial bond (a feeling of specialness) is developed, the infant's attachment to others must grow and deepen for healthy emotional, social, and personality development. According to Brazelton and Cramer (1990) attachment grows over time. The outcome is the detachment and eventual independence of the child. The basis for attachment is the reciprocal adult/child relationship that develops from the time of birth. Four stages in the development of early interactions have been identified (Brazelton & Cramer, 1990). The first stage is during the first week to 10 days. During this period the infant learns to control his **emerging competencies** and gain control of his ability to maintain his attention. The adult's job is to appreciate the emerging competencies and not overwhelm the infant with input. The second stage from about 1 to 8 weeks is **prolonging attention.** With some control achieved, infants can now prolong attention and maintain communication and interaction with their most important adults. They begin to take control as they use smiling, vocalizing, facial expressions, and motor cues to signal the adult that they are ready to interact. The adults learn to match their behaviors to the baby's. The third and fourth months are a **limit-testing** period. Infant and adult test their abilities to communicate and affect the other's behavior. Interaction should become rewarding; there should be a sense of joy in play. The fourth stage should appear around 4 to 5 months with the **emergence of autonomy**. Infants begin to take the lead in the interactions with adults. They take control and begin to move their attention from the adult to other things and people in the environment. The adult needs to respect these initial signs of autonomy and

not try to overwhelm the infant with bids to get attention back again.

Rhythm and Reciprocity

Brazelton and his associates (1977, 1978, 1982, 1990) studied infant and adult reciprocity by observing infants from 2 weeks to 24 weeks of age. The infant is placed in a baby seat and then is given the chance to play with an object, a parent, or a stranger. The cycle of attention to object or person is measured by examining videotapes of the infant and adult made during these play periods.

To check how the baby relates to objects, a small rubber ball is hung about 12 inches from the infant. The child tries to make movements in the direction of the ball. These movements are usually jerky. His attention pattern is marked by sharp periods of attention and then ignoring of the object. A graphic representation of this is curve A (Figure 8–1). When a person he knows (such as his mother) is in front of him, the infant's reaction is different. His cycle of attention is smoother, as in curve B (Figure 8–1). He gradually becomes more attentive and then gradually withdraws attention in a smooth rather than jerky rhythm. He also moves his body forward and back with the cycle. He seems to want the person to approach him. The parent who is in **rhythm** with the child is able to move toward the child and away in tune with the child's attention and movements as shown in curve C (Figure 8–1). It can be seen that the adult is moving in rhythm with the child. When the adult is not in tune with the child, the curves might look like curve D (Figure 8–1). When baby finds he can't get into rhythm with the adult, he may withdraw and even stop trying. If the mother stands in front of him and does not respond at all, the baby becomes jerky, as if relating to an object. If he gets no response, he soon withdraws. He gives up and may play with his own body or his clothing. He seems to display a feeling of disappointment.

Mothers and fathers follow different patterns

| emerging competencies | limit-testing | rhythm |
| prolonging attention | emergence of autonomy | |

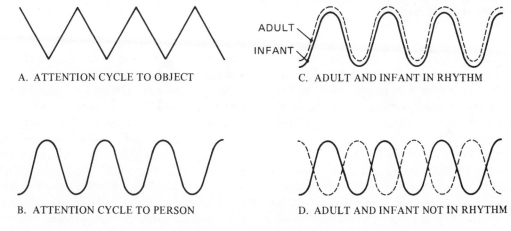

A. ATTENTION CYCLE TO OBJECT

C. ADULT AND INFANT IN RHYTHM

ADULT

INFANT

B. ATTENTION CYCLE TO PERSON

D. ADULT AND INFANT NOT IN RHYTHM

Figure 8–1   **Attention curves**

in their reciprocal interactions with their infant. These patterns develop by 2 or 3 weeks of age. Mothers tend to start out more smoothly and softly and try to find the baby's pattern. Fathers are more playful and try to carry on more of a regular conversation. Their pattern is more sharp and jerky. Baby learns this difference quickly. When Dad approaches, he is more playful and bright eyed, as if ready for action.

When a stranger enters, both infant and stranger may have difficulty finding the right rhythmic pattern. The stranger does not give the infant the expected response; stranger and child may both become frustrated. They may both give up trying to get into rhythm with each other.

Brazelton feels the development of **reciprocity** is absolutely necessary for the development of not only affective, but also cognitive and motor growth. It is through this reciprocal relationship that infants receive the social stimulation they must have. As they receive stimulation, they use their senses, sharpen them, and begin to see themselves as competent persons.

Research comparing preterm and full-term babies has shown differences in rhythm and reciprocity favoring the full-term infants (Lester, Hoffman,

& Brazelton, 1985). Preterm infants and their mothers were not as closely synchronized as full-term infants and their mothers. Lester et al. feel this may happen because the preterm infants are unable to stop and process information quickly enough to change behavior to fit with their mothers'. Term infants also tended to take the lead and dominate the interaction. Mothers of the preterm infants found them hard to follow; it was difficult to figure out what the infants would do next. This tended to frustrate the mother, which may weaken the mother/child relationship.

Rhythmicity within the total family setting has also been studied (Sprunger, Boyce, & Gaines, 1985). All families develop some kind of daily routine that sets the rhythm of daily living. At the same time, the infant develops a rhythm in his daily functions of eating, sleeping, and eliminating. Families with strong routines and an infant with predictable routines had mothers who reported feeling the most competent in their roles.

Rhythm appears to be a basic factor in infant development. It is important in one-to-one relationships and in physiological functioning. The total family functions better and members feel better adjusted if infant and family are synchronized.

KEYTERMSKEYTERMSKEYTERMSKEYTERMSKEYTERMSKEY

reciprocity

Attachment and Reactions to Strangers

Child psychologists have long been interested in the development of infant behaviors that indicate attachment has developed. **Attachment** refers to the relationship of belonging between infant and caregiver. Research shows the infant goes through three steps (Schaffer, 1977). First, the infant learns to tell the difference between humans and objects. This is learned during the first weeks of life. Second, the infant learns to distinguish mother from other humans. This is usually accomplished before 3 months. It is not until the third step, at about 7 months, that the infant becomes upset when mother leaves him and shows signs of missing mother when she is gone. Around 7 to 9 months, the infant may also show signs of fear of strangers or **stranger anxiety.** When the happy, smiling 7-month-old is transferred from mother's arms into the arms of a stranger, the infant is likely to change to a crying, unhappy person. At this point, it can be said that attachment has been accomplished. From this point, baby actively seeks mother (or other primary caregiver) when she is out of sight.

Horner (1980) concludes that when an infant meets a stranger, the development of the relationship takes place more smoothly if the infant controls the meeting. That is, the meeting is more successful if the stranger remains in one place and the infant is allowed to observe and approach when and if the infant wishes to get a closer look or make contact with the new person.

Researchers are very interested in the strength of the attachment relationship and how it relates to other behaviors (Bretherton & Waters, 1985). Research strongly supports the view that the mother's observed sensitivity to the infant's needs during the first months is predictive of the quality of their later relationship. Mother's sensitivity is also related to the child's later reaction in the **strange-situation** naturalistic laboratory setting. This setting is one in which the infant is placed in an unfamiliar room and is allowed to explore some toys either with the mother or a stranger

present. When the mother has been absent and returns, the observed reunion behavior has been found to be related to later behaviors. While most infants greet their mothers happily, some infants reject their mothers and some display anger.

Rejection of the mother was found to be related to early insensitivity and to mothers' dislike of physical contact with their babies during the first 3 months. These babies also tend to display unpredictable aggression periods at home. The mothers of these infants tend to lack emotional expressiveness (Bretherton & Waters, 1985). Osofsky (1989) compared the interactions of teenage unmarried mothers and older, married mothers with their respective infants. The teenage mothers used more inappropriate affective responses, misinterpreted communications from their infants more frequently, gave fewer positive responses and less attention, were more directive, and used less mature language. Pianta, Stroufe, and Egeland (1989) found that mothers under stress were less sensitive to their infants' needs than mothers who had good emotional support or felt satisfied in their relationships.

The evidence seems to indicate that the first 3 months is a critical time for development of an attachment relationship. Strength of attachment at 12 months has been found to be predictive of later attachment (Bretherton & Waters, 1985) and disorganized or disoriented attachment at 18 months is predictive of hostility in preschool children (Lyons-Ruth, Alpern, & Repacholi, 1993) while securely attached children are more likely to be viewed by their teachers as more affectively positive, more empathetic, and more compliant (Bretherton & Waters, 1985). Bretherton and Waters (1985) also noted that research indicates strength of attachment appears to be related to children's functioning. When two-year-olds were challenged with a difficult task, those identified as securely attached sought help and support from their mothers whereas those identified as insecurely attached did not seek help.

In summary, the research indicates that children and mothers who develop a strong positive attachment in infancy will continue to show a positive re-

| Attachment | stranger anxiety | strange-situation |

lationship and the children will display more positive behaviors in preschool.

Sociability at 3 months of age is another behavior that has been studied as it relates to later evidence of attachment to mothers (Lewis & Feiring, 1989). At 3 months infants were rated on whether they were more toy or person oriented. Those who were more person oriented at 3 months showed more secure attachment behaviors to their mothers when observed at one year of age. That is, they showed a preference for mother over continuing to play with toys when put in the strange-situation setting.

Caruso (1989) cautions that we need to look at the interrelationships of attachment, wariness, and exploratory behavior in an ecological context. That is, we have to look at the patterns of behavior to arrive at the whole picture. For example, infants might move away from their mothers to explore toys as an avoidance behavior or because they feel secure with their mothers and feel supported as they move into unknown territory. We will look at the significance of this point of view again in Unit 10 in the discussion of infant child care.

Researchers also looked at the infant's attachment behavior with mother as compared with father (Bretherton & Waters, 1985). It was found that the quality of the two relationships may be quite different. That is, the child may be secure with one parent and not with the other. The relationship with the mother, as principal caregiver, seems to be more predictive of the child's later feelings of security than the relationship with the father.

Concern over separation distress in infants, toddlers, and parents has increased along with the increased frequency of leaving children with a childcare provider (Godwin, Groves, & Horm-Wingerd, 1993). Field et al. (1985) observed infants and parents when the children were brought to and when they departed from a childcare center. Leave-taking distress increased across the two semesters. That is, it appeared to become more difficult for the infants to leave their parent as the year progressed. Girls and their mothers had the most difficulty parting as evidenced by more crying and attention-getting behaviors by the infant and more efforts by the mother to distract the child. Mothers also tended to stay longer than fathers before finally leaving. Field et al. noted that in another study in which parents were questioned, it was found that 75 percent of the mothers but only 35 percent of the fathers expected their infants to cry, and 40 percent of the mothers and none of the fathers were concerned about the infant's response to their departure. This indicates that what parents expect may be what happens. That is, the concerned parent hesitates about leaving and this signals the infant to fuss and cry. It was also found that infants and their parents spent more time interacting before leave-taking than did preschoolers and their parents. It seems as children get older they and their parents can separate more easily.

Another concern relative to child care is the effect that the frequent turnover in childcare personnel may have on infants' attachment security. Raikes (1993) found that the amount of time spent with a high-quality teacher was directly related to infants' attachment security. Nine months appears to be the critical amount of time needed to develop a secure relationship. The results from the studies of early attachment have implications for the adult who works with young children. Hopefully, this will help you understand the possible elements in the child's and parents' early relationships that may affect later behavior. Both Godwin et al. (1993) and Vance and Boals (1985) provide suggestions for helping infants, toddlers, and parents manage separation distress. Vance and Boals (1985) emphasize establishing positive relationships and responding quickly and consistently. Babies need close relationships that can be established not only during feeding but also through singing, talking, reading to, and cuddling the infant. When infants' calls for attention bring consistent and immediate responses, they develop their first feelings of success. Through these early experiences, the infant develops positive expectations about how others will respond to him and thus he develops feelings of self-confidence. Godwin et al. (1993) point out the importance of helping the parents as well as the child. Parents may demonstrate uneasiness due to guilt about leaving the infant. It is important to allow children to be left on a gradual basis, make parents feel comfortable, be reassuring, and keep lines of communication open.

Interactions with Adults and Peers

Researchers are also interested in other aspects of infant/parent interaction. Both mothers and fathers have been the focus of study. Also of interest is how infants respond to peers (that is, other infants).

Interaction forms the basis of communication (Honig, 1982). This mutual give-and-take is the origin of the feelings of trust essential to infant development. As already described, patterns of communication begin at birth. Parent and child develop patterns of reciprocity and rhythm in their exchanges and some degree of synchrony develops. Gazing seems to be an important aspect of this beginning communication. The longer the parent looks, the longer the infant returns the gaze. However, if the infants find they are overwhelmed by too much demand for attention, they may become irritable and withdrawn. Thus, from the beginning, babies develop a share of the control of the interaction.

Feeding (Honig, 1982) is another situation in which communication takes place. Caregivers need to learn to read the infants' signals for pacing the feeding time. Play also proceeds in cycles of engagement and withdrawal. Smiling involves sensitivity to signals. When the caregiver smiles, the baby observes for a while before smiling back. The caregiver needs to withdraw his smile to give the infant a chance for a break before beginning the cycle again. Caregiver and child learn to share experiences. They may gaze at the same object or event—caregiver talks and comments while infant looks and smiles. When the infant begins to babble and vocalize, synchrony and responding by the caregiver is critical for good speech development. Five-month-old infants have shown they are sensitive to adult tone of voice indicating either approval or prohibition directed at themselves or to an adult (Fernald, 1993). A parent's immediate response to an infant's vocalizing encourages the infant to continue. The amount of time spent interacting with the infant, especially verbalizing, seems to be the most critical factor related to the child's later competence. Honig

(1982) notes that boys, especially, seem to need the opportunity to be in situations in which they can control the interaction in order to develop their own sense of power and control.

Imitation is an important element in parent/child interaction (Uzgiris, 1984). Imitation is a form of interpersonal communication. Imitative responses on the part of parent and child can develop into a cycle of turn-taking in which each participant influences the activity of the other. Both vocal and facial expressions are imitated. It may be from these exchanges that the infant begins to perceive the mother as a teacher. Uzgiris (1984) concludes tht imitation is not only a means for developing interpersonal communications but is also an essential element in cognitive growth and development.

Research has broken down some of the stereotyped views of differences between mother and father interactions with infants (Sawin, 1982). On the whole fathers may be just as active participants as mothers in caregiving and affection giving with their infants. Both mothers and fathers tend to give more affectionate attention to the opposite-sexed infant and more attention and stimulation to the same-sexed infants. By 12 months of age, some well-established sex differences have been observed (Snow, Jacklin, & Maccoby, 1983). Fathers used more physical and verbal prohibitions with the boys than with the girls. However, the boys tended to do more acts that would need limitations. Girls tended to stay closer to the father and be held more. Fathers also did more playing with the girls that would keep them away from forbidden objects and thus require less regulation behavior from the fathers. Sex stereotyping in toy use already was evident. Fathers suggested both trucks and dolls to the girls but never suggested dolls to the boys. Fathers did, however, let their sons play with a toy vacuum cleaner, which involved the use of gross motor skills.

Infants also relate socially with other infants (Honig & DiPerna, 1983; Moore, 1978). By 10 or 12 months infants in pairs look at each other, smile, and make friendly sounds. Infants, too, were found to

Imitation

have peer preferences. Infants chosen most often for interaction by other infants are those who initiate contacts, approach by looking at the other infant first, and do very little grabbing of toys away from others. Placing infants in playgroups of just two children seems to bring more positive interaction than placing them in larger groups (Figure 8–2). The duration of infants' interactions with both peers and siblings appears to be related to the quality of inter-actions with their mothers (Vandell & Wilson, 1987). Infants who had prolonged turn-taking social interactions with their mothers also had longer inter-actions with older siblings and with other infants. It seems that the experience with mother transfers to other situations.

Trevarthen (1989) believes that this early in-fant/adult interaction also has a cognitive component. He views it as a precursor of thoughtful message-making and message exchange. By 9 months of age, infants begin to understand there is a mutual agree-ment shared with others about certain objects and people. Trevarthen suggests that this is the beginning of the learning of the signs, symbols, and rituals of the culture.

Infants also learn about themselves during their first year. For example, when shown a videotape of themselves, infants as young as 9 months of age im-itate what they see (Lewis, 1977). They are twice as likely to imitate a tape of themselves as one of a strange infant. Nine-month-olds show that they know themselves when they look in a mirror (Figure 8–3).

Figure 8–3 **By 9 months of age, the infant recognizes her mirror image and enjoys herself.**

After reviewing the research Beverly Gulley (1988) makes several suggestions for the promotion of infant peer interaction. For the youngest infants, toys seem to distract from peer interest. Touching and smiling are usually responses to peer vocalization. Therefore, placing a pair of very young infants side-by-side without toys promotes their awareness and mutual responsiveness. Toys can be introduced dur-ing later infancy. Infants usually take time to get in-volved with each other, so caregivers need to allow them time to become familiar.

Temperament

As already discussed, temperament seems to be an important factor in parent/neonate interaction. Daniels, Plomin, and Greenhalgh (1984) found that the characteristics of emotionality and soothability were associated with the ease of relating to babies. Those babies rated as the most temperamental were also rated as the most emotional and least easily soothed.

Dunst and Lingerfelt (1985) examined the effect of temperament on the learning of two- and three-

Figure 8–2 **Peer relationships begin in infancy.**

month-olds. They found that learning rates were predicted by two aspects of temperament: rhythmicity and persistence. Rhythmicity was a good predictor, as babies who were reported by their mothers to follow predictable cycles in their daily routines learned the most in the laboratory. It may be they have a sense of predictability that aids their learning. Persistence was also a good predictor; babies who paid better attention learned faster.

Researchers have investigated the relationships between parent characteristics and infant temperament. Mangelsdorf, Gunnar, Kestenbaum, Lang, and Andreas (1990) looked at infant temperament, mother's personality, and mother-infant attachment. They discovered a link between maternal personality, maternal behavior, and infant temperament. Those mothers who scored as having positive affective behavior on an affect questionnaire expressed more warmth and provided more security for their nine-month-old infants than mothers who scored low on positive affective behavior.

Although more premature than full-term infants may fall in the irritable, demanding category, there is a range of temperament within the preterm group (Plunkett, Cross, & Meisels, 1989). Plunkett et al. (1989) point out that whereas the unhealthy prematures may fall in the difficult, hard-to-comfort category, the healthy prematures are more usually characterized as excessively active. Overall, Plunkett et al. (1989) found no differences in parent-reported temperament characteristics when comparing full-term with high-risk and low-risk preterm infants.

Emotional Development and Mental Health

By the end of the first year, children usually have displayed the primary emotions of joy, fear, anger, sadness, disgust, and surprise (Lewis, Sullivan, Stanger, & Weiss, 1989). The secondary emotions such as embarrassment, empathy, envy, pride, shame, and guilt appear later when the child has reached a higher level of cognitive development. Malatesta, Culver, Tesman, and Shepard (1989) measured emotional expressions of infants and their mothers at $2^{1}/_2$, 5, $7^{1}/_2$, and 22 months. For the infants, sadness and anger were the most consistently expressed emotions

from observation to observation. For the mothers, total negative emotions were consistent as was the expression of joy. Total positive emotions of mothers and children were strongly correlated across time. The results indicated there is some consistency in emotional expression over time and mothers and infants display similar positive emotions.

Mental health is reflected in infants' emotional well-being. Alice Honig (1993) reminds adults who work with young children that besides providing infants with appropriate toys and good physical care, they need to provide love and warmth. They also need to be tuned in to signs that a baby is not thriving emotionally. For example, dull eyes without sparkle, pushing away rather than cuddling up with an adult, crying inconsolably for hours, and having wild tantrums (Honig, 1993, p. 72). Violence in the family, on television, and in the neighborhood has been identified as a source of post-traumatic stress disorder that can even affect infants (Special report, 1994).

INTERACTION PATTERNS OF MINORITY INFANTS AND THEIR MOTHERS

Theory based on research done predominantly on Anglo majority children may not generalize to children from minority cultures. Cynthia T. Garcia Coll (1990) reviewed research that focuses specifically on minority infants and toddlers. Parental behaviors with their infants do vary from culture to culture. For example, Navajos carry their babies on a cradle board on their backs. The use of the cradle board lowers the infants' levels of arousal and activity resulting in less mutual give-and-take. However, this lower level of interaction does not generalize to the periods when the infants are not on the boards. Navajo infants are less fearful than Anglo infants during the first year but more fearful in the second year. However, there is wide variation within the Navajo population; the more interaction infants have with others, the less fearful they are.

Coll (1990) describes the results of other studies of minority mother-infant interaction. Mexican-American mothers tend to be more tactile and less verbal in stimulating their infants when compared with Anglo mothers. Mothers from various Hispanic groups vary in their behavior with infants: Cuban mothers talked the most and played more teaching games and Puerto Rican and South American mothers talked less and played more social games. Compared with the Hispanic mothers, African-American mothers talked the least and did the least infant game-playing. When questioned, the Cuban mothers expressed the objective of educating their children while the African-American mothers expressed a fear of spoiling the infants by giving them too much attention. Native American mothers and infants were much more silent and passive when compared with African-American and Anglo mothers.

Except for the Native American infants being more passive, there is no information on ways these different styles of interaction may affect infant/caretaker attachment or infant temperament. On the other hand, whereas large group research of a particular culture may indicate certain cultural patterns, individual group members may vary significantly. For example, Brinker, Baxter, and Butler (1994) observed the interactions of African-American mothers and infants who were participants in an early intervention program. Both low socioeconomic status (SES) and middle SES groups were represented, and some of the mothers were drug users. They found a diversity of interaction patterns and concluded that it is important not to stereotype the members of any particular cultural subgroup.

AFFECTIVE BEHAVIOR: THE CAREGIVER

More and more, we are beginning to see it is the quality of the relationship more than who the infant has the relationship with that is most important. As children develop trust during the first year, they also develop the ability to love. To be able to love others when grown up, it is essential that the child learn to love during the first months of life (Fraiberg, 1971). The "mothering" activities can be shared. Baby has an infinite amount of love to give and share (Schaffer, 1977).

Mother has traditionally been considered the primary caregiver. In recent years, just as men have become more involved in the delivery process, they have begun to take a more active role with infants. Middle- and lower-class fathers have been found to show equal interest with mothers in the newborn when observed in the maternity ward. Competence as a parent is a matter of sensitivity to what the infant needs. The competent parent can read the infant's messages correctly and respond appropriately (Figure 8–4).

Research has shown that when observed at home, men generally take on very few regular routine caregiving chores such as feeding, bathing, and diapering the baby (although this may be changing). The man's main role has been to play with the infant. Just as Brazelton has observed differences in interaction, so have others (Sawin, 1982; Parke & Sawin, 1977). When fathers play, they are more physical and rough. Mothers play quieter games, like "peek-a-boo." Children whose fathers spend a lot of time playing with them are found to be better adjusted to strange situations. There is also a positive relationship between father's playing and later cognitive development. The child may get some special benefits from father that are not found with mother.

SUMMARY

Infant competence is enhanced by the development of attachment and a good reciprocal relationship with caregivers. Love and warmth are basic to accomplishing these tasks. A reciprocal cycle of exchange in social interaction is a sign of a positive,

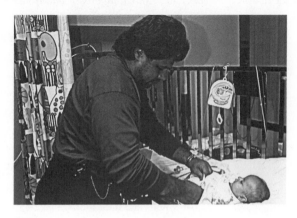

Figure 8–4 **Father is a competent and loving caregiver.**

sensitive relationship. Observation of the reunion between parent and child after parent absence can give clues to the strength of attachment. Interactions with both parents are important, though somewhat different. If given the opportunity, infants are interested in relating to peers as well as to adults. Temperament has some influence on whether the infant is viewed as easy or difficult. Infants, through their responses to their caregivers, control a share of the interaction and influences the caregiver's response. All the primary emotions develop during infancy. Although we know a little about cultural variations in mother/child interactions, we don't know how, or if, these variations might account for cultural differences in temperament and attachment.

FOR FURTHER READING

Belsky, J., & Nezworski, T. M. (Eds.). (1987). *Clinical implications of attachment.* Hillsdale, NJ: Erlbaum.

Brazelton, T. B., Field, T. (Eds.). (1990). *Advances in touch.* Somerville, NJ: Johnson & Johnson.

Buss, A. H. & Plomin, R. (1984). *Temperament: Early developing personality traits.* Hillsdale, NJ: Erlbaum.

Field, T. M. & Fox, N. A. (Eds.). (1985). *Social perception in infants.* Norwood, NJ: Ablex.

Garber, J., & Dodge, K. A. (Eds.). (1991). *The development of emotion regulation and dysregulation.* New York: Cambridge University Press.

Gewirtz, J., & Kurtines, W. M. (Eds.). (1991). *Intersections with attachment.* Hillsdale, NJ: Erlbaum.

Leavitt, R. L. (1994). *Power and emotion in infant-toddler day care.* Albany, NY: State University of New York Press.

Lewis, M., & Haviland, J. M. (Eds.). (1994). *Handbook of emotions.* New York: Guilford.

Lewis, M., & Worobey, J. (Eds.). (1989). *Infant stress and coping.* San Francisco: Jossey-Bass.

Rosenblith, J. F. (1992). *In the beginning: Development from conception to age two.* Thousand Oaks, CA: Sage.

Rovee-Collier, C., & Lipsitt, L. (Eds.). (yearly) *Advances in infancy research.* Norwood, NJ: Ablex.

Weiss, M. J., & Zelazo, P. R. (Eds.). (1991). *Newborn attention: Biological constraints and the influence of experience.* Norwood, NJ: Ablex.

White, B. (1988). *Educating the infant and toddler.* Lexington, MA: Heath.

Wilson, L. C. (1990). *Infants and toddlers: Curriculum and teaching,* (2nd Ed.). Albany, NY: Delmar.

Wolff, P. H. (1987). *The development of behavioral states and the expression of emotions in early infancy.* Chicago: University of Chicago Press.

Zeanah, C., Jr. (Ed.). (1993). *Handbook of infant mental health.* New York: Guilford.

SUGGESTED ACTIVITIES

1. Observe a mother, a father, and a stranger interacting with the same infant for 3 to 4 minutes, each in turn. Describe how the mother, father, and stranger interact with the infant. Write a description of the infant's response to each. What are the similarities and differences in the infant's response to each and theirs to him? Are the responses what you expect from reading the text?

2. Observe two or more infants in a setting where they are free to interact if they wish. Do they seem to notice each other? Do they smile, vocalize, or reach out? If they are mobile, do they seek each other out, touch, exchange toys? Describe exactly what happens. Share your observations in class.

3. Interview four fathers of infants (two fathers of boys and two fathers of girls, if possible). Ask the following questions.
   a. How much time do you spend playing with your baby? When? What do you do?
   b. What kinds of routine tasks do you do for your baby (that is, feeding, changing, bathing, etc.)? How often?

c. How did you feel when you first saw (baby's name)? Did the baby fulfill your expectations? Does the infant fulfill your expectations now?

d. What do you enjoy most about babies? What, if anything, do you find most irritating or frustrating?

Analyze the answers. Compare the fathers' responses. What are the similarities and differences? Are there any differences between the responses of the fathers of boys and fathers of girls?

4. Make an entry in your journal.

REVIEW

A. Match the stages of early interaction in Column I with the descriptions in Column II.

Column I   **Column II**

1. Stage 1   a. The limit testing period during which adult and infant test their abilities to communicate.
2. Stage 2   b. The infant gains control of his emerging competencies and his ability to maintain
3. Stage 3   attention.
4. Stage 4   c. The infant begins to take the lead in his interactions—autonomy emerges.
                 d. The infant can prolong attention and maintain communication and interaction.

B. For each example below, decide whether the infant is most likely interacting with mother, father, or a stranger.

1. Adult approaches infant and says, "Hi Brad, old boy. Did you have a good day?" Brad is bright-eyed and looks like he's ready for fun.

2. Adult approaches saying "Hi, sweetheart." Brad gurgles. Adult bends closer, "Gurgly-goo to you, too."

3. Adult approaches with, "Hi, Brad!" Brad looks at adult with a serious expression. "How about a little tickle, Brad?" Adult tickles Brad's tummy. Brad looks closely. Adult says, "It takes time to get going, doesn't it, Brad?"

C. Describe the two basic types of reciprocal relationships that may develop between adult and infant.

D. List two factors that affect infant/adult rhythmicity.

E. Select all the correct answers:

1. When the mother returns to the strange-situation room most infants are delighted.

2. Infants who reject their mothers when they return to the strange-situation room may have mothers who are insensitive and who do not enjoy physical contact with the baby.

3. There is no indication that the irritable infant is less attached to the mother at one year of age than the happier infant.

4. Attachment can develop anytime during the first year.

5. Securely attached two-year-olds will turn to their mothers when they need help.

6. Fathers observed leaving their children at a childcare center are likely to stay longer than mothers.

7. Positive adult relationships developed in infancy are the basis for later competence.

F. Explain why the five-month-old who would go willingly to everyone, now at 8 months cries when held by anyone but mother.

G. Describe a situation in which infant and parent are developing communication skills.

H. How would you explain the fact that infants have been observed to get along very well with each other?

I. Write the number of each correct statement.
   1. Mothers do a better job of caring for infants than fathers.
   2. Fathers are just as interested in their newborns as are mothers.
   3. Father's play with infants is rougher than mother's.
   4. Both social and cognitive development seem to be given a special lift from time spent with father.

J. Mrs. Clark is very upset with her relationship with two-month-old Sally. Sally is cranky, sleeps in short spurts, and never seems satisfied. Mrs. Clark feels she must be doing something wrong. What do you think?

K. List the primary emotions that appear during infancy.

L. Describe what is known about minority culture mother/child interactions.

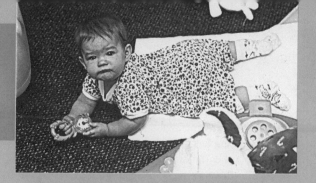

Infancy: Motor and Cognitive Development

OBJECTIVES

After studying this unit, the student should be able to:

■ Apply the rules of normal motor development.

■ Recognize the factors that influence motor development.

■ Describe activities that support motor development.

■ State brief descriptions of the cognitive stages occurring during the first year of sensorimotor development.

■ Recognize factors relevant to infant categorization.

■ Explain why brain lateralization is important to cognitive development.

■ Know the factors that are important in infant object manipulation.

■ Demonstrate knowledge of infant social referencing.

■ Support the need for infants to have time to explore and play on their own, independent of adult intervention.

■ Evaluate infant development using an infant development evaluation sheet.

During the first 2 years, motor and cognitive development are closely related. This relationship was recognized by Piaget in his description of the sensorimotor period. Motor development focuses on the child's increasing control and refinement of his movement activities and sensory development on the increasing control and refinement of his perceptual or sensory (touch, taste, feel, hear, smell) behaviors. However, research designed to consider in detail the processes that relate the sensory and motor development is a new and growing field called **developmental biodynamics.** This new view of motor development focuses not just on the sequence of

developmental biodynamics

motor development but also on how motor development and perception (obtaining information through the senses) interact. Most of the biodynamic research to date has been done during the period from neonate to beginning walking (Lockman & Thelen, 1993). In this unit physical, motor, and sensory development will be examined separately and as they relate to each other.

MOTOR AND PHYSICAL DEVELOPMENT

Motor and physical development are influenced by the interaction of a combination of factors both genetic and environmental. Newborns move in a reflexive manner over which they have no control. The focus of the first 2 years is the development of voluntary motor control. Both internal neurological factors connecting body and brain and environmental factors, such as nutrition and opportunities for sensorimotor exploration, influence how this process takes place for individual children. However, there are normative patterns that most children follow at their own rate.

Motor and physical growth proceed in an organized way from head to toe (**cephalocaudal**) and from the center out (**proximodistal**). When the infant is born, the head is relatively large for the body when compared with adult proportions. The trunk and arms and finally legs and feet eventually catch up in growth. Motorically, the infant first learns to lift the head, then the shoulders, and eventually the trunk, and is thus able to sit up without help. The infant next gains control of the legs as when advancing from crawling and creeping to standing and walking. The development from center out is evident in observing the infant's arm movements. At first, infants move in a rather gross way, moving the whole arm from the shoulder. Gradually, control proceeds from shoulder to hand.

Allen and Marotz (1994) have developed a profile of infant development. They caution that when looking at such a profile it is important to keep in mind that in reality the child who is **normal** in every way does not exist. The profile is a list of developmental guidelines. They will not be an exact fit for every child as there is a wide range of normal development at any age. Some examples of the typical infant characteristics described by Allen and Marotz (1994, Chapter 4) are as follows:

Newborn: Motor activity is mainly reflexive and includes behaviors such as swallowing, sucking, yawning, blinking, grasping movement, walking movement when held upright, and a startle response to sudden loud noises.

One to four months: Average length is 20 to 27 inches and average weight 8 to 16 pounds; can grasp objects with entire hand, can raise upper body and head with arms in prone position, and when lying down can turn head from side to side.

Four to eight months: Gains about one pound per month and 1/2 inch in length; teeth begin to appear with increase in drooling, chewing, biting, and putting things in the mouth; uses finger and thumb (pincer grip) to pick things up; transfers objects from one hand to the other; shakes objects; puts objects in mouth; pulls body up to crawling position; rolls body from front to back and back to front.

Eight to twelve months: Height gains average of 1/2 inch and weight one pound per month; continues to reach for and manipulate objects (stacks, sets side by side, drops, throws); pulls to a standing position; creeps on hands and knees; walks with adult support by the end of the first year.

Motor development is influenced by a number of factors: genetics, status at birth, size, build and composition, nutrition, rearing and birth order, social class, ethnicity, and culture (Malina, 1981).

Neonates who suffer respiratory problems have been found to have delayed motor development, and neonates with lower Apgar scores will more likely have delayed motor development than those with higher scores. In addition, low birth weight and prematurity can lead to slower motor development: sitting, standing, and walking are usually attained later by low-birth-weight infants.

See Figures 9–1 and 9–2 for infant and toddler weight and length charts. The relationships of size, physique, and composition to motor development are complicated (Malina, 1981). It seems to be the extremes (very light and very heavy and/or very long or very short) who are affected. For example, muscular and small-boned or very long infants are most likely to be early walkers.

Undernourished and malnourished children lack the muscle strength and skeletal development necessary for normal motor activity. In addition, central nervous system dysfunction, which is usually present in the undernourished and malnourished child, limits coordination and control. Overweight babies may

also have limited development. With excess weight to move, the infant may not be motivated nor physically able to develop necessary motor skills.

By the age of one, boys have been observed to engage in more physical activities than girls. This may be the result of environmental influences rather than genetic (Malina, 1981). The firstborn in families seem to have some advantage over their siblings, possibly due to receiving more personal attention. "Only" children tend to be slower in motor development, perhaps because they may be overprotected. In general, children reared in more permissive environments with more opportunities for motor activity tend to be advanced.

There is only a small amount of research comparing different races and social classes. The results tend to favor the lower SES group children. It may be that the upper SES children are overprotected and do

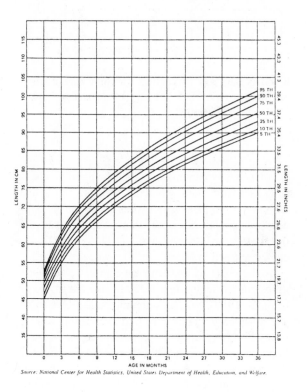

Source: National Center for Health Statistics, United States Department of Health, Education, and Welfare.

a. Length by age percentiles for girls ages birth–36 months

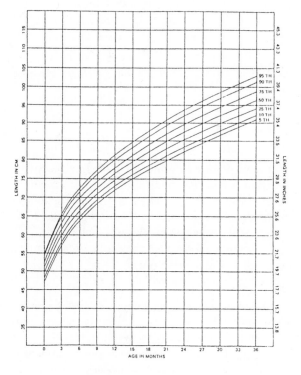

b. Length by age percentiles for boys ages birth–36 months. (From Allen & Marotz, *Developmental Profiles*, by Delmar Publishers)

Figure 9–1

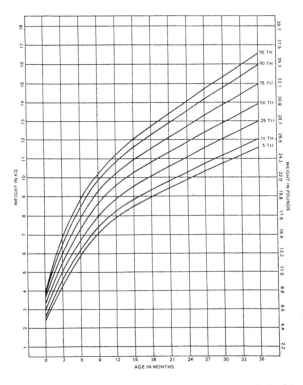

a. Weight by age percentiles for girls ages birth–36 months

b. Weight by age percentiles for boys ages birth–36 months. (From Allen & Marotz, *Developmental Profiles*, by Delmar Publishers)

Figure 9–2

not have as many opportunities for motor activity. African-American children tend to be ahead of European-American children in motor development during the first year, and both have been found to be ahead of Hispanic infants on some motor tasks.

As mobility becomes greater the infant gains a new view of the world (Figure 9–3). By 9 months, the infant can move about.

> Travel changes one's perspective . . . It's when you start to get around on your own steam that you discover what a chair really is. Parents who want a fresh point of view on their furniture are advised to drop down on all fours and accompany the nine- or ten-month-old on his rounds. It is probably many years since you studied the underside of a dining room chair. (Fraiberg, 1959, pp. 52–53).

The infant spends hours practicing newly acquired motor skills.

Once they can move on their own, infants begin to detach from their mothers. They are individuals with their own ideas about what to do. At this point, new problems develop for infant and adults since for the first time, interests conflict. These will be discussed in Section III.

The onset of crawling appears to be related to milestones in cognitive development (Kermoian & Campos, 1988). Now armed with the ability to move, and afforded the opportunity to exercise it, new opportunities open up for exploration and the construction of new knowledge about the world. The more efficiently the infant can move, the more she can learn. Bushnell and Boudreau (1993) believe the development of motor abilities may make it possible for children to use perceptual information such as haptic (touch/feel) and depth perception to learn more about their environment. For example, Kermoian and

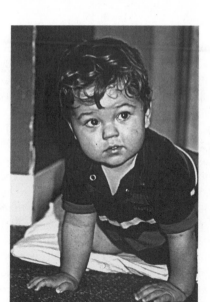

Figure 9–3   **Now that the infant can move on his own, a new world opens up.**

Campos (1988) found that eight-and-one-half-month-olds who could move around on their own were cognitively more advanced than those who couldn't.

"Independent walking is the major developmental task of infancy" (Malina, 1981, p. 214). Walking lays the foundation for the development of other motor tasks. The child can move about without depending on her hands. Her hands are then free to engage in other kinds of motor tasks. Walking at the expected time indicates that nervous system and muscle development are normal (Thelen, 1984). Walking is the landmark that indicates the end of infancy and the beginning of toddlerhood. Esther Thelen (1984) looked very closely at the development of walking. A close examination of infant kicking movements while prone showed that they are the same kinds of movements used in walking. When the infant first becomes a walker there are many deficiencies relative to adult walking. The new walker has a wide stance, cannot stabilize on one leg for very long, has a short stride, and tends to hold his arms out for balance. Holding a steady posture is very difficult. This may be due, to some extent, to immature neurological development but is probably also influenced by body proportion, center of gravity, and muscle strength and tone.

Head, shoulders, hips, and chest grow faster than legs during the first eighteen months. Once legs begin to grow longer and slimmer, gait matures. At the same time, the infant's leg muscles are relatively weak and lack muscle tone. Cognitive development also has some influence on motivating walking. Zelazo (1984) believes there is a spurt in cognitive development that coincides with the onset of walking. He points out that talking and functional (rather than just exploratory) object use begin at about the same time as walking.

The Adult Role in Motor and Physical Development

Malina (1981) emphasizes the significance of movement experiences for young children. The child needs to be provided with opportunities for different kinds of motor exploration, discovery, and practice. These should include both child-selected and adult-directed activities.

Wilson (1990) has developed a curriculum plan for infants. Some examples of her suggestions for infant motor and physical development materials and teaching strategies are the following:

Birth to four months of age:
Appropriate materials would be rattles, yarn or textured balls, and small toys to grasp. To develop muscular control before they are able to turn their own bodies, young infants need to be moved from back to stomach frequently during their waking hours so they can try out different muscle groups. The adults who care for infants can stimulate motor development through simple actions such as holding out toys that they can reach for.

Four months to eight months of age:
Appropriate materials during this period include foam toys, small toys and objects to grasp, toys safe to throw, toys safe to bang and hit, and low things to climb over and under. Infants are beginning to move as they become stronger and better coordinated. They need a safe floor area where they have opportunities to move, to sit and play with toys, and to lie down when they feel tired.

Eight to twelve months of age:

Motor development materials for this period should include very low materials to climb over, sturdy furniture to pull up on and walk around while holding on. Other materials include balls to clutch, objects to stack, nesting toys, a pail with small objects to drop into it and one piece puzzles. Infants continue to need safe spaces for movement with materials they can safely explore. Adults can help by assisting them in their early efforts at walking and supervising their efforts to climb stairs and pull themselves up. Infants now enjoy motor games such as pat-a-cake or playing hide-and-seek with objects.

Of equal importance to indoor play is outdoor play. Both Frost (1992) and Wortham and Wortham (1989) provide guidelines for infant outdoor environments. Wortham and Wortham (1989) warn that it is tempting not to consider outdoor play for infants because of the effort needed to move them from indoors to outdoors and back again. However, infants can benefit from experiences with climate changes, variations in the landscape, the openness of the outdoors, the messiness, wildlife, and the people.

COGNITIVE DEVELOPMENT

Cognitive development is a term used to describe the acquisition of knowledge and the way the knowledge is used. Researchers are very interested in just how much babies know and how they go about learning. As discussed in Unit 7, we now recognize that infants are much more competent than was previously thought. Sensory competencies underlie the infant's ability to progress through the various stages of cognitive development.

Object Permanence and Recognition

During the first year, two major sensorimotor abilities proceed through their first developmental stages (Ault, 1983). One is the concept of **object permanence** and the other, **object recognition.**

"Object permanence is defined as the knowledge that objects continue to exist even when one is not perceiving them" (Ault, 1983, p. 30). Children develop this knowledge through a series of six stages. Four of these stages take place during the first year. During stage one (0 to 2 months) things out of sight are out of mind for the infant. The infant does not search for a hidden object or even show any sign of knowing that it has been hidden. At stage two (2 to 4 months), the infant still does not search. The infant may, however, gaze for a few moments in the direction where a hidden toy was last seen. In stage three (4 to 8 months), the infant searches for an object that is partially hidden. The infant also looks for something that he has caused to disappear, such as a rattle he has dropped. Between 8 and 12 months the fourth stage is reached. If a toy is covered by a cloth or other screen, the infant lifts it to find the toy. However, if the toy is then hidden under something else, the infant looks in the first hiding place before going to the second. The concept of object permanence is starting to develop, but is not completely developed until the middle of the second year. At this point, adult and child can enjoy a game of peek-a-boo.

Many researchers are critical of Piaget's explanation of the development of the object concept (Wishart & Bower, 1984). For example, some researchers found that if the object was put under a transparent cup or placed on top of a box the infant still acted as if it was out of sight. Wishart and Bower (1984) did a large-scale study designed to discover the underlying reason for this apparently inconsistent behavior. Their theory is that the problem concerns object identity rather than object permanence. That is, the infant goes through several stages in developing the concept that an object maintains its identity no matter where it is placed. As an infant moves through these stages, different search strategies are developed for finding the moved object. For the adult who works with young children, this theory suggests that games that involve moving objects to different locations within sight are just as important for the infant as hidden object games (Figure 9–4).

The second sensorimotor ability, object recognition, concerns the features the infant uses to identify

---

KEYTERMSKEYTERMSKEYTERMSKEYTERMSKEYTERMSKEY

| Cognitive development | object permanence | object recognition |

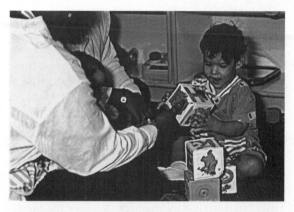

Figure 9–4 Manipulation of objects provides the infant with information that builds cognitive skills.

objects. As infants grow, they learn to use features such as color, shape, size, and texture. They seem to acquire this ability at about 16 weeks of age. The younger infant perceives the differences but does not use the information as an aid in identification.

Communications

Infants are also developing in the communication area. They are able communicators. Condon and Sander (1974) have shown through slow-motion photography that infants move in rhythm with the speech of the adults around them. They also develop a game-like communication system with objects (Watson, 1976). That is, infants chatter happily as they watch their mobiles or bat at a rattle or ball hung from a string. This vocalizing reflects the infant's needs and mood.

As young as 2 months of age, infants discriminate mother's voice from a stranger's voice (Roe, 1990). This difference favors girls whose vocal output to their mothers is at a higher rate than vocal output to strangers. This is mainly found to be the case with females from higher-education-level families. The lower language performance of children from lower education families appears to be evident as young as 2 months of age.

Labeling appears as an important component of cognitive development as early as 10 months of age

before children actually begin to speak conventional words (Baldwin & Markman, 1989). When a new object was labeled for infants between the ages of 10 and 14 months of age, infants attended to the object for a longer period of time than if no label was provided. Labeling would mean showing or pointing to the object with an accompanying verbalization, such as, "See the robot. It's a robot" (Baldwin & Markman, 1989, p. 394). When given an opportunity to play with a group of toys that included a previously labeled toy, they attended longer to the object that had been previously labeled than to the other toys. Verbal labels appear to be facilitative and stay with infants even before they speak their first word. This would indicate that it is valuable for an infant's cognitive development to label objects even though speech has not yet appeared.

Infants seem to have the ability to communicate with nonverbal gestures (Legerstee, Corter, & Kienapple, 1990). Specific hand and arm actions are consistent and convey specific meanings. When infants smiled and gazed at their responsive mothers they gestured with pointing and with open hands. When faced with an inactive mother or a doll, they gazed passively, put their arms at their sides and curled their fingers under. The pointing and open hands appeared to indicate active communication.

Infant speech develops gradually from single vowel sounds at one month of age to vowel/consonant combinations by 8 months, to possibly some single words by 12 months. Understanding develops simultaneously so that by 12 months children usually can respond to simple directions such as "Bring me your teddy bear, please," or "Put your cup on the table" (Allen & Marotz, 1994). Language development is described in more detail in Unit 22.

Categorization

Categorization is another important area of early development. Categorization skills enable us to sort and group items according to similar attributes. For example, a group of toy vehicles consisting of cars, trucks, airplanes, and boats can be sorted according to type, use (used on land, sea, or air), color, or size. Categorizing behavior as it is observed in preschool- and kindergarten-age children is discussed in Units 20 and 21. Only recently have researchers looked at infants to find the beginnings of categorization skills and concepts. Infants were found to be able to recognize categories such as toy stuffed animals, round fruit, human faces, colors, and shapes (Sherman, 1985). What the infants seem to learn and remember are the most obvious, consistent attributes of items in a category. For example, when infants were shown a series of drawings of faces all of which had the same hairline and jaw line and then, after a delay, were shown the same and similar faces, the ten-month-old infants picked hairline and jaw line as the critical features for the category (Sherman, 1985).

Eimas and Quinn (1994) studied the categorization behaviors of three- and four-month-old infants. The infants were shown photographs of natural animals. The target basic categories were either horses or cats. The infants indicated that cats, zebras, and giraffes were not included in the horse category. Horses and tigers, but not female lions, were excluded from the cat category.

Younger (1993) found that ten-month-old infants can exclude items that don't fit in a category of animals they are learning. This indicates that infants actively compare the items presented to them and decide which belong in the group and which do not. Research does not tell us how infants apply this emerging capability in their everyday experiences to develop categories, only that the capability is present. It would suggest, however, that infants can benefit from having experiences with many types of objects (living and nonliving) that can serve as the basis for category building. We will look further at category building as we consider cognitive development in older children.

Planning

Planning is an important human higher-level cognitive ability. Planning enables us to consider ways to solve problems prior to actually embarking on a solution and thus cuts down on time lost with trial-and-error approaches. Planning involves men-

tally going through a sequence of steps leading to a solution before actually trying out the solution. Willatts (Willatts, 1989; Willatts & Rosie, 1989) believes that infants are capable of some primitive planning behaviors and thus some representational thought earlier than Piaget's view of infant cognitive development. Piaget believed that planning ability and representational thought did not appear until the end of the sensorimotor period (around 18 months to 2 years). Willatt's research indicates that infants show planful behavior as young as 9 months of age. Infants can perceive a situation in which it was possible to remove a barrier, pull a string, and obtain an object versus a situation in which the string was not attached to the object. In the first situation, infants removed the barrier and pulled the string to get the object. In the second, they picked up the barrier and played with it. They appeared to figure out under which condition they could or could not obtain the desired object.

Brain Lateralization

Brain lateralization has been the subject of much interest (Brooks & Obrzut, 1981). It was found that each of the hemispheres of the brain controls different types of cognitive and behavioral functions. In right-handed persons, the left side of the brain processes in a sequential, analytic, linguistic mode. The right side processes in a parallel, holistic, spatial, nonlinguistic mode. Research indicates that infants are born with this differential functioning of the two sides of the brain. To function well there needs to be good communication between both sides.

It has been suggested (Brooks & Obrzut, 1981; Cherry, Godwin, & Staples, 1989) that the brain lateralization factor has important implications for parents and teachers. Optimum brain development involves the development of both left and right brain functions and the communication between the two. There is some research indicating that left-side function in the language area can be influenced by environmental experiences. Otherwise, at this point, we have to assume that infants need a variety of experi-

KEYTERMSKEYTERMSKEYTERMSKEYTERMSKEYTERMSKEY

Planning   Brain lateralization ences designed to develop both sides. Activities that should stimulate both sides of the brain include music boxes and wrist bells for auditory stimulation; mobiles and colorful pictures for visual stimulation; bells on booties or low mobiles for stimulation of kicking; plastic keys, balls, and discs on chains for finger dexterity; and nipples for sucking. The right side is often more neglected in these days of back to basics. It is important that infants have time to develop their own ways of dealing with the environment in order to develop their creative side as well as their analytic and verbal side.

The Importance of Object Manipulation

The play of infants is meaningful and meanings can be enhanced with "materials which lend themselves to manipulation, exploration, and multiple uses" (Goldhaber & Smith, 1993). The haptic (touch) aspect of object manipulation provides meaningful information to infants (Catherwood, 1993). The most simple, offbeat materials can capture infant attention. For example, Goldhaber and Smith (1993) dumped crumpled paper on the floor in their infant room. The group, ranging in age from 5 to 14 months, gathered around the paper and explored its properties. The crumpled pieces were picked up, mouthed, shaken, dropped, and observed as they rolled across the floor.

What happens if infants do not have the sensorimotor experiences needed in order to develop cognitively? Ruff, McCarton, Kurtzberg, and Vaughn (1984) compared full-term and preterm infants on their object manipulation skills. In a previous study, Ruff found that infants between 9 and 12 months of age obtained information about objects through three types of manipulations: fingering the surface of the object, looking at the object while they rotate or turn it, and transferring the object from hand to hand. Three groups of children, one full-term and two preterm (one group categorized as high risk and one as low risk according to medical information available), were observed while manipulating small blocks. The high-risk

infants spent the least time manipulating the blocks. The low-risk preterms reacted about the same as the full-term infants. The preterm high-risk group infants are likely to have some central nervous system damage that would lead to a lower level of neuromuscular maturation and deficient fine motor coordination. Thus, they manipulated the blocks much less and received less information about the blocks than the other infants. With less information about objects they are likely to have a deficit in categorization ability, a basic cognitive skill that, as we have already seen, begins to develop during infancy.

Social Cognition

Social interaction and social resources are essential support for cognitive development. Social referencing is used by infants to gain information from others in order to understand and evaluate events and behave in the appropriate manner in a situation (Hornik & Gunnar, 1988). Infants have been observed to seek information and use the information as a guide for behavior. Infants may respond to affective social referencing, that is, the affective expressions of others and to instrumental social referencing, using information about others' interactions with objects or people as a guide to their own interactions with novel objects or people. Positive effect from others facilitates positive behaviors toward novel objects and negative effect promotes avoidance (Hornik & Gunnar, 1988). As an example consider Tony at 12 months of age:

> Tony is seated on the floor next to a cage that contains a rabbit. Tony's mother is seated nearby. Tony moves closer to the cage. He looks over at his mother who smiles and nods. Tony looks back at the rabbit with interest. He appears to want to touch it but holds back. He looks over at her again and she says, "It's okay to pat the bunny." He still holds back. Tony's mother comes over. She reaches in and pats the rabbit, "This is a sweet rabbit. He's soft and smooth. You can pat him too." Tony observes his mother's demonstration. He then leans over the cage and gently pats the rabbit just as his mother did.

KEYTERMSKEYTERMSKEYTERMSKEYTERMSKEYTERMSKEYTERMSKEY

object manipulation   Social referencing

This ability to gain information from others and apply it in new situations is of course essential in getting the most out of future educational and life experiences. Also important is that infants can retain information learned through imitation and apply it in future situations (Meltzoff, 1988).

Play as a Vehicle for Learning

Infant learning focuses on play activities. Play is the major vehicle for cognitive and motor development (Caruso, 1988). Research on infant play indicates that it serves a number of functions in infant learning (Caruso, 1988). Caruso (1988) defines learning as not just remembering, but remembering and understanding. That is, learning occurs when infants make sense out of their experiences. Infant play includes both an exploratory and a playful aspect that sometimes cycle each other and sometimes integrate and become a part of the same actions.

Play behaviors develop in several stages. Infant play consists mainly of mouthing and simple manipulation. Quality of spontaneous play is related to level of cognitive development whereas responses to adult-directed play are not. Therefore, it is extremely important for infants to have plenty of opportunities for spontaneous play in a stimulating environment without adult intervention. Both physical and social stimulation are critical for a responsive environment that enhances the quality of infant spontaneous play. A rich environment affords the infant opportunities to experience objects of many shapes, sizes, textures, and colors with adults who are sensitive to the infants play needs and provide positive responses to the infant's exploratory activities.

The Adult Role in Infant Cognitive Development

Adults provide the interaction and the environment that supports cognitive, motor, social, and affective development. Specific examples of appropriate, supportive interactions have been inserted throughout this unit. The adult role with infants will be discussed in more detail in Unit 10.

SUMMARY

Cognitive development in infancy is closely tied to sensory and motor growth and activities. Infants move through a sequence of physical and motor development toward the time when they can walk without support. Once infants can walk, they leave infancy and enter toddlerhood. Infants also go through a sequence of stages in cognitive development centered on their increasing knowledge of objects in the environment and knowledge of the functions of language. The adult role is to provide the appropriate stimulation through personal interaction and by providing a stimulating environment. Infants need a balance of time with other people and time to play and explore on their own in order to develop to capacity during this first part of the sensorimotor period.

FOR FURTHER READING

Allen, K. E., & Marotz, L. (1994). *Developmental profiles.* (2nd Ed.). Albany, NY: Delmar.

Butterworth, G. E., Harris, P. L., Leslie, A. M., & Wellman, H. M. (Eds.). (1991). *Perspectives on the child's theory of mind.* New York: Oxford University Press.

Caulfield, R. Infants' sensory abilities: Caregiving implications and recommendations. *Day Care and Early Education, 21* (4), 31–35.

Colombo, J. (1993). *Infant cognition: Predicting later intellectual functioning.* Thousand Oaks, CA: Sage.

KEYTERMSKEYTERMSKEYTERMSKEYTERMSKEYTERMSKEYTERMSKEY

Play

Kalverboer, A. F., Hopkins, B., & Gueze, R. (Eds.). (1992). *Motor development in early and later childhood.* New York: Cambridge University Press.

Mehler, J., & Dupoux, E. (1994). *What infants know: The new cognitive science of early development.* Cambridge, MA: Blackwell.

Melkman, R. (1988). *The construction of objectivity: A new look at the first months of life.* New York: Karger.

Moerk, E. L. (1983). *The mother of Eve—As a first language teacher.* Norwood, NJ: Ablex.

Sinclair, H., Stambak, M., Lezine, I., Verba, M., & Rayna, S. (1989). *Infants and objects: The creativity of cognitive development.* San Diego, CA: Academic Press.

Thelen, E., & Lockman, J. J. (Eds.). (1993). Developmental biodynamics: Brain, body, behavior connections. *Child Development* [Special section], *64* (4), 953–1190.

Wellman, H. M., Cross, D., & Bartsch, K. (1988). *Infant search and object permanence: A meta-analysis of the A-not-B error.* Chicago: University of Chicago Press. [Originally published as *Child Development Monographs* #214, *51*(3)]

Wilson, L. C. (1995). *Infants and toddlers: Curriculum and teaching.* Albany, NY: Delmar.

SUGGESTED ACTIVITIES

1. Observe an infant at home or at a childcare site. Use an infant development evaluation sheet, as shown in Figure 9–5. Evaluate the infant's developmental level and rate of development.
   a. Overall, does the infant seem to be average, ahead of normal expectations, or slow in his rate of development?
   b. Are there any areas in which the infant seems to be exceptional, ahead of, or behind in development?
   c. What suggestions do you have for the parents and/or caregiver regarding this infant?

2. Find an infant under 6 months of age and an infant between 9 and 12 months of age. Compare their development of object permanence. Try the following tasks and record their responses. Compare their reactions. At which stage of object permanence would you place each of the infants?
   a. Follow an object through space visually.
      Make a red and white bull's-eye pattern or use a bright plastic toy. Have the infant lie down or sit in an infant seat. Place yourself behind the infant so she concentrates on the object, not on you. Move the object in a circle around the infant's head. Do this five times. Note whether or not the infant tries to follow the object with her eyes and head. If she does follow it, does she follow it smoothly and through the complete circle?
   b. Reaction to a disappearing object.
      Use a brightly colored toy. Be sure infant is looking at it. Move it slowly to a position where it is hidden. Do this three times. Note if the infant follows the object to the point where it disappears; whether she continues to glance at the spot where it disappeared; and whether she seems to be visually searching for the object at the point where it disappeared.
   c. The partially hidden object.
      Use an object (toy, doll, stuffed animal, teething ring, rattle) that infant finds interesting. Hold the object in front of the infant and be sure she is looking at it. Put the object down in front of infant where she can see it. Use a white cloth to cover part of the object. Note whether the infant tries to grasp the object. Does she try to remove the cloth or does she lose interest in the object when it is covered? Does she manage to get the object?
   d. The completely hidden object.
      Pick out a small object that you know the child finds interesting. Be sure she watches as you hide the object completely under the white cloth. Does she lose interest? Does she pick up the cloth and play with it? Does she pick up the cloth and get the object?

Observer _____ Date _____ Time _____ Place _____

Infant's Name _____ Birth Date _____ Age _____

Average Age of Appearance	Behavior	Observed		Comments
		Yes	No	
Birth to Six Months				
Gross Motor				
1 month	Moves head from side to side			
1 month	When lying down makes crawling movements			
1 month	Head held erect when held at shoulder for three seconds			
1 month	When cheek is rubbed turns to same side			
1½–2 months	Turns from side to back			
2–3 months	Held sitting, head is predominantly erect			
2–3 months	Prone, lifts head up			
2–4 months	Prone, lifts head and upper chest well up in midline using forearms as support, legs straight out with buttocks flat			
2½–3½ months	Rolls over			
3 months	Held standing, lifts foot			
5 months	Prone, holds arms extended			
5½ months	Reaches on same side as arm used			
5½–6 months	Stands holding on			
Fine Motor				
1 month	Regards bright object			
1 month	Turns eyes and head toward light			
1 month	When rattle placed in hand, drops immediately			
2 months	Holds rattle briefly			
2½ months	Will glance from one object to another			
3 months	Hands usually open			
3–4 months	Plays in simple way with rattle			
3–4 months	Inspects fingers			
3 months	Holds rattle actively			
3–4 months	Reaches for dangling ring			
3–4 months	Follows ball visually across table			
4 months	Carries object to mouth			
4–5 months	Recovers rattle from chest			
4–5 months	Holds two objects			
5 months	Transfers object from hand to hand			
5–6 months	Bangs in play			
5–6 months	Sits, looks for object			
Cognitive				
1 month	Responds to sounds			
1 month	Vocalizes (other than cry)			
1 month	Cries lustily when hungry or uncomfortable			
2 months	Smiles			
2–3 months	Laughs			
2 months	Visually recognizes mother			
2 months	Coos — single-vowel sounds			
3 months	Vocalizes when spoken to or pleased			
3–4 months	Shows preference for familiar persons			
4–5 months	Turns head to sound of bell			
4–6 months	Turns head to sound of rattle			
4 months	Increases activity at sight of toy			
4½–6 months	Fingers mirror image			
4½–5 months	Discriminates strangers			
5½–6 months	Plays peek-a-boo			
5½–6 months	Shows interest in sound production for pleasure and excitement			

Figure 9–5 **Infant development evaluation sheet (Adapted from *Developmental Guidelines*, compiled by Sprugel and Goldberg under the direction of Merle B. Karnes, Updated mimeograph.)**

Average Age of Appearance	Behavior	Observed Yes	Observed No	Comments
Six Months to Twelve Months				
Gross Motor				
6 months	Sits alone for 30 seconds			
6 months	Rolls from back to stomach			
6 months	Lifts legs to vertical and grasps foot			
6½ months	When on stomach, pivots 180 degrees in order to obtain toy which is kept just out of infant's reach			
6½–7 months	Sits: Briefly, leans forward on hands			
7 months	Lying on back, brings feet to mouth			
7½–8 months	Pulls self to stand			
8 months	Stands briefly with hands held			
9 months	Walks holding onto furniture			
9 months	Attempts to crawl on all fours			
9 months	Stands holding but cannot lower self			
9½–10 months	Sits steadily and indefinitely			
9½–11 months	Walks with both hands held			
9½–10 months	Stands momentarily			
10 months	Creeps			
11–11½ months	Stands alone well			
11–12 months	May walk alone			
Fine Motor				
6 months	Secures cube on sight			
6 months	Follows adult's movements across the room			
6 months	Immediately fixates interesting small objects and stretches out to grasp them			
6 months	Retains rattle			
6½ months	Manipulates and examines an object			
6½ months	Can reach for, grab and retain rattle held in front of him			
7 months	Pulls string to obtain an object			
7½–8½ months	Grasps with thumb and finger			
8–9 months	Persists in reaching for toy out of reach on table			
8 months	Shows hand preference			
8–8½ months	Bangs spoon			
9 months	Searches in correct place for toys dropped within reach of hands			
9 months	May find toy hidden under cup			
10 months	Hits cup with spoon			
10 months	Crude release of object			
10½–11 months	Picks up raisin with thumb and forefinger pincer grasp			
11 months	Pushes car along			
11–12 months	Puts three or more objects in container			
Cognitive				
6 months	Spontaneous social vocal sounds			
6 months	Smiles and vocalizes at image in mirror			
7 months	Vocalizes four different syllables			
7½–8 months	Says "Da-Da" or equivalent			
8 months	Vocalizes single syllables such as _da, ka, ba_			
8½ months	Demands personal attention			
9 months	Vocalizes deliberately as means of inter-personal relationship			
9 months	Babbles tunefully, repeating syllables in strings ("mam-mam," " bibiba")			

Figure 9–5   Infant development evaluation sheet.   (Continued)

Average Age of Appearance	Behavior	Observed		Comments
		Yes	No	
Six Months To Twelve Months				
9–9½ months	Clearly distinguishes strangers from familiars, and requires assurance before accepting their advances; clings to known adult and hides face			
9–10 months	Responds to name and to "no, no"			
10 months	Looks at pictures in book			
11 months	Says one word other than mama and dada – usually one syllable used to designate an object			
11 months	Will find hidden object			
12 months	May have two to eight words besides "mama" and "dada"			
Self Help				
6 months	Lifts cup			
8 months	Reaches for toys out of reach consistently			
9 months	Holds, bites, and chews biscuits			
9 months	Puts hands around bottle or cup when feeding			
9 months	Tries to grasp spoon when being fed			
9 months	Holds bottle to feed self			
11½–12 months	Is able to drink from cup when it is held though may spill			

Figure 9–5   **Infant development evaluation sheet.   (Continued)**

    e. Two hiding places and an object.

This time use two cloths, the white one and another one that is a dull and uninteresting color. Lay the two cloths down on the floor in front of infant. Hide the object under one of the cloths. If infant finds it, then hide it under the other cloth. Does infant look under the correct cloth first or under the one that was used the first time?

    f. Three hiding places and one object.

If infant successfully has found the hidden object with two cloths, then add a third. Note her behavior as the object is hidden under the first, then the second, and then the third. Does she successfully find the object under the third cloth?

3. Go to a store where infant toys are sold. Make a list of the toys and their prices. Decide which infant skills each toy is meant to develop. Design two toys that you could make yourself to serve the same purpose.

4. Make an entry in your journal.

REVIEW

A. Place in order of development each of the following body parts: legs, head, trunk.

B. Put an X by all the correct statements.

    _____ 1. Both heredity and environment influence motor development.

    _____ 2. Children with lower Apgar scores at birth can be predicted to have delayed motor development.

    _____ 3. Size, physique, and body composition have no known effect on motor development.

_____ 4. There is a proven genetic difference in the level of motor skill development of boys as compared with girls.

_____ 5. African-American and Hispanic infants tend to be ahead of European-American infants in motor development.

_____ 6. When the child can walk independently his hands are freed to explore the environment and he can move on to development of other motor skills.

_____ 7. Independent walking is a landmark that is considered the end of infancy and the beginning of toddlerhood.

_____ 8. Walking is most likely not related to growth in the cognitive area.

C. How old is each of the following infants?
   1. Carlos pulls himself up to his feet in his playpen. He loves to eat raisins and picks them up carefully with thumb and index finger.
   2. Betsy sits propped up, turning her head from side to side as she observes the activity in the room.
   3. Clancy sits on the floor rolling a ball back and forth to his sister. He seems to get bored as his glance wanders and he gets on all fours and creeps away.

D. Describe two activities that would be helpful in supporting infant motor development.

E. Select the correct answers.
   1. In Sherman's study, infants viewed drawings of faces that all had the same hairline and jaw line. When shown pairs of faces where one had the previously viewed hairline and jaw line and the other had some other features,
      a. the infants showed no preference for either one of the faces in the pairs.
      b. the infants remembered features other than jaw line and hairline best.
      c. the infants picked hairline and jaw line as the critical features in the pictures.
   2. The results of Sherman's study
      a. show that infants can develop categories.
      b. indicate infants cannot develop categories.
      c. add no information to our knowledge of when children begin to learn to categorize.
   3. The results of Younger's 1993 study and preceding studies indicate that:
      a. By 10 months of age infants can detect and organize category features.
      b. Fourteen months of age is the critical time for developing the ability to organize category features.
      c. The infants became confused when shown a picture of a novel animal.
   4. Willatt's research
      a. Confirms that infants always use trial and error to solve problems.
      b. Confirms that infants can think through a solution to a problem before acting.
      c. Supports Piaget's ideas regarding the age at which we can expect representational thought to be evident in infant approaches to problem solving.

F. Explain the importance of brain lateralization to cognitive development.

G. List the three types of object manipulation that seem to be necessary for the infant to achieve full cognitive capacity.

H. Why might we predict that a high-risk, preterm infant could be delayed in cognitive development?

I. Provide an example of infant social referencing.

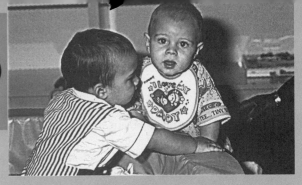

Infancy: Sociocultural Aspects of Development

OBJECTIVES

After studying this unit, the student should be able to:

■ Recognize the factors that indicate a high-quality infant environment.

■ Discuss the pros and cons of day care for infants.

■ Recognize the effects of maternal employment on infant development.

■ List the socioeconomic and cultural factors that may affect infant development.

■ Evaluate infant caregiver behavior using an infant caregiver evaluation sheet.

THE INFANT ENVIRONMENT

The infant needs an interesting and rich environment but one which is not overstimulating. There is a need for responsive adults and exciting objects. However, the objects do not have to be expensive materials intent on educating, especially during the early months (White, 1975). Homemade toys and nontoxic household objects are fine. Washcloth dolls, sock animals, covered foam rubber blocks, stuffed toys, rattles, and mobiles keep younger infants happy. It helps if infants are positioned so they can observe pictures, people, and other things of interest. When infants begin organizing objects between 6 and 12 months, coffee cans with small safe objects to drop in and pour out are fun. Cloth books, spool heads, jar lids, and a soft ball are good play materials.

David A. Caruso (1984) suggests that the infant's need to explore can be enhanced through the social and the physical environment (Figure 10–1). Social environment goals include:

• Allowing each infant enough time for self-initiated exploratory play with things and with people.

• Being alert to, and responding positively to, the infant's self-initiated interpersonal exploration.

• Initiating play for more passive infants and encouraging them to be more assertive and take over their own activities.

The physical environmental goals suggested by Caruso are also important:

• The playroom should be open and equipped with a variety of play areas and toys.

• Toys should be visible and placed on low, open shelves where they are readily accessible.

• Toys should be matched to children's developmental levels.

Figure 10–1   **Infants need space in which to move about and toys they can explore with all their senses. (From Wilson, *Infants and Toddlers: Curriculum and Teaching*, 2nd ed., by Delmar Publishers)**

- Play materials should respond to the baby's natural actions such as banging two items together, kicking, fingering, etc.
- Floors should be carpeted for safe, comfortable crawling.

The importance of quality social interaction between caregiver and child, as pointed out in previous units, must not be underestimated. The child's normal behaviors can be difficult for adults who do not understand their significance. According to T. Berry Brazelton (*Tots . . .*, 1984) the sudden bursts of developmental change that are normal for babies can send caregivers into a spin. Infants become obsessed with each new skill to be mastered. The author once heard her daughter, at 5 or 6 months of age, grunting and groaning in her crib. Upon entering her child's room she found her daughter moving her body around the crib methodically ripping off the elastics that held the crib bumpers. The baby was feeling very powerful while mother felt vexed. Around the same time, baby also asserted her independence by insisting on holding her bottle herself. Mother had to deal

with losing an important parental function. These assertions of autonomy and independence can upset the uninformed parent or other caregiver who may not realize that asserting oneself independently is a part of normal infant development.

Fathers, siblings, and others all play important roles in the lives of infants (Cole & Cole 1989). In the 1980s fathers' roles changed as more mothers were employed and fathers took on more responsibility for infant care. (*Fathers' . . .*, 1984). Ninio and Rinott (1988) did a study that examined the amount of fathers' interactions with infants and its relationship to fathers' estimates of infants' social-cognitive competence. About half of the wives of the men in the sample worked outside the home. The fathers in this study were more likely than those in earlier studies to take responsibility for infant care. However, there was wide variation. The findings indicated:

- The more a father was involved in infant care, the higher were his opinions of infant capacities.
- On the average, fathers attribute less competence to their infants than do mothers.
- The more fathers are involved in infant care, the closer the match between mothers' and fathers' estimates of infant competence (Figure 10–2).

The fathers who spent less than 15 minutes per day with their infants viewed them as the least capable; the fathers who spent an hour or more per day with

Figure 10–2   **In the quality childcare center, each child's daily activities are carefully recorded to inform all the staff and the parents.**

their infants viewed them as more capable. The views of these latter fathers were more congruent with the mothers' views. It may be that the low-interaction-time fathers are men who believe infants in general are not interesting and that children do not require social and cognitive stimulation until they reach an age in which they can communicate and interact in a more adultlike manner. The highly interactive fathers may have beliefs that value the importance of infant stimulation.

Fathers who are the primary caregiver tend to retain their playful attitude. They are also sympathetic and friendly and take pride in parenthood. Thus, male primary caregivers take on the characteristics previously believed to be female but also retains the conventional male characteristics when interacting with the infant (Berk, 1994).

The absent father continues to be of concern. More than 25 percent of our children live in female-headed households. Forty percent of the children in these households haven't seen their fathers in a year or more. With more mothers in the workforce, father love and care is needed more than ever. Having a nurturing father who spends time with the young child provides her with a positive male model for development of caring and compassion (Louv, 1994).

Maternal Employment During Infancy

Since 1990 the percentage of mothers of children under six in the labor force has fluctuated around 60 percent. This is an increase of 50 percent since 1975 (State of America's children, 1994). Some mothers work because of financial necessity, others because they feel the need for a fulfilling career. In either case, the result may be a rather hectic family life.

There is a good deal of concern regarding the effects of maternal employment on child development and parent/child relations. Some research has looked at these factors from the maternal employment view. Other research has looked at these factors from the childcare view. We will look first at the maternal employment view. Infant attachment has been the focus of many studies. Usually using the strange-situation method (as described in Unit 8), researchers have looked at mother-infant and father-infant attachment

in families with employed and nonemployed mothers. First, we will look at the results of study that uses the strange situation as the measure of attachment.

Chase-Landsdale and Owen (1987) examined the effects of maternal employment on infant-mother and infant-father attachment. Ordinarily attachment is built gradually during the interactions of the first 7 months. Therefore Chase-Landsdale and Owen selected mothers who were employed when their infants were very young. The quality of father-infant and mother-infant attachment in mother-employed families was compared with nonemployed mother families. Overall no association was found between mother's work status and quality of infant attachment to mothers or girls attachment to fathers. However, sons of nonemployed mothers were more secure with their fathers than sons of employed mothers. The authors suggest that sons of employed mothers appear to be more vulnerable to feelings of insecurity in two-wage-earner households and may be treated more negatively and less thoughtfully than girls.

Before turning to infant child care, one more maternal employment study merits attention. Zaslow, Pedersen, Suwalsky, and Rabinovich (1989) did home observations of mothers, fathers and their one-year-old infants on weekday evenings. They observed in homes where mothers were employed outside the home and in homes where mothers were homemakers. Comparing their results with the results of other studies the authors noted the following emerging consistencies:

- When observed on weekday evenings, parents in employed-mother families tend to interact less with their infants than parents in home-maker families.

- In mother-employed families there is less play with objects which may in turn result in less than optimum cognitive development for the infants. Boys especially receive less of this type of attention.

It appears likely that the burden of the demands on working parents in the evening (chores, making contacts with spouse, etc.) preclude providing the infant with as much attention as would be optimum. It may be that working parents need to divide labor so one does chores while the other plays with the baby. It is also possible that mothers find it difficult to change from the serious businesslike behavior of the world of work to some of the more playful behavior of parenting. Finally, it may be that infants who have been in **child care** all day are used to being autonomous and prefer independent play thus making it more difficult for parents to interject themselves into the play activity. More research is needed to try to identify the reasons for these differences between evening interactions in employed-mother families as compared with homemaker-mother families.

The Question of Child Care: Effects on Infants

A great deal of research, professional discussion and disagreement has focused on child care for infants. By 1990, more than 6.5 million children under the age of five were cared for by someone other than a parent. Of this number 37.9 percent were in childcare centers, 26.6 percent in family childcare homes, 25.1 percent in the homes of nonparent relatives, 5.1 percent were in their own homes with a nonrelative caregiver, and 5.1 percent were in other settings (State of America's children, 1994). Jay Belsky (Belsky, 1991, 1990; Belsky & Rovine, 1988) has been the leading figure in interpreting the research on infant child care as indicating a number of dangers. Belsky concluded that ". . . extensive infant day care experience is associated with insecure attachment during infancy and heightened aggressiveness and noncompliance during the preschool and early school age years" (Belsky, 1988, p. 235). Belsky noted that observations remarkably consistent with attachment theory can be made. Belsky concludes that nonmaternal care during the first year of more than 20 hours per week presents a risk factor for the infant. Other researchers disagree with Belsky's interpretation (see Philips, McCartney, Scarr, & Howes, 1990; Chess, 1990; and *Early Childhood Research Quarterly, 3* (3), 1988). From her review of the infant childcare research, Carollee Howes (1989) concludes that the effects of child care on infants is related to the quality of the care. She agrees that security of attachment is critical as a basis for future social and emotional development. She believes,

however, that the critical factor, in or out of the home, is the degree of sensitivity and responsiveness of the caregiver to the infant (Figure 10–3).

From their observations of infants with their mothers, fathers, and caregivers Goossens and van Ijzendoorn (1990) note that some children had stronger, more positive attachment relationships with their caregiver than with their parents. Whether a strong infant-caregiver relationship other than with parents can make up for a weak parent-infant attachment is unknown. Goossens and van Ijzendoorn (1990) also noted that the most sensitive caregivers tended to be younger and possibly had more energy for coping with infant demands.

Thornburg, Pearl, Crompton, and Ispa (1990) looked at comparisons of childcare arrangements (no day care, part-time care, and full-time day care) during infancy through age five and the effects on social, intellectual, and motor development. They found no significant negative effects on the social behavior of children who had been in full-time day care as infants. Those children who were in part-time arrange-

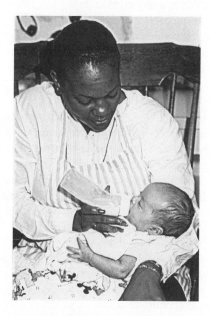

Figure 10–3   **The day-care provider can become a supplement to the family.**

child care

ments had the most social problems in kindergarten. Children who stayed home all five years were the most compliant with adults. African-American children appeared to gain a cognitive advantage from the out-of-home experience as reflected in cognitive assessment test scores. These researchers had no information on the quality of child care received.

The final answer to the question of child care for infants is not yet available. However, with the ever-increasing proportion of mothers of infants who are working, as Chess (1990) suggests, we need to face reality and work for high-quality care for all infants who need it.

Quality Infant Child Care

Korelak, Colker, and Dodge (1993, pp. 1–5) have identified seven key indicators of quality child care:

1. The program is based on an understanding of child development.
2. The program is individualized to meet the needs of every child.
3. The physical environment is safe and orderly, and it contains varied and stimulating toys and materials.
4. Children may select activities and materials that interest them, and they learn by being actively involved.
5. Adults show respect for children's needs and ideas and talk with them in caring ways.
6. Parents feel respected and are encouraged to participate in the program.
7. Staff members have specialized training in early childhood development and education.

Korelak, Colker, and Dodge (1993, p. 11) describe the developmentally appropriate infant room in the childcare center as "warm and homelike" and as being staffed by caregivers who "meet infants' needs consistently, promptly, and lovingly." The caregivers encourage infants to use their developing sensorimotor skills. The environment should look like a comfortable home with pictures at eye level,

room for creeping and crawling, and appropriate materials for the older infants to explore. Family childcare environments should meet the same standards and present a homelike atmosphere.

Infancy is a critical time for children. If an infant must be in day care, the caregivers and the environment must include the basic ingredients proposed. Finding this quality care at an affordable cost is difficult. The need for high-quality care is urgent. Finding competent, quality care can be a hopelessly frustrating task.

Parent Education and Support

Obviously, it is important not only for professionals to know how to design and implement a high-quality infant environment, but it is equally important for parents to have these skills. **Parent education** has become increasingly popular as a major approach to the improvement of life for young children. Parent education can take many forms. It can be a program that is hospital-based and provides information during the prenatal and neonatal periods. It may be a center-based parent/child learning center (Vartuli & Rogers, 1985), or it may be home-based. Parent education includes involvement in the childcare center or early childhood program by attending workshops, making educational materials, volunteering to assist in the class, attending parent-teacher conferences and other related activities.

Parent education is critical for teenage parents who are ill-prepared to care for their infants and whose chances of finishing high school are poor. During the 1980s, 300 schools in 46 states started parenting programs for teens and childcare centers for their children (Kantrowitz, 1990). Through these programs the children are looked after while their mothers attend class and the mothers take child development courses that help them understand their children and how to parent them. Both the mother and the child are provided an opportunity that greatly increases their chances of becoming productive citizens.

Family support has been mandated for infants with disabilities. (See Unit 35.) Parent support groups are a commonly used method of meeting this requirement (Krauss, Upshur, Shonkoff, & Hauser-Cram, 1993). Krauss et al. (1993) suggest being cautious in placing parents in support groups as all parents don't feel equally comfortable discussing their problems in such a public setting. Further, parents who are less educated tend to be less involved in the groups. This may be due to their lack of education, lack of child care, working hours that conflict with meeting times, lack of interest, tending to be from a lower SES level, or lack of transportation to get to the meetings.

Another method of providing for parent education, involvement, and support is the home visit. This approach provides support for parent and child in the place where they feel most comfortable. With home visits, it is especially important to be sensitive to the culture of the family. LaPoint, Boutte, Swick, and Brown (1993) suggest using a bicultural approach. Their approach uses activities that integrate the family's culture and mainstream culture.

Infant Home Environment and Later Development

There is a growing body of research that supports the long-term value of the kinds of environmental features discussed in this unit. For example, Bradley and Caldwell (1984) used the **Home Observation for Measurement of the Environment (HOME)** method in the homes of children when they were 12 and 24 months old. They compared the observational results with some of the same children's first-grade achievement test scores. The relationships were positive. Especially strong was the relationship between having appropriate play materials in the home at 12 and 24 months and higher school achievement. The level of mother's acceptance of the child and mother's encouragement of child development were also strongly related to school achievement. Parental responsiveness did not show as strong a relationship as it did to level of cognitive development at age three. It may be that as children become more independent of adults, the quality of materials available maintains its importance,

whereas maternal responsiveness has its greatest effect during the first three years when the child is more dependent.

The availability and use of school support such as extended family and professionals and the sense of personal control affect how skillful mothers are as parents (Stevens, 1988). Stevens interviewed low income and teen African-American mothers and Anglo mothers. They were observed at home. Stevens obtained ratings of parenting skill, personal control, and amount of informal and formal child rearing support systems. The more skilled African-American teen mothers were those who were willing to recognize they had needs and sought help from extended family members. The more skilled adult African-American mothers were those who expressed more personal control. The more skilled Anglo adult mothers felt higher levels of personal control and sought help from extended family and professionals to solve child-rearing problems. African-American teens who lived with their mothers appeared to have an advantage in having advice-givers close at hand.

Teen parents and infants can also gain advantages from the presence of the teen's father in the household (Radin, Oyserman, & Benn, 1989). Teen fathers often do not have much interaction with their children; thus, these infants are deprived of male interaction. Grandfathers can serve this function. Radin et al. (1989) found that high levels of interaction with nurturing grandfathers enhances infant development, especially for girls. On the negative side (for the teen mothers) the infants by age two favored the grandfathers as sources of attention and were more obedient for the grandfathers than for their mothers.

SOCIOECONOMIC AND CULTURAL CONSIDERATIONS

Socioeconomic Factors

Marian Wright Edelman (The child's defender, 1993) who heads the Children's Defense Fund is a

KEYTERMSKEYTERMSKEYTERMSKEYTERMSKEYTERMSKEYTERMSKEY

Home Observation for
Measurement of the
Environment (HOME)

leading advocate for children's welfare in areas such as health care, teenage pregnancy, violence, and poverty. In a 1993 interview, she discussed the rising problems of poverty that demand our attention and our resources. She also discussed the problem of racial and gender bigotry. As adults, she emphasizes that we all have the responsibility to set an example of fairness and tolerance for our children. She is fearful that our country is becoming more divided into the privileged and the deprived. She also sees a resurgence of racial segregation. In her book, *The Measure Of Our Success: A Letter To My Children And Yours*, she expresses her concern that children are not receiving the support needed to grow up strong:

> . . . we are on the verge of losing two generations of Black children and youths to drugs, violence, too early parenthood, poor health and education, unemployment, family disintegration—and the spiritual and physical poverty that both breeds and is bred by them. Millions of Latino, Native American and other minority children face similar threats. (p. 11)

Further, she points out that millions of Anglo children are sinking also. Of the 406,000 youths who dropped out of school between October 1991 and October 1992, only 36 percent were employed (Youth indicators, 1993, 1994).

A recent study by the Carnegie Corporation (Study says. . . , 1994) substantiates that life for infants and toddlers has not improved but is worse than ever. During the first three years when they should be nurtured, loved, protected, and stimulated, they are neglected. One out of four infants lives at the poverty level in a single-parent family and one out of three is physically abused during infancy. The report recommends more planned parenthood, better salaries that will make employment in child care more attractive, better monitoring of childcare quality, expanded health and nutrition services for infants and children, and more family-friendly workplace policies.

Cultural Considerations

As indicated, our efforts to develop tolerance and understanding regarding the **cultural diversity** in

our country have not yet succeeded to a large extent. Hilliard and Vaughn-Scott (1982) pointed out the negative stereotype of inferiority that goes along with the term *minority* and suggested that each cultural group should be considered relative to its own special qualities. Looking at cultural groups from this view can enable us to see the importance for adults who work with young children and their families to understand their cultures. Gonzales-Mena (1992) describes how to take a culturally sensitive approach in infant-toddler care programs to resolve caregiver/parent conflicts regarding child-rearing practices. Hopefully, a calm exchange of ideas can provide a solution. She suggests that you find out what kinds of goals each parent has for the child, become clear about your own values and goals, become sensitive to anything that makes you feel uncomfortable, build positive relationships, learn to be an effective cross-cultural communicator, learn how to create dialogs, use a problem solving rather than a power approach when conflicts arise, and commit yourself to educating yourself and the parents with whom you work.

It is essential to understand child development within cultural contexts (Bowman & Stott, 1994). Some research has documented cultural differences relative to child behavior and child-rearing practices across cultures. We do know that there are differences in children from different cultures that are observable in newborns from different cultures, which are observable in newborns and their first reactions to the world (Freedman, 1982). For example, Chinese babies are more adaptable to change than Anglo babies. When picked up while crying, Chinese babies stop immediately while Anglo babies stop gradually. Native American babies were observed to be even calmer and more adaptable than were the Oriental babies. Native American mothers and their infants operate very well as a unit. Researchers looked at these differences relative to hereditary versus environmental origins. The diet common to the culture and other environmental factors may affect newborn behavior patterns even prior to birth. Whatever the basis for the differences, infants from different cultures are born with different characteristics (Figure 10–4). The basis is probably in both biology and culture. We know that parents in different cultures interact differently with their children (Paguio, Robinson, & Skeen, 1985). For example, German parents are more strict than American parents, having more rules and allowing fewer choices. Lower socio-economic children are usually more externally oriented for control, and middle and upper economic level children more internally oriented for control.

There is an increasing amount of research being done on a variety of cultural groups by researchers from those cultural groups. Hopefully, these new studies will help us see which kinds of factors generalize to all children and which are culture-specific. Harrison, Wilson, Pine, Chan, and Buriel (1990) placed ethnic minority families in ecological context as suggested by Bronfenbrenner. They considered adaptive strategies, socialization goals, and developmental outcomes of African-Americans. Native Americans and Alaskan natives, Asian-Pacific Americans, and Hispanic-Americans. These cultural groups operate under ecological challenges resulting from a history of oppression and discrimination. The gaps between minority and majority populations on social indicators such as health care, employment opportunities, and housing continue to widen. With the exception of Native Americans, most of these live in urban areas, are younger, and have higher birth rates than majority families.

Each minority cultural group has developed adaptive strategies to promote survival and well-being (Harrison et al., 1990). The extended family is a major strategy for problem-solving and stress-coping. We have seen an example of the power of this system in the support of teen mothers' parenting skills. **Biculturalism** is another adaptive strategy. Cultural groups struggle to maintain their cultural heritage while making the needed adaptations to survive in the majority culture. Minority cultures also cope by holding onto the ancestral world views. That is, they gain strength through long-term beliefs about life. Most minority peoples believe in collectivism (loyalty to the group) rather than the individualism that pervades Arab-European culture. They also tend to have strong religious beliefs that guide their actions.

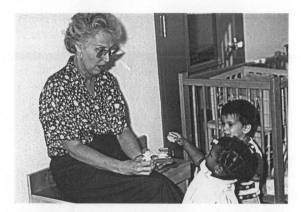

Figure 10–4 **The caregiver needs to become familiar with the child's cultural background.**

While the mechanisms for transmitting the culture are the same in majority and minority cultures, ethnicity determines group patterns of values, social customs, language, perceptions, behavioral roles, and rules of social interaction (Harrison et al., 1990). Minority families have to find the means to maintain ethnic pride in their children while providing the tools they need to function in the majority society. Parents of successful African-American children have been found to emphasize ethnic pride, self-development, awareness of racial barriers, and egalitarianism in their socialization practices. Minority socialization tends to focus on interdependence and cooperation as the route to success. This contrasts with the Western view of competition, autonomy, and self-reliance.

The third area examined by Harrison and her colleagues (Harrison et al., 1990) is the cognitive developmental outcomes of children raised in minority families. Infusion of biculturalism is a major goal in minority families. Achievement of this goal seems to produce children whose thinking is more flexible and who respond well to varied formats for learning. Ethnic minority children attain higher achievement in school if there is continuity between home and school expectations and environments. However, with their bicultural orientation they are sensitive to discontinuities between home and school.

KEYTERMSKEYTERMSKEYTERMSKEYTERMSKEYTERMSKEYTERMSKEY

Biculturalism

Harrison et al. (1990) point out that there is still much to be learned regarding the cultural context of child rearing and child development in ethnic minority families. This unit will close with examples of two studies that look at parents and infants in minority ethnic groups. Harwood and Miller (1989) found that Anglo and Puerto Rican mothers have contrasting views of what can be considered appropriate attachment behaviors. Harwood and Miller (1990) had the mothers respond to examples of the three strange-situation infant responses: A) avoidant, B) secure, and C) resistant. The Anglo mothers believed strongly that the B-type child response was the normal, acceptable response while the Puerto Rican mothers viewed both the B and C responses as being typical of normal infants. Anglo mothers evaluated behavior relative to standards of independence and self-confidence, Puerto Rican mothers looked at behavior as it affected others and the harmony of the situation. They were more geared to harmony and cooperation.

Bornstein et al. (1992) looked at mothers' responsiveness to infants in three countries: the United States, France, and Japan. Researchers found that the infant behaviors were similar in all three cultures and that the mothers responded in a similar manner in all three cultures. There appear to be some behaviors that are universal across cultures. Additional socio-cultural factors will be described in Units 14, 19, 32, and 36.

SUMMARY

Social and cultural factors are very important influences on infant development. The infant needs a rich environment that will challenge his developing cognitive, social/emotional, and psychomotor abilities. Development is influenced by the objects and the people that surround the infant. Both fathers and mothers add important dimensions to infant development. Additional stress on today's families results when both parents are employed outside the home and when single parents must balance work and child-rearing responsibilities. Some experts believe that infants are psychologically damaged if the mother works outside the home during the first year. Others disagree and suggest that if the daytime care is high quality, the baby will thrive normally. The major problem with this view is that high quality day care is difficult to find.

Parent education is increasing in scope. There is a recognition that parents need support and advice on how to parent. A home environment with appropriate play materials and nurturing caretakers provides for the best development.

Socioeconomic and cultural conditions are very important factors in infant development. The lower the income level, the greater the possibility that the family will not have access to appropriate health and nutritional care. Ethnic group is also a critical consideration. Each cultural group has its own set of values and customs and its own view of what is acceptable and unacceptable child behavior. The adult who works with infants must be knowledgeable about each infant's culture and work from a multicultural point of view: respecting each culture but also providing what the infant will need in order to operate in a world that may be dominated by another culture.

FOR FURTHER READING

Bredekamp, S. (Ed.). (1987). *Developmentally appropriate practice in early childhood programs serving children from birth through age eight.* Albany, NY: Delmar.

Clarke-Stewart, A. (1989). Single-parent families: How bad for the children? *Today, 1* (6), 60–64.

Cromwell, E. S. (1994). *Quality child care: A comprehensive guide for administrators and teachers.* Des Moines, IA: Longwood Division, Allyn & Bacon.

Fein, G. G., & Fox, N. A. (Eds.). (1988). Infant day care, Part II: Empirical studies [Special issue]. *Early Childhood Research Quarterly, 3* (4).

Fein, G. G., & Fox, N. A. (Eds.). (1988). Infant day care [Special issue]. *Early Childhood Research Quarterly, 3* (3).

Harms, T., & Clifford, R. M. (1989). *Family day care rating scale*. New York: Teachers College Press.

Harms, T., Cryer, D., & Clifford, R. M. (1990). *Infant/toddler environment rating scale*. New York: Teachers College Press.

Hewlett, B. S. (Ed.). (1992). *Father-child relations: Cultural and biosocial contexts*. New York: Aldine de Gruyter.

King, E. W., Chipman, M. F., & Cruz-Janzen, M. (1994). *Educating young children in a diverse society*. Des Moines, IA: Longwood Division, Allyn & Bacon.

Leavitt, R. L. (1994). *Power and emotion in infant-toddler day care*. NY: State University of New York Press.

LeVine, R., Miller, P. M., & West, M. M. (Eds.). (1989). *Parental behavior in diverse societies*. San Francisco: Jossey-Bass.

Luster, T., & Okagaki, L. (Eds.). (1993). *Parenting: An ecological perspective*. Hillsdale, NJ: Erlbaum.

McAdoo, H. P. (Ed.). (1993). *Family ethnicity: Strength in diversity*. Thousand Oaks, CA: Sage.

Nugent, J. K., Lester, B. M., & Brazelton, T. B. (Eds.). (1990). *The cultural context of infancy: Vol. 2, Multicultural and interdisciplinary approaches to parent-infant relations*. Norwood, NJ: Ablex.

Nugent, J. K., Lester, B. M., & Brazelton, T. B. (Eds.). (1989). *The cultural context of infancy: Vol. 1, Biology, culture, and infant development*. Norwood, NJ: Ablex.

Ogbu, J. U. (1992). Understanding cultural diversity and learning. *Educational Researcher, 21* (8), 5–14.

Wilson, L. C. (1995). *Infants and toddlers: Curriculum and teaching*, (2nd Ed.). Albany, NY: Delmar.

SUGGESTED ACTIVITIES

1. Visit a home- or center-based infant day care site. Observe a full day of activities if possible. Use the evaluation sheet in Figure 10–5 to evaluate the competence of the caregiver(s). Answer the following questions:
   a. Did the caregiver(s) have the desirable characteristics needed by an infant caregiver who is developmentally appropriate?
   b. What were the caregiver's strengths and weaknesses?
   c. In what areas should the caregiver try to improve?

2. Visit a family that includes an infant. Observe the parent(s). Rate the parent behavior using the infant caregiver evaluation sheet. Evaluate the competence of the parent(s) by answering Questions a through c in Activity 1 relevant to the parent(s).

3. Visit a family in which the mother and father share the infant care. Observe each parent separately caring for their baby. Did you note any similarities? Any differences? Repeat your observation in the homes of families with different racial and socioeconomic backgrounds. Again compare parents with each other and with families from different cultures. Do you perceive any differences that you feel are due to cultural differences in personality and/or customs?

4. Many agencies and groups publish pamphlets designed to help parents select high-quality child care settings. Obtain some of these and compare them with each other, particularly regarding the suggestions for choosing infant care. Visit one or more centers and see if you find the suggestions from the pamphlets to be helpful. Design your own guide for parents. To find pamphlets, check with your cooperative extension service, your state department of health, and early childhood education professional organizations such as the National Association for the Education of Young Children (NAEYC, 1509 16th Street, N.W., Washington, DC 20036-1426), the Association for Childhood Education International (ACEI, 11501 Georgia Avenue, Suite 315, Wheaton, MD 20902), or the Southern Early Childhood Association (SECA, P.O. Box 5403, Little Rock, AR 72215-5403), and local childcare resource and referral programs.

INFANT CAREGIVER EVALUATION SHEET

For each infant caregiver behavior or characteristic check whether the caregiver exhibits behavior that is more like the appropriate or more like the inappropriate descriptors.

Appropriate Practice		Inappropriate Practice		Comments
Adult/child interaction	__	**Adult/child interaction**	__	
1. Frequent one-to-one, face-to-face pleasant contact with adults.	__	1. Infants left without adult attention for long periods.	__	
2. Adults speak in pleasant soothing voices, have frequent eye contact.	__	2. Adults speak harshly, shout, or use baby talk.	__	
3. Infants are carried about and spoken to as a means to offer stimulation.	__	3. Silent adults move infants only for convenience.	__	
4. Adults talk to infants as they do routine activities.	__	4. Routines are done silently with no verbal or playful interaction.	__	
5. Adults respond to infant vocal communications.	__	5. Adults ignore infant attempts to communicate vocally.	__	
6. Adults respond quickly to infant distress cries in a warm manner.	__	6. Adults ignore distress signals or respond at their convenience.	__	
7. Playful interactions are done with sensitivity to the infant's needs.	__	7. Adults frighten, tease, or upset the infants.	__	
8. During play adults offer comments, suggest ideas, encourage infant's own explorations.	__	8. Adults interrupt, impose their own ideas, take toys away when child is involved.	__	
9. Lots of language used: talks, sings, reads to infants.	__	9. Little language used. Infants left to entertain themselves or watch TV.	__	
10. Parents and infants warmly greeted each day.	__	10. Infants received coldly.	__	
11. Babies are worked into the group each day.	__	11. Babies are put on the floor or in a crib abruptly.	__	
12. Caregivers provide for individual differences in feeding and sleeping schedules and food preferences and eating styles.	__	12. Rigid schedules are imposed that suit adult convenience.	__	

Figure 10–5 **Infant caregiver evaluation sheet. [based on J. R. Lally, S. Provence, E. Szanton, & B. Weissbourd, Developmentally appropriate care for children from birth to age 3. In S. Bredekamp (Ed.),** *Developmentally Appropriate Practice in Early Childhood Programs Serving Children from Birth through Age Eight***, Washington, DC: National Association for the Education of Young Children.]**

Appropriate Practice		Inappropriate Practice		Comments
Adult/child interaction	__	**Adult/child interaction**	__	
13. Infants are helped to interact positively with each other.	__	13. Infants are either not to play with each other or forced to play when they don't wish to.	__	
14. Adults model positive, warm behavior.	__	14. Adults model harsh, loud, aggressive behaviors.	__	
15. Adults play games like Peek-a-Boo and 5 Little Piggies.	__	15. Games may be imposed when infant isn't interested, to fill time rather than as a learning experience.	__	
16. Routines are viewed as learning experiences.	__	16. Routines are done as quickly as possible to get them over with.	__	
Environment	__		__	
17. Diapering, sleeping, feeding, and playing areas are separate.	__	17. Areas are combined, are noisy and distracting.	__	
18. There are soft elements (pillows, padded walls) and hard elements (rocking chairs, mirrors).	__	18. Sterile or cluttered; lacks variety.	__	
19. Colors are bright and varied.	__	19. Rooms are bland and dull.	__	
20. Each infant has his/her personal crib and feeding and diapering supplies.	__	20. Infants share cribs and supplies.	__	
21. Babies play both indoors and outdoors, on the floor, in cribs, in strollers, etc.	__	21. Play mostly indoors in one location.	__	
22. Mirrors are placed where children can see themselves.	__	22. No mirrors are available for infants.	__	
23. Temperature and humidity are comfortable levels.	__	23. Rooms are too hot or too cold.	__	
24. Rooms are decorated with cheerful pictures of people, animals, plants, etc.	__	24. Rooms are dull and dingy. Decorations are at adult eye level.	__	
25. Enough space so infants can roll and move about as their motor skills develop.	__	25. Space is cramped and not enough for free movement.	__	
26. Floor covering is easy to clean carpet.	__	26. Floor covering is dirty and/or hard and cold.	__	
27. Plenty of safe, washable toys that are too large for infants to swallow are available. Toys range from simple to complex.	__	27. Toys are unsafe and/or not washable. Toys do not provide for different developmental levels.	__	
28. Mobiles are within infant's view but out of reach.	__	28. Mobiles are out of infant's view or where they can be reached.	__	
29. Toys are on low open shelves where infants can make selections.	__	29. Toys are dumped on the floor in piles or out of reach; adults controlling selection.	__	
30. Safe, well padded climbing structures and steps are available for exploration.	__	30. No climbing structures, or unsafe structures.	__	
31. Heavy cardboard books with rounded edges and bright pictures are available.	__	31. No books are available or inappropriate books are provided.	__	
32. A variety of ethnic and nonsexist, pictorial materials are provided.	__	32. Pictures depict cartoon characters and/or ethnic and sex role stereotypes.	__	

Figure 10–5 Infant caregiver evaluation sheet. (Continued)

Appropriate Practice		Inappropriate Practice		Comments
Health, safety, and nutrition	—		—	
33. Toys that have been put in mouths are put aside to be cleaned in a bleach solution.	—	33. Toys are scattered on the floor, bottles are left on the floor and used by anyone.	—	
34. Staff appear to be healthy.	—	34. An obviously ill staff member is working with infants.	—	
35. Children are always supervised by an adult.	—	35. Children are left unsupervised.	—	
36. Safety precautions are taken: electrical outlets are covered, dangerous substances are kept out of reach, extension cords are not exposed.	—	36. Children are told "no" to hazards that shouldn't be present. Rocking chairs are in crawling areas.	—	
37. Clothing is appropriate for weather and activity.	—	37. Clothing is inappropriate for weather and/or activity.	—	
38. Adults wash their hands before and after diaper change and before feeding.	—	38. Handwashing is inconsistently done.	—	
39. Diaper changing area is sanitized after each change.	—	39. Several children may be diapered without sanitizing the area.	—	
40. Only healthy foods are served. Eating is a sociable happy time with enough adults to give each infant proper attention. Infants who are into solid foods are provided with finger foods they can eat on their own.	—	40. Cookies and other high sugar foods are served as treats. Large groups of infants are fed at the same time. No messing with food is allowed. Little or no conversation takes place during eating.	—	
Staff/parent interactions	—		—	
41. Staff work to support parents as the primary caregivers.	—	41. Staff compete with parents and avoid discussion of controversial issues.	—	
42. Pertinent information is shared daily.	—	42. Staff usually talk with parents only at scheduled conferences.	—	
Staff/child ratio	—		—	
43. Staff ratio is no more than one adult to three babies. One main and one auxiliary caregiver relate to each infant on a regular basis.	—	43. Child/staff ratio is more than 3:1. Infants relate to more than two adults each day.	—	
Staff qualifications	—		—	
44. Staff are warm and caring and knowledgeable about child development. Preferably they have had some formal training in infant education and care.	—	44. Infant care is a chore and strictly custodial. They have unrealistic ideas about normal development. No training in infant care and development.	—	

Figure 10–5   Infant caregiver evaluation sheet.   (Continued)

REVIEW

A. Evaluate the following infant care situation.

Ms. Miller is the head teacher with a group of ten infants. She has been in this position for 5 years. She has two assistants, Mrs. Kwan who has been with her for 3 years and Mr. Peterson who has been with her for 1 year. The infant section of the center is divided into two rooms. One room contains cribs and changing tables. The other room contains highchairs, walkers, a couch, and two rocking chairs. About half of the second room is a play area. There is carpeting on the floor and an assortment of play materials such as sock animals, foam rubber blocks, rattles, and stuffed toys. Infants can move the mobile about freely. The adults observe and move in when needed. While changing one of the babies, Mrs. Kwan tickles, sings, and carries on a 'conversation' with the baby. During nap time the three teachers discuss the day's events and plan for the future. Mrs. Miller gives her assistants constructive criticism and compliments them on their skillful handling of their young charges. In the evening as the parents arrive to pick up their children, the teachers greet each one and briefly report on the events of the day for their child.

B. Select the correct statements from those that follow:
   1. The more time a father spends with his infant the higher he is likely to rate the infant's social and cognitive capacities.
   2. Today's fathers are much more involved with infant care than was the case in the past.
   3. If possible, when both parents work, father should share responsibility for household tasks.
   4. Parents are not finding that if both parents are employed that it increases parenting stress.
   5. In the Barglow et al., study it was found that working mothers and their infants were more likely to have poor attachment relationships than at-home mothers and their infants.
   6. Weintraub et al., observed that at home the children of nonemployed mothers were more independent than children of employed mothers.
   7. Weekday evenings in homes where both parents are employed there is less parent interaction with infants than in homes where the mother is not employed.
   8. Jay Belsky is a proponent of sending infants to day care before 3 months of age so that they are not yet too attached to their mothers.
   9. Older women make the most sensitive caregivers for infants.
   10. Plenty of high-quality child care is available if parents will just take the time to look for it.
   11. Currently, parent education is very popular.

C. In your opinion, should an infant be put in a day-care situation? State your reasons pro or con using material from this unit to support your argument.

D. List some factors related to poverty and/or cultural diversity that might influence development of the infant.

Section III

The Toddler: Developing Toward Independence

INTRODUCTION

Who are the typical toddlers? During the second year, children usually enter the toddler period. They usually are walking but their speech is limited. Their understanding of communication is beyond their speech. They are active imitators. The people in their environment serve as models. They want to do what others do. For example, a child whose mother is an accountant is observed using a calculator while mother works with her computer spreadsheet. Toddler may be observed sitting in the laundry basket making motor noises and pretending to drive a car. Toddlers are entranced with their newly found mobility and enjoy all kinds of physical activity: running, lifting, carrying, pushing, pulling, etc. They also enjoy roughhousing and dancing with older children or adults.

Toddlers display many behaviors that may be viewed with delight by adults or cause stress and frustration. Cognitively, they demonstrate an understanding of spoken language but cannot speak yet. They view things and events at face value focusing on the most obvious interpretation. Motorically, they are ahead of their spoken language development. They move about their environment with ease (and frequently with speed), which requires adults to provide constant supervision and guidance.

In this section, we will look at toddlers as they move toward independence: motorically, affectively, and cognitively. Finally, we'll examine the toddler environment.

11

The Toddler: Autonomy and Motor Development

OBJECTIVES

After studying this unit, the student should be able to:

■ Name the two major developmental areas in which a toddler shows the most growth.

■ Recognize five areas of behavior which reflect toddler growth from dependence to independence.

■ Identify major toddler characteristics from the theorists' point of view.

■ Analyze and evaluate toddler gross and fine motor behavior and development.

At the age of 17 months, Kate visits a second grade class that is made up of many of the same students she had visited at the age of 5 months. One child, Shelly, describes Kate in this "toddler action story":

Toddler Kate can walk, talk, smell, and her favorite thing is to climb. Kate can say "pop" and "milk, DaDa, achee, MaMa, cracker." Last year Kate was five months old. But now Kate is seventeen months old and loves to do tricks but her favorite trick to do is roll. The end of Kate's story.

Shelly has noticed two major changes that characterize the toddler: her increased movement (she likes to climb and roll) and her ability to speak. Movement dominates the first year of toddlerhood, with language development dominating the second year. Selma Fraiberg describes the child just entering toddlerhood:

The discovery of independent locomotion and the discovery of a new self usher in a new phase in personality development. The toddler is quite giddy with his new achievements. He behaves as if he had invented his new mode of locomotion (which in a restricted sense is true) and he is quite in love with himself for being so clever. From dawn to dusk he marches around in an ecstatic, drunken dance, which ends only when he collapses with fatigue. He can no longer be contained within the four walls of his house and the fenced-in yard is like a prison to him. Given practically unlimited space he staggers joyfully with open arms toward the end of the horizon. Given half a chance he might make it. (Fraiberg, 1959, pp. 61–62)

"The toddler is a dynamo, full of unlimited energy and enthusiasm. . . . The toddler period begins with the limited abilities of an infant and ends with the relatively sophisticated skills of a young child" (Allen & Marotz, 1994, p. 70).

Toddlerhood is the time when the child begins to move from dependence to independence. T. Berry Brazelton lists five major areas in which the child shows growth from dependence to independence between the ages of one and three (Figure 11–1).

- The toddler learns about independence. He finds out that he can do many things for himself. He is very proud when he can open the kitchen cupboard, take out a box of crackers, open it and help himself. He finds he can decide for himself and practices making decisions. Adults often find him to be negative. One of his first words is usually "no!" Toddler is curious about new people but still attached to the familiar ones. He may be slow to make friends but enjoys a new relationship once he breaks the ice.

- The toddler learns the importance of limits. Adults often meet toddler's new independent actions with a firm "no." Toddler will tease and test just to make sure he is clear regarding limits. Gradually he will begin to avoid forbidden objects and places. By the age of three he begins to have inner controls and does not always need to look for limits to be set on his behavior by others.

- The toddler learns from play and fantasy. He learns more concepts [such as color, shape, and size] as he moves about and engages in more new activities. He also learns about himself and others as he plays. Toddler learns from his wishes and fantasies. He may have an imaginary friend who takes responsibility for his bad behavior thus lightening his feelings of guilt. He also begins to learn the difference between fantasy and reality.

- Toddler learns through identification. Toddler imitates others. He imitates voice, movement, and daily activities of other people. Toddler puts baby doll to bed with the same tender care parents use when they tuck him in for the night. Toddler sits in a box and drives the car just as an adult does. Toddler tries out "being" everyone.

- The toddler learns more and more as he acquires language skills. Toddler moves from one word sentences to sentences several words in length. Toddler's actions are accompanied by more and more speech (Brazelton, 1977, pp. 114–116).

Toddlerhood is the period from 1 to 2$\frac{1}{2}$ or 3 years; it is the time a child grows from infant to preschooler. By 2$\frac{1}{2}$ years, Brazelton feels that children reach a time when they pull all these new skills together and are especially fun to be with as they move toward the maturity of three:

> What fun it is to have made it with a three-year-old who can act for himself, who can think for himself, who can be gay and amusing, who can express his thoughts independently, who is beginning to realize his independence from you! How rewarding to find that at last he can afford to let himself care about you as another person—not just as an extension of himself. (Brazelton, 1977, pp. 114–116)

Figure 11–1   The toddler enjoys her newly developed motor control as she squats, puts the blocks in the container, picks up the container, and carries it off.

Frodi, Bridges, and Grolnick (1985) looked at the development of autonomous behavior in a group of children at the time they were 12 months and again at 20 months. These researchers were interested in how the children's mastery behaviors relate to mothers' control behaviors, attitudes, and sensitivity, and to infant-mother attachment. Children and mothers were observed during laboratory toy play sessions. Children of mothers who supported autonomy, which is growth toward independence, displayed more task-oriented persistence in working with toys at 20 months than did the children of the more controlling mothers. Both strongly attached children and avoidant children (as measured in the strange situation) showed more task persistence than those who were ambivalent. The attached children seemed to be autonomous due to feelings of security. The avoidant children seemed to use the toys as a means of avoiding mother.

Holden and West (1989), having observed mothers and toddlers in the naturalistic setting of the supermarket, moved into the laboratory to observe how mothers of twos and threes deal with their toddlers dynamic behavior. In the naturalistic setting, they observed that the children got into less trouble if their mothers were foresightful and kept the children constructively busy through conversation or having them help with the shopping. Mothers who waited until the children misbehaved before they intervened had children with greater frequencies of undesirable behavior. The mothers' task in the laboratory was to keep the children from playing with attractive forbidden toys. The children were permitted to use less attractive objects. As in the naturalistic study, mothers who behaved proactively had fewer problems than those who behaved reactively. Holden and West also noted that both mothers and children were very creative in finding ways to keep away from the forbidden toys and finding interesting ways to use the less attractive objects. The mothers' creativity took a toll in mental and physical energy. " . . . the truth about the 'terrible twos' may originate in mothers' quite accurate perception of the amount

of effort they expend to make their impulsive youngsters behave as cooperative partners" (Holden & West, 1989, p. 69).

Bullock and Lutkenhaus (1988) studied the development of volitional behavior in children between the ages of 15 and 25 months. By volitional behavior, they referred to acts done in order to achieve a particular outcome or goal. Volitional skills require the child to keep the goal in mind, have the ability to stick to and follow through on the task, and keep track of progress. The toddler period is a transitional time for developing the abilities needed to be volitionally competent. The tasks used by these researchers were building a block tower, cleaning a blackboard, and dressing a doll. The results indicated that children younger than 18 months are primarily activity oriented. That is, they act for the sake of pure action. After 18 months, they begin to be outcome oriented and show pleasure when they achieve goals. By 24 months, they move more directly toward the goal and have a definite stopping point in mind. It is not until about 30 months that toddlers begin to note mistakes and make corrections when in the middle of a task. Younger children might recognize a mistake but not do anything to correct it. The twenty-month-olds showed the greatest discrepancy in recognizing the standards for the task, being able to have the control to meet the standards, and actively involving the self. The authors suggest that this coordination problem underlies the "terrible twos'" typical volatile behavior. That is, young toddlers move and act for the sake of the action itself and not to achieve any specific goal. When children develop to the point where their actions are coordinated and goal directed, the sense of self as an active and competent person begins to form.

The young toddler can be pictured as one who is rapidly developing new competencies in the motor, cognitive, and affective areas. However, as these competencies are in the process of development, his efforts at achievement and at finding out what he can do demand a great deal of attention and energy from the adults who care for him.

THE THEORISTS LOOK AT THE TODDLER

Erikson, Freud, Maslow and Rogers, Skinner, Sears, Bandura, Piaget, Vygotsky, and Gesell each views the toddler from his own perspective. All but Skinner and Bandura place toddlers in a special stage of development relative to growth and learning.

At around 18 months of age, toddlers enter Erikson's second stage in which they must deal with crisis: **autonomy versus shame and doubt** (Miller, 1989). The toddler has a strong drive to push ahead and use newly developed locomotor skills. At the same time, toddlers must also develop self-control and learn to use these skills within the limits set by the environment. They learn they may climb up on the seat of the couch, but they may not climb up on the back and jump off. They learn they are allowed to run outdoors but not in the house. Toddlers need to develop a healthy feeling of shame when they have done the wrong thing. At the same time, if feelings of shame are too strong, toddlers will doubt their own capabilities and be unable to develop a healthy sense of independence. Toddlers can be very defiant (the "No!" stage, or exhibiting much negative behavior) or very compliant (going along with everything without ever asserting themselves). The adult has to guide toddlers through this period in such a way as to encourage autonomous behavior balanced with self-control. During much of this crisis period, behavior centers around toileting—a critical achievement in physical and motor development.

Freud emphasized the importance of the toilet training experience during ages one-and-a-half to three, which he labeled the **anal stage**. He found that adult psychological problems often had their roots in an improperly handled toilet training experience. This is an important concern in our culture. The demand to retain urine and feces is the first demand made on the young child to control biological and physiological needs (Mead, 1978).

Both Maslow and Rogers emphasize the importance of developing **assertiveness**. Assertive behavior reflects a basic feeling of autonomy. At the same time the child becomes more independent, dependence, love, and security are still needed. To develop a strong self-concept, children have to learn to discriminate between adults' feelings about their acts versus their own feelings about themselves. For example, parents may disapprove when the child soils his pants but the child is still loved (Mead, 1978). Toddlerhood is a delicate time relative to the development of the self-concept. The toddler meets many negatives and it is very important that these are perceived as behaviors that society disapproves of for everyone, not just for one particular young child.

Robert R. Sears (cited in Maier, 1978) perceives the toddler as entering a second phase in development that lasts through the preschool years. At around 16 months of age, the toddler enters a stage in which socialization is emphasized. The child must begin to act in accordance with the expectations of society as taught within the family situation. Children learn that to be rewarded with praise and approval from their parents, they must act in certain ways. Sears also emphasizes the importance of imitation as a means of learning expected behaviors. Toddlers learn their sex role (that is, how a boy acts like a male and a girl like a female) by copying what they see older people do. Sears, like Erikson and Freud, views toilet training as a key development during this period. Finally, toddlers must learn when and how to handle aggressive impulses.

From Bandura's point of view, the development of more refined motor skills and higher-level cognitive skills enables the toddler to make better use of the capacity for observational learning (Miller, 1989). The toddler moves from visual to symbolic representations, which enables the child to imitate previously observed behaviors after she is no longer observable. Her more refined motor skills enable the accomplishment of a greater variety of tasks. Commonly the result is finding the toddler trying out mother's makeup, dad's shaving equipment, or mixing up an original recipe in the kitchen.

In Piaget's view, the toddler goes from the latter

KEYTERMSKEYTERMSKEYTERMSKEYTERMSKEYTERMSKEY

| autonomy versus shame and doubt | anal stage |
| | assertiveness |

part of the sensorimotor period into the early part of the **preoperational period**. Between 18 months and 2 years of age, the child passes from sensorimotor to preoperational. Perceptually, children mature to the point at which they achieve object permanence and begin to have mental images more like an adult. Motor development ceases to dominate cognitive growth and language development takes over. Play and imitation are the major vehicles for learning. This idea is consistent with those of Erikson and Sears.

Vygotsky's stages are not defined in as much detail as those of the other theorists (Van Der Veer, 1986). He did recognize that as the child entered his second year and as he started to walk, talk, and show more complex affective behaviors, he was in an important transition period. Vygotsky focused most of his attention on language development. The important development was 'autonomous' speech. For Vygotsky, autonomous speech was verbal pointing. That is, the words often have no meaning out of context. Children commonly make up some of their own approximations that only the immediate family may understand. The meaning of this first speech is context dependent. According to Vygotsky, thought is not yet verbal. We will look further at Vygotsky's view of language and thought in later units.

Gesell views development as continuing through a sequence of behavioral ages and stages. The toddler period is made up of five stages in Gesell's scheme. For Gesell, fifteen months is the critical age for the child in his second year:

> At fifteen months the modern child has usually achieved the upright position; he can attain the standing position unaided; he can walk alone; he prefers to walk; he has discarded creeping and begun to jargon in a manner that promises the most human achievement of all—speech. (Gesell et al., 1974, p. 122)

Gesell also points out the normality of a negative stage during toddlerhood and the importance in our culture of toilet training between the ages of two and three. The toddler's pressured need for activity reaches a peak between two and one-half and three, at which time he tends to settle down a bit.

The right environment is the key to healthy development at any age, from Skinner's point of view. In Unit 14, some specific applications of Skinner's ideas are related to working with toddlers.

As viewed by the developmental theorists, the toddler is normally very active and is beginning to be an independent person. Maturing muscular control enables the toddler to walk, climb, run, and toilet. Language opens up new areas of learning and communication. Play and imitation are major means for learning about the world and of the behavior expected regarding sex role, independence, aggression, differentiating right and wrong, and social actions.

PHYSICAL AND MOTOR DEVELOPMENT

As children leave infancy and enter the toddler period, they are still growing physically at a rapid rate. By the time children reach age three, their rate of growth slows down until they reach adolescence, at which time there is a rapid spurt. The rate of growth of the head is still ahead of the rest of the body so the head is still relatively large. The arms and trunk are more proportional, but the legs are still short in comparison to the rest of the body. When toddlers stand, they appear to be in a hole up to their knees with a large head and trunk and short, chunky legs. Motorically, they are quite skilled and very mobile (Figure 11–2). They are no longer quiet, passive, and content with being in a playpen or crib. They must move at all times: "Motor activity is so vital to the child of this age that interference, restriction of this activity even through another biological process, sleep, is intolerable to him" (Fraiberg, 1959, p. 59).

Toddlers present a rather humorous picture as they move about. They are still clumsy and uncoordinated:

> The eighteen-month-old walks on a broad base, feet wide apart; he runs with a stiff, propulsive, flat gait. He squats a good deal; his abdomen is rather prominent; . . . he uses whole-arm movements in ballplay and

preoperational period

Figure 11–2 **This toddler works on recently acquired climbing skills.**

Figure 11–3 **Toddlers enjoy toys they can push and pull.**

"painting"; his hands are not agile at the wrists; . . . He even has trouble getting his spoon into his mouth. (Gesell et al., 1974, p. 141)

Gross motor movements dominate activity (Figure 11–3). "He lugs, tugs, dumps, pushes, pulls, pounds" (Gesell et al., 1974, p. 141). Toddlers may be seen running about with stuffed animals or dolls held tightly against their chests. Toddlers may dump their toys out of their containers and leave them in a pile on the floor. Toddlers repeat actions over and over, as if practicing to be able to do them perfectly. For the next year and one-half, the toddler gradually becomes more agile and coordinated. The pace slows until at three, as he becomes a preschooler, a great deal more control is evident.

The toddlers' curiosity combined with their developing motor skills makes keeping up with their exploits a challenge to adults.

Toileting

Achievement of appropriate toileting habits is a major physical/motor skill that is expected to be accomplished by the end of the toddler period (about age three). By age two, most children can be dry during the day but many are not daytime dry until age three. Night dryness usually comes even later (Cole & Cole, 1989). The ability to control elimination is dependent upon both muscular maturation and desire (Figure 11–4). That is, children must be able to control their muscles in order to eliminate at the proper

time. They also must want to eliminate in the potty rather than in their pants. They can use muscular control to retain waste until they get off the potty as well as they can retain it until they get on.

Children need not only muscular maturation and desire, but also cognitive maturity. They need to be able to understand and follow instructions and retain the information between eliminations. The more

Figure 11–4 **Learning to toilet requires muscular maturity, desire, and a cognitive level that will enable the toddler to understand and remember what is required.**

casual and relaxed the adults are, the more likely success will be achieved (Honig, 1993).

Fine Motor Skills

While the toddler spends a great deal of time working on his gross motor skills, fine motor skills are not neglected. During the toddler years the child progressively refines hand and finger movements (McGlaughlin & Morgan, 1981). Coordination of thumb and fingers improves and the hands are used with more precision. Small objects are manipulated with increasing dexterity. During toddlerhood, the child learns to eat independently with the fingers and then to use eating utensils (Figure 11–5). Space and movement become coordinated so objects can be reached for and picked up with smooth movements and minimal effort. By 15 months a child can drop objects into and empty them out of containers, hold two objects in one hand at the same time, begin to fit objects together, turn the pages in a cardboard or cloth book, hold a crayon in a whole hand grasp, and build a tower of two or three blocks. During the rest of the toddler period, these skills are further refined. By two-and-a-half the child can hold a pencil in the hand rather than the fist, is beginning to draw, and can pour liquids from one container to another (McGlaughlin & Morgan, 1981).

As discussed in Unit 8 cognitive development during the sensorimotor period is enhanced by the child's opportunities to explore objects. It is usually assumed that the more attention the child gives to this exploration the more information the child obtains (Ruff, 1986). From the age of 6 months, children can be observed to clearly focus their attention on objects for measurable periods of time. The child fingers and turns the object while looking at it with an intent expression. This type of behavior is called **examining**. As fine motor development becomes more precise, the child can handle objects more dextrously during these periods of examination.

Figure 11–5 Toddlers enjoy exploring materials such as shaving cream that offer interesting opportunities for sensory exploration and application of emerging motor competencies.

SUMMARY

Toddlerhood is a crucial period that bridges the time from infancy to preschool. During the period of about age one (or when the child begins to walk) until age three, toddlers develop basic motor, affective, and cognitive skills that enable them to engage in independent activity throughout life.

Toddlers are very active and constantly on the move. To slow down to eat, dress, toilet, or sleep is a difficult task. In this second part of the sensorimotor period, both gross and fine motor development are spotlighted, especially during the second year. By age two-and-a-half, gross motor skills are being applied to achieve goals beyond development of the skill itself. Fine motor skills have been refined to the point where the young child can do many things independently such as feeding, toileting, and dressing, which support the developing self-concept and develop feelings of control and power. Motor skills continue to support cognitive development by enabling the child to experience more precise examination of objects and solve problems using climbing, lifting, throwing, and other gross motor skills.

KEYTERMSKEYTERMSKEYTERMSKEYTERMSKEYTERMSKEY

examining

FOR FURTHER READING

Ames, L. & Ilg, F. L. (1983). *Your one year old.* New York: Dell.

Ames, L. & Ilg, F. L. (1980). *Your two year old.* New York: Dell.

Brazelton, T. B. (1992). *Touchpoints: The essential reference.* Reading, MA: Addison-Wesley.

Kalverboer, A. F., Hopkins, B., & Geuze, R. (Eds.). (1992). *Motor Development in early and later childhood.* New York: Cambridge University Press.

Rosenblith, J. F. (1992). *In the beginning: Development from conception to age two.* Thousand Oaks, CA: Sage.

Thelen, E., & Lockman, J. J. (Eds.). (1993). Developmental biodynamics: Brain, body, behavior connections. *Child Development, 64,* 953–1190. [Special section]

Williams, H. G. (1983). Assessment of gross motor functioning. In Paget, K. D. & Bracken, B. A. (Eds.), *The psychoeducational assessment of preschool children* (pp. 225–260). Orlando, FL: Grune & Stratton.

Wilson, L. C. (1995). *Infants and toddlers,* (3rd Ed.). Albany, NY: Delmar.

SUGGESTED ACTIVITIES

1. Get acquainted with a toddler. After you have seen each other enough so that you are good friends, take him for a walk. A toddler can't go very far, so plan a short but interesting route; or take him to a playground if there is one close by. Answer the following questions based on observations made during your excursion.
   a. Describe who the child is, the child's age, and how you happen to know him.
   b. Write a description of what actually happened on the walk. What did the toddler do and say? Did he do what you expected?
   c. How would you assess his motor skills? Did he walk with ease? Did he stop and stoop to pick things up and manage without falling? Did he have a chance to climb?
   d. Overall what did you learn? Did any unexpected things happen?

2. Interview three or four parents of two-year-olds regarding their experiences with toilet training. Explain that this is an assignment for your child development class and that you have been reading about the toddler and the importance of toilet training during this age period. Record the name, age, and sex of each child. Then ask the following questions.
   a. Do you feel you have been pretty relaxed about toilet training or have you felt pressured to get it done in a hurry?
   b. When did you first put (*child's name*) on the potty? Can you remember how old she was? What happened?
   c. How far along is she now? Does she ever have a daytime accident? How about at night? What procedures have you used for training?
   d. How did you decide how to start and when to start? Did someone give you advice? Did you read about how to do it in a book or magazine?
   e. Do you find that (*child's name*) is into a period where she wants to do everything for herself? Has this carried over into toileting?
   f. What advice would you give to another parent regarding toilet training?

3. Supermarkets, department stores, or any large store with lots of colorful and interesting things to buy are exciting places for a child. The toddler usually finds these places interesting but his desire to explore is balanced by the push for autonomy and his still strong attachment to his parents. Go to a supermarket, discount store, or shopping mall. Observe some children who appear to be between the ages of one and three. Observe at least four parent/child pairs for 5 to 10 minutes each. Note signs of attachment and independence. Write a detailed description of each pair observed. Did the children act as you expected after having read the text? Compare them with each other considering probable age.

4. Observe a toddler at home or at a day-care site. Use the toddler development evaluation sheet (Figure 11–6) to evaluate the toddler's developmental level in the area of gross and fine motor development, self-help, and social development.

    a. Overall does the toddler seem to be average, ahead of normal expectations, or slow in her rate of development?

    b. Are there any areas where the toddler seems to be exceptionally ahead or behind in development?

    c. What kinds of suggestions do you have for the parents and/or caregiver regarding this toddler?

    d. Support all your conclusions and recommendations with data from your evaluation sheet.

5. Make an entry in your journal.

Observer _____ Date _____ Time _____ Place _____

Infant's Name _____ Birth Date _____ Age _____

Usual Age of Appearance	Behavior	Observed		Comments
		Yes	No	
Between 13 and 18 months	**Gross Motor**			
	Pulls a toy attached to a string.			
	Using hands and legs, climbs up ten steps without help.			
	Crawls down ten steps backward, feet first.			
	Walks six steps alone without help.			
	Goes from sitting to standing without help.			
	Walks up steps with a person holding his hand.			
	Fine Motor			
	In imitation, child places one two-inch block on top of another two-inch block.			
	Given a large crayon and large piece of paper, the child scribbles.			
	While sitting in an adult's lap, turns two or three pages in a large book with cardboard pages.			
	In imitation, places three one-inch cube blocks in a six-inch diameter cup.			
	Holds a pencil and makes a mark on a sheet of paper.			
	In imitation, builds a four-block tower with two-inch cube blocks.			

Figure 11–6 **Toddler development evaluation sheet: Fine and gross motor development and self-help skills (Adapted from G. J. Schirmer (Ed.).** *Performance Objectives for Preschool Children.* **Sioux Falls, SD: Adapt Press, Inc. Used with permission).**

Usual Age of Appearance	Behavior	Observed		Comments
		Yes	No	
Between 13 and 18 months	Self Help			
	Picks up one or two toys when adult picks up toys.			
	Opens mouth and allows adult to brush his teeth.			
	Chews and swallows semisolid foods cut in small pieces.			
	Takes off some clothing such as mittens, hat, sox.			
	Indicates that he has a wet diaper.			
Between 18 and 24 months	Gross Motor			
	Toddler walks fast or runs stiffly for a distance of six feet.			
	Balances on his feet in a squat position while playing with objects on the floor for several seconds.			
	Walks backward for four steps without losing his balance.			
	Bends over, picks up an object from the floor, and stands up straight again without falling over.			
	Standing, he kicks a ball without falling.			
	Sits down in a small chair without help.			
	Standing, he throws a ball at least one foot.			
	Standing on the floor, he jumps in place two jumps.			
	Fine Motor			
	Given a piece of unlined paper and a pencil and shown how to draw an arc, the child draws one.			
	Can turn a door knob that is within his reach using both hands.			
	When shown how, unscrews the lid set loosely on a small jar.			
	Places large pegs in a pegboard.			
	Connects and takes apart a pop bead string of five beads.			
	When shown how, he zips and unzips a large sized zipper.			
	Self Help			
	When asked to, toddler removes his shoes and socks without help.			
	Uses a child-sized spoon correctly when eating cereal.			
	Sometimes puts on mittens and cap without help.			
	Child drinks from a small cup or glass by himself.			
	Gradually is able to take off most of his clothing if it is unfastened.			

Figure 11–6   Toddler development evaluation sheet (Continued)

Usual Age of Appearance	Behavior	Observed Yes	No	Comments
Between 18 and 24 months	After 20 months, he uses the toilet or potty correctly most of the time when placed on it by an adult.			
	By two, indicates his need to use the potty occasionally without being reminded.			
The following appear gradually between 25 and 36 months of age. Each item in each section is in approximate sequence of maturity.	Gross Motor			
	Uses a small rocking horse or rocking chair for three minutes without falling off.			
	Carries a small breakable object such as a glass or a plate without dropping it.			
	While standing, throws a small ball two feet.			
	Catches a large ball or balloon which is rolled slowly across the floor.			
	Toddler goes up and down stairs with one foot leading for at least five steps.			
Between 25 and 36 months of age	Fine Motor			
	Puts a small peg into a pegboard hole without help.			
	Unwraps a small piece of wrapped candy.			
	Turns the pages of a cardboard book without help.			
	Puts the pieces in a three-piece formboard correctly.			
	Imitating, puts small objects in a cup and dumps them out.			
	Draws a recognizable "v" with a crayon on plain paper.			
	Builds a six-block tower.			
	Usually strings five large beads on a string.			
	Pours water from a small pitcher into a glass with very little spilling.			
	Self Help			
	Most of the time, feeds himself correctly with a small spoon with very little spilling except with liquids.			
	Puts a fork into meat or potatoes and eats correctly.			
	Indicates his need to toilet one to three times each day.			
	Takes off pants, shirt, socks, and shoes.			
	When given specific directions, puts his toys away about half the time.			
	With help, turns on the water faucet, fills a glass, and turns off the faucet.			
	Completes urination on his own but may need help with wiping and getting clothing on again.			
	When reminded, puts his coat on a hook.			
	Drinks from a glass without spilling.			

Figure 11–6 **Toddler development evaluation sheet (Continued)**

REVIEW

A. What are the two major developmental areas in which the most amount of growth takes place during toddlerhood?

B. T. Berry Brazelton outlined five areas of behavior that reflect the toddler's growth from dependence to independence. Match the areas to the correct examples.

Areas		*Examples*

1. independence
2. limits
3. play
4. identification
5. language skills

a. Janie pulls a stool up to the kitchen counter. She opens the cupboard and takes out a box of crackers and a jar of peanut butter. She climbs down. Then she takes a spoon from the drawer. She is ready to make her own snack.

b. Carlo calls out, "Leche, leche!" Carlo's mother knows right away that he wants a glass of milk.

c. Paul now keeps busy building garages for his toy cars.

d. Dad looks over at Tom. Tom is talking on his toy telephone at his little desk. Dad notices that Tom is holding the phone and sitting at the desk just as he does.

e. Tanya reaches out for Mom's coffee cup. "No, no, Tanya—hot!" says mother.

C. The developmental theorists (Erikson, Freud, Maslow, Rogers, Piaget, Sears, and Gesell) agree on some basic characteristics of the toddler. Write the numbers of the characteristics listed below with which they would all agree.

1. The toddler is quiet, compliant, and not very active.
2. Toddler's maturing muscular control is reflected in much of his behavior: he is very active motorically as he learns to walk, run, and climb.
3. Toilet training is a very important accomplishment for toddler.
4. Play is not very important for the toddler.
5. The toddler learns a great deal through observing others and imitating their actions.
6. The toddler is too young to understand anything about what is right and wrong.

D. Consider the following situations and then evaluate each.

1. Mrs. Wright has a difficult time buying clothes for eighteen-month-old Rodney. She thinks matching shirts and slacks are really handsome. However, if she gets a set with a top that fits Rodney, the pants are 6 inches too long.
2. Theresa Garcia at 15 months is a very busy person. She has just poured the contents of her brother's piggy bank on the floor and is about to take off, clutching the bank tightly to her chest.
3. Mary Lou Carter, age 18 months, has just gotten off the potty chair and has immediately wet her pants. Her mother gives her a good hard spanking.
4. Maria, age 18 months, sits contentedly putting blocks in an empty coffee can and then pouring them out.
5. Chan, age 12 months, sits on a blanket on the floor. He has several small objects: a rattle, a set of plastic toy keys, and a set of nesting cups. He picks each up in turn, appearing by the focus of his eyes to look closely at each as he manipulates it.
6. Nancy, aged two, says, "Do it myself!" as she sits in the bathtub, takes the soap from her mother's hand, and rubs it over her body.

12

The Toddler: Affective Development

OBJECTIVES

After studying this unit, the student should be able to:

■ Explain Vygotsky's and Erikson's views of the toddler.

■ Identify the stages in the development of toddler play.

■ Evaluate affective behaviors of the toddler and toddler caregiver.

■ Analyze and evaluate toddler social behavior.

■ Describe the place of moral development during the toddler period.

T oddler's increasing independence can be seen in their play and social activities. The attachment to a caregiver and the accompanying self-trust and trust of others allows the toddler to move away from adults and try things out.

The social and emotional aspects of child behavior take a leap forward in maturity during the toddler period. Vygotsky (Wertsch, 1985) placed particular emphasis on the importance of social and cooperative behavior in the social context as support for cognitive development. A skilled partner, an adult or older child, supports the child's learning within the **zone of proximal development (ZPD)** (the distance between actual development and potential development at any particular time). Erikson (Miller, 1989) emphasized the emotional aspect of psychological development within a cultural context. Remember he placed the toddler in a crisis of autonomy versus shame and doubt in his ongoing search for identity. During this period, children's temperaments are volatile and unpredictable, and their emotions may be expressed very strongly as they search for a definition of who they are.

In this unit we will look at toddler affective development in the areas of play and social relationships, social sensitivity and self-control, temperament, and self concept.

PLAY AND SOCIAL RELATIONSHIPS

Play

Segal and Adcock (1976) found that children from a variety of socioeconomic and cultural backgrounds engaged in very similar kinds of play activ-

KEYTERMSKEYTERMSKEYTERMSKEYTERMSKEYTERMSKEY
zone of proximal development (ZPD)

ities. In many ways, these toddlers were like small scientists as they explored and experimented in the environment (Figure 12–1).

According to Nicolich (1977) toddlers develop through a sequence of stages in their play, as seen in the following examples:

Stage 1: Rudy picks up a spoon, looks at it, puts it in his mouth, bangs it on the floor, drops it.

Stage 2: Rudy picks up the spoon and pretends to eat.

Stage 3: Rudy uses the spoon to feed a doll.

Stage 4: Rudy mixes up some pretend food in a pan with the spoon. He uses the spoon to put some pretend food in a dish. He then proceeds to eat, using the same spoon.

Stage 5: Rudy goes to the shelf. He takes a plate, cup, and saucer and carefully places them at the table. He returns to the shelf and gets a spoon, knife, and fork with which he completes the place setting. His mother sits at the table. Rudy says, "Soup, Mom." He feeds her with the spoon.

At Stage 1, Rudy explores. At Stage 2, he does a simple pretend act. At Stage 3, he adds the doll to the activity. By Stage 4, he goes through a sequence of activities. At Stage 5, he plans somewhat before acting and uses his newly acquired words.

Simple social play appears before social pretend play (Howes, 1985). Solitary pretend play is evident at about 12 months of age. Interactive social play usually appears during the second year. Social pretend play with peers usually does not appear until the third year. Social play of one-year-olds may involve one child chasing another or two children rolling a ball back and forth. Two-year-old social play is apt to include some role-taking (i.e., baby, parent, firefighter, airplane pilot, etc.). Howes observed toddlers who were ages 16 to 33 months at the beginning of a 4-month period of observation. The children were observed during play in a childcare center. Howes found that about half the children engaged in some simple social pretend play just prior to two and all the children showed some social pretend play activities by 30 months of age. These young children developed some very effective strategies for integrating

Figure 12–1   Toddler play involves the independent exploration of materials such as sand.

pretense into their social play. Children younger than 27 months usually used nonverbal strategies such as recruiting another child by acting out a fantasy and indicating by gaze or facial expression that the other child is expected to do the same. Older children use verbal recruitment such as, "You be the waitress" or "You be a puppy too." In another study of pairs of acquainted toddlers observed playing at home, Howes (1989) found a similar series of developmental stages in their social and social-pretend play.

Peer Relationships

Toddlers are interested in other children their own age and are capable of developing a social relationship (Eckerman, Whatley, & Kutz, 1975). Social activities include imitating the other child, showing the other child a toy, offering the child a toy, accepting a toy from the other child, using a toy with which the other child has finished, taking a toy from the other child (when the other child does not protest), struggling over a toy (when the other child does protest), and taking part in coordinated play. **Coordinated play** involves both children doing something together. They might build a block tower, fill a bucket with water, or take turns adding blocks to a tower and knocking it down (Eckerman et al., 1975).

Toddler-peer relationships are usually characterized as being somewhat stormy (Honig & DiPerna, 1983). Toddlers have been observed to engage in many negative social behaviors such as grabbing other children's toys, hitting, and biting. They almost seem to explore their **peers** in the same way they explore objects. Also, if they are moving toward autonomy, they may find overcoming another child's will to be very fulfilling. It may seem that putting toddlers in a group is asking for trouble. However, studies such as the one by Howes (1985) indicate that if toddlers have the opportunity to be together on a daily basis and get to know each other well, they develop positive social relationships. Toddlers seem to have the most positive interactions in pairs (versus larger groups) (Honig & DiPerna, 1983). This indicates that a toddler playgroup will run more smoothly if it is set up with several areas where one or two children can play, rather than offering limited choices where more than two have to play in the same area. Further, it has been found that interaction is more positive with gross motor equipment than with small toys. Toys should be plentiful enough so that arguments are cut to a minimum. Toddlers like to imitate each other so there should always be duplicate toys. If a toddler can pick up an identical toy and imitate a peer, positive social development is reinforced. If there is no duplicate, the toddler will then try to take the other child's toy. Honig and DiPerna (1983) conclude that it is very important for adults to intervene when toddlers are aggressive. However, besides letting them know that the aggression is not acceptable, adults have to show the toddlers positive alternatives.

By 21 months of age, toddlers have developed a complex communication system (Ross, Lollis, & Elliott, 1982). They have a variety of ways of communicating, depending on the goal they wish to achieve. One group of communications is used for getting involved with another through invitations to play or attempts to join another's play. Included in this group were giving something to or offering something to the other child. Another group of communications is made up of expressive acts and protests. Expressive acts include laughing, smiling, patting, kissing, naming, greeting, etc. Protest actions include screeching,

fussing, whining, verbal "no" or "don't," threatening gestures, or withdrawing self or an object. A third group of communicative actions includes declaratives and shows. **Declaratives** are verbalizations that are meaningful. **Shows** are calling attention to something by pointing, holding up an object, and/or saying "look" or "see."

Positive communications usually bring positive responses from peers, and negative communications usually bring negative responses. The only communications that are often not understood by other toddlers are declaratives. Toddler communication centers mostly on giving, taking, exchanging, and showing objects.

Brownell (1990) observed previously acquainted eighteen-month-old and twenty-four-month-old toddler same or mixed age pairs in a playroom setting. As might be expected, the older children engaged in much more complex social actions. Of more interest was the behavior of the younger toddlers when paired with an older partner as compared with a younger partner. When paired with an older partner the 18-month-old toddlers were "more socially active, socially involved, and affectively enthusiastic" and used more advanced means to engage the older child than they used with the younger child (Brownell, 1990, p. 844). These results would support the value of mixed-age grouping. Brownell and Carriger (1990) looked at the development of cooperation between same-age peers at 12, 18, 24, and 30 months of age. Same-age pairs of peers were placed in a problem-solving situation in which to obtain some toys the children had to work cooperatively. While one worked a lever to make the toys attainable the other could get the toys. The apparatus was designed so one child alone could not accomplish the task. Whereas none of the twelve-month-olds and few eighteen-month-olds could work cooperatively to get the toys, the twenty-four- and thirty-month-olds were much more able to coordinate their efforts.

Adult Influences

Adults can have a strong influence on toddler's social behavior. For example, Howes, Hamilton, and

Matheson (1994) followed a group of young children enrolled in day care as infants up until they were 4 years old. Howes et al. (1994) examined the interrelationships of teacher and peer behaviors as they relate to children's social competence. Toddlers who were more secure in their relationships with their teachers were less aggressive and engaged in more positive play with their peers. Teachers who approached social problems in a positive manner (helping the child initiate contact with a peer, monitoring contact with peers, and explaining peer behavior) tended to have children who were more highly accepted by their peers. That is, direct instruction on how to interact with peers brought positive results.

Fagot, Hagan, Leinbach, and Kronsberg (1985) observed playgroups that included toddlers when they were 13 to 14 months of age and then 9 to 11 months later. They recorded teachers' responses to toddlers assertive actions. The results of the first set of observations showed that teachers were more likely to respond to girls when they sought attention in a calm, low-key way and boys when they used physical means or cried, whined, or screamed. There were actually no differences in the frequencies with which these behaviors were used by boys and by girls. During the second observations there was a significant difference between boys' and girls' attempts to get teacher attention. Girls talked more while boys were more often negative (whine, cry, and scream). During the first observation both boys and girls exhibited equal amounts of assertive behaviors (grab, hit, push, and kick). Teachers were more likely to ignore girls' assertive acts and give some attention to boys'. By the time the second set of observations was made, boys were significantly more negatively assertive than girls. Teachers now responded about the same to both boys' and girls' assertive acts. Peers, however, reacted more negatively to boys' assertive acts than to girls'. It may be that teachers expect boys to be more assertive and are more alert to their negative behaviors while expecting girls to use more positive behaviors, being more alert to these kinds of bids for attention from them. This adult attention seems to maintain these behaviors. It appears teach-

ers need to be alert to treating boys and girls in a non-stereotyped fashion. Although teachers had dropped the **sex stereotyped** reactions by the time the second observations were done, the children seemed to have adopted them in their peer interactions. Parents have also been observed to influence toddler play by selecting sex-stereotyped toys (Eisenberg, Wolchik, Hernandez, & Pasternack, 1985).

Rogoff and Mosier (1993) examined **guided participation** as a vehicle through which the child learns what needs to be learned to function in a particular culture. This point of view grew out of Vygotsky's theory that social and cooperative behaviors between partners (the young child and older, more skilled partner), rather than didactic instruction, supports growth in the zone of proximal development. Rogoff and Mosier (1993) observed and interviewed four toddlers and their families who lived in an urban setting in the United States (Salt Lake City) and four who lived in a Mayan village in Guatemala. Their objective was to observe guided participation in cultural contexts considering the local goals for development. Adults were observed to guide children by adjusting communication and by simplifying tasks and helping them with difficult parts. When toddler and adult disagreed on what to do next, the adults usually respected the child's choice, this was especially true with the Mayan mothers. The Salt Lake City mothers used more complex verbal explanations while the Mayan mothers used more demonstrations reflecting a cultural difference in choice of communication mode. The Salt Lake City pairs had more face-to-face communication although these toddlers moved about more. Salt Lake City parents spent time playing with their toddlers whereas the Mayan mothers encouraged their toddlers to play alone so they could get their work done. In the Mayan culture the children were not viewed as conversational partners as they were in the middle-class Salt Lake City culture. In the Mayan culture the children relied on observational learning to acquire necessary skills; their attention was not managed to the extent the Salt Lake City children's was. The Salt Lake City mothers used a lot of praise and cheering and mock excitement as motivation. Although their specific guidance techniques differed, in both cultures the caregivers and children were collaborators in determining what would happen in a particular situation.

Social relationships with peers and adults are well established during the toddler period.

SOCIAL SENSITIVITY AND SELF-CONTROL

Toddlers have developed sensitivity and emotional expressiveness. As noted in the discussion of peer relationships, toddlers use expressive and protest communications in relating to peers. This increasing sensitivity is apparent also in their family relationships.

Emotional Expression

Remember from Unit 8 that emotional expression is well established in infancy. Malatesta, Culver, Tesman, and Shepard (1989) examined the emotional expressions observed on the faces of two-year-olds and their mothers in both stressful and nonstressful situations during infancy and toddlerhood. The strange situation was used to elicit expressions of emotion. Malatesta et al. (1989) found that two-year-olds have adopted facial expressions such as compressed lips, the knit brow, and lip biting, which indicate efforts to control negative feelings. The mothers of the two-year-olds displayed more expressivity to girls than to boys. In particular, the girls received more smiling. During play boys and girls displayed the same amount of anger. From 7 1/2 to 22 months, the frequency of negative expressions used were significantly correlated whereas frequency of positive were not. Mothers and their children tended to have the same emotional patterns at age two. Mothers who showed appropriate attention to their infant's emotional states had two-year-olds who displayed more positive emotions. Mothers who ignored infant sadness and pain were more likely to have two-year-olds who displayed sadness and anger following reunions. At two, during nonstressful interactions, secure children were more attentive to their mothers. During stressful interactions insecure children were more positive in their attention to their mothers in that they showed more interest but they also showed compressed lips with more frequency. The authors believe this indicates suppression of emotion and vigilance regarding what may happen next. The findings of the Malatesta et al. (1989) study indicates that emotional expressions are under some control by age two and that maternal emotional responsiveness during infancy has influenced children's development of emotional expression.

Sensitivity and Expressiveness

Toddlers can show sympathy toward others. One-year-olds may try to give comfort and help to those in pain or distress. The toddler is very aware when someone else is upset or hurt and often responds in a helpful, sympathetic manner (Figure 12–2).

When firstborn toddlers experience the arrival of a baby brother or sister, the older child often regresses to infantlike behaviors that were previously given up. For example:

Figure 12–2   **Toddlers are sensitive to the feelings of their peers.**

Upon the arrival of her new baby brother, two-year-old Janie's behavior at preschool changes. After snack, she is observed to get into the doll bed, burp, and curl up with her thumb in her mouth.

Children may also display signs of jealousy and a desire to get rid of the new arrival.

A group of four three-year-old boys, all of whom have younger siblings, play firefighter every day. During the course of their activity each day, the baby dolls burn up in the oven.

Dunn and Kendrick (1980) observed some firstborns (ages 18 to 43 months when the study began) and their mothers. The first observation took place when the mother was pregnant. Further observations were carried out when the younger sibling was 2 weeks, 3 weeks, 8 months, and 14 months. It was found that after the sibling's arrival, the mother initiated less playful attention directed toward the older sibling such as comments on what the child was doing. Mothers also initiated fewer verbal games and suggested new play activities less often. The mothers overall gave less sensitive attention. At the same time, there was more negative interaction. Control became dominant to a greater degree in interactions between mother and child.

Dunn and Munn (1985) studied family conflicts and the development of social understanding during the second year as observed in the home. They found that during this year there is an increasing understanding of conflict situations and their emotional aspects. During this period there is an increase in the frequency of either supporting or teasing a sibling or parent when sibling and parent are engaged in a conflict. By 16 to 18 months children show signs of knowing that they recognize forbidden behavior. Toddlers are especially interested in noting wild behavior, rude behavior, or behavior that involves possessions and not sharing. Around 18 months mothers begin to provide more verbal justifications to toddlers in their responses to toddlers' unacceptable behavior. While toddlers showed more understanding of conflicts and the emotions that accompanied them, they also became much more expressive: tantrums,

self-abuse, destruction of objects, and physical aggression toward siblings increases during the second year. This may be a reflection of their increasing awareness of themselves and their efforts to gain autonomy.

Toddlers also react to violence and may evidence symptoms of **post-traumatic stress disorder** such as "re-experiencing" the experience in their play, becoming emotionally subdued and withdrawn, having night terrors, shying away from persons or situations that are similar to the persons or scenes of the violent event, developing signs of anxiety such as troubled sleep, or displaying disrupted eating habits and aggression, developing a limited attention span, and distorting trust relationships (Special report, 1994).

Toddlers are just beginning to develop a sense of success and failure and the emotions that accompany success and failure (Stipek, Recchia, & McClintic, 1992). Before the age of two, the toddlers seemed to have had an intrinsic sense of accomplishment. Around two they began to look to adults for approval. Children who received more praise from mothers tended to express more spontaneous positive emotions (i.e., smiling, clapping, exclaiming) regarding their accomplishments.

Toddlers are sensitive to their own emotions and to the feelings of others. They can provide sympathy and they can show hostility and jealousy. They enjoy feeling good about their accomplishments and learn to look to adults for confirmation.

Attachment

Toddlers (and their parents) can still experience separation distress (Godwin, Groves, & Horm-Wingerd, 1993). In their study of leave-takings and reunions at a childcare center, Field et al. (1984) found that toddlers, protested much more strongly than infants when it was time for the parent to leave. They showed more attention-getting, verbal protest, clinging, and crying behaviors. Parents of toddlers showed more hovering, distracting behaviors and did more sneaking out of the classroom. Children who received a verbal explanation for the leave-taking

KEYTERMSKEYTERMSKEYTERMSKEYTERMSKEYTERMSKEY

post-traumatic stress disorder

tended to protest less and show less stress. Those children who stayed most easily also tended to leave most easily. The adult who works with young children can be supportive of parents by helping them understand that it is normal for toddlers to protest more than infants or preschoolers at being left. Parents need to know that this is a part of normal development. Otherwise, they may feel they are at fault.

Compliance, Self-Control, and Discipline

A great deal of research has been done on the development of compliance, self-control, and discipline during early childhood (Honig, 1985a, 1985b). This research has focused both on parent influence (Honig, 1985a) and the influence of other caregivers (Honig, 1985b). Honig (1985a) points out that since toddlerhood is a time when children are pushing toward autonomy, that even the most cooperative children have a need to assert themselves and will at times be noncompliant to adult wishes. Honig defines **compliance** as "immediate and appropriate response by the child to an adult's request" (Honig, 1985a, p. 50). Adults use various types of **control techniques** to try to modify children's behavior and get them to comply. The goal of control techniques and the teaching of compliance is the development of **self-control.** The development of compliance and self-control appears to have roots in infancy and toddlerhood.

Researchers have looked at early attachment relationships and **discipline** techniques as they relate to later self-control in young children (Honig, 1985a, 1985b). Older infants and toddlers enjoy helping with chores. Through these cooperative activities with adults the toddler learns how to be helpful. Toddlers also enjoy being told what to do. With their growing understanding of language and need to do things themselves, they view this type of activity as a game. Strong, healthy attachment to parents is highly related to later compliance. Parents who use positive suggestions in order to get compliance are more likely to receive compliance than are parents who use commands, prohibitions, and/or reasoning. Toddlers whose mothers use physical force are more likely to be more frequently disobedient. When mothers and toddlers were observed in a situation in which the toddlers had a problem-solving task, securely attached toddlers were more enthusiastic, paid better attention to the task, showed less frustration, said 'no' less often, sought help from their mothers more frequently, and were more accepting of their mother's suggestions than were less well-attached toddlers.

Children who have strong and healthy attachments to parents tend to be more cooperative with other adults. This is a very important factor today when more and more children are placed in the care of nonparental adults. The most serious problem for beginning teachers is dealing with discipline (Honig, 1985b).

The teacher who begins a career with a group of toddlers faces a big challenge. A great deal of understanding, patience, and tolerance of normal negativeness is needed. As with any other behavior there will be a wide range in degree of compliance within a group. Infant experiences have already had a powerful effect on behavior. Further, compliance does not appear to develop in a linear fashion (Schneider-Rosen & Wenz-Gross, 1990) but varies with context and age. Eighteen-month-olds seem to want to please and are more compliant than twenty-four-month-olds, while by 30 months compliant behaviors become more frequent. The most effective approach with toddlers is finding alternative acceptable activities and/or behaviors and giving them positive attention when they are behaving appropriately. Once toddlerhood nears an end and children are into the preoperational period, thinking processes go through a change that enables them to respond very well to reasoning. Positive approaches to discipline with preoperational children are discussed in Unit 29.

Moral Development

A major concern for adults who work with young children is the development of ethical behavior; the development of an understanding of right and wrong; that is, the development of morality. **Morality** grows out of social relationships (Damon, 1988). As adults, we must understand the social world of children in order to understand their special view of morality. Morality is not easy to define. Damon (1988) describes it as including the following (p. 5):

1. Morality is an evaluative orientation towards actions and events that distinguishes the good from the bad and prescribes what is good.
2. Morality implies a sense of obligation toward standards shared by others in the group.
3. Morality includes a concern for the welfare of others. It extends beyond one's own desires.
4. Morality includes a sense of responsibility for acting on one's concern for others. (Acts of caring, kindness, benevolence, kindness and mercy)
5. Morality includes a concern for the rights of others. (Justice and fairness)
6. Morality includes a commitment to honesty.
7. When morality is not lived up to, judgmental and emotional responses occur (shame, guilt, outrage, fear, contempt).

With children we are interested in how their views of morality and their judgments of morality change with time within their unique and nonadult social context.

The early moral emotions are empathy, shame, and guilt (Damon, 1988). We already have seen that toddlers may have the beginnings of empathy or a sensitivity to the feelings of others. However, not all toddlers evidence this emotion. **Shame** is a feeling of embarrassment that may occur when children feel they have not lived up to certain behavioral standards. Remember that according to Erikson toddlers are striving for autonomy, but failure brings shame and doubt. Potty training is often the focus for the toddler's first experience with this feeling. Parents may humiliate the child when success is not achieved. Guilt develops later during the preoperational period.

Toddlers are premoral. They are just beginning to learn about right and wrong and good and bad, and which kinds of acts fall under each label. Their values are usually situation specific. For example, just because they have learned not to pull the cat's tail does not mean they will not pull the dog's tail.

In the classroom, rules develop along two separate lines: moral and conventional. Moral rules are those that apply in every setting and have to do with aggression (i.e., physical harm) and resource violations (i.e., taking someone else's toy). Social conventions are those that are devised to deal with a specific setting and include rules for keeping materials in order and norms for various settings and activities (i.e., not talking during a story, keeping the blocks in a special area). Smetana (1984) found qualitative differences in social interactions relative to the two types of transgressions. Responses to conventional transgressions were much the same for ones and twos. On the whole they paid little attention. Teachers had to repeatedly remind them to attend to basic rules such as not talking during storytime and sitting down while eating. The toddlers were much more responsive to moral transgressions. They responded emotionally and physically at both ages. The older children were also likely to make a statement regarding the harm done. Whereas caregivers tended to provide a rationale for moral transgressions they did not do so for conventional transgressions. The personal nature of moral transgressions (that is, viewing and/or feeling pain or loss) and the reasons provided by caregivers probably support the learning of moral right and wrong earlier than conventional. Also, conventions often seem rather arbitrary from the child's point of view. "Why *not* stand up when you eat?" "Why put things away when you are finished?" Reasons for these rules are not as obvious as the consequences of pulling another child's hair.

TEMPERAMENT

The toddler's temperament traits continue to be distinct at ages one and two (Persson-Blennow & McNeil, 1980). At each of these ages, children display a range of behavior regarding temperament characteristics such as rhythm, mood, attention-persistence, and distractability. By age two, there are no significant differences between the temperaments

Morality   Shame

of boys and of girls even though adults may think that there are sex-stereotyped differences.

In their research Matheny, Wilson, and Nuss (1984) found great variability in temperament characteristics among toddlers. They also found consistent characteristics in individuals as obtained from both maternal ratings and from observations. There is increasing evidence that difficult temperament in infancy may be an indicator of problem behavior later on (Lee & Bates, 1985). Lee and Bates (1985) found that two-year-olds rated by their mothers as difficult were observed to be highly negative in their responses to their mothers' attempts to control them. If this conflict persists into later childhood, these difficult toddlers could be future problem children.

SELF-CONCEPT

Through social interactions and play, young children gradually develop an idea about who they are. This picture of oneself is called a self-concept (Yamamoto, 1972). The feedback received from people and objects met in the environment, no matter what culture, are reflected to the toddler in a self-concept. Each child develops an individual "self" according to the people the child chooses to imitate and the experiences in which the child chooses to participate (Figure 12–3). Play activities help the child develop as an acceptable member of the culture. As children practice what they have learned through observation in their play activities, they find out from the reactions of those around them whether they are acceptable members of their culture. If they get a lot of positive responses such as praise, approval, and accomplishment of tasks, they develop a positive feeling about themselves.

Of primary importance in the development of self-concept is the development of ethnic identity. Ethnic identity evolves through ethnic socialization. "Ethnic socialization refers to the developmental processes by which children acquire the behaviors, perceptions, values, and attitudes of an ethnic group, and come to see themselves and others as members of such groups" (Rotheram & Phinney, 1986, p. 11).

Figure 12–3   **Pretending to be a grownup is an important activity in the development of the self-concept.**

Self-concept and self-esteem are closely tied to ethnic identity and develop through ethnic socialization. During the toddler years, children are probably assimilating some information regarding physical aspects of people such as skin color and hair type and texture. However, it is not until ages three or four that they begin to categorize and compare these differences and to place themselves in a particular category.

SUMMARY

Toddlers have well-established social and personality characteristics. Toddlers play well on their own and can also play nicely with their peers in a supportive setting. Pretend play is in its early stages. Peers are just beginning to be involved. Peer relations are often characterized by being rather volatile, involving aggressive contacts on each other's bodies and play materials. Direct instruction on how to get the attention of others and how to share is helpful for making toddler play more positive. The responses of adults influence toddler behavior. Children tend to repeat behaviors (positive and negative) to which adults pay attention. Toddlers show signs of sensitiveness towards the feelings of others and of understanding what is happening in social conflict situations. As toddlers strive for independence, their dependence on emotional attachment to parents seems to peak. Discipline becomes increasingly important as normal toddler behavior tends to include many negative responses. As negative as toddlers are, they also have a natural compliance when it comes to showing off their emerging skills and knowledge. This facet of their behavior can be used to help develop compliance. Toddlers are in a stage of premoral development where they are learning to categorize right and wrong, especially in terms of what hurts and what does not. Abstract rules mean very little to toddlers. Temperamental characteristics tend to be stable through this period. Toddlers are becoming more and more aware of themselves and developing a broader concept of self.

FOR FURTHER READING

Curry, N. E., & Johnson, C. N. (1990). *Beyond self-esteem: Developing a genuine sense of human value.* Washington, DC: National Association for the Education of Young Children.

Fagot, B. I., & Kavanaugh, K. (1993). Parenting during the second year: Effects of children's age, sex, and attachment classifications. *Child Development, 64,* 258–271.

Greenberg, P. (1991). *Encouraging self-esteem and self-discipline in infants, toddlers, and two-year-olds.* Washington, DC: National Association for the Education of Young Children.

Lewis, M., & Haviland, J. M. (Eds.). (1993). *Handbook of emotions.* New York: Guilford.

Rosenblith, J. F. (1992). *In the beginning: Development from conception to age two,* (2nd Ed.). Thousand Oaks, CA: Sage.

Ross, H. S., & Lollis, S. P. (1989). A social relations analysis of toddler peer relations. *Child Development, 60,* 1082–1091.

Spencer, M. B., Brookins, G. K., & Allen, W. R. (Eds.). (1985). *Beginnings: The social and affective development of black children.* Hillsdale, NJ: Erlbaum.

SUGGESTED ACTIVITIES

1. Observe a toddler at home or at a day care site. Use the Toddler Social Development Evaluation Sheet (Figure 12–4) to evaluate the toddler's social development.
   a. Overall, does the toddler seem to be average, ahead of normal expectations, or slow in developmental rate?
   b. What kinds of suggestions do you have for the parents and/or caregiver regarding this toddler?
   c. Support all your conclusions and recommendations with data from your evaluation sheet.

2. Lead a class discussion comparing toddler social observations. On the chalkboard, make a summary chart showing the range of behaviors observed.

3. Observe a group of toddlers playing on gross motor equipment and compare this behavior with their behavior when playing with small, individual toys. Do you note any similarities or differences when comparing play with the two types of equipment?

4. If you haven't yet made friends with a toddler, do so. Take him to a quiet place away from the other children. Put out six to ten of the toddler's favorite toys. Make up a game where you ask him to do a series of tasks with the toys, e.g., "Bring me your truck." "Put the baby to bed." "Roll the ball." Note how the toddler responds to these requests. Does she comply? If not, what is her response? Does she seem to enjoy the game?

Usual Age of Appearance	Behavior	Observed		Comments
		Yes	No	
	Social			
Between 13 and 18 months	Toddler usually plays with other children if they are available.			
	Prefers help from mother to help from other adults most of the time.			
	When he is in a small group, he enjoys the attention of others.			
	Initiates social contacts.			
	Imitates play activities of others.			
	Plays side by side with another child.			
	Expresses emotions such as joy, anger, and fear appropriately.			
	When suggested by an adult, toddler usually shares food or toys.			
Between 18 and 24 months	Greets other people if asked to.			
	Plays appropriately with a car or a doll.			
	Recognizes emotions in others such as fear, anger, and happiness.			
	More than half of the time, directs his own play activities.			
	Enjoys helping with chores.			
	Begins to sometimes use "please" and "thank you" as he nears age two.			
Between 25 and 36 months	Often watches others to observe how they do things.			
	Pretends a doll is a baby or plays house pretending rooms and roles for about three minutes at a time.			
	Spends 60 percent of his time playing alone.			
	Once in awhile, asks to help with a household chore such as setting the table or folding the laundry.			
	Starts saying the names of his friends.			
	Plays in a small group for up to 20 minutes.			
	Often offers to share toys with his playmates.			
	As he nears three, is able to leave his mother and go to nursery school without a fuss.			
	Initiates contact with other children quite often when in a group setting.			

Figure 12–4 Toddler Social Development Evaluation Sheet (Adapted from G. J. Schirmer (Ed.). *Performance Objectives for Preschool Children.* **Sioux Falls, SD: Adapt Press, Inc. Used with permission.)**

5. Interview one or more parents of twelve- to twenty-four-month-olds who are walking. Ask them the following questions:
  a. What are (*child's name*) favorite play activities?
  b. Does he have the opportunity to play with other children? Are they the same age? What do they do?
  c. Do you find that (*child's name*) ever acts negatively? When has this occurred? Does he ever defy you? Say "No!"? How do you respond?
  d. Do you feel he has any idea regarding what is right and what is wrong? How can you tell?

  Compare the responses you get with the text descriptions and with those of other students in the class.

6. Make an entry in your journal.

REVIEW

A. Explain Vygotsky's and Erikson's views of the toddler's affective development.

B. Nicolich defined a series of stages that the toddler goes through in the development of play behaviors. Match the stage descriptions in Column I with the behavioral descriptions in Column II.

Column I	**Column II**
1. Exploration	a. Maria moves a toy car across the floor making a sound like an engine.
2. A simple pretend act	b. Maria goes to the toy box and gets four cars, two trucks, and a bag of blocks. She takes the materials to the rug, builds a garage, and puts the cars in saying, "Park the car."
3. More complex pretend act	
4. Sequence of activities	c. Maria moves a car and a truck across the floor and parks them side-by-side.
5. Plans and uses speech	d. Maria picks up a toy car, looks at it, tastes it, bites it, and runs her fingers over it.
	e. Maria finds some cars and blocks on the rug. She builds a shelter around one of the cars. Then she takes the car out and pushes it around the floor.

C. Consider the following situations and evaluate each.

    a. Eighteen-month-old Maria plays alone with three stuffed bears. "Mama bear, papa bear, baby bear," she repeats.

    b. Twenty-month-old Liu Pei and eighteen-month-old Maria roll a ball back and forth to each other.

    c. Georgie and Rudy, both two-year-olds, are pulling on the arms of a teddy bear, each shouting, "Mine!"

    d. Mrs. Phung is puzzled. When eighteen-month-old Hien Phung plays with eighteen-month-old Tony he grabs things from him and won't share. When Hien plays with two-and-a-half-year-old Lai he shares nicely.

    e. Ms. Garcia responds more frequently to boys than to girls who seek attention by yelling, screaming, and whining.

    f. Maria, 20 months of age, is trying to put some nesting cups together. Her mother sits next to her. "Maria, find the biggest." Maria finds it. "Good work! Now find the next biggest." Maria finds it and places it in the correct position, "Good Maria, you have the idea."

    g. Dat is also 20 months old. He is trying to figure out what he can do with playdough. His mother pats it and rolls it. He watches her. Then he takes a piece of the dough and pats it.

    h. Mr. Brown is surprised when seventeen-month-old Brian runs over and gently pats two-and-one-half-year-old Emily who has just fallen down and is crying in anguish.

    i. Lai has a harder time letting her mother leave the child care center now at 14 months than she did as an infant.

    j. The next time Kate heads for a flower pot, her mother takes her hand and says, "Let's go play in your sandbox."

    k. Mr. Santos finds Jaimie's behavior is often apparently inconsistent. He jumps up and speaks out during stories, gets out of his chair often during lunch, and bothers other children during nap time. On the other hand, he is very aware of aggressive behavior and how others can be hurt and controls himself well during play activities.

    l. At 18 months Bill was compliant, at 24 months he was negative, and now at 30 months he seems to be settling into a more compliant stage.

D. Explain *morality* and how it relates to toddler affective development.

The Toddler: Cognitive Development

OBJECTIVES

After studying this unit, the student should be able to:

■ Name the Piagetian stages through which the toddler passes.

■ Describe Vygotsky's view of toddler cognitive development.

■ Identify examples of toddler concept learning.

■ Analyze and evaluate toddler speech samples relevant to stage placement and context.

■ Analyze and evaluate examples of toddler cognitive development.

According to Piaget, the toddler is passing through the sensorimotor to the preoperational period of cognitive development. Before toddlerhood, sensory and motor activity are the dominant means for learning. Sensory and motor modes of learning are important all through life; but during the preoperational period, play and imitation are the dominant means for cognitive growth.

Toddlerhood continues through the last two of the six stages outlined by Piaget, which take the toddler from reflexive activity to thinking before acting (Ault, 1983). Between 12 and 18 months, toddlers usually experience the fifth stage. They continue to enjoy repeating actions but also try new ways of doing things. As Ault (1983) describes, the toddler changes from dropping the same toy out of the playpen time after time in the same way, to dropping different toys in different ways. Around 18 months of age, toddlers reach Piaget's sixth and final stage during which representational thought develops. At stage six, the child begins to think before acting, doing what is called **representational thinking**. Children are now able to represent, or think through, a problem in their minds before going into action. Suppose a toddler wants a toy on a shelf that is out of reach. The toddler tries to reach it by stretching but stops when unable to do so and appears to think about the problem. Earlier, the child would have kept trying to climb the shelves and stretch even though to

KEYTERMSKEYTERMSKEYTERMSKEYTERMSKEYTERMSKEY
representational thinking

an adult, it was obvious the attempt would fail. Now, the child represents the next move in her mind's eye. The child stops, thinks, and then gets a small chair to stand on, enabling her to reach the desired toy.

At the same time, toddlers are progressing through the final two stages of object permanence. By 12 months of age, toddlers are able to solve the problem of the toy hidden under a cloth if they see it hidden and if it is always hidden in the same place. Between 12 and 18 months, they develop the ability of finding an object hidden in a series of hiding places as long as they are allowed to see the object being hidden. Around 18 months or shortly after, toddlers can search for objects that have been hidden without having seen which hiding place has been used. During this period, the toddler enjoys playing hidden object games.

From Vygotsky's point of view the toddler is in an important period in the development of language (Wertch, 1985). Toddler are in a critical zone of proximal development for language. Speech is essential for the development of higher mental functioning. That is, speech supports concept development. Scaffolding, support and guidance from adults or older peers, as toddler explores his environment, assists toddler in reaching his cognitive developmental potential.

CONCEPT DEVELOPMENT

Toddlers are busy and active learning about concepts such as size, shape, number, classifications, comparisons, space, parts and wholes, volume, weight, length, temperature, and time (Charlesworth & Lind, 1995). As toddlers move about and work with many things in their everyday environment, they learn about the properties of objects in meaningful ways (Goldhaber & Smith, 1993). For example:

- Raymond tries to hold onto a large beach ball but finds he can hardly stretch his short little arms around it. (size)

- Josie has some play dough. She pounds it, pinches it, and rolls it. (shape)

- When asked how old he is, two-year-old Nathan holds up two fingers. (number)·

- Marnie lines up her green blocks in one row, yellow blocks in another, and red blocks in a third. (classifying by color)

- Alfredo, age two and one-half says, "My apple bigger" as he points at Tanya's apple and his apple. (comparison)

- Lisa tries to stuff her big panda bear into a small box and finds that it does not fit. (space)

- George breaks his cracker into two pieces, saying, "I have two crackers!" (parts and wholes)

- A group of toddlers are gathered around a tub of water. They have containers of many sizes which they fill with water. They fill, pour, and mix (Figure 13-1). (volume)

- Petey tries to lift a box of toys but cannot do it. (weight)

- Bonnie tries to put her doll in the toy crib but the doll is too long. She finds an empty cardboard carton that is just the right size and makes a bed for the doll. (length)

- Maria takes a sip of hot soup and says, "Ouch!" (temperature)

- David says, "Juice time next." (time)

Toddler cognitive development has been studied extensively. Some of the types of characteristics and behaviors that appear to be typical of toddlers are described in the rest of this section. Toddlers will work very hard to solve a problem that challenges them in their zone of proximal development. DeLoache,

Figure 13–1   **Water play helps toddlers learn about volume.**

Sugarman, and Brown (1985) supplied toddlers with a set of nesting cups (a sequenced set of cups designed so each will fit in the next size if they are placed in the correct order). Toddlers tended to focus on the immediate problem of getting one cup into the other, even trying to force larger cups into smaller without considering the relative sizes of the whole group of cups. Toddlers can be very determined in their efforts to solve a problem.

Toddlers are developing a capacity to remember through observing, through acting on objects, and through imitation. When asked to remember where an object was hidden, eighteen- to twenty-four-month-old children showed signs of consciously using strategies to keep the hiding place in mind (DeLoache, Cassidy, & Brown, 1985). They used verbal strategies such as talking about the objects and non-verbal strategies such as glancing at or pointing to the hiding place. The researchers interpreted these behaviors as early examples of rehearsal and self-checking, strategies commonly used at older ages. Objects are superior to just verbal descriptions as memory aids for toddlers (Price & Goodman, 1990). Event sequences are remembered best if they are experienced rather than just explained verbally.

Hay et al. (1985) found that children were more likely to imitate the actions if a verbal explanation accompanied them. Even though children at this age were not very proficient in speaking, the verbal cues seemed to support their imitative behaviors. This suggests that while demonstrating a task or action to a young child the adult should label the actions, i.e. "Look I'm putting the blocks in the box."

Researchers have looked at toddlers' development of other specific concepts. For example, Sera, Troyer, and Smith (1988) studied two-, three-, and four-year-olds' and adults' internal representations of normative size concepts. That is, they were interested when the relative nature of *big* and *little* is understood. Big and little take on meaning relative to the other members of their class (i.e. other insects, airplanes, houses, and cats). Sera et al. found that while two-year-olds could pick out shoes of the appropriate sizes for adults and children, they had trouble with buttons and plates. Fours, on the other

hand, could easily select the correct items. It may be that the more familiar a class of objects is, the more accurately the twos are able to conceptualize the relative sizes.

Toddlers are also beginning to develop concepts in the area of classification and categorization. That is, they are beginning to put things with similar characteristics into groups. Fenson, Cameron, and Kennedy (1988) used an object and picture matching task to get at this concept with twenty-six-month-old children. Perceptual similarity/nonsimilarity was the significant factor in the accuracy of the children's matching of objects to pictures. For each object, the children were shown four pictures from which to select the one most like the specified object. The more similar the picture was to the object and the less similar the other pictures were, the easier it was for the children to make correct choices. There was little difference in their selection of basic and superordinate matches if they were perceptually similar. Two-year-olds may categorize more on looks than on which items really belong together on the basis of function or class group. Classification will be discussed in more detail in Unit 21.

As already mentioned, language development is in high gear during the toddler period and is closely tied to concept development. Waxman and Kosowski (1990) looked at noun-category bias in two-year-old children. Noun-category bias is suggested as a bias that limits the possible meanings young children will assign to a new noun when compared to items in the same class or category. They were specifically interested in whether when given choices of matching a target (e.g., a cow) to four possible choices if the children would select items in the same superordinate category (e.g., animals such as a fox and a zebra) or thematically related items (e.g., milk and a barn). Their results supported that the strong link is between nouns and superordinate category relations. Further evidence for the close relationship between language and concept development comes from a study by Gopnik and Meltzoff (1992). They found that eighteen-month-olds who were able to name more things were more advanced in their abilities to sort objects into groups.

SPEECH AND LANGUAGE DEVELOPMENT

As toddlers approach age two, speech develops at a fast rate (Figure 13–2). Once toddlers say their first words, they enter the **holophrastic stage** of language development (Pflaum, 1986). During this stage, the child speaks in one-word sentences called **holophrases.** These words are usually the names of familiar things, such as body parts. Things that are active are apt to be labeled first: "doggie," "car," or "kitty." Food words or names of other desired items are used in this early speech.

Children also use words that refer to a specific thing but which are not real words. One seventeen-month-old uses "adoo" to refer to water. She also used the approximation "mulk" for milk. Most young children substitute sounds (such as the *i* in milk and the *t* in tummy) or leave out some sounds, such as "minee" for vitamin, or "fust" for first. Context (conveying where or what) is very important at this stage. That is, it is important to know what toddlers are referring to when they use their single-word sentences. For example, "Doggie!" might mean:

"I see a doggie on TV."
"There is a doggie outside."
"I want the dog to come in."
(with tears) "Doggie knocked me down."

Figure 13–2 As speech develops, toddlers say the names of things in picture books.

Since toddlers usually understand more than they can say, adults may use follow-ups such as "Show me," "Take me to ____," or "Point to ____," and so on to find out exactly what the toddler is trying to tell them. Adults also can expand on what the toddler says and note whether the toddler reacts in a way that indicates they have found the right meaning. That is, a toddler may say, "Doggie!" Mom says, "There's a doggie outside?" The toddler runs toward the living room. Mom follows and sees that there is a dog in front of the house. "There is a doggie outside," she repeats as the toddler laughs and points with excitement.

McCune (1989) recorded the vocal development of 10 children from the time they were nine months of age until they were 16 months of age. There was considerable variability in the timing and the number of strong nominals and relationals the children used by 16 months. **Strong nominals** are those nouns which refer consistently to at least two referents ("kitty" to real and stuffed cats); **strong relationals** refer to words that are used consistently for potentially reversible relationships (e.g., "up" for "pick me up"). At 16 months, the range of strong words was from none to twenty-seven. The beginning of the use of such words was from fourteen-months-old on.

Sometime between 18 months and 2½ years, toddlers begin to put two or three words together in sentences. These short sentences, which are still incomplete by adult standards, are called **telegraphic sentences**; this second stage in the development of speech is the telegraphic stage. Sentences at this stage, like a telegram, contain only the essentials:

"More mulk."
"Daddy work."

Context is still important. That is, what is the child referring to when he says, "Hurty pummy"?

"My tummy hurts."
"Teddy bear's tummy hurts."

Like detectives, adults have to look for clues to help them to come up with the response the toddler has in mind.

KEYTERMSKEYTERMSKEYTERMSKEYTERMSKEYTERMSKEY

| holophrastic stage | Strong nominals | telegraphic sentences |
| holophrases | strong relationals | |

Between 18 months and 4 years, sentences become longer and more complete—more like those of an adult. "Daddy work" becomes "Daddy is at work." Two-year-olds vary a great deal in their speech. Some use holophrases, some use telegraphic speech, and some use more adultlike speech.

One of the toddler's unique characteristics is that his comprehension (understanding) of language is ahead of his speech development. Oviatt (1982) was interested in the development of the comprehension of common object names. In particular, she wanted to find out how twelve- to twenty-month-old children learn that an unfamiliar but similar object can have the same name as a now familiar object. Children were picked who were unfamiliar with rabbits or hamsters. Mother and researcher introduced each infant to one of the animals informally. They played and used the animal's name in a way that was intended to be as much like a normal speech situation as possible. Each child was then asked to identify the target animal when it was paired with another animal. Three different types of media were used: stuffed replicas, drawings, or photographs. At all levels there were children who could recognize the target animals, but between 15 and 18 months there was a big improvement. This is consistent with other theory and research that suggests there is a change in the thought processes at around 18 months of age. Adults who work with young children can see from this study that toddlers can learn the names of things through natural conversation centering on the objects. Formal drill and practice are not needed.

By age two children usually use speech along with much of their activity. Furrow (1984) studied two-year-olds' use of private and social speech. Private speech takes place when the child plays alone and social when involved with another person. Furrow was interested in whether two-year-olds use speech to serve the same functions in the private and social contexts. The children were studied during an informal play session in their own homes. The researcher took the role of the child's playmate when needed, letting the child take the lead in the play activity. Furrow found that speech was used differently in social and private contexts. Social speech included more regulatory (telling about something or someone not present), and attentional (seeking attention from the other person) functions. Self-regulatory speech (speech that directs one's own activity) dominated in the private context. Overall a much wider variety of speech functions was used in the social context (Figure 13–3).

Somewhere around sixteen- to eighteen-months-old toddlers become strongly focused on speech. They suddenly lose interest in their toys. They want to be near an adult much of the time demanding verbal interaction. They particularly demand that objects be labeled for them and they watch the adult's mouth as he speaks. During this period, they also may show an increased interest in books. This behavior keeps up until they are using the words effectively in their own speech. This appears to be an important activity for plunging into the period of rapid development of speech and language that takes place from 18 months of age to four (Cawfield, 1992).

While most children are speaking fluently by age four, a considerable number of children experience delay and may still be speaking in one word phrases with very limited vocabularies. **Expressive language delay (ELD)** should be of concern and development, not just left to chance. These children should be evaluated as to speech and social development, hearing. The possibility of learning difficulties

Figure 13–3 **Toddlers use their speech skills in their play.**

Expressive language delay (ELD)

in the family history should be investigated (Paul, 1989; Rescorla & Schwartz, 1989; Whitehurst, Fischel, & Arnold, 1989).

INTERACTION OF CONCEPTS, KNOWLEDGE, AND LANGUAGE

As already mentioned, concept and language development go hand-in-hand and they interact. McCune (1989) has documented a relationship among the development of the object concept, the appearance of representative play and the onset of rapid growth in language. As the toddler learns more language, there is more material to process when thinking and as thought capabilities become more complex language can be used in more complex ways. Through the child's speech we learn much about the child's thought processes. Consider the following examples from the activities of a toddler friend of the author:

> Emmett was going through a period when his interest focused on discovering the many qualities of cellophane tape. He was standing in the kitchen trying to throw some pieces of the sticky tape into the air. Unnoticed by Emmett, the piece of tape fell on the floor. Emmett noticed the tape was gone. He gazed up toward the ceiling and said, "Tape stuck in the sky."

From the example, we get a glimpse into Emmett's reasoning. As for most children his age, the most obvious solution is the answer. If you are trying to throw something sticky into the air and it disappears, it must be stuck in the sky.

Vibbet and Bornstein (1989) examined the relationships among three aspects of mother-toddler interaction and specific toddler competencies in referential language and pretense play. All toddler subjects were 13 months of age. The following interaction domains were studied:

> Social interactions: Affective and interpersonal communication, both nonverbal and verbal.
>
> Didactic interactions: Mothers' efforts to call the toddlers' attention to things in the environment.
>
> Control actions: Degree to which mothers or toddlers initiated and maintained activities.

Naturalistic observations of mothers and toddlers were done in their homes. Toddlers were also assessed individually on language competence and free play competence. Mothers' didactic frequencies were strongly related to infants' noun comprehension and overall language competence. Didactic activities included actions such as pointing out objects, demonstrating how they worked, and elaborating on the properties of objects. Apparently this makes it very clear to toddlers that words stand for things. This didactic activity was accompanied by verbal social praise and encouragement. Purely social conversation does not have this effect, nor does the situation in which the toddler takes dominant control in initiating activities. Other research suggests that by the end of the second year it is more effective if the mother switches to following the child's lead. In the area of skill at pretend play, frequent didactics combined with social interchanges were related to more pretend play skill. Mutual interaction seems to be more important than control in play skill development. The context for learning to pretend may be more casual than that for learning language. Much content of pretend play is learned through observation of everyday activities such as talking on the phone and cooking.

SUMMARY

During the toddler period, the child progresses from the sensorimotor to the preoperational stage of cognitive development. Representational thought appears and the object concept develops. Toddlers are learning about many concepts such as size, shape, color, and space. They are developing problem-solving strategies and memory strategies. Toddlers learn a great deal through imitation and especially from observing demonstrations accompanied by a verbal explanation. Toddlerhood is a period when language skills develop rapidly. One-word sentences grow to four- or five-word sentences. At first comprehension is ahead of expression but expressive language moves ahead during this period. The type of language used in social situations differs from that used in private speech when playing alone. The toddler's primitive level of thought is reflected in his language.

FOR FURTHER READING

Allen, K. E., & Marotz, L. (1994). *Developmental profiles: Prebirth to eight,* (2nd Ed.). Albany, NY: Delmar.

Bloom, L. (1993). *The transition from infancy to language.* New York: Cambridge University Press.

Butterworth, G. E., Harris, P. L., Leslie, A. M., & Wellman, H. M. (Eds.). (1991). *Perspectives on the child's theory of mind.* New York: Oxford University Press.

Gottfried, A. W. (Ed.). (1984). *Home environment and early cognitive development.* New York: Academic Press.

Moerk, E. L. (1983). *The mother of Eve—As a first language teacher.* Norwood, NJ: Ablex.

Rosenblith, J. F. (1992). *In the beginning: Development from conception to age two.* Thousand Oaks, CA: Sage.

Savage-Rumbaugh, E. S., Murphy, J., Sevcik, R. A., Brakke, K. E., Williams, S. L., & Rumbaugh, D. M. (1993). Language comprehension in ape and child. *Monogr. of the Society for Research in Child Development*, *58* (Nos. 3-4, Serial No. 233).

Shatz, M. (1994). *A toddler's life: Becoming a person.* New York: Oxford University Press.

SUGGESTED ACTIVITIES

1. Observe a toddler at home or at a day-care site. Use the toddler cognitive development evaluation sheet (Figure 13–4) to evaluate the toddler's developmental level and rate of development in the cognitive area.
   a. Overall, does the toddler seem to be average, ahead of normal expectations, or slow in his rate of development?
   b. Are there any areas in which the toddler seems to be exceptionally ahead or behind in development?
   c. What kinds of suggestions do you have for the parents and/or caregiver regarding this toddler?
   d. Support all your conclusions and recommendations with data from your evaluation sheet.

Usual Age of Appearance	Behavior	Observed Yes	Observed No	Comments
Between 13 and 18 months	Cognitive			
	When asked, "Where is _____?" looks for missing family members.			
	Listens to nursery rhymes for two–three minutes.			
	Points to an object he wants and vocalizes to indicate need.			
	When asked to point to his body parts, points to at least three.			
	When asked, says his first name.			
	Places a circle or square in the correct space on a formboard.			
	Responds appropriately with "yes" or "no."			
	Carries out a variety of one-step directions.			
	Language			
	Points to familiar objects when asked.			
	Imitates the vowel sounds (a, e, i, o, and u) in words such as cat, bed, lid, dog, and mud.			
	By 13 months, speaking vocabulary is four to ten one- or two-syllable words.			
	Shows by response that he understands some simple phrases.			
	As he nears 17 or 18 months, he uses about 10 words in one day and uses 10–25 different words in a five-day period.			
	At 17 months, names two body parts when asked.			

Figure 13–4   **Toddler Cognitive Development Evaluation Sheet (Adapted from G. J. Schirmer (Ed.).** *Performance Objectives for Preschool Children.* **Sioux Falls, SD: Adapt Press, Inc. Used with permission.)**

Usual Age of Appearance	Behavior	Observed		Comments
		Yes	No	
Between 18 and 24 months	Cognitive			
	When observed for one hour, he uses at least one two-word sentence.			
	Usually points to at least four different body parts.			
	Communicates his needs verbally.			
	Repeats two digits (such as 1–2 or 2–5).			
	As he nears 24 months, he carries out two commands given together, such as "Pick up your Teddy bear. Put him back on the chair."			
	Matches like objects, such as circles with circles or squares with squares or trucks with trucks.			
	Imitates touching ten body parts with no mistakes.			
	Language			
	During free speech the child uses the parts of speech as follows: nouns, 50 percent; verbs, 14 percent; adjectives and adverbs, 18 percent; and pronouns, 10 percent.			
	Responds correctly to simple commands such as "sit down" and "come here."			
	When shown a pile of five or more objects and asked verbally to pick a particular one, toddler is able to.			
	By 24 months during free speech, the child uses the parts of speech as follows: nouns, 39 percent; verbs, 21 percent; adjectives and adverbs, 17 percent; and pronouns, 15 percent.			
Between 25 and 36 months	Cognitive			
	Identifies at least one of the primary colors (red, yellow, or blue).			
	Points to small body parts such as chin, eyebrow, nose, mouth, knee, cheek, and ear when asked.			
	When shown two objects of different size (such as a big ball and a small ball), points to the big and small object.			
	When shown an action (such as jumping, sleeping, sitting) the child identifies it and says it verbally.			
	The child matches four pairs of color samples.			
	Stacks a five-part stacking toy in the correct order.			
	Puts a picture which has been cut in half back together correctly.			
	Right after he hears a simple story, states two ideas about the story in one- or two-word sentences.			
	When asked, "How old are you?" holds up the correct number of fingers.			
	When shown pictures of common objects such as spoon, car, ball, or house, names them.			
	Repeats three digits from memory (such as 4-6-7 or 1-3-6).			

Figure 13–4 **Toddler Cognitive Development Evaluation Sheet (Continued)**

Usual Age of Appearance	Behavior	Observed		Comments
		Yes	No	
Between 25 and 36 months	Language			
	Uses the following sounds with 90 percent accuracy: p, b, m, t, d, n, w, h.			
	Uses more and more two-word sentences.			
	Is beginning to use plurals correctly.			
	Answers simple questions such as "What do you wear?"			
	Identifies basic adjectives such as big, small, good, bad, slow, fast.			
	Over a period of several days, uses adjectives such as small, happy, sad, noisy, big, little, tiny, hot, cold, hard, soft, sweet, sour, fast, and slow in free speech.			
	Without being asked, elaborates on his ideas.			
	During free speech, by 36 months, uses nouns, 23 percent; verbs, 23 percent; adverbs and adjectives, 17 percent; and pronouns, 19 percent of the time.			

Figure 13–4   Toddler Cognitive Development Evaluation Sheet (Continued)

2. Find a toddler between 12 and 16 months of age and one between 18 and 22 months of age. Compare their development of object permanence. Try the object permanence tasks and record their responses. With the younger child, start with part d of the second activity in Suggested Activities for Unit 9. If the child succeeds through exercise f, proceed to the tasks that follow. Begin with exercise a of this activity for the older child. Compare the reactions of the two children. At which stage of object permanence would you place each of them?

The following is a continuation of the object permanence task from the second Suggested Activity, part d, in Unit 9.

a. Object hidden in sequence in three hiding places.
   Find three different hiding places such as a cloth, a box, and a hat. Have the child watch as you take a small familiar object (such as a doll, car, cracker) and hide it first under one object, and then move it between two objects. Move it under the next object, then between the two, and then under the third. Be sure the object is visible between hiding places. Leave it under the third hiding place. Note how the toddler goes about searching for the object. Repeat three times. If the toddler looks under the last hiding place first, he is ready to try a more difficult task.

The next problems involve searching under several screens placed on top of each other.

b. A favorite object hidden under three screens at the same time.
   Put three screens over the object, one at a time. Let the toddler search. If he removes all the screens and finds the object, go on to the next task.

c. Object in a box with screens.
   Put the favorite object in a box with a lid that can be taken off easily. Put two cloths over the box, one at a time. Note how the child goes about his search. If he searches until he finds the object, go on to the next task.

The following problem involves the invisible hiding of an object.

d. Invisible hidden object.
   Put three cloths on a surface that will absorb sound. Use a small object that can be hidden in your hand. Hide the object in your hand. Be sure the toddler is watching. Hide your hand under each of the cloths,

leaving the object under the third one. Be sure that the toddler cannot see the object when your hand is between each cloth. Show the toddler your empty hand. Observe while the toddler searches. Write down what he does. Repeat two or three times. If he looks directly under the last cloth and finds the object, repeat three times, hiding the object under a different cloth each time, but always putting your closed hand under each cloth in turn. If he always starts with the last cloth and searches systematically in sequence, then he has achieved the final stage of object permanence.

3. Go to a store where young children's toys are sold. Make a list of toys that you feel would be good for a toddler. Record the price of each. Make two toys from waste materials that would serve the same purposes but would cost less.

4. Do one of the following activities to get some first-hand information on toddler language development.
   a. Have at least three conversations with a two-year-old. Tape record the conversations each time. Later write down from the tape everything the child said. Label each sentence as holophrastic, telegraphic, or beyond telegraphic (that is, complete sentences). Count how many of each you recorded. Using the information on language development from this unit, describe and evaluate the child's level of language acquisition.
   b. Record on tape a conversation between a mother or father and a two-year-old. Try to get twenty to thirty minutes of talk. Transcribe the conversation later and label each of the parent's speech samples that involve prompting, echoing, or expansion. Count how many of each the parent uses. What does this tell you about the parent/child interaction? (play dough, water, and sand are materials that the parent and child might use to produce conversation.)

5. Put yourself in a toddler's place. Imagine you are in a playpen looking out at a room full of interesting items. Describe what is in the room and how you might be feeling separated from the space around you. Write down what you have thought about and your reaction to taking the toddler point of view. Discuss your report with a small group in class.

6. Make an entry in your journal.

REVIEW

A. Describe Piaget's and Vygotsky's views of toddler cognitive development.

B. In Column I are listed some concepts that the toddler is learning. Match the concepts with the behavioral incidents in Column II.

Column I	Column II
1. size	a. Petey tries to put a square in a round space on a formboard.
2. shape	b. Josie says, "I have more cookies!" as she points to Nathan's cookies.
3. number	c. Marnie tries to curl up in the laundry basket and finds that it is just the right size.
4. color	d. David runs out into the snow without his mittens. Soon he is back crying that he is too cold.
5. comparisons	e. Lisa finds she can pick up a tennis ball easily but a soccer ball is too big for her short arms.
6. space	f. Nathan picks out all the blue crayons.
7. parts and wholes	g. Alfredo is in the sandbox filling containers with sand.
8. volume	h. Bonnie runs through the house in her pajamas shouting, "Bedtime!"
9. height	i. Raymond chants under his breath, "One, two, three. One, two, three."
10. temperature	j. Bonnie cuts her play dough into many small pieces.
11. time	k. Marnie stands next to a tape measure that is glued on the wall and says, "Look! Marnie big girl!"

C. Analyze, evaluate, and comment on each of the following examples of toddler behavior.

1. Maria, eighteen-months-old, is playing with an insert puzzle. She is trying to place a square shape in a circle space. She grunts as she pushes hard not appearing to notice that she's trying to push the shape into the wrong space.

2. Two-year-old Kate has to put her teddy bear on the shelf while she eats lunch. During lunch she often glances at the bear and at one point jumps up and runs over to look at it.

3. Mrs. Quan shows Lai how to use her new toy. Her demonstration is accompanied by an explanation. Mrs. Hopkins demonstrates the use of the same type of toy for Kate but does it without any comments or explanation.

4. Two and one half-year-old Kate's favorite doll is on the kitchen table just out of reach. She tries to stretch and reach it. Then she runs to the other side of the table and tries again. Next she climbs on a chair and leaning across is able to grab the doll's leg and pull it toward her.

5. Lai, age two-and-a-half, is observed retelling the story of *Goldilocks and The Three Bears* using puppets, toy dishes, her little chairs, and some boxes for beds.

6. Chan Mung, 17 months old, refers to real and stuffed animal dogs as "doggie", to all vehicles as "car", and uses "up" to mean "pick me up", "get it off the shelf for me", and "plane in the sky."

7. Sam, 13-months-old, and his mother are playing with an assortment of toys. "Look at the truck, Sam," says his mother pointing at a yellow dump truck. "You can carry your little blocks in the truck." "Your truck has four big wheels that run smoothly."

D. Analyze these toddler speech samples. For each sample, tell which stage the child is in and the importance of context in each case.

1. "Daddy!"
2. "Bad girl!"

E. Put an X next to each statement below that is correct.

_____ 1. Toddler's speech development is ahead of comprehension.

_____ 2. It is expected that toddlers will use private speech (that is, talk to themselves) when playing alone.

_____ 3. Toddler social speech includes a greater variety of language use than does private speech.

_____ 4. There is very little relationship between concept and language development.

14

The Toddler Environment

OBJECTIVES

After studying this unit, the student should be able to:

■ Understand the importance of the sociocultural aspects of the toddler environment.

■ Analyze and evaluate toddler caregiver behavior.

■ Analyze and evaluate toddler environment.

oddlers are curious about the world. They are also developing toward independence. The combination results in a great deal of experimentation. Toddlers have been known to see what might happen if they flush a toy down the toilet, dry a wet stuffed animal in the oven, and mix up a variety of ingredients to make a cake like they have seen adults make. The combination of curiosity and independence provides for a period of development that is a challenge for adults. In this unit, we will look at the toddler environment from four perspectives: sociocultural, home, child care, and the adult relationship.

THE SOCIOCULTURAL ENVIRONMENT

As suggested by Bronfenbrenner (1989, see Unit 2) and described in Unit 10 (see Gonzales-Mena, 1993) children need to be studied and interacted within their community, family, and peer group. The importance of paying close consideration to the growing diversity in our country is a major

focus in the fields of child development and early childhood education (i.e., Derman-Sparks, 1989, 1993, 1994; *Kappa Delta Pi Record*, 1992; Mallory & New, 1994; Sexton, Snyder, Sharpton, & Stricklin, 1993). In Unit 10 we began to look at some of the sociocultural influences on the infant. In this unit the topic will be expanded.

McLoyd (1990) describes the impact of economic hardship on African-American families and their children. African-American children suffer in larger proportion than other groups. By 1985, 41 percent of African-American children lived in **poverty** as compared to 13 percent of Anglo children. According to the 1990 census there was only a minor improvement in the percentages of children under eighteen who are poor: Anglo, 12.5 percent; African-American, 39.8 percent; Latino, 32.2 percent; Native American, 38.8 percent; Asian/Pacific Islander, 17.1 percent; Other, 35.5 percent; Overall in the USA, 18.3 percent (*State of America's Children*, 1994). McLoyd examines psychological distress, parenting, and socioemotional development. She develops four major arguments (p. 311):

KEYTERMSKEYTERMSKEYTERMSKEYTERMSKEYTERMSKEYTERMSKEY

poverty

- Poverty and economic loss diminish the capacity for supportive, consistent and involved parenting and render parents more vulnerable to the debilitating effects of negative life events.

- A major mediator of the link between economic hardship and parenting behavior is psychological distress deriving from excess of negative life events, undesirable chronic conditions, and the absence and disruption of marital bonds.

- Economic hardship adversely affects children's socioemotional functioning in part through its impact on the parent's behavior toward the child.

- Father-child relations under conditions of economic hardship depend on the quality of relations between the mother and father.

Besides the poor nutrition, lack of proper clothing and shelter, and poor health care for children, poverty promotes parental distress, which tends to produce increased use of aversive and coercive discipline such as physical punishment and yelling by parents. This can be an especially significant negative factor for the normally active toddler. Poverty is also associated with children having poor peer relations.

Not all poverty families have these negative characteristics. McLoyd (1990) points out that the negative factors can be mitigated if the parents have a strong social support network. The social support network may give needed psychological support and may temper parents from acting abusively toward their children. The support group can be a source of advice and of role models. Also, if the neighborhood is considered safe and friendly, parents are likely to act more positively toward their children than if the neighborhood is considered unsafe and high risk. In the safe neighborhood there is more daily positive interaction between neighbors. A strong extended family and/or a stable marriage are also associated with less stressed parents who are more emotionally stable and who are less punitive toward their children.

As described in Unit 10, Harrison, Wilson, Pine, Chan, and Bruiel (1990) analyzed the family ecologies of ethnic minority children: African-American, Native American/Alaskan Native, Asian, Pacific Americans, and Hispanics. **Family ecology** is defined as "important family functionings that are a reflection of the interactions between the family as a social system and other societal institutions and systems" (p. 348). Harrison et al. (1990) believe that the family ecologies of minorities will differ from that of the majority because minorities must deal with problems such as prejudice that go along with minority group status. The ecologies of minority families will affect the development of minority children.

Racial/cultural/ethnic families are strongly affected by years of discrimination and poverty. Currently, they live mainly in urban areas, are on the average younger families, and have higher birthrates than majority families. Minority families developed adaptive strategies. For example, the establishment of extended families supports problem-solving and stress coping. Flexible social roles have supported adaptation. For example older siblings or grandparents may take on parenting roles when needed. Biculturalism is another adaptive strategy. That is, the minority members learn to function effectively within the minority and the majority cultures. A major minority-majority difference is that the majority culture emphasizes individualism whereas the minority cultures place more emphasis on collectivism and group harmony and cooperation. These adaptive responses shape the way minorities socialize their children.

As described in Unit 10, Harrison et al. (1990) point out that minority families have the child socialization goal of interdependence rather than individualism. They would encourage cooperation rather than competition, autonomy, and self-reliance. This point of view contrasts with the view presented in the text that the task of toddlerhood is to develop toward independence. While this is the majority view, it is in conflict with the minority views and might present a conflict of values when majority adults are working with minority families. On the positive side, biculturalism, and particularly bilingualism, seems to contribute to cognitive flexibility. That is, bicultural/bilingual children can deal with problems in varied

Family ecology

formats. The cultural discontinuity that minority children meet when they enter school and neighborhood may enable them to develop situational problem solving skills. On the other hand, the more congruent home and school teaching strategies are, the better child achievement is. The information from the review by Harrison et al. underlines the importance of adults becoming knowledgeable regarding the sociocultural background of the children and families with whom they work. It also encourages adults to work with children in a congruent manner while also helping them to learn the skills needed to operate successfully in the majority culture (Figure 14–1).

The study by Rogoff and Mosier (in Rogoff, Mistry, Goncu, & Mosier, 1993) described in Unit 13 is a good example contrasting toddler/parent interaction in two different cultures (a Mayan Indian town in Guatemala and a middle-class urban area in the United States). This study was part of a larger research project (Rogoff, Mistry, Goncu, & Mosier, 1993) that also included observations in a tribal village in India and a middle-class urban neighborhood in Turkey. The universals discovered were that in each culture toddlers and caregivers developed a system of mutual collaboration for learning that included a shared understanding and adjustments to the partner's degree and approach to involvement. Cultural variations centered on differing values and goals. Major community differences were whether or not children were segregated or integrated into adult activities. When segregated, caregivers had to be more formal in directly teaching, especially in the language area. Adults viewed the children as conversational partners. When children were integrated, they were more on their own learning through observation with adult responsive assistance but not planned direct instruction. The middle-class caregiver-toddler interactions were much like those in traditional school instruction. The authors suggest that non-middle-class children could benefit from having their parents learn some of the techniques that work so well at preparing middle-class children for school. On the other hand, middle-class parents and school personnel can benefit children by putting learning in a context in which children have to rely more on their own efforts and their own observational skills. Within our country, we need to be aware that children need to learn how to function in the majority culture without losing the values and customs of their primary culture.

THE HOME ENVIRONMENT

Toddlers can be quite content with simple play materials that help them develop fine and gross motor coordination. For example, Wilson (1990) suggests many homemade toys for toddlers such as the following examples:

Figure 14–1 Through guided participation with adults, toddlers learn the skills and behaviors valued by their culture.

18 to 24 months

Tunnel: Use sturdy long rectangular cardboard boxes large enough for the children to crawl through. Cut out the ends and tape the edges to keep them from scraping children and also to keep the boxes from tearing. Place several boxes end-to-end or in a zig-zag pattern. (p. 250)

24 to 30 months

Soap paint: Use one part soap flakes and one part water. Beat the mixture with a hand egg beater. Skim off soap suds to paint on a table top or shelf or freezer paper. (p. 270)

THE CHILD CARE ENVIRONMENT

The key indicators for quality child care listed in Unit 10 apply to toddler care also (Koralek, Colker, & Dodge, 1993). Koralek et. al (1993) describe the developmentally appropriate toddler program as one that "provides a balance between a toddler's needs for security and independence" (p. 37). The appropriate toddler environment "includes several small, clearly defined interest areas where two or three toddlers can engage in activities such as playing with water or sand, fingerpainting, building with large cardboard blocks, or dancing to music" (p. 37). There is more than one of the most popular toys. There is plenty of room for movement and use of large muscles. Materials are at a level where toddlers can make independent selections. The room is arranged so that caregivers can easily supervise all areas. For more specifics, see also Lally, Provence, Szanton, and Weissbourd (1987).

Wortham and Wortham (1989) emphasize the need for appropriate toddler play space (Figure 14–2). Toddlers like to play with individual toys. They like to pick up, drop, pour, stack, carry, and push and pull. Toys combined with sand is a favorite. Remember, they also enjoy playing alongside each other. Wide slides, sandboxes, and rocking boats provide opportunities for shared fun. Toddler playgrounds should have a variety of surfaces and small safe feeling spaces with a variety of textures enclosed by shrubs or partial walls.

During the infant and toddler period, it is important that the environment be one that makes the children feel comfortable with their own cultures (Whaley & Swadener, 1990). Whaley and Swadener (1990) emphasize that multicultural education begins with infants and toddlers. Teachers need to learn the background and culture of each child to have continuity between home and center. Avoid gender or culturally stereotyped toys, books, puzzles, and puppets but do include dolls, books, music, and other materials that are authentic representations of different cultures. Encourage children to become competent in their first language as well as being exposed to English in a nonpressured way. Put pictures up that show different cultures. Encourage infants and toddlers to

Figure 14–2 **Toddlers need space to move about and a variety of appropriate play materials.**

feel good about themselves, to be empathetic, to share, and respect the feelings of others.

> Early multicultural education is not a curriculum: it is a perspective and commitment to equity, sensitivity, and empowerment. It is something that can and should be built into the everyday experiences of young children. It is not direct teaching, but the integration of many ideas into the play experiences of the infant and toddler. Perhaps most important is the fact that children at this age can be empowered in the areas of self-esteem, acceptance and empathy. (Whaley & Swadener, 1990, p. 240)

THE ADULT AND THE TODDLER

From the toddler's point of view, the adult, determined to socialize the toddler, is a major interference in what could be a delightful time of life. Selma Fraiberg describes the toddler point of view as follows:

> . . . They [adults] urge him to part with treasures he discovers in his travels, the rusty bolts, charred corncobs and dried up apple cores that are so difficult to find unless you know where to look for them. They send unsolicited rescue parties to prevent him from scaling marvellous heights, from sloshing through inky puddles, or pursuing the elusive tail of the family dog. . . . They are there to interfere with the joys of emptying garbage cans and wastebaskets; and, of course, they bring in proposals of naps and bedtime at the most unfortunate moments and for reasons that are clear only to them. (Fraiberg, 1959, pp. 62–64)

The toddler soon gets a reputation for being negative, as he resists this adult interference with his plans. From the adult's point of view, there are some things that are really dangerous for the toddler's health and safety and for the adult's mental health. Somehow the toddler has to begin to learn what is acceptable and what is not, while at the same time having some freedom to explore.

Two concepts to consider when working with toddlers are prevention and behavior modification. Prevention involves making the environment healthy and safe for the child and minimizing the need for excessive restraint. For example, electric light sockets should be covered, and poisonous substances put out of reach. Valuables that cannot be replaced if broken can be put away for awhile out of sight. Some delicate but replaceable items can be left out to use as teaching tools to show the toddler how to handle things with care.

Prevention can also be viewed as being proactive rather than reactive. A proactive style foresees potential problems and prevents them from happening. A reactive style waits until the problem occurs and then reacts.

Skinner's Theory: Behavior Modification

B. F. Skinner's theory of learning has been used as the basis for a technique called behavior modification. Remember, toddlers understand speech to a greater extent than they can speak themselves. In behavior modification, a combination of verbal and nonverbal actions are used to help the toddler learn desired behavior and give up undesirable behaviors (Figure 14–3). As a first step, the toddler is rewarded for doing the appropriate thing.

A smile, a pat, and/or an attentive look can be given when toddler is doing something appropriate, such as playing nicely.

Toddlers soon learn which activities bring positive attention and comments, and they repeat those activities. A second technique of behavior modification involves the use of substitution and redirection.

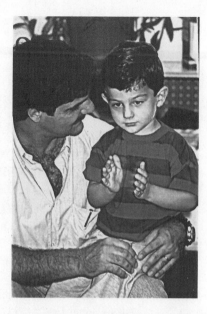

Figure 14–3 **Talking to the toddler in a pleasant tone of voice reinforces the child's cooperative behavior during play.**

With substitution, toddlers are directed to do something that makes it impossible for them to do the undesirable activity. For example:

Toddler likes to open drawers and cupboards. Each time he opens one which adult doesn't want opened, adult gently helps toddler close it, saying, "Close it, that's a good girl/boy."

Redirection with toddlers involves physically changing their course of action. As a toddler moves toward an adult's bookshelf, the adult gently turns the toddler to head to the child's own bookshelf (Figure 14–4).

Other Factors That Influence the Effectiveness of Guidance Strategies

Helping the toddler become a socialized preschooler is not easy. It requires a great deal of patience and positive behavior on the part of the adults.

KEYTERMSKEYTERMSKEYTERMSKEYTERMSKEYTERMSKEY

Prevention   behavior modification

Figure 14–4 The toddler can be directed into helping with household chores as a positive way to explore adult materials.

This is not new information. The findings of the classic study by Sear, Maccoby, and Levin (1957) indicated that punishment alone does not help in the long run to develop self-regulation and compliance. As described in Unit 11, positive guidance is more effective in the long run.

Howes and Olenick (1986) compared family and childcare influences on toddlers' compliance. Since the period between 18 and 36 months is believed to be critical for the development of compliance and self-regulation, Howes and Olenick studied families with children in this age range. They looked at families with toddlers in high-quality day care, low-quality day care, and not enrolled in day care. They were interested in the relationships among several factors: father involvement, family integration into social support networks, maternal role satisfaction, and quality of child-care placement. Previous research indicated that father involvement has a positive relationship with optimum toddler development, that integration into a social support network relates positively with mother's effectiveness in interaction and quality of attachment to the child, and that mother's role satisfaction has a greater impact on child development than employment itself.

The quality of the father's relationship with the toddler is also critical (Easterbrooks & Goldberg, 1984). Easterbrooks and Goldberg (1984) found that high involvement by the father was related more strongly to cognitive than to emotional development. For fathers, the amount of time spent in play activities with the toddler seemed to be more important than involvement in routine caregiving such as feeding, diapering, and bathing. When observed in a problem-solving situation, the toddlers who performed most positively tended to have fathers who were sensitive in the situation and allowed toddlers to be autonomous, were encouraging, and provided age-appropriate cues. Sensitive fathering appears to be as important as sensitive mothering.

It has become increasingly apparent that fathers need to be more involved than just at the level of basic responsibility such as providing financial support and seeing that children's health and welfare are provided for (McBride, 1989). Fathers also need to be involved in direct interaction and be directly accessible when needed. McBride (1989) describes the program at The Center for Young Children (CYC) at the University of Maryland, which provides help for fathers so they can learn how to be more involved with their young children. Fathers and children meet at CYC on Saturday mornings for a combination of play group and discussion activities that help the fathers learn more about child development and how to solve problems in discipline, sibling rivalry, the influence of television, etc. The children benefit from the interaction with their fathers and the long-term benefits of increased father involvement.

Parents and other caretakers must learn positive guidance techniques. Miller (1990) points out that children will not develop in a positive direction with no guidance, but on the other hand they cannot be molded like clay. Adults must recognize that each child comes "equipped with individual personalities, likes, dislikes, interests, and motives" (Miller, 1990, p. 50). Miller sums up the adult role as follows:

> The role of the adult is to guide, assertively and respectfully, never forgetting that even the youngest child is truly a person with all the rights befitting any other human being (even the right to be negative and recalcitrant on occasion). In the developmental interactionist perspective, child guidance is intended to give children feedback about the realities of their world, to allow them choices within reasonable limits, and to help them con-

front the logical consequences of their own actions, (Miller, p. 50)

SUMMARY

Burton White (1975) formulated conclusions regarding the first three years of life that summarize the critical features of the environment and the adult role. White views the first three years as the most critical in the child's life. As a result of the research he and his colleagues have done, White concludes that there are two critical times during toddlerhood.

- Around 12 to 15 months when the child begins to walk. Children who had more freedom of movement, fewer restrictions of gates and playpens, and greater opportunity for motor activity at this age were better developed at age three than children who were more restricted.

- Around 24 to 27 months when language is developing at a rapid rate. Mothers of well-developed children encouraged exploration and curiosity, listened to their children's conversations, and made high demands for cooperation from the child.

A great amount of basic learning occurs during the toddler period. The environment the adult arranges and the way the adult interacts with the child appear to be critical in promoting the best development possible as the child grows toward the preschool period.

The toddler is both enjoyable and frustrating. A toddler's constant movement can wear down even the strongest and more patient adult. The adults in a toddler's life must be in close contact with the toddler, allowing a certain amount of freedom but expecting the child to conform to necessary rules and regulations.

FOR FURTHER READING

Azrin, N. H. & Foxx, R. M. (1974). *Toilet training in less than a day.* New York: Simon and Schuster.

Brazelton, T. B. (1992). *Touchpoints: The essential reference.* Reading, MA: Addison-Wesley.

Castle, K. (1983). *The infant and toddler handbook.* Atlanta, GA: Humanics, Ltd.

Coakley, B., & Kopp, M. (1991). *Guide for establishing and operating day care centers for young children.* Edison, NJ: Child Welfare League of America.

Committee for Economic Development. (1993). *Why child care matters: Preparing young children for a more productive America.* New York: Author.

Cromwell, E. S. (1994). *Quality child care: A comprehensive guide for administrators and teachers.* Des Moines, IA: Longwood Division, Allyn & Bacon.

Daniel, J. E. (1993). Infants to toddlers: Qualities of effective transitions. *Young Children, 48*(6), 16–21.

Essa, E. (1995). *A practical guide to solving preschool behavior problems.* (3rd Ed.). Albany, NY: Delmar.

Galinsky, E., & Friedman, D. (1993). *Education before school: Investing in quality child care.* New York: Scholastic.

King, E. W., Chipman, M. F., & Cruz-Janzen, M. (1994). *Educating young children in a diverse society.* Des Moines, IA: Longwood Division, Allyn & Bacon.

LaPoint, S. A., Boutte, G. S., Swick, K. J., & Brown, M. H. (1993). Cultural sensitivity: How important is it for effective home visits? *Day Care and Early Education, 20* (4), 11–14.

McAdoo, H. P. (1993). *Family ethnicity: Strength in diversity.* Thousand Oaks, CA: Sage.

Miller, D. F. (1990). *Positive child guidance.* Albany, NY: Delmar.

Phinney, J. S., & Rotheram, M. J. (1987). *Children's ethnic socialization: Pluralism and development.* Newbury Park, CA: Sage.

Rothenberg, B. A., Hitchcock, S., Harrison, M. L., & Graham, M. (1983). *Parentmaking.* Menlo Park, CA: Banster.

Schrank, R. (1984). *Toddlers learn by doing: Toddler activities and activity log for parents and teachers.* Atlanta, GA: Humanics, Ltd.

Segal, M. (1985). *Your child at play—Birth to one year.* New York: Newmarket.

Segal, M. & Adcock, D. (1985). *Your child at play—One to two.* New York: Newmarket.

Segal, M. & Adcock, D. (1985). *Your child at play—Two to three.* New York: Newmarket.

White, B. R. (1984). *First three years of life.* New York: Avon.

Wilson, L. C. (1995). *Infants and toddlers: Curriculum and teaching.* Albany, NY: Delmar.

SUGGESTED ACTIVITIES

1. Visit a home- or school-based toddler day-care site. If possible, observe a full day of activities. Use the evaluation sheet in Figure 14–5 to evaluate the competence of the caregiver(s). Answer the following questions:
   a. Does the caregiver have the kinds of characteristics needed to be a competent toddler caregiver?
   b. In which areas is the caregiver strong, average, and weak?
   c. Where would you recommend that improvements be made? What advice would you give this caregiver if you had the opportunity?

2. Visit a family that includes a toddler. Observe the parent(s). Rate the parent behavior using the toddler caregiver evaluation sheet. Evaluate the competence of the parent(s) by answering questions a through c in Activity 1 that are relevant to the parent(s).

3. After having had some experience in observing or interacting with one or more toddlers, consider your own reaction to toddlers and their approach to life. How would you feel about being with toddler(s) 8 hours each day? How would you go about relating to them? Share your reactions and ideas with a small group in class.

4. Discuss the following questions with small groups in class:
   a. Would it be easy for a parent to feel like a failure in dealing with a toddler? How and why?
   b. What are the differences between the toddlers with whom you have interacted or observed? What are the similarities?

Caregiver Characteristic	Specific Behaviors	Rating			Comments
		Strong	Average	Weak	
Positive Toward Life	Pleasant appearance – smiles, seems happy				
Enjoys Young Children	Shows pleasure in the activities and antics of the toddlers. Comments on how much she likes children of this age.				
Energetic and Giving	Moves with energy from child to child. Always seems ready to help each child and to find needed play materials or give physical aid and comfort. Spends extra time planning, obtaining materials, preparing, contacting parents, etc.				
Patient	Shows an understanding of toddler's need to achieve autonomy: allows him to make mistakes, try out new skills, etc. Gives each child ample time to explore each activity without undue interruptions.				
Tolerant of Messes	Encourages toddler to feed, dress, wash, and toilet himself in spite of the mess he may make in the process. Has materials for toddler to pour objects in and out of containers. Provides activities and materials for water and sand play, Play Doh and finger painting.				
Casual Regarding Minor Risks	Allows toddler to perform motor activities that are a challenge. Allows toddler to use tools such as hammers and scissors as soon as his fine-motor coordination allows for their use. Supervises use.				
Serves as a Consultant	Doesn't hover over child but is always available to help. Observant of children; doesn't ignore them.				
Designs an Appropriate Environment	Encourages large-muscle movement: climbing, walking, running, rolling, ball playing, pushing, pulling, lifting, and carrying. Space and materials are provided for these activities. Provides material for small-muscle activity: simple puzzles and pegboards, blocks, beads, Play Doh, crayons, containers, and objects. Tables, chairs, sinks, toilets (and/or potties), coat hooks, toy shelves, etc. are designed for toddlers to help themselves.				
Is a Good Listener	Listens to what the toddler has to say with interest.				
Sets High Standards for Cooperation	Makes the rules clear and expects toddler to learn those rules by about two or two and one-half.				

Figure 14–5   Toddler Caregiver Evaluation Sheet (Adapted from D. L. White, *Experiences and Environment*. Vol. 2 by Prentice-Hall. Used with permission.)

c. To what degree did the different caregivers you observed meet individual children's needs?

d. What advice might be given to a caregiver in a day-care home who had one or more toddlers in her group?

5. Make an entry in your journal.

REVIEW

Consider the factors discussed in Units 11, 12, 13, and 14 regarding the toddler's physical and motor, affective, and cognitive development; the toddler environment; and the adult role with the toddler. Then analyze and evaluate the toddler development center described here.

Mrs. Sanchez discovered that there was a need for day care in her neighborhood for one- to three-year-old children. There were enough facilities for infants and a fine center for children three and older. She found an empty store in the neighborhood and converted it into The Toddler Development Center. With the help of others in the neighborhood, she was able to obtain help in remodeling the store and getting money to buy equipment. Some of the people in the neighborhood contributed their time and skills to build needed partitions, install new plumbing, and build play equipment. The big window in the front of the store was kept. The children can look out at the busy street and the people in the neighborhood can look in. In back of the store, a former parking lot was converted into an outdoor play area.

A visit to the center after it is underway finds the following activities in progress. As we enter, we find ourselves in a large area where several children are busy with large-muscle activity. Some are going up five steps and then sliding down a small slide. Others are crawling under the slide as if it were a tunnel. Some of the two-year-olds are loading big blocks in wagons which they push or pull across the floor. A one-year-old is pulling a dog with wheels on a string. In the corner, there is a pile of cushions and pillows of many sizes and some of the children are rolling and jumping on them, stacking them, and doing just about everything one could do with such materials.

Children go freely in and out of another room in the back where there is quieter activity. In one area, three children are sitting on a rug working with simple formboards, puzzles, and bead stringing. One child has a big laundry basket full of small rubber balls. He has a number of containers that he fills with the balls and then pours into the laundry basket and fills again. Other activities available include working with play dough, paint and crayons, and paper and scissors. There is a corner at the back with a rug and some shelves filled with books. The sturdy cardboard books are on the lower shelves and the more delicate books on the higher shelves. The opposite side of the room has been designed as a small house. Neighbors have built a small stove, refrigerator, and sink from wood. There is a table with chairs and three cribs, also handmade. There are many rag dolls with clothes that can be put on and taken off. One of the teachers is having a pretend dinner which two of the children have made for her. Another child is feeding a "baby" which he finally tucks carefully into a crib.

One child reaches for another's play dough. The teacher in the area, Mr. Smith, notices and places a glob of play dough in the first child's hand, saying, "Here's some play dough for you, Charlie." Mr. Smith glances at the children playing with the puzzles and beads. He says, "You children are really working hard today." All the teachers give smiles, hugs, and pats on the head as they supervise the children's activities.

Some of the children are wearing diapers while others are in training pants and some in regular underpants. In the bathroom there is a changing table, two small toilets, and two portable potty chairs. The staff appears to let each child proceed at his own pace as to whether he uses the potty or toilet.

When one child falls down and scrapes his knee, several other children gather around as the teacher comforts him. One runs off and asks another teacher for a bandage while another child runs for a clean, damp cloth with which to wipe the "hurty."

There is quite a bit of talking going on. Sentences from the children range from word approximations such as "adoo" for "water," to "truck" as a child points to a toy he would like to use, to "more milk" at snack time.

Section IV

Physical and Motor Development from Preschool to Primary

INTRODUCTION

On the north side of the city we visit Carver Elementary. Carver is located in a lower socioeconomic section. Most of the families are headed by single mothers and are supported by welfare allotments. All the children are eligible for the federally funded free lunch and breakfast program. The school houses two four-year-old classrooms, four kindergartens, and three each of first through fifth grade. Observing at recess on the kindergarten playground we see one teacher on duty supervising the 78 kindergartners. The children have a selection of balls and jump ropes to use but no climbing equipment, swings, or sandbox. Mostly they run randomly in small groups pretending to be superheroes or heroines or persons in distress. Inside we interview "Coach," the physical education teacher. He explains that he only has time to work with the prekindergarten, kindergarten, and primary children one hour per week. During that time, he works with them on basic skills such as throwing, catching, and kicking balls or running from one fixed point to another. With the primary children, he introduces simple games with rules, such as dodge ball.

After school you have an opportunity to meet with the principal and some of the teachers. You ask them what kinds of things they do to promote health and nutrition in the school. They explain that they have become increasingly concerned about the health and physical development of their students. Just providing breakfast and lunch and one period of physical education per week is not enough. Therefore, they are gradually developing a physical fitness curriculum that includes daily teacher-directed movement activities and instructional units on good health and nutrition practices. They have communicated their objectives to the parents. The children and teachers are planning a health fair for the spring as a vehicle for getting parents more involved and concerned about their children's health, nutrition, and motor development. Through the local medical society, they have located two doctors who are willing to volunteer half a day per month to provide health education activities and consultation for parents and children. The principal and teachers are very excited about this new program and believe it will have a positive impact on the students and their families.

A few days later we visit Westchester Elementary located in the Eastern section of the city. The area is middle- and upper-middle socioeconomic level. No students are eligible for federally supported breakfast and or lunch programs. Most of the families have two parents in the home. About 60 percent of the mothers work full-time. The school houses six kindergartens, and four or five classes at each grade level up through fifth. Many of the students are enrolled in a before-and-after school program conducted at the school. The program was started by the parents and is run by a parent board. There is a tuition fee for this service. You visit the primary playground, which you note has some excellent permanent equipment purchased with a combination of money from Parent Association fund-raising activities and donations from businesses in the community. The mass of students are supervised by three teachers, one teacher from each of the primary grades who is performing his or her assigned playground duty for that day. Some children are observed in vigorous physical activity: climbing, jumping, and running. Most are engaged in some sociodramatic play, pretending that the playground equipment is a spaceship or a house. They are active but do not engage in a sustained physical activity. Some children sit on benches and watch their more active peers. You talk with the physical education teacher Mrs. Phillips. She also can meet with each class only once each week and follows the same program as Coach.

You meet with the principal and some of the kindergarten and primary teachers after school. They voice their concerns about the physical fitness of their students and the health care they receive. Many of the parents are very health conscious and make sure their children eat nutritious food, have regular medical and dental checkups, and get plenty of outdoor exercise. On the other hand, many are either ignorant or too busy to monitor their children's

health. They send them to school hungry or with a nonnutritious breakfast picked up at the local donut shop. At home they watch TV for hours. Many attend a nearby childcare center before they enter kindergarten at Westchester. The center is convenient but offers no teacher-planned physical activity nor any nutrition and health education curriculum. They have suggested that the after-school program might provide some adult-directed physical activities but most of the parents are not interested. They have their children enrolled in the local soccer league in the fall and winter and T-ball or softball in the spring and summer and believe that is enough. The teachers are concerned that some of the coaches are pushing the children too hard—making them overuse their developing muscle and bone structures and sending them back onto the field of play without checking that injuries are completely healed. They are considering the development of a physical fitness program at the school.

We have just visited two elementary schools in two different neighborhoods. The schools are fictitious, but the situations described represent what is happening with our young children today. Consider what we learned from our observations and our discussions with the principals and teachers. Reflect on some of the problems that seem to be present as threats to the health and welfare of the students. After reading this section, look back at these descriptions and evaluate what is going on in each of the two settings. Explain where you feel the schools are on the right track and where you feel they could be doing a better job.

15

Physical Growth, Safety, Health, and Nutrition

OBJECTIVES

After studying this unit, the student should be able to:

■ Identify examples of the basic principles of growth.

■ Use a growth chart to determine if a child's height, weight, and body proportions are within the normal range.

■ Discuss the effects of a good diet and good health care on a child who has suffered malnutrition.

■ List the health and nutrition problems that low-income children may have when they enter school.

■ Assess safety factors for young children.

■ Evaluate situations involving adults' and children's attitudes toward illness and nutrition.

■ Describe the basic parts of a nutrition, health, and safety education program for young children.

As the number of young children living in poverty continues to increase (State of America's Children, 1994), adults who work with young children have an ever-increasing need to provide the proper conditions to support physical growth, health and nutrition in a safe environment. Marotz, Cross, and Rush (1993) state that "Health, safety, and nutrition are closely related because the quality of one affects the quality of the others" (p. 7).

Poor health and physical condition weaken the child's appetite. Poor nutrition can affect alertness and lead to inattention and increased chances of accidents. All three factors can affect the course of normal physical development.

Physical development is a critical aspect in the lives of children. If children proceed at a normal rate, they will be able to keep up with the activities of their peers. We have seen in earlier units that children who experience poor prenatal conditions, are low-birth-weight and/or preterm start out with a strike against them. The need for optimum safety, health, and nutrition continues throughout childhood in order to support physical and mental growth.

Every child goes through the same basic patterns of physical growth, but there is a wide range of normality. Through toddlerhood, the child has a relatively large head and short trunk and legs. By the time the child reaches age three, head growth slows down and the trunk and legs begin to catch up. Proportions become more like an adult's. Whether or not certain children proceed at a normal rate of growth and achieve their capacity depends on a number of factors: heredity, socioeconomic status, exposure to substance abuse, diet, physical exercise, amount of stress, the level of safety and sanitation in the environment, and the quality of the nutrition provided (Marotz et al., 1993).

Adults who work with young children have a number of responsibilities related to children's physical growth, nutrition, safety, and health care. First and foremost, they must provide a safe physical environment. Overall, they monitor the children's general growth and health. In some early childhood programs, the director and/or teachers arrange for medical and dental examinations. Sometimes there is a nurse on staff who arranges for the examinations. The early childhood teacher may plan and prepare a daily snack. In an all-day program breakfast, lunch, and snacks are served. The director and/or teachers should have input into the menu planning although this is probably not as likely if the class(es) are part of a larger school that goes up through the elementary grades (in contrast to a childcare center serving prekindergartners or pre-first graders). Finally, early childhood teachers have a responsibility for planning safety, health, and nutrition education programs for students and parents.

PHYSICAL GROWTH

Physical growth follows several basic principles (Maxim, 1980, pp. 105–108). These principles fall into seven general categories:

1. directional growth
2. general to specific growth
3. differentiation/integration in growth
4. variations in growth
5. optimal tendency in growth
6. sequential growth
7. growth during critical periods

Directional Growth

Direction of growth is from head to toe (cephalocaudal) and from the center out (proximodistal). Head-to-toe growth is outlined in Figure 15–1.

The sequence of growth from head to toe can be seen in the gradual change in proportions from the prenatal period to adulthood. Muscular growth is reflected in the progression of lifting the head, then the shoulders, and finally the trunk, as the infant learns to sit without aid in a step-by-step sequence. Eventually, she is able to stand and finally to walk as her trunk-to-toe development matures to the point at which her legs and feet can hold her up and she can coordinate the muscles necessary for walking. The sequence from center out is reflected in the development of arm movements that are at first from the shoulder. Gradually, the child controls her arm at the elbow, then the wrist, and then the hand and the fingers.

General-to-Specific Growth

General-to-specific development is exemplified in the large, gross movement of the arms and legs seen in the infant to the specific movements used in walking or drawing a picture.

Differentiation/ Integration in Growth

Differentiation refers to the process the child goes through as he gains control of specific parts of his body. Younger children often have trouble locating parts of their bodies. For example, a three-year-old is lying flat on the floor and is told, "Lift your head." Very likely, he will lift his shoulders and his head. If a five-year-old is asked to perform the same task, he usually lifts his head, leaving his shoulders still on the floor.

Once the child has differentiated (or found) the individual parts of his body, he can develop **integrated movements**. That is, he can combine specific movements in order to perform more complex activities such as walking, climbing, building a block tower, or drawing a picture. Many integrated movements develop naturally with no special instruction. That is, if the environment allows the child the freedom to try, he will crawl, walk, sit, and grasp on his own. Other types of integrated movements, such as opening a door, skating, or riding a bicycle, may require special help.

KEYTERMSKEYTERMSKEYTERMSKEYTERMSKEYTERMSKEYTERMSKEY

| Differentiation | integrated movements |

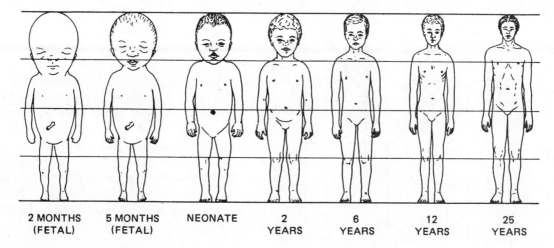

| 2 MONTHS (FETAL) | 5 MONTHS (FETAL) | NEONATE | 2 YEARS | 6 YEARS | 12 YEARS | 25 YEARS |

Figure 15–1 **Changes in body proportions: prenatal to adult**

Variations in Growth Rates

Children vary in their growth rate. That is, some grow faster than others. Girls grow faster than boys until adolescence. In addition, different parts of the body grow at different rates.

Optimal Tendency in Growth

Growth always tries to fulfill its potential. If growth is slowed down for some reason, such as lack of proper food, the body will try to catch up when it again has adequate food.

Sequential Growth

Sequential growth refers to the set order in which growth proceeds. For example, sitting comes before crawling, crawling before creeping, and creeping before walking, due to the sequence of growth of the necessary bones and muscles.

Growth During the Critical Periods

The concept of **critical periods** refers to the idea that growth in certain areas may be most important at particular times, such as described in the prenatal period. An example is Burton White's contention that the first three years are the most important in the development of intellectual competence (White, 1975). Another general characteristic of growth that may relate to critical periods is that it has four cycles: two of slow growth and two of rapid growth (Hurlock, 1978). The first period of rapid growth goes from conception until age 6 months. The rate gradually slows down during the toddler and preschool periods and levels out until puberty. At puberty, there is another rapid growth spurt followed by a leveling off until adult growth is achieved. This growth curve is shown in Figure 15–2.

Parents are often quite concerned about their child's growth rate. They wonder if he is too tall or too short, too thin or too fat. Pediatric growth charts, Figures 15–3 and 15–4, help to answer these questions. To use the charts, follow these steps.

1. Pick the chart for the child you wish to assess: boy or girl.

2. From the two charts for each sex, pick the one for the characteristic of interest: height or weight.

3. Place your finger on the bottom of the graph until you come to the child's age.

KEYTERMSKEYTERMSKEYTERMSKEYTERMSKEYTERMSKEY

Sequential growth   critical periods

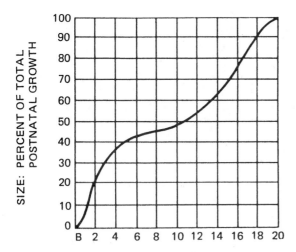

Figure 15–2   **General growth curve: Birth to age 20**

4. Run your finger up the vertical line until you come to the child's height (or weight).

5. Move both fingers toward the center of the chart, the left hand horizontally and the right hand vertically until they meet. Make a mark with pen or pencil.

6. Follow the nearest curved line to find the child's weight or height percentile. The percentile tells you where the child is compared with other children his age. The fiftieth percentile denotes that 50 percent (or half) the children of that age are bigger and half smaller. The tenth percentile indicates that 10 percent of the children that age are smaller and 90 percent are larger.

If a child's height or weight is below the fifth percentile or if his weight is above the ninety-fifth percentile, then he is considered at high risk relative to good health. This child should be seen by a doctor.

Measurements must be taken as carefully as possible. The child should have his shoes off and no more than underpants on. The scale should be accurate. When measuring height, the child should stand against a wall.

The average size of people in North America has been gradually increasing over the years. Improved environmental conditions have most likely enabled the children of immigrants to this country to achieve their growth potential (Roche, 1979). Whereas people in this country who have been able to reap its full environmental benefits have reached their growth potential, some groups at the lower socioeconomic levels have not had this opportunity. Poor nutrition is probably the greatest contributor to stunted growth among the lower socioeconomic groups (Rosser, 1977). In the past, it was thought that African-American children grew more slowly than European-American children during the first year. Research (Rosser, 1977) indicates that when matched for economic level, there is no significant difference between the two groups in height and weight. There is a difference between the two groups in body proportion, however.

SAFETY

A safe environment is a prerequisite for optimum child development. Marotz et al. (1993) outline the basic elements of an environment that promotes healthy physical, cognitive, and psychological development. Licensing and accreditation standards are designed to ensure that the environment is physically safe (Marotz et al., 1993). High-quality environmental standards should be met relative to building facilities, outdoor play areas, staff qualifications, group size and composition, staff-child ratios, program content, health services, and transportation.

Environmental standards include allowing adequate space for the number of children, meeting fire department safety standards, having adequate sanitary facilities, safety glass in low windows, good lighting, sturdy furniture, easily cleaned walls and floor coverings, safety electrical receptacles, and telephones located conveniently for emergency use. Outdoor space also needs to be adequate in size. It should be fenced and have a latched gate; have a variety of sturdy, safe play equipment; contain no poisonous plants or shrubs; and be well supervised at all times. A well-trained and competent staff is needed to see that standards are met and maintained (Marotz et al., 1993). See Marotz et al. (1993) for a safety checklist (pp. 160–62).

Young children may be involved in many types of accidents including, most often, motor vehicle accidents, burns, drownings, falls, and poisoning (Marotz et al., 1989). Most accidents in early child-

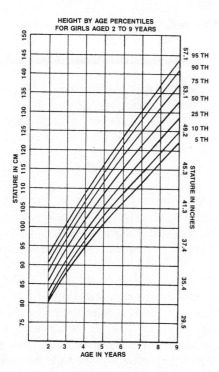

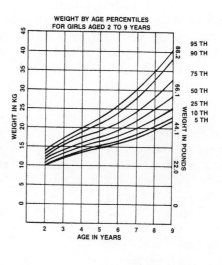

Figure 15–3   Height and weight charts for girls, ages 2–9 (Courtesy of National Center for Health Statistics, United States Department of Health, Education and Welfare)

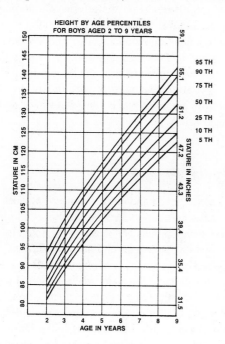

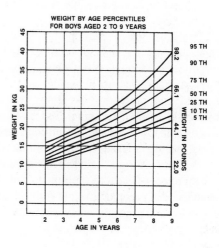

Figure 15–4   Height and weight charts for boys, ages 2–9 (Courtesy of National Center for Health Statistics, United States Department of Health, Education and Welfare)

hood settings occur during outdoor play activities; swings, 34 percent; climbing apparatus, 33 percent; slides, 21 percent; and other apparatus, 12 percent. Looking at severity of injury, Aronson (1983) found climbers were by far the most dangerous equipment, followed in order by slides, hand toys, and blocks, other playground equipment (excluding swings, sandboxes, seesaws, and gliders), doors, indoor floor surfaces, motor vehicles, swings, pebbles or rocks, and pencils. Early childhood educators need to take care in choosing safe equipment, providing close supervision, and teaching children to use the equipment in a safe manner. Accidents can be prevented if adults are knowledgeable about child development and plan accordingly by following four basic principles: "advanced planning, establishing rules, careful supervision, safety education" (Marotz et al., 1993, p. 183). Details on ways to implement these principles are described by Marotz et al. (1993).

There also is increasing awareness of numerous environmental hazards, such as pesticides, tobacco smoke, toxic art materials, lead, stale air, and asbestos. Many of these factors can be controlled by the alert adult. Others, such as building construction, power line location, lead content of soil and water, and pesticides and herbicides, may not be under our direct control; but, we should be aware and investigate the presence of any possible health and safety hazards (Gratz & Boulton, 1993).

Safety education is very important for both parents and students. Parents can become involved in safety education through newsletters, parent meetings, observations, class participation, assisting with field trips, and presenting programs themselves (Marotz et al., 1993). Children need to know the rules and regulations for the use of equipment and materials and the rationale for the rules and regulations. Units on safety can include a focus on occupations that protect us, such as firefighters, police officers, and medical personnel. Young children can also learn about bicycle/tricycle safety, pedestrian safety, vehicle safety restraints, dangerous substances, and home safety (Marotz et al., 1993).

Today we also need to be concerned with young children and sports injuries (Micheli, 1990). Organized sports have worked their way down to the primary grades replacing free play and sandlot sports.

Dr. Lyle E. Micheli, Director of Sports Medicine at Boston Children's Hospital since 1974, has noted an increase in children with types of injuries that previously only professional athletes had. These injuries are due to overuse (that is, playing when hurt) or to overtraining. These injuries may develop slowly in growing children but result in permanent problems. Many volunteer coaches are not trained in safe training techniques. Parents need to be sure that coaches are certified before letting their children participate in organized sports.

The safety of our children must be foremost in our minds. Brooks and Roberts (1990, p. 1) note that ". . . the major threat to children's health and welfare in the U.S. comes not from disease but from a large and seemingly miscellaneous collection of so-called 'accidental' injuries and deaths—drownings, poisonings, automobile and bicycle collisions, pedestrian injuries, electrocutions, burns, falls, and the swallowing of foreign objects." When all these injuries are grouped together they are the single greatest threat to children. "They account for 40% of child mortality between the ages of 1 and 4, 50% between 5 and 14, and 75% between 15 and 19." (p. 1) Brooks and Roberts (1990) report on the efforts of a number of groups around the country who are working to make the public including parents, children, and caregivers more aware and affect public policy to strengthen preventive measures and protect children from needless injury. Some examples of specific areas of concern are fire and burn prevention, gun safety, and car passenger safety.

NUTRITION

General health and nutrition have long been recognized as important factors affecting children's physical development and behavior. Providing adequate nutrition for young children is a serious problem in the United States. "Among the current generation of U.S. children are many whose potential will be limited in some fashion by inadequate nutrition, either before birth or during their infancy or childhood" (State of America's children, 1994, p. 45). During fiscal year 1992, over 13 million children received food stamps, 12 million received free and reduced-price school lunches, and 4.3 million received free and reduced-price breakfast (State of America's children, 1994). Summer food programs are growing in number to fill the gap when schools are not in session.

"*Nutrition* [italics ours] is the science of food and how it is used by the body" (Endres & Rockwell, 1994, p. 1). Determination of which nutrients enter the body is tied in with social, economic, cultural, and psychological factors associated with eating. Young children need foods that provide nutrients for growth and energy (Marotz et al., 1993). Foods are needed from the Basic Four Food Groups (Marotz et al., 1993, p. 293):

- Milk and milk products (milk, yogurt, and cheese group)
- Meat and meat alternates (meat, poultry, fish, dry beans, eggs, and nuts)
- Fruit and vegetable group
- Bread and cereal group (bread, cereal, rice, and pasta)

Lack of a proper balanced diet can lead to serious problems (Figure 15–5).

A study done by Super, Herrera, and Mora (1990) demonstrates the effects of providing supplementary food to infants and their families at risk for malnutrition. Super et al. (1990) assigned two hundred eighty Columbian infants at risk for malnutrition to four different experimental groups. These groups were formed by the presence or absence of two different interventions:

1. Food supplementation for the entire family, from mid-pregnancy until the target child was 3 years old.

2. A twice-weekly home-visiting program to promote cognitive development, from birth to age three.

All the families in the study received free medical care. The four experimental groups were designed as follows:

Figure 15–5 **A nutritious lunch give these boys the energy they need for the rest of the day.**

A. Obstetric and pediatric care only.

B. Medical care and family food supplementation from the time the target child was six months old until 36 months of age.

C. Medical care and food supplements from pregnancy until the target child was 6 months old.

D. Medical care and full supplementation from the twenty-sixth week of pregnancy until 36 months of age.

A1. As A above plus home visits.

D1. As D above plus home visits.

At ages three and six, the children who received the full food supplementation were larger than those who did not; those who also received home visits were even better developed.

Children are affected most harshly by undernutrition and malnutrition during the early years. Remember, the head grows first, with 70 percent of adult brain weight being attained by the age of two and full brain growth by age six. Therefore, to be effective, supplementary nutritional help must be available as early as possible (Kunjufu, 1980). For example, the effects of poor nutrition show up in early infancy relative to weight, length, and cognitive performance (Rose, 1994). This does not mean that food provided after six does not have a positive effect. Although previous damage cannot be corrected, further damage can be avoided. The best procedure, however, is to provide adequate nutrition from the beginning.

A study done by Pollitt, Gorman, Engle, Martorell, and Rivera (1993) followed children into adolescence who were given supplementary nutrition from birth to 7 years of age. Compared with children who had a minimal supplement and those who had none, the adolescents who had received the supplement from birth through age seven performed significantly better on a number of cognitive tasks. These results support the long-term benefits of early supplementary nutrition.

As evident in the Supra et al. (1990) study and a study by Grantham-McGregor, Powell, Walker, Chang, and Fletcher (1994), it is difficult to separate the effects of malnutrition and sensory deprivation as the two often go hand in hand. Programs that provide both food and sensory stimulation are the most effective. Further, it is important to keep in mind that the general health environment is also important. Those who live in poverty are often living in crowded housing with poor sanitation and may not have easy access to the best medical care.

After reviewing the research done in this country and other countries on **malnutrition** and child development, Stevens and Baxter (1981) found the following implications:

- Even though the relationships are not completely clear, it is clear that adequate nutrition definitely supports optimal child development.

- We need to continue comprehensive nutritional programs and include education for parents so they are well informed on optimal nutritional practices.

- Early childhood educators need to be working with nutritionists to establish nutrition education programs.

- Early childhood screening programs should include nutritional screening.

- We need much more research telling us how comprehensive child development programs that include a nutrition component affect child development and nutritional status.

- We need to be political advocates for the maintaining of child nutrition programs such as those for day care and residential facilities; school lunch, breakfast, and supplemental milk programs; Head Start; WIC (a program that provides special supplemental food for women, infants, and children); food stamps; and food distribution.

GENERAL HEALTH

Adults who work with young children should be concerned with all aspects of children's health. According to the Children's Defense Fund, children's health has become more and more in danger as health care coverage has dwindled (State of America's children, 1994). Pregnant women and young children are being denied the most basic preventive care. In 1992, 8.65 million nonpoor children were without private health insurance. As costs rise, the number of uninsured children rises. In this section, physical fitness, disease and illness, substance abuse, and mental health will be discussed.

Physical Fitness

Physical fitness is of great concern. Adults are watching their diets, running or walking on a regular basis, and enrolling in formal exercise and fitness programs. Children, on the other hand, are being neglected (Javernick, 1988). The trend toward more sit-still programs for young children with no formal exercise program is increasing the prevalence of obesity. While freeplay time outdoors is not enough since obese children are likely not to be very active, at least they had the opportunity for some physical activity. The possibility for motor activity has disappeared from many early childhood programs. Javernick (1988) suggests simple activities that any teacher could initiate (p. 22):

KEYTERMSKEYTERMSKEYTERMSKEYTERMSKEYTERMSKEY

malnutrition

- Jog around the playground with the children before freeplay time begins.

- Do ten minutes of calisthenics to music each morning with the children.

- Set up a supervised obstacle course.

Adults might also invest in one of Arnold Schwarznegger's books or videos, *Arnold's Fitness For Kids* published by Doubleday. The books are available in three levels: birth to five, six to ten, and eleven to fourteen. Schwarznegger encourages parents to do some exercise with their children. It doesn't have to be complicated. For example, for the two- and three-year-old he suggests running, piggybacking, climbing, jumping around, and sliding. For four- to five-year-olds, he suggests a large ball and a laundry basket. At first, the child can drop the ball in the basket, then gradually back off and throw it in. For five- and six-year-olds, he suggests tag games. He advises limiting TV time and encouraging children to be active (Hellmich, 1993). In the school setting a variety of appropriate, safe equipment promotes physically active play (Henniger, 1993/94 and 1994).

The research done by Pellegrini and Perlmutter (1988) and others supports the value of allowing closely supervised rough-and-tumble play on the playground. Rough-and-tumble play consists of "laughing, running, smiling, jumping, openhand beating, wrestling, play fighting, chasing, and fleeing" (p. 14). This is happy activity, not aggressive, hostile activity. Pellegrini and Perlmutter observed kindergarten, second, and fourth graders during rough-and-tumble play on the playground. They discovered that rough-and-tumble play was positively related to social competence. They found it often led to children's involvement in cooperative games with rules and reduced the frequency of aggressive play. It had especially positive effects on boys. Pellegrini and Perlmutter believe teachers should help boys who do not get involved in rough and tumble to do so. Rough and tumble, while providing some needed physical activity, also serves an important function in social development.

In 1988 the American Academy of Pediatrics provided a list of physical fitness facts (Physical fitness facts, 1988) that indicated a need to focus on physical fitness for children. Some of the facts identified in national studies are that:

- The level of physical fitness among children in the United States is declining.

- Up to 50 percent of American children are not getting enough exercise to develop healthy hearts and lungs.

- Forty percent of five- to eight-year-old children show at least one risk factor for heart disease (e.g. high blood pressure, high cholesterol, or lack of physical activity).

- Forty percent of boys six through twelve and 70 percent of girls six through seventeen cannot do more than one pull-up.

- One-third of boys ages six through twelve and 50 percent of girls cannot run a mile in less than 10 minutes.

- More than half the nation's schools do not have physical fitness testing.

- Only Illinois requires that students in all grades take physical education every day.

Prevention and Identification of Disease and Illness

Those who work with young children need to know both the signs of normal occasional illnesses and long-term or chronic illnesses (Marotz et al., 1993). They need to be able to recognize and attend to the more common problems such as colds, diaper rash, diarrhea, earache, sore throat, stomachache, toothache, vomiting, and fever while being alert to the possibility that any of these symptoms could be indications of a more serious, chronic condition. For example at least 71 percent of children have a serious ear infection before the age of three, and 33 percent had three or more (Watt, Roberts, & Zeisel, 1993). Ear infections can seriously impair hearing and interfere with the normal course of language development. If chronic health conditions are not diagnosed and

KEYTERMSKEYTERMSKEYTERMSKEYTERMSKEYTERMSKEY
Rough-and-tumble play

treated, they can interfere with learning. Abnormal fatigue or poor posture can be indicators of underlying problems. Seizures caused by abnormal electrical impulses within the brain are symptomatic of problems such as the effects of high fever, brain damage, central nervous system infection, and others. The greatest single cause of health problems among young children is allergies. Signs of allergic disorders include symptoms such as frequent colds and ear infections; chronic runny nose, cough, or throat clearing; headaches; frequent nosebleeds; unexplained stomach aches; hives, eczema, or other skin rashes; etc. Sickle cell anemia is an inherited disorder found most often among black populations. Early identification can indicate to parents that medical care is needed. Many of the problems mentioned go by unnoticed by parents who have not had experience with other young children and do not have knowledge about normal child development and behavior.

Alexander and Vincent (1989) did a study to determine whether childcare staff members were confident in their ability to recognize and prevent common health problems of children in their centers. They asked staff from forty childcare centers to respond to a questionnaire indicating whether they had taken classes in health education, family relationships, and/or child development and to rate their confidence in recognizing contagious disease, recognizing and reporting child abuse, providing first aid, and preventing the spread of disease. Although over 50 percent responded affirmatively in each area, many staff felt the need for more classes, especially in child abuse, first aid, and preventing the spread of disease. The study supported a need for more involvement by health professionals in childcare programs and the education of childcare professionals.

The increase in group care for young children has brought an increase in the prevalence of various childhood diseases (Kendall, 1983). After reviewing the research in this area Kendall (1983) recommends the following practices:

- Require very careful handwashing procedures for both children and adults.
- Post procedures for diapering and feeding and be sure areas are sanitized after diapering and toileting.

- Do not feed and diaper in the same areas.
- Rinse diapers immediately.
- Place children in diapers in small groups for safety and in small centers for better health monitoring.
- Separate children in diapers from those who do not wear diapers.
- Provide paid sick leave so staff can fully recover before returning to school after an illness.
- Keep in touch with medical professionals in the community in order to be informed and to consult on health issues.

A major concern for those who work with young children is the advent of acquired immune deficiency (AIDS) in young children. In most cases, the virus was acquired from the mother during gestation with a small number being the result of blood transfusions with contaminated blood (Marotz et al., 1993). The incurability of AIDS has engendered emotional discussion and strong fear (Kirp & Epstein, 1989) even though the human immunodeficiency virus (HIV) is not transmitted through casual contact but only through sexual contact and blood transfer (Marotz et al., 1993). School systems and childcare centers need to educate staff regarding AIDS and HIV and develop policies before AIDS and HIV children arrive.

There may be a positive side to the less severe childhood illness. In his presidential address to the Society for Research in Child Development in 1985, Arthur Parmelee (1986) discussed the potential benefits of children's illnesses. Parmelee views the common childhood illnesses such as colds and gastrointestinal upsets as important socialization events. The handling of these experiences by families can be a positive growth experience for everyone. Colds, coughs, runny noses, nausea, vomiting, and diarrhea occur most often in young children between the ages of one and five. Through these experiences young children learn what it means to be ill and learn how other family and community members act and react. Children develop a concept of illness and wellness. They learn about caregiving and nurturance and how to act toward an ill person.

Substance Abuse

The damaging effects of substance abuse were described in Units 4 and 5. Drug abuse, alcohol abuse, and passive smoke inhalation continue to be sources of serious problems for young children. As mentioned in the earlier units, we don't have enough solid data to substantiate all the claims that are made regarding the effects of these substances. On the other hand, we can't ignore the possibilities.

For example, Rist (1990) reported that in 1990 the first crack cocaine babies entered kindergarten. They were characterized as not easy to teach. They usually are born with birth defects and frequently are abandoned or go home to a crack environment. They seem unable to cope with too much sensory stimulation and are unable to respond when asked to do a complex task. Placed in the stimulating environment of the classroom, these children tend to either withdraw or become wild and difficult to control. Schools need to be prepared to handle these damaged children. They need an emotionally supportive, structured school/care environment beginning in infancy to counteract the chaos at home. In a program in Hillsborough County, Florida (Henry, 1990), kindergarten teachers attended workshops to learn how to work with these students. Teachers learned to structure the environment. For example, they learned to use masking tape to create workspaces and to glue footprints on the floor to show where to line up. They were told to keep classroom decoration at a minimum and to limit the number of activity options offered in order to keep the stimulation level minimal. Crack children need to know the daily schedule and exactly what will happen next or they may become very upset. In Hillsborough County, they are trying to plan ahead so these crack children can function in mainstream educational settings.

Lilian Katz (1994) warns that some materials being produced for use by teachers of young children for drug-abuse education are not appropriate and may be confusing and even misguide them. For example, can a preschooler or kindergartner perceive the difference between an adult who drinks an occasional beer and one who is an alcoholic? How will the child who comes from a home where illegal drugs are used accept that his family and their friends are doing something bad? As we will see later in this text, preschool and kindergarten students are not at a level in their mental development where they can understand the relativity underlying these situations. Rather than subjecting a whole class to inappropriate instruction Katz suggests that early childhood teachers try to obtain assistance for individual children and families as problems are perceived. Meanwhile, there is a need to find methods of drug education that fit the limits of young children's understanding.

Mental Health

Mental health was mentioned previously as an important concern for infants and toddlers. This concern is, of course, important for children of all ages. Jacobs (1990) has identified some of the problems in child mental health. Services are most frequently inadequate and inappropriate and usually uncoordinated with social, medical and educational service areas. As poverty increases so does the need for mental health services. A report from a survey in a county in Wisconsin is probably not untypical: more child abuse is being reported, more emotionally disturbed children are being placed in residential treatment centers, and the number of children in emergency detention at state mental hospitals is increasing. Congress has initiated the Child and Adolescent Service Program (CASP) to attempt to provide solutions to these problems. Meanwhile, for those who can obtain the services, great strides have been made by psychiatrists, psychologists, and social workers in the treatment of mental disturbance in infants and young children (Gelman, 1990). Early intervention strategies can now begin in infancy. Infant depression and other problems can be successfully treated.

Mental health should also be a concern for early childhood teachers in considering their classroom practices. Research by Burts, Hart, Charlesworth, and Kirk (1990) and Burts, Hart, Charlesworth, Fleege, Mosley, and Thommasen (1992) indicates that in some kindergartens, developmentally inappropriate instructional practices are used, such as having students sit still for long periods in large group activities and/or doing workbook/worksheet activities with a focus on abstract concepts such as learning numerals, the alphabet, and phonics out of context. When these practices are the major means of instruction, significantly more stress behaviors are observed than in kindergartens where developmentally appropriate practices are used, such as limiting the time spent in large group activities, allowing students to move about the room, and using concrete materials rather than abstract. A further danger to mental health is the use of group administered paper-and-pencil standardized achievement tests with young children. Fleege, Charlesworth, Burts and Hart (1992) observed kindergarten students before, during, and after spring standardized testing sessions. The frequency of observed stress behaviors increased significantly during the testing period.

THE ADULT ROLE IN NUTRITION AND HEALTH CARE

Adults who work with young children and their families can support the children's physical and mental development by supporting good nutrition and health care. At the school or center nutritious meals and snacks should be provided. Routines such as handwashing by children and staff should be emphasized. A health and nutrition education program should be developed for the students and their families.

Marotz et al. (1993) describe the need for good nutrition as the basis of good health. The adults must have knowledge about proper nutrition to serve as good models. They need to know that nutrients are needed to provide energy, materials for growth and maintenance of body tissue, and regulation of body processes. Each day the body requires minimum amounts of nutrients obtained from the four basic food sources: dairy, protein, fruits and vegetables, and grains. **Recommended daily dietary allowances (RDA)** can be used to determine which foods to purchase and to monitor daily food intake. An RDA table can be found in Marotz et al. (1993), p. 300–303 or can be obtained from Food and Nutrition Board, National Academy of Sciences, National Research Council, Washington, DC.

Adults can support good child nutrition by offering the children only nutritious foods. Sweets and other junk foods should not be on the early childhood menu.

Meals should be happy, pleasant times. Serving family style can promote a pleasant atmosphere and provide for children an opportunity to develop independence (Bomba & Knight, 1993). Young children develop gradually in their eating behaviors and their approach to eating should be respected (Figures 15–6 and 15–7). For example, the younger toddlers will do mostly finger feeding and commonly may turn the spoon upside down on the way to the mouth. Around two, the appetite decreases and food preferences develop. Adults need to be patient with children during this period. The two-year-old enjoys self-feeding but still uses fingers along with utensils. Finger foods should be provided. From three on, the appetite usually improves along with the use of utensils but finger foods can still make eating easier. By three, children enjoy helping with food preparation. Children have small stomach capacities and use up a lot of energy. A nutritious snack such as cheese cubes, fruit slices, raw vegetables, or fruit juice should be provided between meals.

Adults often use food as a reward for appropriate behavior. For example, a child picks up his toys

Figure 15–6   **These infants are just learning to feed themselves with finger foods.**

NUTRITION AND HEALTH EDUCATION

Figure 15–7   The toddler still enjoys food he can handle with his fingers but he is also learning to use utensils.

and is given a cookie or a piece of candy. Using food in this way increases its preferential status (Birch, Marlin, & Rotter, 1984). Food is also used as a contingency leading to a preferred activity, for example, eating green beans and then being allowed to go out to play. When used in this way food becomes even less liked (Birch et al., 1984). In practice, this implies that using food as a contingency is not the way to get children to like that particular food.

Adults who work with young children are observers and appraisers of their health status. Marotz et al. (1993) suggest a scheme for health appraisal. First, there are everyday observations of the children that give an opportunity to gather information on their energy levels and motivation. Changes in activity level may indicate a problem. Daily health inspection requires only a minute or two but is very important. General appearance, scalp, face, eyes, nose, etc. can be looked at for signs of any suspicious changes. Parents should remain with their children until the inspection is complete. This policy involves the parents and ensures that they are present if anything of special concern is noted. Health education is also important. Marotz et al. suggest that parents and children need information on topics such as toy safety, the importance of eating breakfast, nutritious snacks, the benefits of exercise, cleanliness, dressing appropriately for the weather, and dental hygiene.

Once the normal eating patterns are understood and the necessary foods for young children are identified, the next step is to educate both children and parents regarding these factors. Further, in schools for low-income children, whether full-day or part-day programs, supplementary food may be served to the children. This may include just snacks or one or more meals.

National attention has been drawn to nutrition and the necessity of nutrition education for teachers, parents, and children. Research has shown that young children are capable of learning the basic concepts of good nutrition (Paguio & Resurreccion, 1987). An example of such a study is one done by Marilyn Church (1979) at the University of Maryland Center for Young Children. The children were pretested regarding their food preferences. Following the pretest, a program of nutrition education was carried out that involved children and parents. The purpose of the program was to increase the children's and parents' knowledge about foods and to broaden the children's food choices. Following the program, the children were tested again. It was found that their food knowledge had increased significantly. There was also a trend toward broader food selection. The researchers found some incidental reactions such as:

> Children seemed to take a genuine interest in new foods and enthusiastically participated in their preparation. Mothers were pleased and surprised to see results in the child's actions at home. (Children actually asked for asparagus and ate broccoli!) (Church, 1979, p. 64)

Children were observed talking about food during their play activities. They also often asked the teachers if particular foods were good for them.

Church concluded that young children definitely are capable of acquiring new knowledge and attitudes regarding food. She suggests that programs for young children should include multisensory experiences that involve children in looking, tasting, touching, preparing, and eating a variety of foods (Figure 15–8). In addition, there should be games, films, books, and trips to support food experiences. Charlesworth and Lind (1995, Units 22, 26, and 37)

Figure 15–8 **Children enjoy helping with food preparation. In this case, the teacher reviews the pictograph recipe with the children before they start their baking project.**

Figure 15–9 **With a sink at his level, a toddler can wash his hands independently but is still fascinated by the feel of the water running over his skin.**

provide examples of ways food experiences can be integrated into the early childhood curriculum through dramatic play, math, science, and social studies activities. Children especially enjoy participating in food preparation experiences (Figure 15–8), studying food sources and tasting foods or reading about foods from different cultures.

The basic concepts of health, hygiene, and safety can also be learned by young children. Nutrition education contributes to knowledge about healthy living. In addition, young children can learn basic health habits and routines such as brushing teeth, hand washing, bathing, toileting and dressing appropriately for the weather. Hand washing is especially critical (Figure 15–9). Germs can be spread from dirty or poorly washed hands. Young children can learn appropriate hand-washing procedures. They can also perform science investigations that demonstrate that hands do carry germs. For example, Charlesworth and Lind (1995, Unit 37), outline an investigation using two peeled potatoes. A child who has not washed his hands for several hours handles one potato, which is then put in a jar labeled "unwashed hands." Another child washes his hands, handles the second potato and puts it in a jar labeled "washed hands." The children then observe the day-by-day physical changes that take place.

SOLVING THE HEALTH CARE PROBLEM

As already mentioned, an increasing number of children, both poor and nonpoor, are without proper medical care due to lack of medical insurance. Whereas the poor can receive care under Medicaid, they often are lacking in the means to get to the hospital or clinic. Gylys (1971) found that economic factors were an important element in making decisions about seeking professional medical help. Low-income people valued medical care as much as those in the middle-income level but lack of money, distance from available facilities, waiting time at the clinic, and lack of a babysitter often impeded their obtaining needed medical attention. The low-income child is more likely to enter school not only undernourished and hungry but also lacking in necessary medical care and attention.

There are comprehensive approaches to family health care. Grace Dixon (1980) describes a family health care center in Cleveland, Ohio, which emphasizes maintenance and prevention in contrast to the usual crisis approach to health care for low-income families. A team of professionals including internists, pediatricians, nurse practitioners, social workers, laboratory technicians, radiologists, pharmacists, and two child development professionals work together. Besides medical services, the following child development services are offered by the center:

- **Waiting Child Service.** Supervised playrooms are available in which children can play while they wait for an appointment or while they wait for a parent who is receiving treatment.
- **Assessments.** Both informal and formal assessments of the child's development are done by child-development workers while the child is in the playroom.
- **Child Education.** Children are helped to deal with the stress of medical treatment. They also receive nutritional snacks.
- **Education in Parenting.** This takes place through informal conversations with parents, demonstrations done during planned visits to the playroom, and parent group meetings. In the afternoons, a child development expert is available for questions on a drop-in basis.

The center also maintains a working relationship with other agencies involved with young children, such as Head Start and Home Start. This approach to child development and health care integrates services for the whole family beginning with infancy and continuing through early childhood and school age.

Efforts are being made to solve the health and nutrition problems that we are facing as we move toward the twenty-first century (State of America's children, 1994). At the time of this writing, health care reform is on top of the agenda in Washington, DC. The goal of reform is for every American to have health insurance that cannot be taken away. Meantime, individual states have moved to expand and improve children's health insurance coverage. Beginning in Fall 1994, all poor children will be eligible for federally funded vaccinations from their preferred physician.

In the areas of hunger and nutrition, reforms are also being made (State of America's children, 1994). The food stamp system has been revised to enable more needy families to meet the eligibility requirements. Child nutrition programs are gradually being expanded. Funding for the school lunch program, the Child and Adult Care Food Program, Summer Food Service Program, and the Special Supplemental Food Program for Women, Infants, and Children (WIC) has

been maintained. More work needs to be done at the community level to ensure that all needy children and adults receive the assistance to which they are entitled.

Adults who work with young children need to know each child's health history and support the family in finding the best health care available in the area. They must also try to work hand in hand with health care personnel.

SUMMARY

Good health and nutrition are basic to proper physical development, as well as to cognitive and affective growth. Physical growth follows several basic principles and proceeds through four cycles. The growth rate of the preschool child slows down after the rapid pace of the prenatal and infant periods. Concerns about a child's size relative to others his age are quickly answered through careful measurement of height and weight and comparison of the results with U.S. Government weight charts.

Adults are responsible that an environment is safe from hazards that may cause illness or injury for young children. Young children should not participate in organized sports if they are pressured to overuse growing bones and muscles. Physical fitness is important but physical education programs should be developmentally appropriate.

During prenatal, infancy, and early childhood, food supplements in combination with cognitive stimulation can improve the prognosis for good physical health and cognitive growth in future years for children who live in poverty environments. These children also need access to medical care.

During the eighties, a number of new dangers to child health were spotlighted: children affected during pregnancy by crack- and alcohol-addicted mothers, and AIDS-infected mothers; children as infants and older endangered through passive smoke inhalation; and threats to mental health.

The child who is malnourished or in poor physical health because of illness or disease cannot function either physically or mentally to capacity. The adult who works with young children needs to be well informed regarding nutrition and other health facts. She also needs to be involved in nutrition and health education for the whole family.

FOR FURTHER READING

Andersen, R. D., Blackman, J. A., Bale, J. F., Jr., & Murph, J. R. (1993). *Infections in children: A sourcebook for educators and child care*. Gaithersburg, MD: Aspen.

Bell, K. N., & Simkin, L. (1993). *Caring prescriptions: Comprehensive health care strategies for young children in poverty*. New York: Center for Children in Poverty.

Child Health Alert. Published monthly. P.O. Box 338, Newton Highlands, MA 02161.

Child Health Talk. Quarterly health newsletter published by the National Black Child Development Institute, 1463 Rhode Island Ave., NW, Washington, DC 20005.

Child Welfare League of America. (1991). *Our best hope: Early intervention with prenatally drug-exposed infants and their families*. Edison, NJ: Author.

Child Welfare League of America. (1991). *Serving children with HIV in child day care: A guide for center-based and family day care providers*. Edison, NJ: Author.

Dixon, S. (1990). Talking to the child's physician: Thoughts for the child care provider. *Young Children, 45* (3), 36–37.

Eddowes, E. A. (1989). IDEAS! Safety in preschool playgrounds. *Dimensions, 17* (2), 15–18.

Fletcher, J., and Branen, L. (1994). Making mealtime a developmentally appropriate curriculum activity for preschoolers. *Day Care and Early Education 21* (3), 4–8.

Frost, J. L. (1992). *Play and playscapes*. Albany, NY: Delmar.

Goldberg, E. (1994). Including children with chronic health conditions: Nebulizers in the classroom. *Young Children, 49* (2), 34–37.

Hendricks, C. M. (Ed.). (1992). *Young children on the grow: Health, activity, and education in the preschool setting*. Washington, DC: ERIC Clearinghouse on Teacher Education.

Huston, A., McLoyd, V. C., & Coll, C. G. (Eds.). (1994). Special issue: Children and poverty. *Child Development, 65* (2).

Jessee, P. O., Nagy, M. C., & Poteet-Johnson, D. (1993). Children with AIDS. *Childhood Education, (70)* (1), 10–14.

Lecca, P. J., & Watts, R. D. (1992). *Preschoolers and substance abuse*. Binghampton, NY: Haworth Press.

Leppo, M. L. (Ed.). (1993). *Healthy from the start: New perspectives on childhood fitness*. Washington, DC: ERIC Clearinghouse on Teacher Education.

Manna, A. L., & Symons, C. W. (1990). Promoting student health through children's literature. *Educational Horizons, 69* (1), 37–44.

Moukaddem, V. (1990). Preventing infectious diseases in your child care setting. *Young Children, 45* (2), 28–29.

Noll, R. B., Zucker, R. A., & Greenberg, G. S. (1990). Identification of alcohol by smell among preschoolers: Evidence for early socialization about drugs occurring in the home. *Child Development, 61*, 1520–1527.

Oyemade, U. J., & Washington, V. (1989). Drug abuse prevention begins in early childhood (And is much more than a matter of instructing young children about drugs!). *Young Children, 44* (5), 6–12.

Rothlein, L. (1989). Nutrition tips revisited: On a daily basis, Do we implement what we know? *Young Children, 44* (6), 30–36.

The speech and hearing project. (1992). *The Kamehameha Journal of Education* (Special issue), *3* (1).

SUGGESTED ACTIVITIES

1. Weigh and measure a number of young children. Divide the children's data into four groups: three-year-olds, four-year-olds, five-year-olds, six-year-olds and seven-year-olds. Add the heights and weights for each group. Divide the totals by the number of children in each group to obtain the average. Compare your data with the averages on the charts in Figures 15–3 and 15–4. This is a good group project.

2. Follow one or more three- to eight-year-olds through the day, keeping a record of what they eat. Evaluate their daily food intake. Did they eat foods in the recommended food groups? Did they eat fatty or high cholesterol foods? Did they eat foods with high levels of sugar or sodium?

3. Keep a record of your food intake for a week. Categorize each item to see if you have eaten food from all four of the basic food groups. Give yourself one point per day for each group from which you ate each day (for a possible 28 points). Share your results with the rest of the class by making a distribution of scores for the totals and for each food group. Where do people seem to be lacking the greatest amount? Which groups seem to be eaten by everyone with regularity? How much so-called junk food did people eat? Would you all be good models for young children?

4. Visit four or more early childhood centers or schools where children are fed at least one meal each day. Try to divide your visits between centers and schools that serve lower and middle/upper economic level populations. Interview the directors/principals/teachers regarding their nutrition program. Record the date, the name of the school/center, the type of school or center (i.e. publicly or privately funded, provides child care, is an elementary school), number of children eight or under enrolled. Some questions you might ask:
   1. Does your school serve breakfast? Snacks? Lunch? If so, how are the meals financed?
   2. Who plans the menus? Purchases the food ingredients? Prepares the food? What are their qualifications? Can you give me a copy of your menus for the week?
   3. Are the children ever involved in any of the food planning and preparation? If so, how?
   4. Is nutrition education included in your curriculum? If so, what major concepts do you teach? Can you give me some examples of learning activities that you use? Have your students provide you with any evidence of change due to your program? (for example, increased attendance, more alert behavior, more knowledge about food and nutrition, trying a wider variety of foods, etc.)
   5. Do you have any nutrition education included in your parent education program? If so, describe what you do. What is the parent response?
   a. Summarize your results.
   b. Do you feel the programs have good nutrition education components? If not, what do you feel are the weaknesses? What improvements could be made?

5. Interview four parents of three- to eight-year-old children. Find out what kind of health care they have for their child (children) and themselves. Use the following questions and any others you feel would be of interest.
   1. Record the date, the child's name and age, and the person interviewed (mother, father, etc.)
   2. Think back. Can you remember when you began prenatal care with <u>child's name</u>? Did you have a private obstetrician or did you go to a clinic?
   3. Since your child was born do you go to a family physician, a pediatrician or a clinic? Do you take your children for regular checkups or just when they are ill? Have you found that medical care for your child(ren) has been convenient, reasonably priced, and competent? Do you feel your child has had the personal attention he(she) should have?
   4. What about medical care for yourself? Do you get a yearly physical or just see a doctor when you are ill? Do you have a personal physician or use a rotating staff of physicians? Do you feel your available medical and health care is convenient, reasonable, and competent? Would you make any changes if you could?
   a. Summarize your information.
   b. Does medical care seem to be adequate for the families from whom you obtained information? If not, what seems to be the problem?
   c. How does the care received by those you interviewed compare with the family center described by Grace Dixon in this unit?

6. Make an entry in your journal.

REVIEW

A. Match the examples in Column II to the basic principles of growth listed in Column I.

Column I	**Column I**
1. cephalocaudal	a. Rudy learns to ride his tricycle.
2. proximodistal	b. At age three Kate's rate of growth slows down.
3. general to specific	c. Maria is able to lift her head and then her head and shoulders.
4. differentiation	d. Derrick is just beginning to be able to separate two fingers from the rest for counting.
5. integration	e. Now that she is nearly five Isabel can control her arm movements from the shoulder, elbow, and wrist and also has good control of finger movements.
6. sequential growth	f. Juan's legs are just beginning to grow longer; his proportions look more adultlike and his appearance is less squat.
7. growth goes through cycles	g. At first, the infant seems to flail his arms wildly but soon begins directing them for specific purposes such as grasping a toy.
	h. Maria has just learned to walk.
	i. Three-year-old Bill tries to hop on one foot. His five-year-old sister Kate has no problem, but Bill can't seem to keep one foot off the floor while he jumps on the other.

B. For each of the following examples, use the growth charts in Figures 15–3 and 15–4 to find each child's percentile rank on height and weight. Decide whether each child is normal, heavy, thin, short, or tall compared to other children his age. Describe the child's proportions.

1. Kate is four years of age. Her height is 35 inches.
Her weight is 30 pounds.

2. Jason is five years of age. His height is 43 inches.
His weight is 45 pounds.

3. Rudy is three years of age. His height is 41 inches.
His weight is 43 pounds.

4. Thuy Phung is seven years of age. Her height is 43 inches.
Her weight is 44 lbs.

C. Evaluate the following situation relative to the safety factors discussed in the text.
The kindergartners at John Dewey Elementary School share playground facilities with the first and second graders. Equipment consists of wooden seat swings, a ten-foot-high jungle gym, and a twelve-foot-high slide. The playground is surfaced with asphalt. There are a total of 125 children in five kindergartens. Two or three classes use the playground at the same time and are supervised by one or two teacher aids.

D. If a young child is malnourished during the prenatal period and infancy but is then given a proper diet, what would you predict will happen in terms of achieving his capacity in height and weight, school achievement, and IQ scores?

E. List the health and nutrition problems that the low-income child might have when he enters school.

F. Evaluate the following situations and/or comments.
1. "It doesn't matter what the child eats as long as he eats a lot."

2. The children's dining room is noisy. Adults are yelling at children, "Watch what you are doing!" "Don't spill your food!" "Eat what's on your plate!"

3. Two-year-old Joey's appetite seems to be diminishing. His mother is concerned.

4. Rudy, age three-and-one-half, is eating lunch and says, "I don't like peas!" His mother, exasperated, responds, "But, Rudy, peas are your favorite!"

5. It does not matter if a basically well-nourished child is overweight or underweight. It will not affect school performance.

6. We must protect young children from even the most common illnesses such as upset stomachs and colds.

7. The coach for Mary's soccer team has a high-win record. He has the children run laps before practice and encourages them to keep on playing even when they suspect a minor injury. He says that the best soccer players are tough.

8. While adults are concerned with their own physical fitness, children have been ignored.

9. Most child care providers are knowledgeable about health, safety, and nutrition.

10. AIDS is easily passed on to others through casual contact.

11. Today's teachers are all well prepared to work with crack children in their classrooms.

12. Young children do not need mental health care. They are too young to have emotional or social problems.

G. Describe what you would include in a safety, health, and nutrition program for young children. Why is such a program important?

H. Describe what you would include in a safety health and nutrition program for parents of young children. Why is such a program important?

I. Discuss your feelings about a family health care center as described by Grace Dixon.

Unit 16

Motor Development

OBJECTIVES

After studying this unit, the student should be able to:

■ Explain the relationship between physical and motor development.

■ Recognize the critical factors in gross and fine motor development.

■ List twelve gross motor skills.

■ Analyze and evaluate a child's readiness for formal handwriting lessons.

■ Recognize the developmental sequence for drawing.

■ Explain why assessment of the young child's motor skills is important.

■ Describe how the young child learns motor skills.

Closely allied to physical growth is the development of motor skills. As the body grows physically, muscles develop and mature and the child is able to perform new motor acts. The preschool/kindergarten period is a time when the differentiation of the various parts of the body is completed and when integration becomes the primary focus (Figure 16–1).

Motor responses develop following the same patterns for physical development described in Unit 15. The cephalocaudal, proximodistal, and mass-to-specific developmental patterns are also apparent in motor development. Gross motor development usually comes before fine motor development. For ex-

ample, eye movement, which involves small-muscle coordination, does not mature until 6 or 7 years of age. This is an important factor in the timing of the introduction of formal reading instruction. Gradually, the child learns not to use excess movement but to do things in the most efficient way. For example, a young preschool child may throw a ball while moving his whole body in what seems to be a rather distorted way. The older child coordinates the body in a smooth sequence of movement which is all directed at moving the ball accurately through space. Motor development takes place in an orderly fashion, parallel to physical development. Hand preference also develops gradually. Infants tend to be bilateral in that

Figure 16–1   Both large- and small-muscle development are critical for the young child.

they tend to move both sides of the body at the same time. Gradually, they become unilateral and can move one side without moving the other.

THE IMPORTANCE OF MOTOR BEHAVIOR

Michael G. Wade (1992) points out the importance of perceptual-motor development and play in the overall development of children. The motor cortex leads the way in the earliest stages of neural development. Wade (1992) believes this factor suggests ". . . movement will be the primary vehicle of discovery for the developing child" (p. 1). As described in earlier units, the infant is born with basic reflex movements that gradually develop into voluntary motor movements; motor development is closely tied to sensory development. According to Wade (1992) motor activity and play should be more than just vehicles for letting off excess energy but should be recognized as forerunners of the more formal intellectual and cognitive areas of development.

Children learn many basic concepts through movement. For example:

- **Space:** Theresa and Jason climb into a packing box which they are pretending is a cave. Theresa comments, "This is just the right size for us."

- **Word meaning:** Rudy, pretending he is Superman, comes flying across the playground.

- **Abstract symbols:** Mrs. Ramirez has made some large numerals on the floor with tape. The

children are barefooted and are moving along each tape numeral repeating the names as they go.

- **Social studies:** "Pretend you are a firefighter putting out a fire. Show me what you would do."

- **Science:** "We've been talking about lungs and how they work. Look at the bottle again with the balloon. Now pretend you are a lung, filling and emptying. Show me how you would move."

Movement is also one of the vehicles for developing representational competence (Raines, 1990). That is, actions can be used as symbols for communication. Rudy, pretending to be Superman, is telling us that he would like to be big, strong, and fast. He is also showing us how well coordinated he is. As the children pretend to be balloons, they demonstrate their body control and their ability to symbolize an idea through action.

GROSS MOTOR DEVELOPMENT

The motor development of the infant and toddler have already been described. From the end of infancy until about age six or seven, fundamental motor skills develop. These skills include "locomotor skills such as running, jumping, hopping, galloping and skipping, and object control skills such as throwing, catching, striking, kicking and dribbling" (Burton,

1992, p. 3). These **fundamental motor skills** are learned by everyone and serve as the foundation for more specialized motor skills that will be learned later. Beyond early childhood, specialized skills are developed relative to each person's particular needs and interests. Examples of these **specialized movements** would be learning a variety of ways of pitching a baseball, spiking a volleyball, or serving a tennis ball (Burton, 1992). By ages six or seven, children can begin to integrate two or more skills. That is, they can run and throw, stand on one leg and bend and pick something up, or hit a ball with a racket while maintaining their grip and balance.

Several factors affect the timing of the emergence of a particular skill. These factors include body size and physical growth, strength relative to body weight, and the maturity of the nervous system. According to Burton (1992) the maturity of the nervous system is probably the most critical factor. The nervous system is responsible for controlling each unit of movement and eventually enables the child to move smoothly without having to think about each movement. The degree to which an environment offers opportunities and encouragement for movement may also affect timing and competence level in the development of motor skills.

The first objective for the child is to gain control of each fundamental movement skill (Halverson, 1971). Once control is gained, the child can refine the quality of movements so they are correctly sequenced, well coordinated, and rhythmical. For example, when a child learns to bounce a ball, the first objective is to keep the ball near the body. "His adjustments are basically to the object, and his problems range from bouncing too hard to too far, to bending over and being hit in the nose by the bouncing ball, to chasing and trying to catch up with the ball that 'got away'" (Halverson, 1971, p. 29). When the child has mastered keeping the ball near, he then tries variations such as bouncing it fast or slow or bouncing it under his leg. These variations are qualitative refinements. The development of fundamental skills and their refinement is very dependent on the child's perceptual development. For example, to

bounce a ball, the child must perceive the rate of speed and position of the ball relative to the rate, speed, and direction of movement of his body. Developing motor skills is more than just eye-hand coordination (Halverson, 1971).

A review of the research on the development of motor skills led Betty Flinchum (1975, p. 12) to conclude there is strong support that there is a ". . . progression in the development of patterns from simple arm and leg action to highly integrated total body coordination." The progression in throwing, for example, is from elbow to shoulder. The progression in catching is from arm and body to catching with the fingers. That is, the younger child tends to throw from the elbow while the older child throws with movement from the shoulder. The younger child grasps the ball to the body, while the older child catches it in the hands. Kicking also proceeds in a progression. First, there is no back swing. Next, there is a swing from the knee, then the hip, and last, a full-leg swing (Flinchum, 1975).

A movement pattern that follows an appropriate sequence has three phases: preparation, acting, and follow-through. Note the kicking sequence in Figure 16–2. The child lifts her leg back (preparation), kicks the ball (action), and lets her leg go forward with the

Figure 16–2   **A movement pattern involves a sequence of three phases: preparation, action, and follow-through.**

momentum from the kick (follow-through). In the throwing sequence, the arm with the ball goes back (preparation), the arm moves forward and the ball is released (action), and the arm moves through an arc back down to the body (follow-through).

As with other areas of development, there are guidelines for determining if a child is progressing normally. Figure 16–3 lists norms for gross motor activities. Each skill usually develops sometime during the period listed. All children of the same age do not have exactly the same skills.

The major caution as discussed in Unit 15 is not to allow them to overuse their developing muscles or damage their growing bones (Micheli, 1990). Simultaneously, as children begin to coordinate more than one movement, they also enter the concrete operations period. Now they can apply those motor skills to playing action games with rules. Jack Maguire (1990) has published a collection which includes the rules for games such as hopscotch, baseball, cops and robbers, drop the handkerchief, duck duck goose, dodge ball, jump rope, red rover, and other old favorites.

FINE MOTOR DEVELOPMENT

Kate, age five, is carefully stringing beads. She places each one carefully using both hands in a coordinated manner.

Rudy, age three years, is building a block tower. It has eight blocks and it is getting higher.

Isabel, age four, takes her painting and, using clothespins, hangs it on the line to dry.

These children are all involved in fine motor activities that are typical for their age. When their behavior is compared with the selected skills listed in Figure 16–4, it can be seen that it fits the normal expectations. Kate at age five should be able to string beads. Theresa at five-and-a-half should be able to make a clay object with at least two small parts. Rudy, at three, should be able to build an eight-block tower. Using clothespins to hang up her painting is probably a slightly advanced skill for four-year-old Isabel. Printing his first name and copying words is expected for a five-year-old like Jason.

Developing Handwriting Skills

Fine motor development is basic for the eventual mastery of handwriting skills (Lamme, 1979). Handwriting is being taught to children at earlier ages, with the result that many children are faced with learning to write before they are ready. That is, they may be pressured to write before they have all the prerequisite skills. Linda Lamme (1979) identifies six areas of prerequisite skills:

1. small-muscle development
2. eye-hand coordination
3. ability to hold a writing tool
4. ability to make basic strokes
5. letter perception
6. orientation to printed language

The first four skill areas in the list involve fine motor development.

Before children can use a writing tool, they must have control of their small muscles. That is, they must be able to control wrist and finger muscles. They can gain this control through the use of manipulative materials such as jigsaw puzzles, construction toys, and snap beads. Children also can gain control of small muscles through play with small toys such as peg dolls, cars, trucks, and dollhouse furniture. Materials that can be molded such as clay, sand, dough, and mud support small-muscle development. Zipping, buttoning, and using scissors, crayons, and other art materials help develop finger dexterity.

Once children have developed small-muscle skills, they can coordinate the hand and eye. Most of the activities already mentioned also promote eye-hand coordination skills. The child who hammers nails straight, builds a block tower without it falling over, or copies complicated parquetry designs probably has attained the eye-hand coordination needed for handwriting.

Some tools for writing are easier to use than others. Markers and felt-tipped pens are easiest for the child to use because they require very little pressure to achieve the desired results. Chalk is the next easiest, then crayons, and last, pencils. Contrary to

Skills Expected During Three Age Periods

Between 37 and 48 Months	Between 49 and 60 months	Between 61 and 72 Months
Throws ball underhanded (4').	Bounces and catches ball.	Throws ball (44' boys; 25' girls).
Pedals tricycle ten feet.	Runs ten feet and stops.	Can carry a 16-pound object.
Catches large ball.	Pushes/pulls/wagon/doll buggy.	Kicks rolling ball.
Completes forward somersault (aided).	Kicks 10'' ball towards target.	Skips alternating feet.
Jumps to floor from 12''.	Carries 12 lb. object.	Roller skates.
Hops three hops with both feet.	Catches ball.	Skips rope.
Steps on footprint pattern.	Bounces ball under control.	Can roll ball to hit object.
Catches bounced ball.	Hops on one foot four hops.	Rides two-wheel bike with training wheels.

Figure 16–3 Normal expectations for the development of selected gross motor skills (Selected from G. J. Schirmer (Ed.), *Performance objects for preschool children*, pp. 69–72, by Adapt Press. Used with permission.)

Skills Expected During Three Age Periods

Between 37 and 48 Months	Between 49 and 60 Months	Between 61 and 72 Months
Approximates circle.	Strings and laces shoe lace.	Folds paper into halves and quarters.
Cuts paper.	Cuts following line.	Traces around hand.
Pastes using pointer finger.	Strings ten beads.	Draws rectangle, circle, square and triangle.
Builds three block bridge.	Copies figure X.	Cuts interior piece from paper.
Builds eight block tower.	Opens and places clothespins – (one handed)	Uses crayons appropriately.
Draws 0 and +.	Builds a five block bridge.	Makes clay object with two small parts.
Dresses and undresses doll.	Pours from various containers.	Reproduces letters.
Pours from pitcher without spilling.	Prints first name.	Copies two short words.

Figure 16–4 Normal expectations for the development of selected fine motor skills (Selected from G. J. Schirmer (Ed.), *Performance objectives for preschool children*, pp. 74–75, by Adapt Press. Used with permission.)

popular belief large diameter pencils are not necessarily easier for young children to use. Carlson and Cunningham (1990) found that some preschoolers handled large diameter pencils better and some handled small diameter pencils better. Therefore, they recommend that both be available and students be allowed to select the size they can grip and control most easily. Children need opportunities to experiment with these tools for drawing before they are asked to use them for writing. Children should also have time to use paintbrushes, kitchen utensils (such as spoons and spatulas), garden tools, sieves and strainers, and woodworking equipment. All these materials help the child learn how to hold a tool and use it to perform some act that cannot be done with the hand alone. According to Lamme, the beginning writer should be given markers and felt-tipped pens for his first efforts. When a child begins to select a pencil for writing he then can be helped to hold it correctly.

> The pencil should be loosely gripped with the fingers above the shaved tip to about an inch from the tip. Only the index finger should remain on top of the pencil, not two or three fingers. (Lamme, 1979, pp. 22–23)

Lamme cautions that the young writer should not be pressured too much about grip. He may become discouraged. Lamme suggests that the child who is having difficulty can be spotted by two indications:

- He holds his pencil too tightly, tires quickly, and is not able to write for very long. The pencil should be loose enough in the child's grip to be pulled right out.
- He clenches his teeth and presses hard, leaving a deep impression on the page. Or, he may write so lightly that it can hardly be seen. Pressure should be even.

By observing the child's drawing, the adult can determine whether or not the child is able to make the basic strokes needed for writing. Look for straight lines, circles, and curved lines. Do the lines join each other when houses, cars, people, or other figures are drawn? These strokes should not be taught during art activities; they are allowed to occur naturally. Eventually, when formal handwriting lessons are introduced,

the strokes for writing are taught. The child goes through the transition from drawing to writing slowly and gradually. Lamme (1979) suggests five guidelines to use in deciding if a child is ready for handwriting:

1. The child repeats patterns (or letters or words) over and over.
2. The child goes from left to right and then return sweeps to begin again at the left.
3. The child realizes that letter elements can recur in variable patterns.
4. The child lists all of the letters (or words or symbols) he knows.
5. The child perceives likenesses and differences among letter elements, concepts, letters and words. (Lamme, 1979, p. 23)

Handwriting, of course, does not involve only small-muscle coordination. It also involves perception. The child must perceive similarities and differences, shapes and sizes, and direction. These perceptions are then integrated with small-muscle control to produce writing. It is important that children be shown standard letter models. They should also begin writing on unlined paper and continue until they have achieved a uniform size. Reversals are commonly made by beginning writers and are quite normal for the preschool and kindergarten child. Letters such as *b* and *d*, and *p* and *q* are easily confused. Some children may write many symbols in reverse.

Finally, Lamme indicates the child needs to have an orientation to printed language. That is, children must understand that printed language stands for spoken language. Children need to use their early writing skills to make books, greeting cards, and signs, and to label pictures.

Figures 16–5, 16–6, 16–7, and 16–8 are examples of early handwriting. At age four-and-one-half, Kate imitates a shopping list (Figure 16–5). She makes letterlike forms that appear to her to be like an adult's. At age five-and-a-half, she sits in the kitchen and copies words off cereal and detergent containers (Figure 16–6). At five-and-a-half, she also writes freehand (Figure 16–7). Note the repetition and the reversals. Also at five-and-a-half, she writes a caption on her picture (Figure 16–8).

Figure 16–5 **A four-and-a-half-year-old makes a shopping list.**

Figure 16–6 **A five-year-old enjoys copying print from things in the environment.**

By age three, most young children express an interest in name writing. Both Hildreth (1936) and Harste, Woodward, and Burke (1984) have documented the developmental sequences in name writing from ages three to six. The three-year-old uses scribbles that look like pretend cursive or mock letterlike forms. Fours usually combine letterlike forms with real letters. Fives usually can write their names correctly including the correct letters in the right sequence but may use all capitals or mix capitals and lowercase letters. By age six, most children can print their names correctly with an initial capital followed by lowercase letters. Young children enjoy learning to write their names if given time and encouragement. They also enjoy experimenting with other words as seen in Figures 16–5 through 16–8.

Developing Drawing Skills

A concern for parents and other adults focuses on the question of teaching children conventional printing (as used in this book and in most children's textbooks and storybooks) or teaching them a slanted manuscript alphabet such as the **D'Nealian alphabet.** Proponents of the slanted alphabet believe use of this type of alphabet for beginning writing makes the transition to cursive writing much easier. Graham (1993, 1994) reviewed the research on this question and came up with three reasons that the slanted alphabet may not be a good choice for young children. First, he found no evidence that use of the slanted manuscript makes it easier for children to learn to make the transfer to cursive. Second, both parents and teachers have to learn about the new alphabet and teachers have to learn to write it. Finally, the most important factor probably is that before coming to kindergarten most children have begun to write using traditional manuscript. Learning a new alphabet means they have to make an extra transition that doesn't appear to be beneficial. Graham (1993, 1994) does not recommend using a slanted alphabet in kindergarten and the early primary.

The development of drawing skills parallels development of writing skills. For the most part, younger preschoolers are in the prewriting prerepresentational experimental stage. Just as they use scrib-

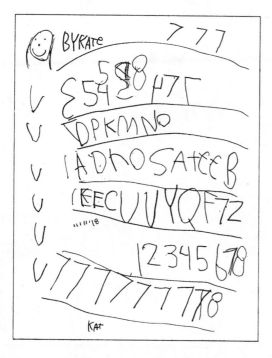

Figure 16–7   **A five-year-old likes to practice writing.**

Figure 16–8   **A five-and-a-half-year-old puts a caption on her picture.**

bles in their writing, they also use scribbles in their drawing. The preschooler goes through two main phases or stages in his use of materials (Sevigny, 1979). The first is the *manipulatory-exploratory* stage. This is a process stage in which the child experiments to discover what can be done (and not done) with the materials. The child's objective is to gain some control over the materials. Children's drawing at this stage is referred to as scribbling. They do not name what they make but strictly experiment to find out what can be done. The **communicative phase** begins when children name and label their drawings. Now children know what can be done with the material and look for configurations they can name (Sevigny, 1979).

The first stage in the development of art is seen in the **random scribble**. Young children enjoy exploring the movement of their arms and shoulders and the resulting patterns on the paper. Gradually, the

movement becomes more controlled. Children then proceed to "controlled pattern movement, to controlled line, to controlled shape, to named shape, to symbolic shape to art" (Sevigny, 1979, pp. 3–4). The first three stages are straight line control, circular control, and curved line control. All three of these stages of control are basic to handwriting skill development.

When children have achieved these three levels of control, they can then combine lines, curves, and circles to make shapes. They have then reached the shape control stage. They are still not trying to make anything, but simply exploring shape. Eventually, the shapes begin to remind the child of something he has seen earlier. The child gives the shape a name after finishing it. The child works with these presymbolic shapes, gradually working into symbolic shapes or representations of real things.

communicative phase   random scribble

The young child needs plenty of time to explore materials in order to pass through these stages with the natural maturational development of muscle, bone, and conceptualization. Sevigny (1979) feels that dittos and coloring books should never be given to young children. They need big paper and room to move.

By the fourth or fifth year, the preschooler uses some symbols. These symbols are quite primitive, with the symbol for a person being most common. A figure is usually made with circles and lines; usually, it is made up of a circle for a head with lines connected for limbs. Gradually, their drawings become more like what they see in the world, but they still include only the essentials. It is not until the sixth year that more details and more realistic proportions appear. Figures 16–9 and 16–10 show drawings by a four-and-a-half-year-old girl. Note the simplicity of

Figure 16–10 In this drawing of two girls on a horse, the child has used basic shapes and includes just the most essential details.

the three girls; yet there is no doubt that they are girls. The long hair and the dresslike bodies are clear clues. The girls are riding on an animal (a horse, according to the artist) in Figure 16–10. We don't know if they are bareback riders or if this is just the child's sense of perspective.

Figure 16–11 includes pictures of families as drawn by preschoolers, kindergartners, and first graders in the fall of the school year. The author selected an immature and a mature drawing from each level to show the wide range of development within each group as well as the increase in complexity from preschool to first grade as more body parts and clothing details are added to the drawing.

When one considers handwriting, a concern with **handedness** usually surfaces. There is concern regarding whether the right-hand dominant have an advantage over the left-hand dominant and over the children

Figure 16–9 The young child's drawings contain just the essentials.

a. a mature prekindergartner

b. a less mature prekindergartner

Figure 16–11 **These drawings demonstrate the wide range of motor development found in prekindergarten, kindergarten, and first-grade students.**

c. a mature kindergartner

d. a less mature kindergartner

Figure 16–11 (Continued)

e. a mature first grader

f. a less mature first grader

Figure 16–11 **(Continued)**

who do not seem to have settled on a preference. In order to learn more about handedness and its relationship to motor competence in preschoolers, Tan (1985) identified two groups of four-year-olds. One group was identified as left-handed and the other as having no hand preference. Tan developed the PHI (Preschool Handedness Inventory) to assess handedness. The PHI requires the child to do tasks such as opening and shutting a packet of pens, drawing, cutting with scissors, catching and throwing a bean bag with one hand, and others. A standardized test in combination with a fine motor inventory devised by Tan were used to assess level of motor development. The left-handed children were not found to be weak in motor development. They did just as well as right-handers on the motor assessment tasks. Tan suggests that left-handed children often may be judged as lacking proper motor development because they look different when they are engaged in motor activity. On the other hand, the children with no preference did have below-average motor skills. Most of these children were boys. It is important that the adult who works with young children identify these children and help them to strengthen their motor skills through developmental activities.

THE ASSESSMENT OF MOTOR SKILLS

Mature performance in certain kinds of motor skills has been shown to be predictive of readiness for kindergarten and first grade. For this reason, it is important that the adult working with preschoolers be aware of these skills and how to assess them.

Assessing

An informal motor skill inventory was developed by Harriet G. Williams (1975) of the University of South Carolina. This instrument assesses four areas of perceptual-motor capacity:

1. **Gross Motor Control:** running, hopping, jumping, skipping, throwing, and catching (Figure 16–12).
2. **Fine Motor Control:** cutting, pasting, manipulating objects, clapping, and using such instruments as pencils and crayons.

Figure 16–12 **This playground invites young children to work on the development of gross motor skills.**

3. **Visual Perception:** coordination of eye and hand, perception of figure and ground, form constancy, position in space, and spatial relations.
4. **Body Awareness:** awareness of position in space, hand preference, right and left, and knowledge of body parts.

Activities are suggested that aid the child's development in each area.

Williams (1983) has identified a number of other motor assessment tools that are appropriate for four-, five-, and six-year-olds. She warns that motor diagnosis should be made with caution. Young children often do a motor task incorrectly due to lack of understanding of the instructions rather than inability to accomplish what is asked. Before a formal motor assessment is administered, children should be observed during play activities and assessed with an informal checklist.

Assessing Fine Motor Skills

The Gesell readiness tests are more formal developmental measures that have several items focusing on fine motor skills. These include copying forms (such as circle, cross, and square), completing a picture of a man, name printing, and copying block constructions (Figure 16–13). Items concerning right and left, visual perception, and general information are also included. Claims have been made that the Gesell tests have been found to be highly predictive of school readiness (Carll & Richard, n.d.). Gesell adherents find that they have been very useful as prekindergarten and pre-first grade placement measures. Each child is given a developmental age score that indicates whether placement should be in prekindergarten, kindergarten, pre-first grade, or first grade. There has been a great deal of criticism regarding using the Gesell as a gatekeeping instrument (Meisels, 1987). For example, Lichenstein (1990), after studying the predictive value of the Gesell, cautions that it should not be used as the primary determinant of grade placement. It can provide some valuable information about the child that could supplement other observations in making placement decisions. Lichenstein found that the Gesell predicted that over 50 percent of the children in his sample were not ready for first grade while other measures indicated the group had average capability. He also found that the more Gesell training teachers had, the more likely they were to rate children as unready for first-grade placement. He found that the test was not an accurate one. For example, ratings of child performance by independent raters had unacceptably low percentages of agreement. The developmental philosophy of the Gesell ignores environmental factors such as lack of experience with pencil and paper and blocks and puts too much emphasis on inherited developmental time schedules as a determinant of readiness for learning. A validity study with the Gesell school readiness tests done by Graue and Shepard (1989) showed similar misidentification results.

The adult who works with preschool children needs to be aware of each child's skill level in both the gross and fine motor behaviors. Gross motor skills should develop as a prerequisite to the fine motor skills, which are essential for communication of knowledge.

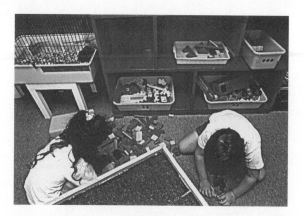

Figure 16–13   **Young children are offered the opportunity to try out a variety of activities involving fine motor skills.**

LEARNING AND MOTOR DEVELOPMENT

As already described in Unit 9, the relationship between sensory and motor development is being studied in more detail than in the past in the emerging field of developmental biodynamics. Evidence indicates that the development of motor abilities enables young children to receive more sensory information and thus learn more about their environment. Researchers in this area hope to shed light on the exact relationship between motor, perceptual, and intellectual development and functioning. Meanwhile, it does appear that multisensory experiences are most likely to enhance children's learning.

Poest, Williams, Witt, and Atwood (1989) had parents and teachers of preschool children enrolled in nursery schools and day-care centers respond to questionnaires designed to find out the types and frequencies of physical activities the children engaged in. They discovered that most preschool children engage in very little of the high-intensity physical activity that stimulates the heart and promotes good health and optimum motor development. Although they may have excellent selections of playground equipment, most of their active play is low intensity. Children left on their own used the equipment for sociodramatic play that involved low intensity activity which did not meet the standards of vigorousness needed to promote physical fitness. Very little time was spent in teacher-directed motor activities. Teachers with child-development training did more motor instruction than those with elementary training. Children whose parents engaged in more physical activity also engaged in more physical activity. The authors conclude that more physical fitness and motor development instruction is needed in preschool and day-care centers.

Poest, Williams, Witt, and Atwood (1990) suggest that a motor development program should include three major categories of focus: fundamental movement skills, physical fitness, and perceptual-motor development. Fundamental motor skills that preschool children are neurologically ready to develop include "walking, running, leaping, jumping, hopping, galloping, sliding, skipping, climbing, and tricycling; the manipulative or ball skills of throwing, kicking, punting, striking, volleying, bouncing, dribbling (hand), dribbling (foot), rolling, catching, and trapping; and the balance skills of bending, stretching, twisting, turning, swinging, upright and inverted balances, body rolling, dodging and beam walking" (Gallahue, 1982 as cited in Poest et al., 1990, p. 4). Poest et al. (1989, 1990) believe children should not be just left on their own to develop these skills; they need adult-directed practice and instruction to ensure optimum development. Physical fitness (discussed in Unit 15) "refers to the level of health development and functional capacity of the body" (Poest et al., 1990, p. 5). According to Poest et al. (1990), to be physically fit, children must maintain an adequate level of cardiovascular endurance, muscular strength, muscular endurance, flexibility and body leanness. Perceptual-motor development involves taking information in through the senses and making a motor response. Perceptual-motor development includes "body, time, spatial, directional, visual, and auditory awareness" (Poest et al., 1990, p. 6).

Poest et al. (1990) make a number of suggestions for the improvement of large muscle time. First, planning is essential. Each of the fundamental motor skills should be methodically addressed. Equipment should be set up to offer challenges for each skill. Physical fitness activities should be planned daily. Poest et al. (1990) advise that group calisthenics or exercise routines are not appropriate for young children. Perceptual-motor activities include copying movements (like *Simon Says*) in touching body parts will develop body awareness. Time awareness can be developed through marching to a beat or to rhymes or chants. Spatial relations can be developed through the use of obstacle courses.

There is evidence that young children's overall learning is enhanced by using a motoric (versus an abstract) approach. For example, Herman, Kolker, and Shaw (1982) found that kindergartners' memory for location of objects in an unfamiliar environment is enhanced by motor activity. This supports having young children carefully rehearse all the routine activities at school rather than just telling and/or demonstrating the procedures.

SUMMARY

Motor skills develop in a sequence parallel to that of physical growth. Motor development supports concept development, perceptual development, and representational competence. Gross motor development includes activities that use the large muscles: throwing, running, jumping, and pulling. Gross motor skills precede fine motor skills. The critical time period for the development of fundamental motor skills begins with toddlerhood and continues until about age six or seven.

Fine-motor activities make use of the small muscles, such as those in the wrist and the hand. Fine-motor activities such as bead stringing, building with construction toys, drawing, and clay modeling serve as the basis for developing the skills that will be needed for handwriting. The adult who works with young children should be cautious and not push them into formal writing lessons too soon.

Since the preschool period is a critical time for the development of fundamental motor skills, the adult who works with young children should be alert to each child's developmental progress in order to assess how well each child is doing. It is important for young children to be engaged in informal teacher-planned and teacher-directed motor activities to be sure all children have the opportunity to develop fundamental skills.

FOR FURTHER READING

Allen, K. E., & Marotz, L. (1994). *Developmental profiles*, (2nd Ed.). Albany, NY: Delmar.

Block, S. D. (1977). *Me and I'm great: Minneapolis, MN*: Burgess.

Curtis, S. (1984). Joy of movement. *Day Care and Early Education*, *12* (1), 18–21.

Frost, J. L. (1992). *Play and playscapes*. Albany, NY: Delmar.

Henniger, M. L. (1994). Planning for outdoor play. *Young Children*, *49* (4), 10–15.

Hirsch, E. S. (Ed.). (1984). *The block book*. Washington, DC: National Association for the Education of Young Children.

Hoppert, R. (1985). *Rings, swings, and climbing things: Easy to make play equipment*. Chicago: Contemporary Books.

Kalverboer, A. F., Hopkins, B., & Geuze, R. (Eds.). (1992). *Motor development in early and later childhood: Longitudinal approaches*. New York: Cambridge University Press.

Macfill, R. A., Ash, M. J., & Smoll, F. L. (1982). *Children in sports*. Chicago: Human Kinetics.

Munson, E., & Sorenson, M. (1989). *Motor development and physical education activities for young children*. St. Paul, MN: Minnesota Department of Education.

Stinson, S. (1988). *Dance for young children: Finding the magic in movement*. Reston, VA: American Alliance for Health, Physical Education, Recreation, and Dance.

Thelen, E., & Lockman, J. J. (1993). Developmental Biodynamics: body, brain, behavior connections (Special section). *Child Development*, *64*, 953–1190.

Weikart, P. (1987). *Round the circle: Key experiences in movement for children ages 3 to 5*. Ypsilanti, MI: High/Scope Press.

Weiller, K. H., & Richardson, P. A. (1993). A program for kids: Success-oriented physical education. *Childhood Education*, *69*, 133–137.

SUGGESTED ACTIVITIES

1. With a small group in class, see if you can remember the physical activities you enjoyed in preschool and kindergarten. List the activities on the chalkboard or on a piece of chart paper. Can others in the class think of any that your group hasn't mentioned?

2. Are there any students in the class who are left-handed? Did this pose any problem for them? If you are left-handed, you might want to look in the library for articles on handedness and note suggestions for working with a child who is left-handed.

3. Observe some young children when they are on the playground or elsewhere involved in a variety of large-muscle activity. In class, list all the gross motor skills you observed. List yours on a piece of chart paper or on the chalkboard. Have other class members add others. An alternate activity: divide the class into two or more teams. With a time limit of three minutes, see which team can list the most gross motor activities.

4. Moving from preschool to kindergarten to primary usually means moving from concrete activities to more paper-and-pencil activities. Suppose you are a preschool teacher and you have helped build the children's fine motor skills through the use of manipulative toys and other fine-muscle materials. At the same time, you have been teaching them a variety of concepts with concrete materials. Suppose there is a child who has some knowledge that he can express through concrete means but not with paper and pencil or workbook. What should you do to help him ready himself to change to paper and pencil? Review the following questions with a small group in class to arrive at an answer.

   a. Make photocopies of the following examples so each person in the group has one. Look at the examples carefully and, pretending you are a child, decide which skills and concepts are needed to complete each task.

Which item is a different size from the others? In each box, make a green *X* on the one that is a different size.

In each box, one item is different from the others. Put a purple line under the item that is different.

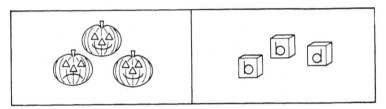

Draw a black circle around the object that looks just like the one in the square box.

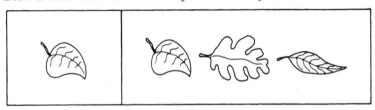

In each box, draw a red line from the numeral to the picture that shows how many articles there are in that circle.

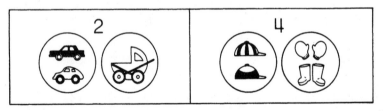

   b. What could you do if you feel that some of the children in your group are not able to handle tasks like those in 4a? How would you begin to help? What might happen if you didn't take action?

5. Visit a nursery school, child development center, kindergarten or primary classroom. Obtain permission to try the following tasks with 4 three-year-olds, 4 four-year-olds, 4 five-year-olds, 4 six-year-olds, or 4 seven-year-olds or with one or more children from each age level.

TASK 1: Throwing and Catching a Ball

Materials: A ball about 10 inches in diameter.

Instructions:

a. Stand four feet from the child. Say, "I'm going to throw the ball to you; you catch it." Throw the ball. Note the child's response to catching.

b. Be sure the child has the ball. Say, "Now you throw the ball to me." Note the child's response.

c. Give the ball to the child. Say, "Now throw the ball as far as you can." Note how far the child throws before the ball hits the ground. Note also how the child throws.

TASK 2: Running and Stopping

Instructions: Measure off ten feet. Ask the child to run the ten feet and stop. For example, you might say, "See the chalk lines on the sidewalk. Stand at this line. Now run to the other line as fast as you can and then stop."

TASK 3: Copying Shapes

Materials: Using a black marking pen, draw on three-inch by five-inch cards the following shapes: a circle, a square, a triangle, and a rectangle.

Instructions: One at a time, ask the child to copy each shape on a piece of plain white paper using a black felt pen. Say, "Look at this shape. You draw one just like it on your paper."

TASK 4: Stringing Beads

Materials: A lace and twenty preschool beads.

Instructions: Give the child the lace. Say, "Here is a pile of beads. See how many you can put on your lace." (Help him with the first one if he seems in doubt as to what to do.)

If you wish, make up some more tasks using Figures 16–3 and 16–4 as a guide. After you have your data, compare the children's performances with the norms in Figures 16–3 and 16–4. How did each of the children with whom you worked compare? How did they compare with each other?

6. If you are interested in learning more about the development of children's art, check the library for references and select a book for reading. Prepare a report for the class on *Children's Art: Its Development and Relationship to Perceptual and Motor Growth*.

7. Make an entry in your journal.

REVIEW

A. Explain the relationship between physical and motor development.

B. Write the number of each correct statement.
1. Action is the basis of the child's intellectual development.
2. Motor success gives the child confidence in her own skills.
3. Motor development integrates all our senses.
4. Children learn basic concepts through movement.

C. List twelve gross motor skills.

D. Select the correct answer(s) to the following. There may be more than one correct answer for some of the questions.
1. The appearance of a particular skill is dependent on
   a. maturation only.
   b. environment only.
   c. the interaction of maturation and environment.
2. The environment can offer the young child ways to make the most of his emerging motor capabilities by
   a. having the adults teach him how to use materials and equipment.
   b. having adults give him positive reinforcement for attempting to use his motor skills.
   c. stepping in and helping him when he needs assistance.
   d. being sure he has equipment such as balls, bean bags, wagons, doll buggies, and ladders available.

3. When learning to bounce a ball, the young child goes through the following sequence:
   a. gains control; refines the quality of the movement; plays basketball.
   b. gains control so that the ball stays near him; tries variations such as bouncing the ball fast or slow.
   c. drops and catches; drops and bounces; bounces ball.
4. The critical time for the development of motor skills is
   a. age 3 years to age 6 years.
   b. 24 months to 48 months.
   c. 18 months to 60 months.
   d. 36 months to 60 months.
5. There are several phases in a movement pattern that follow an appropriate sequence. In order, these phases are
   a. preparatory; follow-through; and action.
   b. preparatory; approach; action; follow-through.
   c. approach; action; follow-through.
   d. preparatory; action; follow-through.

E. Read each of the following examples. Decide if the child is progressing normally, slowly, or faster than average. Use the chart in Figure 16–3.
   1. Paul is five years old and is just learning to ride his tricycle.
   2. Joe is three years and three months old and can throw a ball underhanded six feet.
   3. Mary has just turned five and can skip quite well.
   4. Nancy is four years old and can hop two hops on one foot.
   5. Paul can pull a wagon full of blocks.
   6. Joe can catch a bounced ball.
   7. Mary has just started riding a two-wheeled bike with training wheels.
   8. Nancy can bounce a ball under control.
   9. Paul can bounce a ball but still has trouble catching it.
   10. Mary is learning to roller skate and does quite well.

F. Using the chart in Figure 16–4, decide if each of the following children is progressing normally, slowly, or is advanced for his or her age in fine motor skills.
   1. Mary is 5 years of age. She can print her first name, fold paper into halves and quarters, and trace around her hand.
   2. Nancy is 4 years old. She can pour from a pitcher without spilling, cut on a line, and copy the figure *X*.
   3. Paul is five. He can barely approximate drawing a circle, he has difficulty cutting, and every time he tries to pour from a pitcher at snack time, he spills some of the drink on the table.
   4. Joe is 3 years old. He can draw a circle, cut paper, and build an eight-block tower.

G. Match the prewriting skill in Column I with the correct example in Column II.

Column I	**Column II**
1. small-muscle development	a. A child can hammer nails straight and copy complicated block designs.
2. eye-hand coordination	b. This child's drawings include lines, curves, and circles.
3. hold a writing tool	c. A child sits with an open book in his lap, pretending to read it.
4. do basic strokes	d. This child recognizes and names all the letters of the alphabet.
5. letter perception	e. These children are using construction toys, peg dolls and little cars, and clay and sand.
6. orientation to printed language	f. This child can hold a pencil well with a loose grip.

H. Decide if six-year-old Bill appears to be ready for first grade. Bill likes to use writing tools. He sits for long periods repeating patterns and letters on his paper. He always goes from left to right and begins again at the left when he reaches the end of a line. He realizes that the same letters can be rearranged to make new words, such as *pan* and *nap*. He can write almost all the alphabet from memory, plus about six short words. He doesn't get any letters mixed up and can discriminate the few sight words he knows.

I. In what skill does the child develop from random scribbler to a controlled movement pattern, to controlled line, to controlled shape, to named shape, to symbolic shape?

J. Why is it important for the adult who works with young children to assess the children's motor development?

Learning: From Preschool To Primary School

Of major concern to those who work with young children is discovering how they learn and in what kinds of settings they will be able to reach their potentials for achievement. As you already know, the National Association for the Education of Young Children (NAEYC) has developed guidelines for developmentally appropriate practices in programs serving children from birth through age eight (Bredekamp, 1987). We have already examined how infants and toddlers learn and related their learning to the NAEYC guidelines. In this section, we will look at how children ages four through eight learn. Instruction should fit the children's individual learning styles and developmental stages and ages. Our knowledge of child development should guide instruction in the classroom. As you read the classroom descriptions that follow, think about whether these classrooms are developmentally appropriate.

KINDERGARTEN OBSERVATIONS

Excerpts from observations by Donna Jolly

A Public School: Woodhaven Elementary

There were 21 children and one teacher in the classroom. Learning centers were arranged throughout the classroom predominantly on the perimeter areas. They contained an abundance of highly meaningful concrete materials, which children were able to pursue, manipulate, and actively explore.

The environment was print rich. Each center was labeled; in the reading center there were books made by the children containing many of their drawings and writings, and there was a writing center equipped with many materials the children could play with and learn about concepts of print.

The day began with a group activity. The class was working with the letter *T*. A large *T* cutout was spread out in the center of the floor. Each child had brought an object from home that began with the letter *T*. The children and the teacher were seated around the letter. The children placed their objects on the *T* and said the name. Mrs. A wrote the name on a big chalkboard for all to see. The children all participated in handling and talking about the objects.

Then they did a movement exercise, pretending their bodies were *T*s.

Next, the children got their *t*oothbrushes and a graph was made of colors of the *t*oothbrushes. This large-group activity integrated reading, language, mathematics, physical, and social development tasks. During the discussions and the following center time, Mrs. A used many open-ended questions. She accepted more than one answer when posing questions to her students. She also asked individuals and groups questions pertaining to their work. She often initiated questions that required complex ideas and thinking strategies.

Particularly impressive was the science center. It was abundant with materials. Scales and other measuring devices, rocks, charts, terrariums, a bone collection, a preserved snake collection, and many other materials were available for the students' investigations.

The children were provided with many opportunities daily to develop social skills. Their group time was a cooperative venture in which all were an active part. The tables and chairs were arranged so that areas were provided for children to work together and share materials. Both child-initiated and teacher-initiated activities took place. Children made many of their own decisions and choices. The prevailing atmosphere was one of curiosity, exploration, and peaceful appreciation for the teacher and each other and from the teacher toward the children.

Private School: Montessori Children's Center

The Montessori class included nineteen children ranging in age from 2.5 years to 5.9 years. There were three teachers. Mixed age groups are characteristic of a Montessori classroom.

The children seemed totally absorbed and very actively involved in their activities. Some examples of activities I observed were: three children completing a puzzle of North and South America, a child working on a large numeral game board where num-bers were placed in order from 1 to 100, another working with blocks and pegs, others using red rods, some using dressing frames, several children working at the practical life table, one painting on an easel outdoors, and a child working on addition with sets of chips. Most of the materials were very sensory oriented and required active involvement.

I was amazed at the concentration these children exhibited. One young three-year-old attended to his math game for over 20 minutes. Another pursued addition with one of his teachers for a long period of time.

Many opportunities existed for fine motor skill development. There were dressing frames, tweezers and tongs used to place small objects into cupcake tins, devices for pouring and spooning rice and corn in various containers, clay to use with cookie cutters and rolling pins, pin pricking pads, and lacing beads.

It was evident that children in this prepared environment have been instructed in how to do certain activities, that is, that there is a certain procedure to follow to use the materials. For example, before going out to paint, a teacher reinstructed a number of children first on where to get the paper that is stored for painting, then to put on a smock, and lastly to come outdoors to the easel. Mrs. D focused on instructing another child on the steps to follow in a practical life exercise.

After free selection time, a large-group reading period was held. Stories and poems were read by a teacher. If a child chose not to participate, he could go to the adjoining room and listen to tapes or read a book silently.

During the self-selection time the teachers participated actively with the children. They asked questions and provided opportunities for dialog. They introduced individual children to many problems to solve. Opportunities were present and support was also given for cooperative small group projects. Children worked on puzzles together, shared the dressing frames, cooperated on a math game, interacted in the practical life environment, painted together outdoors, and even worked in a workbook together. Peer teaching was also observed.

Parochial School: Parker School

There were twenty-one children and one teacher in this classroom. This program used a prescribed structured, teacher directed, workbook program. Rote memorization and drill were used with abstract curriculum materials. I observed the teacher instructing the children about the letter *R*. Through a visual on the board, each child was given the opportunity to sound out this letter and the consonant blends made with each vowel. Dittoed worksheets were then distributed following the large-group activity time. These again pertained to the letter *R* and allowed for only one correct response. Upon completion of this task, Mrs. E checked each child's paper for accuracy and they were then allowed to select a book from the reading center. No other activities were available.

Next, a music teacher came into the class to instruct the children. The TV was used to lead the class in a few songs as they sat quietly in a group on the floor.

There was no opportunity for any social interaction during the time I observed. Although Mrs. E was warm, loving, and positive, there were very few opportunities for communication in friendly informal ways about the children's interests. There were a few learning centers in the room which were used in the afternoon during play time. They were a fill-in-the-gap type of activity instead of being viewed as places for truly meaningful learning experiences.

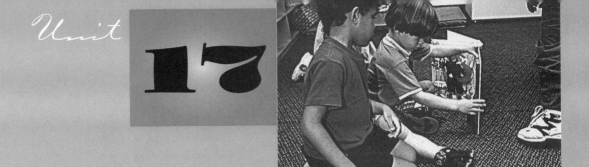

17

How Learning Takes Place

OBJECTIVES

After studying this unit, the student should be able to:

- Define learning, perception, reflex, and memory.

- Discriminate between the developmental and behaviorist views of learning.

- Apply the concepts of perception, learning, and memory.

- Recognize examples of perceptual, learning, and memory concepts.

- Understand the importance of action and concrete sensory experiences in young children's learning.

Learning may be defined as behavior change that results from experience. Learning experiences involve many kinds of activity, as the following examples show.

Four-year-old: Kate, age four, points to a small creature that is walking on the sidewalk and asks "Dad, what is it?" "That's a big red ant," answers her Dad.

Three-year-old: Chan grabs Ginger's truck. Ginger hits Chan. Mrs. Clark steps over and says, "Wait a minute. This has to stop." She puts an arm around each of them and looks at each in turn explaining, "Taking other people's toys is not allowed but hitting is not allowed ei-

ther. Chan, next time you ask Ginger to let you use the truck when she is done with it. Ginger, when someone takes something from you, you ask for it back. If they won't give it back, come and ask Mrs. Clark for help."

In the experiences described, each of the children involved has learned a new behavior. Kate has learned to name a red ant. Chan and Ginger have been told how to solve problems peacefully. Future behavior will demonstrate if they have learned how to do it.

Different theorists have different views of learning. The developmentalists emphasize the interaction between growth and learning.

KEYTERMSKEYTERMSKEYTERMSKEYTERMSKEYTERMSKEY

Learning

Behaviorists emphasize the effect of the environment on learning. Kate learned "red ant" because she has a responsive father who answered her question. Chan and Ginger learn how to negotiate because they want Mrs. Clark's approval.

The developmentalists emphasize stages and readiness for learning. They view learning as an active process that takes place as the young child acts upon the environment and constructs his own knowledge (DeVries & Kohlberg, 1990; Kamii, 1986) (Figure 17–1). They view changes as part of a process more than as an end product. Behaviorists emphasize the end product (or the behavior that is learned) and view the process as the same, no matter where the child is in terms of age and developmental stage. This author takes the position that both points of view have something to offer to adults who work with young children. As Ruth Ault (1983) points out, the process and product approaches have some similarities and some differences, but both points of view can be useful to parents and educators. Unfortunately, traditional education, especially past the kindergarten level, has taken a behaviorist view and ignored the constructivist view (Larkin, 1993; Lauritzen, 1992).

This unit describes some basic processes in learning with applications from both the developmentalist and behaviorist points of view. Unit 18 provides more detail on the adult's role in the young child's learning.

Figure 17–1 Children construct their own knowledge about the class guinea pig as they observe its daily activities.

PERCEPTION

"In its simplest sense, perception is the brain's interpretation of physical sensations.... Sensation is what happens when physical stimuli are translated into neural impulses that can then be transmitted to the brain and interpreted" (Lefrancois, 1992, p. 225).

The senses of taste, touch, sight, hearing, smell, and proprioception (messages from within the body, such as a muscle contraction) bring messages to the brain. The meaning of these messages to each individual is different, depending on individual perception of the information. For example, Melissa tastes some beans that have a lot of hot pepper sauce in them. She frowns, says "Awful," and runs for a glass of water. Mario takes a bowl of beans from the same pot. He tastes them. He smiles with satisfaction and says, "Bueno, bueno!" Melissa and Mario each have a different interpretation of the taste of hot pepper sauce.

The importance of perception is emphasized by seeing what might happen if messages were interpreted in ways that are very different from the way other people in the culture interpret them. For example, consider the following incident:

Richie looks at the word *cat* and says "That says 'bat.'"

Perception is related to the processes of learning, cognition, and language. A child with a problem in perception has difficulty in other areas.

Up until about age five, children tend not to perceive the totality of the available information (Cole & Cole, 1989). Younger children become distracted and lose their train of thought when presented with stimuli that are loud and flashy. They also tend to explore new things in an unsystematic way and thus miss some of the details. Often they miss the most important and relevant information. In addition, they may overestimate the effects of specific sensory experiences (O'Neil & Astington, 1990). For example, O'Neil and Astington (1990) asked children to decide whether sight or touch would have to be used to answer a question about a hidden object. The under fives overselected feeling as the means to solve the problem. We have already discussed how infants and toddlers, in the sensorimotor period, favor their senses of touch and taste in exploring new materials. This need to touch seems to carry over through the early preoperational period.

Attention

Attention is a critical aspect of perception. Attentional processes involve ignoring irrelevant information and finding relevant information (Ault, 1983). At first, infant attention is captured by whatever is novel in the environment. Soon attention becomes voluntary. That is, infants can choose what they wish to attend to. As children grow older, they become increasingly skilled at being able to ignore what is not important and to attend to what is important. As they become more adept at attending and avoiding distractions, their attention span for any specific task increases.

Learning Through Sensory Involvement

Since young children seem to favor and appear more skilled at learning through touching and feeling than through vision, it would appear that this is a characteristic that could be used to advantage. Maria Montessori (Morrison, 1991) noted this characteristic of young children and applied it to instruction. The materials designed by Montessori all involve manipulation of objects as a means to develop all the senses. Materials used in this approach encourage perception of color, shape, size, texture, sound, and other attributes through the manipulation of concrete materials. In **sensory involvement**, all the senses are

used as a bridge from the concrete to the abstract. For example, children trace sandpaper letters and numerals while saying the name of each one, thus making use of touch, sight and sound at the same time. Montessori was very creative in developing multisensory materials for young children (Figure 17–2).

Those who support the Piagetian cognitive developmental view also believe that children learn best through manipulation of objects. Williams and Kamii (1986) point out that young children's manipulation of objects is not mindless but involves mental as well as physical action. For example, Isabel puts another block on her block tower because she thinks it will balance. Jason rolls his clay because he thinks he can make it look like a snake. No one has told these children what to do. They have figured it out for themselves.

LEARNING

When there is a change in behavior as a result of experience, it can be said that learning has taken place. Reflexes such as blinking the eyes, pulling back from a hot flame, or crying are not learned although experience may increase or decrease the frequency with which they occur. Some learning is dependent on maturation. For example, a newborn cannot walk, talk, play tag, or do arithmetic problems. We will look at several aspects of learning: classical conditioning, operant conditioning, observation and

Figure 17–2 **Young children learn actively through their firsthand sensory experiences.**

Attention   sensory involvement imitation, some specifics of learning, adult and peer support of learning, and activity and learning.

Classical Conditioning

In **classical conditioning**, learning takes place through the association of a stimulus and a response. For example, a child will startle to a loud noise. If something else is paired with the loud noise, the child may also learn to respond with a startle to the new stimulus. In Watson's classic experiment with the infant Albert (cited in Miller, 1989, p. 216), Albert was naturally startled by a loud noise. Albert was not afraid of white rats. However, when Albert was shown the white rat along with the loud noise, he became afraid of the white rat. Much learning takes place through these simple and usually accidental associations. For example, baby says, "Mama" when mother happens to be around. Mother responds with a smile and a hug. *Mama* becomes associated with Mother.

Operant Conditioning

Learning also takes place through **operant conditioning**. Through operant conditioning, behavior is shaped by careful use of reinforcements (rewards) for appropriate behavior. At the same time, inappropriate behavior is ignored so that it is not rewarded with attention. In Unit 14, it was suggested that operant conditioning (behavior modification) techniques are especially useful with the toddler. For the preschooler, there is a wider variety of choice for managing behavior.

Observation and Imitation

In previous units, the importance of observation and imitation as vehicles for learning were described. Throughout the preoperational period, much of the child's learning is achieved through these processes. The child can learn through imitation in two ways.

Children can act at the same time as the adult and receive an immediate reward. They also can learn when they seen someone else (a model) receiving a reward for a behavior. The following is an example of the first type of learning.

> Mark comes into the bathroom. His Dad is brushing his teeth. Mark says, "I want to do that, too." Dad responds, "We have a little toothbrush we've been saving for you." He gives it to Mark, saying, "Now watch me and do what I do." Mark watches. He then does what he saw his Dad do. Father says, "Good for you, Mark. You're a big boy."

Next is an example of the second type of learning.

> Isabel notices that other children in her preschool class are complimented for sharing. She decides to share, also.

In the first example, Mark copies simultaneously what his Dad does and receives an immediate reward. In the second example, Isabel's peers serve as models. She sees what brings approval to other children and then does the same thing on her own. She has the expectation that she will also receive a compliment from the teacher.

Some Specifics of Learning

What is learned in one situation may be applied later in another situation (Figure 17–3). There are several basic features of learning (Yussen & Santrock, 1978). Some of these features are generalization, discrimination, shaping, extinction, and habituation. **Generalization** is the process of finding similarities among things. For example, balls, tires, and coins are round. Or, girls and boys and moms and dads are people. **Discrimination** has to do with perceiving differences. One ball is red and one is blue. One tire is big and the other is small. One person has long hair and another has short hair.

Shaping has to do with gradual acquisition of a learned behavior. This is done through **successive approximation**, or gradual learning. For example, it is not unusual for a child new in a group situation to

KEYTERMSKEYTERMSKEYTERMSKEYTERMSKEYTERMSKEY

| classical conditioning | Generalization | Shaping |
| operant conditioning | Discrimination | successive approximation |

Figure 17–3 **As children work with a variety of materials, they note similarities and differences.**

refuse to join in large-group activities. The first day or so, he sits apart from the group and may even do another activity. The next day, he sits near the group but just watches the activity. Soon, he moves into the group but is not an active participant. Finally, he participates along with the other children. **Extinction** has to do with unlearning. If a behavior is not rewarded, it gradually is no longer used. **Habituation** is a feature of getting used to something. That is, when an event is novel or infrequent, the child is more likely to pay attention to it immediately than if it occurs frequently. If an adult who never speaks sharply to a child does so suddenly, the child attends immediately. The child who is frequently spoken to sharply becomes accustomed to the harsh tone of voice and does not pay much attention.

Classical conditioning, operant conditioning, and observational and imitative learning are behavior-oriented approaches to explaining how learning takes place. Piaget (Miller, 1989) has developed a theory of how learning takes place that makes some guesses

about unseen behavior—that is, what is going on in the mind as learning occurs. He views learning as a continuous process of adaptation. The child adapts through the processes of assimilation and accommodation. **Assimilation** is an incorporation process. New ideas and concepts are fit into old ideas or concepts. For example, the child knows that the big, red, round object is a ball. He sees a small, blue, round object that he also assimilates as *ball*. **Accommodation** is the means for changing the old concepts to fit a new piece of learning. He sees another big, red, round object that he calls *ball*. He is told that this object is a *balloon*. Accommodation enables him to modify his concept of ball and add a new concept, balloon. Through adaptation, the child maintains equilibrium or balance between himself and the environment. A balance between assimilation and accommodation brings about **equilibration**. The child can, to his satisfaction, make sense out of the world.

Adult and Peer Support of Learning

In previous units, Vygotsky's view of the importance of adult support for learning in the zone of proximal development has been described (Wertsch, 1985). Adult support (or scaffolding) is always critical for children's learning. That is, at the right moment when the child is ready to move ahead, the adult can support development through asking the right questions and providing appropriate materials and explanations. While, as described next, active learning through child-initiated activities is essential, so is skillfully initiated adult support and guidance. Peers (other children) can also have effects on each other if encouraged to work together toward common goals (Cannella, 1993; Tudge, 1990).

Activity and Learning

An appropriate environment for young children supports active learning. It includes many opportunities for child-initiated learning (Bullock, 1990). Children do not wait around for an adult to arrive before they en-

KEYTERMSKEYTERMSKEYTERMSKEYTERMSKEYTERMSKEY

| Extinction | Assimilation | equilibration |
| Habituation | Accommodation | |

gage in learning. They are continuously acquiring knowledge. "They are busy trying to make sense out of everything they encounter" (Kamii, 1986, p. 71). According to DeVries and Kohlberg (1990), the Piagetian **constructivist** view perceives the roots of educational practice "in his theory of the role of action in development" (p. 19). Spontaneous activity is the foundation of mental development. DeVries and Kohlberg (1990) summarize Piaget's point of view in the following three "interdependent characteristics of early education aimed at fostering development" (p. 20).

1. Methods appeal to the child's spontaneous mental activity.

2. The teacher acts as a companion who minimizes the exercise of adult authority and control over children and as a guiding mentor stimulating initiative, play, experimentation, reasoning, and social collaboration.

3. Social life among children offers extensive opportunity for cooperation (including conflict) in situations inspiring children to desire coordination with others (p. 20).

The third characteristic cannot be overemphasized. Social interaction is extremely important as a vehicle for learning. Cooperation for Piaget is not mindless submission but refers to individuals operating with each other in both harmony and conflict (Figure 17–4).

MEMORY

Memory is the retention of what is learned over a period of time (Yussen & Santrock, 1978). "When we encode and store some aspects of an experience and then, after a period of time, retrieve part of that stored representation, we have engaged in a process called memory" (Ault, 1983, p. 107).

Four types of memory are recall, recognition, paired associates, and reproductive. Recall is remembering something pulled directly the mind's storehouse.

"What is your name?" "My name is Carlos."

"Who are your friends?" "Sam, Stephanie, Justin, Maria, and Mark."

"How old are you?" "Four."

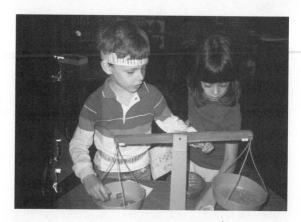

Figure 17–4 **These two children are learning through interactions with each other and with the materials.**

Recognition is easier than recall in that the choices are given, such as, "Are you three or four years old?" "Look at those animals. Pick out the dog." "Show me which child is your friend, Sam." Paired associates involves placing two things together, such as a name with a face or an object with a color or shape, or some other characteristic, as in, "This is my friend, Sam." "The red sweater is mine." or "Triangles have three sides; rectangles have four sides." Reproductive memory is more difficult than simple recall. In this case, what is recalled must be reproduced. For example, Kate writes her name, draws a picture of her friends, and holds up four fingers to represent her age.

Memory can be aided by a number of factors. The more senses involved in the original learning experience, the easier it is to remember. The Montessori method is an example of learning through more than one sense at a time. Learning through experience is another example. The child is told that a small cup holds less water than a large cup. The child remembers better if he can pour water from cup to cup and experience through sight and action the fact that the small cup holds less.

Memory is best when the items to be remembered are meaningful. Three is more easily remembered as an amount if you are 3 years old or looking forward to being 3 years old, or if three objects are explored and held while someone says, "There are three rocks: 1, 2,

3." If a child likes long hair, she will remember the names of people with long hair more easily than those with short hair. As the child reaches the preschool years and learns more about categorizing or grouping things, he also can use this skill to aid memory.

Metamemory, or one's knowledge about memory, has been of interest to researchers (Lefrancois, 1992). Researchers have been interested in finding out at what age people begin to have some idea about how they remember things, what kinds of things are easiest to remember, and how well they memorize. Young children tend to have faulty views about how things are remembered; they use inefficient strategies to help them memorize (Fabricus & Cavalier, 1989).

LEARNING STYLES

All children do not learn the same way. There are many **learning styles**. Each child has strength in different modalities. Fagella and Horowitz (1990) describe seven styles identified by Howard Gardner in his book *Frames of Mind* (discussed in Unit 25). Two contrasting examples are the linguistic (language) learner compared with the bodily/kinesthetic learner. Children who learn best through words do well in our schools as the curriculum is currently set up because they like to read and write, are good at memorizing, and learn best by saying, hearing, and seeing words. In contrast, the bodily/kinesthetic learner does poorly in the sit-still classroom. Bodily/kinesthetic learners like to move around, touch, and talk. They are good at physical activities and crafts and learn best through touching, moving, and interacting with space, and process knowledge through their bodily sensations. Some children learn best on their own, others work better in a group. Style is an extremely important variable in school learning.

THE DESIRE TO LEARN

An important task for those who work with young children is being sure these children are assisted in every way to maintain the desire to learn. They require encouragement to learn, unlike infants and toddlers for whom it is so natural. Honig and Lansburgh (1990) emphasize the task of encouraging young children "to learn to strive and strive to learn" (p. 4). At any age success breeds success. Failure destroys the will to try. Honig and Lansburgh (1990) list three rules for helping young children maintain feelings of competence:

1. Keep in tune with the child.
2. Do not ignore the child.
3. Do not overload the child.

Teachers need to be careful that each student receives equal attention. Some studies have indicated that the more competent students get the most attention, thus increasing their good feelings about themselves while the poorer students get less attention, thus increasing their feelings of failure. They may give up and never achieve any success.

Katz (1993) recommends that adults need to maintain children's disposition to learn. This disposition can be defined as the motivation to master or learn new things. These students are oriented toward "developing new skills, trying to understand their work, improving their level of competence, or achieving a sense of mastery based on self-referenced standards" (p. 1). After reviewing the research, Katz (1993) concludes that children will benefit most and maintain the highest motivation from a combination of individual and cooperative learning goals.

Graham (1994) reviewed and examined the research on motivation in African-Americans. She found, contrary to several commonly held stereotypes "African Americans appear to maintain a belief in personal control, we have high expectancies, and enjoy positive self-regard." We are left with the questions of why so many low SES African-American children fail when their motivation to learn is strong. Some of the difficulty may lie in the match between learning styles and school instructional practices.

Providing programs that fit learning styles and make children feel good about themselves has been increasingly difficult as early childhood instruction has become increasingly less developmentally appropriate. Unfortunately, instruction has become more

learning styles

paper and pencil/workbook/worksheet oriented so as to fit with standardized tests. Madaus (1988) refers to this type of curriculum as 'measurement driven'. Hopefully some of the current efforts at assessment reform (which will be discussed later in the text) will take hold. The curriculum for young children should be designed to fit the child's level of development and learning style rather than the child reshaped to fit the curriculum (Charlesworth, 1989).

SUMMARY

Young children learn through their experiences. They learn through constructing knowledge as they interact with the environment and through various forces that exert outside controls on their activities.

Young children perceive the world differently from older children and adults. They use all their senses but tend to be selective in the information they take in. They learn best through manipulation and handling of concrete objects in contrast to passive listening or using workbooks or worksheets.

Learning may occur through classical conditioning, operant conditioning, and observation and imitation, combined with interaction with the environment. Young children are still in the process of developing memory strategies. Their memory processes are relatively inefficient, but they do remember more if the input has been from real concrete experiences rather than abstract instruction.

Other critical factors in learning include adult support- and activity-based learning in an appropriate environment. Opportunities to work with peers also enhance learning. Through instruction that fits their learning styles children can achieve greater success and maintain their desire to learn.

FOR FURTHER READING

Arnheim, R. (1993). Learning by looking and thinking. *Educational Horizons, 71* (2), 94–98.

Astington, J. W., Harris, P. L., & Olson, D. R. (Eds.). (1988). *Developing theories of mind.* New York: Cambridge University Press.

Butterworth, G. E., Harris, P. L., Leslie, A. M., & Wellman, H. M. (Eds.). (1991). *Perspectives on the child's theory of mind.* New York: Oxford University Press.

Dawson, G., & Fischer, K. W. (1994). *Human behavior and the developing brain.* New York: Guilford.

Gardner, H. (1991). *The unschooled mind.* New York: Basic Books.

Hearst, E. (1991). Psychology and nothing. *American Scientist, 79,* 432–433.

Piaget, J. (1985). *The equilibration of cognitive structures.* Chicago: University of Chicago Press.

Rogoff, B., & Mistry, J. (1985). Memory development in cultural context. In M. Pressley & C. Brainerd (Eds.) *Cognitive learning and memory in children* (pp. 117–141). New York: Springer-Verlag.

Schneider, W., & Pressley, M. (1988). *Memory development between 2 and 20.* New York: Springer-Verlag.

Siegel, J., & Shaughnessy, M. F. (1994). An interview with Howard Gardner: Education for understanding. *Phi Delta Kappan, 75,* 563–566.

Siegel, L. S., & Ryan, E. B. (1989). The development of working memory in normally achieving and subtypes of learning disabled children. *Child Development, 60,* 973–980.

Wood, D. (1988). *How children think and learn.* New York: Basil Blackwell.

SUGGESTED ACTIVITIES

1. One aspect of perception is visual discrimination and watching. Find out how skillful children are at some visual discrimination tasks. Try the tasks on at least three young children. Three children of the same age may be used to get an idea of the variation in skill at one age. Or, pick children at different ages (e.g., one three-

year-old, one four-year-old, one five-year-old, and/or one six-year-old) to get some idea of developmental differences. The following tasks may be used.

Warm-up task: Concept of *same*

To accomplish the following skill tasks, the child must be able to understand and use the concept "same." show the child a group of three familiar objects (such as a cube block, a penny, and a toy animal). Have an exact duplicate of each object. In turn, show the child each duplicate object.

Say, "What is this?" (If he can't name it, you name it and respond, "This is a block. Now you tell me what it is.")

Hold up the block, point to the three objects and ask, "Which one is the same as this?" (If he does not answer correctly, show him which is the same. Then have him show you.)

Repeat with the other two objects. If the child does not understand "same," going on to the skill tasks would be frustrating and meaningless. If he does understand "same," go on to the following skill tasks.

Skill 1: Shape—Keep color and size constant, varying shape only.
    a. Present three shapes and ask, "Which is not the same?"

    b. Present a square to the left and a square, triangle, and circle to the right. Point to square #1, and ask, "Which of the other shapes is the same as this one?"

        Present a circle on the left and repeat.

Skill 2: Color—Size and shape are kept constant and only color varies.
    a. Present three objects and ask, "Which is not the same?"

    b. Present three objects.

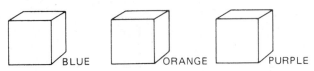

        Show the child a fourth object that matches one of the three, and ask, "Which is the same?"

Skill 3: Size—Shape and color are kept constant with only one size varying.
 a. Present three objects, asking, "Which is not the same?"

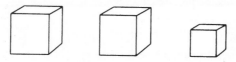

 b. Present three objects of different sizes.

Show the child an object that is the same as one of the three, and say, "Find one that is the same as this one."

Skill 4: Detail
 Card a.

   "Which is not the same?"

 Card b.

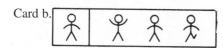   "Which is the same as this one?"
(Point to the figure on the left.)

Contrast and compare the responses from each of the children. What were the similarities and differences? Did you find any reflections of age difference? Compare your results with those obtained by other students in the class.

2. Examine visual memory by using the following tasks. Find three children (between three and seven) either all the same age or three different ages.

 Task 1: Real Objects

 Have a collection of eight to ten common objects (such as toy car, small dolls and animals, buttons, crayon, pencil, and spoon). Include some duplicates.
 a. Have the child name each object.
 b. Put the duplicates aside.
 c. TASKS
  1. Show the child four objects. Show him a duplicate of one, saying,
   "I'm going to hide this." (Hide it.)
   "Find one like I showed you."
   Task can be increased in difficulty by using more and similar objects.
  2. Show the child three objects. Say, "I'm going to hide one. Cover your eyes (or turn head)." Hide one. "Open your eyes. What is missing?"
   Task difficulty can be increased by showing more objects and hiding more.
  3. Show the child two or more objects. Say, "Look carefully before I hide them." Cover (or remove) the objects. Say, "Name as many as you can remember."

 Task 2: Pictures
 Administer the same tasks, using pictures instead of objects.

Task 3: Sequence

Place pictures of objects in a simple sequence on a card. Let the child study the sequence and then hide the pictures. Say, "Name the pictures in order."

Contrast and compare the responses from each of the children. What were the similarities and differences? Were there any differences according to age? Compare results with those obtained by other students in the class.

3. Auditory memory can be examined using a digit span task. Present the child with several numbers (such as 1-3-5-9) and ask the child to recall the numbers in the order presented. Work with a three-year-old, a four-year-old, a five-year-old, a six-year-old, and/or a seven-year-old. Present the following sets of digits each in turn. Say to the child each time, "Listen carefully to what I say because I want you to repeat some numbers after I say them."

Warmup task: "One. Now you say 'One.' "
"Four. Now you say 'Four.' "

Task 1: 2-5-8
Task 2: 1-4-5-9
Task 3: 3-5-7-9
Task 4: 1-3-5-7-9
Task 5: 5-1-9-4-2

Were there differences in the number of digits recalled by each child? Did the children seem to have any special way of trying to remember the number sequences? Write a description of each child's response to the tasks.

4. Children can learn through watching other children being rewarded for some behavior. Arrange to work with two groups of four-, five-, six-, or seven-year-olds. Have four children in each. Work with one group at a time. Give each child paper and crayons. Say to them, "Draw a picture of things you see outdoors." With the first group, wait until everyone is working and approach one child and comment on his picture (e.g. "What nice clouds," "What a nice tree" or "Pretty flowers"). Say nothing else to either group during the drawing sessions. Count how many in each group drew the object you reinforced in the one child's picture. In which group's pictures did that item appear more often? Did it appear more often in the pictures of the group that was reinforced? Did the individual whose picture was commented on respond (such as by drawing more of the item mentioned)?

5. Make an entry in your journal.

REVIEW

A. Match each of the terms in Column I to their correct definitions in Column II. Put the answers on a separate sheet of paper.

Column I

1. learning
2. perception
3. reflex
4. memory

Column II

a. an inborn, unlearned behavior
b. retention of what is learned over a period of time
c. a change in behavior that occurs as the result of experience
d. the interpretation of what is sensed

B. Write the number of each statement that describes a part of the developmentalist view of learning.

1. The process of learning, rather than the product, is emphasized.
2. The interaction between growth and learning is emphasized.

3. Learning is emphasized more than growth.

4. The product of learning (what is learned) is emphasized more than the process.

5. Stages of growth and readiness to learn are viewed as key factors.

6. The child constructs his own knowledge.

C. Read the following description. What seems to be the problem?

Johnny is working on a task that involves sorting letters of the alphabet into different piles. He has put all the *p*s and *b*s in the same pile.

D. Label the types of learning that Pablo and Terry experience in the following story.

Pablo is four-and-a-half years old and attends an all-day child development center program. Pablo is working with a puzzle. Terry is working with Tinker Toys. Mr. Carter stops by. He smiles and says, "Good work, Terry." Pablo glances up at Terry as Mr. Carter speaks. Pablo puts aside his puzzle and starts to build with Tinker Toys. Pablo says to himself, "I need more of those orange things." The lights flicker twice. This is the signal to clean up for lunch. Pablo suddenly feels hungry.

E. Decide which of the following are examples of generalization, discrimination, shaping through successive approximation, and extinction.

1. One of the mothers brings the family dog to school to visit. He is a friendly basset hound who loves children. Most of the children are delighted to pat him and hug him. Patrice runs into the bathroom and refuses to come out. Her teacher finds out from her mother that Patrice has been afraid of dogs since a big dog jumped on her when she was two years old.

2. The next time Hound visits school, Mr. Hernandez encourages Patrice to sit where she can see the other children playing with him. A couple of weeks later, the dog returns. This time, Mr. Hernandez is able to get Patrice to sit closer to the other children. When the dog visits again, Patrice is willing to let him come within two feet of her. With each step that Patrice takes closer to the dog, Mr. Hernandez commends her for being so brave. Eventually, she sits next to Mr. Hernandez while he pats the dog. Finally, when Hound returns for his final visit of the year, Patrice pats him on the head.

3. After that, Patrice never runs away at the first sight of a dog although she is still cautious until she is sure the dog is friendly.

4. Patrice tells Mr. Hernandez that Joe's dog, Hound, is nice. She says, "He's not mean like the dog that jumped on me."

F. Name the three processes that, according to Piaget, enable the child to adapt to and make sense out of his environment.

G. Match the types of memory listed in Column I with their descriptions in Column II. Put the answers on a separate sheet of paper.

Column I	**Column II**
1. recall	a. "Name all these animals for me." (A bear, a mouse, and a deer are on the table.)
2. recognition	
3. paired associates	b. "Here are three animals. Now, I'll cover them with a cloth. Next, I'll show you one and put it back. Okay, now I'll take off the cloth. Which animal did I show you?"
4. reproduction	
	c. "Now, I'll cover the animals again. Draw a picture of one of the animals."
	d. "With all the animals covered, tell me what kinds there are under the cover."

H. Mrs. Jones is teaching the children the concepts of hard and soft. She shows them a piece of cotton, a ball of Play-Doh,® a piece of fur, a piece of wood, a cube of metal, and a plastic box. She asks which are hard and which are soft. How could this experience be improved to help the children remember hard and soft?

Unit

The Adult Role in Learning: General Characteristics

OBJECTIVES

After studying this unit, the student should be able to:

■ Observe adults and children and describe the adults' roles in the children's learning.

■ State the two basic roles of the adult in children's learning.

■ Identify the adult role in learning as it might be defined by Piaget, Vygotsky, Erikson, Freud, Maslow, Rogers, Gesell, Skinner, and Sears.

■ Discriminate between the characteristics of a Piagetian teacher role and a behavioristic teacher role.

■ Evaluate whether an adult is using behaviorist techniques well.

■ Identify the behaviors and comments of a teacher that help children think and learn.

■ Develop activities that promote cooperative learning.

Adults have a critical role in learning, both from a theory and a practice point of view. There are two basic aspects to the adult role: interaction with children as they go about their daily lives and provision of the physical environment in which children operate. The two most prominent views of the adult role are those inspired by Piaget, Vygotsky, and behaviorist theory. In this unit, we will look at these views. We will also consider the effects of rewards on learning, the responsibilities of adults to provide opportunities for children's thinking and problem solving skills to develop, and some ideas regarding the characteristics of the effective adult.

APPLYING THEORY TO PRACTICE

Each of the theorists Piaget, Vygotsky, Erikson, Freud, Rogers, Maslow, Gesell, Bandura, Sears, and Skinner view the adult role in learning a little differently. From the Piagetian cognitive-developmental point of view, the adult takes the role of a guide and sets the stage for learning. The adult questions the child to encourage the development of thought, and to assess the stage of development of the learner. The adult then provides appropriate learning experiences. From the Vygotsky-based cognitive-developmental view the adult takes a more prominent and somewhat directive point of view in providing the scaffolding children need to move through each zone of proximal development to reach their learning potential (Figure 18–1). Interaction with others is essential to learning in both cognitive-developmental views.

From the psychoanalytic point of view (Erikson, Freud, Rogers, and Maslow), the adult is also a guide but there is more emphasis on emotional and personality development than on cognitive. The adult is emotionally supportive; an interpreter of feelings, motives, and actions; and assists the child in solving social problems. The adult assesses the emotional make-up of the child and his progress through each developmental crisis.

The maturationist (Gesell) sees the adult as a guide who supports the child through the cycles of growth. The adult support is considered especially important in getting through rough spots. The adult is understanding, tolerant, and calm. The child's development in the cognitive, affective, and psychomotor areas is assessed to supply him with experiences at his developmental level.

Behaviorists Skinner and Sears both emphasize the importance of the environment to learning. Sears, however, is not as sure as Skinner that adults can learn to control the child's behavior in a manner that applies behaviorist techniques well (Maier, 1978). In contrast to the cognitive-developmental, psychoanalytic, and maturationist views, Skinner perceives the adult as a director rather than a guide. The adult sets the stage, dispenses reinforcements and punishments, and manages observable behavior.

Bandura refers to his theoretical point of view as "social cognitive theory" (Perry, 1989). From Bandura's perspective adults serve an important function as models of appropriate behavior. They are also a resource, at a more abstract level, for instruction on how to accomplish the tasks needed to survive and thrive in the social world (Miller, 1989). The cognitive label is meant to emphasize the importance of the mental work needed to coordinate and integrate various aspects of learning. For example, children

Figure 18–1   From Vygotsky's point of view, the supportive adult provides the scaffolding that assists the child to higher levels of development.

learn to throw and catch a ball, bat a ball, and how to run. They also learn the rules for baseball. To play the game they have to mentally integrate the skills and the rules of the game. Much of this learning takes place simultaneously through observation of older children and/or adults playing baseball. However, not every child will choose to play baseball because they may not be interested or motivated to become involved. Observing and learning particular social behaviors does not guarantee that children will perform them. They also need the motivation to do so.

The environment provided by the adult is viewed differently relative to each of the theoretical positions. Common to all the developmental approaches is the importance of some degree of freedom. For the cognitive-developmentalist, there is freedom within limits. Choices are offered. Concrete materials and experiences are the basic learning activities. There are opportunities for social interaction and the child is encouraged to observe, study, and manipulate the environment.

From the psychoanalytic view, the environment has a somewhat therapeutic aspect. There are outlets and avenues for expression of feelings such as hostility, doubt, shame, pride, and happiness. The maturationist emphasizes that the limits be broad enough to allow room for growth. It is considered important that activities available fit the particular behavior stage. For the behaviorist, the environment allows for maximum positive reinforcement of appropriate adaptive behaviors. The environment provides the control and the behavioral models.

THEORY-BASED APPROACHES

Piaget's constructivist, Vygotsky's view, and the behaviorist points of view have been the most widely applied to the development of approaches to the role of the adult relative to young children's learning. We will now examine these approaches.

Piaget's Constructivist View of Learning

The applications of Piaget's views of cognitive development to practice are numerous. For Piaget (1971, pp. 151–157), "To educate means to adapt the individual to the surrounding social environment. The new methods [referring to open education], however, seek to encourage this adaptation by making use of the impulses inherent in childhood itself, allied with the spontaneous activity that is inseparable from mental development." Piaget indicates the child is capable of diligent and continuous research, springing from a spontaneous need to learn (Figure 18–2). Intelligence is an "authentic activity." For Piaget, ac-

Figure 18–2 **The teacher can sit back, observe the children solving problems on their own, but join in when needed.**

tivity, both physical and social, is the key to learning and development. Spontaneous play is the vehicle for this activity.

As already pointed out in earlier units, many early childhood educators have adopted Piaget's concept of **constructivism**. Constance Kamii (1986) and Rita DeVries (DeVries and Kohlberg, 1990) are two outspoken constructivist early childhood educators referred to in Unit 17. For Kamii and DeVries (DeVries & Kohlberg, 1990) in defining the role of the teacher it is first assumed "the teacher is child-centered, relates well to children, knows how to manage a classroom smoothly and how to provide traditional nursery school [or other early childhood level] activities" (pp. 83–84). In addition the teacher's role includes:

1. Creating an atmosphere conducive to learning. The atmosphere promotes positive child development through encouraging independence and initiative so the child can speak out, ask questions, and experiment and explore.

2. Providing materials and activities and assessing what the children are thinking. Children are encouraged to explore materials on their own. When new ideas are needed the teacher models ideas that flow naturally into what the children have been doing. The adult picks up on the children's interests and follows their lead rather than imposing ideas on them.

3. Encouraging children to keep trying and to construct their own knowledge rather than imposing one "right" answer.

4. Helping children extend their own ideas.

Rather than trying to modify young children's preoperational thought, Kamii and DeVries (DeVries & Kohlberg, 1990) value it, plan for it, and teach in terms of it. Kamii (1986) states that **autonomy** is the goal of education envisioned by Piaget. That is children will be able to explore and think through problem solutions and construct knowledge independently through their own actions.

constructivism   autonomy

Vygotsky's View of Learning

Moll (1990) outlines Vygotsky's view of the adult role in children's learning. Vygotsky's theory of cultural transmission joins development and learning. Vygotsky viewed education not only as central to cognitive development but also as the core sociocultural activity of humans. His work focused on the social origins and cultural bases of individual development. Vygotsky saw the cooperative relationship between adult and child as the main part of the educational process.

For Moll (1990) the zone of proximal development (ZPD) is the concept at the heart of Vygotsky's theory. The concept of the zone is not just an outline for a simple sequence of instruction from establishment of a level of difficulty, to provision of adult assistance, to evaluation of independent performance. For Vygotsky, applying the ZPD to instruction was a complex social process. It is too easy to focus the ZPD on rote learning of skills. Vygotsky viewed learning as a holistic process within the ZPD with a major focus on the development of meaning and understanding. His ideas are in line with the whole language approach to literacy (discussed in Unit 24). Vygotsky believed that meaning comes out of everyday activities.

Vygotsky didn't specify particular forms of adult social assistance to learners. However, according to Moll (1993), he did mention collaboration and direction, and assisting children through demonstrating, asking leading questions, and introducing ideas for beginning to move toward a problem solution. Vygotsky suggested that children changed (or transformed) the help they received from others and internalized this help to be used to guide their independent problem-solving.

> The focus is on the *social system* within which we hope children learn, with the understanding that this social system is mutually and actively created by teacher and students. This interdependence of adult and child is central to a Vygotskian analysis of instruction. (Moll, 1990, p. 11)

From Vygotsky's view "a major goal of schooling is to create social contexts (zones of proximal development) for mastery of and conscious awareness in the use of these cultural tools" (Moll, 1990, p. 12). These cultural tools are our means of communication: reading, writing, and speech.

Change takes place within the ZPD when a child demonstrates she can do something independently today that she could not do yesterday except with assistance. Vygotsky viewed classroom learning as being intertwined with the relationship between thinking and the social organization of classroom instruction. "The role of the adult is not necessarily to provide structured cues but, through exploratory talk and other social meditations such as importing everyday activities into the classrooms, to assist children in appropriating or taking control of their own learning" (Moll, 1990, p. 13). Learning is a joint experience between adult and children, not just transmission of knowledge from adult into the heads of the children.

Behaviorist Views of Learning

Behaviorist approaches, usually called behavior modification or behavior analysis, have been applied to changing the behavior of children in many preschool classrooms (Moore, 1977). The behaviorist approach is based on the following general principles (Sheppard, Shank, & Wilson, 1973):

- People are taught to behave the way they do.
- People teach each other.
- To learn is to change.
- Teachers are people who change learners.

For the behaviorist, "The single most important factor in learning a behavior is what happens immediately following the behavior" (Sheppard et al., 1973, p. 5). If we want to increase the number of times the child behaves in a certain way, a positive consequence must follow each time the child behaves in that way. Positive consequences that are likely to increase positive behavior are called **rewards** or **reinforcements**. Adults who are skilled at behavior

rewards   reinforcements

change are constantly alert for opportunities to follow up desired behavior with positive consequences. These include verbal and nonverbal approval and praise, physical contact, activities, and privileges or material objects. This increases the frequency of the occurrence of desirable behaviors. Undesirable behaviors are generally ignored unless they are dangerous in nature. Behavior modifiers also use techniques such as shaping and substituting an incompatible behavior. A whole classroom system called behavior analysis (Bushell, 1982) has been developed using behaviorist principles.

The Effects of Rewards on Child Behavior

A growing body of research indicates we need to proceed with caution in our use of **extrinsic rewards** (both concrete and social). Our goal has been to develop a desire within the child to learn through the development of **intrinsic rewards** or internal motivation. In discussing the infant and toddler, we have seen they have this internal drive to find out about the world. During the preschool and kindergarten years, it is important to keep that natural curiosity alive. Gottfried (1983) after reviewing research on intrinsic motivation concluded that it is important to encourage intrinsic motivation during the early years as the basis for later academic motivation. She further suggests that the early childhood learning environment should be as anxiety free as possible since high anxiety is associated with low motivation. In a more recent review of research focused on praise and reward, Cannella (1986) found that research indicates that concrete rewards (such as prizes or stickers) actually lower motivation for previously preferred activities. In addition she found that effective praise must be task specific, that is, focus on a specific accomplishment. For example, "You had a hard time figuring out how to make your building as tall as you wanted it, but you did it." versus "I like the way you are building with blocks." Too much praise puts the teacher in a position of authority, increases student dependence on the teacher

and inhibits self-motivation and initiative. Both Gottfried (1983) and Cannella (1986) make some suggestions for adults who work with young children. First, Cannella warns:

- Rewarding a child for participation in an activity already enjoyed will lower his future interest in the task.
- Giving the child positive information will increase motivation; negative information will decrease motivation.
- Only young, low ability, low SES children seem to benefit from high praise. Older, higher ability and upper economic level children already know their capabilities and don't need to be overwhelmed with praise.
- Too much praise may produce too much dependence on the teacher and serve as a behavior control which lowers self-motivation.

Cannella advises:

- Let children solve social as well as intellectual problems themselves.
- Help children develop their own self-evaluation skills by evaluating their own work and making their own decisions about which center to work in or which project to work on next.

Hitz and Driscoll (1988) suggest that rather than using the term *effective praise*, **encouragement** is a clearer term to use in referring to the types of social rewards that are motivating and promote autonomy. Encouragement involves making specific statements. That is, rather than "Your picture is beautiful" (general statement), use specific statements such as "I noticed you use a lot of yellow in your picture" or "You worked for a long time on your picture" (specific statements). Encouragement should be given in private, not in front of the whole group. Encouragement is not evaluative. "Good job" or "Well done" are evaluative statements. Encouragement statements are specific such as "You worked a long time with the blocks today" or "You read the word *cat*." Encour-

| extrinsic rewards | intrinsic rewards | encouragement |

agement should be given in a normal pleasant voice; not deadpan and not overenthusiastic. "I" statements such as "I like the way you . . ." are not appropriate because they promote looking to the valuing of others rather than self valuing. More appropriate would be "You looked proud . . ." or "You looked excited . . ." Encouragement does not promote comparisons and competition. Children are encouraged relative to their individual accomplishments, such as, "You sorted those pictures faster than you did yesterday" or "You put all the art materials away neatly in the right places." Note the action that is actually happening or has happened and be specific in your comments. Hitz and Driscoll (1988) conclude, "Encouragement, on the other hand, fosters autonomy, positive self-esteem, a willingness to explore, and an acceptance of self and others" (p. 13).

Selecting Theory for Practical Application

In Unit 1, examples were provided to demonstrate how different theories can be applied to different problems. Teachers often avoid adopting theory as a tool because promoters of particular theories usually support only one point of view and leave the practitioner the problem of making a choice. Teachers are frequently left in a state of confusion as they try to sort out the claims made for each theory as the guide to instruction. When theories are viewed as complementary, rather than contradictory they can be used to develop a framework to guide instruction. This is not a new idea but one that each new early childhood educator needs to consider. Cowles (1971) summed up the view that no one theory answers every educational question by suggesting that theories "are in many ways far more complementary than competitive, in the same way that neither the trunk or the leg describes the whole elephant." Honig (1986) suggests that theories can be most useful if they are mixed and matched.

> Don't become wedded to one theoretical model or another. Be flexible and perceptive. (Honig, 1986, p. 10)

Keep in mind that each theory addresses a different aspect of development. We might first want to consider the problem to be dealt with, then choose the theory that seems to apply best to that problem. Look back at the examples in Unit 1 and you will see how this approach works.

THINKING AND PROBLEM SOLVING

The focus for learning should put an emphasis on the importance of children developing thinking and problem solving skills in contrast to an emphasis on acquiring specific skills such as counting a specific number of objects, memorizing the alphabet letter names and sounds, or writing alphabet letters and numerals to fit specific models. It requires teachers to give up didactic, lecture-type, instruction and provide children more time for exploration and experimentation. Campbell and Arnold (1988) point out that a majority of questions asked in classrooms are literal. That is, they ask for direct informational feedback that requires memory skills but not the exercise of thinking skills. The developmental approach to questioning suggested by Campbell and Arnold involves going step-by-step from simple to complex questions. Start at the literal "What is?" level. Then move on to "What else?" questions which associate the new information with previous information. Next move on to the cause and effect with "What?" and "Why?" questions. These questions take the children further from the immediate situation. At the next level the imagination is brought into play with "What if?" questions. These questions take the children's thinking into the possible and provide room for a variety of responses. There is no 'right' answer.

Vygotsky's concept of scaffolding supports the value of good questioning for children's learning (Cassidy, 1989). Questions such as "How can we find out?", "What will happen when we . . . ?", "What should we do to . . . ?" open the way for children to think and to solve problems. Carr (1988) specifically addresses critical thinking skills. She points out that students need to learn how to question, analyze, and to look beyond the obvious to find possible answers. However, critical thinking skills should not be taught as isolated skills but should be an integral part of everyday learning in all areas of the curriculum. Barbour (1988) also warns that thinking skills are not developed through a packaged curriculum but are developed through opportunities to solve problems through physical and verbal exploration. Children need time to talk over and try out different ways of doing things during their daily play activities. The curriculum should permit "children the freedom to discuss, agree, argue, inform, regulate and imagine with each other" (p. 68), not just with teachers or other adults.

Problems may be specifically defined with a specific logical answer or open-ended with a number of possible solutions available (Brown, 1988). It is the open-ended problems that children need more opportunities to tackle. Whether the problem is social (i.e. who gets to try the new puzzle first) or conceptual (i.e. how can two sandwiches be divided among three children), first the problem must be identified and defined. Then brainstorming can be used to identify as many possible alternative solutions as possible. Finally, various solutions can be tried to see how they might work out. Tudge and Caruso (1988) found that cooperative problem solving can enhance young children's cognitive development (Figure 18–3). That is, in line with Piaget's thinking, when children work together to solve problems their cognitive growth is supported. In the natural situation there is usually one or more experts and one or more novices in the group. Tudge and Caruso were interested in what would happen when children paired on the basis of their levels in problem solving were presented with a balance beam problem to solve through a paired effort. Tudge and Caruso found that when they paired a higher level

Figure 18–3 **One important aspect of the adult role is to provide children the opportunity to work cooperatively in small groups.**

and lower level child, and the higher level child was sure of the solution, the lower level child moved up. If the higher level child was unsure, the lower level child did not change and sometimes influenced the higher level child to select the lower level solution. If the children were allowed to try out their predicted solutions, they improved in further problem-solving situations whether or not their partner was at the same or a different level. Tudge and Caruso suggest a number of ways teachers can ensure that true cooperative problem solving occurs in their classrooms. These include (pp. 50–51):

1. Plan activities in which children have a shared goal. For example, encourage them to plan together how to build a zoo for the toy animals.

2. The goal should be intrinsically interesting to the children. Encourage children to figure out how to solve problems they have selected such as how to share the available blocks or how to fill the water table.

3. Children should be able to achieve their goal with their own actions. They need to have the opportunity to try out their solutions.

4. The results of the children's actions should be both visible and immediate. Then if they are not satisfied with one solution, they know right away and can try another way.

5. The teacher's role is to encourage and suggest, not to direct.

6. Encourage children to interact with each other by introducing activities as problems that need to be solved by two or more children working together.

7. Help the children clarify or adapt their shared goals. The teacher can help the children think through what they plan to do before they act by rephrasing their solution and giving them time to reflect on whether that is really what they want to do.

8. Help involve children who are less likely to initiate, that is, the quieter more reserved children, to contribute to the discussion.

Tudge and Caruso point out that problem solving may occur in any curriculum area. It may occur during play or during open-ended activities designed by the teacher. By encouraging cooperative problem solving, teachers can greatly enhance cognitive development.

SUMMARY

Whichever theoretical position is examined, adults have a definite role in children's learning. The major difference among theories is the degree to which adults serve as guides as compared to serving as directors. The Piagetian or constructivist and the behaviorist views have been the most widely applied to education. The constructivist sees the adult as a guide who sets up the environment and supports the children's active construction of their own knowledge. The behaviorist views the adult as a director who directly shapes the child's behavior and gives him specific knowledge, which the adult believes to be important.

For the behaviorist, extrinsic rewards shape behavior and gradually give way to intrinsic rewards for learning. For the constructivist, the child is by nature a learner and acquiring knowledge is intrinsically rewarding. Research indicates that rewarding children for things that they already like to do can decrease their performance. It has also been found that specific encouragement is more effective than general praise.

While theorists in every camp may tout their own points of view, the most practical approach to the selection of a theoretical framework appears to be to fit the theory to the problem. Not one theory can answer every question.

A vital aspect of the adult role is supporting children in the development of their thinking and problem-solving skills. Provision of open-ended activities, asking open-ended questions, providing needed scaffolding, and encouraging group discussion and cooperative problem solving in all areas of the curriculum are essential support for children as they reach their learning potentials.

FOR FURTHER READING

Ayers, W. (1989). *The good preschool teacher: Six teachers reflect on their lives.* New York: Teachers College Press.

Ayers, W. (1993). *To teach: The journey of a teacher.* New York: Teachers College Press.

Bredekamp, S. (Ed.) (1987). *Developmentally appropriate practice in early childhood programs serving children from birth through age eight.* Washington, DC: National Association for the Education of Young Children.

Confrey, J. (1990). What constructivism implies for teaching. In R. B. Davis, C. A. Maher, & N. Noddings (Eds.). Constructivist views on the teaching and learning of mathematics, *Journal for Research in Mathematics Education, Monograph number 4* (pp. 107–122).

Essa, E. (1995). *A practical guide to solving preschool behavior problems,* (3rd. Ed.). Albany, NY: Delmar.

Gardner, H. (1991). *The unschooled mind.* New York: Basic Books.

Goffin, S. G. (1989). Developing a research agenda for early childhood education: What can be learned from the research on teaching? *Early Childhood Research Quarterly, 4,* 187–204.

Moll, L. C. (Ed.). (1990). *Vygotsky and education: Instructional implications of sociohistorical psychology.* New York: Basic Books.

Peters, D. L., Neisworth, J. T., Yawkey, T. D. (1985). *Early childhood education: From theory to practice.* Monterey, CA: Brooks/Cole.

Rogoff, B. (1989). *Apprenticeship in thinking: Cognitive development in social context.* New York: Oxford University Press.

Schifter, D., & Fosnot, C. T. (Eds.). (1993). *Reconstructing mathematics education: Stories of teachers meeting the challenge of reform.* New York: Teachers College Press.

Vasta, R. (Ed.). (1992). *Six theories of child development.* London and Philadelphia: Jessica Kingsley.

SUGGESTED ACTIVITIES

1. The objective of this activity is to look at the teacher's role as one who provides an environment for learning. Some classrooms offer opportunities for the child to express his individuality, to explore, and to experiment. Other classrooms are very highly structured and offer little room for the child to act as an individual. Visit a preschool, kindergarten, or primary classroom and categorize the environment in its physical, social-emotional, and intellectual aspects and decide if it is one that promotes children's learning. The following learning environment checklist, adapted from Harms (1970, pp. 304–308), can be used.

   a. Write a description of the room you visited.
   b. Write a summary of everything you saw.
   c. Write a summary of what you learned using the learning environment checklist.
   d. Do you feel the teacher(s) do a good job in their role(s) as provider(s) of a learning environment? Why?

LEARNING ENVIRONMENT CHECKLIST

Characteristic	Yes	No	Comments
The Physical Environment			
Is there a place for quiet and noisy activities to go on at the same time?			
Are a variety of materials available and easy for children to obtain?			
Is it clear where each type of material may be used?			
Can children choose to use material alone or in groups?			
Are children allowed time to explore, experiment, and discover?			
Do the adults remain in the background, stepping in only to expand an activity by adding material, asking a question, making a suggestion, or helping to settle a dispute if necessary?			
The Interpersonal Environment			
Is there a feeling of mutual respect between adults and adults, adults and children, and children and children?			
Do the adults spend more time observing and interacting with the children than setting limits?			
Do the adults have specific objectives for each child's learning?			
Is cooperation rather than competition reinforced?			
Do the adults model the kind of behavior they wish the children to learn?			
Do the adults give ample appropriate positive reinforcement?			

Activities	Yes	No	Comments
___ art ___ books ___ games ___ music ___ animals ___ trips ___ puzzles ___ manipulative toys ___ cooking ___ dramatic play			
Are there materials of different difficulty levels?			
Do the children do some of the planning?			
Do the teachers pick up on the children's interests?			

2. Read descriptions of four Head Start/Follow-Through model programs or other early education program models. Compare the descriptions of the teacher's role in each model. Which do you feel is best in promoting learning? Why?

3. Imagine yourself as a teacher of young children. Which roles would you adopt? Why? What do you see as biases that you would have to work on? How would you describe your style?

   To guide your self-analysis, review the list of roles that follow and write why you would or would not take on each one. When you have finished, write a summary picture of you as a teacher as you see yourself now.

   Roles:
   A. Guide
       1. emphasis on cognitive
       2. emphasis on affective
   B. Director
       1. emphasis on cognitive
       2. emphasis on affective
   C. emphasis on freedom within limits
   D. development of an environment that allows maximum positive reinforcement of appropriate adaptive behavior as described in this unit
   E. emphasis on questioning
   F. emphasis on promoting activity
   G. emphasis on collaborating and encouraging
   H. observer of children
   I. provider of materials, experiences, and problems to solve
   J. supporter of individuality and self-awareness
   K. one who responds to children's play activities

   Look at your summary. Are there any biases that appear or should appear to complete the picture? Discuss your style with a small group in class. What are their reactions? How do they view themselves?

4. Make an entry in your journal.

REVIEW

A. What are the two basic roles the adult has in the child's learning?

B. Match the theorists in Column I with the adult roles in learning described in Column II.

Column I	**Column II**
1. Piaget	a. The adult guides the child through the cycles of growth and gives support when the child goes through a difficult stage.
2. Vygotsky	
3. Erikson, Maslow, Rogers, Freud	b. The adult is more of a director than a guide. The environment controls learning.
4. Gesell	c. The adult is more of a director but feels most humans cannot master the skills needed to do a top-quality job.
5. Skinner	
6. Sears	d. The adult guides the child's healthy emotional, social, and personality development and assists the child through his developmental crises.
7. Bandura	
	e. The adult guides the child through the stages of mental development by providing the appropriate environment, the right kinds of questions, and an opportunity for exploration and discovery.
	f. The adult is a model of appropriate behavior.
	g. The adult provides support for the child through the zone of proximal development.

C. Write a *P* for each statement that describes a Piagetian teacher role and a *B* for the statements that describe a behaviorist teacher role.
   1. Teachers are people who change learners.
   2. What the teacher does immediately following a behavior is a critical factor in determining whether or not the behavior is learned.
   3. The teacher asks questions that help the child solve the problem on his own.
   4. The teacher needs to be alert so she can follow up desired behaviors with positive consequences for the child.
   5. The teacher provides a variety of experiences in which the child is encouraged to explore and experiment.
   6. The teacher feels free to stand back and let the child discover for himself.

D. Read the following description of teacher behavior. Decide if this teacher is using good behaviorist techniques by reinforcing only desired behaviors and using a variety of reinforcers.

   Paul R. is the head teacher for a group of four- and five-year-olds. The children are busy in several learning centers set up around the room. Julie comes in, goes to her cubby, hangs up her coat, and comes over to greet Paul. He gives her a hug and tells her to look around and decide what she would like to do this morning. Paul moves about the room, smiling at children as they work. Throughout the observation period, we note that Mary Lou always lets Paul know when she needs something by yelling across the room, "Teacher! Teacher! I need you." Paul always goes to her immediately. Each time he reminds her not to yell.

E. Describe an activity that promotes cooperative problem solving.

The Adult Role in Learning: Parental and Social Factors

OBJECTIVES

After studying this unit, the student should be able to:

- Analyze and evaluate his or her own feelings about parenting styles, parent education, and parent involvement.

- Identify competent adult caregivers and teachers.

- Evaluate whether an adult caregiver or teacher has a positive or negative teaching style.

- Discuss multicultural and anti-bias education.

- Discuss why adults must adopt different roles and behaviors when they work with children and parents from different social and cultural backgrounds.

Both parents and others in society have profound influences on young children. In this unit, the role of parents in young children's learning is examined relative to parent/child interaction, nonparental care, and parent education and involvement. Also discussed are sociocultural factors, ethnic/racial effects on learning, and culturally relevant educational practices and materials.

THE ROLE OF PARENTS

Parents of young children play a critical role in their learning. There are several ways to consider this role: how parent and child interact, how parents can be helped to be more effective, and how parental care compares with nonparental care.

Parent/Child Interaction

Burton White and his colleagues did some interesting and valuable research on the precursors in early childhood of competent behavior in children at the time they enter the elementary grades at age six. After observing many children in school settings, this group of researchers defined the characteristics that indicate the behavior of a **competent six-year-old** child. They consider a competent six-year-old to be one who can manage well in the school situation both socially and cognitively (White & Watts, 1973).

White et al. (1973) studied a sample of children from infancy through preschool age. Using their criteria, they determined that the mothers of the best-developed children tended to be positive toward life,

KEYTERMSKEYTERMSKEYTERMSKEYTERMSKEYTERMSKEY

competent six-year-old

enjoyed young children, gave of themselves, and did not devote 100 percent of their time to their infants. They were energetic, patient, tolerant of messes, casual regarding minor risks, consultants to the child, designers of the environment, and on call when needed.

The following is an example of interaction between a highly competent mother and her children (Carew, Chad, & Halfar, 1976, pp. 71–72, used with permission).

> Mother is doing the laundry and the dryer comes to a stop. Recognizing the signal, Matthew says, "I'll get the jammies (pajamas) out," and scrambles down from his mother's lap. Mother: "Okay. You get the jammies out." Matthew: "Me take them out," as he opens the dryer door and starts pulling out the clothes. His brother, Ernie, runs over and they both pull the clothes out calling, "Me get them out!"
>
> They continue pulling out the clothes. Ernie: "It's on! You better come out of there!" (The dryer has in fact stopped.) Matthew continues poking his head in the dryer searching for any clothes that might be left. Mother calls from the pantry, "Did you get it all out?" Matthew gathers up an armful of clothes and walks to the pantry. Mother: "Give them here." Matthew: "I got to throw them in here," and tries to put the clothes into the washer. Mother: "They already went in there. They're washed already." She takes the clothes from Matthew.

The preceding example is in sharp contrast to the following example from the observations of Diana.

> Mother asks Diana if she'd like an egg. Diana: "Yeah!" as she puts a toy bottle in her mouth. Diana calls, "Can we get the toaster out?" Her brother joins in: "Can we get the toaster out?" Bobby carries the toaster from the pantry to the kitchen table and hands it to Diana. Mother intercepts and takes the toaster away. Diana: "Can we get the toast (bread) out?" She runs to the refrigerator and looks in: "Hey, Mom, where's the toast?" Mother: "I'll get it." Diana: "Where's the eggs?" Mother scolds: "Get out of there. Stay out." Diana follows her mother to the table.

Mothers of highly competent children participate with their children in activities as a guide and a partner and allow their children to actively explore household materials, even though it might be messy and not very convenient. Mothers of competent children show a high degree of trust in their children and their children's capabilities (Figure 19–1).

White and Watts (1973) summarize the behavior of the mothers of competent children as follows. These mothers:

- Talk to the child a lot at his level.
- Show an interest in the child's accomplishments.
- Provide a diversity of materials and activities.
- Promote independence but give help when needed.
- Present the child with imaginative suggestions.
- Strengthen the child's intrinsic motivation to learn.
- Make the child feel it is important to do a task well.

While the child has freedom to explore, the mother is secure enough to say "no" when necessary and to be consistent and firm regarding rules and regulations.

Figure 19–1   "Good, you can do it for yourself." The adult helps the child to be independent and responsible.

These researchers found that competent behaviors were established in infancy and toddlerhood. The role of the mother in the child's development before age three was found to be crucial.

Since the studies by White et al., other research has supported the basic findings that positive, cooperative interactions between parent and child when completing a task at the preschool level predict higher academic achievement in elementary school (i.e., Epstein & Evans, 1979; Hess, Holloway, Dickson, & Price, 1984; Hess & McDevitt, 1984). Studies have also indicated that sons receive more helpful support than daughters. That is, mothers tend to be more directive with their daughters (Hess & McDevitt, 1984; Weitzman, Birns & Friend, 1985).

Shared book reading is a parent/child activity that has been closely examined. Pellegrini, Perlmutter, Galda, and Brody (1990) found that low SES African-American mothers used the same kinds of strategies as the middle-class mother/child pairs in previous studies. The mothers seemed to operate in the zone of proximal development as they demanded higher-level cognitive responses when engaged with a familiar book than with a new book.

Hyson, Hirsh-Pasek, Rescorla, Cone and Martell-Boinske (1989) found that upper-middle-class mothers' beliefs regarding mastery were related to their interactions when working on a problem-solving task with their children. Those mothers who believed strongly in skill mastery were much more directive than those whose beliefs about skill mastery were less strong.

Okagaki and Sternberg (1993) found differences in beliefs regarding school performance among parents from different cultures. Immigrant parents from Cambodia, Mexico, the Philippines, Vietnam, and native born Anglo-American and Mexican-American parents were questioned regarding their beliefs about child rearing, what should be taught in first and second grades, and what characterizes an intelligent child. The immigrant parents favored conformity over autonomy while the American-born parents favored autonomy. Anglo-American parents related cognitive characteristics such as problem-solving skills, verbal ability, and creative ability to intelligence. The other groups placed more importance on noncognitive characteristics, such as motivation, so-

cial skills, and practical school skills. This latter view is not the traditional American teacher view although efforts are being made to incorporate the affective aspects into instructional goals. Okagaki and Sternberg (1993) suggest that the immigrant parents' emphasis on conformity, while negatively related to school performance, is probably a practical approach for children who must learn to live in a new culture.

The context of the instructional task appears to be an important factor in how mothers go about teaching. If they believe the task to be more school related (versus game related), they are much more directive and more concept oriented even though the two tasks may actually involve the same skills. Mothers also may not interpret the task in the same manner as the educator, indicating that educators need to be very specific with parents regarding the purposes of school related tasks (Sonnenschein, Baker, & Freund, 1993).

Most studies have focused on the mother's role in learning. What about the father's role? Observations of father/child interaction suggest that the father's role is similar to the mother's; that is, there are more role similarities than there are differences (Weintraub, 1978). The same kinds of maternal techniques that have positive effects will have positive effects when used by fathers. Today, fathers are more involved with their young children right from birth than they were in the past, as described in Unit 6. Radin (1982) interviewed mothers and fathers of three- to six-year-olds in families where the father took the predominant role in child care. Compared to fathers in families that were more traditional, these fathers provided much more cognitive stimulation for their children. Both boys and girls were provided with more educational materials. However, boys received more direct instruction from their fathers than did girls. Both boys and girls received intellectual benefits from this nontraditional child care arrangement. Father involvement with children and their schooling not only has positive effects on academic achievement but also on self-concept and moral and social development (Swick & Manning, 1983).

Nonparental Care

The concerns about and characteristics of out-of-home care and caregivers for infants and toddlers has already been discussed in previous units. The out-of-home caregivers also have an influence on the older child's learning. Alison Clarke-Stewart (1984) has done extensive research in this area. Clarke-Stewart identified a continuum of childcare arrangements that ranged from full-time at home with parents to full-time in a childcare center. In addition she identified an arrangement in which children were cared for part-time at a nursery school and part-time at the caregiver's home or their home. Seven childcare arrangements were identified:

1. At home with parents
2. At home with parents and siblings
3. At home with baby sitter
4. Childcare home
5. Nursery school, part-time
6. Childcare center, full-time
7. Nursery school and baby sitter

Children were observed in this variety of settings and mothers, fathers, and caregivers were interviewed. Clarke-Stewart found that center-care children were more competent than children in the other types of situations in interactions with parents, with strangers, and with unfamiliar peers. They were also ahead in intellectual abilities and social knowledge. Childcare center children were also more independent of their parents. The center-based childcare settings tended to have more highly trained caregivers than did the other settings. The results indicated that high-quality, out-of-home care can have beneficial effects on child development.

As discussed in earlier units Thornburg, Pearl, Crompton, and Ispa (1990) found that full-time day care had no apparent detrimental effects on children's social and intellectual development as measured when they were in kindergarten. Childcare attenders tended to be somewhat more aggressive than non-day-care attenders but not to the point of being viewed as problem children by their teachers. African-American children appeared to receive some intellectual benefits from having attended childcare programs. Burchinal, Lee, and Ramey (1989) found that African-American lower socioeconomic level children who were enrolled from infancy in a high-quality intervention childcare

program were significantly ahead in cognitive development when compared with similar children who attended lower quality community child care, who were ahead of similar children who experienced little or no child care. Caughy, DiPietro, and Strobino (1994) found this same protective factor for impoverished children who entered child care as infants. Phillips, Voran, Kisker, Howes, and Whitebook (1994) reporting the results of a national childcare study, found that upper-class children received the highest quality care, middle-class children the least quality care, and lower-class children more variable care (that is, some of the best and some of the worst). Most of the low SES programs are government funded and thus there is a government responsibility to evaluate some of these programs and provide for increased quality. Support is increasing that quality child care during early childhood is not only nondetrimental but can enhance the development of young children.

Parent Education and Involvement

Research has demonstrated that some kinds of parent/child interactions are effective in enhancing children's learning while others may thwart normal development. Therefore, early childhood educators have sought means to help parents become more effective teachers of their young children. A great deal of attention has focused on parent education and on parent involvement. The Head Start program (Celebrating Head Start's 25th Anniversary, 1990) has effectively included both the educational and the involvement components. Head Start focuses as much on the education and the involvement of parents as on the education of the children. While preschool educators have long recognized the value of parent education and involvement, educators at the elementary and secondary levels are just beginning to recognize the importance of getting parents more involved in the education of their children (Epstein, 1991).

Fitzgerald and Goncu (1993) point out the importance of the parent/teacher relationship being a collaborative one in which both teachers and parents contribute to decisions regarding what children learn and how they learn it. They believe this is especially important for low-income parents and children whose backgrounds are different from the school personnel. In their study of parent involvement in low-income urban public schools, they found there was very little collaboration. The school personnel set the agenda for parent involvement, deciding what forms it should take, where it should take place, and what the focus should be. Fitzgerald and Goncu (1993) suggest it is essential that school personnel stop viewing themselves as the experts who tell parents what is best for their children and learn to respect parents' opinions and negotiate with parents regarding what is best for their children.

SOCIAL/CULTURAL FACTORS

We cannot assume all children are the same and they will react the same way to every adult or to the same adult at all times. The United States is a diverse nation with a variety of cultural groups. We have always been a nation of immigrants and continue to be so today (Seefeldt, 1983). Our nation also varies greatly in terms of locales (rural, urban and suburban) and social classes (West, 1986). All these factors affect the adult role in the child's learning. Each adult will view children differently relative to that adult's cultural group, social class, and locale. Children will react differently relative to the same factors.

The social/cultural aspects of children's learning are extremely important considerations when they enter an out-of-home setting, whether for pre-elementary school child care or for more formal schooling. Adults need to be informed to avoid stereotypes and misconceptions (Slaughter-Defoe, Nakagawa, & Johnson, 1990). Lack of cultural understanding can lead to misinterpretation of children's language and cognitive competence (Hilliard & Vaughn-Scott, 1982). For example, Bloch, Tabachnick, and Espinosa-Dulanto (1994) present a picture of some of the unfair assessments made regarding children's academic progress and social behavior based on teachers' incomplete and biased information. Even the best intentioned teachers "still had too little knowledge of all of their children's back-

grounds to understand all of the different ways in which children's competencies could be utilized in the classroom and [in] their learning" (p. 245). Bloch et al. (1994) found there were school norms that did not leave room for the strengths that might be found in the non-European-American students. They believed there was too much pressure for assimilation and not enough openness to the strengths and talents the non-European-American children brought with them to school.

Perez (1994) called for diversity to be responded to with respect. He proposed that schools look upon diversity not as a problem but as an opportunity to experience other peoples and cultures. He suggested several steps that could be taken. For example, children's names should be respected by learning to pronounce them correctly as given rather than changing them to English equivalents. Further, students' primary languages can be respected. Teachers can't become fluent in all the languages currently represented in our schools, but they can learn at least a few basic terms and phrases of the languages of the students in their classrooms. Students should be free to speak their primary languages at school if English is not a particular focus of the instruction. Teaching English should be viewed as adding a second language, not as replacing the primary language. Finally, teachers can demonstrate respect for the students' cultures. Students' cultural beliefs, values, histories, and experiences can be integrated into the curriculum. This should not be done in a fragmentary way, but there should be a real integration that looks at different cultural perspectives on various issues.

In education, we face a number of problems in our efforts to respect the diversity within our culture. The term **multicultural education** has become the goal we strive for but it has also brought about some concerns that are not yet answered. Knutson (1993) points out two multicultural challenges. First, there is the problem of "teaching *to* diverse populations—migrants, immigrants, refugees and minorities," and second there is the problem of "teaching *about* these populations". Clabaugh (1993) describes a third problem. In our quest for multiculturalism how far do

multicultural education

we go? For example, if a student comes from a community that does not value education, do we have the right to encourage that student to pursue her studies? If a student comes from a culture in which corporal punishment is the norm for misbehavior or in which women are looked upon as property, do we have the right to propose alternatives? A fourth problem is put forth by Ryan (1993). Ryan's concern is that a peril of multiculturalism is that schooling to the group may bury individuality. Multiculturalism can perpetuate stereotypes overlooking that members of a cultural group each have their own individuality. Ryan believes that multicultural education should focus on both integration (what needs to be done to network and relate to others who are different) and differentiation (what are the individual's talents, skills, strengths, weaknesses, likes, and dislikes). While teachers need to be aware of some of the prevalent attributes of diverse cultures (as for example, described in this unit and others), they also need to be aware that not every member of a group will fit these attributes exactly. A final consideration is the question of balancing our respect for diversity with the major mission of our schools, which is to promote (Rozycki, 1993, p. 127):

1. the non-exclusive distribution of power, i.e., democracy,

2. the reduction of stereotyping, i.e., destroying prejudice, and

3. equal opportunity for all persons to any role in society.

Rozycki (1993) points out that this apparent inconsistency is very confusing to immigrants who have come to this country to become American. Hilliard (1994) believes that questions of race, socioeconomic status, and gender equity should be treated as political rather than educational and pursued on that level. On the other hand, Hilliard sees culture as something real that includes the shared creativities and experiences of groups of people. For most people, socialization and learning begin in a primary culture. It is this cultural diversity that should be understood and inform educational decision making to provide the best education for each individual. Hilliard believes to accomplish this goal educators

must distinguish between what is political and what is educationally relevant.

Keep in mind that every cultural group is represented by a diverse collection of individuals, and we need to avoid stereotypes. At the same time, there are some cultural attributes that need to be understood and considered by adults to work with young children and their families from a culturally respectful point of view. We will look next at some of the unique characteristics of the major cultural groups in the United States.

Hispanic-Americans

Our largest group of Hispanics are Mexican-Americans. Baecher (1977), Castillo, and Cruz (1974), and Saracho and Hancock (1983) feel that teachers of Mexican-American children should have special competencies and use some special strategies. The most important role according to Castillo and Cruz is that of an authority figure who builds confidence in the child by showing confidence in the child's ability to learn. Mexican-American children are especially sensitive to the authority figure's feelings about them. Since most Mexican-American children work best in a cooperative situation with their peers, they need teachers who provide opportunities to learn through cooperative work. Both Baecher and Castillo and Cruz list three areas or domains in which teachers of Mexican-American children need special skills:

- The teacher enhances the verbal and interactional behavior of the Mexican-American children. For example, she is fluent in English and Spanish and uses both as teaching languages.

- The teacher develops curricular activities that build a positive self-concept and self-esteem in Mexican-American children. Activities include the child's cultural background, community, and home as a basis.

- The teacher is a liaison between school, parents, and child. The teacher welcomes parents into the school as visitors or volunteers. She communicates in the parent's preferred language.

Saracho and Hancock (1983) suggest some specific strategies based on Chicano or Mexican-

American culture. For example, Mexican-American foods can be prepared in class (Figure 19–2). Further, children always enjoy playacting stories and fables. Mexican-American children should have an opportunity to listen to and role-play fables and stories from their own culture that teach their cultural values.

The Chicano or Mexican-American mother has a different teaching style and takes a different role with her child than does the Anglo-American mother, according to a study done by Luis M. Laosa (1977). Mexican-American mothers use more non-verbal communication; Anglo-American mothers use more verbal communication when they teach their children a task. However, within the Mexican-American group, the more schooling a mother had, the more questions she used, the fewer commands she gave, and the more freedom she gave the child to solve the problem on his own. Moreno (Scholar, 1994) had seventeen Chicano and twelve Anglo-American mother/child pairs videotaped teaching their children to tie their shoes. He found that whereas Chicano mothers used more commands

than Anglos during the first 3 minutes of instruction, this number decreased over the next 6 minutes observed and turned out to be less overall than exhibited by the Anglo mothers. While Anglo mothers increased their praise over time, Chicano mothers use of praise was constant. Moreno concluded that Chicano mothers don't actually overuse commands as has frequently been reported. Within any cultural/ethnic group, there is variation. For example, research comparing the views of child development of Mexican-American mothers who had various degrees of acculturation into mainstream culture found that different groups within the Mexican-American culture varied in their views of how children develop (Gutierrez & Sameroff, 1990; Gutierrez, Sameroff, & Karrer, 1988).

By the year 2020 the size of our country's Hispanic population is predicted to be beyond the size of the black population (Hyland, 1989). It is our fastest growing minority population. Hispanics are the most undereducated group, have the highest dropout rate, and are the most segregated (Hyland, 1989). The

Figure 19–2   **These children enjoy preparing one of their favorite foods.**

greatest problem for Hispanic Americans is becoming fluent speakers of English. Finding ways to help them to retain their heritage and their first language while learning English is a major challenge for adults who work with young Hispanic children.

Native Americans

Lee Little Soldier (1992) describes how Native American preschoolers have been observed to be enthusiastic and talkative in their informal Head Start preschool classes in contrast to their uncommunicative behavior in most kindergarten and elementary classrooms. The pressure for individual achievement and performance demanded in the traditional elementary school are in conflict with Native American family values. Native Americans grow up in an extended family with a strong group orientation. Individual public attention makes them feel uncomfortable. When working with Native American children, several sets of values should be respected (Foerster & Little Soldier, 1978):

- They respect and value the dignity of the individual.
- They value cooperation.
- They value sharing.
- They view time as having no beginning and no end.
- They are taught to listen to the wisdom of their elders and to be independent.

They respond poorly to both a traditional structured situation with the teacher as the director and a completely free situation where the teacher is always in the background. "Teachers are there to offer assistance when needed but should encourage the children to be self-reliant" (Foerster & Little Soldier, 1978, p. 56).

Little Soldier (1992) cautions that beyond these core values not all Native American families fit one stereotype. There are more than two hundred fifty recognized tribes in the United States. Each tribe has its own history, culture, and language. Within each tribe there are diverse levels of acculturation and education that determine what Native American children bring to school and what level of comfort they will feel in the school. To succeed academically, they may accul-

turate to school expectations and even become alienated from their primary culture. Eventually, they may find that although they act like non-Native Americans they are not accepted as equals and thus find themselves alone, angry, hostile, and frustrated. Schools need to help Native American children learn to live comfortably in both cultures, that is, to be bicultural.

Little Soldier (1992, p. 18–20) suggests five value areas where home and school may conflict:

1. Direct personal criticism and harsh discipline that might negatively influence a child's self-esteem is avoided at home.
2. Native Americans may feel indifference to acquiring material goods.
3. Many Native Americans tend to view time as flowing and relative; things are done as the need arises rather than by the clock or according to some future-oriented master plan.
4. Not all children, certainly not all Native American children, learn best in the logical, linear, and sequential teaching style typical of today's elementary school.
5. Physical modesty should be considered; the need for privacy in toileting, dressing/undressing and showering in physical education classes must be taken into account.

Little Soldier (1992, p. 21) concludes that "We have to begin where children are and not where we feel they ought to be," which is, of course, a basic position in early childhood education.

Curriculum materials and activities can be geared to the Native American culture. For example, Borenzweig and Wilmshurst (1981) developed learning kits geared to the Native American children with whom they worked. The kits are used by parents with their children. The kits are designed to teach concepts such as object permanency, understanding of physical properties of materials, etc. Of course, the bottom line is to learn about the Native American culture whether you have Native American students or not. Both Jane Billman (1992) and Denise Shaffer (1993) suggest guidelines and resources for instituting an authentic Native American curriculum.

African-Americans

Carol Brunson Phillips (1994) promotes an interactive approach to African-American child development. From this view, the social, political, and economic characteristics of the school interact with what the children bring from home. African-American children bring some specific core values and experiences to school. For example, they bring a personal orientation that comes from their infant experiences. As infants, they are held and played with rather than a wide array of toys, they are encouraged to play with their caretaker's face, thus developing a close interpersonal relationship. African-Americans have developed some unique language usage, which results in verbal performances through narration of myths, folktales, sermons, joke telling, and other special kinds of talk. Talk is used to learn about life and the world and to achieve group approval and recognition. African-Americans have also developed a unique language system, which has continued the African language traditions as adapted to European English. Thus, African-American children enter school equipped with these and other cultural attributes. The school traditions and values have grown from a different historical tradition with its basis in European culture which stresses individuality and competition. Thus, African-American students are placed in a conflict situation between home and school values and traditions. As with other cultural groups, they either fight the system and fail, give in and acculturate completely, or learn to operate in both styles fitting their style to the setting. Teachers can support children in making the transition into school and into a bicultural mode by learning more about African-American history and culture and by capitalizing on the learning styles they bring to school and by discussing openly the conflict situation in which they find themselves.

African-American children enter school with a style of learning that can be capitalized on to bring about success. They tend to have a relational cognitive style that contrasts with the analytical cognitive style of most European-American middle-class designed schools (Hale, 1982). That is, African-American children tend to thrive where freedom, variation, creativity, novelty, uniqueness, and affective and other humanistic patterns describe the school situation. Children with an analytic cognitive style fit into situations that emphasize rules, standardization, conformity, regularity, precision, and other factors that support a strict structure for learning. African-American children are oriented more towards other people than to things and need a lot of interpersonal interaction in their learning. Many African-American children enter school with energy and enthusiasm that is often labeled as hyperactivity and is then squelched (Hale, 1982). School becomes sterile and boring. The African-American child's assertive style of problem solving tends to be viewed negatively by teachers (Holliday, 1985) so that by age nine or ten "we speculate that teacher attitudes transform young black children's achievement efforts into learned helplessness" (Holliday, 1985, p. 128).

Vann and Kunjufu (1993) believe that African-Americans should have an Afrocentric, multicultural curriculum. That is, they should not have just a European-American viewpoint but also an African-American, Native American, Asian-American, and any other relevant viewpoint in every area of the curriculum. Janice Hale-Benson (1990) reported on a preschool program designed specifically for African-American children and their special characteristics. Visions for Children ". . . offering a teaching method and curriculum which encourages children to learn the information and skills necessary for upward mobility, career achievement, and financial independence in the American mainstream" (p. 199). The curriculum also teaches ethnic cultural pride and the importance of contributing to the development of African-American people. The curriculum is infused with black history and culture while at the same time emphasizing cognitive skills such as reasoning, memory, problem solving, creativity and language. Expressive language skills are a major focus. The daily schedule has a balance of teacher-directed and child-selected activity periods. The Visions for Children Program is paired with a quality conventional childcare center as a control group. Various self-concept, cognitive, and attitude measures will be administered at regular intervals as the children progress through both programs.

As a group, African-American mothers have high aspirations for their children (Washington, 1988). They want their children to be learners and to have a good education. Washington (1988) suggests African-American mothers need to learn to appreciate and apply the people orientation and the movement orientation of young African-American children to enhance their learning at home just as is suggested for enhancing school instruction.

Asian- and Pacific Islander-Americans

Our country's Asian and Pacific Islander population is rapidly increasing. The 1980 census results revealed that the number of people in our population with Chinese, Filipino, Japanese, Korean, Vietnamese, Hawaiian, and Samoan ancestry was double what it was in 1970 (Kitano, 1982). Other groups that have increased in number include Cambodian, East Indian, Guamanian, Hmong, Indonesian, and Laotian (Pang, 1990). Included by the 1980 census in a category of all other Asians were Bangladeshi, Bhutanese, Bornean, Burmese, Celbesian, Cernan, Indochinese, Iwo-Jiman, Javanese, Malayan, Maldivian, Nepali, Okinawan, Sikkimese, Singaporean, and Sri Lankan (Pang, 1990). The Asian and Pacific Islander group is our fastest-growing minority group. "In 1985, the Asian-American population was estimated to be 5.1 million and projected to increase to 10 million by the year 2000, approaching four percent of the national population" (Pang, 1990).

Just as with other ethnic groups, Asian-Americans represent a wide cultural variability. Some pride themselves on being highly assimilated and may even refuse to speak their ancestral language or practice any of their ancestral customs. Others may take a more bicultural approach by maintaining pride and involvement in their ancestral language and customs while also appreciating the need to adopt the mainstream culture in order to move up socioeconomically. Families with longstanding roots in this country may be at odds with new immigrants or with immigrants from other Asian countries. For example, Pang (1990) describes an incident where a Cambodian-American student would not accept help from a Vietnamese-American student because of a long-time an-

tagonistic relationship between Cambodia and Vietnam.

Kitano (1982) cites one study that looked at the learning characteristics of preschool-age Asian-American children. With the exception of the Filipinos, the Asian-American children were as field independent as Anglo-American children. This indicates that they were as task-oriented as the Anglos. The Asian-Americans tended to be reflective in their approach to problem solving. That is, they didn't jump right in with a response but thought their answers through first. Their perceptual-motor development was good. Visual discrimination was also good as far as discriminating forms, figures, letters, and numbers. They didn't know as many letter and number names in English as the Anglo children. Their quantitative concepts were generally as good or better than Anglos'. Kitano (1982) formulated the following conclusions:

- The Asian American cultures are not all the same.
- Within and between groups background experiences differ and teachers must treat each child individually.
- Group achievement rather than competition should be emphasized.
- Korean children seem to possess a low self-concept.
- Learning styles differ between groups, with Samoans and bilingual Chinese children tending to be less creative, Filipino children more field dependent, Chinese more reticent about answering questions posed individually in front of the class, and Vietnamese children more passive.
- Overall the Asian American preschoolers rank well on school readiness.
- Teachers need to keep in mind that each Asian group has its own culture and customs (they do not fit one stereotype).

Research such as that reported by Holloway (1988), and Stevenson and Lee (1990) indicates that the higher achievement levels of students in Japan and Taiwan relative to American students may be related to parental beliefs and practices. Not only do Japanese and Chinese parents tend to set higher standards for achievement, they also tend to believe that effort is just as important, if not more important, than native ability. In this country parents tend to believe native ability to be more important than effort. There is also a tendency to believe that Asian-Americans are all high achievers. Pang (1990) cautions that this assumption does not hold because within each group there is wide variability. All Asian-Americans are not "whiz kids." Also, all Asian and Pacific Islander-Americans do not hold the effort-over-ability belief. Mizokawa and Ryckman (1988) reported a study done in the Seattle public schools comparing the beliefs about school achievement effort and ability held by Chinese, Filipino, Japanese, Korean, Vietnamese, and other Southeast Asian-American students. They also found that overall, Asians attributed success more to effort than innate ability. However, when broken down into the various subgroups they did not fit into one global stereotype. Koreans attributed significantly more to effort than the other groups. All except the Japanese attributed more of their successes to effort than they did failures to lack of effort. The lower socioeconomic level students seemed to find more value in working hard to achieve success. On the other hand they also were more likely to perceive math/science failure as due to lack of ability. The authors of this study emphasize the variability that pervades the Asian cultural groups relative to their beliefs about academic achievement.

Currently we are gaining a better understanding of our Southeast Asian immigrants. Before the 1970s we had very few Thai, Laotian, Cambodian, and Vietnamese immigrants (West, 1983). West agrees with others that teachers need to be aware that Southeast Asians cannot be considered as one homogeneous group. Each group is a separate culture with different languages, customs, and religious beliefs. Morrow (1989) describes the cultural importance of Southeast Asian names. Each of the groups he describes (Vietnamese, Cambodian, Laotian, and Hmong) have distinctive rules regarding how names are sequenced and used. An understanding of name customs would be a good first step in learning the cultures and customs of Southeast Asian students.

Despite the many differences among the Southeast Asian cultures, West (1983) suggests some generalizations that can be made regarding Indochinese customs and beliefs and the school. Teachers need to be aware of the following factors:

- Males and females do not make physical contact of any kind in public.
- Indochinese custom does not permit a person to be patted on the head.
- Teachers are held in great reverence. There is not the informality we tend to have in this country.
- Parents are accustomed to not being involved in their child's education at the school level. They would not think of telling the teacher what to do. PTA and other types of parent involvement would seem strange to them.
- Because Indochinese are used to the lecture method, group activities and independent projects are also new and strange.
- They appreciate compliments from the teacher if given privately.
- Listening is emphasized more than speaking (so they may appear shy).
- Problems are not supposed to be communicated to those outside of the family, so they may seem to be uncommunicative.

As with other cultures, they may be integrated into the classroom by sharing their culture with others. (Figure 19–3). Foods, folklore, and holiday customs may be brought into school. The critical aspect, however, is the teacher's attitude of acceptance.

European-Americans

Historically, European-Americans have been the dominant group in our society. Howard (1993) proposes that it is time for European-Americans to rethink their role in a multicultural country and in the development of multicultural education. European-Americans do share with other Americans that we all came from somewhere else originally. However, we also need to consider that there is great diversity within the European-American culture. Many of our diverse European-American cultural groups were pressured to take on the Anglo-Saxon Protestant image to be "real" Americans. Howard (1993) points out that as the dominant group, they

Figure 19–3 **Parents from different cultures can share their experiences and enrich the diversity of the classroom.**

were not forced to learn about the minority group cultures to survive. Now times are changing and they need to honestly face the inequities of the past and look forward to supporting changes in the future. Howard (1993) further suggests that European-Americans must become more humble and not insist they know it all. They should stop forcing their ideas onto other groups. Further he believes European-Americans need to develop respect for other groups and their right to be themselves. Howard's first suggestion for European-Americans is that they find themselves and define who they are as a people. Then they can begin to become a part of the new multicultural partnerships.

It is important also to recognize that within the European-American culture is contained what is still the largest nonmainstream group that lives at or below the poverty level: the lower-socioeconomic status (SES) Anglos (Garber & Slater, 1983). These Anglo families are under constant economic threat. Their income is always insecure due to the changing economy and due to employment in seasonal industry (such as construction). Their children's cognitive style, language patterns, and motivation make it difficult for them to meet the challenges offered by the middle-class mainstream.

Interracial Children

As the multicultural population increases, so does the population of interracial children (Wardle, 1987; Pang, 1990). According to Wardle (1987) the 1983 census counted 632,000 interracial marriages of which 125,000 were African-American/Anglo. There are also many Asian-American/Anglo and Native American/Anglo children. Other intermarriages include Eurasian, Asian/Latino, Asian/African-American, and Asian/Native Americans according to Pang (1990). Also, many children conceived during the Vietnam war have emigrated to the United States (Pang, 1990).

According to Wardle (1987) we know very little about interracial children and their families. Interracial couples have resisted being studied and their children have conventionally been forced to select the racial identity of one parent. However, parents of the sixties took a broader view and encouraged their interracial children to be proud of their whole heritage. We do not know the degree to which having interracial parents affects the young child's learning. It is especially important to get acquainted with interracial families to understand their beliefs, values, attitudes, and behaviors and help them feel comfortable and welcome in the school setting.

Connecting Cultural Style and Education

In the previous discussion in this unit, the varying learning and teaching styles suggested as being applicable to our various ethnic/racial groups have been described. Asa G. Hilliard, III (1989) discusses the conflict posed between consideration of **cultural styles** and not **stereotyping** our students. Hilliard suggests that we think of style as the personality of a group. His definition of style is "consistency in the behavior of a person or of a group that tends to be habitual" (p. 67). Hilliard suggests the following general points can be made regarding style:

1. Styles are learned, not innate.
2. Like other learned behaviors, styles can be changed.
3. A person can learn to use more than one style and switch when appropriate.
4. Style is deeply rooted and generalizes to cognitive, learning, and behavioral attributes that follow the same rules of style. (p. 67)

Hilliard goes on to explain his belief that children are failing in school not due to a mismatch between teacher and student styles but due to poor teacher delivery of whatever style is used. For example, teachers tend to demand less from students they believe to be low achievers, wait less time for them to respond to questions, provide less support through repeating questions, giving clues, or asking a new question, and a number of other ways treat them differently than those students perceived as high achievers.

Hilliard (1989) believes that style becomes a problem when teachers misread style differences as signs of poor potential or when style differences cause problems in communication. Misreading style differences may result in the teacher "teaching down" to the children and not providing an opportunity for them to fulfill their potential. Teachers need to understand style differences that are not stereotyped but

are based on firsthand observation and use this information to better understand and communicate.

Irvine (1990) lists several areas in which teachers need to develop:

1. Teachers need to be reflective practitioners who are open-minded, observe their students, and make informed decisions.
2. Teachers need to understand the cultural knowledge of their students and use their prior knowledge and culture in their teaching.
3. Teachers need to show caring support for their students through behaviors such as eye contact, facial expression, and body posture.
4. Preservice teachers must have opportunities to observe and teach in model classrooms with minority students where they can use interactive and cooperative teaching methods.
5. Preservice teachers should have opportunities to interact with minority students in non-school settings (i.e., churches or recreational programs) where they can study the culture, interact in a more relaxed way, and face any fears they may have relative to student personal styles of interaction.
6. Teachers need to study the cultures, language, and history of their minority students and capitalize on their students' strengths.
7. Teachers need to include their students' parents and community in the education process.

Teachers also must help their students, no matter what their cultural backgrounds, to view our nation in its pluralistic nature. The social and cultural diversity in our country's population has mandated a multicultural approach to education at all levels. The early childhood educator needs to be aware of the pluralistic nature of our society and to incorporate multicultural education into the curriculum. Ramsey (1982) suggests that teachers first become aware of their own cultural backgrounds and how they relate to the rest of society. Further, they need to face their own biases and prejudices and learn to accept each child individually without im-

KEYTERMSKEYTERMSKEYTERMSKEYTERMSKEYTERMSKEY

cultural styles	stereotyping

posing stereotypes. Once adults have dealt with their own feelings, they are then ready to help children gain a multicultural perspective (Ramsey, 1982). Teachers can help young children enhance their self-concepts and cultural identities by starting with a study of the group or groups represented in their own classroom. They can also stress cooperation and working together. Finally, Ramsey (1982) suggests that young children be made aware of other cultures through concrete experiences such as introducing clothing, food, work, music, and so on from other cultures into the classroom. Stress the similarities rather than the differences among cultures. That is, all cultures have shelter, clothing, food, work, language, and so on.

Multicultural education is not a "topic" presented one week and then forgotten. It is an attitude and an instructional approach that should pervade the whole early childhood program and serve to enhance child development, especially in the areas of self-concept and social concepts. Derman-Sparks (1989, 1993, 1993/1994) point out that young children are already aware of cultural biases (p. 1):

- They notice differences and construct classificatory and evaluative categories very early.

- There are identifiable tasks and steps in the development of identity and of attitudes.

- Societal stereotyping and bias influence children's self-concepts and attitudes toward others.

The early childhood curriculum needs to be not only multicultural, but also anti-bias. "Bias is any attitude, belief, or feeling that results in, and helps justify, unfair treatment of an individual because of his or her identity" (Derman-Sparks, 1989, p. 3). Anti-bias (Derman-Sparks, 1989, p. 3) is defined as follows:

Anti-bias: An active/activist approach to challenging prejudice, stereotyping, bias, and the "isms." In a society in which institutional structures create and maintain sexism, racism, and handicappism, it is not sufficient to be nonbiased ... , nor is it sufficient to be an observer. It is necessary for each individual to actively intervene, to challenge and counter the personal and institutional behaviors that perpetuate oppression.

The anti-bias curriculum uses the ideas of the multicultural curriculum but goes beyond the "tourist" approach in addressing all types of prejudice and working directly with children's developing identity and attitudes by dealing directly with stereotyping, bias, and discriminatory behavior. The anti-bias curriculum is not an add-on but is an integral part of the regular curriculum.

SUMMARY

Competence has its roots in infancy and early childhood learning. Parents and other caregivers are critical parts in supporting optimum child development. Adults vary in their styles of teaching young children. Some approaches enhance learning more than do others. Children seem to thrive when taught in a positive manner with clear communications, high expectations for achievement, mature language, rule-based discipline, and self-regulated control. Both mothers and fathers tend to offer more cognitive stimulation to boys than to girls. As more and more mothers work, fathers are taking a greater part in child care. Parent education and parent involvement are becoming increasingly important.

Cultural and social variations also influence the young child's learning. The adult who works with young children must be knowledgeable regarding their social/cultural background and incorporate this knowledge into curriculum and instructional planning. Our major cultural groups include Anglo-Americans, African-Americans, Hispanic-Americans, Asian- and Pacific Island-Americans and Native Americans. Within and between groups, variation is increased due to specific regional background, length of time in this country, socioeconomic status, and local differences.

Teachers need to understand style differences and incorporate these differences into their instruc-

FOR FURTHER READING

Ambert, A. N., & Alvarez, M. D. (1991). *Puerto Rican children on the mainland*. New York: Garland.

Ayers, W. (1993). *To teach: The journey of a teacher*. New York: Teachers College Press.

Banks, J. A. (1993). Multicultural education: Development, dimensions, and challenges. *Phi Delta Kappan, 75*, 22–28.

Berger, E. H. (1991). *Parents as partners in education*. New York: Merrill.

Boutte, G. S., LaPoint, S., & Davis, B. (1993). Racial issues in education: Real or imagined? *Young Children, 49* (1), 19–22.

Bundy, B. F. (1991). Fostering communication between parents and preschools. *Young Children, 46* (2), 12–17.

Carrasquillo, A. L. (1991). *Hispanic children and youth in the United States: A resource guide*. New York: Garland.

Cath, S. H., Gurwitt, A., & Gunsberg, L. (Eds.) (1989). *Fathers and their families*. Hillsdale, NJ: Analytic Press.

Celebrating diversity and Focus on multicultural teaching. (1992). *Kappa Delta Pi Record, 29*.

Chiang, R. A. (1994). Home-school communication for Asian students with limited English proficiency. *Kappa Delta Pi Record, 30*, 159–163.

DeVillar, R. A., Faltis, C. J., & Cummins, J. P. (Eds.). (1994). *Cultural diversity in schools*. Albany, NY: SUNY Press.

Dunn, R., Dunn, K., & Perrin, J. (1994). *Teaching young children through their individual learning styles: Practical approaches for grades K-2*. Des Moines, IA: Longwood Division, Allyn & Bacon.

Epstein, J. (Ed.) (1991). Parent involvement [Special section]. *Phi Delta Kappan, 72* (5), 344–388.

Escobedo, T. H. (1993). Curricular issues in early education for culturally and linguistically diverse populations. In S. Reifel, Ed., *Advances in early education and day care: Perspectives on developmentally appropriate practice* (Vol. 5) (pp. 213–246). Greenwich, CT: JAI Press.

Gestwicki, C. (1992). *Home, school, and community relations: A guide to working with parents*, (2nd Ed.). Albany, NY: Delmar.

Gullo, D. F. (1992). *Developmentally appropriate teaching in early childhood: Curriculum, implementation, evaluation*. Westhaven, CT: National Education Association.

Hewlett, B. S. (Ed.). (1992). *Father-child relations: Cultural and biosocial contexts*. New York: Aldine de Gruyter.

King, E. W., Chipman, M. F., & Cruz-Janzen, M. (1994). *Educating young children in a diverse society*. Des Moines, IA: Longwood Division, Allyn & Bacon.

Koralek, D. G., Colker, L. J., & Dodge, D. T. (1993). *The what, why, and how of high quality early childhood education: A guide for on-site supervision*. Washington, DC: National Association for the Education of Young Children.

Luster, T., & Okagaki, L. (1993). *Parenting: An ecological perspective*. Hillsdale, NJ: Erlbaum.

Mallory, B. L., & New, R. S. (Eds.). (1994). *Diversity and developmentally appropriate practices*. New York: Teachers College Press.

McAdoo, H. P. (1993). *Family ethnicity: Strength in diversity*. Thousand Oaks, CA: Sage.

McLean, S. V. (1990). Early childhood teachers in multicultural settings. *Educational Forum, 54* (2), 197–204.

Multicultural education bibliography. (1994). *Kappa Delta Pi Record*, (Summer issue).

Phinney, J. S., & Rotheram, M. J. (Eds.) (1987). *Children's ethnic socialization*. Newbury Park, CA: Sage.

Ramsey, P. G. (1986). *Teaching and learning in a diverse world: Multicultural education for young children*. New York: Teachers College Press.

Rogoff, B. (1989). *Apprenticeship in thinking: Cognitive development in social context*. New York: Oxford University Press.

Slaughter, D. T. (1989). Who gets involved? Head Start mothers as persons. *Journal of Negro Education, 58* (1), 16–29.

Slavin, R. E., Karweit, N. L., & Wasik, B. A. (1994). *Preventing early school failure: Research, policy, and practice.* Des Moines, IA: Longwood Division, Allyn & Bacon.

Sleeter, C. E. (Ed.) (1990). *Empowerment through multicultural education.* Albany, NY: SUNY Press.

Spencer, M. B., Brookins, G. K., & Allen, W. R. (Eds.). (1985). *Beginnings: The social and affective development of black children.* Hillsdale, NJ: Erlbaum.

Vold, E. B. (Ed.). (1992). *Multicultural education in early childhood classrooms.* West Haven, CT: National Education Association.

Voyat, G. (1983). *Cognitive development among Sioux children.* New York: Plenum.

SUGGESTED ACTIVITIES

1. The purpose of this activity is to aid students in analyzing their feelings about parents and what parents should do and not do. Complete the following activities. Compare and discuss your responses with a small group in class.
   a. Write a short description of an ideal parent or parents.
   b. Write a description of the way your parents interacted with you. How did they support your learning? Were they active participants? What kinds of rewards did they use? What kinds of punishments? Did they have positive or negative styles?
   c. Compare your two descriptions. Are they the same or different? In what ways?
   d. Write a description of yourself as a parent (as you are or as you think you would be). Write a reaction to your description.

2. Visit a home in which there are one or more preschool/kindergarten/primary children. Observe the mother for 30 minutes and the father for 30 minutes. If the father is not available, observe the mother for one hour. Write down everything the parent and child do when they interact. Analyze and evaluate the material relevant to the Burton White competence categories by looking for the occurrence of the following behaviors:
   a. Does the parent participate in activities as a guide and partner?
   b. Is the child allowed to explore household materials (such as play with pots and pans or a tub or sink of soapy water, or help cook a meal)?
   c. Does the parent trust the child to try things (cut some fruit or a carrot with a sharp knife, climb a ladder, pour his own milk, do a simple errand)?
   d. Does the parent talk to the child a lot and listen to what the child has to say?
   e. Does the parent show an interest in the child's accomplishments?
   f. Does the parent provide a variety of materials and activities?
   g. Does the parent encourage the child to do things on his own but give help when needed?
   h. Does the parent present imaginative suggestions to the child when he runs out of play ideas?
   i. Does the parent reward the child for learning and for doing tasks well?
   j. Does the parent set clear and consistent limits?

   Write a summary profile of each parent observed. If two were observed, compare the behaviors observed. Were there any differences? What were they? Would you conclude that these parents are competent and have a well-developed child?

3. Find four mother/preschooler or father/preschooler pairs with whom to work. Visit them at home and have each pair do a structured teaching/learning task such as those used by Epstein and Evans. For example, you could bring the ingredients and have each pair bake cookies, or you could bring a new puzzle the child has never seen before and ask the parent to teach the child to put the puzzle together. While the parent and child complete the task, write down everything they do and say. Afterwards, assess whether the parent has a positive or negative way of interacting. A positive style with the puzzle task is one in which the parent helps the child by expanding on what he says, asks questions that help him think about what to do, and encourages him

to solve the problem on his own. A negative style is one in which the parent says "no" and "don't" a great deal and tells the child what to do. A positive approach in the cookie-baking task is one in which the parent and child work cooperatively and talk constantly about many subjects, or in which they work cooperatively but talk centers on the baking task activities. A negative style is one in which the child is passive: neither parent nor child says very much and the child has little if anything to do in making the cookies; the parent does most (or all) of the work while the child watches. Categorize the information obtained from each observation.

a. Which parents use positive styles?

b. Which use negative styles?

c. Which children do you feel will do best in first grade in terms of learning? Which will be the lowest achievers?

4. Brainstorm some ways to involve working parents in their child's educational program.

5. Using the information in this unit and some further reading on multicultural and anti-bias curriculum, devise a list of criteria that indicate a classroom is multicultural and anti-bias. Visit several preschool, kindergarten, and primary classrooms. In each classroom note which cultural/social groups are represented. Using your multicultural/anti-bias criteria, note any evidence that the class curriculum is multicultural and anti-bias. If possible, interview each teacher regarding how multicultural and anti-bias curriculum is included in planning for instruction.

a. Evaluate the multicultural and anti-bias curriculum in each classroom.

b. Compare the classrooms. Which met the greatest number of your criteria? Which met the least number of your criteria? Overall did you find teachers had cultural and bias awareness?

6. Make an entry in your journal.

REVIEW

A. Decide which of the following comments are by people competent in their adult role in children's learning. (See White and associates' and Carew's list of characteristics.)

1. "Don't bother me when I'm working. You get in my way."

2. "Would you like to help me clean? Here, I have an extra sponge for you."

3. "You can help me cut the carrots."

4. "Do you need some help? I'll be right with you."

5. "Play in your room quietly where you won't bother me."

6. "What a beautiful picture you drew. I'll tape it on the refrigerator where everyone can see it."

B. Decide whether the following examples are positive in teaching style or negative in teaching style.

1. Mother is trying to teach Matt how to put his trousers on correctly. "First, find the front." Matt turns them backwards. "How do you know which is front and which is the back?" Matt examines the trousers. "Oh, the zipper is in the front." "Good, Matt, that's right. Now put your legs in." He gets both legs in the same pant leg. "What happened, Matt?" He looks at the situation and pulls one leg out and puts it into the other pant leg.

2. Mother is trying to teach Mark how to put his trousers on correctly. "This is the front," she reminds him. Mark starts to put them on backwards. "No, Mark! Not that way. The zipper goes in the front." Mark gets both legs in the same trouser leg. "Don't do it that way, Mark. Here, let me do it for you."

3. Dad is showing Patty how to hammer in a nail. Patty hits the nail and it bounces out. Dad says, "No, Patty, you must hold the nail like I showed you. Don't do it that way again."

4. Mother and Mario are making pizza. Mario watches as mother rolls out the dough and puts the sauce and the other ingredients on.

5. Dad and Johnny are making biscuits for Sunday breakfast. "This is a two-cup measure, Johnny. Measure out two cups of flour while I get the milk and the baking powder." Dad returns with the milk and baking powder.

   Johnny: "O.K., Dad."

   Dad: "Yes, great. Pour it in the bowl."

   Go back to the negative comments and suggest alternative ways to handle each situation.

C. Discuss your opinion of multicultural and anti-bias education. Do you feel that adults have to take on different role behaviors in teaching children from different cultural/social groups? Apply the ideas discussed in the unit.

Cognitive Growth and Development from Preschool to Primary

In this section, we will look at children's cognitive development in more detail: how they think and remember, and how they learn to speak, read, and write. We will also look at the question of intelligence and creativity. Young children are especially fascinating because they view the world so much differently than older children and adults. As preview to this section, we will meet Ramona Quimby, a fictional child who typifies the kinds of behaviors that make young children so special. We will meet Ramona at ages four, five, and eight.

RAMONA AT AGE 4

At age four Ramona is characterized as a big problem by her big sister "Beezus" (Beatrice) who is 9 years old. Ramona's character illustrates some typical four-year-old thinking and behaviors. Ramona is fixated on the book *The Littlest Steam Shovel*. She refers to the main character as "my Scoopy." She demands to have it read over and over. Her mother and

father have found ways to avoid these repeated readings so Beezus gets the brunt of the requests. Ramona has the story completely memorized word for word and if Beezus makes any changes she immediately corrects her. Beezus decides to take Ramona to the library to get another book. Much to Beezus's dismay Ramona selects *Big Steve and the Steam Shovel*—another steam shovel book!

Beezus intends to check the book out on her card but Ramona wants a card. Beezus explains that she has to be able to write her name to get a card. Ramona claims that she does know how to write her name, so the librarian fills in the necessary information. Ramona signs:

She has watched Beezus write *Beatrice* and from her four-year-old point of view signing your name means making some wavy lines with dots and cross lines. Ramona's behaviors are vexing but, as we shall see, make sense in terms of what we know about how four-year-olds think and reason and how they apply their cognitive skills to an emerging knowledge of written language.

Another four-year-old characteristic demonstrated by Ramona is imagination. Her mother comments, "Oh, you know Ramona. Her imagination runs away with her" (Cleary, 1955, p. 40). Ramona sits in the middle of the livingroom in her empty plastic wading pool pretending she is in a boat in the middle of a lake. Ramona walks along with a string dragging behind. On the end of it is Ralph, her imaginary green lizard. Ramona uses marshmallows as powder puffs to powder her nose like a grownup woman would. Sometimes her imagination and her literal view of things leads to what, from an adult view, is faulty reasoning. For example, pretending that she is Gretel (*Hansel and Gretel*) and her doll is the witch, she pushes the doll into the oven in which a cake is baking. Needless to say, the result is disastrous for both the cake and the doll.

To sum up, Ramona at age four views the world at face value, is showing signs of an interest in reading and writing, has a vivid imagination that is reflected in her dramatic play, and tries the patience of her sister and parents.

RAMONA AT AGE 5

At five, Beezus views Ramona as not just an annoyance but as a full-blown pest. At age five, Ramona is very excited as she is entering kindergarten. She has also just learned to skip. She skips around the livingroom, singing as she waits to leave for school. For Beezus, this behavior is immature and she views Ramona as a pest.

Ramona is still a literal thinker, taking everything at face value. Her kindergarten teacher, Miss Binney, tells her, "Sit here for the present." Of course, Miss Binney means "temporarily" while Ramona assumes she is a special person who will receive a gift. "Ramona wondered if her present would be wrapped in fancy paper and tied with a ribbon like a birthday present" (Cleary, 1968, pp. 17–18). The class learns a new song about "the dawnzer lee light." Ramona is puzzled because she is not sure

what a "dawnzer" is. Miss Binney reads *Mike Mulligan and the Steam Shovel* to the class. Mike and his steam shovel spend the whole day digging the basement for the town hall. During the discussion after the story, Ramona has an important question. She asks, "Miss Binney, I want to know—how did Mike Mulligan go to the bathroom when he was digging the basement of the town hall?" (Cleary, 1968, p. 23). Miss Binney is rather taken aback while the other children all seemed to have the same question in the back of their minds.

RAMONA AT AGE 8

At age eight, Ramona is into a new stage of development. She is about to enter the third grade at a new school. Reading, writing, and arithmetic are well in hand. However, Ramona's thinking, although more abstract, is still not completely out of the literal stage. She's still very concrete in her view of things. In fact, she is now overboard in the degree of accuracy she demands.

> Ramona had reached the age of demanding accuracy from everyone, even herself. All summer, whenever a grown-up asked what grade she was in, she felt as if she were fibbing when she answered, "third," because she had not actually started third grade. Still, she could not say she was in the second grade since she had finished that grade last June. Grown-ups did not understand that summers were free from grades.

She can now understand the nuances of adult speech. When her teacher Miss Whaley says the label she has made for her fruitfly jar is 'neat' Ramona knows she means extra good, not tidy.

Ramona is industrious when it comes to creative projects. When given the assignment of giving an oral book report that sells the book, she writes a TV commercial and constructs props for the presentation.

Now Ramona is stuck after school with playing with four-year-old Willa Jean. Willa Jean does all the things Ramona did that annoyed Beezus when Ramona was four. Ramona is driven to distraction by repetition.

Ramona is now concerned with acting grown-up and mature. She has reached a level of cognitive development in which she can understand some of the problems now faced by her family. Her father has changed to part-time work so he can attend college, and her mother has gone to work full-time. She is also more on a level with Beezus now. They can discuss their concerns and develop mutual decisions.

In the following units, we'll look at cognitive development from preschool to primary. As you read each unit, keep Ramona in mind.

The Ramona books are authored by Beverly Cleary:

(1955). *Beezus and Ramona*. New York: Yearling. (Ramona, age four)
(1968). *Ramona the Pest*. New York: Yearling. (Ramona, age five)
(1981). *Ramona Quimby, Age 8*. New York: Yearling. (Ramona, age eight)

Unit

20

The Cognitive System

OBJECTIVES

After studying this unit, the student should be able to:

- Define cognition.
- Identify cognitive behaviors.
- Recognize parts of the cognitive structures and cognitive process.
- Name Piaget's stages of cognitive development and identify the major characteristics of the sensorimotor and preoperational stages.
- Recognize and explain examples of centering.
- Draw a model of the cognitive system.
- Describe metacognition and provide an example of instruction that enhances metacognitive thought.
- State the significance of right and left brain functioning.

The term **cognitive** has already been used numerous times in this text in referring to certain types of child behavior. In this section, the term will be defined and described in more detail and applied to the preschool, kindergarten, and primary child's concept and language development. In this first unit, the term *cognitive* is defined and various views of cognition described. The cognitive system, which includes cognitive development, structure, and functioning, is examined. Finally, the significance of brain development and functioning is considered.

COGNITIVE DEFINED

Cognitive pertains to the mind and how it works. The cognitive system is made up of three parts.

KEYTERMSKEYTERMSKEYTERMSKEYTERMSKEYTERMSKEYTERMSKEY

cognitive

- **Cognitive functioning** describes how the cognitive system works.
- **Cognitive structure** includes all the parts of the cognitive system.
- **Cognitive development** refers to changes in cognitive structure and functioning that may take place over time.

The term refers both to what is in the mind (what the child knows) and how the mind works (how the child thinks). Of course, we cannot see directly into the mind; so we must guess what is happening in the child's mind from what he does. For example:

> Three-year-old Bill is playing with some small blocks. The blocks are several colors. Bill says, "This one is blue, this one is red, this one is green." He looks up at his mother, saying, "These blocks are all different colors."

From Bill's behavior, we can guess that he had formulated in his mind some idea about color. First, he can match the names blue, red, and green to the correct block. Second, he knows that blue, red, and green are all colors (Figure 20–1). In Bill's mind are stored the ideas of blue, red, and green in a place for "color"; this is an example of cognitive structure. The idea of each color enters Bill's mind first. Next, the idea of color enters and becomes the place in which to store the ideas of red, blue, and green.

In the example of Bill and the blocks, cognitive functioning denotes what happens as each color idea enters Bill's mind, is stored for future use, remembered when needed, and applied to some problem Bill wishes to solve. In this case, he matches the color names to the blocks with which he is playing.

Copple, DeLisi, and Sigel (1982) reviewed the history regarding the different theoretical views of cognitive development. Up until the middle of the twentieth century, learning theory and psychoanalytic theory served as the basis for our view of cognitive development. The learning theory view of cognitive development saw cognitive growth from childhood to adulthood as a change in quantity of knowledge but not quality. That is, children and adults learn in the same way; their behavior just

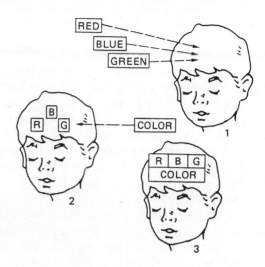

Figure 20–1   **Bill learns that red, blue, and green are all colors.**

changes as new learning takes place. Learning theory was clear-cut and easily adaptable to education and, therefore, became the popular point of view.

Psychoanalytic theory recognizes qualitative differences in learning during different periods of development. Emphasis is on personality development and the development of a strong self-concept. With a strong self-concept the child is free to learn, solve problems, and know (Copple et al., 1982).

Also during this century, the testing movement became popular. Intelligence tests were developed, designed to measure cognitive development and compare each child with other children of the same age. The work of Jean Piaget brought still another view of cognition into focus. Piaget worked in the laboratories of Binet when the early intelligence tests were being developed. Piaget became fascinated with children's wrong answers and why they came up with these answers. Piaget developed the clinical interview method to find out how children's thinking changed as they grew and developed. The purpose and format of the clinical interview is much different from that of the intelligence test (Copple et al., 1982). We have already looked at the types of tasks Piaget developed to study the cognitive development

KEYTERMSKEYTERMSKEYTERMSKEYTERMSKEYTERMSKEY

Cognitive functioning   **Cognitive structure**   **Cognitive development**

of infants and toddlers. In this section we will examine the clinical interview methods used with the preschool, kindergarten, and primary age child.

Language development is an important part of cognitive development. In the late 1950s and early 1960s, Noam Chomsky (Copple et al., 1982) contributed new ideas on the development of language that went beyond the then current learning theory view. The study of language changed from just the study of grammar to the study of language meaning and language use. These areas will be discussed in Unit 22.

The development of the computer has also had an impact on our view of cognitive development. The computer gives us a model for looking at complex cognitive processes (Copple et al., 1982). With the computer, we can study some of the complex functioning involved in input, transformation, storage, retrieval, and output processes. Information processing approaches to cognitive development have grown out of the studies of computer models of cognitive processing (Klahr, 1989). A model of this type will be discussed later in this unit. More recently, Vygotsky's and Bandura's views of cognitive development have come into more prominence. These theories will also be discussed.

COGNITIVE DEVELOPMENT

Piaget found the child uses his mind in a different way in each period of cognitive development. He identified four periods of cognitive development (Figure 20–2). Between the ages of three and eight, children pass through the preoperational period and enter the concrete operational period. Young children usually enter concrete operations some time between the fifth and the eighth year. The **formal operations period** usually does not appear until early adolescence, around 11 or 12 years of age.

The sensorimotor period was discussed in Sections II and III. It is during this period that sensory and motor modalities dominate learning. The child also develops and learns through motor activity. Skills such as grasping, crawling, creeping, standing,

and walking develop during this period. Once he can move, the sensorimotor child is everywhere exploring busily (Figure 20–3).

The toddler is passing from the sensorimotor into the preoperational period. This period may last from around the age of two until about seven. Between ages five and seven, there is a transition period or time of change during which the child is moving into the next period. A child may reach concrete operations at five or at seven or sometime in between. During the **preoperational period**, the focus of development changes from sensory and motor to language and speech. The child develops almost all the speech skills he will use through the rest of his life. After the preschool period, language becomes more complex but by four the child usually has developed most of the basic skills.

The preoperational child learns through pretend play. He views the world from his own point of view and believes only what he sees in the way he sees it. Although his mind works more like an adult's than does an infant's, it is still operating differently. The child comes up with many ideas that seem wrong to adults but are right within the limits of the way the young child can think. For example:

- Two-year-old Kate calls all small, furry animals "ki-ki." This includes cats, dogs, rabbits, and squirrels.
- Three-year-old Bill pours his milk from a short, squat glass into a tall, thin glass, "Now I have more milk." The milk looks taller so there must be more of it (even though it is actually still the same amount).

During this period, the child learns new skills through the imitation of others. He also begins to use one thing to represent something else. For example, he may use sand as food, a doll as a real baby, or a stick as a gun in his play. As the child matures, the child can pretend that an object is there and does not need a real or a substitute object. He can eat from imaginary plates, sleep in imaginary beds, and play with imaginary friends. Also, as the child moves to

formal operations period   preoperational period

Age	Period
Birth to two	Sensorimotor
Two to five	Preoperational
Five to seven	Transition: preoperational to concrete operations
Seven to eleven	Concrete Operations
Eleven through adulthood	Formal Operations

Figure 20–2   **Piaget's periods of cognitive development.**

the later stages of the preoperational period, he moves from simply imitating the actions of others to "becoming" the person he is imitating. That is, he *is* the soldier, the father, or the grocer. Along with this comes play acting long, involved themes such as going on a trip or buying things at the shopping mall. Lillard (1993a) suggests that between ages two and four children's pretend representational play provides a zone of proximal development in which they participate in nonreal activities and places. They do not yet view these realities as being housed in the mind but take the behaviors and activities at face value.

The **transition period**, from five to seven, is very important (Gardner, 1982). During this time, the way the child thinks changes from preoperational to **concrete operational period**. We only know when this change takes place through observation of and interviews with children. This is the time when most children start school. Just how ready a child is for the first grade depends on whether or not he has passed through the transition. The adult working with young fives and sixes must help them through the transition. During this period of shift from preoperational to concrete operational thought, a number of changes take place. The child uses language to direct his own activities and the activities of others. He is able to see another's point of view and to consider it along with his own. He is no longer as easily fooled by the way things look as he was before.

- At age five, Kate recognizes and names many kinds of small, furry animals correctly and knows that they all fall under the label "animal."

- When Bill, now six, pours his milk into a taller, thinner glass he knows and can tell that, "The glass is taller but it is also thinner—there is the same amount of milk."

During kindergarten and the primary grades we can expect that children will be in the transition stage from preoperational to concrete operational ways of thinking (Figure 20–4).

Figure 20–3   **The child in the sensorimotor period enjoys experimenting with objects.**

transition period   concrete operational period

Figure 20–4   In the concrete operations period, children can keep two or more things in mind at the same time and are able to play games with rules. (From Charlesworth and Lind, *Math and Science for Young Children*, ©, Delmar Publishers)

Supporting Cognitive Development

Support for cognitive development may come in several forms this author finds complementary. From the Piagetian point of view, the child constructs his own knowledge from within. The adult acts as a guide and supplies the necessary opportunities to interact with objects and people (Kamii, 1986). Vygotskian theory emphasizes the importance of scaffolding by an adult or older child in the zone of proximal development (Wertsch, 1985). Comparing the two theories, Brown (1988) notes that Piaget and Vygotsky value both individual and social aspects of knowledge acquisition. Bandura's social cognitive theory adds a further perspective (Perry, 1989). Bandura's theory supplies a framework for " . . . how children operate cognitively on their social experiences and how these cognitive operations, in turn, influence the child's behavior and development" (Perry, 1989, p. 3). All three theorists view the child's increasing ability to handle symbols as the crux of cognition. Children learn through constructing knowledge through acting on the environment, as a result of adult support at the right time, and through observing what others do.

COGNITIVE STRUCTURE

The content of the child's mind and the way it is organized is called the cognitive structure. Within the child's mind, there are units of thought. Large units of thought are concepts. These units of thought are the bits and pieces that are used in the child's thought processes. Simple units that start to develop in infancy were called **schema** (plural: *schemata*) by Piaget. He believed these are partial pictures of what the infant actually sees and experiences. A schema includes the highlights of what the infant perceives. For example, if he has seen a circle once, he will show signs of recognition when he sees it again, but may not realize it is the same shape. As the child stores more schemata in his mind, he gradually develops preconcepts and then concepts. A preconcept or a concept ties several schemata or events together.

During the late sensorimotor and early preoperational periods, the child's schemata join into preconcept groups. Preconcepts may be **overgeneralizations** or **overdiscriminations**. When the child overgeneralizes, he encounters a new thing and places it in his mind in the area where there is something like it. For example, Kate has in her mind a small, furry, four-legged thing she calls "ki-ki." We call it a cat. She sees a new thing that is small, furry, and four-legged (a rabbit) and calls it "ki-ki." She then sees a skunk and next a squirrel. She calls each one "ki-ki." Another child puts a paper bag on his head, saying, "Hat." Then he puts a boot on his head and then a cardboard box. Each time he says, "hat."

While the child overgeneralizes with some things, he overdiscriminates with others. He cannot seem to find a place for certain things that do not look the way they are expected to. For example, John meets his teacher in the supermarket. He looks shocked, hangs back, and clings to his dad. For him this is not the same person he sees each day at nursery school. Mentally, he cannot accept his teacher out of context.

By the time the child is in the late preoperational period, he has acquired some simple concepts. That

schema   overgeneralizations   overdiscriminations is, he has begun to tie his schemata together into groups that have common attributes. These concept groups somewhat resemble those of adults. He begins to store round things together, furry and feathery things together, things with wheels together, and so on. For Kate, ki-ki becomes kitty and belongs with cats. She learns "dog" is associated with furry creatures that bark, jump on you, and lick your face. Both are animals and both are pets. Some kinds of cats are not pets—these are wild animals. Cat, dogs, pets, animals, wild animals are all concepts.

The same thing happens with the concept of animals just described. Look at Figure 20–5. As an infant, the nine schemata enter the infant's mind (1). During the preoperational period, these nine schemata develop into preconcepts (2) and then into concepts such as the three groups in (3): dogs, house cats, and wild cats. Finally, these three concepts group under the broad concept of "animals." These concepts, the raw material that the child uses for thought, make up the cognitive structure (Figure 20–6).

An interesting area of research is called metacognition (Copple et al., 1982). Metacognition refers to knowledge and thinking about cognition.

> "In this game I'm going to move some things while you are out of the room and you have to remember where they were. The first thing will be the blue truck." Chan immediately looks over at the blue truck.

In this example, Chan shows that he knows something about cognition. He realizes that if he wants to remember something it will help to note carefully everything he can about it. Children are much more limited than adults in the breadth of their understanding of the thought processes of themselves and others.

Lillard (1993a) reviewed the research on young children's pretend play and the relation of pretend play, especially representational play, to children's knowledge of the mind. As already mentioned, pretend play appears to be a bridge to an understanding of how the mind works. However, preoperational children don't appear to make the connection between pretend and mental representation. That is, they look at action at face value without an under-

standing that, for example, when a person is pretending a banana is a telephone they have a mental representation (or picture) in their mind of the banana as food and as a pretend telephone (Lillard, 1993b).

Memory is another important area of metacognition. Around the age of four, children seem to be able to understand the relationship between time and memory (Lyon & Flavell, 1993). That is, the longer one is separated from an object or an activity, the harder it is to recall the object or activity. Flavell, Green, and Falvell (1993) found that when young children were asked if the brain is doing anything when a person is sitting still they believed that the brain is essentially empty. Even a large percentage of six- and seven-year-olds did not perceive that the mind is continuously thinking. Young children can be helped to develop better and more efficient cognitive strategies through training in memory strategies and practice in reflecting on their ideas.

Examples of metacognitive research and practice based on metacognition research are described by Berliner (1990) and Casanova (1990). Berliner (1990) states that the research on metacognition shows that when people are more aware of how they are thinking during the instructional process they learn better and remember more. Berliner (1990) describes an experiment of comparison done with children ages five to seven in which one teacher used metacognitive dialogues, another teacher taught facts, and one taught using a project approach. The metacognitive dialog was developed by the teacher asking questions such as what had the children learned from a specific experience; what new things had they learned that morning; how did they know they had learned something new; and what different sources of information had they used to learn about the topic of study. At the end of the unit, the teacher divided the class into small groups and asked each group to prepare materials that they could use to teach others about the topic they had studied. When the children in all three groups were asked about what they had done during the unit, the children from the dialog group showed an awareness that the purpose of the activities was to learn about the

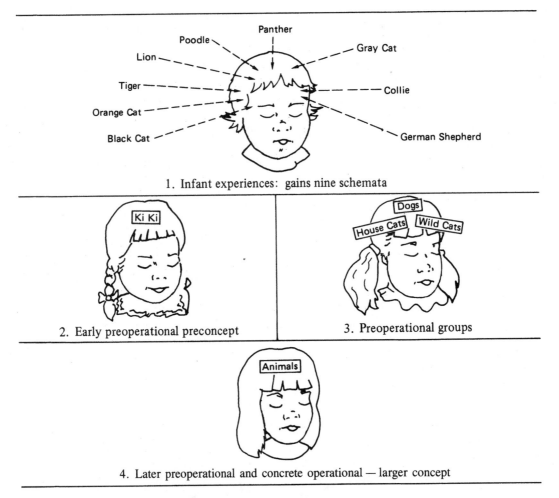

1. Infant experiences: gains nine schemata

2. Early preoperational preconcept

3. Preoperational groups

4. Later preoperational and concrete operational — larger concept

Figure 20–5   Kate's thinking develops from schemata to preconcepts to concepts.

topic. The other children tended to view the activities as ends in themselves.

Casanova (1990) makes some suggestions for practice that can help students think about what they are learning and thus be more efficient learners. For example, suppose a child comes into class with an insect specimen and asks the teacher what it is. Instead of just telling the children or looking it up herself, the teacher can first ask if any of the children know what the specimen is. Then she can ask how they might confirm or disconfirm their ideas. The children might suggest looking it up in a book, asking their parents, etc. Finally after discussing the possibilities, the teacher could as-

sign finding out the insect's name as homework. In this manner, the children learn to think about how to obtain information, they weigh alternatives, obtain information, and eventually decide on an answer. When the children plan, organize information, and make decisions, they are using their metacognitive skills.

COGNITIVE FUNCTIONING

Cognitive functioning refers to the way cognition works. The usual way to picture cognitive functioning is as a sequence that involves a stimulus and then some sort of activity in the mind followed by a

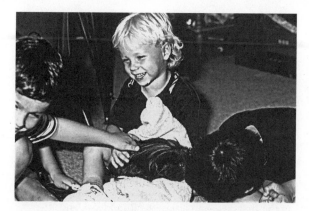

Figure 20–6 Eventually, the child's cognitive structure will find a space other than "kiki" for all small, furry creatures.

response. We can observe the stimulus and the response but not the activity in the mind. All this unobservable activity is cognition. This is an information processing point of view. The stimulus is the **input**, the response is the **output**, and the internal activity is **processing**.

The model of cognitive functioning in Figure 20–7 shows there is a fourth aspect to cognitive functioning—feedback. Following the response or output, there is a response (either external or internal) that serves as another stimulus (or input). At the bottom of the diagram are definitions of input, processing, and output. Input is acquired through perception, which is the interpretation of what is sensed. Once perceived, information is processed. Processing may involve recall, thinking, reasoning, organizing, associating, problem solving, or combinations of all these processes. Output is always some kind of motor expressive activity such as speaking, writing, gesturing, or making facial expressions.

If any of the three aspects of cognitive functioning does not work as it should, a malfunction results. For the child in the preoperational stage, perception works differently than for the older child and the adult. The preoperational child cannot attend (pay attention) to all aspects of the information before him at the same time. This results in the receiving of only part of the available information. Thus, he often comes up with problem solutions that seem

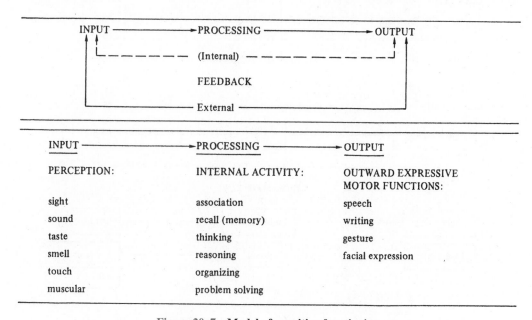

INPUT	PROCESSING	OUTPUT
PERCEPTION:	INTERNAL ACTIVITY:	OUTWARD EXPRESSIVE MOTOR FUNCTIONS:
sight	association	speech
sound	recall (memory)	writing
taste	thinking	gesture
smell	reasoning	facial expression
touch	organizing	
muscular	problem solving	

Figure 20–7 **Model of cognitive functioning.**

KEYTERMSKEYTERMSKEYTERMSKEYTERMSKEYTERMSKEYTERMSKEY

input   output   processing

wrong from the adult point of view. Piaget refers to this process of being overwhelmed by one aspect (such as height) as **centering**. As the child gains more experience perceiving things, he learns more details and gains a more complete overall picture for each schema. As he develops into concrete operations, he is able to attend to, perceive, and process more and more bits of information at the same time.

To show how cognitive function works, consider the following example. A college student, working with three-year-old Celina, gives her a digit-span test, Figure 20–9:

> . . . I utilized a digit span of 2-4-6, followed by 2-4-6-8-1, and the seven-digit span was 2-4-6-8-1-3-5.

I began the activity with Celina. She was able to correctly repeat the first span. The second span was confusing for her. After a few seconds of deliberation she responded with 1-8-6-2. I observed a mild reaction of embarrassment. The seven-digit span was totally lost.

Celina looked amused and offered her own span of 8-9-10. The last digit span seemed to go right over her head, as if she wasn't paying attention.

The input in this case, the three series of digits, was auditory. Processing involved mainly memory (recall), and output was the repeating of the digits (Figures 20–8 and 20–9). There appears to have been some internal feedback as evidenced by the look of embarrassment after her second response and the look of amusement after the third. That is, Celina perceived her own mistakes and responded with embarrassment in the first case and amusement in the second.

In Piaget's scheme, assimilation and accommodation are the functional aspects of cognition. Assimilation is the input aspect and accommodation is the processing aspect.

Problem-solving approaches to learning support more complex cognitive functioning. Berliner's (1990) and Casanova's (1990) examples of metacognition based teaching can be categorized as a prob-

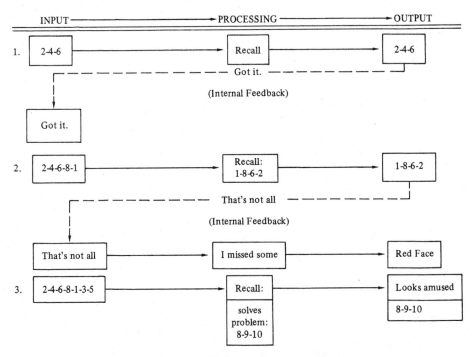

Figure 20–8 Celina's cognitive functioning when presented with three digit-span problems.

Figure 20–9   The preschool child's output may combine verbal and symbolic representation that reflects input and processing. This example shows the child's concept of germs on the teeth.

lem-solving approach. Critical thinking is another name given to problem-solving approaches (Szabo, 1990). Problem solving requires that students be creative and construct their own rules, rather than have rules provided by someone else. Szabo (1990) describes how she applied the theory of critical thinking to her first graders' experience with *The Three Little Pigs* story. First, the children heard several different versions of the story. Then, they retold the story with puppets they made. Next, they analyzed the characters and the situation and the problems that each character had. The children were given the problem of devising puppet shows in which the identified problems were solved. They could change any part of the original story but had to retain the same problems. Finally, they presented their shows to the other first grade classes.

THE BRAIN AND COGNITION

A great deal of interest has focused on how the brain functions in cognitive processing and learning (Languis, Sanders, & Tipps, 1980; Cherry, Godwin, & Staples, 1989). Researchers have been especially interested in how different parts of the brain function in controlling different types of cognitive, sensory, and motor activity. Left- and right-side brain function has been of special interest. Each side of the brain

processes in a different way. In addition, the left side of the brain controls the right side of the body and the right side the left side of the body.

The brain's left side reacts to input in an analytic way. Left-brain processing is logical and organized. It is basic to learning logical ideas and skills such as the rules of speech, reading, and math. The brain's right side controls orientation in space, creative talents, awareness of the body, and face recognition (Ornstein, 1973). The hemispheric functions can be divided as follows (Cherry et al., 1989, p. 13):

HEMISPHERIC FUNCTIONS

Left Brain	Right Brain
• analyzes	• responds to intuition
• uses logic	• uses impulses, spontaneous
• is aware of time	• temporal unawareness
• deals with events in sequence	• random, lack of sequence
• reduces to parts	• holistic — no concern about separate parts
• assembles a whole from parts	• nonverbal: associates words by touching object, not by viewing picture
• systematic	
• verbalizes and processes language	
• sorts and organizes	• diffuses information
• mathematical	• recognizes faces, three dimensional shapes, patterns
• pragmatic	
• cognitive	• responsive to tones, sounds
• factual	• originative, concerned with ideas
• concrete	• sensory
• abstract	• processes imagery, visual
	• symbolic, representational

When input is taken in, each half of the brain perceives it in a different way (Languis et al., 1980; Cherry et al., 1989):

Rudy is painting a picture. The left side of his brain reacts in a logical fashion: the tree must have a brown trunk and branches and green leaves. The right side of his brain reacts emotionally: the paint colors are bright and warm and his arm is moving in motions that feel good and bring a pleasing result on the paper.

If both sides are working together in a complementary fashion, Rudy will paint an original but realistic-looking tree. If the left side dominates, he may be obsessed more with logic than originality and satisfaction. The result might be a realistic but stereotyped tree. If the right side of the brain dominates, logic may be left behind and the tree may have a yellow trunk, purple leaves, and other original looking features.

Languis and associates (1980) point out that educators often emphasize left-side learning and ignore right-side learning. Complete understanding involves integrating both kinds of perception and processing. To tap total creative potential, educators must provide experiences that utilize both sides of the brain.

SUMMARY

The term *cognitive* refers to the mind and how it works. Piaget's view of cognition is widely accepted in early childhood education and development. Other complementary views are those of Vygotsky, Bandura, and Information Processing. Piaget's theory of cognitive development provides four periods of mental growth. From preschool to primary children pass from the preoperational period, through a transitional phase, and into the concrete operations period.

The cognitive structure is made up of bits of knowledge such as schemes, preconcepts, and concepts. Metacognition, or thinking about thinking, is an area of great interest. Research indicates that those who can think about thinking can learn more efficiently and remember more. Cognitive functioning refers to the way cognition works. Information processing models can help us picture how cognitive functioning takes place. Problem solving methods of instruction use metacognitive strategies that make the learners think about how they are learning. Another important aspect of cognition is the theory of left and right brain function. Left-brain function is analytic and organized and applies language to solving problems. Right-side function is more sensory and creative. School learning is conventionally dependent on left-side kinds of functions. The person who is right-brain dominant may have difficulty in adjusting to a left-brain focused curriculum.

FOR FURTHER READING

Astington, J. W. (1994). *The developing child: The child's discovery of the mind*. Cambridge, MA: Harvard University Press.

Baker-Ward, L., Gordon, B. N., Ornstein, P. A., Larus, D. M., & Clubb, P. A. (1993). Young children's long-term retention of a pediatric examination. *Child Development, 64*, 1519–1533.

Britz, J., & Richard, N. (1992). *Problem solving in the early childhood classroom*. Westhaven, CT: National Education Association.

Brown, J. S., Collins, A., & Duguid, P. (1989). Situated cognition and the culture of learning. *Educational Researcher, 18* (1), 32–42.

Butterworth, G. E., Harris, P. L., Leslie, A. M., & Wellman, H. M. (Eds.). (1991). *Perspectives on the child's theory of mind*. New York: Oxford University Press.

Carnine, D. (1990). New research on the brain: Implications for instruction. *Phi Delta Kappan, 71*, 372–377.

Demetriou, A., Efklides, A., & Platsidou. (1993). The architecture and dynamics of developing mind. *Monogr. of the Society for Research in Child Development, 58* (No. 5–6, Serial No. 234).

Elkind, D. (1993). *Images of the young child*. Washington, DC: National Association for the Education of Young Children.

Inhelder, B., de Caprona, D., & Cornu-Wells, A. (Eds.) (1986). *Piaget today*. Hillsdale, NJ: Erlbaum.

Molfese, D. L., & Segalowitz, S. J. (1989). *Brain lateralization in children*. New York: Guilford.

Nelson, C. A. (Ed.). (1994). *Memory and affect in development*. Hillsdale, NJ: Erlbaum.

Pressley, M., & Brainerd, C. J. (Eds.). (1985). *Cognitive learning and memory in children*. New York: Springer-Verlag.

Rogoff, B. (1989). *Apprenticeship in thinking: Cognitive development in social context*. New York: Oxford University Press.

Sternberg, R. J. (1990). Thinking styles: Keys to understanding student performance. *Phi Delta Kappan, 71*, 366–371.

Sternberg, R. J. (Ed.) (1989). *Advances in the psychology of human intelligence, Vol. 5*. Hillsdale, NJ: Erlbaum.

Sternberg, R. J., & Smith, E. E. (Eds.) (1988). *The psychology of human thought*. New York: Cambridge University Press.

Sugarman, S. (1987). *Piaget's construction of the child's reality*. New York: Cambridge University Press.

SUGGESTED ACTIVITIES

1. Observe a child between the ages of three and eight in nursery school, kindergarten, a primary classroom, or during playtime at home. Write down every behavior that indicates the child is using or learning a concept. Some concepts that might be observed are size, shape, number, classification, comparisons, space, part/whole, volume, weight, length, temperature, and time. (Refer to Units 13 and 17 for examples of these concepts.) What do your results tell you about the cognitive structure of this child? Compare your results with those of other students in the class.

2. For 30 minutes during free playtime observe two different preschool groups consisting of children ages two to three and three to four or five. Also, observe a kindergarten class of children ages five and six. Observe 15 minutes each in two of the following areas:

   a. housekeeping
   b. sand or water play
   c. manipulative toy play (puzzles, construction toys, etc.)
   d. blocks

   Make up a chart as shown.

Class age _____		Date _____	
School _____		Time _____	
Symbols Used			
Blocks	Housekeeping	Sand/Water	Manipulative Toys

List each instance of the use of a symbol (the use of something to represent something else). Report the results in class. Which area in the chart showed the most symbolic play? What kinds of symbols were used in each area? What, if any, age differences were noted in terms of the number and kinds of symbols used?

3. Observe one or more toddlers (ages eighteen months to twenty-four months) and one or more two-and-a-half to three-and-a-half-year-olds for 30 to 60 minutes for each age group. Note any instances of overgeneralization or overdiscrimination. Compare the reactions of the age groups. Discuss your observations with other members of the class.

4. Follow a child's activities for 15 minutes. Diagram his cognitive function. (Refer to Figures 20–7 and 20–8.) In your own words, write a description of how the child's cognitive system was functioning during your observation. Refer to your diagrams as you write.

5. Visit the library or contact your instructor for a list of resources. Find a book or an article on children's cognitive development. After reading the article, write a short summary and your reaction to the article. Include the complete bibliographic information:

      title of the article or book
      author(s)
      name of the publication (journal, magazine, book)
      publisher (for books)
      dates
      page numbers

Make copies of your summary for the class and discuss the article during class discussion time.

6. Make an entry in your journal.

REVIEW

A. Write a definition of cognition.

B. Read the following example. Explain your estimation of Mary's cognitive development.

    Two-year-old Mary is playing quietly alone in the kitchen. She has put all the contents of one drawer on the floor and is busily moving objects around and putting them in different piles. She has the long-handled cooking spoons in one pile and short-handled serving spoons in another. A red plastic cork, a set of red plastic measuring spoons, and a red funnel are in another pile. Another pile contains several metal cookie cutters and still another, a wooden rolling pin, a wooden spoon, and a wooden salad fork and spoon.

C. Indicate whether the following examples illustrate (a) cognitive functioning or (b) cognitive structure.

  1. color
  2. a car and a bus
  3. "That animal is a dog."
  4. schemata
  5. thinking
  6. concepts
  7. preconcepts
  8. memory
  9. problem solving
 10. perception

D. Write an *S* for sensorimotor, a *P* for preoperational, and a *C* for concrete operational.

  1. The child learns through pretend play.
  2. The child learns mainly through taste, smell, sight, and touch; and through grasping, crawling, creeping, walking, and climbing.
  3. The child can see another's point of view as well as his own.
  4. The child is an explorer.

5. The child begins to use symbols such as sand for food.
6. The child can coordinate two or more aspects of a problem at the same time.
7. The child learns through imitation.

E. Describe how the concept of *horse* might develop from schema to preconcept to concept.

F. Write the number of each of the following that is an example of centering. State on which attribute the child has centered.
   1. George looks at two groups of blocks. There are five blocks in each group. One group is pushed close together and the other group is spread out. George says there are more blocks in the bunch that is spread out.
   2. A furry creature runs through Mary's yard. Mary has a gray kitten named Jet. Mary calls out, "Jet." The creature (a squirrel) keeps on running. Mary runs after it, crying.
   3. Jane meets Mrs. McGee and her mother, Mrs. Clark. Mrs. Clark is several inches shorter than her daughter. Jane thinks Mrs. McGee is the mother.

G. Read the following behavior description. Diagram the child's activities using the cognitive functioning diagram. Tell which aspects of the description might be labeled cognitive structure. At which stage of cognitive development is this child?

   Ronald is sitting at a table. It is snack time. He reaches for a pitcher of juice, picks it up, and pours some into his cup. Some juice spills on the table. Ronald frowns. He takes his napkin and wipes up the juice.

H. Explain metacognition and how metacognitive skills may enhance learning. Provide an example of a problem-solving approach that makes children think about thinking.

I. Study the following behavioral description. Categorize Kate's behaviors as right brained and/or left brained.

   Kate is a kindergartner. She is very quiet in class, saying very little. She chooses dramatic play and art as her favorite activities. She doesn't care for teacher-directed structured activities or tasks that involve workbook/paper and pencil. She prefers to develop her own learning experiences.

Concept Development

OBJECTIVES

After studying this unit, the student should be able to:

- List the highlights of Piaget's developmental theory.

- Identify the cognitive characteristics of the preoperational child.

- Identify the cognitive characteristics of the concrete operational child.

- Analyze and evaluate a child's behavior when engaged in a concept activity.

- Recognize teaching practice that is consistent with Piaget's theory.

- Explain how Vygotsky's theory helps us understand how young children develop concepts.

"*Concepts* [italics ours] are the cognitive categories that allow people to group together perceptually distinct information, events or items (Wellman, 1982). Concepts form the basic parts of the young child's cognitive structure. Compared to the concepts of older children and adults, young children's concepts seem incomplete and even incorrect. Therefore, they may come up with responses that seem wrong to adults but are right from the children's viewpoints. For example:

A young boy is trying to get his mother to buy him an ice cream cone. The mother is saying no. The boy wants to know why. The mother explains that she does not have enough money. Using child level logic, the boy asks, "Why don't you get some money from the wall?" (that is, the bank money machine) (Goodman, 1991)

The concept that money has to be given to the bank before we can go to the 'wall' and get it back is too abstract for a preschooler. It is not until second or third grade that children can begin to understand where we get money and what we can do with it.

Gelman (1982) proposed that rather than comparing young children's concepts with older persons as if the young children's concepts were in some way

KEYTERMSKEYTERMSKEYTERMSKEYTERMSKEYTERMSKEY

Concepts

deficient, we should look at where young children are developmentally, question them using tasks designed to meet their conceptual level, and appreciate just how much they really do know. Wellman (1982) agrees that preschoolers should be studied in their own right and suggests the following guidelines:

- Compare preschoolers of different ages (versus comparing preschoolers with older children).

- Use measurement tasks which utilize materials and content with which young children have had firsthand experience.

- Develop assessment methods designed for younger children that require less verbal knowledge and cooperation than we expect from older children.

Each concept has various aspects to it. What we want to find out about young children is how far along they are in understanding the parts and putting them together.

THE BASIC CHARACTERISTICS OF PREOPERATIONAL THOUGHT

Piaget's view of early concept development is the most thorough created thus far. It is meaningful to adults who work with young children and applicable to teaching and understanding the young child. Some basic concepts the young child learns (size, shape, number, classification, comparison, space, parts and wholes, volume, weight, length, temperature, and time) have been mentioned. There are also theories concerning concepts as they fit into the broad picture of concept development.

The child who is in the preoperational period, thinks in a manner characteristic of that period. As the child enters the preoperational stage at age two, he has acquired object permanence and has had his first real thoughts and insights. His rate of motor development has leveled off, as he can now walk, run, and climb and he has fairly good small-muscle skills

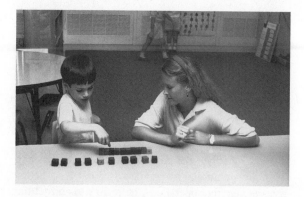

Figure 21–1 **The preoperational child centers on the most obvious evidence and decides the long row has more cubes. The concrete operational child realizes that both groups have the same number of cubes.**

(such as feeding himself, and using a crayon). Acquiring language becomes a major focus of development; representational or symbolic play becomes an essential activity.

The preoperational child's view of the world has been referred to as **egocentric**, meaning that he centers his perception on the most obvious and is bound by what he sees (Figure 21–1). He also tends to feel that seeing is believing. Physical operations cannot be mentally reversed. For example, if some pennies are moved in space, such as from a row to a pile, the preoperational child cannot reverse the moving of the pennies back to the row in his mind. Everyone does not agree with Piaget's conclusion that preoperational children are egocentric (Black, 1981; Gelman, 1982; Lee, 1989) as young children do appear to see another's point of view in certain situations (such as when someone is hurt, they offer sympathy). Lee (1989) suggests that they perceive differently in social than in physical situations. In social situations they seem more able to decenter than in physical situations.

Preoperational thinking is reflected in the young child's everyday actions. Cause and effect are the most obvious associations, such as in "Juanita gave me candy. She is a nice girl." Or "John won't share the clay. He is a bad boy." A person's value (good or bad) is determined by his most immediately observed actions. What the preoperational child sees is what he believes. When something happens to shake that belief, the child is cognitively unable to accept it. Bobby sees a male kindergarten teacher on television. He denies the possibility, thinking, "At my school all the kindergarten teachers are ladies—that's the way it is supposed to be." That is the way he saw it in real life, and that's the way it is to him. The discrepancy is impossible to accept.

At age five, the child may already be passing from preoperational into concrete thinking. As he arrives at concrete operations, he begins to correct the illogical ways (from the adult point of view) of thinking typical of the preoperational period.

THE BASIC CHARACTERISTICS OF CONCRETE OPERATIONAL THOUGHT

As the child enters and proceeds through the concrete operations period the child is able to mentally reverse transformations (such as in the conservation problems that follow). She relies less on the most obvious aspect of a problem and can retain several variables in mind at the same time (Figure 21–2). This period runs from about ages seven to eleven. It is not fully achieved until age eleven or even beyond (Miller, 1989).

Operations are actions that take place internally as part of the organized cognitive structure. Mathematics operations, when presented through concrete tasks, are easily observed. Each step from putting sets in one-to-one correspondence, to operations such as addition, subtraction, multiplication and division grows through the gradual building of a system of mental actions. As we shall see in later units social actions also change as the child enters and proceeds through the concrete operations period (Miller, 1989). Now children can reverse thought, they can decenter, and their thinking is more in line with that of adults. It is very important for adults to keep in mind that "the concrete operations are still 'con-

Figure 21–2 The child who has reached concrete operations can keep more than one attribute in mind and can solve a multiple classification problem. (From Charlesworth and Lind, *Math and Science for Young Children*, © by Delmar Publishers)

crete.' They can be applied only to concrete objects—present or mentally represented. They deal with 'what is' rather than what 'could be' " (Miller, 1989, p. 64). At best, when young children are entering the primary grades they are only in the beginning stages of the concrete operational period.

SOME BASIC CONCEPTS

Classification

One of the most important cognitive skills is the ability to classify and categorize items in the environment. Children learn which items are red, which we use to cover our bodies, which are cars, and which are toys. They also learn that an item may belong to more than one category, such as *red*, *sweater*, and *wool*. **Classification** is also basic to understanding math and science. In math, the concept of sets or groups is fundamental. The child must understand the concept of *apples* and the concepts of *red* and *green* to use these concepts in a problem-solving situation, such as three green apples plus two red apples equals five apples. In science, categorizing is also a basic operation. For example, in geology, minerals are identified by attributes such as color, hardness, and smoothness.

The toddler and the preschool child spend a great deal of time moving objects into different groups. The following examples, noted by two university students, show the contrast between a three-year-old's sorting behavior and that of a five-and-a-half-year-old. Bill is three and Kate is five.

> Bill was given four squares, four triangles and four circles, one each of blue, green, yellow and red. When asked to sort the shapes into a group he sorted them by shape. When asked to divide them another way he spent several minutes reorganizing and came up with the same pattern.

> Kate had been given the same set of shapes. She also piled them first according to shape. When asked to sort them another way she promptly sorted them by color.

Bill, being a typical preoperational thinker, sorted the shapes one way and remained centered on shape when asked to try another criteria. Kate, on the other hand, moving toward concrete operations, could decenter and change to color with ease.

Underlying the ability to classify is knowledge of a number of basic concepts:

- color, shape, and size

- material (such as paper, cloth, wood, and plastic)

- pattern (such as dots, stripes, or plain)

- function (Items share a common use such as all are things to eat with or to write with.)

- association (Items are related to each other but do not perform a common function: milk goes in a cup; matches are for lighting the candle; but you buy them both at the store.)

- class names (such as food, animals, tools, people)

- common elements (All have wheels, all have long hair, all have T-shirts on.)

Conservation

With his inability to decenter, the preoperational child is not yet what Piaget labeled a conserver. The attainment of **conservation** involves the acquisition of the ability to understand the transformation of materials without being fooled by appearances. For example (Figure 21–3). A bunch of pennies is placed in front of the child. Then a transformation is made; that is, the positions of the pennies are changed. In this case, they are spread out. When asked if there is still the same number of pennies or if there are more, the preoperational child will answer "more." The preoperational child centers on the amount of space used and not on the actual number of pennies. Also, she cannot reverse the transformation in her mind. The concrete operations child, on the other hand, says, "There is still the same number, ten." He can reverse the operation in his mind and is not fooled by the amount of space used in each case. He can think about two things at once: the number of pennies and the amount of space.

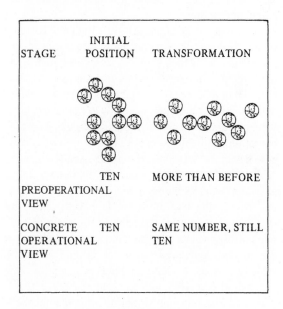

Figure 21–3 **A change in thinking takes place from the preoperational to the concrete operations period.**

The first conservation concept that develops is usually that of number, around age six or seven (Dyrli, 1971). To find out if the child can conserve number, he is first shown one row of ten objects (seven at a minimum) and asked to make a row with the same amount, as shown in Figure 21–4. If the child is unable to construct an equal row, he has not developed the concept of **one-to-one correspondence** and the interview proceeds no further. The younger preoperational child spends long hours of playtime working on one-to-one correspondence. In Figure 21–5, a child lines up some containers and places a horse on each one, one horse for each container. In the task described first, the child who has not developed one-to-one correspondence is likely to produce a row such as the following:

Original Row

Preoperational Child's Row

The child has centered on just length rather than length and number.

Look again at Figure 21–4. If the child demonstrates he does have the concept of one-to-one correspondence, he is then shown a series of transformations such as in 2A, B, and C. In each case, he first agrees that there are two equal rows. Then a transformation is made and he is asked, "Do both rows have the same amount or does one have more?" The preoperational child answers that the longer row in each case has more. When asked why, he usually answers, "cause it's longer." The concrete operational child answers, "There's the same amount. You just moved one row." The transitional child has to check by counting or by putting the pennies back into one-to-one correspondence. As the child moves further into the concrete operations stage, he is able to handle transformations of additional kinds of materials such as a ball of clay made into a pancake or snake; water poured into a tall, thin or short, fat container; or a straight path made into a curved path. In preparation for the time when he can conserve, the preschool child works on the concept of one-to-one correspon-

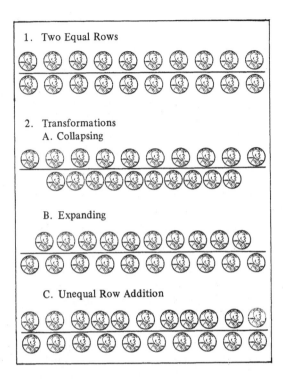

Figure 21–4 **One-to-one correspondence (1. Two equal rows) and three transformations (2. A, B, C).**

dence between objects; on parts and wholes with clay; on volume with water and sand; and on *more*, *less* and *the same* with many kinds of materials.

Although the preschool child cannot solve the number conservation problem, he does have some knowledge of mathematical concepts (Ginsburg, 1980; Gelman & Gallistel, 1983; Charlesworth & Lind, 1995). For example, by age three, he has an understanding of *more* and *less*. When shown two groups of pennies (such as six versus four or five versus nine), he can tell which group has more. By four or five years of age, after agreeing that two groups of pennies have the same amount, when the pennies are hidden in two boxes and one or two pennies are added to one box, he realizes that there are now more pennies in one box than in the other. When a four-year-old is shown two small groups of objects such

Figure 21–5 **The preoperational child spends time matching objects so they pair up in one-to-one correspondence.**

as three blocks and two blocks and asked how many there are altogether, he should be able to solve the problem by using some form of counting. Thus, he demonstrates the beginning of an understanding of addition.

Seriation or Ordering

Preschool children spend much of their time putting things in order according to some criteria such as size, age, or color. This is called **seriation** or ordering. They begin with simple comparisons of big and little, old and young, and light and dark. They then move on to small, middle-sized, and large (big). They delight in stories such as *The Three Bears* and *Three Billy Goats Gruff*, which make use of these concepts. Eventually, the child becomes capable of ordering four or more items. For example, Bill and Kate were asked to order some circles of different sizes.

The next task was seriation. I gave Kate seven circles and asked her to show me the biggest and smallest. She had no problem doing this. When I asked her to put them in order by size from largest to smallest she put them in the following order:

and when I asked her to put them from smallest to largest:

Each time she had the largest and smallest right next to each other.

With the seriation activity for Bill came the most interesting observation. I gave him three circles, a big one, a

seriation

medium one and a small one. He pointed to the biggest and smallest ones correctly when I asked him to but when I asked him to put the three circles in order by size starting with the largest and going to the smallest, he picked up the smallest one and hid it under the largest one. (He did this when asked to try the task another time, also.)

Bill seems to be at the comparison stage at which he can handle only two sizes at once. Kate can see the two extremes in size but cannot yet attempt to put all the midsize circles in sequence. Another common response is the following, in which the child gets the shortest and longest sticks placed correctly but mixes up the sticks in between. The child centers on the ends of the sequence.

1 2 7 4 3 9 5 8 6 10

Space

Development of **spatial concepts** also takes place during early childhood. Spatial concepts include concepts such as in, on, over, under, into, together, beside, between, on top, inside, outside and below. Infants and toddlers begin to develop these concepts as they move their own bodies about and as they experiment with objects. Reifel (1984) suggests that using blocks is an excellent activity for learning about space. The toddler starts with soft spongy blocks that he grasps, tastes, stuffs in containers, places next to each other, and eventually places on top of each other. Preschoolers can use wooden unit blocks as they progress from rows and piles to surfaces, enclosures, and eventually symbolic representations (such as a house or a skyscraper) (Figure 21–6). As structures become more and more complex children experiment with more spatial concepts placed in various combinations.

Figure 21–6   **Unit blocks provide an opportunity for children to work with spatial concepts and informal measurement.**

Causality

Young children ask us many "why" questions. Piaget points out the importance of asking children about their view of why things happen as they do in the world from his research on **causality** (Charles, 1974). Piaget found young children progress from realism to objectivity. Realism refers to the inability of the young child to clearly distinguish between herself and the others around her. As the child sees *I* as separate from the rest of the world, she reaches objectivity. The child who has not yet reached the objective stage will use animism and artificialism relative to things in the world. **Animism** involves giving human characteristics to nonhuman things such as cars, trees, wind, or the sun. **Artificialism** refers to the young child's feeling that everything in the world is made for people. The sun exists to give us light and warmth (rather than, we exist because we have the sun). The three- to five-year-old may answer "why" questions in a number of ways that seem wrong from an adult point of view. For example:

1. He may attribute human-type motivation as the cause of events. For example, we get hurt because we have been bad or it snows because someone wants us to be cold.

KEYTERMSKEYTERMSKEYTERMSKEYTERMSKEYTERMSKEY

spatial concepts	Animism
causality	Artificialism

2. If things are close together in time or space, they are viewed as in a causal relationship.

3. Things are because they are. Dogs have tails because they are part of dogs. The rain falls because it falls from the sky.

4. A person's gestures, thoughts, and words may affect another person. Saying something bad to someone will actually hurt them.

5. Things happen because they have to happen. Airplanes fly so they won't crash. Night must end so day can begin.

The example that follows illustrates a young child's causal reasoning abilities.

Adult	Kate, age four-and-a-half
Are you alive?	Yes.
Why?	Because that's the way God made us.
Is a cloud alive?	Yes.
Why?	Because God made that too.
Is a bicycle alive?	No, because it doesn't talk.
Is a car alive?	Yes, because it runs for real.
Is a tree alive?	No, because it sits there on the grass.
Is a gun alive?	No, because it doesn't talk.

Kate refers to a higher authority as a reason for the existence of herself and clouds. In considering the man-made items and the tree, she has a somewhat animistic interpretation. She decides whether each item is alive or not relevant to the human characteristics of being able to talk or run.

Sophian and Huber (1984) examined children's understanding of the causes of movements of train cars under various conditions. The judgments of three-year-olds and five-year-olds were compared. It was found that children were consistent in the types of rules they used to select which car moved the others. The older children had a much better grasp of the place of time in cause and effect, that is, that cause happens before effect. As a whole, the children did not seem to have the concept that the engine usually caused the train to move by pulling. They just as often decided that the caboose pushed as that the engine pulled. The three-year-olds tended to rely more on these concrete types of cues than the five-year-olds

who used time factors more often in making causal decisions. In a second experiment using different situations, Sophian and Huber found that five-year-olds could benefit from training in solving causal problems whereas three-year-olds could not. Their studies supported that fives are in a transitional stage where they can begin to think in more abstract terms.

Mathematics, Science, and Social Studies

The ideas and examples just described illustrate some of the basic concepts of mathematics, science, and social studies (Charlesworth & Lind, 1990). Price (1982) reviewed the research in all three areas. Later reviews (Castenada, 1987; Hinitz, 1987; Forman & Kaden, 1987) looked independently at each area. The Piagetian view of cognitive development has served as the basis for a great deal of this research. We will look first at mathematics, then science, and finally social studies.

A number of researchers have tried to accelerate mathematics learning through special training while others have tried to show that if assessed in a different way, children actually know more than Piaget gave them credit for knowing (Price, 1982). There is disagreement as to whether the same concept is being tested if you change the tasks you give the children. For example, Gelman and Gallistel (1983) simplified the number conservation task for two-, three-, and four-year-old children. They used much smaller groups of items (such as two to five) and showed that very young children do have some concept of one-to-one correspondence and counting. However, to be conservers of number, children must be able to work with sets of ten or more.

Many young children can understand simple addition and subtraction if allowed to use counting strategies to arrive at an answer (Price, 1982). They can also solve simple verbal problems long before they are acquainted with written mathematical symbols. Understanding of geometric and spatial concepts seems to be related to having an opportunity to talk about and use the language that relates to the concepts.

A great deal of the research with young children has focused on their counting skills more than on their understanding of number (Castenada, 1987). A developmental sequence for counting skills and the eventual application of counting skills to addition and subtraction has been identified. Although counting skills are important tools, they are not the sum total of early childhood mathematics. Not only are other important fundamental concepts such as number sense (an understanding of what oneness, twoness, threeness, etc. mean), conservation, classification, and seriation in the process of development but more important than just rote learning is the development of an understanding of mathematics (Charlesworth & Lind, 1995).

As described in Unit 19, significant research has been done looking at how children in different cultures develop mathematics concepts and at the factors that promote mathematics achievement in school. Both cultures within the United States and cultures in other countries have been studied and compared. Researchers have been particularly intrigued at the advanced mathematical achievement of Asian elementary students both here and in their native countries (i.e., Stevenson & Lee, 1990, and studies mentioned earlier in the text). Ginsburg et al. (1989) found that within this country it appears that upper middle class Anglo American and Asian American four-year-olds tend to be ahead, while African Americans and Hispanic Americans and middle class Anglo Americans tend to be about equal in mathematical knowledge before they enter school. Ginsburg et al. (1989) did their assessments using concrete materials that were familiar to the children. In the Ginsburg et al. studies, all the four-year-olds had rudimentary mathematical knowledge such as being able to count into the teens and do concrete addition and subtraction problems. Saxe, Guberman, and Gearhart (1987) documented the variety of mathematical activities that are included in the everyday social interactions of preschoolers at home.

Entwisle and Alexander (1990) assessed the beginning of first-grade mathematics status of large comparable samples of African-American and Anglo-American students; the assessment took place in Baltimore and was measured by the California Achievement Test (CAT), administered in the fall of first grade entrance. There were no significant differences between the two racial groups at that time. By the end of the year, the Anglo-American students had moved ahead. The researchers concluded that there is something happening in school that results in this disparity. There was also a social class difference with improved performance in children whose parents had more economic resources. Parents' expectations were also a potent force in level of achievement (as was discussed in an earlier unit).

Forman and Kaden (1987) define **child science** as the child's gradual acquisition of the knowledge that some constants exist in the world and that there are reasons for these constants. Forman and Kaden (1987) take a cognitive-developmental point of view regarding developmental theory, learning theory, and instructional theory. From this point of view of science instruction, children explore and construct ideas while the teacher supports their endeavors. The children are immersed in a rich problem-solving environment that encourages them to reflect on their own thinking (Forman & Kaden, 1987).

Studies have emerged that look at young children's concepts of heat, ordering, causality, levers, weight, length, earth and heaven, time, gears, and life and death (Price, 1982; Forman & Kaden, 1987). There is still much to be learned regarding the developmental stages underlying the understanding of science concepts. Research on science instruction supports the superiority of the hands-on approaches compared to the didactic textbook approaches (Forman & Kaden, 1987).

Those in social studies education perceive it as the dominant theme that underlies the curriculum (Hinitz, 1987). All the basic concepts can be constructed through social studies activities (Charlesworth & Miller, 1985). Economic concepts, geography and spatial relations, history and temporal relations, and sociology have all been the focus of early childhood social studies research (Hinitz, 1987). Social behavior and social thinking has been the focus of more research than content areas such as history, geography, anthropology, political science, economics, and sociology. Research on social behavior and social thinking is the focus of Section VII of this text.

APPLICATION OF THE CONCEPT DEVELOPMENT THEORY

This overview of concept development has outlined many of the concepts that are developing during early childhood. In this final part of the unit, we will look at how the concept development theories of Piaget and Vygotsky are related to educational practice.

Applications of Piaget's Theory to Instruction

There are a number of ways Piaget's ideas may be applied to teaching young children. There may be applications for teaching (what the teacher does), for curriculum planning (what children can learn), and for diagnosis (where the child is at a certain point in his development). These applications come in the form of guiding principles rather than as specific ways to teach specific skills and concepts. Ginsburg and Opper (1979) recommend the following principles based on what they feel Piaget's work suggests for teachers:

- Education should be child centered. It should be designed from the child's point of view rather than from the adult's. Adults need to remember that children see things differently.
- Learning occurs best when it comes from self-initiated activity. This should include the use of real objects and the use of thought. We learn most from our reactions to our own activity. That is, the child who spends hours placing her blocks in rows and putting a peg person on each one, learns one-to-one correspondence from the activity itself and from her reactions to it. For example, finding that she has the same number of blocks as she has people, she will repeat the activity over and over as if to confirm that this is true. She may then label the colors of the blocks and count the number of blocks and peo-

ple. Children should have opportunities for guided discovery.

- There is a wide range of development within a group of children. This underscores the need for individualized approaches to teaching and learning. Teachers need to find out where the child is to plan learning experiences that fit his level of development. The child needs a chance to work on his own.
- Social interaction assists the child in modifying his egocentric point of view. Through his interactions with other children, he finds that everyone doesn't have the same opinion as he does. He also learns that if he wants to convince others that he is right, he must develop a clear, logical argument.
- The child's learning is limited by the stage in which he happens to be. The stage also indicates which concepts the child should know or be in the process of learning.
- The interview techniques which Piaget has developed tell us how the child thinks. The Piagetian interviews tell us which stage a child is in relative to concept development.

As described by Roopnarine and Johnson (1993), Piaget's work has inspired a number of approaches to teaching practice in a constructivist framework. Leaders in this field are Constance Kamii, Rita DeVries, George Forman, and Loris Malaguzzi (Reggio Emilia in Italy). They each have their own interpretation of constructivism. Their basic differences focus on how directive the adult can be and how specific the materials and activities can be geared. They all agree that children should work with concrete materials and should be encouraged to reflect on their actions in order to develop real understandings.

Applications of Vygotsky's Theory to Instruction

From Vygotsky's theory, as already discussed, we obtain a theoretical perspective for the importance of social interaction as support for children's learning (scaffolding) and for providing the right kind of support at the right time (the zone of proximal development). To the Piagetian perspective of inner construction of knowledge is added an emphasis on the adult and/or other children providing support for concept development and acquisition. Vygotsky's theory provides a perspective for adding a structure to children's experience and knowledge. Vygotsky provided us with the view that the adult-child interdependence is central to instruction (Moll, 1990). Vygotsky's theory has been applied to instruction in preschool literacy instruction, writing instruction, instruction in the home, science instruction, and instruction for mildly retarded and learning disabled children (Moll, 1990). Combining the Piagetian-inspired views and the Vygotskian-inspired views into a post-Piagetian approach to instruction has added recommendations for "specific interactions and interventions in the process of children's knowledge construction, though they [Piagetians and post-Piagetians] similarly favor 'active methods' because of their shared constructivist view (Inagaki, 1992). This post-Piagetian approach to constructivism, as compared with the purely Piagetian constructivism, provides for more teacher direction such as using open-ended questions and providing materials that lend themselves to particular kinds of actions.

SUMMARY

Concepts are the cornerstones of thought. Young children actively construct basic concepts such as classification, conservation, ordering, space, and causality.

The theories of Jean Piaget and Lev Vygotsky help us to understand young children's concept development and acquisition. Piaget's ideas have been especially helpful in offering many ideas that can be applied by adults to their work with young children. Piaget's theory of constructivism and his periods of cognitive development have become increasingly popular as guides in the designing of early childhood education programs.

Figure 21–7   Sand and/or water offer open-minded experiences that can be explored by the child in their own ways.

The preschool child from ages two through four is in the preoperational period. During this period representational activities are critical for concept development. Between five and seven, children progress into a transition period which takes them into concrete operations. During each period these children have unique ways of thinking that are different from those of adults or older children. To move through each stage at the pace his capacities allow, young children need to be active in their own learning processes. Adults must provide a rich environment for exploration where children are free to construct their own knowledge (Figure 21–7).

Research in the development of mathematics, science, and social studies concepts during early childhood provides us with some insight into how children develop their understanding in these content areas. Piaget's theory has inspired the development of a number of curricular approaches. Vygotsky's conceptualizations of the zone of proximal development and scaffolding are becoming important guides in our consideration of young children's concept learning.

FOR FURTHER READING

Backscheider, A. G., Shatz, M., & Gelman, S. A. (1993). Preschoolers' ability to distinguish living kinds as a function of regrowth. *Child Development, 64*, 1242–1257.

Barrett, S. E., Abdi, H., Murphy, G. L., & Gallagher, J. M. (1993). Theory-based correlations and their role in children's concepts. *Child Development, 64*, 1595–1616.

DeVries, R., & Kohlberg, L. (1990). *Constructivist early education: Overview and comparison with other programs*. Washington, DC: National Association for the Education of Young Children. (Original work published 1987)

Fabricus, W. V. (1993). Two roads diverge: Young children's ability to judge distance. *Child Development, 64*, 399–414.

Forman, G. E., & Hill, F. (1984). *Constructivist play: Applying Piaget in the preschool*. Menlo Park, CA: Addison-Wesley.

Fuson, K. C. (1988). *Children's counting and concepts of number*. New York: Springer-Verlag.

Ginsburg, H. P. & Russell, R. L. (1981). Social class and racial influences on early mathematical thinking. *Monographs of the Society for Research in Child Development, 46* (6).

Inhelder, B., de Caprona, B., & Cornu-Wells, A. (Eds.) (1988). *Piaget today*. Hillsdale, NJ: Erlbaum.

Kamii, C., & DeVries, R. (1978). *Physical knowledge in preschool education: Implications of Piaget's theory*. Englewood Cliffs, NJ: Prentice-Hall.

Kohn, A. S. (1993). Preschoolers' reasoning about density: Will it float? *Child Development, 64*, 1637–1650.

Lave, J. (1988). *Cognition in practice: Mind, mathematics, and culture in everyday life*. New York: Cambridge University Press.

Marzolf, D. P., & DeLoache, J. S. (1994). Transfer in young children's understanding of spatial representation. *Child Development, 65* (1), 1–15.

Neisser, U. (Ed.) (1988). *Concepts and conceptual development*. New York: Cambridge University Press.

Peters, D. L., Neisworth, J. T., & Yawkey, T. D. (1985). *Early childhood education: From theory to practice*. Monterey, CA: Brooks/Cole.

Rogoff, B., & Lave, J. (Eds.) (1988). *Everyday cognition*. Cambridge, MA: Harvard University Press.

Scholnick, E. K. (Ed.) (1983). *New trends in conceptual representation: Challenges to Piaget's theory?*. Hillsdale, NJ: Erlbaum.

Soja, N. N. (1994). Young children's concept of color and its relation to the acquisition of color words. *Child Development, 65*, 918–937.

Thomas, H., & Lohaus, A. (1993). Modeling growth and individual differences in spatial tasks. *Monogr. of the Society for Research in Child Development, 58* (9, Serial No. 237).

SUGGESTED ACTIVITIES

1. With a group of fellow students, pool items taken at random from your purses or pockets. Study the items. Pretend you are a young child. Group the items according to the categories of classification. What are the bases for your groupings? (You might use color, material, pattern, function, association, class names, or common elements.) Compare your choices with the other students in your group. See how many different kinds of groups can be developed by grouping and regrouping. What is the difference between what you would do as a young child and what you do as an adult?

2. Think about how Piaget's ideas relate to your past, present, and future work with children. Discuss your ideas with a small group in class. Develop some questions to clarify your ideas. List the questions on the blackboard or on a large sheet of newsprint or chart paper. Present the questions to the instructor and other class members for a response.

3. Try the following basic concept interview tasks with two or more young children. Compare the responses from each. In which Piagetian stage would you place each child? Why? Report your results in class. Your report should include:
   a. the questions asked/tasks presented to each child
   b. the child(ren)'s specific responses
   c. results and conclusions:
      1) What did you learn about each child?
      2) Which stage is each child in?
      3) How did you feel about the whole experience?

PREKINDERGARTEN BASIC CONCEPT INTERVIEW TASKS

TASK 1: CLASSIFICATION

Instructions: Place in front of the child twelve objects: 2 red, 2 blue, 2 green, 2 yellow, 2 orange, 2 purple. Use at least four or five different kinds of things. For example:

Color	Object 1	Object 2
red	bead	block
blue	ball	block
green	ball	block
yellow	bead	car
orange	comb	car
purple	barrette	bead

Provide the child with several (six to eight) small containers (bowls, boxes, or cups). Tell the child, "Put the toys in the (bowls, boxes, or cups)."

Evaluation: Note how many groups the child makes and the criteria (color, category, shape, etc.) used.

TASK 2: SERIATION

Instructions: Present the child with two or more objects that differ in one dimension such as height or width. For example, cut some drinking straws so that the shortest is two inches, the next two-and-a-half, the next three inches, etc. Start with two for a two-year-old, three for a three- or four-year-old. See Task 3 for the kindergarten/first-grade child in Activity 4.
   a. For two straws. Place them in front of the child. Say, "Find the longer (taller) straw. Find the shorter straw."
   b. For three or more items: Say, "Find the tallest (or shortest) straw. Put the straws in order from shortest to tallest."

Evaluation: For a., note if child can identify short and tall. For b. note if the tallest and shortest (or largest and smallest) are placed correctly and if the middle sizes are mixed up or in order.

TASK 3: NUMBER

Instructions: Have a supply of twenty identical objects (such as coins, chips, cube blocks). Ask the child to do the following:
   a. For this rote counting task no objects are needed. Tell the child, "Count for me. Count as far as you can."

Evaluation: Note if the number names are in order and how far the child can count correctly and how far incorrectly. Note the types of errors made.
   b. Place sets of objects in front of the child. Start with two, then one, then four, then three, then five. Ask, "How many of these are there?"

Evaluation: Note if he can apply the number names in order, if he uses one-to-one correspondence, and if he can tell you how many are in each group.

 c. If the child has rote counted over five a. previously, make all the objects available. Say, "Count as many of these things as you can."

Evaluation: Note if he can apply the number names in order, if he uses one-to-one correspondence, and if he can tell you how many there are when he finishes.

4. Follow the instructions given for Activity 3.

KINDERGARTEN/FIRST-GRADE CLINICAL INTERVIEW TASKS

TASK 1: CLASSIFICATION

Materials: eight squares (four large and four small with one of each size red, yellow, blue, and green) eight triangles (four large and four small with one of each size red, yellow, blue, and green) eight circles (four large and four small with one of each size red, yellow, blue, and green)

Instructions: Present the child with the cardboard shapes piled at random in front of him. Say, "Sort (pile) these shapes in groups any way you want to." After the child has done one sort say, "Now sort (pile) these shapes in another way."

Evaluation: The preoperational child normally sorts one way (such as by color, shape, or size) and avoids trying any of the others. The concrete operational child will try another way.

TASK 2: CONSERVATION OF NUMBER

Materials: 25 cube blocks, chips, coins, or any other small object, all the same size.

Instructions: Set up a row of nine objects. Have the rest in a pile to the side. Say, "You make a row just like this one." (point to yours)

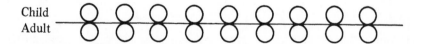

Ask the child, "Does one row have more blocks or do they both have the same amount? How do you know?"

If the child agrees to equality, go on to the transformations that follow.

Transformation 1
Say, "Now watch what I do." (push yours together)

Ask the child, "Does one row have more blocks or do they both have the same amount? Why?" Say, "Make them have the same amount again." (If the child has given a conserving answer tell him, "Line them up like they were before I moved them.")

Go on to the other transformations, always being sure the child agrees to equality first.

Transformation 2

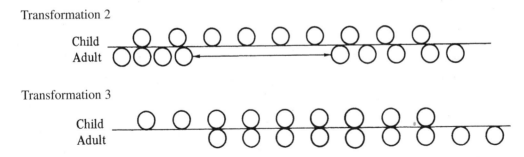

Transformation 3

Evaluation: The child who is not yet a conserver will center on one aspect of the problem such as length. For transformation (1) he will say that he has more because his is longer or that the adult's is shorter. The transitional child will be inconsistent, that is, he may conserve on one task and not on another. At a more advanced stage, he may appear unsure of his conserving answers and have to count or do one-to-one matching to be sure there is still the same number in each row. The conserver will tell you with confidence that there is still the same number in each row and is even likely to say, "You just moved them."

TASK 3: SERIATION

Materials: Items of the same shape, but in graduated sizes such as ten sticks or ten circles as shown.

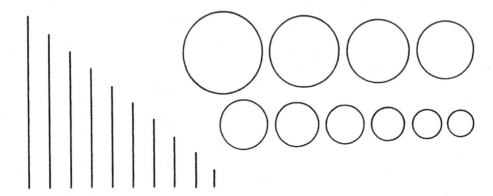

Instructions: Put the items in random order in front of the child. Start with five items. If this is too difficult, go back to three. If five is easy, try all ten. Tell the child, "Start with the largest (biggest, tallest, fattest, longest) and make a row from largest to smallest (tallest to shortest, fattest to skinniest, longest to shortest)."

Evaluation: The preoperational child will order the sticks in an approximate way such as already shown in the unit. He usually focuses on the two extremes and has the middle sizes out of order. The concrete operational child can decenter and put the objects in the correct order.

TASK 4: CAUSALITY

Materials: The following list of questions.

Instructions: Ask the following questions. Give the child plenty of time to answer. Respond with "yes," "uhuh," and other nonevaluative comments. Ask, "Why" or "Tell me some more" to see if he can expand. Try to get the child's reasons.

    a. "Are you alive?"

        "Is a cloud alive? Why?"

        "Is a bicycle alive? Why?"

        "Is a car alive? Why?"

        "Is a tree alive? Why?"

    b. "What makes clouds move? Why?"

        "How does the sun move? Why?"

        "Why don't the clouds fall down? What keeps them up?"

        "What keeps the sun up in the sky?"

Evaluation: Note the kinds of reasons the child gives for his answers. Note whether he uses animism or artificialism. As the child moves into concrete operations, he will give a more realistic answer to the questions about life. His answers to the questions about the things he cannot touch himself (such as the clouds and the sun) will still be illogical.

5. Make an entry in your journal.

REVIEW

A. List the highlights of Piaget's developmental theory.

B. Select the correct answer(s) to the following. There may be more than one correct answer.

    1. During most of the preschool period, the child is in the

        a. sensorimotor stage.

        b. preoperational stage.

        c. concrete operations stage.

        d. formal operations stage.

    2. Developmentally, the preschool child

        a. has acquired the object concept.

        b. has real thoughts and insights.

        c. has a rate of motor development that is leveling off.

        d. is acquiring language, which is a major focus of development.

    3. The preschool child's activity is characterized by

        a. little evidence of representative or symbolic play.

        b. learning through imitation.

        c. a lack of egocentrism.

        d. a focus on the most obvious parts of a problem.

    4. As the young child goes into the concrete operations stage, she

        a. integrates her old ways of thinking into the new.

        b. attains reversibility.

        c. is more egocentric.

        d. can conserve.

C. Look at each of the examples that follow. Analyze each one according to the child's probable Piagetian stage, his age, the concept or activity in which he is engaged, the adult response if there is one, and the evidence for your decisions. Apply the following list of terms as appropriate to each situation:

one-to-one correspondence	reversibility
seriation	transformation
conservation (conserver)	symbolic
classification (categorizing)	representational
causality	animism
preoperational	artificialism
concrete operations	concept
egocentric (centering, decentering)	

* * * * * * * * * * * * *

1. Joe, age four, is playing with some strings of various sizes. He lines them up.

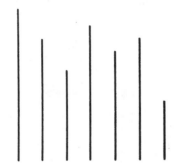

2. Doug, age five, is shown a row of ten pennies. He is then asked to, "Make a row that has the same number as this one." He does so:

First Row
Second Row

Adult says, "Now watch what I do." (One row is moved):

First Row
Second Row

"Do both rows have the same or does one row have more?" Doug points to the first row, saying, "That row has more." "Why, Doug?" "Because it is longer," says Doug.

3. Tanya, age three-and-a-half, is playing with some sticks and stones in the backyard. She arranges the sticks and stones like this:

"Each dog has a bone," she says.

4. Roger is six years old. He is shown two rows of ten chips. He agrees that each row has the same number of chips. One row is then expanded:

(1)
(2)

Roger is asked, "Does one row have more or do they both have the same amount?" "The same," says Roger. "At least I think they do. Maybe I better count them to be sure."

5. Derrick, age four, is asked the following questions:

Question	Derrick's Answer
Are you alive?	Yes.
Why?	We have blood.
Is a cloud alive?	Yes.
Why?	Everything has blood.
Is a bicycle alive?	No.
Why?	It has a motor.
Is a mountain alive?	No. Because it stays wherever it is.
Is a tree alive?	No. Because it only moves if someone chops it down.

D. In which of the following situations are adults applying Piaget's theories to practice? In which are they not? Give reasons for your answers.
   1. Mrs. Tanaka laughs to herself as she hears Derrick tell Bill, "The rain comes so it can water our gardens."
   2. "I teach to the average child in the group. Then, at least, everyone learns something."
   3. Today Mr. Santos brought in more containers for water play as he has noticed the children becoming more interested in measuring and pouring and playing with water.
   4. Mrs. White Bear gives her three- and four-year-olds many materials they can use for sorting and classifying.
   5. "No Tim, you are not allowed to draw a dog. Everyone is drawing oranges today."
   6. "Johnny, you didn't copy the pegboard design correctly. It's all wrong."
   7. "Kate, I noticed you started copying the pattern for the pegboard design just like it is and then changed it. Why?" Kate: "Oh, I didn't have enough green pegs so I used blue instead."
   8. Mrs. Brown notices that the unit block structures are getting larger and more complex. She decides to make the block area larger.

E. Give an example of how concept learning is basic to math, science, and social studies.

F. Explain how Vygotsky's theory helps us understand how young children develop concepts.

Language Development

OBJECTIVES

After studying this unit, the student should be able to:

■ Identify definitions and examples of the major kinds of language rules.

■ Explain the current points of view regarding how language is learned.

■ Analyze language samples according to developmental stage, semantic component, and rate of development.

■ Recognize examples of normal speech development such as pragmatic usage, use of phonemes, dialect, thought as reflected in speech, a language relationship between child and adult, and baby talk.

■ Explain how cultural and socioeconomic factors affect language development.

■ Explain the important factors in the adult role in the child's language development.

L anguage is a complex and important area in child development. It is necessary in several ways. Language

- is a major means for transmitting our culture to the next generation. It is an important tool in education
- is involved in our mental processing (such as thinking, problem solving, and memory).
- serves as a means of communication

Language symbols are arbitrary. That is, language symbols are agreed upon by a group to have certain meanings that can then be used for communication. The English, Chinese, Egyptians, Spanish, and other cultural groups developed their own languages, which are the dominant forms of language in certain geographic areas. Language takes a number of forms: oral, written, gestural, facial expressions, and physical position. Certain languages do not rely on oral communication but use other senses. For example, the sign language used by the deaf is visual; braille used by the blind is tactile.

An amazing aspect of language is the speed with which it develops. The average child has nearly adult language facility by the age of four.

WHAT IS LANGUAGE?

Language is a well-ordered system of roles that each adult member of the language community tacitly comprehends in speaking, listening, and writing (Yussen & Santrock, 1978, p. 245). Our knowledge of language is basically unconscious. That is, it is something we learn through the natural course of everyday life (Figure 22–1).

There are three types of language rules. Some rules deal with the units we use; that is how sounds are put together in a meaningful way. For the English speaker, the string of sounds "gato" is not a meaningful one. For the Spanish speaker, it is. While the

Type of Rule	Aspect of Speech That is Governed
Phonological	The use of phonemes, the smallest units of speech.
Morphological	The use of morphemes, the smallest meaningful units of speech.
Syntax	The way words are put together into acceptable phrases and sentences.
Semantic	Determines the correct use of words in context and relative to the referents used.
Pragmatic	The degree to which language is used appropriately and to the best advantage in a particular situation.

Figure 22–2 Language is a system of rules that is accepted as correct by a language community.

English speaker does not respond to "g-a-t-o," he does respond to "c-a-t." If the three units were put together as "a-t-c" or "t-c-a" they would not be organized in a way that would make sense to an English speaker. The rules that tell us which sounds to use and how to sequence them deal with units called **phonemes** and **morphemes**. A second set of rules has to do with the way words are placed in sequence to make an acceptable sentence or phrase. This is known as **syntax**. The third set of rules defines what language means and how it can be used most appropriately in specific situations. This set of rules refers to **semantics** and **pragmatics** (Figure 22–2).

Phonemes

Phonemes are the smallest units of language. In English, there are 36 individual speech sounds. These are the phonemes of English. There are specific rules in English that are used to combine sounds. For example, look at the following sound

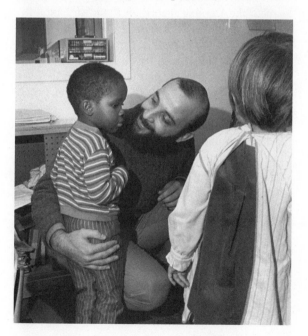

Figure 22–1 Language development proceeds through the same stages in every culture.

KEYTERMSKEYTERMSKEYTERMSKEYTERMSKEYTERMSKEYTERMSKEY

| Language | morphemes | semantics |
| phonemes | syntax | pragmatics |

combinations and decide which follow English rules and which do not:

> *aq   kz   kl   bc   br*

If you said yes for *kl* and *br* and no for *aq*, *kz*, and *bc*, you were correct. However, note that *kl* and *br* carry no meaning on their own.

Morphemes

Morphemes are strings of sounds that do have meaning. They are the smallest meaningful units in a language. Look at the following examples and decide which are morphemes:

> *a   gpa   car   drw   pre-   -ing*

The morphemes are *a*, *car*, *pre-*, and *-ing*. The others, *gpa* and *drw* are not meaningful in English.

Syntax

The syntax of a language is the set of rules for producing acceptable phrases and sentences. For example, "dog a it is" is not an acceptable English sentence. "It is a dog." and "Is it a dog?" are acceptable. Young children first invent their own syntax or rules for putting words into meaningful context (Genishi, 1987). An early rule might be as simple as noun + another word: e.g., "Milk gone," "Daddy bye-bye," "Water hot."

Semantics

Semantics is the study of meaning. It refers to words used in the correct context and attached to the appropriate referent. Is a dog referred to as *dog* and a table as *table*? Are sentences put together in meaningful ways?

1. The dog ate the bone.
2. The house ate the dog.

The first sentence uses words in a meaningful way. The second does not. As children grow into the elementary years, they begin to understand some of the more subtle meanings, i.e., although candy and a person can be sweet, thin and skinny are similar, but they are subtly different (Genishi, 1987).

Pragmatics

Pragmatics has to do with the rules for using language appropriately and to advantage. Which example shows good use of pragmatic rules?

1. Open the door, please.
2. (Gruff voice) Open the door!

The first example shows good social use. The request (1) is more likely to be granted than is the command (2).

HOW ORAL LANGUAGE IS LEARNED

There are three views of how language is learned: the learning theory view, the structural-innatist view, and the interactionist view (Cole & Cole, 1989). The **learning theory** approach puts emphasis on the environment, the structural-innatist emphasizes hereditary factors, and the interactionist views language acquisition as an interaction between heredity and environment.

The learning theory view explains language acquisition through the mechanisms of classical conditioning, operant conditioning, and imitation. Through classical conditioning and simple associations, vocal and visual become attached. The child imitates what he hears and is rewarded when he makes a sound that sounds to others like the name of an object. Baby's first "words" may be approximations of the real word which only those in his family understand. An example of approximation is the following:

17 months	*21 months*	*24 months*
adoo	wadder	water

At first the child is probably restricted by a limited use of phonemes and an incomplete recall of what he has heard (Figure 22–3). However, because everyone

learning theory

Figure 22–3 **With his not-fully-developed use of phonemes, the young child seems to speak his own language.**

in the family responds to his "adoo" with a glass of water, filling the bathtub, or turning on the hose, depending on the context, he continues to use "adoo" until gradually he is able to say, "water." Children learning to speak also use groups of sounds that have even less relationship to the real word than "adoo" does to water. The same child who used "adoo" used "pow" for pacifier. This term continued to be used by not only her, but by the whole family until the time when the last pacifier was gone. All normal children go through the same stages: from cooing to babbling to one-word, two-word, three-word and then complete sentences. The specific language the child learns is determined by the environment in which he lives.

The **structural-innatist theory** explains language acquisition as a more complex process. It is felt that the human is born with a biological need to develop rule systems for language, while reinforcement and imitation give feedback and build vocabulary. The need to have rules is inborn, as is the sequence of development the child goes through before he masters his own language. This newer view came about for several reasons:

- Children devise sentences that they have never heard. That is, rather than learning each sentence separately, they learn rules. If they learn, "The bird is on the branch." they can apply the same rules to put together the sentence "The cat is on the fence."

- Repeated drill does not change a child's stage of development. He will change when he is developmentally capable:

  Sandy: Want milk!
  Mother: Oh, you mean, "I want milk."
  Sandy: Want milk!
  Mother: Can you say, "I want milk."
  Sandy: Want milk!
  Mother: Sandy, please say, "I want milk!"
  Sandy: *Want milk!* (Yussen & Santrock, 1978, p. 251)

  Sandy is in the two-word telegraphic stage and no amount of pleading on mother's part can change what nature has set up.

- Children get positive reinforcement for incorrect or immature sentences.

  That is, they do get positive responses to sentences such as:

Maria (20 months)	*Mr. Sanchez, her father*
"Daddy, dog big."	"Yes, the dog is big."
"More milk."	He pours her a glass of milk.
"Car blue."	"Yes, the car is blue."

Even though children get these positive responses for sentences that use incorrect syntax, they continue to expand and eventually develop the more sophisticated syntax of adult language.

The **interactionist theory** is the most recently developed. There is an interaction between biological and environmental factors. The sequence and timing of speech development is biologically determined, while the specific language the child learns is determined by the environment in which he lives (Genishi & Dyson, 1984). Some interactionists emphasize the cognitive, i.e., language grows out of sensorimotor thought and is mainly learning how to use words to get what you want (Cole & Cole, 1989). Learning the rules of the language is a by-product of learning to communicate more clearly. Other interactionists emphasize cultural context. Children reinvent language but they have people who already know the language who guide the acquisition process (Cole & Cole, 1989).

THE SEQUENCE OF SPEECH DEVELOPMENT

Figure 22–4 outlines the development of speech from birth to school age. Every normal young child passes through the major stages shown in the chart. The ages given in the outline are for the average child and thus may vary from child to child. Note that the child's language develops from the simple to the complex: from individual sounds, to syllables, to one-word sentences, to two- and three-word sentences, and then to more complex and complete sentences. The column headed Semantic Elements refers to the meaning attached to the child's vocalizations. It had been felt that until the child said his first meaningful word, usually between twelve and eighteen months of age, there was no meaning, as such, attached to his vocalizations. However, this idea is now being questioned. At this point, semantic element during the prelinguistic period will be considered as the type of meaning conveyed to adults by the child's preword vocalizations.

KEYTERMSKEYTERMSKEYTERMSKEYTERMSKEYTERMSKEY

structural-innatist theory	interactionist theory

AGE	LANGUAGE CHARACTERISTICS	SEMANTIC ELEMENTS
Birth	Reflexive crying	None; reflex
1 Month	Differentiated cry	Sleepy, hungry, angry, or hurt
6 Weeks	Cooing—vowels (squealing, gurgling)	Comfort
6–7 Months	Babbling: one-syllable vocalizations build into strings.	Pleasure, vocal practice
10 Months	Seems to be trying to imitate.	Vocal practice
12 Months	First word or wordlike combinations of sounds	Now has a referent.
12–18 Months (begins)	Holophrases; one-word utterances Usually the names of familiar objects which act and react	Referents; context is critical
18–30 Months (begins)	Telegraphic speech; two- to three-word sentences which contain only the essentials	Referents; context is very important
About 2½ years to 4 years	Sentence length increases to four or more words.	Clearer to adult listener. More detail is included.
By four years	Syntax is like that of adults. Articulation may not be fully developed.	Thought is still preoperational and is reflected in speech.

Figure 22–4   **The development of speech (Adapted from S. R. Yussen & J. W. Santrock, *Child Development*, ©1978 by W. C. Brown)**

At birth the child's cry is reflexive, but within a month becomes differentiated. That is, there are different cries to indicate the infant is sleepy, hungry, angry, or hurt. By six weeks the child is using vowels and is giggling. These vowel sounds are called cooing. They indicate the child feels comfortable and happy. Around six to seven months of age, the child is vocalizing syllables that he builds into strings:

Syllable	*Strings*
ma	mamamamama
mu	mumumumumu
did	did-did-did
aba	aba-aba-aba-aba

Eventually, syllables are alternated and more varied such as "aba-da-da-ba-ma-ma-dadi." This babbling seems to denote pleasure and also seems to be a kind of vocal practice. Around 10 months, the infant begins

to try to imitate speech. There is usually a slowdown in output at this point until the first wordlike combinations, which have a referent appear. That is, sounds are no longer made just for fun but refer to something. For example, Michael Halliday (1975) collected samples of his son Nigel's early vocalizations. At age one he collected samples such as the following:

Nigel's Word	*Referent*
dada	Daddy
da	dog
ba	birds
aba	a bus
ka	car

Then the child moves into the linguistic period. That is, he begins to use meaningful speech. In the semantic elements, context is very important. When the child uses one-word sentences, "where" and "what" are essential to the meaning. For example, "tummy" may mean "My tummy hurts," "This is my tummy," or "Does your tummy hurt?" When the child puts two or three words together in the telegraphic stage, his message only contains the most essential words. The context continues to be important. "Hurty tummy" may mean "My tummy hurts," "Your tummy hurts," or "His tummy hurts."

During the holophrastic and telegraphic periods, it is not unusual for a child not to articulate every sound in the English language. He may substitute sounds or omit them. Try to figure out what is missing or what is substituted in the list on the left below. Check the list on the right. The samples are from a twenty-three-month-old girl.

Child's Word	Real Word
1. greem	green
2. kik	kiss
3. Chrik	Chris
4. Hena	Helena
5. Printess	Princess
6. yove	love
7. glakkes	glasses
8. bwony	bologna

It can be seen that /m/ is substituted for /n/; /k/ for /s/; /t/ for /s/; /y/ for /l/; and /l/ is omitted in two cases. Sometime between age two-and-one-half and four, sentences increase in length until they are complete. Meaning becomes closer to that of the adult listener so that the context is understood from the sentence itself. For example, "No bed" becomes "I no go bed," then "I don't want to go to bed." By age four syntax is usually almost like that of an adult.

INDIVIDUAL DIFFERENCES

The information discussed so far describes the general course of normal oral language development as adults describe it. However, children learning to speak do not consciously break language down and label the parts; we adults do that for descriptive purposes. Each child lives in a unique language environment to which he brings unique genetic characteristics. Katherine Nelson (1982) discusses some of these differences. She notes that two main types of beginning speakers (that is, one- and two-year-olds) have been identified: referential and expressive. Each type of speaker has unique characteristics:

- Referential speakers are mainly nouns with some verbs, proper names, and adjectives while expressive speakers use much more diverse speech that includes a large number of combinations such as "stop it" and "I want it."

- Referential speakers use mainly nouns while expressive speakers use pronouns extensively.

- While referential children do lots of object labeling, expressive children tend to use many compressed sentences: one or two words, usually stuck together, stand for a longer sentence.

- Early speakers may use both styles but in different situations, such as referential during story time and expressive during social play.

These differences may be accounted for neurologically (brain hemisphere dominance), relative to environmental conditions (i.e. how the parents interact with the child), and in light of whether language learning is mainly a cognitive task for the child or whether the child also learns to use the language appropriately in different contexts. Whatever the reasons for these individual differences, the important point is to be aware of them when evaluating the speech development of a particular child.

Oral language development can be evaluated formally or informally: through individual questioning or through observations during daily activities. Individual questioning involves eliciting language responses from the child through specific language tasks such as those described in Activity 3 of this unit. For example, if we asked a twenty-month-old to name specific body parts, we would expect that about eight body parts would be named. We would also expect a fifteen- to twenty-month-old to use two-word combinations (Capute et al., 1980). Caz-

Referential speakers   expressive speakers

den (1981) suggests evaluating language proficiency while playing games such as lotto with small groups of older (three- to five-year-old) children. Three levels of language can be checked during this type of activity.

- The child can visually match a card to the card the teacher holds.
- The teacher can verbally describe a card and the child locates it.
- The child can describe the card.

Genishi and Dyson (1984) favor informal evaluation methods such as checklists and anecdotal records as the means for recording information during observation of children in their regular activities. Structured interview tasks can be used to obtain information that may not show up during regular activities. Interviews can be open-ended questions or questions designed to get specific information (such as the child's knowledge of singulars and plurals or ability to label objects). It is very important for teachers to observe the language behavior of their students and use the information they obtain to plan instruction and encourage expansions of language (Goodman, 1985; King, 1985). Other guidelines for observation and evaluation will be discussed in Units 23 and 24.

THOUGHT AND LANGUAGE

Those who study language have been interested in how language and thought relate. Those who take the environmental-learning perspective believe that much of human thought is dependent on language. Words aid in communication, but they also help children understand the world and the things in it better. Therefore, the more words the child knows, the more advanced his cognitive development will be (Cole & Cole, 1989).

Piaget's theory serves as the basis for the interactionist view. At the end of infancy, a new mode of representation grows out of sensorimotor schemas. Language reflects thought from the Piagetian view. Language then does not affect thought, thought determines language. Early speech, like early thought would then be egocentric, that is, it would center on

the most obvious and would ignore what others have to say (Cole & Cole, 1989).

The structural-innatists disagree that speech grows from sensorimotor cognition. They believe a built-in device in humans acquires language. Language is used to express thought but language and thought are not interdependent (Cole & Cole, 1989).

Vygotsky developed a theory that looks at the language and thought relationship from the cultural-context point of view. Vygotsky believed that from the beginning the child's language development is determined by the social context. Children first develop speech as a form of social communication. Eventually, they develop inner speech, which interconnects thought and language. Vygotsky's studies indicated that what Piaget identified as egocentric speech does have, from the children's point of view, a communicative function. Vygotsky believed that during the first 2 years language and thought developed in a parallel fashion so there is language without thought and thought without language. At two they begin to join each other. Language becomes intellectual and thinking verbal. Language, even when used individually, has its roots in the social context (Cole & Cole, 1989).

Which theory is correct in its view of the language/thought relationship? This question is still not answered. However, they are certainly related and when the two most popular theories (Piaget's & Vygotsky's) are compared, a great deal of common and complementary aspects are found, especially after the first two years (Lucy, 1988). Piaget concentrated more on the representational nature of language and Vygotsky more on the social nature. At the practical level, both are certainly important.

Thought Reflected in Language

Whatever our views of the relationship of language and thought development, listening to children is one of our major means of learning about their thinking processes and their concept development. Thinking is still preoperational at age four, while in many ways speech is very adult like. That is, four-year-olds have an extensive vocabulary and their grammar is adultlike. These factors should be kept in mind when trying to communicate with young children. While their speech may be quite articulate, their reasoning is still preoperational as evidenced in the following example from a child who is nearing age three (*Growing Child*, 1973):

> John wants to ride along in the car when his sister goes to school. Dad explains that it's not their turn today: they belong to a car pool and their turn is tomorrow. The next day John wants his swimming suit. When asked why, he replies, "You promised we were going in a pool."

This example reflects the preoperational "seeing is believing" approach to problems. Children take language in its most literal sense and do not have the more abstract concepts that they will acquire as they approach adulthood. Children make up their own interpretations. This literal interpretation by young children must be kept in mind when communicating with them. The adult and child may be using the same words with different meanings.

Keep in mind the vocabulary of preschoolers may be behind their ability to understand and their reasoning may be ahead of their ability to communicate clearly. Young children frequently seem to be oblivious to the finer nuances of language. For example, in a study by Flavell, Speer, Green, and August (1981), it was found that kindergartners didn't perceive when they were given incomplete directions to follow. Flavell et al. (1981) presented to kindergartners and second graders a series of tasks in which they had to follow tape-recorded directions to try to build block structures. For several of the tasks, the directions were purposely incomplete and unclear. The kindergartners showed little if any recognition that some of the directions were inadequate. Even those who seemed to realize during the building process that something was wrong with the instructions always said the instructions were fine when questioned after completion of the task. Flavell et al. concluded "it appears that children may often not understand what they see, hear, or read and yet be totally oblivious to this state of affairs" (p. 53). This research implies that adults who work with young children must be very careful in providing instructions to them and be tolerant of their lack of recognition of their own lack of understanding.

There is an increasing interest in children's awareness of language, that is, their ability to think about the structure and the functions of language (Grieve, Tunmer, & Pratt, 1983). Research indicates this awareness begins to develop in early childhood. Young children have demonstrated the following signs of language awareness:

1. Young children can make judgments about language such as:
   - Four-and-a-half-year-olds know that they should show interest in getting a piece of candy from an adult by saying, "I would like a piece of candy." rather than "I want a piece of candy."
   - Children as young as four can adjust their speech by using appropriate voices for different dramatic play roles and by simplifying their speech when talking to younger children.
   - Five-year-olds realize that adults use more complex sentences than children use.
   - Very young children can recognize that they may not articulate correctly (such as the words in the list presented in an earlier part of this unit).

2. Young children can apply language rules:
   - They can add /s/ for more than one of something.
   - They can add /ed/ to show past tense.

3. Young children can correct language:
   - They may show that they realize they have made a mistake by adding a word, changing a word, or changing word order on their own.
   - They may respond to adult prompts. That is, the adult indicates that a different word is expected and the child figures out what the word should be.

4. Young children can define words by their function:
   - Broom is for sweeping.
   - Ball is for throwing.

5. Young children can identify a part of a word or a part of a sentence if the task is presented in a simple and appropriate manner.

6. From the time, as infants, children find they can control the sounds they make, they enjoy practicing and playing with words through repetition, chants, rhymes, and plays on words.

Grieve et al. (1983) suggest some important implications for practice. First, the evidence suggests children know a great deal about language before they enter school. Secondly, language awareness may be an important prerequisite to learning to read. The relationship between language awareness and beginning reading was reviewed by McGee, Charlesworth, Cheek, and Cheek (1982). There is a growing body of research that suggests that story knowledge is an important prerequisite to learning to read. Awareness of how events and characters are common to all stories is essential. Children remember stories better if they have a basic concept that stories have a beginning, a middle, and an end. Kindergarten seems to be the critical time for development of story concepts such as:

• Stories have a beginning, a middle, and an end.
• Stories have characters.
• Stories have a setting.
• Stories have a theme.
• Stories have a plot.

The kindergarten curriculum should include activities that will help students develop story knowledge.

CULTURAL ASPECTS OF LANGUAGE

It is well documented that speech development proceeds in the same sequence around the world (Slobin, 1972). That is, children proceed through the cooing, babbling, one-word, two-word, and three-word stages on their way to adultlike speech. The differences between and within countries have to do with the actual sounds used and the rules for combining sounds (Munroe & Munroe, 1975). A problem arises for the adult who works with young children when a child arrives in school with language that is different from that used in the school or understood by the teacher. Differences seem to take three main forms:

• Nonstandard dialect. The child speaks the language of the area but uses some rules that are different from those used by other people in the area. The dialect called Black English (BE) has been the subject of much study and controversy.

• Non-English speaking, or speaking English as a second language. A large segment of our population speaks Spanish as a first language. A large influx of immigrants from Southeast Asia and a constant influx of children from other countries in smaller numbers increase the number of non-English speaking children.

• Differences in language are associated with socioeconomic status. The language use of children and parents from different social classes has also been studied.

Nonstandard Dialect

A **dialect** is a variation of the standard speech of a language. There has been particular concern with English as spoken in the United States by African-Americans (Cazden, Baratz, Labov, & Palmer, 1981). Black English (BE) is a uniform dialect in that it is spoken with a consistent grammar from place to place. That is, the basic rules of BE are standard in a wide variety of geographic areas. The following are some differences between BE and standard English (SE). Note the sounds omitted and substituted and the ways of indicating tense and possessives. In the following example a second grader, Freddie, is helping check math problems.

| *Freddie, BE* | *Standard English* |
| O kay boys and gur, take out you math bookses. We gona' check ours work. Numba' one twenty-fo, two is fo plus nine is thuteen. Don't you be getten out you set. | Okay boys and girls, take out your math books. We are going to check our work. Number one-twenty-four, two is four plus nine is thirteen. Don't you get out of your seats. |

In BE, relative to SE, verb tenses differ, sounds are omitted, and sounds are substituted in a consistent rule-governed way. Adults who work with young children who speak Black English should support that BE functions as an acceptable language. They must confront the misconception that BE speakers are not good thinkers (Bartlett, 1981). Another myth to watch for is that BE is ambiguous or vague. It is just as clear as any other form of English to the person who speaks it and/or understands it.

The controversy that arises over the place of Black English in the school program centers around whether it should be used in school; and when, how, and if Standard English should be taught to BE speakers. There are differences of opinion centering around this issue. Cazden, Bryant, and Tillman (1981) questioned three groups of black adults in the Roxbury section of Boston regarding their feelings about BE and school. Parents were against the use of BE in school. They felt the school's job was to teach the standard dialect that the child would need to make it in the Anglo-dominated culture. A group of community leaders favored the use of BE. They felt that BE was an important cultural element that gives the African-American child psychological strength as well as an acceptable form of speech. Teachers, on the other hand, felt more conflict. They could see the importance of BE in the preservation of the culture, but could also see the need to master SE for survival through joining the mainstream culture.

Granger (1976) in a later, more extensive survey, found parents and teachers were supportive of the need for competence in their own dialect first. They saw the need for SE to be developed by the time the child reached the age where he would seek employment. Granger further cites research indicating that, in seeking employment, what the person says is more important than how he says it. Granger feels that the young child's dialect should be accepted as a fully credible language. The child should be helped to make full use of his nonstandard speaking skills. With the presence of standard speaking models, he feels children acquire SE slowly and naturally without losing their facility in BE. The child should be viewed as having a language difference rather than a language deficit. He has found no evidence that directive teaching of SE makes any measurable change in dialect (Figure 22–5).

Njeri H. Nuru (1980) states the need to support a **bilingual (bidialectic)**/bicultural approach to the African-American child's language development. To succeed in a white-dominated society, African-American children need to know and understand the white language and culture. At the same time they need to preserve their own language, culture, and values. Critical to the success of bilingual/bicultural education for African-American children is respect from their teachers, both African-American and white. African-American teachers and administrators have the responsibility of:

Figure 22–5   "Say it with me. 'This is a bear.'" Directed teaching of standard English may increase vocabulary, but whether it generalizes to their situations is questionable.

bilingual (bidialectic)

- looking at policy from an African-American perspective
- assessing their own attitudes toward language and culture
- compensating for the language/cultural bias in standardized tests
- keeping up with current developments and literature
- keeping up with new educational trends
- being sure to share knowledge and ideas relevant to the African-American perspective with Anglo colleagues who teach African-American children

Nuru also lists a number of things African-American parents can do to help their children maintain African-American culture and language. Some of these include having African-American publications in the home, being models of culture, showing appreciation for African-American language, demonstrating the necessity of bilingual/bicultural living for survival, teaching standard American-English as an alternative language system, reading as a model for children and to broaden knowledge of African-American culture, being sure to keep in touch with their child's teachers, and feeling free to question test scores regarding cultural bias.

When the Language in the Home Is Not English

Many young children in our country do not learn English at home. At home, Mrs. Sanchez reads:

Esta es una casa grande.

Aquí vive la familia Raton.

También vive aquí un gato grande. (DeHoogh, 1978, p. 1)

At school Isabel Sanchez may hear:

This is a big house.

The Mouse family lives here.

A big cat lives here too.

There is no question that if Isabel is to survive in this country, she must learn to speak English. There is, however, a good deal of difference of opinion regarding when and how Isabel should learn English.

A review of research on bilingual/bicultural young children and their education by Soto (1991) explains some of the misconceptions about young children and second-language learning, describes successful bilingual education approaches, and suggests how research can be applied by early childhood educators. Soto (1991, p. 31) believes that, "Based upon existing bilingual research and what we know about how young children develop, a supportive, natural, language-rich environment, affording acceptance and meaningful interaction, appears optimal." Too frequently, bilingual education is set up on a deficit model, which views the children as lacking language competence rather than recognizing their strength in their first language. Garcia (1986, pp. 15–16) provides a definition of early childhood bilingualism, which includes the following conditions:

1. Children are able to comprehend and produce linguistic aspects of two languages.

2. Children are exposed "naturally" in the form of social interaction, to the two languages as they are used during early childhood. This condition requires a substantive bilingual environment. This may be through family, extended family, or travel experiences.

3. Development must be simultaneous in both languages. This is in contrast to the native speaker of one language, who after mastery of that language, begins on a course of second language acquisition.

Garcia applies this definition to dual language acquisition during the first five years. Soto (1991) describes the variety of terms used to label second language learners (p. 32):

Linguistic minority student: speaks the language of a minority group.

Linguistic majority student: speaks the language of the majority group.

Limited English proficient (LEP): has a limited amount of English as a second language.

Non-English proficient (NEP): speaks the native language only.

English only (EO): refers to monolingual English speakers.

Fluent English proficient: speaks English and another language at home.

Soto points out that some of these terms such as LEP emphasize the children's weaknesses rather than their strengths. Too frequently programs for these students are treated as compensatory rather than enriching.

Soto (1991) identifies several misconceptions commonly held regarding young second-language learners. First, young children do not learn a second language more quickly than adults. People may get this impression because young children are less inhibited, have more frequent social interactions, and have an easier time with pronunciation. Second, there is no evidence that the younger the child, the easier it is to learn the second language. However, the earlier the start, the more likely the person will eventually be more proficient. Thirdly, it is believed by some that there is a single best way to acquire a second language. Individual differences must be considered as in any other type of instruction. Generally, second language learning should be learned naturally, not in a fixed package of lessons.

Soto (1991) describes successful approaches to bilingual instruction. The three most frequently used approaches are the transitional, the maintenance/developmental, and the two-way bilingual. Transitional approaches begin with instruction in the native language and move as quickly as possible into instruction in English. The maintenance/developmental approach builds language skills in the native language while simultaneously moving toward mastery of English. The two-way approach is designed for both language minority and language majority speakers with the expectation that both groups will be academically successful and become bilingual. Overall, the research evaluating bilingual early childhood programs indicates that children from programs that develop proficiency in both languages hold the advantage in achievement in both languages and in the development of divergent thinking ability and cognitive flexibility.

Soto (1991, pp. 34–35) offers seven suggestions for application to instruction by teachers of young children:

1. Be aware of individual differences—do not push children too fast into becoming second-language proficient.

2. Be accepting of whatever the children say. Opportunities for trial and error are very important. Children should have time to converse in both languages. Adults should not dominate the conversation but should listen and support the efforts of the children. There should be plenty of opportunities for informal conversation during dramatic play, stories, cooking, etc.

3. Use an additive approach. That is, add on new language skills while maintaining and enriching first language skills.

4. Provide a stimulating developmentally appropriate curriculum, not teacher-directed scripted instruction.

5. Include experiences that would be culturally responsive to any child.

6. Informal observation should be used to obtain information needed for planning.

7. The classroom should have an environment that is accepting and values culturally and linguistically diverse young children.

Soto (1992) advocates supporting bilingual education in spite of the English-only proponents. Children are at a great advantage intellectually if their education is bilingual and if their primary language and culture are maintained at home, in the community, and in school.

Learning English becomes more complex in a multilingual setting, i.e., where several native languages are spoken. In this case, teaching in the native languages and English is usually not possible. For example, Solorzano (1986) describes a school in Falls Church, Virginia, where fifty-five different languages are spoken. In this setting bilingual education as described by Soto (1991) is impractical. In this type of situation, an English as a Second Language (**ESL**) or an immersion program are the only possibilities. These approaches can be successful if there is ample time for informal conversation in English;

KEYTERMSKEYTERMSKEYTERMSKEYTERMSKEYTERMSKEY
ESL

not just rote teacher-directed activities. Genishi, Dyson, and Fassler (1994) have observed that children in multilingual and bilingual classrooms develop communication proficiency rapidly in a climate where conversation with both peers and teacher is encouraged continuously.

Zheng He, a native of the People's Republic of China was interested in observing in an ESL class attended by a kindergartner whose primary language was Chinese. He was concerned because her English was not improving very rapidly. The following excerpts are from his observations.

There are ten children in the class. They come from ten different countries. There is a teacher and an assistant. They use an immersion approach which utilizes small group and one-to-one activities for instruction. The small group activities are teacher directed. The program uses a six-stage ESL program for children. The program has a Sesame Street theme.

For the first part of the daily whole-class lesson, the teacher asks the children to close their books and prepares them for what they will see and hear on the page. Picture cards are presented to introduce new vocabulary.

In the second part of the lesson, the children are asked to open the books and look at the assigned page. The teacher describes the pictures for the children. The teacher points out certain objects and characters and helps the children review vocabulary. Four steps are used in each lesson. The first is listen, look, and point. As the children listen to a tape or the teacher they point to the appropriate pictures. The second step is to speak in a chorus repeating a song, chant, conversation, poem, or story line by line after the teacher. In the third step, the children are grouped into pairs and practice the conversational exchanges they have just learned. For the fourth step, the pairs role play the conversation.

For the third phase of the daily lesson, children are provided opportunities to relate the new language to themselves and their daily lives through games, role playing, and art projects. They also work on individual worksheets. In one-to-one activity the teacher and the aide help each of the children read their books individually according to their reading levels. They correct pronunciation and intonation and explain what the book is about. The children spend 50 minutes in the group activity and 30 minutes in the one-to-one and games, role playing, and art projects. There is no time for play with concrete materials or for the informal spontaneous conversation that facilitates learning a second language as documented by Genishi et al. (1994).

In some cases, a teacher may have only one or two students who speak a language other than English at home. Just as in the bilingual and multilingual groups, the teacher needs to provide plenty of time for informal conversation and trial and error and encourage everyone to be a good listener. The author had the opportunity to observe a Vietnamese child who had never spoken English enter a regular kindergarten class in January and by May read to the rest of the class in English. The teacher and other students were welcoming, accepting, and supported her efforts to learn English and she was very successful.

Courtney Cazden (1990, November) provided the following description of what is done by teachers who are helpful to young second-language learners:

1. They engage the children in one-to-one conversation.

2. They adapt the conversation to the children's stages of English language development.

3. They include the children in structured activities with English-speaking peers.
   a. repetitive rhymes, songs and fingerplays
   b. literacy activities, i.e., picture book reading
   c. manipulative activities (i.e., puzzles, construction toys, clay) with an adult who used the activity consistently with consistent accompanying language

4. The teacher shows appreciation for the children's language learning strategies. Second-language learners go through a distinct set of language acquisition stages:
   a. They try what they have and if it does not work, they drop it: a trial and error approach.
   b. When their first language does not work they lie low and do some guessing.
   c. They begin to communicate using gestures and approximations.

d. They learn useful things to say (important labels and phrases) and try to communicate with peers.

e. If their efforts are accepted and get results, they keep on talking.

Keeping these developmental stages and techniques in mind, a teacher can feel at ease with second-language learners enrolled in her classroom.

Socioeconomic Differences in Language Development

An important consideration for the adult who works with young children is socioeconomic status differences in language development and language use. Since the 1950s many experimental model early childhood programs have been developed with the major objective of improving the language skills of lower socioeconomic level children. The published versions of a number of these programs have been reviewed and evaluated by Bartlett (1981). Joan Tough (1982a) cautions that packaged programs are not the whole answer to the language curriculum for children from lower socioeconomic levels. Research indicates that lower SES children have a good command of language but have deficiencies in language use that can only be developed through teacher/child spontaneous dialogue (this approach is described in Unit 23).

The British sociologist Basil Bernstein (1972) calls attention to some of the cautions that must be taken when developing programs for lower socioeconomic level children. He contends that we were too quick to coin terms such as "culturally deprived, linguistically deprived, and socially disadvantaged" (p. 135). The whole concept of compensatory education, he feels, implies that there is a deficit or lack of something within the child's family that makes the child unable to benefit from education. This in turn leads to pressure for the child to drop his cultural identity. Bernstein cautions that we must not assume that the lower-class child is deficient in language-development just because he uses language differ-

ently than do middle- and upper-class children. The lower-class child has developed language that is useful within his culture, family, and community and yet has difficulty in school (Walker, Greenwood, Hart & Carta, 1994). Says Bernstein, "It is an accepted educational principle that we should work with what the child can offer. Why, then, don't we practice it?"

THE ADULT ROLE IN LANGUAGE DEVELOPMENT

The basic role of the adult is to provide the scaffolding for the young child's language development. Vygotsky suggested that young children need adult guidance to support them until they reach understanding. This guidance enables the young child to proceed through the stages of language development as easily and as rapidly as his capacity allows. The adult serves as model, provider of language experiences, and interactor as she participates in the give-and-take of conversation. According to Tough (1982b) the adult provides an environment that promotes thinking through the use of meaningful dialog between teacher and children. Through the use of divergent questions (questions that do not have one right answer) the adult encourages the child to construct concepts through his own language experiences. Adults need to let children know that they are interested in what the children are thinking. Adult/child interaction has been the focus of extensive research. Researchers have examined the roles of adult and child from a number of different points of view and at a variety of ages and stages during infancy and early childhood.

These critical roles begin in infancy. The infant responds to speech from the first day of life (Condon, 1979) when he can be observed synchronizing his body movements into rhythm with adult speech. Further, infants whose mothers always respond to their early vocalizing have been found to be at an advantage in speech development at age two (Freedle & Lewis, 1977). From about age one to age four, adults use what is called **baby talk (BT)**. BT is a simplified form of speech with short, simple sentences and simple vocabulary that is within the child's realm of experience. It is often rather high pitched and consists of a lot of questions and commands. BT has been found to be used everywhere in a variety of cultures. It seems to serve several functions in language acquisition (Ferguson, 1977, pp. 209–235):

- BT enables good, clear communication, and self-expression.
- It is suited to teaching language to a young child in the early stages of speech development.
- Children learn social values through the frequent use of words such as *pretty*, *good*, *bad*, and *dirty*, etc.
- The child learns socially acceptable "cute" terms for referents which may be taboo, such as for some body parts.

Throughout the developmental period, the adult's listening behavior serves as reinforcement for the child's increased use of speech. White and Watts (1973) found that mother's attention and acceptance of the young child's speech around twenty-four to twenty-seven months of age was a critical factor in the child's later development of competence. Newport, Gleitman, and Gleitman (1977) found that even responses such as "mm-hmmm" seem to serve as powerful reinforcers of the child's speech. The "mm-hmmm" signals the child that what he has said is worth listening to (and thus worth saying).

Children do not learn language in the same way in every community. Each community has its own expectations and customs. Shirley Brice Heath (1983) studied language development environments in two communities. Trackton was an all-black community of two-family rental homes. It was made up of those who considered themselves "respectable" and on the way up and the transients who settled for a short time while waiting to go up north or move into a public housing project. Most of the residents of Trackton worked at decent-paying but seasonal jobs. While the outside of their homes looked rundown, inside they were comfortably and nicely furnished. Roadville was a neighborhood of small, individually owned homes inhabited by white mill workers. The homes were neat and well kept up. Although their incomes were fairly good, having the right appliances and other material goods were valued and usually kept the families on a financial tightrope.

Roadville parents felt it was important for the baby to have his own space, if possible his own room. The first year was spent in a colorful environment with many toys and many opportunities for language and literacy experiences. The infant heard nursery rhymes and played with many objects that provided experiences with color, shape, and texture. Conversations with infants were frequent. So-called baby talk was commonly used. Mothers were cautioned not to pick up their babies too soon or too much and they learned to listen for sounds that told them the infant really needed something. Babies were given time alone to explore and to play with sounds. Mothers listened closely for any sound that approximated the first word. Mothers were home alone a great deal of the time and spent a lot of time talking with their infants. As soon as word approximations were picked up by adults, the adults addressed verbal responses to the infant using these words. They also began to label items for the infant, such as "Milk, say milk." Toddlers developed their own vocabulary that was picked up by the adults. Infants were encouraged in their monologs and adults expanded and extended what they heard the children say. Adults picked up on nouns used by children and use each noun as the topic of a lengthy discourse. Adults viewed themselves as language teachers for their young children and used every opportunity to teach labels, ask questions, and expand on the child's vocalizations. From the age of two and on, boys and girls were segregated in their play and provided with sex-stereotyped toys. Adults and older children played social games such as pat-a-cake and peek-a-boo. Most adult/child play centered on a book or a toy. By four, this play activity ended and most children went to nursery school for their educational activities. Moral education became dominant at home after four and children learned that there is one right way for everything. Thinking about alternatives was discouraged.

In contrast to Roadville infants, Trackton infants were surrounded by adults and older children night and day. They were almost never left alone to coo and babble on their own. They were constantly held and were in the midst of conversation and other household noises except when everyone went to bed. They were in the midst of communication between and among others, but communication was rarely, if ever, directed at them. They were talked about but not talked to. Adults felt that infant vocalization was not meaningful and that it was not necessary to respond to it. Adults believed that when a child was ready he would talk; you could not teach children to talk. Even when infants began to make their wants and needs known with meaningful sounds adults ignored them, believing that they (the adults) could best determine the infant's needs.

Toddlers were watched while they explored. Adult vocalizations usually were warnings of danger ("do's" or "don'ts"). Toddler boys had special status and were included in adult conversations because conversational skill was considered of special value for males. Boys were teased and taunted by adults and between sixteen and twenty-four months usually picked up a special phrase that they used to respond to their tormentors. For example, sixteen-month-old Teggie used "Go on, man" to mean "No," "Give it to me," and so on. Early on, Trackton children learned to judge from nonverbal behaviors just what role they should take with others. Posture and gesture were very important means of communication, as they told the child whether to tease, defy, boss, baby, or scold. In problem situations they were often provided with a question, "What you gonna do if . . . ?" and forced to think of their own solution.

In Trackton young children were not viewed as conversational partners. Children were not information givers; they were knowers. That is, they paid attention and learned. Toddler vocalization usually consisted of repetition of parts of the conversation going on around them. Eventually, these vocalizations developed into monologs parallel to the conversation they heard. Eventually, young children attempted to become conversationalists by breaking into the adults' conversation. Trackton parents did a lot of correcting and never used simplified speech or clarifications (such as talking slower). Girl talk followed the same stages as boy talk but at a later time

for each stage. Boys started trying to enter conversations around fourteen to eighteen months while girls began to participate around twenty-two months. Girls were not included in challenges but were included in female interchanges called **fussing** and in playsong games with older children. Playsong games are spontaneous rhymes and chants. They are much like nursery rhymes and guessing games middle-class mainstream adults play with their infants and toddlers. Young children were not expected to ask questions. Adults asked them questions. The most frequent questions were analogies designed to see if the child could transfer information from one situation to another: "What's dat like?" Trackton children centered on the smallest details of what they experienced. For example, when sorting items they tended to focus on some tiny detail like a slight blemish rather than on color, shape, or size. They could not answer questions regarding why they sorted as they did. Adults seldom asked them *why* questions. Most of the children's questions to adults had to with context: "Whose is this?" "You buy dese?" etc.

In both communities, children learned to talk but in vastly different language environments. Trackton infants "come up" while Roadville infants are "brought up." Trackton infants are surrounded constantly by others and have no particular routine while Roadville infants spend most of their time alone or with their mothers and follow a predictable daily routine. Roadville parents converse with their infants and toddlers and use direct instruction; Trackton parents talk about their children and expect them to learn on their own.

When enrolled in a preschool program, both groups presented language-related problems to their teachers. Both groups had dialects which did not fit the teachers' standards for speech. However, this did not bother the teachers as much as the ways children used language. Teachers could understand the words but not the meanings. The Trackton children did not answer questions and the Roadville children gave very minimal answers. On the children's part both groups had some difficulty in understanding indirectly stated rules such as, "Is this where the scissors belong?" vs. "The scissors belong in this basket."

KEYTERMSKEYTERMSKEYTERMSKEYTERMSKEYTERMSKEY

fussing

During group discussions the Trackton children interrupted and chatted with their neighbors. Teachers recognized that they had to take on new role behaviors in order to successfully teach these children. For example, they learned to give directions in direct ways and to be very specific. They based questions on children's own experiences and things in their neighborhoods. As teachers changed, so did the children, and everyone felt more satisfied and involved in school.

Heath's research documents how important it is for effective teachers to understand the language environment of their students' community and to find methods to work with what the children bring to school. Home values and methods may not prepare children for the usual mainstream, middle-class-oriented expectations. Heath documented this in another aspect of her research (Heath, 1982). Heath observed the classroom teachers at home interacting with their own children. She found that questions dominated their conversations with their preschool-age children. As parents the teachers felt that this was the only way to insure a response from the children, and they achieved success. It was no wonder that they proceeded with the same strategy in the classroom.

Snow, Dubber, and DeBlauw (1982) suggest this lack of school language preparation for non-mainstream children might stem from variations in parents' values regarding the kind of verbal facility that is important, lack of time and energy to work closely with the child during the early stages of language development, and/or use of different teaching styles. Research supports that an interactive style is the best preparation for school. The role of the parent is to take turns interacting with the child in what Snow et al. refer to as routines. Snow et al. describe three types of routines: formal games played by mothers and infants (such as peek-a-boo), instructional games played by mothers and infants during the second year (such as pointing to body parts and asking "What's this?"), and joint book-reading during the third year (accompanied by particular types of question asking by the mother). Snow suggests that the most language value comes from these routines when they are played over and over to the point where the child takes over and controls the game.

Schachter and Strage (1982, p. 10) have identified several strategies that adults use when they speak to beginning language learners:

1. To get and maintain the child's attention, the adult speaks in a high-pitched voice or addresses questions to the child.

2. Adults simplify speech: sounds, meanings, grammar, conversational patterns.

3. Adults repeat and rephrase their own speech.

4. The adult repeats or rephrases the child's speech, such as expanding a child's short verbalization ("More milk" becomes "You want more milk?")

5. The adult attaches words to the child's current experiences. For example, the adult describes what the child is doing or what the child wants. ("You are building with blocks" or "You want to climb on the chair?")

6. The adult speaks for the child by assuming adult and child roles in the conversation. For example, adult answers his or her own questions: "You want milk?" "Yes, you do want milk."

7. Adult responds to child's attempts at conversation, such as continuing with child initiated-topic rather than starting a new topic.

Mothers who are unaware of how to enrich their children linguistically can be trained to use language-enrichment activities with their young children. For example, in a study by McQueen and Washington (1988) a group of African-American adolescent mothers were given extensive training, which included the following activities:

• The mothers enrolled in classes in mathematics, English, child development, and parent education; they were taught methods of working with their children and served as teaching assistants in their child's classroom at the parent-child center (PCC).

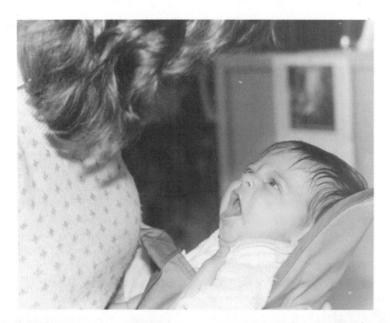

Figure 22–6   a, b, & c) **Conversation is essential to good language development from infancy, through preschool, kindergarten, and into first grade. Conversation begins with an adult and develops into an activity shared with other children.**

- Mothers and children met at the PCC and worked together making toys such as puzzles, felt boards, and musical instruments. Verbal mother/child conversation was stimulated during these sessions.

- At the PCC mothers read stories to their children and learned to follow-up by asking questions and listening to the answers, discussing the story with the children, and having the children retell the stories to their classmates.

This intensive parent education program had significant positive results on the children's performance on language tests as compared with children whose mothers had less extensive or no training in how to support children's language development. All these strategies encourage the child to become a conversationalist and engage in the give and take of dialog (Figure 22–6).

Genishi and Dyson (1984) describe the kinds of teacher talk that fosters oral language development for preschoolers, kindergartners, and primary-age children. For example, the teacher can step into preschoolers' dramatic play and ask a question that will make the children think of ways to expand and extend their activity:

- Tell me about .....
- What's going on here?
- Maybe you need .....
- That's a good idea.
- Call me when you are finished so I can see .....
- What does a ..... do?
- How can you fix the ..... ?

Teachers can also answer informational questions posed by children.

Kindergartners can apply language even further. Kindergartners also enjoy spontaneous conversation (Genishi & Dyson, 1984). Adults need to offer opportunities one to one, in small groups, and in large groups in order to fit each child's preferred setting for talk. Even in more formal, teacher-directed discussions there needs to be an informal, conversational tone that allows for each child's contribution. As with preschoolers adults can insert questions and comments into dramatic play activities. Science and mathematics provide opportunities for children to observe and to describe, analyze, and predict—all activities that enhance language development.

By the primary grades, children can become very skillful in communicating orally (Genishi, Dyson, & Fassler, 1994; Genishi & Dyson, 1984). Teachers only need to create situations that promote talking. At this age children can communicate well with each other and can be paired into teams with one child helping another. They can also work in small groups if given a clearly focused task. Large group discussions demand skillful teaching. Teachers need to ask open-ended questions: "Why?" "How do you know?" "Tell us what you mean" questions.

In Unit 23 we will examine children's use of language and adult techniques for enhancing language use in more detail. The development of competence with written language will be discussed in Unit 24.

SUMMARY

Children are born with the ability to develop language competence in a sequence of steps that go from the simple to the complex. The rate at which the child progresses through these steps is dependent upon inborn capacity and the response from the environment. As speech develops, what the child says reflects what he seems to be thinking. The adult who works with young children must be knowledgeable regarding the implications of cultural factors such as nonstandard dialect, if the child's first language is not English, and socioeconomic status in viewing the language development of the young child. The adult's role in language development is to provide the scaffolding experiences that support language development. The adult serves as a language model and provides language experiences and language interaction. The give-and-take conversation with a competent adult and with peers seems to be the most critical feature in successful early childhood language development.

FOR FURTHER READING

Ambert, A. M. (Ed.) (1991). *Bilingual education and English as a second language: A research handbook 1988–1990.* New York: Garland.

Bates, E., Bretherton, I., & Snyder, L. (1987). *From first words to grammar.* New York: Cambridge University Press.

Cazden, C. B. (Ed.). (1981). *Language in early childhood education* (rev. ed.). Washington, D.C.: National Association for the Education of Young Children.

Diaz, R. M. (1985). The intellectual power of bilingualism. *Quarterly Newsletter of the Laboratory of Comparative Human Cognition, 7* (1), 16–22.

Fletcher, P., & Garman, M. (1986). *Language acquisition.* New York: Cambridge University Press.

Franklin, M. B. (Ed.) (1987). *Child language: A reader.* New York: Oxford University Press.

Heath, S. B. (1983). *Ways with words: Language, life and work in communities and classrooms.* New York: Cambridge University Press.

Hyltenstam, K., & Obler, L. K. (Eds.). (1989). *Bilingualism across the lifespan.* New York: Cambridge University Press.

Jaggar, A. & Smith-Burke, M. T. (Eds.) (1985). *Observing the language learner.* Newark, DE: International Reading Association & Urbana, IL: National Council of Teachers of English.

John-Steiner, V., Panofsky, C. P., & Smith, L. W. (1994). (Eds.). *Sociocultural approaches to language and literacy.* New York: Cambridge University Press.

Levy, Y., Schlesinger, I. M., & Braine, M. D. S. (Eds.) (1988). *Categories and processes in language acquisition.* Hillsdale, NJ: Erlbaum.

Lindfors, J. W. (1987). *Children's language and learning.* Englewood Cliffs, NJ: Prentice-Hall.

Locke, J. L. (1993). *The child's path to spoken language.* Cambridge, MA: Harvard University Press.

McLaughlin, B. (1984). *Second language acquisition in childhood. Vol. 1: Preschool children (2nd ed.).* Hillsdale, NJ: Erlbaum.

McLeod, B. (Ed.). (1994). *Language and learning: Educating linguistically diverse students.* Albany, NY: SUNY Press.

Melendez, S. (1989). A nation of monolinguals, A multilingual world. *NEA Today, 7* (6), 70–74.

Merriman, W. E., & Bowman, L. L. (1989). The mutual exclusivity bias in children's word learning. *Monographs of the Society for Research in Child Development, 54* (3–4, Serial No. 220).

Nelson, K. E., & Reger, Z. (Eds.). (1994). *Children's language* (Vol. 8). Hillsdale, NJ: Erlbaum.

Neuman, S. B., & Roskos, K. A. (1993). *Language and literacy in the early years: An integrated approach.* Fort Worth, TX: Harcourt Brace.

Odlin, T. (1989). *Language transfer.* New York: Cambridge University Press.

Pellegrini, A. & Yawkey, T. (Eds.). (1984). *The development of oral and written language in social contexts.* Norwood, NJ: Ablex.

Reynolds, A. G. (Ed.). (1990). *Bilingualism, multiculturalism, and second language learning.* Hillsdale, NJ: Erlbaum.

Rice, M. L., Schiefelbusch, R. L. (Eds.). (1987). *The teachability of language.* Baltimore, MD: P. H. Brookes.

Slobin, I. (Ed.). (1986). *The cross-linguistic study of language acquisition.* Hillsdale, NJ: Erlbaum.

Snow, C., & Conti-Ramsden, G. (Eds.). (1990). *Children's language.* Hillsdale, NJ: Erlbaum.

Speidel, G. E., & Nelson, K. E. (1989). *The many faces of imitation in language learning.* New York: Springer-Verlag.

Vasquez, O. A., & Pease-Alvarez, L., & Shannon, S. M. (1994). *Pushing boundaries: Language and culture in a Mexicano community.* New York: Cambridge University Press.

Wells, G. (1985). *Language development in the preschool years.* New York: Cambridge University Press.

SUGGESTED ACTIVITIES

1. Discuss the following language samples with a small group in class. Analyze them and decide what stage the child is in by labeling each part of the sample according to its developmental level. Decide whether the child is vocalizing appropriately for her age. On a sheet of large chart paper or newsprint or on the chalkboard, list the characteristics found for each sample. Compare your results with those of the other student groups. Note

any differences and discuss them. Be sure to decide on the kind of role the adult takes in those samples that include an adult.

Sample 1. Child is 2 months old. She is in her crib watching a mobile and rattling a toy elephant. She bumps the mobile with her arm which flails with excitement as she observes the mobile.

> Igh* ee ee igh a
> a a a a
> (guttural, like a growl) a a a
> a e a
> a a a
>   *rhymes with sigh

Sample 2. Child is 5 months and 3 weeks of age. She is crawling around the living room.

Mother	Child
e-he ba-ba boo-boo	
Hi Hi Kate Hi	
The elephant goes keetsch keetsch	e-we
	ab awa
	aw aba
No No	ub ha
	h ma-ma
No No	uw uw he-e
No No	he we he me-he
She's after the light plug hole.	

Sample 3. Mother and child are in the living room. Mother is trying to get child to speak. Child is now nineteen months old.

Mother	Child
What's this? Where's your shoe? Where's your shoe?	my shoe
Shoe. Yes, shoe.	shoe
What's this? What's that?	ka
Car	ka ka
Another car, yes.	nother, ka, ka
What's this?	baby, muk
Milk, yes. Very good.	muk
Milk, yes.	digh digh digh
Let's look in here, Kate	
What's this?	bee
What are those?	kee
Key, key, yes. Hey, who is this guy? What is that?	beebee
Who is it?	beebee
Beebee (baby), yes. Let's see now. Let's look in here.	
Who is this?	kighkiki
A kitty, kitty, yes.	

Sample 4. Child is now 3 years and 8 months of age. She is in the bathtub with an assortment of toys.

Mother	*Child*
	Do you like the House on the Prairie?
Yes, I like it. I like those little girls.	
	Well, this is on the TV.
Okay. What time is it on?	And it's on.
Oh, what time is it?	The little girls are going in the old plane and they are good and the old plane is going to crash.
Ah! Oh gosh!	And then they are gonna be dead.
Oh, No!	But their daddy and mommy and the little girls are gonna be in it.
Um.	And the pilot is gonna say hi to the mommy and daddy and the little girls.
Uh hum.	But he doesn't know that the pilot cooks something bad.
Oh!	They don't know.
Oh. They won't go in then.	Yes and they will fall in this wastebasket.
Uh hum.	And then he will say Oh Oh Oh what did I put in food. I don't like it. He will say that.
Uh hum.	He will throw it out for them.
Uh hum.	The people, the Little House on the Prairie, will give them the food.
Oh, I see.	And they don't get bad food now.
Oh.	They don't got more bad food. They don't got more bad food. They but they don't got more bad food.
I see.	But you got bad food. Do you got bad food?
No.	Well you got bad food.
Ummm.	And I don't want to eat it.

Sample 5. Child is 3 years and 7 months of age. She is in the bathtub with a bunch of toys—dolls, a boat, furniture. She's playing house with a Barbie doll and some horses.

The horses are gonna eat here, Lisa.
The horse, the horse.
That's a good girl.
And now you horse.
That's a good girl.
Now you horse, okay?
Good girl, horse.
And now you horse. Yeah, now you, now you Blackie.
I want some.
No you don't want some.
You sit on a chair.
I'm eating.
Okay.
(Shouts) I'm putting—I'm putting my dolly on a chair.

Barbie, Barbie, Barbie, Barbie ... (sings this)
(high pitched) 'Cause my mommy is washing my hair today.
So I know how to do it.
I'm closing my eyes.
(High pitched) I'm not closing my eyes.

2. With another student, plan and present a debate on the merits of teaching dialect-speaking and/or non-English speaking young children using a programmed drill method versus an activity-centered method. As preparation do some additional background reading on the pros and cons of each method. Have a third student serve as moderator. After each of you has spent 10 minutes presenting a case for each side of the issue, open the floor to questions and comments from the class. Each debater should then give a three-minute summation. Finally have the class members vote on which method they feel is best.

3. Visit a nursery school, day-care center, kindergarten, or a child at home playing with his neighborhood friends. The child observed should be about four to five years old. Observe for about half an hour, taking down verbatim as much as possible of what the child says. Be sure the child is engaged in play activities. If you have a choice, pick a child who is known to talk a lot while playing.

After your observation, on the same day or another day (with the teacher's or parent's permission) interview the child to find out how he acts in a more structured language situation. Use the following tasks. Be sure to prepare the needed materials ahead of time and be sure you have practiced the instructions.

Task 1: Labeling Objects
Place four common objects or pictures of four common objects in front of the child. Say, "What is this?" (Point to each object in turn.)

Sample of objects (pictures):

Task 2: Describing Objects
Show the child each of four common objects or pictures of four common objects one at a time. Say, "Tell me about this."
Note: name, color, use, shape, parts, composition, etc.

Task 3: Story Telling
Present the child with some interesting objects and/or pictures. Ask him to tell a story (tape record it, if possible). Write a report considering the following.
(1) Include at the beginning of your report:
    a. the child's name,
    b. the child's age, and
    c. where the child was observed and where he was interviewed.
(2) Include a record of everything the child said during your observation and in response to the interview tasks.
(3) Analyze the classroom observation considering the following aspects:
    a. length of sentences used,
    b. dialect of non-English words used,

    c. ability to use sounds (note if any sounds were substituted or omitted),

    d. size of vocabulary and correct use of words, and

    e. use of language in appropriate ways.

(4) Analyze the interview task responses:

    a. Consider whether complete sentences, phrases, or single words were used when responding.

    b. Note length of sentences used.

    c. For the specific tasks:

        Task 1: How many of the objects did he label correctly? Did he say anything besides the names of each object?

        Task 2: Count how many descriptive terms the child used for each object.

        Task 3: Do the same analysis you used for his talk during play. (See Task 3 above.)

(5) Evaluate the language used during the play observation and during the interview tasks. Compare average sentence length used and the percentage of phrases and complete sentences in each situation. What similarities and differences are there? How do you account for them?

(6) Overall, what did you learn about this child's language development? Were you surprised or did he respond as you would expect for a child his age?

4. Visit a preschool, kindergarten, and/or first-grade classroom. Observe the teachers in each setting and record everything they and the children say. Use a tape recorder with the teacher's permission. Analyze the verbalizations of the teachers and the children relative to the factors discussed in this unit regarding the adult role. Which techniques did the adults use? Was there give-and-take dialog? Is there conversation? If possible, observe a parent and child at home, record the language used, and analyze it. Compare your results with those of other students in the class.

5. Make an entry in your journal.

REVIEW

A. Match the definitions in Column I with the terms in Column II. Some of the terms may be used more than once.

Column I	Column II
1. A well-ordered system of rules that every member of a language community tacitly comprehends in speaking, listening, and writing.	a. phoneme (phonology)
2. These two types of rules deal with how sounds are put together in a meaningful way.	b. morpheme (morphology)
3. Examples of these types of sounds are *bar* and *-ed*.	c. syntax
4. These types of rules are used to put words in the proper order to make acceptable phrases and sentences.	d. semantics
5. According to this type of rule, it is more socially acceptable to say, "Please pass the salt" than to say, "Pass the salt!"	e. pragmatics
6. *Dog* refers to a four-legged fur-covered animal that barks and is usually a house-hold pet.	f. language
7. Some examples are /a/, /b/, /c/.	
8. Examples of this type of rule used correctly in English are *br, cl, fr.*	

B. According to the current view, how is language learned?

C. For each of the following vocal samples, identify the developmental age/stage, identify the semantic element, and evaluate whether the child is developing at a normal rate relative to his age.
1. One-month-old Tony is crying. Mrs. Smith comes in and says, "I know that cry; you are hungry."
2. Twelve-month-old Maria says, "Muk, muk." Mrs. Sanchez gives her a cup of milk.
3. Kate, age two, holds her dolly tenderly, saying, "Hurty tummy, hurty tummy."
4. Rudy, age three, says, "Mama, I want a trike for Christmas."
5. Angela, age 7 months, lies in her playpen gazing at a mobile and chattering, "Aba-abi-abi-bi ma-mu-ma-mum."
6. Larry, age four, says, "Airplane go up!"
7. Bobby, age 17 months, says, "Doggy bark!"

D. Evaluate each of the following examples:
1. Two-year-old John sees a cat run across the yard. He says, "Wabbit! Wabbit!"
2. Mary walks up to Laurie and says, "Give me that dolly right now!" Janie says, "No, Laurie, please give me the dolly." Laurie gives Janie the doll.
3. Two-year-old Janie has a vocabulary that includes some of the following strange-sounding words:

Doy (joy)	see (sheep)
how (cow)	hoay (horse)
du (duck)	yeow (meow)
bea (bear)	boo (spoon)
pea ba (peanut butter)	bamma (grandma)

4. George inquires, "Mommy, why doesn't Daddy like pizza?" Mommy responds with the question, "Why do you say that Daddy doesn't like pizza?" After this Georgie replies, "Daddy isn't home. He comes home late when we eat pizza" It happens that on Friday evenings when George's father works the late shift the family eats pizza (*Growing Child*, 1973).
5. Derrick, age five, shouts, "I wanna go to ta park."
6. Since Alfredo was a baby his mother has always spoken to him in English and his father in Spanish. Alfredo speaks well in both languages.
7. Mother: "What's this? Where's your shoe? Where's your shoe?" Child: "My shoe. Shoe." Mother: "Shoe. Yes, shoe. What's this? What's this?" Child: "Ka." Mother: "Yes, car."
8. Mary sticks her hand into the dough mother is making. "Bad girl, Mary. Wash your hands first," Mother says. Mary runs to the bathroom and washes her hands. Mother responds, "Good girl. Clean hands."

E. If you should find yourself teaching children from a culture and/or SES level different from your own, what would you need to do to ensure a successful experience for yourself and the children?

F. What are the important factors in the adult role in relation to child language development?

Language in Everyday Use: Oral Language

OBJECTIVES

After studying this unit, the student should be able to:

- Recognize some of the aspects of early childhood language use established by current research.

- Categorize children's language samples using the category systems developed by Michael Halliday and Joan Tough.

- Know how to expand children's oral language use.

- Explain how play supports academic achievement.

- Discuss the relationship of play and language use.

Each year a teacher friend of columnist Jack Smith (Smith, 1991, January 23) sends him a compilation of her kindergarten students' word definitions. These definitions provide insight into how young children decide on the meaning of new words. For some of the words, they use the word in the definition. For others, they relate to a word they already know that sounds the same or similar. For example:

Language—When you say a bad word, someone says, "Watch your language."

Adore—You go through it so you can go in and out.

Bachelor—You can flip things over with it; the things that you take off cookies with.

Marriage—You like that person and you fall in love and you get married.

Analogy—It's a germ; you get the flu; you get sick; it's your mind.

Brain—You keep your words that you want to say in there; in your head there's this thing that makes you think.

Catherine Garvey (1990) describes the nature of children's talk. Talk is the oral aspect of language. Talk is a natural activity that takes place in the due course of biological development just like walking or playing. Talk is the vehicle through which children learn language. Language develops as the child listens to others talk and as the child talks. Most talk takes

KEYTERMSKEYTERMSKEYTERMSKEYTERMSKEYTERMSKEYTERMSKEY

Talk

place in social settings, but important talk events also take place when the child is alone. It is by listening to children's talk that we infer much regarding how they use language. Talk is the active aspect of language and goes hand in hand with learning social action and interaction. Conversation is a cooperative task in which each party has expectations as to what the other party means and what kind of response is appropriate when each party has his or her turn. The situation within which the talk takes place is very important relative to the talk's meaning to the participants.

Young children gradually learn rules for forming words from sounds and sentences from words. They learn to attach words or approximations of words to referents that are understandable to other people. They learn how to communicate in the variety of situations they find themselves in each day. Young children learn to use talk to protect their rights and justify their actions, to direct the behavior of others, and to obtain needed items. Eventually talk is used to tell about the past, present, and future; to solve problems logically; to ask questions; to develop imaginative situations; to maintain social relationships; and to express feelings. Talk is an important part of young children's play. Adults have a crucial role in supporting the child's increasing skill as an oral language user.

THE INFANT'S USE OF LANGUAGE

It is well documented that infants develop different cries for expressing their need for food, relief of pain, and sleep. However, there is some question as to whether the other kinds of sounds that infants make are meaningful in any way. Several questions have been asked by those who study infant vocalization and its development:

- If infant vocalizations are meaningful, at what age do they begin to be so?
- Are there situational variations for infant vocalizations?
- Are infant vocalizations like later vocalizations, or do they consist of a unique infant sound system?

There has been a great deal of research on adults' (and especially mothers') speech behavior

relative to infants but less on infants' vocal behavior as directed toward humans or objects. The following are some basic facts that have emerged from some of the research on infant vocalization:

1. There does seem to be a direct relationship between the phonetic aspects of infant vocalization and the phonology of later speech (Oller, 1977; Stark et al., 1975). That is, the sounds that an infant makes are like the ones he will use when he learns to speak.

2. Meaning develops from the situations in which the infant is placed (Freedle & Lewis, 1977). That is, the amount and kind of vocalizing the infant does depends on where he is; floor, mother's lap, playpen, or infant seat. For example, infants were observed to do more intense vocalizing when in the infant seat communicating with mother than when seated on mother's lap.

3. Infants carry on a gamelike conversation with objects (such as mobiles and toys) as well as with people (Watson, 1972). For example, a four-month-old is in her playpen "talking" to her toy rubber dog:

   > e-e ma a
   > e-e-e a
   > e-e a
   > hav
   > he-e-e
   > he e-he

4. Infants respond to speech from the first day of life (and possibly in utero). They have been observed to synchronize their body movements in rhythm with adult speech (Condon, 1979). Mothers address preverbal infants with identifiably differentiated "melodies" that communicate their intent to the infant (Fernald, 1989).

5. Meaning enters infant vocalization by the middle of the first year (Halliday, 1979). The infant develops both verbal and nonverbal signs that carry specific meaning. For example, Halliday's son Nigel at eight months expressed the following:

Meaning	Expression
I want that. I don't want that. Do something with that for me to watch.	Nonverbal: Grasps an object momentarily and then lets go Touches object lightly for a moment Touches object firmly for a longer time
Let's be together. That's interesting.	Vocal: A distinct vowel sound with a low falling tone A distinct vowel sound with a mid-falling tone

Halliday found that by nine or ten months, his son Nigel was rapidly constructing a protolanguage. A **protolanguage** consists of meaningful sound combinations that are not words. At this point the child is able to use verbal communication intentionally (Smolak, 1986). That is, the infant realizes that sound patterns can be used to influence the behavior of others.

6. In certain situations each normal child makes very similar noises (Ricks, 1979). Distinct vocalizations are made that adults can interpret as a:

   • request.

   • frustrated noise.

   • greeting noise.

   • pleasantly surprised noise.

7. Before the development of speech, infants develop mouth movements that resemble smiles, sneers, rage. Other emotions are also expressed (Trevarthen, 1979). They also move their lips in speechlike movements that may be imitations of what they see. Further, they have been observed to try to get others to respond to them. When their conversation is interrupted they will wave their arms, grimace, and otherwise try to regain the center of attention. The infant is often the one in control in its vocal exchanges.

There is, then, some research indicating that speech, in a real sense, begins to develop gradually starting at birth and continuing through early primitive communications to some apparently consistently meaningful vocalization by 5 or 6 months of age.

THE TODDLER'S USE OF LANGUAGE

Many studies have examined the period around ten to eighteen months of age when the child says his first word. The following are some of the results that have come from this research:

1. When an analysis was made of the first fifty words acquired by a sample of children between the ages of one and two (Nelson, 1973), it was found that beginning language usually involved the naming of objects that were acted upon by the child, such as a ball, or acted upon by others, such as a car.

2. Children continue in their first talk to speak about objects and their ideas regarding these objects (Bloom, Lightbown, & Hood, 1975).

3. As children move into two-word combinations there seem to be some consistent patterns that they use (Braine, 1976), such as:

   • Patterns that draw attention to something.
       See + _____ (See dog, See car, See doll)

   • Patterns that refer to specific properties of objects:
       Big/little + _____ (Big dog, Little doll)

   • Patterns concerned with having something happen again:
       More + _____ (More milk)

   • Patterns concerned with disappearance:

Allgone + _____ (Allgone milk, Allgone Dad)

- Patterns expressing the negative:
No + _____ (No milk, No bath)

- Patterns that request:
Want + _____ (Want milk, Want cookie)

Through this study of his son, Nigel, Michael Halliday (1975) looked at the meaning of language as it functions for the child; that is, the purpose to which the child puts his developing language skills. Halliday views language as developing in three phases from the age of around 12 months to the adultlike speech of the two-year old:

- Phase I: The child develops his own language. By 16 1/2 months, Nigel has 12 meanings. By 18 months, he has 150 meanings and is ready to enter phase II.

- Phase II: Transitional stage, which begins between 12 and 18 months of age. The following examples were collected by the author of this text:

	Daughter
Mother	*(17 months)*
Hey, who is this guy?	bee-bee
Who is that?	
Who is it?	bee-bee
Beebee (baby), yes. Let's see now. Let's look in here. (Opens book) Who is this?	kighkiki
A kitty kitty, yes.	

- Phase III: Adultlike stage, which starts around age two-and-a-half. The following examples involve the author of this text and her daughter at age two years and ten months. Daughter is playing with a doll (Michael) in the bathtub.

| *Mother* | *Daughter* |
| No, not yet. | Michael can have some (water). Michael can have some. He could have some drink, some, some pop for me to drink and this is Kate's. |

An amazing change has taken place in just seventeen months. Language before about eighteen months is very much children's own. They may or may not imitate exactly what they hear an adult say. After 18 months, they rapidly develop adult words.

Halliday developed a category system to describe the functions of language during phases I and II prior to adultlike usage. The seven categories are:

1. Instrumental: The child demands service or materials. Examples: "I want." "Where's mine?" "Give me that."

2. Regulatory (See Figure 23–1): The child uses commands or requests to control the behavior of others. Examples: "Do that." "Let's go." "Pick me up."

3. Interactional: Language is used to interact: to greet, call by name, respond to another. Examples: "Me and you." "Look at this." "This is for you."

4. Personal: Language is used to express uniqueness and self-awareness (such as personal feelings, interest, disgust, complaint, surprise, joy). Examples: "I'm going to." "I am . . ." "That's my . . ."

5. Heuristic: The child asks and acknowledges questions. Examples: "Tell me why." "What's that (called)?"

6. Imaginative: The child creates his own environment, makes up stories, plays let's pretend, and recites jingles, rhymes, or chants.

Figure 23–1   "That one," says the toddler, as he uses the regulatory function of language.

7. Informative: Gives some information that is not known by others. Examples: "I've got something to tell you."

Halliday found that prior to 18 months of age, Nigel developed the following pattern: categories 1 through 4 were used up to 12 months of age; category 6 between 15 and 16-and-a-half months of age; and all but the seventh appeared by 18 months. Personal use occurred most often followed by instrumental and regulatory use. Interactional use occurred less often and the amount of heuristic and imaginative use was very small.

Figure 23–2 gives the results in a chart. Nigel at 18 months is compared with the author's daughter at two-and-a-half to three-and-a-half years. It can be seen that for the older child there is much less instrumental use, about the same regulatory use, more interactional and less personal use, and an increase in heuristic and imaginative use. Informative use has appeared. The language used by the older child is less self-centered. Conversations have more give and take.

LANGUAGE USE FROM PRESCHOOL TO PRIMARY

Halliday's work offers evidence of the variety of language use the child develops by the time he reaches the preschool stage. It is interesting to compare the child's use of language with that of an adult, another child, or with himself when he is playing alone. Some examples from research on the preschool to primary child's use of language are:

1. The child modifies his speech to fit the age of the listener (Shatz & Gelman, 1973). For example, the child uses longer sentences when speaking to an adult than to a child. The child seems to have some idea of what the audience expects and can understand.

2. During free-play time after age three, talk becomes less self-centered and more collaborative. Middle-class children are more likely to assert themselves and seek help from the adults in school than are lower-class children (Schachter et al., 1974).

3. Young children's talk is more advanced when the child is conversing about a familiar topic than about a nonfamiliar topic and when the child is engaged in dramatic play that centers on a familiar theme. A theme in which the child knows the roles, objects, and sequence of activities elicits higher level speech than does an unfamiliar theme (French, Lucariello, Seldman, & Nelson, 1985). Thus, to assess the child's real oral language capability, data needs to be obtained when the child is talking about a familiar topic or playing a familiar role.

4. Children's use of language is reflected in their talk about books and about their artwork. Book experiences elicit questions and answers. Artwork elicits a description or a story (Genishi & Dyson, 1984).

5. Dramatic play is the setting for rich communication (Genishi & Dyson, 1984).

Child	Percentage of Each of Halliday's Categories Used						
	1. Instrumental	2. Regulatory	3. Interactional	4. Personal	5. Heuristic	6. Imaginative	7. Informative
Nigel* (18 months)	21.4%	20%	11%	42.07%	2%	3%	0%
Kate (30–42 months)	1.56%	27%	29.6%	18.6%	14.8%	12.5%	4.4%

Figure 23–2 **Comparison of the language use of an eighteen-month-old with that of a child between two-and-a-half and three-and-a-half shows the development toward more variety and the appearance of the more mature uses. (*Nigel's data from M. A. K. Halliday,** *Learning how to mean: Explorations in the development of language*. **London: Edward Arnold)**

6. Kindergartners take part in complex conversation while engaged in open-ended activities such as dramatic play, art, science, and math (Genishi & Dyson, 1984). Children seem to rely on the concrete referents (such as being able to view each other's drawings) to support their conversation (Ramirez, 1989).

7. Young children often engage in private speech, that is, speech that takes place when they are alone and that seems to be addressed to themselves or to no one in particular. Most private speech is used for self-guidance, but it can also be used for word play, fantasizing, and some affect expression. In addition, private speech is used for "verbal stimulation; play and relaxation; to express feelings and emotionally integrate thoughts and experiences" (Berk, 1985, p. 49). The amount of private speech used when performing a new task is positively related to the degree of success on the task in the future (Behrend, Rosengren, & Perlmutter, 1989). Thus private speech appears to support learning.

8. Young children often don't realize when they have sent or received an inadequate message (Beal & Belgrad, 1990; Robinson & Robinson, 1983; Sodian & Schneider, 1990).

9. Children's speech during instructional sessions reflects the emphasis made by their teachers during instruction (Lawton & Fowell, 1989).

10. Children's verbalization can affect the curriculum through opportunities to ask questions, engage in discussion, report information, and teach peers (Kessler, 1989).

11. Through dialogues with parents children learn the strategies needed in order to maintain dialogues with peers (Martinez, 1987).

12. During their third year children learn to monitor family conversations and intrude with relevant questions and information (Dunn & Shatz, 1989). These young children are already learning how to link into an ongoing dialogue between an older sibling and the mother.

Joan Tough (1977) did some of the most extensive research on the use of language by young children. She sampled the language of some children in England at ages three, five-and-a-half, and seven-and-a-half. At age three, the sample was obtained while the child played with a friend using a standard set of play materials for 45 to 60 minutes.

Tough found that Halliday's categories did not make fine enough distinctions for the complex talk of three-year-olds. She came up with four categories or functions of child speech (Figure 23–3). A **function** in terms of child speech is a means by which a child achieves some purpose through the use of language. Within each function there are subcategories or uses. The four functions according to Tough (1977, pp. 47–69) are:

1. Directive Function: The child is concerned with directing actions and operations.
   a. Self-directing language such as:
      Jimmie: This car goes down here . . . the little car.
      Pushing it down here . . . the little car.
   b. Other directing language such as:
      James: Put your brick right on top. Be careful . . . don't push it . . .

Function	Use
1. Directive	a. Self-directing b. Other directing
2. Interpretive	a. Reporting on present and past experiences b. Reasoning
3. Projective	a. Predicting b. Empathetic c. Imaginative
4. Relational	a. Self-maintaining b. Interactional

Figure 23–3 **Tough's language categories**

2. Interpretive Function: The child communicates the meaning of events or situations. He is concerned with present experiences or memories of the past. He uses logical reasoning.
   a. Reporting:

   Mark: That's a dog and that's an cat.
   Tim: I saw a big ship . . . and it was going on the sea.
   Tom: The garage is too small for the car to go in.

   b. Reasoning:

   Jane: And the ice cream was soft because we forgot to put it in the fridge.
   Andrew: People don't like you if you take their things . . . I don't do that.

3. Projective Function: The child talks about situations in which he is not presently involved. He speaks of things in the future; things that haven't happened and might never happen.
   a. Predicting:

   Jill: Wait until she is four or eight and then she'll go to school and she'll be a new person to go to school.
   Meg: My mom'll be cross 'cos I've got my sleeves wet.

   b. Empathetic:

   Tim: The boy wouldn't like going up and down on the see-saw . . . it would make him feel sick.

   c. Imagining:

   Tom: The building's all on fire . . . a man at the top . . . can't get down . . . fire engine comes . . . er-er-er-er . . . get out the ladder . . . put it up . . .

4. Relational Function: The child relates himself to others through his use of language.
   a. Self-maintaining:

   "I want a biscuit."
   "Can I have a sweet?"
   "Go away you're hurting me."
   "I want a red crayon so I can draw my picture better."

   "I don't like your picture."
   "If you spoil my castle I'll have to tell the teacher."

   b. Interactional:

   "Would you give me my car back now 'cos I'm going home."
   (A more thoughtful, less self-centered relationship than self-maintaining)

Tough analyzed the samples of spontaneous speech of three-year-olds that she collected. She found that the amount of talk from the lower- and upper-middle-class children was about the same but that the variety was quite different. The language of lower socioeconomic class children, she indicated, "tended to be limited to the ongoing present experience and to monitoring their own activities." The upper-middle-class children used language more often for:

- Analyzing and reasoning about present and past experiences, and recognizing overall structure;
- Projecting beyond the present experience to future events, possible alternative courses and consequences, and into the feelings and experiences of others;
- Creating imagined scenes for their play which were dependent on the use of language for their existence for others.

Tough concludes (1977, pp. 165–166) "[The lower socioeconomic class] child's disadvantage in school seems to stem more from a lack of motivation to think in these ways, from lack of experience in thinking in these ways and from his general lack of awareness of meaning of this kind." The problem does not stem from a lack of language resources.

LANGUAGE USE IN PLAY

Young children spend most of their time in play activities. Play situations have proven to be a rich source of information on language use during early childhood. Research has provided the following kinds of data:

1. Observations of two- to five-year-olds indicated that during dramatic play older children's talk reflects a more in-depth knowledge of the

various roles and factors in the real-life setting that they are dramatizing. The older children carry on more mature conversations. They had better strategies for settling disagreements (Sachs, Goldman & Chaille, 1985).

2. Dramatic play is a vehicle through which young children develop the ability to construct stories that demonstrate narrative competence: that is, they can tell or retell a story that ". . . combines an appropriate setting with characters that react to a central problem through a sequence of events that move to a logical conclusion" (Galda, 1984, p. 105).

3. Children who use the most complex talk during play also use the most complex talk in oral recall of familiar stories. This indicates that language used in dramatic play and language used in story telling follow the same developmental path (Guttman & Frederiksen, 1985).

4. The skills learned in preschool dramatic play are applied by kindergarten and primary students to inform others during "Show and Tell" times. Kindergarten children tend to focus on action statements that tell what they do or what an object does (Evans, 1985).

5. Valuable experiences during dramatic play include the opportunity for exchange and turntaking in language use, for taking another's point of view during conversation, and for modification of language to fit a partner's age level (Yawkey & Miller, 1984).

6. Planning is an important part of sociodramatic play. Two-year-olds have been observed to never plan their dramatic play roles ahead; three-and-one-half-year-olds spend a lot of time planning their roles (often due to disagreement regarding who will get a most desired role), and 50 percent of their talk has to do with planning action usually regarding who would use particular play objects; five-year-olds decide on roles quickly, settle disagreements more easily, use more complex action-planning talk, and

more complex plots. For sociodramatic play to be successful, children have to be able to pretend (Figure 23–4), take on a role, know about the theme of the play, carry out actions that go with the theme, communicate ideas, and resolve conflict. Language capability is essential to success in all the competencies, while engaging in these activities provides practice in use of language (Sachs, Goldman, & Chaille, 1984).

Communication is a critical part of dramatic play. As children get older their pretend play becomes more complex and each episode lasts longer (Farver, 1992).

7. Dramatic play centers such as the kitchen area promote higher level fantasy play and accompanying conversation (Asquith & French, 1989). This type of communication through conversation requires good listening skills which are in turn necessary for literacy development.

8. Language level is affected by the setting in which the communication takes place. For example, Benedict (1994) found that kindergartners displayed more advanced oral lan-

Figure 23–4 **To sustain sociodramatic play roles, children must have highly developed language skills.**

guage facility during dramatic play than during other activities and more advanced oral language facility in a whole language as compared with a basal-based classroom. Isbell and Raines (1991) found differences in fluency when comparing preschool children's use of language in block, housekeeping, and thematic centers. The children were most fluent in the block center, next in the thematic center, and least in the housekeeping center.

9. As mentioned earlier, children's private speech is also an important language aspect of dramatic play when children are alone or with others (Berk, 1985).

10. Children's use of language in sociodramatic play is based upon the language used in their culture. For example, when three-and-one-half to five-year-old African-American girls were observed while engaged in family sociodramatic play, mother was dominant in language production, with twice as many utterances as other pretend characters. Mothers' talk reflected both strictness and nurturance. Daughter/big sister players spoke much like mother and changed to less complex talk when speaking to baby (versus mother). Overall the talk was an accurate reflection of real-life talk in the African-American family (McLoyd, Ray, & Etter-Lewis, 1985).

11. Strategies for second language acquisition have been observed during sociodramatic play. For example, from observations of a preschooler who spoke Korean as a first language and was in the process of learning English through her experiences in nursery school, it was found that the dramatic play dialog the child had observed was the basis of much of her initial English talk. She tried out the dialog when playing alone and then would attempt to apply what she learned during cooperative play. Her first successes were in establishing the theme, naming characters, and setting a goal. However, she couldn't negotiate with her peers in English.

She turned to pretend reading to her dolls for English practice before returning, with more success, to cooperative dramatic play (Heath, 1985). Peer relationships among a group of four Korean-speaking preschoolers supported their participation in a classroom in which the teacher and the other children were English speakers. Being free to communicate in their primary language and to imitate during the normal classroom activities allowed them to become active participants in these activities (Meyer, Klein, & Genishi, 1994).

These examples demonstrate the value of sociodramatic play for oral language learning and oral language practice.

THE ADULT'S ROLE IN EXPANDING THE CHILD'S USE OF ORAL LANGUAGE

As already described in Unit 21, there are many ways adults can foster young children's language development. Adults can begin in infancy with a conversational give and take that should continue all through early childhood. They also provide peers with whom the young child can practice and expand oral language skills. Finally, adults provide many social and informational experiences that give children something to talk about in situations such as sociodramatic play, dialog with adults or other children, and school discussion settings such as Show and Tell. Young children must learn to use language for a variety of purposes. Adults can help children become reflective and carry on an inner dialog. They can help children think aloud and help them extend their imaginative play through language. Adults can offer opportunities for children to report, to go beyond the observable, immediate situation by use of imagination, and to reason and solve problems. Adults assess where the child is in the development of language use, that is, the zone of proximal development, and provide the experiences that serve as the scaffolding that enables the child to move to the limits of the current zone of proximal development.

Joan Tough (1973) offers some specific strategies for extending the variety in the child's talk. She offers three basic suggestions: invite the child to talk (Figure 23–5), help him to talk in order to think, and help him use his language in contexts of imagination.

Jeffrey Trawick-Smith (1994) describes the importance of having authentic dialog with children, that is, a dialog in which "children and adults talk to each other about interesting, relevant matters" (p. 10). Trawick-Smith believes these conversations provide natural opportunities for adults to model language that is slightly beyond the children's current ability. Trawick-Smith describes some critical features of "teacher talk." Responding is critical as long as it is geared to the meaning of the children's talk and not to the form (i.e., correcting grammar). The adult should expand on the topic of the children's remarks, not correct them or change them. Verbal elaboration that is carefully done can also be valuable. Adults can make comments or ask questions regarding the children's activities that invite responses, not make statements or ask questions designed to control the activity. Questions also can facilitate language development if they are open-ended (versus closed, one answer questions). It is important to allow time for children to think through their answers. **Adult-to-child language (ACL)** is a special form of speech that adults use when speaking with children. It tends to be slower and more deliberate and contain shorter sentences than adult-to-adult language. It should be just beyond the children's current complexity level in their own use of language.

While Tough, Trawick-Smith, and others emphasize the importance of conversation in developing oral language competence, Berk (1985) suggests some ways adults can promote the child's use of private speech as an aid in problem solving:

1. Provide for play in social contexts, since private speech emerges out of social situations.

2. Provide guidance and direction in problem-solving until children feel confident in going ahead on their own.

3. Supply the children with questions that they can use in future problem-solving situations.

4. Provide clues, rather than giving answers. For example, when doing a puzzle, "Which space is the same shape as this piece?"

5. Let children vocalize when they are working. Private speech helps children through changes and assists them in arriving at solutions to problems.

Another critical factor under the control of adults is the way the classroom is set up (the room arrangement and the materials and activities available). Pellegrini (1984) observed the language behavior of two-, three-, and four-year-olds as they involved themselves in various activity centers provided in their preschool classrooms. He categorized the children's talk using Halliday's categories. Housekeeping centers and blocks elicited a large amount of imaginative language. There was also a great deal of social interactional and multifunctional language use in the housekeeping center, which supported group sociodramatic imaginary themes. In contrast, in centers such as art and water play the activity is individual and conversation is not needed to sustain it. Isbell and Raines (1991) also found that the type of center in which a dialog took place affected language production.

Pellegrini also looked at the effect of adult pres-

Figure 23–5 The first step in expanding the child's use of language is the invitation to talk.

KEYTERMSKEYTERMSKEYTERMSKEYTERMSKEYTERMSKEYTERMSKEY

Adult-to-child language (ACL)

ence in the centers. While the presence of adults increased younger children's talk, it decreased the older children's talk. It may be that the older children had reached a level where they could sustain their own play and no longer needed adult support. For the two's and three's the adult presence was necessary. The results of this study suggest that dramatic play centers are essential for providing opportunities to use language fully. It also suggests that teachers should be cautious about involvement in older children's sociodramatic play. If the play is proceeding well and the children are using imaginative and multifunctional language, the adult should stay out.

Pellegrini's classroom conclusions are supported by research focusing on parent scaffolding. Behrend et al. (1989) found that parental interactive style had a strong effect on children during a researcher-designed play session. Stronger parental control seemed to be helpful to the three-year-olds while it lowered the level of performance of five-year-olds.

Adults also take the role of assessor of language use. Through observation adults can obtain samples of child language and find out if children are using language for a variety of functions. Genishi and Dyson (1984) suggest several ways adults can record and assess young children's language development: handwritten notes, tape recordings, observation forms and checklists, and specific language interview tasks. Lane and Bergan (1988) looked at the effects of instructional variables on the language ability of preschoolers enrolled in Head Start. They found that the students who received more direct language instruction and whose teachers did the best job of assessing what they needed when they planned instruction evidenced the highest levels of language competence.

It is clear that adults can enhance the oral language competence of young children through making an assessment of where the child's strengths and weaknesses are and planning for a variety of oral language experiences with adults and with peers.

Cultural Diversity and Language Use

In Unit 22 the options for adults working with children from diverse cultures have already been described. The importance of providing a variety of op-

portunities for conversation for all children is extremely important. As mentioned previously, in many settings a bilingual (BL) approach will work well in a setting where there is a large number of minority language (ML) speaking students and a teacher who speaks their primary language. On the other hand, Necochea and Cline (1993) point out the dangers of taking BL as the only approach to promoting oral language use. First, there are not enough bilingual teachers to meet the needs of all ML students. Secondly, in the majority of classrooms these students are the minority and many speak low-incidence languages such as Hmong, Vietnamese, and Laotian. Necochea and Cline believe that many English-speaking teachers feel helpless in the shadow of the bilingual philosophy and give up on ML students believing that they can't be effective. On the other hand, Necochea and Cline describe creative and effective practices that teachers have developed for working with ML students. The best of these practices emphasizes integration and inclusion "for ML students plus the modification of the delivery of instruction to provide comprehensive input, thus allowing students to participate in the core instructional mainstream program" (p. 407). African-American students and lower socio-economic students can also benefit from a rich language environment. For example, Benedict (1994) found that low SES African-American kindergartners were as advanced in oral language use as middle SES European-American kindergartners when both groups were enrolled in a whole-language kindergarten and also more advanced than comparable African-American children enrolled in a basal-based kindergarten.

SUMMARY

Meaningful speech seems to develop gradually from early infancy. By the middle of the first year, children make nonword meaningful sounds. Between ages one and two toddlers' language develops rapidly. They use it for a variety of purposes. By two-and-a-half, the children's speech is very adultlike. Children learn to use language for various functions. They begin with demands, commands, and interactional talk. They gradually add questions, imagination, and informative uses. By the time they enter kindergarten, they should be able to use language for higher-level functions such as prediction, empathy, and reasoning. Sociodramatic play settings are rich in language use. In these settings, children learn how to use language functions and how to apply them in order to sustain social relationships. Adults have a critical role in developing children's abilities to engage in talk. The adults provide an environment that promotes talk and also provide the initial conversational experiences. With infants, toddlers, two's, and three's, adults need to make a conscious effort to engage in conversation and promote the give and take of dialog. With four's and five's the adult pulls back, observes, and lets the children take over their own talk. However, if the children are not displaying multifunctional language in their talk, the adult may step in and provide the spark to conversation. Children from diverse cultures can expand their oral language use through extensive experiences with conversation.

FOR FURTHER READING

Bates, E., Bretherton, I., & Snyder, L. (1987). *From first words to grammar.* New York: Cambridge University Press.

Britton, B. K. & Pellegrini, A. D. (Eds.) (1990). *Narrative thought and narrative language.* Hillsdale, NJ: Erlbaum.

Franklin, M. B. (Ed.) (1987). *Child language: A reader.* New York: Oxford University Press.

Galda, L. & Pellegrini, A. D. (Eds.). (1985). *Play, language, and stories: The development of children's literate behavior.* Norwood, NJ: Ablex.

Gallas, Y. (1994). *The languages of learning.* New York: Teachers College Press.

Heath, S. B. (1983). *Ways with words: Language, life and work in communities and classrooms.* New York: Cambridge University Press.

Hecht, M. L., Collier, M. J., & Ribeau, S. A. (1993). *African American communication.* Thousand Oaks, CA: Sage.

John-Steiner, V., Panofsky, C. P. & Smith, L. W. (Eds.). (1994). *Sociocultural approaches to language and literacy.* New York: Cambridge University Press.

Kamii, C., Manning, M., & Manning, G. (Eds.). (1992). *Early literacy: A constructivist foundation for whole language.* Westhaven, CT: National Education Association.

Locke, J. L. (1993). *The child's path to spoken language.* Cambridge, MA: Harvard University Press.

McLeod, B. (Ed.). (1994). *Language and learning: Educating linguistically diverse students.* Albany, NY: SUNY Press.

Neuman, S. B. & Roskos, K. A. (1993). *Language and literacy in the early years: An integrated approach.* Fort Worth, TX: Harcourt Brace.

Pellegrini, A. & Yawkey, T. (Eds.). (1984). *The development of oral and written language in social contexts.* Norwood, NJ: Ablex.

Saravia-Shore, M., & Arvizu, S. F. (1991). *Cross-cultural literacy: Ethnographies of communications in multiethnic classrooms.* New York: Garland.

Wells, G. (1985). *Language development in the preschool years.* New York: Cambridge University Press.

SUGGESTED ACTIVITIES

1. Collect language samples from different children at a variety of age levels between 18 months and 3 years. Tape record them if possible. Transcribe the results. Number each phrase or sentence as in the sample cards below.

Card 1. Age: 2 years, 9 months.
 Child is in the bathtub.
   1. Oh, Monster (blows into water),
     I swallow you.
   2. I'm fis (fish).
	Card 2. Age: 2 years, 9 months.
	 Child is in the bathtub.
	   1. You go visit Michael.
	   2. Go there.
	   3. See the Mommy.

Categorize each phrase or sentence using Halliday's category system. Try to get at least twenty-five samples from each child. Bring all the data to class. Figure out the percentage of each category used by each child. Compile the results on the blackboard by listing each child in order from youngest to oldest down the board. Across the board put the numbers from one to seven and fill in the proportions of each category used by each child:

Child	Phrase/ Sentence Number	Halliday Categories: Percentages Observed						
		1	2	3	4	5	6	7

Do you find the same kind of developmental progression as in the example of Kate and Nigel in Figure 23–2? Evaluate your sample compared to what would be expected.

2. Collect language samples from a variety of children between ages three and six years. Tape record them if possible. Transcribe the results. Number each phrase or sentence as in Activity 1. Categorize each phrase or sentence using Tough's category system. Try to obtain at least twenty-five samples from each child. Bring all the data to class. Figure the percentage of each category used by each child. Compile the results as described in Activity 1, only use Tough's categories:

Child	Phrase/ Sentence Number	Tough Categories: Percentages Observed								
		1a	1b	2a	2b	3a	3b	3c	4a	4b

3. See if you can validate the research on the uses of language in play. Observe one or more children during sociodramatic play and during art or water play. Record and transcribe the conversations. Categorize each phrase or sentence using Tough's and/or Halliday's categories. Are more language functions used during sociodramatic play than during an art activity or water play?

4. Make an entry in your journal.

REVIEW

A. Select the correct answer(s) to the following. There may be more than one correct answer.
1. Research has shown the following regarding infant vocalization:
   a. The sounds that an infant makes are like the ones he will use when he learns to speak.
   b. Infants engage in about the same amount of vocal behavior no matter what situation they are in.
   c. Infants carry on conversations with objects.
   d. Even on the first day of life, infants respond to speech.
   e. Meaning does not enter infant vocalization until at least 11 or 12 months of age.
   f. Adults can identify meaningful vocalizations in infants.
   g. Before the development of speech, infants develop mouth movements that imitate emotions but not speech.
   h. Intentionality usually appears in infant verbal communications by 9 or 10 months of age.
   i. The melodic qualities of the mother's speech communicates her intent to the infant.

2. Research has shown the following regarding toddler speech:
   a. First words are usually the names of objects that the toddler acts upon, but seldom does he use a word that is something acted upon by others.
   b. Most of the child's first talk centers on ideas about objects.
   c. Examples of some of the consistent patterns used by toddlers when they begin to put words together are: "See dog, Big dog, Hot milk, More cookie, Allgone kitty, No bed, Want juice."
   d. During Halliday's phase I of language development, the child develops his own language; during phase II the child makes wordlike vocalizations that serve as a transition to phase III, when the child's language becomes more like an adult's.

3. Research shows the following regarding preschool/ primary children's speech:
   a. Preschool children talk to themselves while engaged in motor tasks.
   b. The child uses about the same kind of speech no matter to whom he is talking.
   c. The child talks in shorter sentences to children than to adults.
   d. After age three the young child's speech becomes more self-centered.
   e. Lower socioeconomic class children are less likely to assert themselves and seek help from adults in school than are middle-class children.
   f. Middle-class children exhibit a greater variety of language use than do lower socioeconomic class children.
   g. The child's real language capabilities can be observed during sociodramatic play activities.
   h. Art activities elicit little, if any, valuable talk.
   i. Dramatic play elicits no more talk than other types of play.
   j. Private speech is used mostly for self-guidance.
   k. Young children do not realize when they have not been given enough information to solve a problem.
   l. Private speech distracts the child from the learning task.
   m. The things children say can affect the curriculum.
   n. Parental dialogues with children have no relationship to children's capabilities in carrying on dialogues with peers.
   o. Having an older peer in the family can squelch the young child's capability to link into an ongoing conversation.
   p. The opportunity for conversation through dramatic play, such as in the kitchen area, can enhance the ability to communicate.

B. Following are some child language samples. Categorize each, first using Halliday's category system and then Tough's.

   1. They say, "Go out little piggies."
   2. And Daddy and the Big Bad Wolf was there.
   3. Where's his mommy?
   4. Gonna drink it up. (pretend drink)
   5. Michael can have some.
   6. Rain is coming down.
   7. You're going down.
   8. Laura says we're gonna cook.
   9. I want that toy.
   10. What's that, mom?

C. You are a kindergarten teacher. Several parents are critical of you because you have a dramatic play center in your room. They feel that dramatic play is a waste of time for kindergartners—they should spend their time on more academics. Develop an argument to support the cognitive value of sociodramatic play.

D. Explain how adults can support child talk.

Written Language: Development and Everyday Use

OBJECTIVES

After studying this unit, the student should be able to:

■ Be able to describe examples of reading and writing activities that are appropriate for young children.

■ Recognize statements that describe normal early childhood literacy development.

■ Do informal assessments of young children's reading and writing knowledge.

■ Discuss the adult role in the literacy development of young children.

■ Evaluate whether adults are promoting or discouraging young children's literacy development.

In schools reading and writing have been taught as if they were assumed to develop separately from oral language. Today, it is recognized that written and oral language develop as a whole. According to McGee and Richgels (1990) the traditional view of literacy learning operated under four assumptions (pp. 6–7):

1. Reading and writing were difficult to learn. Whereas oral language developed naturally, specific instruction was needed for reading and writing.

2. Children were not considered to know anything about reading and writing until their products appeared to be like those of adults.

3. Reading required readiness. A benchmark of 6.5 years became the rule for beginning to teach children how to read. Prior to 6.5 years children engaged in so-called readiness activities such as learning the letters of the alphabet, matching and discriminating shapes, and matching and discriminating sounds.

4. Writing was learned after reading. It was believed that children had to learn to recognize and spell words before they could compose.

Today research has demonstrated that the traditional assumptions are false. McGee and Richgels (1990) point out three areas of research that demonstrated traditional assumptions were not correct (pp. 8–10):

1. Studies of children who could read before they entered formal schooling revealed that reading could be learned naturally without formal instruction.

2. Writing may occur before reading. It was found that some preschool children could spell words in systematic ways that adults could recognize. Children who were not readers in the traditional sense could invent spellings. For example, the following spelling was used by a kindergartner:

   WAS A PON A TIME TAR
   WAZ THREE GRLS
   (ONCE UPON A TIME THERE
   WAS THREE GIRLS)

3. Reading and writing are viewed as language processes. That is, learning to read and write is a process similar to learning to speak. All language learning is an interrelated process of learning to communicate.

Out of this research emerged the new psychosociolinguistic view of literacy learning. McGee and Richgels (1990) describe five new assumptions derived from the psycholinguistic point of view (pp. 29–30):

1. Even very young children are knowledgeable about written language. Teachers can no longer assume that children begin school without literacy knowledge. Teachers can find out what children have learned prior to schooling and build on it.

2. Young children's reading and writing may be different from adults' reading and writing, but it is no less important. Adults must accept and appreciate whatever children produce and not force them to conform to an adult model.

3. Reading and writing are similar and interrelated activities. What is written is then read. Literacy knowledge appears in talking, drawing, and play.

4. Young children acquire literacy knowledge as they participate in meaningful activities. For example, in Figure 24–6 children have written letters, applying their knowledge of writing to a meaningful communication activity.

5. Young children acquire literacy knowledge as they interact with others. Interest and acceptance of young children's literacy activities by peers and adults support their learning.

If the environment is print-rich and there are supportive people available, children gain concepts about reading and writing through naturalistic activities. National demands for educational improvement have called attention to the weaknesses in our instructional system and called for reforms. It is imperative that early childhood educators become familiar with literacy as a developmental process and the significance of this process for reading and writing instruction to stem the tide of inappropriate practices.

THE WHOLE-LANGUAGE VIEW OF READING AND WRITING

Out of the research mentioned above developed the **whole-language approach** to reading and writing. The whole-language philosophy places the children and their needs at the center of the curriculum (Reutzel & Hollingsworth, 1988). Children are viewed as actively involved in their own learning. Whole language fits the cognitive-developmental or constructivist point of view. Language is considered as a whole and not cut up into parts (i.e., reading, writing, spelling, speaking). Rather than beginning to learn through letter names and sounds, children learn naturally through stories, poems, and environmental print (e.g., signs, labels on cereal boxes and other containers, etc.).

In the whole-language classroom, children are learning in many different settings. Some are sitting on chairs at tables, others may be in a pillow-filled bathtub, others sit on a carpet using lapboards, and some are seated on an old couch. Writings and drawings are all over the walls. In the whole-language classroom, learning takes place in learning centers, which focus on topics of interest. Children read and write about what they are interested in. The process rather than the product is stressed. Children are sharing ideas and reviewing each other's work. Assessment is done through observation, interviews, discussions, video or audio taping of children reading, and selected samples of children's work. The teacher is a guide and an active participant and model who spends time engaged in her own reading and writing.

The contrast between whole language and traditional instruction can be seen in the following examples:

Spelling taught traditionally	*Invented spelling encouraged*
the snake is green.	WAS A PON ATIM
the pig is white.	TAR WAS A
the fish is orange.	HRNINT HWS TAR
George.	WAS A LITL GOST
	AND TAT LITL
	GOST WOTIDI SAM
	WAN TO PLA TAT
	LITOL GOST GOT
	SUM WAN TO PLAY
	WIT
	JOHN

George plays it safe. He uses only words he is sure about. Note the careful use of periods. John is a risk taker. He is involved in the process of telling his story and feels free to spell words as they sound to him. What does his story say? In case you haven't figured it out:

ONCE UPON A TIME THERE WAS A HAUNTED HOUSE THERE WAS A LITTLE GHOST AND THAT LITTLE GHOST WANTED SOMEONE TO PLAY THAT LITTLE GHOST GOT SOMEONE TO PLAY WITH

Cannella (1988) compared the writings of kindergarten through third-grade students under two conditions: **teacher-imposed structure (TS)** and **child-initiated structure (CS)**. The products produced under both conditions were equally advanced and creative. The TS writings were more legible (in this condition they were reminded to be careful with capitalization and punctuation and to be neat). Under the CS condition the children enjoyed the writing more and took more risks. The kindergarten children under the CS condition were more advanced, more creative, and more legible. When allowed to make their own decision about what to write, children were more free and enjoyed themselves more. The study results showed the contradiction in expecting a child's writing to appear technically perfect and wanting the child to express ideas freely and fluently and enjoy the writing process. In the following sections we will examine some of the specifics young children know about reading, writing, and print and how they learn written language.

WHAT THE YOUNG CHILD KNOWS ABOUT READING

Identification of words in the environment appears to be the first step in learning to read. In a literate society like ours, most children grow up surrounded by print. In homes there are books, magazines, letters, food and other containers, phonebooks, television ads, and other print materials. Only children living in very impoverished and isolated areas with parents who are illiterate may not come in contact with some environmental print during early childhood.

Research indicates that young children are very much aware of environmental print. They pay attention and can identify to what the print refers. They are especially aware of logos associated with frequently visited businesses (such as their favorite store or fast-food restaurant) and frequently used products (such as their toothpaste or favorite cereal). This recognition of words in the environment seems to be the first level in the development of learning to read (McGee et al., 1986) (Figures 24–1 and 24–2).

Young children who have contacts with printed material learn some of the conventions (rules) of print use. For example, in English we read left to right and from top to bottom, and we read books from front to back. It has been found that by kindergarten entrance, many children have these conventions well in mind. Whereas a toddler might be observed looking at a book that is upside down and may turn the pages from back to front, a five-year-old will usually hold it correctly and turn the pages from front to back.

By primary age children can describe accurately what is involved in the process of reading, that is, what it means to read, what reading is used for, and how reading proceeds. Most younger children are still in the process of developing these concepts at a conscious level (McGee et al., 1986). Researchers have found that (McGee et al., 1986):

- Many five-year-olds, if given a book, can explain that the print, not the pictures, is what we read and can explain that words and letters are associated with print.

- Children as young as 3 years of age know that print carries a message.

- Young children believe that to be read, print must have at least three different letters.

- Whereas six-year-olds realize that special eye movements are needed for reading, four-year-olds do not discriminate between reading and just looking at the page.

Figure 24–1   Children can learn about written language through activities with words and letters, such as this collage made up of the names of favorite products advertised in magazines.

Figure 24–2a & b   Shopping centers are a rich source of environmental print for young children.

- Whereas three-year-olds can label common print materials such as phonebooks, grocery lists, letters, and maps and tell something about how they are used, six-year-olds can give specifics about what the print in each piece of reading material is for.

It is commonly believed that letter recognition is a major prerequisite to reading. Certainly it is an important part, but whether it is actually a prerequisite has been the subject of investigation. Research indicates that letter naming is only one of many skills that underlie reading and that children begin to develop concepts about print at the same time they are beginning to recognize letters. Teaching letter names does not in itself ensure reading success (McGee et al. 1986). McGee et al. conclude:

One finding which emerges from studies detailing what young children know about reading is that they seem to learn about reading by participating in reading events. Children learn to read environmental print by observing print in all its complexity. They begin to notice how reading and writing operate in environmental print as well as in other print forms (books, directions, etc.) before and at the same time they learn to recognize letters.

WHAT A YOUNG CHILD KNOWS ABOUT WRITING

Researchers are interested in when and how young children learn that certain kinds of marks have meaning and communicate to other people. Researchers have examined the relationships between drawing and writing, between language used during play and written language development, between the forms used in writing and attempts to use writing to communicate, and the development of alphabet writing.

Young children enjoy drawing and spend many happy hours in drawing activities (Figure 24–3). Although in the early stages their drawing and writing may look the same to the adult eye, young children seem to recognize that there is a difference from a fairly early age. Writing and drawing seem to develop in a parallel fashion from scribbling to representational drawing and making of real letters. Some researchers feel that the drawing supports the writing and others that the writing supports the drawing. Both are symbolic or representative; the drawings represent things and writing represents speech, but researchers are not sure at what point children are able to make this distinction (McGee et al., 1986) (Figure 24–4). Karen Gallas (1994), a first- and second-grade teacher, has documented the power of talking, writing, and drawing in providing a view of children's thinking.

In Unit 23 the importance of sociodramatic play to oral language development was discussed. The relationship between make-believe play and writing has also been studied. Play is also a symbolic activity. There is some evidence that being able to carry on a dramatic play theme is enhanced by experience with story reading, which familiarizes the child with story text and story knowledge. Dramatic play, on the

Figure 24–3 **A message written in conventional letter/word symbols is surrounded by drawn symbols representing germs. Note that may of the basic shapes that are found in letters appear in the germs.**

other hand, affords children the opportunity to develop narratives in formats that could be used later in writing. These experiences also provide knowledge that is helpful when children are introduced to school textbooks (McGee et al., 1986).

Children gradually develop the concepts that writing is linear and continuous and begin writing with their own names. Names are very personal, and writing one's own name is a highly motivating objective. Usually by age five children can write their own names fairly well (McGee et al., 1986). However, within any group of fives there will be a great deal of variation. For example, Figure 24–5 includes examples of signatures of older fours and young fives written the summer before kindergarten entrance.

Besides learning to write letters and words, young children learn that different types of messages have different formats (Figure 24–6). That is, lists, letters, stories, etc. are each set up in a special way. For example, young children have been observed to differentiate between the formats of letters and envelopes. Children can learn to recognize and write al-

phabet letters naturally as they explore these various forms of written communication, rather than through alphabet-copying activities done out of the context of composing (McGee et al., 1986).

WHAT YOUNG CHILDREN KNOW ABOUT PRINT

Another type of question researchers have been interested in is to what degree young children are consciously aware of units of language such as individual sounds (phonemes), syllables, and words. This area is of interest because it is a type of knowledge that is not needed for speaking and listening but is necessary for reading and writing. Three areas have been investigated: (1) children's awareness of words as units of speech, (2) the relationship of such knowledge to reading ability, and (3) children's awareness of word units in print (McGee et al., 1986).

Overall, young children have been found to be confused regarding units of orally presented words.

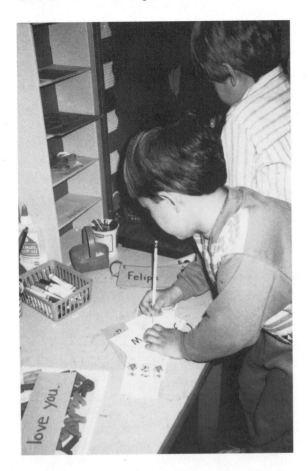

Figure 24–4 In the writing center, children experiment with producing different kinds of messages using a variety of media.

However, there does seem to be a transitional period during kindergarten and into first grade in which individual children begin to be able to make these auditory discriminations. Further, ability to make these distinctions is positively related to level of reading ability (McGee et al., 1986).

Young children seem to have some awareness of words in print before they begin to read. However, researchers have not as yet come up with a satisfactory measuring device. A method that is promising is the analysis of young children's spellings. Children invent spellings that reflect an understanding of how English phonology works. It is probably an unconscious knowledge, but it is there. Figure 24–7 is a Halloween picture

by a kindergartner. Zach has written his own name, copied October from the calendar, and spelled *bat* conventionally on his own. He has invented spellings for two other words: *wich* (for witch) and *grav* (for grave). Zach has an excellent sense of phonology, only omitting the silent letters. In a study of preschoolers' and kindergartners' letter recognition, sound association knowledge, and invented spellings, Richgels (1986) found that conscious awareness of letter/sound correspondence had no relationship to the ability to invent spellings. On the other hand, knowledge of letter names did aid in the ability to spell, probably because letter names may be used as clues for spelling. For example, "U R MI FRND" for "You are my friend."

Richgels (1986a) describes an invented spelling test that he suggests is superior to the usual standardized tests used for assessment of first graders' readiness for formal reading instruction. Richgels suggests that if adults can be tolerant and accepting of children's spellings such as those in the examples, we can learn a lot about children's knowledge of phonology through encouraging them to write using their own spellings.

It is evident that children acquire a great deal of knowledge about written language without much, if any, formal instruction. Examination of their invented spellings is an excellent means for finding out what they know.

HOW YOUNG CHILDREN LEARN ABOUT WRITTEN LANGUAGE

Young children do not learn about print just because it is around. Reading and writing are learned because they can be used to achieve goals. What happens in the context of social learning that promotes literacy development? Print is used as a contact between family members and friends.

- Lists of friends are made.
- Notes and letters are written to friends and family members.
- Signs are made for a lemonade stand.

Heath (1980, 1983) studied a group of professional class families. They used reading in the ways already mentioned plus in a critical/educational way. They read to increase knowledge. When they read,

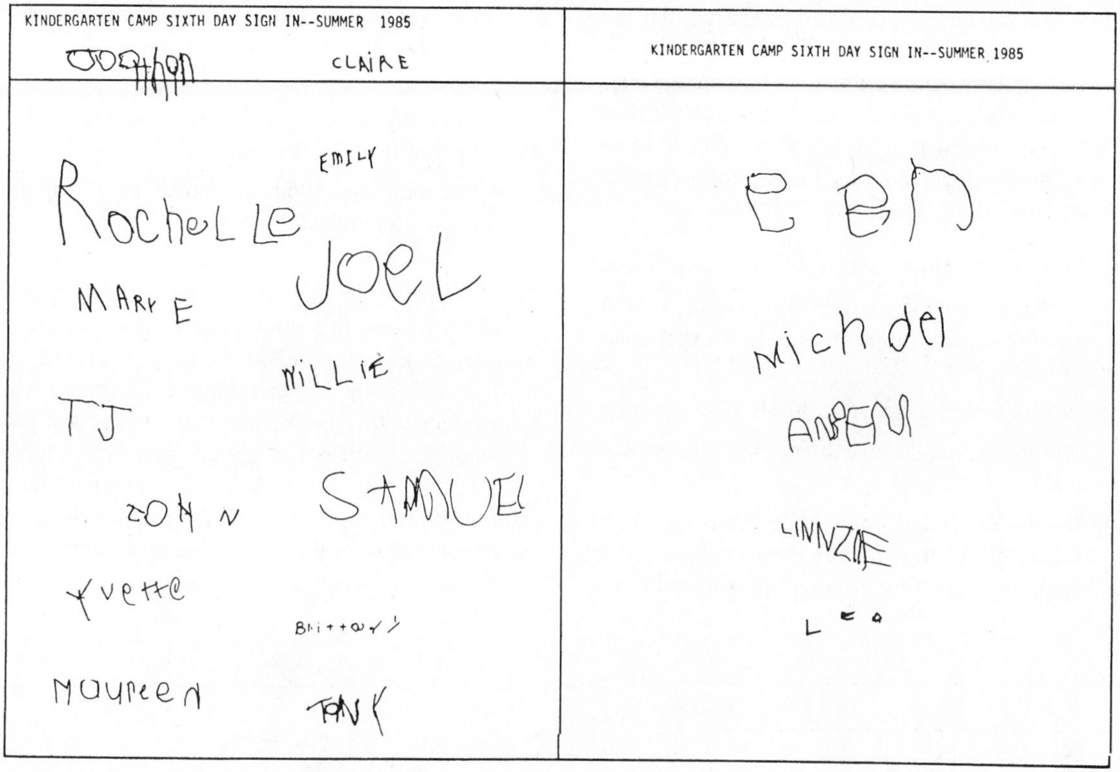

KINDERGARTEN CAMP SIXTH DAY SIGN IN--SUMMER 1985

Figure 24-5 **Young children usually begin writing with their own names. These signatures are from some entering kindergartners.**

they expanded the story-reading activity by relating the story to past activities. The adults also made many comments about the stories and encouraged the children, when old enough, to do the same. Other researchers have found that parents encourage literacy by encouraging children in written language activities and developing in them an interest in books and written language in general. Young children learn about print through supportive literacy experiences with family and friends (McGee et al., 1986). Look back at the letters in Figure 24-6. These letters were sent and delivered through a classroom mail system by children the summer before entering kindergarten. The children were very inspired to write through this exchange of letters. They were thrilled when they received a letter, and they were just as excited when the recipient received theirs. The writing achieved the goal of making a social contact with a friend.

Children have developed strategies to learn about writing while they are writing. Children usually talk before, during, and after writing. They may use talk to get information they need for their writing, to comment while they are writing, or to read what they have written. Children seem to enhance their writing by talking with each other and reading their writing to each other. They also apply what they have learned in other language situations, both oral and written, to their writing. Most important, for young children to write they have to be willing to take risks and experiment. After all, most adults do not look upon writing as a task for preschoolers and kindergartners and thus do not encourage this experimentation. Note that early readers and writers always have an older person in the home that encourages their early literacy efforts. If adults can be accepting of invented spellings and nonconventional sentences (as they are with oral language), children will learn on their own how to manage written language (McGee et al., 1986; Bissex, 1985).

Researchers have attempted to find out the characteristics of adult-child interaction that seem critical to the encouragement of literacy development. A review of this research indicates that the following factors are supportive (McGee et al., 1986):

- Warm-up questions asked before a book is read.
- Verbal interactions during story reading that relate the content of the story to past experiences of the child.
- Positive reinforcement of the child's responses.
- Asking evaluative questions after the book is read.
- Beginning dialog during book reading in infancy before the child is even capable of responding, treating infants' prelinguistic re-

sponses as if they were conventional responses, and then rewarding approximations and finally conventional words used for labels.

- In dialog with infants, mothers labeling important parts of the illustrations.
- Encouraging infants to model their responses from what the adult does.

These type of interactions seem to offer a strong basis for success in school literacy activities. The behaviors listed are more likely to be observed with professional and upper-middle-class parent/child pairs than with working-class or lower-class pairs. Lower-class mothers use less talk and a more limited vocabulary than do middle-class mothers during story reading. Both story reading and writing sessions seem to be of the most value to children if there is reciprocal interaction and reinforcement of the

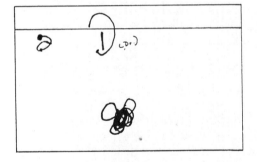

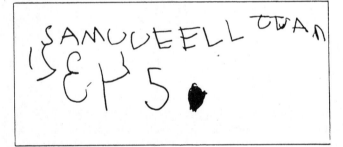

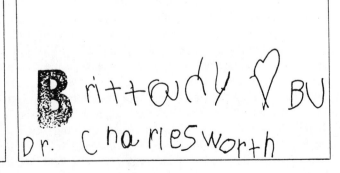

Figure 24–6 **a variety of letters were delivered to each person's mailbox during a summer program for entering kindergartners. Note the range of development. Examples a, b, c, and d were authored by kindergarten campers to Dr. Charlesworth and one from Samuel to Juan, Summer 1985. Examples e, f, g, and h were authored by Mary, who is more advanced in her note writing. Examples i and j were done by Vanessa, a child in a kindergarten for gifted children.**

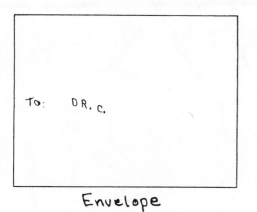

Envelope

Note

Figure 24–6   (Continued)

Figure 24–6 **(Continued)**

child's use of both oral and written language and encouragement of the child's experimentation rather than directions and criticism from the adult.

As mentioned numerous times in this unit, question asking is a critical factor in the development of literacy (Figure 24–8). Questions from readers to nonreaders have been described. Also important are the questions of children directed toward readers. Children ask questions about many aspects of print (McGee et al., 1986):

- They ask about letters. (What is this letter?)
- They ask about words. (What does this say?)
- They ask for information. (Do people come from eggs, too?)
- They ask about print. (Where does it say _____ ?)

There has been some speculation regarding why children are prompted to ask these questions. One reason may be that this is how the children were introduced to reading during infancy and toddlerhood and therefore they are modeling adult behavior. Also, book illustrations often have prominent print, such as a road sign or a sign on a building, that may catch children's attention. Further, as they learn some letters they may be drawn to these in the text and wonder what words say that have these known letters.

THE ADULT'S ROLE IN LITERACY DEVELOPMENT

After reviewing the research on the early stages of learning to read and write, McGee et al. (1986) conclude that children need a multitude of print ex-

Figure 24–7   **A beginning kindergartner combines drawing and writing in his Halloween picture.**

periences to support emerging literacy. They need more than identifying and discriminating sounds and letters, learning rhymes, and developing oral language skills. Early childhood educators need to develop curricula for home and school that include many kinds of print experiences (i.e., Dickinson and Tabors, 1991; Holmes, 1993; Marvin and Mirenda, 1993; McMackin, 1993; Neuman and Roskos, 1993; Rosow, 1994/95). McGee et al. (1986, pp. 63–65) suggest the following:

1. Call attention to the conventions of print while writing down children's dictation.

2. Point out the uses of print materials (such as phone books, storybooks, shopping lists, greeting cards, menus, and magazines) as children use these materials in dramatic play.

3. Model reading behavior by reading when the children are reading (such as during a library or rest period).

4. Have children read signs during field trips.

5. Read children's dictation and have them read their dictation.

6. Encourage writing and drawing and label the products.

7. Draw attention to letters in context such as when writing the child's name, labeling a picture, or taking dictation (Figure 24–9).

8. Provide a variety of writing implements and materials (lined and unlined paper, large and small paper, pens, markers, pencils, chalk and chalkboard, paint and paint brushes).

Figure 24–8   Questioning, labeling, and discussion before, after, and during the story enhance written language development.

A real sun and Roz and Kate and a real house and a puppy is inside the house.

Figure 24–9   Seeing her picture labeled with her own words is a positive literacy experience for Kate.

9. Encourage children to write and accept their products no matter how distant they are from conventional writing.

10. Provide props and print materials that will stimulate role-playing and story re-enactments.

11. Encourage cooperative social interaction during play and during writing activities.

12. Provide moveable letters and encourage experimentation (matching, sorting, sequencing, etc.).

13. Motivate children by encouraging them to write words that are personally important to them (e.g., their own names, names of friends and family members, names of their pets, or favorite play materials).

14. Provide opportunities to write letters, make greeting cards, lists, labels, and captions and to write stories.

15. Call attention to print in familiar stories by pointing to the words as they are read.

16. Write messages to children (e.g., "I like you," "You are a good helper," "Thanks for playing nicely today," "Time to wash your hands").

17. Let the children see adults using written language (making lists, writing captions and notes).

18. Encourage questions and discussion during story reading, especially by relating story content to the children's past experiences.

19. Enlist the aid of parents, volunteers, and older children to be trained as story readers to provide individual story reading time.

20. Develop a parent education program designed to provide parents with techniques for enhancing learning at home.

21. Provide opportunities for and encourage "pretend" reading by modeling easy-to-learn stories, such as are found in predictable books and pattern books.

22. Provide an abundance of reading material including children's literature, wordless picture books, newspapers, telephone books, catalogs, cartoons, menus, coupons, junk mail, and children's magazines.

The materials and activities listed will provide a print-rich environment for young children. Applying the information in this unit in such a print-rich environment, adults can enhance literacy development by encouraging children to construct their own concepts of print and their own reading and writing skills (Figure 24–10).

Sociocultural Considerations and Written Language Use

As with other areas of development, the social and cultural factors that influence written language development must be considered. For example, documented cultural differences in home literacy activities should not be used to excuse the schools' failure to educate particular groups of children (Dyson, 1993). Dyson (1993) points out that, especially in classrooms that include children from diverse backgrounds, "what and how children learn depends upon children's relationships with teacher and peers" (p. 415) within the classroom culture. A major challenge to children is not just to master how to read and write but how to use written communication to control and manage relationships. Dyson (1993) provides examples of how children attach their own social meanings to spelling and

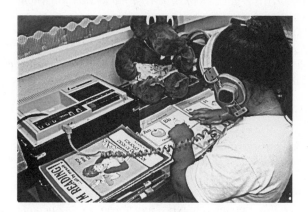

Figure 24–10   The listening center provides an opportunity to connect print with oral language.

writing. This factor is also evident in a study by Mosley (1992) that documents the personal nature of kindergartner's writing and drawing and the nature of social sharing of ideas as children worked side-by-side in small groups. Gallas (1994) provides examples of how the writing and drawing of her diverse groups of primary students helped her to see into their innermost thoughts. Another important aspect of written language development is providing literature that is not only culturally relevant but also not culturally offensive. For example, Cornell (1993) points out that some of the wording in traditional rhymes and folktales may lack meaning, promote prejudice, present stereotypes, support unlawful acts, or be too scary for young children, especially those who are new to the mainstream culture. As an example, Cornell points out that in *Hansel and Gretel* the following social concepts and behaviors are included: absence of parental love, child abuse, child abandonment, trespassing, breaking and entering, gluttony, association of elderly women with evil, fraud and deception, assault and kidnapping, illegal imprisonment, cannibalism, deceit, murder, and a cover up of the children's wrongdoing. These brief examples illustrate the importance of considering the development of written language knowledge and understanding in a social and cultural context.

SUMMARY

Research has informed our view of how young children develop and use their knowledge of written language. It has become recognized that understanding and use of oral and written language develop together rather than, as believed in the past, first oral and then written language. It has also been substantiated that written language development is enhanced through a whole-language approach that integrates reading, writing, spelling, and oral language.

When a child enters school, he or she already knows a great deal about written language that teachers can capitalize on, just as they can capitalize on what the child has learned about oral language. The early childhood classroom should be a print-rich environment in which children are encouraged to construct their own knowledge about reading and writing. Children from print-rich homes come to school recognizing environmental print, knowing how to handle books, recognizing all or part of the alphabet, being able to write their own names and probably some other words, and knowing the use and format of letters, notes, lists, and other printed material. They have had many story-reading sessions at home, during which they were asked questions and encouraged to ask their own questions. A print-rich classroom can move these children ahead toward conventional reading and writing. For those children who enter school with little print experience, the print-rich classroom can introduce the world of reading and writing in the naturalistic way that other children have experienced at home.

Another new point of view has come from research on children's writing. We now realize that writing and reading go together (rather than read first and write later) and that writing (composing, not penmanship) is an important part of the early childhood curriculum. Children as young as three can "write" notes, greeting cards, picture captions, and signatures at a primitive level. Accepting their scribbles as writing will encourage young children to continue their experimentation, which will develop naturally into conventional writing. Sharing ideas about what to write and reading each other's writing helps to build an understanding of print and provides a social and cultural context for literacy development.

FOR FURTHER READING

Allen, J. B., & Mason, J. M. (Eds.) (1989) *Reducing the risks for young literacy learners*. Portsmouth, NH: Heinemann.

Bird, L. B. (1989). *Becoming a whole language school*. Kutonah, NY: Richard C. Owen.

Brock, D. R., and Green, V. P. (1992). The influences of social context on kindergarten journal writing. *Journal of research in childhood education*, *1*, 5–19.

Clay, M. M. (1993). *An observation survey of early literacy achievement*. Portsmouth, NH: Heinemann.

Dyson, A. H. (1989). *Multiple worlds of child writers*. New York: Teacher College Press.

Goodman, K., Goodman, Y. M., & Hood, W. J. (Eds.) (1989). *The whole language evaluation book*. Portsmouth, NH: Heinemann.

Hoot, J. L., & Silvern, S. B. (Eds.) (1988). *Writing with computers in the early grades*. New York: Teachers College Press.

John-Steiner, V., Panofsky, C. P., & Smith L. W. (Eds.). (1994). *Sociocultural approaches to language and literacy*. New York: Cambridge University Press.

Kamii, C., Manning, M., & Manning, G. (Eds.). (1992). *Early literacy: A constructivist foundation for whole language*. Westhaven, CT: National Education Association.

Manning, M., Manning, G., Long, R., & Kamii, C. (1993). Preschoolers' conjectures about segments of a written sentence. *Journal of Research in Childhood Education*, *8*, 5–11.

Mills, H., & Clyde, J. A. (Eds.) (1990). *Portraits of whole language classrooms*. Portsmouth, NH: Heinemann.

Morrow, L. M., & Smith, J. K. (Eds.) (1990). *Assessment for instruction in early literacy*. Englewood Cliffs, NJ: Prentice-Hall.

Neuman, S. B., & Roskos, K. A. (1993). *Language and literacy in the early years: An integrated approach*. Fort Worth, TX: Harcourt Brace.

Petrick-Steward, E. (1994). *Beginning writers in the zone of proximal development*. Hillsdale, NJ: Erlbaum.

Raines, S. C. (Ed.). (1995). *Whole language across the curriculum: Grades one, two, and three*. New York: Teachers College Press.

Raines, S. C., & Canady, R. J. (1990). *The whole language kindergarten*. New York: Teachers College.

Schickendanz, J. A. (1990). *ADAM'S RIGHTIN REVOLUTIONS*. Portsmouth, NH: Heinemann.

Schrader, C.T. (1990). *Symbolic play as a curricular tool for early literacy development*. Early Childhood Research Quarterly, *5*, 79–103.

Taylor, D., & Dorsey-Gaines, C. (1988). *Growing up literate: Learning from inner-city families*. Portsmouth, NH: Heinemann.

Temple, C. A., Nathan, R., Temple, F., & Burris, N. (1993). *The beginnings of writing* (3rd ed.). Des Moines, IA: Longwood Division, Allyn and Bacon.

Vernon, S. A. (1993). Initial sound/letter correspondences in children's early written productions. *Journal of Research in Childhood Education, 8,* 11–22.

Walker-Dalhouse, D. (1993). Beginning reading and the African American child at risk. *Young Children, 49*(1), 24–28.

SUGGESTED ACTIVITIES

1. Divide the class into groups. Have the members of each group look through issues of one of the journals listed from 1980 through the current issue. Students should look for articles describing activities that promote literacy development in early childhood classrooms. Have each group select ten activities to share with the rest of the class, set up the activities in the format given, and provide a copy for each member of the class.

FORMAT FOR LITERACY ACTIVITIES

AREA: Literacy

ACTIVITY:

OBJECTIVE:

MATERIALS:

PROCEDURE:

Journals to search: *Young Children, Dimensions, Day Care and Early Education, Childhood Education, Reading Teacher*, and *Language Arts*.

Discuss the following questions in class:

a. Which journals seemed to have the most useful articles?

b. How many suggested activities did you find that were based on the ideas in the unit?

c. Did you find any activities that you feel are inappropriate?

d. Look over all the activities. Which do you think are best? Why?

2. Try out the informal test of beginner's spelling abilities devised by Donald Richgels (1986a; 1986b) with several kindergartners and first graders. Compare the responses of each child with the others. Note indications that the children have begun to develop concepts of how letters and sounds fit together to make words.

Test Instructions

MATERIALS: A set of moveable letters (such as Fisher-Price magnetic letters or those developed for Montessori classrooms)

PROCEDURE: Interview each child individually. Say a word and give the child the meaning clue, having the child fill in the blank with the word and then spell the word using the moveable letters. Record the child's spelling while the child puts the letters back in the pile. Then go to the next word.

Invented Spelling Test Words

Targeted Word	Meaning Clue
1. JAR	Peanut butter comes in a _____.
2. PIE	One of my favorite desserts is apple _____.
3. DIRT	If I crawl around on the playground a lot, when I come inside my knees will be covered with _____.
4. NOSE	In the middle of my face is my _____.
5. FEET	At the end of my legs are my _____.
6. CRY	When I am very sad, I _____.
7. EAST	The opposite of west is _____.
8. TABLE	When I eat, I sit at a _____.
9. HAT	If my head is cold, I should wear a _____.
10. KITTEN	A baby cat is called a _____.

Scoring

There are 31 possible phonemes. Give the children one point for each one represented even if it is not conventional (such as using a letter name for a sound or putting in an extra letter if it makes sense). The phonemes to look for are: j/a/r, p/ie, d/ir/t, n/o/se, f/ee/t, c/r/y, ea/s/t, t/a/b/le, h/a/t, k/i/tt/en. Give credit if the phoneme is in the right place and is any spelling that conventional English spelling uses to represent that sound (such as /C/ for /K/, /Y/ for /I/, etc.). Extra letters are all right as long as they make sense.

a. Report your results to the rest of the class.

b. Show them the spellings and describe the range of scores.

c. Compare your results with those of other students who did this activity.

3. Collect writing samples from three-, four-, five-, and/or six-year-olds. Provide plain white paper and black Flair pens (so the products can be photocopied and the originals returned to the young authors). To obtain the samples arrange with the teacher(s) to sit at a table in the classroom(s) and invite students to come and write. Use the following questions adapted from those suggested by Harste, Woodward, and Burke (1984, p. 235):

1. Write your name for me.

2. Now write, or pretend to write anything else.

3. (To keep the child going) Can you write anything else?

4. Read me what you wrote. Show me what you wrote.

As you observe each child writing, note the following as adapted from Genishi and Dyson (1984, pp. 185–186):

The Message

a. Does the child believe he has written a message?

b. What is the message? Can the child read it?

c. Did the child create the message or copy it?

d. What is the length of the message?

e. Is there a picture on the page? How do message and picture relate?

Writing System

f. Can you read the child's message?

g. Does the child seem to have a systematic way of writing (arrange the letters or letterlike forms in a certain way to make words)?

h. Does the child use letter names for sounds, omit vowels, or have some other systematic way of spelling?

The Written Product

i. Do the child's written symbols look like letters?

j. Does the child write from left to right?

k. Are the letters arranged in an organized way or haphazardly?

The Purpose of the Writing

Was there a purpose such as:

- to write a message (he may not know what the message is)

- to show which letters he can write

- to add a symbol needed to complete a picture (such as a number on a house)

- to label

- to write a particular thing such as a letter, a list, or a story

- to practice how letters might fit together to make words

- to write dialogue for a character in a picture the child has drawn.

Take the writing samples to class and report on your analysis.

4. Lea M. McGee (1985) combined questions from Clay (1972) and from Goodman and Altwerger (1981) into a task designed to find out what children know about the rules that are used in written language and reading. Try an adaptation of this task with some young children of various ages from three to six.

Conventions of Written Language and Reading Task

MATERIAL: a children's storybook

PROCEDURE:

a. What is this called? (book)

b. What do you do with this? (read)

c. What is inside this? (words, letters, story)

d. Show me the front of this.

e. (Open to a page with words and a picture.) If I were to read this to you, what would I read? (picture vs. print)

f. Show me where to read on this page. (Repeat on another page.)

g. Put your finger exactly where I should begin reading. (left top)

h. Where should I go next? Next? (a left-to-right sweep)

i. Point to one word.

j. Show me one letter.

k. What is this? (period, question mark)

l. Now, I want you to take this book and show me how you would read it. (Note if the child uses book language, that is, speaks with the inflections and intonations that go with reading vs. those that go with talk.)

Note if the child(ren) seems to have a good concept of how to handle and read a book.

5. Find out what some young children know about environmental print. Collect eight to ten samples of items with well-known logos such as Coca Cola, Sesame Street, McDonald's, K-Mart, and Crest and pictures of scenes with words often seen on streets and buildings such as stop, go, in, and out. Also write each word on a plain white card without the identifying logo or other environmental clue (such as *out* on a door). Show these to several children between the ages of three and six. First show the items with the environmental clues and then the words written on the plain white cards. As you show each item ask:

    a. What do you think this says?

    b. What things do you see that help you to know what this says?

    c. Tell me some of the things you know about this (Harste et al., 1984, p. 233).

Note any age differences in the words recognized and the cues used to aid recognition. Report your findings in class.

6. Find out what young children know abut the functions of common print items. Collect several print items such as a letter, a list, a telephone book, a *TV Guide*, a map, a coupon, and/or a magazine. Ask several young children at various ages from three to six the following questions as you show them the items one at a time.

    a. What is this? What do you call it?

    b. What is this used for?

    c. What might it say in (on) this?

    d. Show me how you would you use this _____. (Let the child demonstrate.)

7. Make an entry in your journal.

REVIEW

A. Select the statements that correctly describe young children's literacy development.

    1. Prior to age six-and-one-half children are able to learn very little about reading and writing.

    2. Oral language must be fully developed before written language can be at all understood.

    3. Contrary to earlier beliefs it is now known that reading and writing develop together in a supportive fashion.

    4. There is now research that supports the view that reading and writing can be learned in a natural way just as oral language.

    5. Identifying environmental print is an early step in learning to read.

    6. Letter recognition is a necessary prerequisite to beginning reading and writing.

    7. Literacy develops through interacting with print in a purposeful way.

    8. By age three most children are naturally interested in writing and will experiment with it if given adult acceptance and encouragement.

    9. Research supports that penmanship and spelling are equal in importance with composition for young children.

    10. Young children should be encouraged to invent their own spellings even though they may be incorrect by conventional standards.

B. Discuss the following statement. "The major role of the adult in the young child's reading and writing development is to provide a print-rich environment, to encourage the children's writing and reading efforts in accepting ways, and to stand back and to observe the literacy process."

C. Read the situations below and decide if the adults are promoting or discouraging the literacy development process. Give a reason for your choice.

    1. Mrs Gray Fox observes five-year-old Jason as he writes a story to go with the picture he has drawn of Superman. He writes:

Sprman svz the good gIz. Here he

cms now. I lIk hm the bst.

Mrs Gray Fox asks "Please read me what you have written, Jason." Jason reads, "Superman saves the good guys. Here he comes now. I like him the best." Miss Jones, the student teacher, looks surprised. "Mrs. Gray Fox, shouldn't we make him spell the words correctly?"

    2. It's writing time in the four-year-old group at Mrs. Miller's Child Care Center. All the children are seated at tables. Mrs. Miller has Isabel and Derrick pass each child a pencil and a ditto sheet with an uppercase B and a lowercase b at the top. The paper is lined. She explains that today they are going to practice writing B's.

Intelligence and Creativity

OBJECTIVES

After studying this unit, the student should be able to:

- **Identify the characteristics of the psychometric, cognitive developmental, information processing, triarchic, multiple intelligences, and ethological views of intelligence.**

- **List the criticisms of the use of IQ tests and IQ scores in the assessment of young children.**

- **Recognize the attributes of nondiscriminatory testing.**

- **Describe how the adult who works with young children can have a long-term effect on their school success.**

- **Evaluate the creative aspect of adult and child interaction.**

- **Discuss the relationship among intelligence, creativity, and giftedness.**

Thus far, we have examined cognition as reflected in concept development and in oral and written language development. Intelligence and creativity have an overall effect on cognitive development and cognitive processes. The adult who works with young children needs to be aware of how intelligence is defined, what kinds of criticisms have been leveled at the use of IQ tests for measurement of intelligence, and the role of environmental influences in young children's intellectual development. It is also important to be aware of the creative aspects of young children's development and work in appropriate ways to support creative growth and development. Further, there needs to be an understanding of the relationship among intelligence, creativity, and giftedness. In this unit we will look at various aspects of intelligence and creativity.

WHAT IS INTELLIGENCE?

In the broadest sense, **intelligence** is the ability to benefit from experience, that is, the extent to which

KEYTERMSKEYTERMSKEYTERMSKEYTERMSKEYTERMSKEYTERMSKEY
intelligence

a person is able to make use of his or her capacities and opportunities for advancement in life. Among those who have tried to measure, define, and study intelligence there are a number of different points of view. These views include the psychometric (American); the information processing (mental representation and processing); the cognitive developmental (Piagetian); the triarchic (Sternberg); the theory of multiple intelligences (Gardner); and the ethological (naturalistic).

The **psychometric approach** stresses the measurement of individual differences, that is, the comparing of one person to others. It also stresses acquired knowledge and language skills as those behaviors to be measured in arriving at an estimate of the individual's intelligence. The **information-processing** (or cognitive science) **approach** attempts to identify all the steps taken in a problem-solving task. Rather than looking at problem solving in a global way, the information processing view studies in great detail the steps an individual takes to try to solve a problem. For example, the information processing psychologist might seek to find exactly what mental steps are used to arrive at the answers to IQ test questions or to solve a Piagetian conservation task. The ultimate goal is to able to simulate an individual's problem-solving tactics on a computer. The **cognitive developmental approach** stresses stages in the development of logical thinking, reasoning, and problem solving as the indicators of the growth of intelligence. The ethological view considers intelligence as the degree to which the individual is able to cope with and adapt to life. The **triarch approach** developed by Sternberg (1984a, 1984b) is similar to the ethological view in that it focuses on coping; however, it pinpoints more specifically certain areas to be evaluated using the information-processing approach to evaluation. The **theory of multiple intelligences** developed by Gardner (1984, 1983) is, like Piaget's, biologically based, but it views intelligence as being potentially divided into a number of different types.

These six views are outlined in Figure 25–1. They are outlined relative to definition, how measure-

ment is done, the major emphasis of each, and what is measured. Looking across the chart, notice the overall differences among the views: the theories range from tightly structured and specifically defined samples of behavior in the psychometric and information processing approaches, to more open-ended samples in the cognitive-developmental, triarchic and multiple intelligences approaches, to the total adaptation of the individual to his everyday life in the ethological approach.

The Psychometric Approach

An example of the psychometric approach is the situation in which a young child is taking a standardized intelligence test. Child and examiner are seated at a small table. One at a time, the examiner presents the child with a series of tasks. The tasks might include building a block tower, identifying parts of the body, or discussing what is seen in some pictures (Ambron, 1978). The child is given credit according to how correct each of his answers is relative to acceptable types of answers as described by the test developers. The child is then compared with other children his age by the use of the IQ (intelligence quotient) score he receives. An IQ score between 90 and 110 means he is average according to the test results. A score above 110 indicates he is above average and a score below 90 that he is below average.

The Information-Processing Approach

The information-processing approach is an attempt to overcome a major weakness in the psychometric and Piagetian measurement of intelligence (Siegler & Richards, 1982). Information processing emphasizes the process the individual uses to try to solve problems. Memory processes and problem solving, itself, have been the focuses of information processing research. Memory factors such as capacity, strategies, organization, and so on are studied. Prob-

The Six Views

Aspect of Intelligence	Psychometric	Cognitive Developmental	Ethological	Information Processing	Triarchic Theory	Multiple Intelligence
Definition	What intelligent people do	Adaptations to new situations child constructs	The disposition to behave intelligently: to adapt through problem solving	Intelligence is derived from the ways people represent and process information.	The ability to modify the environment so it will better fit one's adaptive skills	Intelligence is composed of seven intelligences: • linguistic • logical-mathematical • bodily-kinesthetic • interpersonal • intrapersonal • musical • spatial
How and where measured	Measured through a structured series of tasks in a controlled situation	Measured in a controlled setting using open-ended questions	Observed in the environment as the person goes through his daily life tasks	One to one in a laboratory setting	Tests which assess how well one manages oneself, others and one's career; individually administered tasks designed to measure real world coping skills	Unobtrusive measures used in the natural or naturalistic setting
Emphasis	Individual differences	Commonalities at each developmental stage of logical thinking	Identification of cognitive skills needed for adaptive problem solving	The most minute and elementary units of information processing; man's manipulation of symbols	Real world performance: • internalized world • external contexts • experience	Through development achieve different levels in each area. Match individual to activities appropriate to intellectual strengths
What is measured	Acquired knowledge and language skills	Reasoning and problem-solving skills	Adaptive level is evaluated through observation of daily activities.	Intelligent functioning in precise, testable steps relative to memory and problem solving	Real world coping skills (problem solving, verbal, practical/social) measured using tasks relevant to coping skills	Multiple intelligences as they comprise parts of total intelligence

Figure 25–1 **Six views of intelligence**

lem solving is examined in terms of task analysis, or breaking a task down into each substep. For example, children might be observed while trying to solve the Piagetian conservation of number task described earlier. Does the child examine the groups and decide that the group that takes up more space has more objects? Does he use one-to-one correspondence to check? Does he count each group to check? Does he just know that changes in arrangement do not affect the number of objects present? Emphasis is on how the child arrives at a solution rather than the solution itself.

The Cognitive Developmental Approach

Examples of the cognitive developmental approach are the Piagetian clinical interviews described in Unit 21. At the University of Montreal's Institute of Psychology, some psychologists (Pinard & Sharp, 1972) worked on the development of tests of intelligence using Piaget's tasks. One of the tests involves the floating and sinking of objects. Examiner and child sit at a small table. On the table is a small tank of water. There are various small objects available. Pinard and Sharp (1972, pp. 66–67) describe the task given to the child. An interview might go like this:

> The examiner picks up the nail, lets the child feel it if he wants to, and says, If we put this nail in the water, will it go to the bottom, or will it remain on the water?
>
> Child: It will go to the bottom.
>
> Examiner: Explain to me, why do you think it will?
>
> Child: It's heavy.
>
> Examiner: Now you may put the nail in the water and see what happens.
>
> Child puts the nail in the water and it sinks to the bottom.
>
> Examiner: Why does it go to the bottom, do you think?
>
> Child: The nail pushed itself down.

The child is given several objects. Each time he is asked to predict what will happen before he puts the object in the water. He is always asked to give his reason. There are no right or wrong answers as in the psychometric test. In the Piagetian test, the child is just assessed to find out where he is in the sequence of developmental stages. In this case, this child of four-and-a-half gives a typical preoperational response.

The Triarchic Approach

Sternberg (1985) proposed a triarchic approach, which divides intelligent behavior into three areas: the internalized world of the individual, the external world of real-life contexts, and the person's life experiences. He emphasizes that intelligence should be measured relative to these real-life situations. In contrast to the psychometric approach, he feels measurement of intelligence should be done without speed as a factor, without an emphasis on prior knowledge, and in a setting where anxiety is kept at a minimum. Although Sternberg emphasizes the importance of measuring intelligence in a real-life context, the actual situations he uses involve very specific tasks designed to simulate real-world problems that are analyzed using an information processing approach. Although his basic definition of intelligence is much like the ethological, his approach to measurement is more like the psychometric.

The Theory of Multiple Intelligences

Howard Gardner (1983) proposed a theory of multiple intelligences. Gardner believes that while each person has an overall intelligence, this intelligence can be broken down into seven intelligences, each contributing a part to the whole. The seven intelligences are:

- Linguistic intelligence: mastery of language.
- Musical intelligence: degree of musical talent.
- Logical-mathematical intelligence: mastery of the world of objects and the actions that can be performed upon objects (such as counting and ordering).
- Spatial intelligence: ability to perceive the world accurately, to transform and modify one's initial perceptions, to be able to recreate what one has

learned through the visual modality, even without the visual stimuli present.

- Bodily-kinesthetic intelligence: being able to use one's body in skillful ways and to handle objects skillfully.
- Personal intelligences:
  a. Intrapersonal intelligence: access to one's own internal feelings (such as discriminating pleasure and pain).
  b. Interpersonal intelligence: the ability to notice and make distinctions among other individuals (to recognize other's moods, temperaments, motivations, and intentions).

Measurement takes place in the naturalistic setting through observation of children's behavior (Hatch & Gardner, 1986; Gardner & Hatch, 1989; Gardner, 1993). Gardner's premise is that standardized tests are severely limited in that they measure mainly language and logic skills. Therefore, a new method of assessment is needed that taps all areas of intelligence during culturally familiar naturalistic activities.

Gardner's proposals have been put into effect in three projects (Gardner & Hatch, 1989; Gardner, 1993). Arts PROPEL is looking for ways to assess growth and learning in the arts at the secondary level; at the elementary level the Key School project in Indianapolis is attempting to develop assessments of all the intelligences; while Project Spectrum located at Tufts University has developed assessments that fit the child-centered curriculum of preschools and kindergartens. Project Spectrum assessment is done through specific activities designed to tap the multiple intelligences (Gardner, 1993; Krechevsky, 1991). The activities are set up as learning centers within the regular classroom structure. Activities range from the specific—like taking apart and assembling a meat grinder—to the open ended such as the science discovery center. Growth is documented using many methods such as score sheets, observation checklists, portfolios, and tape recordings. The Spectrum assessment system includes several unique dimensions (Gardner, 1993; Krechevsky, 1991).

1. The line between curriculum and assessment is blurred so that assessment is integrated into normal everyday activities.

2. Assessment is embedded into meaningful, real-world activities.

3. The measures used are "intelligence fair." Intelligences beyond just language and logic are tapped.

4. Children's strengths are emphasized.

5. Children's "working styles" are considered (e.g., persistent vs. frustrated, reflective vs. impulsive, confident vs. tentative; responds to visual/auditory and/or kinesthetic cues).

Spectrum classrooms are being developed in some first grades with at-risk populations in Somerville, Massachusetts. Gardner's objective is to free children from the narrow standardized test perspective and help them discover their own intelligences and use the information as a guide to vocational and recreational choices so they can find roles where they feel comfortable and productive.

The Ethological Approach

In the ethological approach, rather than an examiner, there is an observer. Rather than a small room with a table and two chairs, the child is evaluated in her natural environment. The observer stays in the background taking note of the child's behavior. The observers might be looking for some specific kinds of adaptation such as how the child copes with problem-solving situations (Charlesworth, 1978). Or, they might be looking for general behaviors that seem to indicate good adaptation.

Many people contend that the psychometric approach gives an unfair picture of the child's intellectual capacity (Vernon, 1979). They also believe that intelligence test scores have been used in ways that have hurt children and kept them from reaching their potential (Figure 25–2).

KEYTERMSKEYTERMSKEYTERMSKEYTERMSKEYTERMSKEYTERMSKEY
ethological approach

Figure 25–2 Assessment can be done through teacher observation of children during regular classroom activities with children's classroom work being a rich source of information for assessment.

IQ SCORES: CRITICISMS AND CAUTIONS

Criticism of IQ tests and the uses of IQ scores has developed for several reasons (Vane & Moha, 1980):

- Although the IQ scores predict school success, they don't consider coping skills.

- IQ scores have been used and misused to label children as developmentally disabled who really were not; they may just have poor test-taking skills.

- IQ test content is unfair to children who may not have the English language skills nor the knowledge and experiences necessary to give correct answers on the tests.

- The young child is inconsistent in his test responses from one testing to another.

There has been a great deal of controversy over whether there are racial differences in intellectual capacity (i.e., Gould, 1982; Jensen, 1985; Moore, 1982, 1985) or whether the low scores obtained by minority and low SES children reflect biases in the intelligence tests (i.e., McGowan & Johnson, 1984; Cole & Washington, 1986). Constance Kamii and others (1990) believe that cultural bias is a major factor limiting the usefulness of standardized tests of any kind with young children, especially if some important educa-

tional decision such as grade retention or admission to a special program rests on the results. Considering the nature of young children and their yet to be developed capacities, adults who work with them must be very cautious in using and interpreting intelligence test and other standardized test scores. Multiple measures should be reviewed before making any decisions regarding placement or retention.

INTELLIGENCE: ENVIRONMENTAL INFLUENCES

The adult who works with the young child needs to consider the question of assessing the intellectual capacity of the child to plan and evaluate an instructional program. The teacher has to consider classroom, home, and neighborhood performance along with any information from formal or informal testing. The Council for Exceptional Children (Policy, *Exceptional Children*, 1977) has formulated suggested policies for nondiscriminatory evaluation of individual children. Some of the suggested policies include:

- Assessment instruments shall be appropriately adapted when used with children of impaired sensory, physical, or speaking skills and must consider each child's age and socioeconomic and cultural background.

- Specialists implementing evaluation procedures must be familiar with local cultural, language, and social patterns and practices.

- Tests and similar evaluation materials shall be administered in the child's primary language, wherever appropriate.

- Interpreters, in the native language, and/or in sign language may be used throughout all phases of the evaluation.

- All communication with parents and the child shall be in the native language of the home.

- Instruments shall be administered only by trained personnel according to the producer's instructions.

- Instruments shall assess specific abilities, not merely produce a single IQ score.

- No one result shall determine placement.

Evaluation of groups of children (classrooms or schools) can also go beyond IQ scores and make better use of informal interviews with children, checklists, classroom observations, and portfolios of children's work (Isenberg & Jalongo, 1993; Kamii, 1990; Shelly & Charlesworth, 1980). Information for authentic assessment should be obtained when children are engaged in their regular daily activities rather than in artificial individual or group testing situations, Figure 25–2a; through examination of developmentally appropriate student work, Figure 25–2b; or during individual interviews where developmentally appropriate tasks are used. (See Unit 2.) For future guidance see the NAEYC/NAECS/SOE position statement (1991).

An important consideration for teachers of young children is long-term effects. Teachers of young children deal with the child in the child's first school experience. Will or can the teacher have an effect on a child in the long run? Will the child be able to cope with life any better than if he had not received the early educational experience? The long-term follow-up on children who participated in the infant and preschool programs of the fifties and sixties and further studies of those and other models look very encouraging (i.e., Bracey, 1994; Campbell & Ramey, 1994; Farnsworth et al., 1985; Frede & Barnett, 1992; Lazar et al., 1982; Miller & Bizell, 1983; Miller & Bizell, 1984; Schweinhart & Weikart, 1985; Schweinhart, Weikart, & Larner, 1986; Schweinhart, Barnes, & Weikart, 1993). For example, these children have had less special education placement during their school careers. They were also less likely to be retained in a grade than children who had not had a preschool experience. The children had short-term IQ score gains that held through third grade. It may be that the preschool programs taught the children the language and concept skills they needed in order to cope successfully with the early years of school. This also enabled them to go through school with a better set of reading, writing, and arithmetic skills. The adult who works with young children can be confident that the child is being taught some basic skills and attitudes that will help in dealing with future school experiences.

Four-year-old Derrick and two friends have built a hideout with some large blocks and planks. "Now, how do we get in?" asks Kevin. "There's no door." "Easy," answers Derrick. "Through the **trap** roof." He slides one of the roof planks over carefully and the friends climb in slowly, pulling the roof plank back into place above them.

Isabel rolls the play dough. Then she cuts it in half with a popsicle stick which she uses like a knife. She sings while she cuts, "I have a donut." She cuts off several pieces. She hands a piece to Bill and says, "Here's a hot dog."

Figure 25–3   Are these young children creative?

WHAT IS CREATIVITY?

Are the children in the examples in Figure 25–3 creative? How about Kate's drawing in Figure 25–4 of a girl riding a horse? Are young children really creative in the same sense as an older child or adult, or do they just seem creative because of their preoperational view of the world? **Creativity** is an aspect of behavior

Figure 25–4   Children are being creative when they draw what to them is original, such as this "girl on a horse."

KEYTERMSKEYTERMSKEYTERMSKEYTERMSKEYTERMSKEYTERMSKEY
Creativity

that reflects originality, experimentation, imagination, and a spirit of exploration (Figure 25–5).

Both Piaget and Vygotsky have contributed to the theoretical understanding of the concept of creativity (Ayman-Nolley, 1988). Both viewed creativity as emerging from children's imaginative play. Children's imaginative play pulls away from reality and is a reflection of the distortions caused by their pre-formal operational way of thinking. According to Piaget and Vygotsky, true creative imagination develops when abstract thinking and conceptualization are possible in adolescence and adulthood. Both theorists apply their ideas to artistic behavior but say relatively little about scientific inventions. Imagination and fantasy are the two key creative elements that are present in early childhood (Isenberg and Jalongo, 1993). "**Imagination** is the ability to form rich and varied mental images or concepts of people, places, things and situations not present. . . . **Fantasy** is a particularly vivid use of the imagination to create mental images or concepts that have little similarity to the real world" (Isenberg and Jalongo, 1993, p. 7). As with other areas of cognitive development the environment must be one that nurtures creative behaviors to ensure their development.

Creativity can differ in degree depending on the extent to which the result of the creative actions (Torrance, 1983, p. 510):

1. Shows novelty and value (for the child or the culture).
2. Is unconventional in that it diverges from previously accepted solutions.
3. Is true, generalizeable, and surprising in light of what the child knew at the time.
4. Required persistence in going beyond previous performances.

Any of these examples of child behavior may be considered creative but just how creative depends on how well the behaviors fit the criteria for degree.

According to Torrance (1983) young children naturally have creative ways of learning. By age two or three they have experienced learning by "questioning, inquiring, searching, manipulating, experimenting, and playing to find out in their own way the truth about things" (p. 510). Young children learn creatively because they have long attention spans, a capacity for organization, are capable of seeing things in different perspectives, explore before formal instruction, use silence and hesitation, take a "closer look" at things, use fantasy to solve developmental problems, and use storytelling and make believe (Torrance, 1983).

What is Giftedness?

There has been increasing interest in identification of young children who are gifted and development of programs for them. Currently, the number of programs available for this population does not meet

Figure 25–5 Creativity is reflected in the young child's imaginative, original explorations of materials.

Imagination   Fantasy

the demands. This is especially valid for the lower SES groups (Stile, Kitano, Kelley, & Lecrone, 1993). According to Karnes and Schwedel (1983), the definition of **giftedness** is hard to pin down. The definition selected by Karnes and Schwedel (1983, p. 475) is that gifted preschoolers are "children who show evidence of advanced skill attainment relative to their peers." According to Karnes and Schwedel (1983, p. 475), intellectually gifted young children tend to be characterized as follows:

- have accelerated language development.
- understand cause-and-effect relationships more quickly than other children.
- see humor not perceived by other children the same age.
- generalize learning more readily than others.
- are more curious.
- ask more questions.
- are adept at solving problems.
- tend to learn academics at an earlier age.
- have longer task persistence than their peers.
- are more creative in their thinking.
- are more resourceful.

Defining and measuring giftedness is a controversial problem (Hoge, 1988). Selecting the best measure for deciding who is "gifted" and who is "not gifted" presents many difficulties. There are problems in defining giftedness and problems in finding valid and reliable means for identifying the gifted child. While definitions of giftedness may include constructs such as motivation and creativity, actual selection usually rests on an IQ test score ignoring other qualities, which may be equally indicative of giftedness and ignoring the weaknesses of the IQ tests. Jackson and Sacks (1994, April/May) point out that in twenty-five of our largest cities the majority populations are culturally diverse and in a large percentage non-English speaking. The procedures for identification of gifted students has not kept up with these changing populations. According to Jackson and Sacks (p. 8) the iden-

tification of gifted African-American and Hispanic children has been held back for several reasons: "1) preponderantly narrow definitions of giftedness; 2) a heavy reliance on IQ test scores or achievement test scores; and 3) many school personnel's low expectations of these students in predominantly European American school districts." A survey of twelve predominantly nonwhite school districts revealed that minority students were under-represented in the gifted programs. Jackson and Sacks recommend that before minority low SES children are tested, they receive an infusion of intellectual stimulation designed to develop their thinking skills and better prepare them to demonstrate what they can really accomplish.

Creativity, Intelligence, and Giftedness

It can be seen that there is an overlap in the definitions of creativity and giftedness. However, the two do not necessarily go hand in hand. That is, a person may be highly intelligent but not very creative, or highly creative but not of outstanding intelligence. Children may also be low in both creativity and intelligence. They can be gifted in one area but not in others.

Creativity and intelligence, then, do not necessarily go hand in hand. Each child must be looked at individually and helped to develop creatively in his own way in whatever areas he finds of interest

Creativity, Curiosity, and Problem-Solving

Problem-solving skills and curiosity behavior are important elements in the definition of creativity. Torrance (1983) identified several types of creative thinking skills that he believes all children develop to some degree by the time they enter school. Creative-thinking skills are skills through which children develop new combinations and relationships in organizing symbols, objects numerals, people, places, words, etc. Natural curiosity extends children's knowledge as they develop more mature question asking skills. These thinking skills support the young child's curiosity and problem-solving activities. If placed in an environment with peers who are explorers, children's exploratory behavior is increased (Moore, 1985). The presence of a supportive adult also helps to bring out the natural inquisitiveness of young children (Schmidt, 1985).

Early childhood classrooms can provide impetus to exploration by offering a rich array of interesting materials for both spontaneous and planned activities. Changing the environment often will excite children's curiosity and entice them to explore and find out what's new. Science investigations lend themselves to exploration of questions such as:

- How long does it take a bean plant to sprout from a seed?
- Which kinds of objects are attracted by a magnet?
- Where does steam come from?

Adults must be sensitive regarding when to intrude with a question and when it is best to leave children alone to work on their own projects and problems (Clark, 1985).

Artistic Development

According to R. Craig Sautter (1994), integrating the arts into the school curriculum can encourage positive changes in the curriculum. Whereas the arts are conventionally an integral part of prekindergarten and kindergarten programs, from the primary grades and beyond, school becomes more and more textbook driven and drill and practice oriented. Opportunities to create through writing, music, art, drama, and dance can greatly enhance student motivation and provide an outlet for the creativity that is evident in all children at five. Creativity seems to disappear by six or seven when opportunities for application are not available and appears again in adult artists (Davis, 1993; Gardner, 1993).

Creativity is a broad characteristic that can surface in any area. Artistic development as reflected in drawing is an area that has been examined closely. Martha Taunton and Cynthia Colbert (1984) reviewed the research on artistic development of children ages four to six years of age.

Artistic behavior is always intriguing to adults because the child's products give us something tangible that reflects planning, perceptual and conceptual development, and communication skills (Taunton & Colbert, 1984). Drawings have been studied a great deal. As already described in Unit 16, the first stage in drawing consists of scribbles. At this stage the child explores the implements and enjoys the kinesthetic experience as much as the tangible results of the activity. Between the ages of three and five, representational drawings usually appear. The first ones are usually human figures with just a head and leglike appendages (Figure 25–6a). Young children seem to focus in at first from the top down in reconstructing their mental image of human figures. Figure 25–6 compares human figures drawn by kindergarten and first-grade students. All are capable of drawing representationally, but the developmental differences are wide within grade and there is overlap in development between the children at the two grade levels. Overall the first-graders' drawings are more mature. Pictures inspire descriptive verbalizations and, as mentioned in Unit 24, drawing also develops along with written language.

How the Adult Can Foster Creativity in the Young Child

The Association for Childhood Education International (ACEI) has developed a position paper on the child's right to the expressive arts (Jalongo, 1990). The paper presents the arguments for including the expressive arts of music, art, drama, dance, and writing in the curriculum. The expressive arts foster **reflective learning** (*from the inside out*). They enhance symbolic development, growth in all areas of development, and view the child as one who constructs and makes meaning. The expressive arts can be integrated into all the content areas, providing a means for the child to create and construct. The adult role is to provide the materials and the impetus for the children to feel free to use them.

Adults can foster children's creativity by encouraging their personal expressions and providing materials, time, space, and support (Moyer, 1990). For the

Figure 25–6a   **Kindergartners' drawings of their fathers: from early representational to more mature representational.**

Figure 25–6b   **First graders' drawings of their fathers: from early representational to more detailed, proportional versions.**

beginning artists, adults can provide a variety of materials so that children can select the kind of material over which they believe they have the most control. The objective of much early artwork is finding out what can be done with various kinds of materials. Children should be encouraged to decide on their own topic and should have plenty of time to work at their own pace, experimenting and exploring the material without feeling bound by the need to produce a specific product. Teachers may comment as the children work, discussing concepts such as color, line, mass or volume, pattern, shape or form, space and texture. Ditto and pattern art are not appropriate because they devalue the children's ideas, making them afraid to take risks and express themselves. For young children it is the artistic process, not the product that is the focus of creativity (Edwards & Nabors, 1993). "Creativity is feeling free to be flexible and original, to express one's *own* ideas in one's *own* way" (p. 79) not following a teacher's step-by-step directions in a craft-type project. Artwork created and selected by the young artists should be the predominant display material in their classrooms.

When children are well into the representational stage (usually around age five), teachers can suggest topics that integrate art into unit topics as a means for students to represent what they have learned and experienced, still allowing plenty of opportunity for children to work on a sudden inspiration. Nancy Smith (1982, 1983) has developed an approach for providing a topic that still leaves children free to be creative. Smith's point of view is that as children become skilled at representational drawing and have experimented with various media extensively so that they have a feeling for the process, the teacher no longer has to stay in the background. Smith's procedure is designed to promote observational art for children who are ready for it. That is, children age five and above. She has found that children can produce more detailed artwork if they are encouraged to observe the object of their drawing rather than having to draw completely from recall. Figure 25–7 contains some observational drawings done by kindergartners (Koenig, 1986). The models were the type of plastic animals commonly available for dramatic play in preschool and kindergarten classrooms and a real crawfish. Before having the children draw, the adult discussed the visual characteristics of the animals with the children: the contours, the shapes, the body parts, etc. The resulting drawings are very detailed and representational. Compared with data collected by Smith, these children were quite advanced, including many kinds of details usually found mainly in drawings done by older children.

Creativity is nurtured by social interactions. The seeds of original ideas often come from interactions with peers and adults (Wolf, 1989). Mosley (1992) observed that kindergartners shared ideas about basic graphic elements such as birds, rainbows, houses, and people but incorporated the elements into their drawings in original ways. Thompson (1990) reviewed the theory and research on children's talk and drawing development. Before three the act of learning what the implement can do usually takes all the child's attention. From around age three and beyond, children talk about their drawings. It is at this point that the adult and child can enter into discussion centered on the artwork. This adult support enhances the children's development as artists (bringing us again to Vygotsky's concept of scaffolding). Adult comments should be responses to child comments and should focus on shape, color, texture, etc., not on an interrogation regarding the topic or on pressure to tell a story. Examples of appropriate comments would be: "You must like bright colors"; or "You must like to make circles."

Also ask children questions that promote creative thinking such as:

- What if an elephant had no trunk?
- What would you do if you looked out the window in the morning and there was a dinosaur in your yard?

Encourage imagination. When the child says "There's an alligator in my bedroom," go along with it. Ask him questions such as, "What is he doing? Is he hungry? What's his name?" This type of game taps the child's creative potential and encourages him to use his imagination. Keep the children curious, allow them to explore, and guide them to discover answers on their own. Every child has some capacity for creativity; the adult who looks for it will find it.

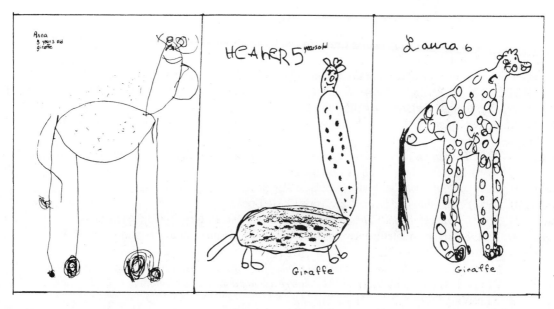

Figure 25–7a   **Observational drawings of a giraffe by three kindergartners illustrate three levels of development in moving from stick drawings to drawings with shape, contour, and pattern.**

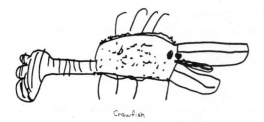

Figure 25–7b   **An observational drawing of a crawfish by a kindergartner shows unusual attention to detail for a child of this age.**

SUMMARY

Six views of intelligence were described in this unit. These views are: the psychometric, the information processing, the cognitive developmental, the triarchic, multiple intelligences, and the ethological. The first three view intelligence as reflected in responses to standard questions. The theory of multiple intelligences and the ethological view look at intelligence as reflected in everyday normal life activities.

The triarchic theory views intelligence as the response to everyday living but attempts to measure it in standardized situations. Many critics feel that the psychometric approach (use of the IQ test) is an unfair assessment of intellectual capacity. IQ tests are felt to be especially unfair to the minority child because of cultural biases and different language experiences. Test scores should be used with caution and combined with other measures and observational materials when a child or program is being evaluated.

Creative behavior is usually defined in terms of originality, high levels of curiosity, and frequent problem seeking. Giftedness refers to advanced intellectual and/or creative abilities relative to one's peers. Creativity may accompany high intelligence, but this is not always the case. Children of lower intelligence may be creative and children of high intelligence are not necessarily creative. The gifted individual may be advanced intellectually or creatively or both. The adult who works with young children can encourage creative behavior by providing an environment in which original and unusual ideas can be pursued.

FOR FURTHER READING

Cohen, S. (1994). For parents particularly: Children and the environment—aesthetic learning. *Childhood Education, 70,* 302–304.

Cox, M. (1993). *Children's drawings of the human figure.* Hillsdale, NJ: Erlbaum.

Dunn, R., Dunn, K., & Perrin, J. (1994). *Teaching young children through their individual learning styles.* Des Moines, IA: Longwood Division, Allyn and Bacon.

Franklin, M. B., & Kaplan, B. (Eds.). (1993). *Development and the arts: Critical perspectives.* Hillsdale, NJ: Erlbaum.

Gallas, K. (1994). *The languages of learning: How children talk, write, dance, draw and sing their understanding of the world.* New York: Teachers College Press.

Gardner, H. (1980). *Artful scribbles.* New York: Basic Books.

Gardner, H. (1982). *Art, mind and brain.* New York: Basic Books.

Gardner, H. (1983). *Frames of mind: Theory of multiple intelligences.* New York: Basic Books.

Lohman, D. F. (1989). Human intelligence: An introduction to advances in theory and research. *Review of Educational Research, 59,* 333–373.

Mugny, G., & Carugati, F. (1989). *Social representations of intelligence.* New York: Cambridge University Press.

Renzuli, J. S., Reis, S. M., & Smith, L. H. (1981). *The revolving door identification model.* Mansfield Center, CT: Creative Learning Press.

Runco, M. A. (1991). *Divergent thinking.* Norwood, NJ: Ablex.

Runco, M. A., & Albert, R. S. (Eds.) (1990). *Theories of creativity.* Newbury Park, CA: Sage.

Russ, S. W. (1993). *Affect and creativity: The role of affect and play in the creative process.* Hillsdale, NJ: Erlbaum.

Sameroff, A. J., Seifer, R., Baldwin, A., & Baldwin, C. (1993). Stability of intelligence from preschool to adolescence: The influence of social and family risk factors. *Child Development, 64,* 80–97.

Sapon-Shevin, M. (1994). *Playing favorites: Gifted education and the disruption of community.* Albany, NY: SUNY Press.

Schirrmacher, R. (1993). *Art and creative development for young children.* (2nd Ed.). Albany, NY: Delmar.

Siegel, J. & Shaughnessy, M. F. (1994). Educating for understanding: An interview with Howard Gardner. *Phi Delta Kappan, 75,* 563–566.

Smilansky, S., Hagan, J., & Lewis, H. (1989). *Clay in the classroom.* New York: Teachers College Press.

Sternberg, R. J. & Berg, C. A. (Eds.) (1992). *Intellectual development.* New York: Cambridge University Press.

Sternberg, R. J. (1984). *Beyond IQ: A triarchic theory of human intelligence.* New York: Cambridge University Press.

Sternberg, R. J. & Wagner, R.K. (Eds.). (1986). *Practical intelligence.* New York: Cambridge University Press.

Sternberg, R. J. (1990). *Metaphors of mind: Conceptions of the nature of intelligence.* New York: Cambridge University Press.

Sternberg, R. J. (Ed.) (1988). *The nature of creativity.* New York: Cambridge University Press.

Tegano, D. W., Moran, J. D., III, & Godwin, L. J. (1986). Cross-validation of two creativity tests designed for preschool-age children. *Early Childhood Research Quarterly, 1,* 387–396.

Venn, M. L., Wolery, M., Werts, M. G., Morris, A., DeCesare, L. D., & Cuffs, M. S. (1993). Embedding instruction in art activities to teach preschoolers with disabilities to imitate their peers. *Early Childhood Research Quarterly, 8,* 277–294.

SUGGESTED ACTIVITIES

1. Can you remember ever having your intelligence tested when you were child? Can you remember why? Compare your experiences with those of other members of the class.

2. The class is divided into two groups. One group develops as many reasons as they can think of for heredity having a stronger effect than environment on intelligence. The other group thinks of as many reasons as they

can why environment has a stronger influence on intelligence than heredity. Each group lists its reasons on a large piece of newsprint (or the chalkboard). One person from each group is chosen to debate both points of view. Three guests can be invited to be judges of the debate. After the debate, the judges can present an award to the side they feel has made the best case.

3. With a small group in class, discuss the statement, "Intelligence testing of young children does more harm than good." Report your decision to the rest of the class.

4. In the library, find an article on intelligence testing. Write a report using the following format:
   a. Bibliographic information: author(s), title, name of periodical (or book), volume number, publisher, date published, page numbers.
   b. A short summary of the article: the main point the author(s) is (are) trying to make and the support they present for their point of view.
   c. A reaction that tells your opinion of the material presented in the article. Does the material have any practical applications? What are they? Do you agree with the ideas presented? Why or why not?

5. Discuss with a small group in class: which would be best, to be highly intelligent or highly creative? Why? Discuss the advantages and disadvantages of both. What is your personal preference? Are you now stronger on intelligence or creativity?

6. Visit an early childhood classroom. Record all the creative acts you observe during a 45-minute period. Group them according to the areas in which each creative act took place (i.e., Social Studies, Science, Mathematics, Writing, Art, Blocks, Dramatic Play, etc.). Discuss activities that you could develop that would promote creativity.

7. Choose an activity from a book of creative activities for preschool children (see Further Reading). Obtain whatever materials are needed and try the activity with a small group of preschool children (three to six children). Write a description of what each child does during the activity. Evaluate each child's degree of creativity using the following scale.

CREATIVITY SCALE

1	2	3	4	5
Low Creativity		Somewhat Creative		High Creativity
(Lacks originality, flexibility, curiosity, willingness to explore — may look to see what others are doing and copy exactly.)		(Has some characteristics of creativity but not all.)		(Demonstrates originality, flexibility, curiosity, willingness to explore — does what he wants to do — not influenced by others.)

If possible, try another activity with the same children individually. Rate their degree of creativity. Were any differences observed when each child worked alone as opposed to when he worked with a group? What were these differences? What seemed to make the difference?

8. Make an entry in your journal.

REVIEW

A. Match the view of intelligence in Column I with the correct definition in Column II.

Column I

1. psychometric view
2. cognitive developmental view
3. ethological view
4. information processing view
5. triarchic theory
6. multiple intelligences

Column II

a. Intelligence is reflected in adaptations to new situations.
b. Adaptations through problem solving.
c. The behavior of intelligent people.
d. Intelligence is made up of seven types of different intelligences.
e. Intelligence is derived from the ways people represent and process information.
f. Intelligence is the ability to modify the environment so it will better fit one's adaptive skills.

B. Decide for each of the following examples whether the assessment is psychometric (P), cognitive developmental (CD), ethological (E), information processing (IP), triarchic theory (TT), or multiple intelligence (MI).

1. Adult: Here are some cups and some saucers. Is there a saucer for each cup? (There are ten cups and nine saucers. They are lined up in two rows so the rows are of equal length.)

    Rudy: Yes.

    Adult: How do you know?

    Rudy: My mother told me.

    Adult: (Concludes that three-year-old Rudy is in the early part of the preoperational stage of intellectual development since he is fooled by appearance and cannot give a logical reason.)

2. Adult: (Speaking to child seated across the table from him) Point to your nose.

    Derrick: (Points to his nose.)

    Adult: (Marks *correct* on his scoring sheet.)

3. Adult: I have a bunch of blocks over here. I want you to count them for me.

    Hien

    Phung: (He starts out taking one block at a time.) One, two, three, four, five, six, seven, eight, nine, ten, twelve, fourteen, sixteen, seventeen, . . . that's as far as I can go.

    (Adult notes that Hien Phung has the concept of one-to-one correspondence, proceeds in an orderly manner, and knows when he has reached his limit.)

4. Adult: Take these blocks and build a tower just like mine.

    Child: (Builds structure but it does not match the adult's.)

    Adult: (Marks *incorrect* on his scoring sheet.)

5. Adult: (Watches as Theresa struggles to reach a toy on a high shelf. After no success, Theresa gets a small chair, puts it by the shelf, and climbs up. She gets the toy.)

    (Adult notes that Theresa has managed to cope with a problem situation and find a solution on her own.)

6. Mrs. Brown observes each of the children carefully as they go about their activities in her preschool classroom. She notes that each child has a unique pattern of intellectual strengths. She will use this information in planning her instructional program.

7. Adult: Sorry, Kate, you can't play with that glass bowl. You will have to find something else to do.

    Kate: I just want to look at it. Could you hold it and I could look?

    Adult: Good idea, Kate. Here, I'll get it.

    (Adult notes that Kate was able to arrive at a solution that was agreeable to the adult and to herself.)

C. List the criticisms of the use of IQ tests and IQ scores.

D. Write the number of each statement that is consistent with suggestions for nondiscriminatory testing developed by the Council for Exceptional Children.
1. Every assessment instrument used must be one that is adapted to each child's socioeconomic, cultural, and language background.
2. A single IQ score can be used for decision making as long as the test is administered by a qualified examiner.
3. Assessment should be broad-based and look at each area of child development.
4. Communication with parents and child could be carried out in the family's language.
5. It is not necessary for those who set up assessment programs to be familiar with the local culture and customs.

E. Can the adult who works with young children have a long-term effect on that child's school success? What evidence is there to support your answer?

F. Decide whether the adult is promoting creativity in the following situations. Give a reason for your answer.
1. The teacher passes out a ditto sheet with a picture of a fish on it and asks each child to color his in carefully, using orange as the main color.
2. The teacher puts paint, crayons, paper, glue, and other materials on the table. She tells the children to think about their trip to the Tropical Fish Shop and then create a picture of the kind of fish they would like to have.
3. Derrick says he doesn't want to make a fish. He liked the snails best. Mrs. Chen says, "Good idea, Derrick."

G. Discuss the relationship among intelligence, creativity, and giftedness.

Section VII

Affective Growth and Development from Preschool to Primary

This section will look at children's affective development in more detail: how they develop in the areas of emotions, personality, and social behavior. Young children's development in the affective areas is closely tied to their development in the cognitive areas. Their views of their own feelings, of themselves, and of others are different from those of adults and older children. As preview to this section we will again meet Ramona Quimby and introduce several other fictional children who typify the kinds of affective thinking and behavior that makes young children so special.

Let's look at Ramona first. At age four young children are just beginning to incorporate a sense of right and wrong and with their preoperational logic may do things that appear to be misbehavior but which really reflect that they are victims of their immature logic. For example, Ramona doesn't want to return *Big Steve and the Steam Shovel* to the library. From her preoperational point of view the library *gave* her the book and she writes her name on every page to prove it.

From preschool to primary, young children learn the limits of their initiative. Having grappled with autonomy they can take on more specific projects. For example, Peter (Keats, 1964) wants very much to be able to whistle so he can whistle for his dog Willie. He views being able to whistle as a sign of maturity and even puts on his father's hat so he will feel more grown-up. He keeps trying and eventually reaches his goal.

Young children are just learning to deal with strong feelings. Alexander during his terrible, horrible, no good, very bad day is faced with a variety of problems and disappointments from waking up with gum in his hair to having his best friend change to some other best friends to lima beans for supper (Viorst, 1972). From preschool to primary is a time when young children learn to face a variety of fears. Monsters may lurk anywhere but grown-ups may not understand. Harry's mother goes into the basement even though Harry knows there is something terrible down there (Gackenbach, 1977). It was left

357

up to Harry to protect his mother from the Terrible Whatzit. Since it is also important to be strong and brave Harry manages to overcome his fears and overcome the Terrible Whatzit.

Peer relationships are very important to young children. Ramona has her best friend Howie. They have their ups and downs but maintain their friend-ship. In kindergarten Ramona chases Davy around the school yard threatening to kiss him. She can't re-sist pulling Susan's curls and finds herself in trouble.

In the following units we'll look at affective development from preschool to primary. As you read each unit, keep Ramona, Peter, Alexander, and Harry in mind.

Books referred to:

Cleary, B. (1955). *Beezus and Ramona*. New York: Yearling. (Ramona, age four)
Cleary, B. (1968). *Ramona the Pest*. New York: Yearling. (Ramona, age five)
Gackenbach, D. (1977). *Harry and the terrible whatzit*. New York: Scholastic.
Keats, E. J. (1964). *Whistle for Willie*. New York: Viking.
Viorst, J. (1972). *Alexander and the terrible, horrible, no good, very bad day*. Hartford, CT: Athenium.

The Nature of Affective Development

OBJECTIVES

After studying this unit, the student should be able to:

- Define affective.
- Recognize the interests of ten major theorists in the affective area.
- Identify affective behaviors of a young child.
- Identify the major areas of each of the ten theorists discussed in the unit.
- Discuss the importance of ego development during early childhood.

Affective is defined as the area that centers on the development of social, emotional and personality characteristics and the self-concept. Each of the major theorists discussed earlier has some interest in affective growth. For Freud, Erikson, Sears, Rogers, and Maslow, affective growth is the center of attention. Freud's theory is concerned with personality development. Erikson's theory centers on social and personality development within the social context. Rogers' theory emphasizes self-concept development. Maslow also emphasizes self-concept development through self-actualization. Sears' theory concerns social learning and social behaviors such as dependency, aggression, and sex-role identification. Bandura's social learning theory focuses on the emotional and motivational aspects of thinking (Miller, 1989). Piaget's theory centers on the cognitive aspects of affect in the areas of play, communication, and the child's concept of right and wrong (Figure 26–1). Vygotsky's theory emphasizes the importance of the social context and culture with an emphasis on the role of parents and teachers as guides (Miller, 1989). Gesell has collected descriptive norms of the young child's affective development.

As previously discussed, in infancy, a bond is formed that is the basis for attachment and future independence. Between ages one and three, the toddler is off on his own. As he interacts with others, he demonstrates an interest in social activity, a need to develop positive self-regard, and even shows kind feelings toward those in trouble or in pain. Thus, the

KEYTERMSKEYTERMSKEYTERMSKEYTERMSKEYTERMSKEY

Affective

Figure 26–1a & b **Affective behavior is seen in the expression of both positive and negative feelings.**

preschool child has already developed through two stages of affective development.

THEORETICAL VIEWS

To Freud, children ages three to six are in the **Phallic Stage**, during which the child concentrates on sex-role identification and conscience development. In Erikson's view the period from three to six is the time for working through **Crisis III: Initiative versus Guilt**. Rogers and Maslow emphasize the importance of the child's personal experience and its effect on self-concept development. For Sears the child continues through phase II: secondary behavioral systems. In the Piagetian system, the child is in the latter part of the preoperational stage and for Vygotsky the stage of Early Childhood. Gesell identified a sequence of stages from age three to five at half-year intervals characterized by equilibrium at three, four, and five and disequilibrium at three-and-a-half and four-and-a-half. For Skinner there is no special stage of affective development during the preschool years; the child merely continues to learn and to have his behavior modified by environmental forces. For Bandura increased cognitive skills affect how the child uses social knowledge.

Freud

Freud's theory (Mead, 1976, Chapter 2) describes five stages through which children pass as they develop from birth to adolescence. As already described, the infant is in the Oral Stage and the toddler in the Anal Stage. The three- to six-year-old is in the Phallic Stage. The seven- to twelve-year-old is in the Latency Stage. These four stages are outlined in Figure 26–2. During the Phallic Stage, according to

Stage	Age	Focus
Oral	Infancy	Emotional facets of the feeding experiences.
Anal	1½–3 years	Emotional facets of the toilet-training experience.
Phallic	3 to 6 years	Sex-role identification and conscience development.
Latency	7 to 13 years	Consolidation of previous stages of development.

Figure 26–2 **Freud's stages of early childhood personality development. The important facet developmentally is that the young child learns to handle the kinds of problems presented in each stage in a positive way.**

Phallic Stage   Crisis III: Initiative versus Guilt

Freud, the child becomes aware of himself (herself) as male (female) and must successfully deal with the identification process. Through this process the child takes on the behaviors of the same-sex parent. The young child also develops a conscience, the sense of right and wrong, as his superego develops (this will be discussed further in the description of Erikson's theory), Figure 26–3.

Erik Erikson

Erikson's theory (cited in Maier, 1978, pp. 71–132) includes eight stages through which each person passes as he develops from birth through old age. As already described, the infant deals with the crisis of Trust versus Mistrust and the toddler with the crisis of Autonomy versus Shame and Doubt. The preprimary child is in the third stage where he faces the crisis of Initiative versus Guilt. During the primary years, children enter **Crisis IV: Industry versus Inferiority**. Each crisis has its roots in infancy and continues to affect future development. Erikson's stages of early childhood are listed in Figure 26–4. None of the crises are ever resolved; the conflicts stay with us throughout life. The person who copes successfully at each step learns to handle these conflicts in a positive and healthy way.

Figure 26–3   **When young children feel tired or under stress they may revert to previously comforting behavior from the oral stage.**

Stage	Conflict That is Faced
I. Infancy	Basic Trust Versus Mistrust
II. Toddlerhood	Autonomy Versus Shame and Doubt
III. Preprimary	Initiative Versus Guilt
IV. Primary	Industry Versus Inferiority

Figure 26–4   **Erikson's theory centers on the eight stages through which people progress during the life span. Each stage presents the person with a new conflict to be handled. Each conflict has its beginning in infancy and continues to influence the person's behavior throughout life. The three stages of early childhood are listed here.**

The preprimary child now has a sense of purpose in what he does. He plans and then attacks a task for the sake of the activity. He loves to investigate and explore, but at the same time he has to learn the limits of his initiative. He must begin to detach himself from his parents and do things independently. Independence is given gradually by adults; the young child must learn what is considered acceptable and unacceptable behavior. The conscience, or sense of right and wrong, begins to develop during this stage. The ego or self-concept works on perfecting basic skills in the psychomotor, perceptual, communicative, and social areas. Children thus become increasingly independent and do more things for themselves, such as dressing, getting their own snacks, and making projects using wood, clay, and other materials. At the same time, they begin to develop inner control of their behavior.

During the preprimary period the foundations of the child's sex-role identity are built. Boys learn who they are in relation to being male and girls in relation to being female. Play is the young child's major activity. Play serves as a means for trying out dreams and working through conflicts. Through play the child can carry out activities that are not available to him otherwise. He can do what adults do through dramatic play and stories. He becomes very aware

Crisis IV: Industry versus Inferiority

that adults have privileges he does not have. Through activities with toys and tools or through responsibilities for younger children, preschool children practice some of these adultlike behaviors.

The preprimary child who passes through this period successfully learns how to take initiative within the limits of society. He develops a conscience but is not so overwhelmed by guilt at his desire to do grown-up things that he is not able to do anything. His new sense of control helps him stay within realistic boundaries.

As children enter the primary years they also enter the stage of Industry vs. Inferiority. Success and productivity are necessary in order for them not to develop feelings of inferiority. They seek to be productive through, not only the cognitive activities such as those in the school setting, but also through projects such as crafts and collections, through physical activities such as sports and dance, and artistic endeavors such as in art and music.

By the preprimary period, the child's personality has developed three major structures: the id, the ego, and the superego (Figure 26–5). The **id** is present at birth and contains the person's unconscious motives and desires. It operates on the pleasure principle; that is, it is concerned with the comfort and well being of the child. At birth, the **ego** begins to develop. The ego develops as the child begins to discover he is separate from his environment. The ego is characterized by reason and common sense and operates on the reality principle; that is, the ego interprets reality to the child. The **superego** begins to develop around the age of four. This is the conscience—the part of the personality that holds on to the moral values of society.

The ego, id, and superego are in constant conflict. The id tells the child to go ahead and enjoy himself: take the cookie even though mother said not to; grab a toy from another child because you want to play with it now. The superego says be good: don't get angry; don't take the cookie; never take someone else's belongings. The ego must mediate between the two so that the child is not dominated by one or the other. Through the ego, the child develops a sense of self so that he can take initiative with confidence but not overstep society's boundaries. At one extreme id-dominated children think only of their own pleasures and desires and behave accordingly. While at the other extreme, superego-dominated children may be so fearful of doing wrong that they are afraid to take chances and as a result don't develop a sense of purpose and initiative.

Robert R. Sears

For Sears (cited in Maier, 1978, pp. 133–164) the preprimary child is in the latter part of stage II: Secondary Behavioral Systems, during which time social learning usually centers in the family. Around three the child begins to **identify** with the parent of the same sex. That is, the girl sees herself as being like her mother and the boy sees himself as being like his father. The young child imitates what he sees adults do and thus begins to learn what it is like to be an adult. Through identification processes, the child takes on the sex-role behaviors that society says are appropriate for him (or her).

Sears also emphasizes the importance and value of play for the young child. Through play, children explore the world and try out behaviors they would otherwise not be able to experience.

Self-control begins to develop during this period. Children behave in ways that will bring the approval of the adults with whom they have formed attachments. Thus, dependency and self-control are closely tied. These first dependent relationships lay the groundwork for later caring relationships with people outside the family.

Aggression develops during the early years as a response to frustration. The child wants a toy; he cries; he gets the toy. The child learns he can achieve his goals through aggressive actions. By the time the child reaches the preprimary period, he usually knows just what the rules are regarding aggression; that is, when, where, and how he can be aggressive. One of the most difficult things for the young child to

KEYTERMSKEYTERMSKEYTERMSKEYTERMSKEYTERMSKEY

| id | superego |
| ego | identify |

Personality	Age at Which Development Begins	Characteristics	Example When in Control
ID	Present at Birth.	• Unconscious motives • Pleasure principle • Acts in terms of most basic desires such as hunger and comfort.	Child is hungry. Takes a cookie, although he has been told that he can take fruit if he wants a snack, because he likes cookies better.
EGO	Begins to develop right after birth.	• Reason and common sense • Reality principle • Mediates between id and superego; tries to keep both under control.	Child is hungry. Wants a cookie but knows that he is only allowed to take fruit. He chooses an apple.
SUPEREGO	Begins to develop around four years of age.	• Conscience; incorporation of society's moral values.	Child is hungry. Afraid to take any food without checking with adult first. If adult is not available, continues being hungry rather than taking the initiative.

Figure 26–5   **The structure of personality: psychoanalytic view**

learn is how to inhibit or redirect aggression in appropriate ways. If the adult is extremely permissive of aggression, the child will continue with aggressive acts. If the adult is very strict about not allowing expression of aggression, the child probably will hold it all in in that situation but may let it out elsewhere. Somehow, a delicate balance needs to be found, allowing for expression of aggression within socially acceptable boundaries. During the primary period, children enter Stage III, Secondary Motivational Systems. By this time their focus leaves the family and centers on outside social structures of which the school is foremost. Primary children are expected to balance dependence and independence and know how to control their aggressive impulses.

In summary, Sears' theory centers on social behaviors such as identification and sex-role acquisition, dependency, play, aggression, and self-control (Figure 26–6).

Rogers and Maslow

As discussed in Unit 1, Rogers and Maslow are not stage theorists. Both focus on the process of achieving a positive self-concept. The child moves toward self-actualization supported by love from parents and positive peer interactions. Since between three and six children begin the move from a focus on parents to a focus on peers, the interactions with peers take on more importance than previously for these two theorists.

Rogers emphasizes the importance of the child focusing on personal experiences. Children need to make full use of their physical and mental faculties to get the most out of their daily experiences. Rogers and his followers emphasize counseling approaches to child rearing, that is, approaches that involve discussing the problem. Emotionally healthy people can see their emotions and the emotions of others clearly; they can bring them to the symbolic level and can speak about them. Parents are in a critical position. They need to learn to accept themselves and their feelings about their children. They have to accept that it is all right not to be "perfect." They have to accept that it is all right not to always feel positive and accepting toward everything their child does.

Maslow also emphasizes self-knowledge. He developed a **hierarchy of needs** that the person must

hierarchy of needs

Figure 26–6   **These children are learning how to share a limited amount of space.**

deal with and satisfy to be self-actualized. Each lower-level need must be satisfied to reach the upper-level needs. The needs include (starting with the lowest and most basic):

1. *Physical/Organizational*
   - Survival — to be able to eat, breathe, and live.
   - Security — predictability, assurance that tomorrow will come.
2. *Affiliation/Social*
   - Belonging — being part of a group.
   - Esteem — being valuable and unique.
3. *Achievement/Intellectual*
   - Knowledge — wanting to know about things, symbols, etc.
   - Understanding — putting small bits of knowledge together into a larger picture.
4. Aesthetic
   - Aesthetic — a sense of order, balance, and beauty; love for all.
5. *Self-Actualization*
   - Being a fully functioning person.
   - Being one's true self.

It can be seen that affective needs are the most basic after survival. Both these sets of needs need to be fulfilled before the child will be motivated to seek knowledge and understanding, essential motivations when he enters school.

Jean Piaget

Piaget's theory of cognitive development (cited in Maier, 1978, pp. 12–70) was reviewed in earlier units. Although Piaget has not delved into affective development with the diligence that he has delved into cognitive development, he sees the two as following parallel developmental sequences. Social learning involves the same adaptational goal as does cognitive development. We seek emotional as well as cognitive equilibrium. Piaget and his followers have studied play, moral development, and social cognition (how we view others) and how they relate to affective development.

Piaget believed that during the preoperational period children focus on reciprocity of feelings and the development of moral feelings (ideas about rules, accidents, lying and justice) (Wadsworth, 1984). When children develop representative thought, the past can be remembered and reconstructed and serve as the basis for reciprocity of values and attitudes. Children begin to like each other because they share the same attitudes and values. They also can begin to anticipate that affective experiences will be positive or negative. Morally the preoperational child is still at a premoral stage (described in Unit 29).

During concrete operations children begin to be able to apply abstract symbols and ideas to concrete experiences. For example, they can consider both sides of a disagreement at the same time, consider what is fair or not fair in a particular situation, and consider the other person's point of view when making a decision.

Lev Vygotsky

Vygotsky's concern with the social components of learning and development have already been described. The adult's role in providing scaffolding which supports the child through the zone of proximal development has been described in previous units.

Arnold Gesell

Gesell's theory (Gesell et al., 1974) applies to all behavior, which he divides into the motor, adaptive, language, and personal-social areas. Personal-social behaviors include personal reactions to other people and the social culture. For Gesell there are unique behavior patterns at each age.

The work of Gesell and his colleagues is a rich source of descriptive material regarding the young child's affective development. For example:

The three-year-old "... tries to please and to conform. Evan asks, 'Do it dis way?' ... He is susceptible to praise and he likes friendly humor.... If a group of parents should again cast a secret ballot, to decide on the most delightful age of the preschool period they would choose the three-year-old."

The three-and-a-half-year-old is characterized by refusing to obey. "It sometimes seems to his mother that his main concern is to strengthen his will by going against whatever is demanded of him."

The four-year-old " ... has meager appreciation of disappointment and the personal emotions of others. He is inquisitively interested in death but has scant comprehension of its meaning.... His words often outrun his knowledge."

The five-old-year " ... wants to do what is right and so he loves to ask permission." The five-year-old is usually very dependent on his mother.

B. F. Skinner

Skinner's operant-conditioning theories have been used to develop ways to modify the behavior of young children. They have been particularly useful when used to stop unwanted behaviors such as temper tantrums and aggression, and to increase the frequency of positive behaviors such as sharing and cooperation.

Albert Bandura

Bandura's theory provides a framework for the acquisition of appropriate affective behaviors. Observing others provides knowledge of expectations for appropriate emotional, personality, and social behaviors (Miller, 1989). Children create some of their own environment through their behavior and their choice of activities. Children who are kind and generous with others receive reciprocal responses from others while those who are hostile and selfish are ignored or treated negatively by others. Children who watch television see different models than those who spend more time with other children. As children mature cognitively and are able to manipulate symbols, they can also manipulate mentally the social roles they have observed and coordinate the behaviors into their own particular way of behaving. Imitation is not necessarily a one-to-one correspondence to what is observed. Cognition also serves a role in the degree to which children perceive themselves as competent in dealing with the environment. Children must not only have the skills to accomplish specific tasks but also view themselves as capable of using their skills to achieve mastery.

Conclusions

Each of these theorists has some interest in affective development. The affective area encompasses the development of the self-concept, ego and superego, sex-role identification, aggression, dependency, moral judgment, social behavior with peers, and the content of play activities. Psychoanalyst Selma Fraiberg (1959) believes that at the center of the development of the child during the early years is the development of "I." For the child to reach age six with good mental health, he must have an ego that is capable of dealing with conflict, tolerating frustration, adapting, and finding solutions to problems that satisfy both his inner needs and outer reality. "These qualities of the ego are the product of the child's bonds to his parents, the product of the humanizing process" (Fraiberg, 1959, p. 302).

SUMMARY

The affective area of development can be defined by examining the theories of several psychologists: Sigmund Freud, Erik Erikson, Robert R. Sears, Carl Rogers, Abraham Maslow, Jean Piaget, Lev Vygotsky, B. F. Skinner, and Albert Bandura. The descriptive work of the maturationist Arnold Gesell adds additional breadth to the picture. During the early years, affective growth centers on the development of the child's picture of himself. By the age of six, he is ready to begin to look at others and society as they relate to himself and to each other.

FOR FURTHER READING

Baldwin, A. L. (1980). *Theories of child development*, (2nd. Ed.). New York: John Wiley.

Kostelnik, M. J., Stein, L. C., Whiren, A. P., & Soderman, A. K. (1993). *Guiding children's social development* (2nd. ed.) . Albany, NY: Delmar.

Lomax, E. M. R., Kagan, J., & Rosenkrantz, B. G. (1978). *Science and patterns of child rearing*. San Francisco: W. H. Freeman.

Maier, H. W. (1978). *Three theories of child development*, (3rd. ed.). New York: Harper and Row.

Mead, D. E. (1976). *Three approaches to child rearing*. Provo, UT: Brigham Young University Press.

Miller, P. H. (1989). *Theories of developmental psychology*, (2nd. Ed.). New York: Freeman.

Moll, L. C. (Ed.). (1990). *Vygotsky and education*. New York: Cambridge University Press.

Rogers, C. (1983). *Freedom to learn for the 80's*. Columbus, OH: Charles E. Merrill.

Vasta, R. (Ed.). (1992). *Six theories of child development*. London & Philadelphia: Jessica Kingsley Publishers.

Wadsworth, B. J. (1984). *Piaget's theory of cognitive and affective development*, (3rd. Ed.). New York; Longman.

SUGGESTED ACTIVITIES

1. Before studying the affective behavior of the preschool child, take a look at yourself. Consider each of the items in the Affective Self-Assessment Checklist. Decide how each statement relates to your self-concept. The abbreviations in the columns are:

   SA: Strongly Agree; yes I do feel this way now.

   A: Agree, I feel somewhat that way or have in the past.

   N: Neutral; sometimes I feel that way or have in the past.

   D: Disagree; I don't feel that way now although I may have in the past.

   SD: I've never felt that way.

Affective Self-Assessment Checklist

	Statements About Myself	SA	A	N	D	SD
1.	I feel close to other people and have many warm ties.					
2.	I have at least one person in whom I can confide and share my deepest feelings.					
3.	I relate easily to authority figures.					
4.	I relate well to my peers.					
5.	I relate easily to those in lower ranks.					
6.	My family has always been fair with me — never too demanding or too pressuring.					
7.	I don't take offense when others tell me what to do.					
8.	Even when others are inconsiderate of me, I try to be cooperative, respectful, and nice to them.					
9.	For the most part, people are fair and don't try to take unfair advantage of me.					
10.	Sometimes people expect more of me than my capabilities allow.					
11.	I feel good about myself as compared with others.					
12.	I'm not afraid to look at myself objectively and understand what makes me "tick."					
13.	I have no problem showing my feelings — whether of happiness, love, anger, fear, etc.					
14.	I have a firm set of values regarding right and wrong.					

When you have finished, review your responses:

1) In which, if any, areas do you feel you could be stronger?
2) Try to remember back as far as you can into your childhood. Do any of these feelings go back to those times?
3) If possible, discuss your responses with a small group in class. How do you compare with others? Do they find the roots of present feelings in their early years? How would each person in the group react to a young child who:
   a. can't relate well to other children.
   b. is being pressured too much to achieve and to be well behaved and is not handling the pressure well.
   c. doesn't seem to be taking on appropriate sex-role characteristics.
   d. always seems to be feeling angry.
   e. resents being told what to do.
   f. always seems to be striving to be like someone else instead of accepting himself and making the most of his own strengths.
   g. seems overly controlled; always trying to hold his feelings inside.
   h. is continuously searching for someone he can be dependent upon.
   i. can't seem to understand what is right and wrong; he's always testing limits.

2. Make an entry in your journal.

REVIEW

A. Define *affective*.

B. Match each of the theorists in Column I with their interest from Column II.

Column I	**Column II**
1. Robert R. Sears	a. social and personality development within the social context
2. Arnold Gesell	b. dependency, aggression, and sex-role identification
3. B. F. Skinner	c. self-actualization through the satisfying of a hierarchy of needs
4. Jean Piaget	d. Observational learning of affective-related behaviors
5. Erik Erikson	e. descriptive norms of affective behavior
6. Carl Rogers	f. cognitive aspects of social behavior
7. Abraham Maslow	g. modification of behavior, including affective
8. Sigmund Freud	h. The role of the adult in supporting the child's development so that the child reaches his or her potential
9. Lev Vygotsky	i. personality development, especially the development of sex-role identification and conscience
10. Albert Bandura	j. self-concept development

C. Identify the affective behaviors in the following example from a case study of a five-year-old preschool child named Sean.

> When he played alone he was quiet and fully involved, yet he just didn't seem as happy as the other children. Later when Sean began playing associatively with children he smiled more, laughed more, and even began to talk more.

> From the beginning Sean has been willing to share and take turns with others. He is very patient and considerate. Sean has extremely good manners and courtesy. Although Sean is a good listener, especially to adults, he lacks skill in communicating with others.... He also seems to find it hard to stand up for his own rights, as can be seen in the many times Sean passively allowed another child to take his toy, his chair, or his tricycle. He seemed to fear other children and would not use any type of skills to ease the situation.

> He shows pride in his accomplishments, and can get the attention of adults in socially acceptable ways. Sean will express feelings of hostility to peers occasionally, but will never express affection. I did not note a single time when Sean expressed either hostility or affection to adults. Sean never destroyed anything or used any acts of physical or verbal violence toward another child. Like many four- and five-year-olds Sean shows dependency by seeking approval and attention. Many times he has exclaimed, "See what I did!"

> Sean has demonstrated fear by withdrawing. He will not answer questions and speak to the teachers in a natural, relaxed way. He withdraws when he is uncomfortable or in unfamiliar surroundings.

D. Write the number of each correct statement.
1. For Erikson the preschool period is a time during which the child must deal with Crisis III: Initiative versus Guilt.
2. Gesell has found that the preschool child enters a stage of disequilibrium at the age of three-and-a-half and four-and-a-half.
3. The crises that Erikson describes are never resolved but are handled successfully if the child is able to deal with them in a positive way.
4. Maslow's hierarchy of needs is based on the belief that some needs are more basic than others and therefore must be satisfied first.

5. During Erikson's Stage III, the conscience, or sense of right and wrong, begins to develop.

6. Normally, in Erikson's scheme, the child would not develop much in the way of independent behaviors until he is of school age.

7. Freud's stage theory runs parallel to Erikson's stage theory and includes the same theory of personality structure: id, ego, and superego.

8. The child who successfully completes Crisis III knows how to take initiative and do things on his own without overstepping the boundaries and limitations set up by society.

9. The id operates on the pleasure principle and the ego on the reality principle.

10. The moral values of society are held in the ego.

11. The child's understanding of his personal experiences is critical to Rogers' theory.

12. Vygotsky is more concerned with the cognitive than the social aspects of the adult's interaction with the child.

13. For Bandura the cognitive aspects of observational learning are not important.

14. Being too strict regarding aggressive behaviors is dangerous, while being too permissive is good for the young child's development.

E. Discuss why ego development is important during the period from ages three to six.

Unit 27

Emotional Development

OBJECTIVES

After studying this unit, the student should be able to:

- State why the young child has a "right to feel."

- Identify the major aspects of attachment.

- Recognize examples of dependence and independence.

- Describe the relationship between independence and responsibility.

- Explain what might be done to handle children's fears and reduce stress.

- Discuss what the child must learn about handling angry feelings.

- Know the developmental aspect of the recognition of emotions.

What kinds of feelings do I have in relation to other people and in relation to things? How do I express these feelings? What purposes do these feelings serve? The answers to these questions are found in the study of the area of emotional development. The emotional area includes feelings such as anxiety, fear, sadness, anger, happiness, love, and affection. Young children have a well-developed set of emotional responses by the time they reach the preschool period. These responses come from feelings children have within themselves about other people, things, and events in the environment. For children's mental health it is important that they have opportunities and methods for expressing their feelings. They also need to learn that having feelings is normal. Adults in our culture often deny feelings and may lead children to hold their feelings in check. As Fraiberg expresses it, the young child has "the right to feel" (Fraiberg, 1959, p. 273).

For example, Fraiberg describes an incident in which a mother wants to buy a substitute hamster before her son finds out that his hamster is dead. Fraiberg feels that the boy has a right to experience the feeling of loss. "In our efforts to protect children from painful emotions we may deprive them of their own best means of mastering painful experiences" (Fraiberg, p. 274). She feels that if the child can experience mourning a hamster, it will help him when the time comes to face the loss of a friend or a family member. Further, holding feelings inside is not mentally healthy. He will also be able to work through his feelings about death and dying.

Lewis and Michalson (1983) did an in-depth study of emotions and their development in early childhood. Whereas emotional and cognitive development are conventionally viewed as separate processes, Lewis and Michalson suggest a model that interrelates the two areas. They choose to view emotional behavior and feelings as cognitive processes. The model they propose is much like the Model of Cognitive Functioning shown in Figure 20–8 of this text. According to the model in Figure 20–8, there would be some internal or external event that would be perceived as input, processed internally in a way such as to develop an internal response or feeling, followed by output through facial expression, vocalization, posture or gesture and/or motor behavior. Internal and/or external feedback would set the sequence moving again.

For example:

Anger:

1. Jason accidentally knocks down the unit block building he has been working on for 20 minutes. (External event)
2. Jason feels his elbow hit the building and sees it topple over. (Tactile and visual perception)
3. Jason thinks, "Oh no! It's falling!" (Processing)
4. Jason feels hot and his body feels stiff. (Internal response)
5. He throws himself to the floor, flailing and crying. (Output, external response, motor and vocal)

Dealing with emotions is an important aspect of working with young children. Adults must be aware that children have had different experiences that will shape their individual emotional reactions and behaviors and be prepared to act accordingly (Elkind, 1993).

The emotions and their development in the young child discussed in this unit include attachment, dependency, fear and anxiety, hostility and anger, and happiness. Also discussed is the recognition of emotions and the adult's role as an observer of emotionally based behavior.

ATTACHMENT

Attachment is a lifelong commitment between child and caregiver that builds from birth and evidences specific features around 6 months of age when the infant perceives the caretaker as a special person (Stroufe, 1991). (Refer to Units 8 and 12.) Terri Smith (1991) describes some of the effects lack of secure attachment may have on children's social behavior. Four-year-old best friends have been found to have a more happy and harmonious relationship if both were securely attached to their mothers. Insecurely attached six-year-old boys were rated by teachers and peers as less competent, less well liked, and as having more behavior problems than securely attached boys. Siblings who have secure attachments also have better relationships. It is important for those who work with young children to assist parents in developing secure attachments and to provide that secure attachment if they are working with young children in a caretaking/instructional role. The various aspects of emotional development described in the discussion that follows are of equal importance and are an integral part of the cognitive developmental factors described in Section VI.

DEPENDENCY

Newborns are completely dependent on the other people in their environment to fulfill all their needs. Two types of dependency develop. One type is an **emotional dependency** that springs from the development of attachment. The other type is a **physical dependency**.

Physical dependency involves basic needs, such as nourishment, comfort, and elimination. The young infant is totally dependent on others to care for his needs. However, physical dependency changes rapidly with age. The child enters a helpless stage, then a stage during which he cooperates and accepts help, and finally, a stage in which he does it himself. By the time the child is a preschooler, he has become independent in regard to eating, toileting, building, and walking and is on his way to becoming independent in dressing. During the preschool period his play and social behaviors become increasingly independent.

Emotional dependency develops in a different way than does physical dependence (Figure 27–1). Whereas hugging, kissing, and clinging are acceptable behaviors for an infant or toddler, as children develop through the preschool period it is expected that the form through which they show and receive affection and love will change. That is, they are less public in their expression and decrease their clinging behavior. From wanting to be picked up and hugged when coming home from nursery school, the preschooler develops toward a verbal greeting, smiling, and maybe a quick hug. Cuddling is saved for the privacy of home. The objective is not to make the child independent of emotional attachments but to change the way the child shows love. Further, children are encouraged to widen their emotionally dependent attachments to others: to peers, relatives, and teachers,

for example. To get reassurance that they are still loved, preschoolers turn more and more to verbal attention seeking:

> "Look what I can do!" (as he tries a somersault)
> "Look at my picture!" (as she holds up a drawing she has just made)
> "Help me, please." (as he tries to rearrange the furniture in his bedroom)
> "Isn't this a pretty dress?" (as she comes in wearing a new outfit)

Some adults feel it is not good to reinforce dependent behavior. However, the child's emotional needs continue to require fulfillment. This requirement is accomplished by giving attention when the child is independently performing a physical act. Punishment for dependency may only increase children's desire for it and the frequency with which they seek attention, reassurance, and affection.

The development of physical independence enables children to develop responsibility for their own actions (Veach, 1979). This is accomplished through offering the child the opportunity to make more and more complex choices.

Independence supports increasing feelings of competence. Lewis and Michalson (1983) define competence as "the ability to participate in a set of age-related tasks, which is accompanied by a positive feeling" (p. 344). Research indicates that these feelings may begin to appear as early as 10 weeks of age. Once feelings of competence (or its opposite, helplessness) are established, they seem to stay with the child as he enters each new situation.

FEAR AND ANXIETY

Young children normally develop fears and anxieties as they proceed through the preschool period (Robinson and Gladstone, 1993). Robinson and Gladstone (1993) found that monsters were the fears mentioned most frequently by three- to five-year-olds. School-related fears appear around 4 or 5 years of age. Children in the Robinson and Gladstone study mentioned fear of not learning to read, of not being able to talk in class, and of being sent to detention. Overall, eighty different feared objects were mentioned. Young

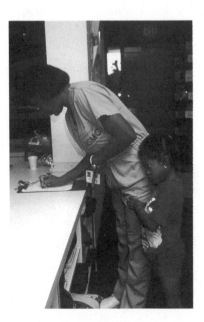

Figure 27–1 **The preschool child becomes physically independent but remains emotionally dependent on adults.**

children are concerned about monsters in the closet and goblins under the bed (Figure 27–2). They may be afraid of going down the bathtub drain or being sucked into the toilet. They may be afraid of new situations and new people. Wind, thunder, and lightning may also be frightening. Working through these fears enables the child to be a mentally healthy person. By working through these childhood fears, he strengthens his feelings of power in relation to the world. The young child has the mental equipment to deal with danger. If adults teach him how to use that mental equipment in dealing with goblins and witches, he will be able to apply those skills later when he meets real danger. He will also learn how to handle things that are realistically anxiety and fear provoking, such as having a tooth filled, getting an injection at the doctor's office, or wondering what happens when an animal or a person dies.

Fear develops most likely through a combination of genetic and learned factors. Fears have been shown to be acquired through conditioning and observational learning. Fear may also depend on the child's perception of the fearful person as a real person or not. For example, infants who have been around a lot of people and thus realize that people come in many sizes and shapes are less likely to develop a fear of strangers.

The normal fears of the young child can be handled by facing them and not pretending they do not exist (Hyson, 1979; Robinson and Gladstone, 1993; Smith, Allen, and White, 1990). Hyson (1979) makes the following suggestions:

- Talk about the fears. Help the child put the fear into words and/or pictures.

- Provide opportunities for dramatic play. Sometimes by taking the role of one who is feared (the doctor, the bad wolf, or the witch) the child can lessen his anxiety.

- Use desensitization or gradually build up to the feared object or experience. Have the child play with a puppy if he is afraid of full grown dogs; let him play in a small swimming pool if he is afraid of a big one.

- If the child's fear is centered on a need of his own, it may work best to work on that need. For example, the child who is afraid of a monster may really have a problem of needing to be aggressive himself.

- Help the child learn skills for coping with fear. For example, prepare through books and dramatic play for a trip to the hospital. Don't tell him that "It won't hurt" when it will.

Death is an especially difficult concept with which to deal. Most young children encounter death in some form whether a dead bug, a pet, or a relative. These experiences provide a component of understanding and feelings about death (Essa & Murray, 1994). Essa and Murray (1994) reviewed the research on children's understanding of (the concept level) and feelings about (the emotional level) death. Understanding the concept of death is more advanced if children have experienced a death event.

Children younger than five or six have a restricted view of death. It is during the five-to-seven transition period to concrete operations that a clearer concept develops. During the elementary years, children begin to understand that everyone will eventually

Figure 27–2   **The young child normally goes through a period when he is afraid of monsters.**

die; but they don't see the personal relevance. Understanding of death includes four basic components:

Finality. Death cannot be reversed. Preschoolers frequently believe that magic or medicine can reverse the process.

Inevitability. All living things will eventually die. Young children tend to believe that death can be avoided.

Cessation of bodily functions. Death ends movement, feeling, thought, etc. Preschoolers may view death as a type of sleep.

Causality. Understanding how death may occur. Younger children tend to focus on outside factors such as guns or accidents, while older children perceive that internal factors such as illness or old age may be the cause.

The first three factors usually become understood between five and seven. Causality seems to be a more difficult concept and is understood later.

Other factors that must be considered besides cognitive development are culture, experience, and environment. Seeing characters on television rise from the dead may distort young children's concepts of death. Different cultures may vary in their views of death. For example, some cultures view death as a "deathman." Children who live in an environment that is war-torn or who live in a violence-prone inner-city neighborhood have early first-hand experiences with death (Essa & Murray, 1994).

At the emotional level, mourning and grief are normal reactions but so are anxiety and fear. As children get older, it is not unusual for their anxiety to increase. The death of a close friend or relative provokes deep emotional reactions in young children. They may even withdraw from and/or deny the fact. Adults have the responsibility of handling these situations in a sensitive and supportive ways (Essa & Murray, 1994).

The threat of war can also cause confusion and fear for young children. During the 1980s, nuclear war was of great concern to children (Beardsley and Mack, 1986). Television news and programs may depict the nuclear threat and be very frightening to children. Understanding of nuclear threat appears to develop in a sequence parallel to that of death. Children ages four to six can be frightened without really understanding what the phenomenon is while by third or fourth grade they begin to understand and need accurate information in order to come to terms with their concerns. Young children can be reassured, but extensive explanations will only confuse them (Children's Nuclear Fears, 1984).

Today war can be with us in our livingrooms through on-the-spot live action reporting. The Gulf War of 1991 demonstrated the power of modern communications technology. It also brought to adult attention the fearful nature of war as perceived by young children. Well-known experts (e.g., Brazelton, 1991; Rogers & Sharapan, 1991) were called upon to offer advice on dealing with children's fears. The most important thing for adults to do is to be honest about the danger and reassure children that we will do all we can to take care of them and keep them safe. It is also more important to listen to children and help modify their misinterpretations than to offer long explanations that may only confuse and frighten them. Through discussion and dramatic play, young children's fears regarding the danger of war can be calmed. Finally, television viewing and radio listening should be kept to a minimum so that children are not overwhelmed by the apparent nearness of the conflict.

STRESS

An element closely related to fear and anxiety is **stress** (Honig, 1986; Mills & Spooner, 1988; Swick, 1987). Stress has been defined in various ways (Honig, 1986, p. 51) such as *nonspecific response of the body to any demand that exceeds the person's ability to cope, a person-environment relationship that threatens or taxes personal resources, and a mental state in response to strains or daily hassles.* Stressors may come from illnesses, fear of failure, being teased about physical appearance, fear of loss of love, poverty, catastrophe, hospitalization, disasters (such as a storm or an earthquake), nuclear threat, war, terrorism, birth of a sibling, death, separation and divorce, step families, etc. Each child reacts differently to the same or similar stressors depending on what the stressor means to the child personally (Honig, 1986). The stress response is made up of several stages (Honig, 1986):

1. Stage of alarm. Physiological changes such as changes in blood pressure or heart rate come with the initial feeling of not being able to cope. Frequently, psychomatic symptoms develop into illness so that stressed children may get sick more often than other children.

2. Stage of appraisal. The same event may or may not be identified as stressful by different children, depending on their beliefs and previous experiences.

3. Stage of searching for a coping strategy. Some strategies are adaptive and some are not. Tears and tantrums are not very adaptive. Ignoring, finding a compromise, or finding a substitute activity are adaptive.

4. Stage of implementing coping responses. Coping responses are the means used to deal with stress. They can take on different forms:
   a. Defensive strategies may be used to distort or deny that there is something disturbing the child. They may act compulsively or rigidly.
   b. Externalization is a process where children attribute control to fate or to other people. They cope with stress by lashing out and blaming others for their problems.
   c. Problem solving may be used to try to find a way to lessen the stress.
   d. Instrumental coping involves using skills and knowledge to try to improve the situation.

Adults can help children by protecting them (reducing stress in the environment) and by facilitating children's learning about how to deal with stress when it does occur (Cadiz, 1994; Honig, 1986).

Today's young children are exposed to numerous stressors at home, in the community, and at school. Since stress has a cumulative effect, as Honig (1986) has suggested, we need to try to eliminate as many stressors as possible. Research by Burts, Hart, Charlesworth, and Kirk (1990) and Burts, Hart, Charlesworth, Fleege, Mosley, and Thomassen (1992) indicates that developmentally inappropriate instructional practices (as defined in Bredekamp, 1987) produce significantly more observed stress behaviors (e.g., laying on the desk, playing with body parts or clothing, playing with objects) in kindergartners than does more developmentally appropriate instruction. That is, the workbook/worksheet curriculum is more stressful than the hands-on/concrete experiences curriculum. Additional stress is added by the use of inappropriate assessment practices that require young children to take standardized group paper and pencil tests (Fleege, Charlesworth, Burts, & Hart, 1992). This research suggests that the elimination of developmentally inappropriate instructional and assessment practices could greatly reduce school-based stress for young children.

Adults who work with young children can assist them to develop the resilience to cope with the stress and trauma in their lives. Children who survive stressful childhoods and traumatic events either have families or other adults, such as teachers, who provide needed support and understanding (McCormick, 1994).

HOSTILITY AND ANGER

Hostility and **anger** are the emotions that underlie aggressive behavior. Feelings of this kind seem to appear shortly after birth (Sears et al., 1957). Of course, we do not know the baby feels anger in the same way as the older child or adult does but he appears, at least, to be angry. "There are the flailing limbs, the blasting cry, the scarlet face and hoarse breathing" (Sears et al., p. 222). The behavior appears much like that which may appear later as a temper tantrum. The problem for the young child is to learn to control the expression of these angry, hostile feelings. Of course, the child has the right to feel anger, but it is necessary to learn the socially acceptable modes of expression. Dealing with hostility and anger is discussed further in Units 29 and 30.

An increase in violence in the lives of young children has brought about an increased need to look at how living in a violent environment affects children's emotional and social development. For many children, their foremost worry is that a loved one will be the victim of a violent crime (State of America's children, 1994). Gun violence has particularly affected young children. Data collected up until 1994 indicated that 801 children ages 1 to 14 died of both accidental and deliberate gunshot injuries in 1991. In 1993, NAEYC published a position paper on violence in the lives of children (NAEYC, 1993). Efforts are being made to teach children at an early age that there are peaceful alternatives to solving problems with violence (Bernat, 1993; Parry, 1993).

Research on anger has looked at the factors that make some children react negatively when hostile feelings are aroused while others act in a positive manner. Strength of emotionality and controllability of emotions and actions have been studied. Eisenberg et al. (1994) examined constructive and nonconstructive factors in the anger behavior of middle-class preschoolers. Children who had overall constructive ways of coping with problems and who reacted with low-intensity emotions were more likely to use verbal methods of dealing with their anger. Those children who used nonconstructive coping strategies and reacted with strong emotions were more likely to react to anger with aggression.

HAPPINESS AND HUMOR

Happiness is the expression of positive emotions such as pleasure, joy, and delight (Lewis & Michalson, 1983). Smiling is the most popular cue to happiness. We have already described the development of the smile. Whether early smiles are really a reflection of happiness, we do not know, but they definitely give the caregiver a positive signal. About a

month to as long as 12 months after smiling, laughing usually appears. Lewis and Michalson did not find any developmental trend in happiness: it was either there or not there. Children older than 19 months showed more happiness than younger children. Hestenes, Kontos, and Bryan (1993) found that children in higher-quality childcare centers with teachers who displayed more appropriate caregiving behaviors displayed more smiling and laughing with greater intensity than children in lower-quality centers.

Understanding **humor** (jokes, riddles, etc.) requires a higher level of cognitive development than that required as a response to tickling and peek-a-boo games that provoke laughter in infants (Honig, 1988). However, infant smiling and laughter builds a foundation for later responses to jokes and riddles. Honig (1988) describes how the appreciation of humor appears to develop in stages beginning with the smiling and laughing that results from infant play with adults and/or older children. Toddler humor may center on purposefully mislabeling objects, such as putting a foot through the armhole of a shirt and labeling it "shoe" (accompanied by laughter). Preschoolers enjoy absurdity (such as a bicycle with square wheels) and play with words (often body parts and bodily function words). Between five and seven children begin to enjoy riddle jokes and once they are into concrete operations their humor becomes quite complex. Humor can brighten children's lives if it is appropriate for their cognitive developmental level. Adults should take the children's leads and couch humor in their style.

RECOGNIZING EMOTIONS

Developmentally, children learn to recognize their own emotions before learning to interpret those of others. Children also recognize positive emotions before negative. Just which emotion is displayed in the child's behavior is a function of context. For example, a mask that frightens a child when worn by a stranger may bring laughter when worn by father (Honig, 1988).

Happiness   humor

Lewis and Michalson (1983) found when children as young as 2 years of age were requested to make faces that would indicate specific emotions, they could make several different kinds of faces (happy, sad, angry, and surprised). By age four they could make happy, sad, angry, funny, surprised, and scary faces. The difference may reflect that two's have less well-developed muscular control, that they have fewer labels, and/or they become bored with the game sooner than the four's. The two's could also identify pictures of happy, sad, angry, and disgusted faces as they fit a story they were told. Lewis and Michalson conclude that by age six children know well when and how to express emotions.

Carroll and Steward (1984) investigated the role of cognitive development in children's understanding of their own feelings. They looked at the relationship between performance on classification and conservation tasks and understanding of feelings with four- and five-year-olds and eight- and nine-year-olds. The children were asked questions such as, "How do you know when you are feeling happy?" and "How do I know when you are feeling happy?" Carroll and Steward found that preoperational children explained feelings in situational rather than more generalized terms. That is, preoperational children saw happiness as having an ice cream cone while concrete operational children would refer to more situations and to inner feelings. Younger children with high verbal intelligence also gave more sophisticated answers.

Kuebli (1994) describes four processes through which children's emotions are socialized (p. 44):

1. chiding or praising children's immediately prior emotional behaviors;
2. giving direct instruction regarding social conventions for expressing emotion ("girls don't brag about their successes")
3. modeling emotional states, expressions, and events—children watch and imitate; and
4. communicating expectancies, verbally or nonverbally, directly to the child or within his hearing ("when I was your age I was afraid the first time I slept away from home").

Discussing emotions is probably the key to understanding. Through discussion, children learn to interpret their feelings relative to the norms and expectations of their culture.

SUMMARY

Early childhood is a crucial period in emotional development. Young children are learning to feel for themselves and recognize in others emotions such as anxiety, fear, sadness, anger, happiness, and love. The attachments they make to others serve as a foundation to take the initiative and move toward independence. Children experience many kinds of fear such as fear of monsters and goblins, death, and war. Coping with imaginary fears helps them gain the skills needed to cope with fears that have a basis in reality. Young children have to learn how to handle their emotions in socially acceptable ways. Research indicates that throughout early childhood children are gradually learning how to label, define, and understand their own emotional behavior and that of others.

FOR FURTHER READING

Campos, J. (1994, Spring). Directions: The new functionalism in emotion. *SRCD Newsletter*, 1, 7, 9–11, 14.

Eisenberg, N., Fabes, R. A., Bernzweig, J., Karbon, M., Poulin, R., & Hanish, L. (1993). The relations of emotionality and regulation to preschoolers' social skills and sociometric status. *Child Development*, *64*, 1418–1438.

Eisenberg, N. (Ed.) (1989). *Empathy and related emotional responses.* San Francisco: Jossey-Bass.

Garabino, J., Dubrow, N., Kostelny, K., & Pardo, C. (1992). *Children in danger: Coping with the consequences of community violence.* San Francisco: Jossey-Bass.

Harris, P. L. (1989). *Children and emotion.* Cambridge, MA: Basil Blackwell.

Kostelnik, M. J., Stein, L. C., Whiren, A. P., & Soderman, A. K. (1993). *Guiding children's social development* (2nd ed.). Albany, NY: Delmar.

Lazarus, R. (1991). *Emotion and adaptation.* New York: Oxford University Press.

Leavitt, L. A., & Fox, N. A. (Eds.). (1993). *The psychological effects of war and violence on children.* Hillsdale, NJ: Erlbaum.

Lewis, M., & Haviland, J. M. (1993). *Handbook of emotions.* New York: Guilford.

McCracken, J. B. (Eds.) (1986). *Reducing stress in young children's lives.* Washington, DC: National Association for the Education of Young Children.

Saarni, C., & Harris, P. L. (Eds.) (1989). *Children's understanding of emotion.* New York: Cambridge University Press.

Saylor, C. F. (Ed.). (1993). *Children and disasters.* New York: Plenum.

SUGGESTED ACTIVITIES

1. Organize a group discussion on childhood fears. On the chalkboard or on a sheet of chart paper, group members can list the childhood fears that they can remember and/or fears that their friends or relatives might have had. The list is divided into those fears that were imaginary and those that were real. How were the fears handled? Are there any lasting effects? Consider each of the following ways to handle a child's fears. Which would be the best? The worst? The group can then rank these alternatives from best to worst.
   a. Force the child to face the fear straight on. That is, make him hold a snake or put him in the swimming pool.
   b. Point out to the child that if he wants to be "grown up" that he must stop being afraid.
   c. Help the child by developing experiences that enable him to gradually experience the fearful situation or object.
   d. Be a strong model. Demonstrate that you are not afraid.
   e. Ignore the fear. Say, "It will go away."
   f. Explain to the child which dangers are realistic and which are imaginary dangers.

   Develop a rationale for the decisions.

2. Read articles and/or books that explain how to handle the subject of death with the young child.

   Organize a small group discussion. Have the students discuss the following list of ways to tell a young child that his grandmother has died. Have the group members rank each method from best to worst. From your reading you should be able to help them see why some of the methods might even be dangerous to the child's emotional development:
   a. Grandmother got very old and she died.
   b. Grandmother went to heaven.
   c. Grandmother died, just like your pet kitten died.
   d. Grandmother went to sleep forever.
   e. Grandmother has gone on a long trip.
   f. Grandmother was very sick and then she died.

3. Observe a young child at home or a group of young children at a nursery school, childcare center, kindergarten, or primary classroom. Observe for 60 minutes. Write a description of any behaviors that indicate children are experiencing emotions such as fear, anger, sadness, happiness, etc. Write a summary of the kinds of emotions you observed. What kinds of events seemed to bring about each type of emotional reaction? What kinds of behaviors gave you the clues needed to label each emotion? If you observed in a group setting, did you notice any differences between male and female behaviors?

4. Make an entry in your journal.

REVIEW

A. Why does the young child have a "right to feel"? What does a "right to feel" mean?

B. Write the number of each correct statement.
1. The smiles of newborns are reflexive.
2. Children laugh and smile more often if they receive a lot of positive responses from others when they display joy and pleasure.
3. Smiling and laughter are of minimal importance in the development of attachment.
4. These early attachments are needed for the child to be socially successful later.
5. Even cognitive development seems to be affected by the strength of attachments.

C. Indicate which of the following examples illustrate physical dependence (*PD*), physical independence (*PI*), emotionally dependent immaturity (*EDI*), and emotionally dependent maturity (*EDM*):
1. Eighteen-month-old Maria drinks from a cup on her own with no help.
2. Five-year-old Jason greets his mother with a smile and shows her the picture he painted in preschool today.
3. Two-year-old Kate cuddles up on mother's lap for a story.
4. Infant Tony is picked up by Mr. Smith and carried to the car.
5. Three-year-old Carlos clings to his father and refuses to go into the day-care group by himself.
6. Four-year-old Isabel puts on her own coat, hat, and boots before going outside.
7. Two-year-old Carmelita says, "No! No! Do it myself."
8. Three-year-old Rudy stops to give his teacher, Mr. Santos, a hug before going off to build with blocks.

D. How are physical independence and responsibility related?

E. What should the adult do in each of the following situations?
1. The child's pet kitten is run over and killed while the child is at preschool.
2. Derrick, age four, runs in the house every time he sees the neighbor's big dog outside. The dog is friendly and loves children.
3. Rudy, age three, wants a night-light left on in his room to scare off the ghosts and goblins.
4. Seven-month-old Karen is introduced to a new babysitter. Mother has taken her to the sitter's home.
5. Rudy, age three-and-one-half, is about to go to the hospital for minor surgery.
6. Three-year-old Rudy's grandfather has passed away. Rudy asks, "When will Grandpa be back? Do you think he misses us?"
7. Derrick, age four, is sitting with his father watching the evening news. The reporter is telling about a disaster at a far-away nuclear power plant. That night Derrick has a nightmare about the local nuclear plant blowing up.
8. A child attends a kindergarten that is pressuring the students to use math and reading workbooks and do them correctly. She becomes cranky, has frequent tantrums, and comes down with more colds than usual.

F. Discuss the statement: "The child must learn not to become angry."

G. Recognition of emotions is a developmental occurrence.
a. Can the young child recognize others' emotions as early as he can recognize his own?
b. Which does the young child recognize first, positive or negative emotions?
c. By age six what milestones would you expect in the child's understanding of emotions?

Personality Development

After studying this unit, the student should be able to:

■ Recognize the major factors in the acquisition of sex-role standards and sex-role behaviors.

■ Determine what stage a child is in regarding his knowledge of sex and birth.

■ Provide developmentally appropriate knowledge regarding sexuality and sex roles.

■ Identify the major factors in the development and description of the self-concept.

■ Discuss whether or not there are cross-cultural differences in personality characteristics.

Characteristics such as cute, funny, happy, well adjusted, confident, aggressive, shy, feminine, and masculine are what we usually think of as **personality traits.** These traits develop from initial genetic temperament characteristics (see Unit 8) as children experience their environment. In this unit, we will examine several characteristics and areas of development that contribute to personality development: sex roles and sex typing, sexuality, self-concept, and cultural differences in personality development.

SEX ROLES AND SEX TYPING IN THE YOUNG CHILD

A major aspect of the individual's personality is reflected in how he or she perceives him/herself as either male or female. Maier (1978) states that "young individuals begin to notice sex and other role differences among those in their environment which affect both their own self-definition and the course they must pursue according to the social demands of their society." The girl must identify with the female and the young boy with the male. Each has to take on the behaviors society says are appropriate for males and females.

The development of sex roles is a complex process. We will examine the development of sex role standards or stereotypes, sex differences, and sex-typing.

Sex-role standards are those behaviors society regards as appropriate for males and females. Since the 1970s, there has been a growing concern that expectations for males and females are stereotyped; that is, that society has set up pictures of males and females that are not necessarily true, fair, or needed. For example, the male stereotype is independent, assertive, dominant, and competitive and applies these characteristics to being the ideal father and family bread winner. The female stereotype is passive, loving, sensitive, and supportive in social relationships and applies these characteristics to being the ideal wife and mother. During the 1970s and 1980s women led a movement to break down these stereotypes and to open more options for careers and combining careers with parenthood.

Jalongo (1989) reviewed the research on career education and sex-role stereotypes. She found that sex-role stereotypes in career awareness take hold in early childhood and become stronger as children grow older. By second grade, boys were found to be more knowledgeable regarding their fathers' occupations and were able to identify twice as many career options as girls. Although older girls are aware of many career options, they tend to perceive themselves in more stereotyped positions. Maternal employment influences females' perceptions of career options. Mothers who are satisfied with their careers tend to have daughters who have higher career aspirations. Fathers are also influential. By the end of high school, both boys and girls tend to identify with the career attitudes of their fathers. Brookins (1985) found that African-American children whose mothers worked had a more egalitarian view of sex roles than comparable children whose mothers were not employed. Children whose mothers were in higher-level occupations expressed a broader range of occupational choices than children of mothers in lower-

level occupations. Jalongo (1985) concludes that career education should begin with preschoolers and be integrated throughout the educational process. There appears to be a need for more efforts at breaking down stereotypes and encouraging boys and girls to survey the variety of choices available not only occupationally but also in other interests and activities.

Sex differences have been examined from a variety of aspects to determine which are biologically and which are socially determined. Shapiro (1990) interviewed current researchers regarding their most up-to-date findings. The longstanding differences in verbal behaviors (favoring girls) and mathematics (favoring boys) have been narrowing in recent years. Some differences do seem to be holding up. Boys, for example, tend to be more active, but the differences are very small during the early preschool years. However, by four or five, children seem to adopt stereotypic roles no matter how hard their parents may try to leave all avenues open to them. Boys work out their aggressive impulses through active gun play; girls by using verbal put-downs and being socially cruel (i.e., "We don't want to play with you"). The case for a biological basis for gender differences is very strongly disputed. A special focus has been the stereotype that females are naturally more nurturant and males more aggressive. There is little evidence that "biology makes women kinder, gentler people or even equips them specifically for motherhood" (Shapiro, 1990, p. 59). The only difference that seems to hold up is that females are better at identifying the emotions of others and even in this area some research indicates this difference may relate to mothers reacting differently to baby girls' emotional expressions than to male emotional expressions by allowing boys more latitude in the display of anger.

It is difficult to separate the effects of societal forces on male and female behavior. For example, when it comes to aggression, girls are more likely to receive a verbal explanation while boys are more likely to be punished with no explanation. This factor might account for the fact that boys misbehave more frequently than girls. Even in book reading, gender

KEYTERMSKEYTERMSKEYTERMSKEYTERMSKEYTERMSKEYTERMSKEY
Sex-role standards

differences have been observed; parents use more emotion words with girls than with boys. While the study of women has been very popular, it may be men that are in need of study. Males are more aggressive as evidenced in the higher rates of male homicides and homicide victims. An emerging body of research indicates that the parental model may be the key. Where fathers take an equal or even full-time role in the nurturant aspects of child-rearing, the boys are more nurturant and the girls have a broader view of the roles they can aspire to in the future.

Several studies have documented that sex labels influence how adults treat babies (Honig, 1983). Infants are treated differently according to whether they have a male or female name or are wearing stereotyped male or female clothing (Honig, 1983). In one study, for example, the same infant was dressed in pink and identified by a girl's name and then dressed in blue and identified by a boy's name. Each adult who played with the baby viewed him/her as definitely showing typical male or female characteristics depending on the identifying name and outfit. When adults thought a baby was a girl, they would offer her dolls to play with, comment on the baby's "femininity" and sweetness, and be more nurturant. When adults thought the baby was male, they would comment on the baby's strength and size, not offer dolls to play with, and give more encouragement for physical activity. Adults who work with preschool children in child-care centers were observed to behave in the same way as the adults in the laboratory setting. For example, they offered more nurturance to girls and encouraged boys to be more physically active.

By the time children reach the age of three, there is gender segregation in nursery school playgroups (Maccoby & Jacklin, 1985). By age six it is almost impossible to find pairs of cross-sex friends, even in the neighborhood setting. Maccoby and Jacklin (1985) observed toddlers and preschoolers in nursery schools. At eighteen months children of both sexes still made contact with each other. By two years and four months, two-thirds of girls' contacts were directed to other girls while boys still showed no preference. By age five-and-one-half, boys directed three-quarters of their contacts to other boys. Maccoby and Jacklin believe that adults were not directly responsible for this sex segregation. They suspect that the adult's responsibility was more indirect. It may be possible that parents provide sex-stereotyped play materials and experiences so that by the time children enter nursery school they seek out those familiar kinds of materials and activities and meet others of the same sex.

It has been documented that as children move through the elementary grades, boys and girls are treated differently by their teachers. Gradually boys' self-esteem increases and girls' decreases. Girls, it appears, are being short-changed. For example, boys get more specific, helpful comments on their work; boys are encouraged to use computers while girls are not; boys demand more attention and get it while girls tend to sit back in silence (Chira, 1994).

Awareness of self as a male or female, exhibiting interest in masculine and feminine activities and behaviors, is observable in the child's earliest years. A two-year-old girl may want to use mommy's perfume and lipstick and wear dresses with lace trim. A boy of the same age may confine his play to trucks, cars, and blocks. In these earliest years, children go back and forth in their interests but usually move gradually toward the behaviors expected by society as they reach ages six or seven. A number of forces shape the child's sex-role behavior. These forces come from family, television, teachers, and peers. From the time the blue booties are put on the boys and the pink booties on girls, boys and girls are treated differently by adults and reinforced for imitating same-sexed models (Figure 28–1).

Figure 28–1   In an accepting environment young girls and boys will play together.

SEXUALITY

The development of the child into an adult who feels comfortable and satisfied in his or her role as a male or female begins in infancy (Lively & Lively, 1991). "**Sexuality** is the term that includes the biological nature of the person, the physical aspects of sex relations, and many other aspects of sex-linked behavior" (Lively & Lively, 1991, p. 21). Learning about anatomy and reproduction are important aspects of the child's developing sexuality. Lively and Lively (1991) emphasize that the primary focus for the adult in supporting the development of children's sexuality is taking a positive and natural approach that demonstrates love and acceptance to the children, not on specific sex instruction (Figure 28–2).

Anatomy is ordinarily learned in the home as the child sees other family members when they are not wearing clothes. If not, it may be learned at nursery school or from neighborhood playmates. In preschool groups, there are usually some very curious children who consistently follow their peers to the bathroom for observation. In a group of two-year-olds, a crowd of children will gather each time a child has to be changed after wetting his pants. This is normal and natural behavior for this age, based on curiosity.

Around age three, children become interested in reproduction. It is around this age that they will ask,

Figure 28–2 Many activities are enjoyed by both girls and boys.

"Where did I come from?" or "How do people get babies?"

Anne Bernstein (1976) asked sixty boys and girls, all of whom had younger brothers and sisters and all of whom were white and middle or upper class, the question, "How do people get babies?" One-third of the children were preoperational three- and four-year-olds, one-third were concrete operational seven- and eight-year-olds, and one-third were eleven- and twelve-year-olds who were just entering formal operations. The children answered her question at six developmental levels as outlined in Figure 28–3. Most of the preschool children were at level one, geography, or level two, manufacturing.

The child at level one answers the question as if it was a geography question. That is, his explanation is in terms of where he thinks babies are located. Some examples from Bernstein (1976, p. 32) include:

- "You got to go to a baby store and buy one."
- "From tummies."
- "From God's place."

The level one child believes that each baby has always existed somewhere, just as he feels all the people he is acquainted with have always been around (and this includes himself). He knows babies grow in mothers' tummies but seems to have a picture of babies moving from one stomach to another as they are needed.

The level two child sees babies as being manufactured just as a car, a stove, or a toy is. He now realizes that a baby hasn't always existed. For example:

> When people are already made, they make some other people. They make the bones inside, and blood. They make skin. They make skin first and then they make blood and bones. They paint the blood, paint the red blood and the blue blood. (Bernstein, 1976, p. 33)

Being still egocentric, they can only solve problems in terms of their own experience. They know that a "seed" gets into the mother's stomach, grows and comes out as a baby. They often adopt the **digestive fallacy**. That is, they feel the baby is swallowed, develops in the mother's stomach, and then is

Sexuality   digestive fallacy

Age Years	Stage	Parallel Piaget Stage	Characteristics
3–4	Geography (Level One)	Preoperational	Babies are in locations such as a store, a stomach, or "God's place." They have always existed.
3–5	Manufacturing (Level Two)	Preoperational	Babies are put together or manufactured just like appliances, cars or toys. They may be perceived as placed in the mother's stomach by the father.
5–7	Transitional Physiology and Technology (Level Three)	Transitional	Realize that love and marriage, sexual intercourse and union of sperm and ovum are involved but can't get the whole process put together.
8–12	Concrete Physiology (Level Four)	Concrete Operations	Can explain conception but don't understand why it happens the way it does.
8–12	Preformation (Level Five)	Concrete Operations	Try to explain conception but feel the baby comes preformed from one of the germ cells (the baby is sometimes thought to be the sperm itself which is fed and sheltered by the egg).
12+	Physical Causality (Level Six)	Formal Operations	Everything starts to come together for the child. He begins to realize that both parents contribute genetically to the baby and that conception can take place without marriage.

Figure 28–3 **Anne Bernstein found six stages in the development of children's understanding of sex and birth. (From A. C. Bernstein, (January 1976), How children learn about sex and birth.** *Psychology Today*, **31–35+.)**

eliminated—a process just like the one their food goes through. At this level, the child may begin to bring the father into the picture but cannot conceptualize how he gets the seed into the mother's stomach to unite with the egg. He thinks that somehow the father unzips or unbuttons the mother's stomach and puts the seed inside.

At level three, children are in a transition from preoperational to concrete operational thought. They might reach this level at age five, but more likely will reach it around six or seven. At this stage they realize that "social relationships such as love and marriage; sexual intercourse; and the union of sperm and ovum" (Bernstein, 1976, p. 33) are involved but they cannot put all this information together into one coherent picture.

Preschool and kindergarten children demonstrate curiosity about reproduction, but their understanding is quite limited due to their preoperational thinking. For this reason the adult must be careful not to give the young child more information than he can handle. Too many details just confuse him and give him more to distort. Bernstein recommends than the

adult first respond with questions to find out where the child is in his thinking:

- How do people get babies?
- How do mommies get to be mommies?
- How did your daddy get to be your daddy?

She feels that children can be given explanations that are one level above their understanding. It is important not to laugh or make them feel stupid when they give their mixed up explanations. For the preoperational child, what they say is perfectly logical from their point of view. Bernstein suggests the following approaches for the level one and level two child:

Level One Child: He believes that babies have always existed. He might be told, "Only people can make other people. To make a baby person, you need two grown up people, a woman and a man, to be the baby's mommy and daddy. The mommy and daddy make the baby from an egg in the mommy's body and a sperm from the daddy's body."

Level Two Child: He believes babies are manufactured. He could be told, "That's an interesting way of looking at things. That's the way you make a doll. You could buy a head and some hair and put it all together. But making a real live baby is different from making a doll or a cake or an airplane." It can then be explained that the ingredients for making the baby are inside the mother and father's bodies. The child can also be asked to consider whether the father could really put his hand into the mother's stomach or whether there might be some other method to bring about the meeting of sperm and egg.

Bernstein cautions regarding the use of some of the available sex education books with the preoperational child as the child often becomes confused by the amount of detail presented.

Knowledge of reproduction also comes from first-hand experiences with pets. At home or at school, mice, gerbils, dogs, cats, rabbits, or fish can offer first-hand experience with the processes of conception, pregnancy, and birth. The most important factor is to answer the young child's questions honestly and simply and accept his interpretations as normal for his age. Honest discussion of sex roles, sex differences, anatomy, and reproduction help the young child develop healthy feelings about him/herself as male or female.

Some topics are not easy to deal with. Communicating about masturbation, sex talk, and sex play is not easy (Kostelnik, Stein, Whiren, & Soderman, 1993; Lively & Lively, 1991). Parents should be the major sex educators but teachers also have to deal with these problems at school. Communication must be open and honest. Punishment and scolding for masturbation can cause feelings of anxiety and fear for the young child. Masturbation is not physically harmful but may hurt the child psychologically. Occasional masturbation can be ignored. Frequent masturbation may be a sign of an emotional problem that warrants professional help. Adults are also concerned with "sex talk" and "sex play" (Lively & Lively, 1991). Adults can make it clear in an honest,

straightforward manner that is not punishing, that certain words are not acceptable at school. While at three, an interest in the anatomy of others is natural curiosity and expressed openly, by five or six children learn adults find their interest in comparing anatomy unacceptable and they will try to conceal their activities (Lively & Lively, 1991). When caught in the act of exploring each other's bodies, children should not be made to feel guilty. It is best to just suggest another activity. This might also be an opportunity to explain that some parts of the body are private and should not be looked at or touched by others. Teachers can assist parents in their task of promoting the development of healthy sexuality in their children by offering help and advice when needed and by providing an accepting and healthy environment at school.

THE YOUNG CHILD'S SELF-CONCEPT

Shirley C. Samuels (1977) points out that early childhood is a critical period for self-concept development. The young child is still open regarding his feelings, and the adults who work with him can assess more easily how the young child feels. As children get older they mask their feelings and it becomes harder to get underneath and find out what is really going on. Adults can help young children to develop a positive **self-concept**; that is, they can help them to feel good about themselves.

The way the child handles development in the emotional and personality areas adds bits and pieces to his concept of himself. Samuels divides the self-concept into several dimensions.

- Body Image—how the child views himself; how he looks physically and how his body reacts and acts.

- Social Self—the racial, ethnic, cultural, and religious self.

- Cognitive Self—the self as viewed in the child's mental development and aptitudes.

- *Self-Esteem*—how the person evaluates his self-concept; how much respect the person has for himself.

Curry and Johnson (1990) expanded the view of self-esteem. They view **self-esteem** as a life-long developmental process. "How children feel and think about themselves is integrally tied to their physical, social, moral, emotional, cognitive, and personality development" (Curry & Johnson, 1990, p. 5). Just as children are viewed as constructors of their cognitive side, they are now also viewed as actively involved in constructing their sense of self. Their view of themselves causes them to behave in certain ways. Behavior brings a response from the environment which in turn is interpreted by the child and incorporated into the self concept. Preschoolers have consolidated a sense of self during infancy and toddlerhood and are in a period where they are testing and evaluating that self as they strive for acceptance, power and control, moral worth, and efficacy and competence. Kindergarten and primary students are entering a new era. They are entering concrete operations and the stage of industry versus inferiority. Relationships become more complex as they venture out into the neighborhood and as they become involved in sports, scouts, camps, hobbies, and lessons. The search for power, competence, acceptance, and moral worth become much more complex as the child strives to meet the demands of formal schooling. We will look more closely at the primary child in Unit 31.

Self-evaluation underlies self-esteem. How one feels about one's competencies affects motivation to achieve. Stipek, Recchia, and McClintic (1992) did a series of studies designed to examine the development of self-evaluation of achievement in children aged 1 to 5 years old. They were interested in finding out just when children begin to evaluate their own competencies and when they develop emotional responses (that is, feeling good or feeling bad). They found that self-evaluation appears to develop in three stages. In the first stage, children are not yet self-reflective and don't anticipate others' reactions to their accomplishments. They may smile when they suc-

ceed but don't show any response that would suggest pride. Just before age two they enter a second stage in which they begin to anticipate adult reactions to their performance. They seek praise for their successes and try to avoid negative reactions to failure. At the third stage, sometime after age three, children gradually internalize external reactions to their successes and failures. They begin to evaluate their performance and react at an emotional level independent of what they may expect from adults. Stipek et al. suggest that since children seem to have some concept of success and failure by the age of 2, that adults should be careful not to impose rigid standards that might lead to young children developing a low self-evaluation that could lead to a lack of motivation to achieve.

There is a great deal of concern in the schools about enhancing children's self-esteem. Formal programs have been developed that are specifically designed to build self-esteem. Katz (1993) suggests these programs tend to provide young children with an unrealistic and out-of-context view of themselves by providing superficial flattery and rewards (such as stars and happy faces). According to Katz (p. 1), "Esteem is conveyed to children when adults and peers treat them respectfully, consult their views and preferences . . . , and provide opportunities for children to make decisions and choices about things that matter to them." Self-esteem is built through everyday constructive activity that provides opportunities to deal with both success and failure. These experiences at school are especially critical for children who are not having positive self-esteem built at home.

Racial and Social Class Factors and Self-Concept

Samuels (1977) found in looking through available research that by age two-and-a-half, children have developed a racial consciousness and a sense of racial identity. The acquisition of feelings of positive self-esteem at home can give the child from the minority racial group and/or lower-class status group the strength to counter the prejudice he may meet outside the family. Teachers can help these children achieve their potential by supporting and maintaining their positive feelings about themselves. Social class may be an even more significant factor relative to self-concept than race. For example, lower-class African-American children seem to have higher self-esteem than middle-class African-American children.

It may be that as the child becomes integrated into the mainstream society, he begins to make comparisons he would not have the opportunity to make if he remained segregated. It may also be that his cultural roots are diluted and/or ignored. This implies an especially strong need for giving support to minority group children in integrated settings. The minority child can easily become lost in the crowd in a setting where it is most important that his cultural pride be reinforced. In studying the interaction patterns of African-American middle-income fathers and their children, McAdoo (1979) found the fathers were for the most part warm, supportive, and nurturant and their children had positive self-esteem. McAdoo (1979) believes that for black children to maintain their self-esteem and achieve their potential, African-American fathers should have more input into their children's preschool programs.

Respect for the culture of the child must include not only language and customs but also the cultural self-concept. The self is a part of the view of one's group. For example, the American African-American has his roots in the African perspective regarding the self. In this culture, there is not the emphasis on individuality that there is in the mainstream culture of North America. Nobles (1977, p. 164) states the contrast as follows:

> Self-awareness or self-conception is not, therefore, limited (as in Euro-American tradition) to just the cognitive awareness of one's uniqueness, individuality and historical finiteness. It is, in the African tradition, awareness of self as the awareness of one's historical consciousness (collective spirituality) and the subsequent sense of "we" or being One.

Richard Rodriguez (1975) writes movingly how he shed his Chicano self and became Mexican-American to get through the educational system. That is he gave up his original culture in order to get through

the system. As an adult, he had to go through a reculturalization process to try to pick up that part of himself that was lost in his childhood.

Cross (1985) points out the importance of the distinction between personal identity and identification with a reference group. Early studies using measures of reference group identification of African-American children came up with a negative self-concept. More recent studies have used personal identity measures, and the results have been in favor of a positive self-concept for African-American children. The most recent approach is to look at both types of identity as they contribute to self-concept. The results indicate that the two types of identity are not directly linked. That is, African-American children with high self-esteem (personal identity) could be identified more with the African-American or the European-American reference group or equally with both. The troublesome factor in the findings from ethnic identity research is that minority group children tend to show a preference for white skin (Spencer and Markstrom-Adams, 1990). Very young children appear to perceive white as being of more value. Spencer and Markstrom-Adams (1990) cite research where young African-American children were trained to a pro-African-American bias; an Anglo experimenter was more effective than am African-American experimenter. They conclude that intervention is necessary to develop a pro-African-American bias.

Another factor that needs to be considered in measuring children's concepts regarding racial identity is their cognitive developmental level (Semaj, 1985 & Spencer, 1985). Currently it is felt that the negative results from the early studies of African-American children's self-image resulted from neglecting the cognitive developmental factor, that is, not considering how preoperational children think. In these early studies children were usually asked if they would prefer to play without a dark-skinned or a light-skinned doll with considering the child's reasons for his/her choice. Alejandro-Wright (1985) used a cognitive-developmental approach to examine how young black girls develop racial categories. She designed her study from a Piagetian developmental perspective. She looked at children's spontaneous grouping in addition to researcher-imposed groupings. The children were asked to group photos of European white, African black, and Asian people by putting together the people whom they felt belonged together. The three-, four-, five-, and six-year-olds tended to use criteria other than color for their groupings. When the researcher asked them to group by black, Negro, white, and Chinese the three- and four-year-olds picked only the darkest-skinned people (although there were darker-skinned people that adults would identify as black). The five- and six-year-olds broadened their categorization to include medium-complected people but called these people brown. The three- to six-year-olds used only color as a criteria, ignoring hair texture and facial features. Negro was sorted in a similar way, although the three's and four's did not seem to be familiar with the term. Not until age ten did children show an understanding of these labels in the biological/physiological sense. For these young children, white included Asians and some light-complected African-Americans. All except the three's could pick the Chinese correctly but could not verbalize a reason for their choice. Until age eight, they perceived the Chinese as an Anglo subgroup. There was a clear developmental sequence from purely color identification through a transitional phase to an adultlike understanding. Young children seem to look at racial identity in a qualitatively different fashion than adults, guided in their understanding by their preoperational way of perceiving the world.

Racial stereotypes (both positive and negative) are already imbedded in European-American preschoolers' thinking (Bigler & Liben, 1993). Bigler and Liben found that when preschoolers were presented with counterstereotyped material, they tended to distort it to fit their preconceived stereotype. Bigler and Liben conclude that just presenting children with nonstereotypic material is not enough to break down stereotypes and may even confirm the stereotype in their minds. Their research supports the need for an antibias approach (as described in Unit 19) by all caregivers during the child's earliest years to avoid negative stereotyping.

CROSS-CULTURAL DIFFERENCES IN PERSONALITY DEVELOPMENT

In Unit 19 social/cultural factors and the adult role in learning were described. Some of these factors are reviewed briefly here since they include apparent personality differences.

African-American children have been characterized as having a strong self-concept, strong motivation to achieve, and a strong religious orientation. They are people-oriented and sensitive to feelings and emotions. Thus, they may respond best to a learning process that stresses human interaction rather than interaction with objects (Hale, 1978, 1982). They also need a setting that will accept an assertive personality style.

Because they are reared to show courtesy to others and respect for authority figures, Mexican-American children may tend to be quiet and unassertive in school. They are affectively oriented and learn best if they like what they are doing. They work best cooperatively rather than competitively. Mexican-American children have also been characterized as "field sensitive." That is, they are unusually sensitive to the environment and those in it (Cortes, 1978).

The Native American personality is characterized as self-confident, serene, and nonaggressive. This personality contrasts with the assertive, independent one emphasized in Anglo culture. Emotionally, Native Americans learn that shame as embarrassment (rather than guilt) is the punishment for bad behavior. Their learning style is affective; teaching is by example and through cooperation and emphasizes readiness. Native Americans respond best to private rather than public recognition and a child-centered approach (Burgess, 1978).

Another cultural complication occurs when children move from one culture to another. Minoura (1993) describes the difficulties experienced by to Japanese children who spent their elementary years in the United States. When they returned to Japan to live they found that they had problems relating to their Japanese peers and teachers. It is the Japanese custom to provide indirect communication that seemed ambiguous to the Americanized Japanese while the more direct communication of the Americanized Japanese seemed too assertive and impolite to the Japanese.

Lower socioeconomic-level Anglos are a group about which we know relatively little. They seem to have a different cognitive style; they have different language patterns; and their motivation is different from that of middle-class Anglos.

As pointed out in Unit 19, all these descriptions are, of course, very general. Within any one cultural group, there is a wide variation and many subgroups. There are many Hispanic and Latino groups. Within the Native American group are many tribes, each with its own unique life-style, language, and values. We must also be aware of individual differences within cultural groups and be careful about making assumptions about individuals based on their membership in a cultural group.

SUMMARY

The personalities of young children are re-

flected in their sex-role learning experiences and in their self-concepts. The early years are critical ones in the development of sex-role behaviors. Sex education includes the acquisition of acceptable (though non-steorotyped) sex-role behaviors, sex-role standards, and awareness of self as male or female. The young child also gains knowledge of anatomy and reproduction.

Preschool children's self-concepts continue to develop. Their racial and social class membership affects the way they perceive themselves. The adult who works with the preschool child needs to demonstrate respect for the child's unique racial and cultural

FOR FURTHER READING

AAUW Report: How schools shortchange girls. (1992). Annapolis Junction, MD: American Association of Women.

Carter, D. B. (Ed.) (1987). *Current conceptions of sex roles and sex typing: Theory and research.* Westport, CT: Greenwood.

Golombok, S., & Fivush, R. (1994). *Gender development.* New York: Cambridge University Press.

Kagan, J. (1994). *Galen's prophecy.* New York: Basic Books.

Liben, L., & Signorella, M. L. (Eds.). (1987). *Children's gender schemata.* San Francisco: Jossey-Bass.

Mack, J. E. & Ablon, S. L. (Eds.). (1984). *The development and sustaining of self esteem in childhood.* Independence, MO: International Universities Press.

Phinney, J. S., & Rotheram, M. J. (Eds.) (1987). *Children's ethnic socialization: Pluralism and development.* Newbury Park, CA: Sage.

Saracho, O. N. & Spodek, B. (Eds.). (1983). *Understanding the multicultural experience in early childhood education.* Washington, D.C.: National Association for the Education of Young Children.

Spencer, M. B., Brookins, G. K., & Allen, W. R. (Eds.). (1985). *Beginnings: Social and affective development of black children.* Hillsdale, NJ: Erlbaum.

Whiting, B. B., Edwards, C. P., et al. (1988). *Children of different worlds.* Cambridge, MA: Harvard University Press.

SUGGESTED ACTIVITIES

1. Think back to your early childhood years. Who do you think had the most influence on your sex-role development? Was it your parents or brothers and sisters? If you had siblings of the opposite sex, did your parents treat you differently? Did they have different rules and different expectations? Compare your experiences with those of other students in the class.

2. Make three columns on a sheet of paper. In the first column, list three gifts you might buy if you were going to a baby shower before the baby was born. In the second column write down what you would buy if you knew the baby were a boy. In the third column, write down what you would buy if you knew the baby were a girl. Compare your lists. Are there any items that are the same in the three lists? With a small group in class

compile your lists by writing the items in three columns on the chalkboard or on a sheet of chart paper. Decide if, as a group, you use sex stereotypes in choosing gifts.

3. Many experts believe that education has tended to support sex-role stereotypes too strongly. Do some reading on the topic and formulate a report for the class on "Sex-Role Stereotyping and Early Childhood Education."

4. Interview some young children regarding their knowledge of sex and birth using the questions suggested by Anne Bernstein. Interview five three-year-olds, five four-year-olds and five five-year-olds. If you don't know enough children at each age level, collaborate with some other students in the class and combine information. Ask each child individually:

   "Where do babies come from?"

   If the first question doesn't get a response, try:

   "How do people get babies?"

   "How do mommies get to be mommies?"

   "How did your daddy get to be your daddy?"

   Write down or tape record what each child says. Compare each child's response with Bernstein's stages. Do the children you (and your classmates) interviewed fit into Bernstein's stages? Were there any problems in assigning a stage to the responses? Were any of the children ahead of what Bernstein found from her interviews? Any behind? What did you learn from this experience?

5. Make an entry in your journal.

REVIEW

A. Write the number of each correct statement.
   1. It is not important for boys and girls to take on the approved sex-role behaviors defined by society as a whole.
   2. Those behaviors that society says are appropriate for males and females are referred to as sex-role standards.
   3. In this country, standards for males and females are not very different.
   4. It is usually expected that females be more passive, loving, sensitive, and supportive.
   5. Sex-role stereotypes that set up male and female standards that have no common elements have been highly criticized in recent years.
   6. Sex-role stereotypes in career awareness do not appear until around twelve years of age.
   7. Logically, it is impossible for a person of either sex to be both warm and nurturant and be assertive and competitive—the characteristics just don't mix.
   8. Research now indicates that the difference in favor of boys relative to girls on math achievement is disappearing.
   9. Of great concern relative to sex differences is the increasing incidence of men's aggression resulting in murder.
   10. There is strong research evidence that in early childhood, girls are more dependent, fearful, timid, and anxious than boys.
   11. Boys have been found to have higher achievement motivation and to be more competitive than girls.
   12. The female role in our culture is more clearly defined than the male role.
   13. Lower-class children take on the stereotyped male and female sex-role behaviors earlier than do middle-class children.

14. It appears that children whose mothers are employed may have a broader view of the career possibilities open to them.
15. Most people tend to treat boys and girls exactly the same.
16. We can expect to find kindergarten girls playing with girls and kindergarten boys playing with boys.
17. The most feminine girls usually play with each other.
18. Gender-segregated play during nursery school and kindergarten is detrimental to girls' adjustment in first grade.
19. Evidence of male- or female-type behavior does not usually appear before the age of four.

B. Match the stages in Column II with the children's answers in Column I. The children have been asked "Where do babies come from?" Each stage may be used more than once (or not at all).

Column I

1. You go to the store and buy the head, legs, arms, body, hair, and everything and then put it together.
2. The mother swallows the seed and it finds the egg in her stomach. Then it comes out.
3. God sends one down when you need it.
4. The baby is in the sperm. The sperm gets to the egg and then the baby can stay there and grow.
5. You go to the hospital and buy one.
6. You get married and then the father puts the sperm in the egg some way—I'm not sure just how.

Column II

a. geography
b. manufacturing
c. transitional
d. concrete physiology
e. preformantion
f. physical causality

C. A three- or four-year-old asks you, "Where do babies come from?" Describe how you would respond.

D. Select the correct answer to the following. There is only one correct answer for each.
1. How the child views himself physically and motorically is referred to as
   a. social self.
   b. cognitive self.
   c. body image.
   d. self-esteem.
2. How the person evaluates his self-concept is referred to as his
   a. social self.
   b. cognitive self.
   c. body image.
   d. self-esteem.
3. The racial, cultural, ethnic, and religious self is called the
   a. social self.
   b. cognitive self.
   c. body image.
   d. self-esteem.
4. In comparing race and social class and their effect on self-esteem
   a. social class may be a stronger factor than race.
   b. race may be a stronger factor than social class.
   c. race and social class are about equal in their effects.
5. Black children may have a unique self-concept due to
   a. the struggle that blacks have had in this country.
   b. their African heritage.
   c. their desire to not be white.
6. Past studies of African-American children's self-concept have been criticized because
   a. only reference-group identity was considered.
   b. only personal identity was considered.
   c. reference group and personal identity were considered.

7. Recent research that examined young African-American children's concept of race from a cognitive-developmental point of view
   a. indicates that African-American children view race differently than Anglo children.
   b. indicates that young children view 'African-American' as referring to very dark skin color rather than to a particular group.
   c. demonstrates that by six years of age children understand the biological/physiological basis of race.

8. Sometimes a minority group child may be forced to disregard his cultural inheritance to succeed in the educational system.
   a. This never happens.
   b. Usually the child is allowed to carry through with both cultures.
   c. This often does happen.

E. Discuss whether you feel that there are real cross-cultural differences in personality characteristics. Support your position.

29

Social Development

After studying this unit, the student should be able to:

- Identify and use Parten's and Smilansky's play categories.

- Identify and use the Hartup-Charlesworth System.

- Recognize aspects of social strategies, positive and negative social responses, and how children become friends.

- Identify characteristics of sibling relationships.

- Recognize ways of helping unpopular children.

- Recognize moral realism and moral autonomy.

- Recognize and categorize examples of prosocial and aggressive behaviors.

- Know how to help children improve their social skills.

- Identify methods of supporting the moral development of young children.

Young children are both sociable and becoming socialized. They spend as much time as they can with other children if they are available. During the preschool period, young children develop enhanced oral language skills that they can use to facilitate social interactions. They become more capable of getting others to comply with their desires.

THEORISTS VIEWS OF SOCIAL DEVELOPMENT

Erikson, Sears, Piaget, Maslow, and Rogers have all focused on the social development of the young child from one or more aspects. For Erikson (cited in Maier, 1978), the child in stage III centers his or her activity on play. From Erikson's point of view, play serves as a vehicle for children to work through their feelings about life. The major social task of preschool children is to develop their relationships with others. They become less socially dependent on their families and move out into the neighborhood and very often into a preschool group. Sears (as cited in Maier, 1978), as already mentioned, focuses attention on aggressive behavior and the development of the conscience. He also recognizes the importance of play as a vehicle for exploration of the world through trial and error. Piaget (as cited in Maier, 1978) also looks at play as an important vehicle of learning for the young child. According to Piaget, play is the preschool child's major means for assimilating and adapting. Confrontations with other children are of major importance for the child's cognitive development in that they help him or her move out of his or her egocentric view of incidents. That is, confrontations force the child to see the other person's point of view.

Vygotsky (Musatti, 1986) believed that social interaction had a critical part in the young child's learning. Vygotsky focused on the adult as the provider of cultural knowledge and was not specifically concerned with the role of peers. However, he did believe that play was related to the development of representational abilities and that play created a zone of proximal development that stimulates the child to overcome cognitive limitations (Musatti, 1986). Since so much of play time is spent with peers, there must be a relationship between the social interaction that is included in play with peers and cognitive development.

Moral development of the young child is also seen as critical by Piaget. It is during the preoperational period that the child's conceptions of good and bad and right and wrong take shape. While young children may at times do what they know to be wrong, they still look upon adults as the ultimate authority and they respect that authority.

Maslow and Rogers (Mead, 1976), like Erikson, view early childhood as a time when children strive for autonomy but have difficulty giving up dependence. They still need love, acceptance, and security from adults. Social interaction is essential for young children to work on the development of a healthy self-concept. As children learn to adjust to others, they begin to realize that they, themselves, are not the only ones in the world: the points of view of others need to be considered.

In recent times some researchers from the disciplines of developmental psychology, social psychology, anthropology, and sociology have attempted to apply theory from cognitive psychology to social development. From this interest has developed an area called social cognition, made up of researchers interested in children's understanding of social events (Ruble, Higgins, & Hartup, 1983). The social cognition point of view is constructivist (refer to Piaget). That is, it is believed that children take an active role in their own social development. Social cognition attempts to relate the social situation to social understanding (cognition) to the resulting social behavior. The focus is on the children's views of social situations and the reasoning that leads to their behavioral responses.

PEERS

Peers are those persons of equal status (i.e., age, grade, developmental level) with whom we interact on a regular basis. For the child in school, they are usually children of the same age. At home and in the neighborhood, they may be older, younger, or the same age. Peers serve as play companions, reinforcers, models, and friends. Learning how to enter peer groups and be accepted and attain popularity are important skills that children explore from preschool to primary. Peers can serve as models of acceptable and unacceptable social behavior. Peers are very important to young children (Figure 29–1). When a child is unpopular and/or socially isolated, it is usually a cause for concern. Siblings (brothers and/or sisters) also have a role in peerlike social development.

It was thought at one time that peers were children only of about equal age. More recently, peers have been defined as children who interact at about the same developmental level in their play. The preschool child, confined to his neighborhood, may play with a wider range of children than the school-aged child who meets a variety of children of the same age in school.

Hartup and Moore (1990) provide a rationale for the importance of peer relationships and their

Figure 29–1   **Peer interaction and activity are of major importance in the social developmental of young children all over the world.**

contribution to child development. Unlike relationships with adults, child-child relationships are fairly egalitarian. That is, there is always the possibility of being dominant as well as submissive, whereas in the adult-child relationship, the adult always has the last word. Child-child interaction provides wider opportunities to deal with a variety of social behaviors and situations such as cooperation, competition, aggression, disagreement and negotiation that may not be available in adult-child relationships. The first two years are spent mainly in learning to relate to adults, while from two on, peers take on increasing importance as resources not only for fun but for learning about how to get along in the social world. Longitudinal studies indicate that childhood friendships and good peer relations are necessary precursors of later mental health and adjustment.

The Contexts of Play and Peer Group Entry

Interaction with peers takes place within a play context. Kenneth H. Rubin and his colleagues have done research on the developmental **context of play** from two points of view:

- **Social Participation:** They used M. B. Parten's (1932) play categories to distinguish the

amounts of social interaction children have during play activities.

- **Cognitive Level of the Play Activity:** They used the Piaget-based categories developed and used by Smilansky (1968).

Rubin and his colleagues developed a two-dimensional category system (Figure 29–2). The play categories defined by Parten (1932) are as follows:

- **Unoccupied Activity:** The child is not playing. He may glance around, not focusing on any one activity for very long; he may play with his clothing; wander around; or follow the teacher. Overall, he shows little interest in and gives little long-term attention to any one activity.

- **Onlooker Activity:** The child observes other children as they play. He may speak to the other children but doesn't get involved in their activity. This type of activity differs from the unoccupied in that the child's attention is strongly focused on a particular activity and he is physically close enough to see everything and to participate verbally.

- **Solitary Play:** The child plays alone and is independent of other children. He uses materials that are different from those of any children around him.

KEYTERMSKEYTERMSKEYTERMSKEYTERMSKEYTERMSKEY

context of play

Social Participation	Cognitive Level of Play Activities			
	Functional	Constructive	Dramatic	Games With Rules
Unoccupied and Onlooker	No	No	No	No
Solitary	Yes	Yes	Yes	No
Parallel	Yes	Yes	Yes	No
Associative	Yes	Yes	Yes	No
Cooperative	No	Yes	Yes	Yes

Figure 29–2   **Play categories used when observing free play activity: Possible combinations**

- **Parallel Play:** The child plays independently but is with other children and is using the same or similar kinds of play materials as his neighbors are. He does not try to control what the other children are doing in any way.

- **Associative Play:** Children play with each other. They talk about what they are doing: they exchange play materials; follow each other around; and there is some controlling of whom is allowed in the group. Everyone is doing a similar type of play activity; there is no division of labor or working together toward some goal or end product. Everyone does pretty much whatever he wishes to do. The group comes together because of a common interest in the materials or activity, not because they want to work together.

- **Cooperative or Organized Supplementary Play:** The child is in a group that is organized for a particular purpose such as making some product, achieving a goal, dramatizing some aspect of life, or playing a formal game. There is definitely a situation of belonging to the group or of not belonging to the group. There are one or two leaders who control the group's activities. Children take different responsibilities and/or roles within the group. The group is organized and controlled by children.

It can be seen from the definitions that during unoccupied activity, solitary play, and parallel play activities, there is by definition no interaction with peers. During onlooker, associative, and cooperative play, peer interaction does take place.

As described by Rubin (1977) the cognitive play categories are broken down as follows:

- **Functional Play:** Simple repetitive muscle movements with or without objects.

- **Constructive Play:** Manipulation of objects to construct or to create something.

- **Dramatic Play:** The substitution of an imaginary situation to satisfy the child's personal wishes and needs.

- **Games with Rules:** The acceptance of pre-arranged rules and the adjustment to these rules.

The categories are listed developmentally from functional play, which is seen in infancy, to games with rules, which usually appear in the concrete operations stage. Peer relationships can develop during any of these four types of play if the child is at the same time involved in associative play or cooperative play activity. The possible combinations can be seen by looking again at Figure 29–2. The activities are listed from top to bottom as the least social to the most social, and from left to right as the lowest to highest cognitive level play.

Through collecting observational data on lower- and middle-class four-year-olds in a preschool setting, Rubin and his colleagues found that the lower socio-economic class child's play tended to be at a lower level both socially and cognitively. When they compared preschool and kindergarten children, they found a developmental difference in free-play behavior. Probably the older children's less egocentric view allows them to engage in more reciprocal, give-and-take kinds of activity. As children participate in more social play, peers become more important and vice versa.

Researchers have been especially interested in how children enter cooperative and associative play groups and how relationships are maintained in these contexts. For example, peer relationships can be examined as settings for social problem-solving situations. "Social problem-solving (SPS) behaviors are attempts to achieve personal goals within social interaction" (Krasnor, 1982, p. 113). For example, when playing together, children will often want to change the theme of the play. To achieve this goal they may try any number of strategies, such as threatening to leave the scene, offering a bribe (i.e., sharing a prized possession), making a polite request, crying, or hitting. The strategy chosen is probably influenced by the child's previously used strategies and by the particular situation. A child who is capable of accurate processing of social information will probably show more variability in strategies as situations vary.

Group entry techniques have been the focus of much study (Hart, McGee, & Hernandez, 1993). Children who gain entry with ease are those who have techniques relevant to what the group is already doing. The most successful group entry tactic is to hover for a short time and then move in copying the behavior of the group members. Classrooms of children form unique cultures that develop their own patterns for successful social group entry and participation (Kantor, Elgas, & Fernie, 1993). For example, object sharing will be successful only if the object offered is of value to the group and is used with "the appropriate gesture, tone, and language" (Kantor et al., 1993, p. 143). Socially competent children are skilled at interpreting the social positions of their peers, are good at reading peer social cues, and can readily pick up social-cultural knowledge.

Peer Reinforcement and Peer Popularity

Peer reinforcement plays a critical role in children's social behaviors. Giving positive reinforcement not only shapes the behavior of others but also is associated with degree of **peer popularity**. Two related studies, one by Charlesworth and Hartup (1967) and one by Hartup, Glazer, and Charlesworth (1967), defined social reinforcement and collected information on its frequency and power. Both positive and negative reinforcement categories were defined and used (The Hartup-Charlesworth System, 1973).

POSITIVE REINFORCEMENTS

I. Positive attention and approval. Examples: "Here, Bobby, it's coming" as Ronnie pushes a toy care to Bobby. (giving directions)

Ronnie smiles at Bobby. (smiling or laughing with no accompanying verbalization)

II. Giving affection and personal acceptance. Examples: Ronnie sits between Bobby and Derrick. Bobby puts his arm around Ronnie and kisses him. The three all have their arms around each other and Ronnie hugs Derrick. (physical attention and acceptance)

Ronnie says, "I like you, Bobby." (verbal affection)

"You can be the boss." (verbally giving status)

III. Submission. Examples: Ronnie gets an idea to put the ramps a different way. Bobby agrees with him. (accepts another's idea)

Ronnie drives his car with the steering wheel. He shows Bobby and Bobby does it, too. (imitation)

Ronnie and Bobby work together to build a garage for their cars. (cooperation)

IV. Giving tokens. Example: Bobby gives Ronnie two cars. (voluntarily and spontaneously gives a toy to another child.

NEGATIVE REINFORCEMENTS

V. Negative reinforcements. Examples: Ronnie and Chuck won't let Bobby and David play. (noncompliance: rejection, denies an activity to another)

Andy, frustrated and angered, says, "Get off" and "Stand up." He pulls the boys off his block building. (rejects and attacks)

Building with blocks, Andy says, "This is not the door, David." (derogation: disapproval)

It was found that four-year-olds gave more positive reinforcements than did three-year-olds (Charlesworth & Hartup, 1967). This is not surprising, since younger children engage in less social play with peers than do older children. The older children also gave reinforcements to more different children than did the younger children. Girls tended to reinforce girls, and boys reinforced boys. Those who gave the most positive reinforcement received the most. More positive reinforcement was given during dramatic play than during other types of activities (Figure 29–3). The least positive reinforcement was given during participation in table activities (such as art or playing with manipulative toys) and when a child was just wandering around the room.

Giving of positive reinforcement was linked to popularity (Hartup et al., 1967). That is, the children who gave the most positive reinforcement were likely to be very well liked by their peers. Overall, relatively little negative reinforcement was given compared to the amount of positive reinforcement. It is clear from this research that by the preschool period, reinforcement from peers becomes a powerful social factor.

Going beyond the classroom, some researchers have felt the playground provides a more natural and less restrictive context for the study of children's social behavior (Hart, 1993). Ladd and Price (1993) describe a number of studies that looked at the playstyles of accepted and rejected children on playgrounds. Popular preschoolers appear to be those that start the year as skilled cooperative players. Preschoolers who begin the year in an argumentative fashion tend to be more likely to be rejected throughout the year. Older children follow a similar pattern. Those children selected on a sociometric measure by peers as most liked demonstrate more cooperative and social play on the playground. Those who are rejected by peers on the sociometric measure tend to spend more time on the playground in unoccupied behavior.

Popular children are better at negotiating disagreements with peers. Black (1989) found that the children who were most often selected as *liked* by their peers, also used positive negotiation strategies in their social interactions during laboratory play sessions. Positive strategies included such acts as agreeing to and extending peer ideas, soliciting clarification of peer suggestions, and explaining ongoing play to newcomers. Liked children were able to insert their own ideas by attaching them to peers' ideas rather than rejecting the peers' ideas outright and insisting on their own.

Ladd (1990) investigated the relationship between kindergartners' peer relationships during the first 2 months of school and their attitudes toward school and degree of academic success at the end of the kindergarten year. Ladd found those children who achieved the most satisfactory peer relationships, that is, formed some solid friendships upon school entry were more successful academically and had more positive attitudes toward school. Children who were rejected early were more likely to have negative views of school and to experience less academic success. The results indicate that if children can be placed in kindergartens with preschool friends they have a better chance of maintaining those old friendships and making a good adjustment to school. The results also point out the importance of making social skills development an integral part of the kindergarten curriculum.

Figure 29–3 **During cooperative dramatic play, children give each other a great deal of positive social reinforcement.**

Friendship

Friendships are special relationships that develop with other people. Friendships serve special functions for young children. Young children's friendships center on enjoyment, entertainment, and satisfaction. The goals are stimulation and excitement through high levels of fantasy play. Children repeat the same themes (such as danger-rescue) over and over again. They learn to develop means for communication, management of conflicts, negotiation, and other-perspective taking as they engage in dramatic play (Hart et al., 1993). Friendships serve four major functions (Hartup, 1991, pp. 1–2):

1. As emotional resources relative to having fun and for adapting to stress;

2. Cognitive resources for both problem solving and knowledge acquisition;

3. Contexts in which basic social skills are acquired or elaborated;

4. Forerunners of subsequent relationships (as reported by Ladd above).

Friendships may be viewed relative to the child's view of friendship, developmental changes with age, conflict resolution, and effects on peer status.

Selman and Selman (1979) explored the development of children's ideas regarding friendship. Younger children tend to be egocentric and cannot see the other person's point of view. They have difficulty separating and seeing both a physical action and the intention behind it. When someone grabs a toy from young children, they cannot comprehend that the other person may feel that he has the right to take the toy.

> Friends are valued for their material and physical attributes, and defined by proximity. As one child told us, "He is my friend." Why? "He has a giant Superman Doll and a real swing set." (Selman & Selman, 1979, p. 71)

The child at this stage looks at what seems to adults as the most obvious physical characteristics in deciding whom he likes:

- Girls with long hair are nice.
- My teacher is nice because she has a cat.
- He's my friend because he gives me candy.

As children move to a higher level, they can begin to differentiate between their point of view and the point of view of others but still may not understand the need for give and take. A good friendship usually involves one person doing what the other person wants him or her to do:

> Said one child, "She is not my friend anymore." Why? "She wouldn't go with me when I wanted her to." (Selman & Selman, 1979, pp. 71–72)

Considering that the preschool child is in the beginning stages of forming friendships, it is not surprising to find young children's friendships characterized by:

- one person taking the lead and another following more often than there being a real give-and-take relationship.
- breaking down of friendships when the follower decides not to follow.
- difficulty on the part of the young child in understanding the other person's point of view.

Berndt (1983) looked at social cognition (how children view friendship) and social behavior. Sharing and helping seem to be critical factors in marking the difference between friendships and nonfriendships. Sharing and helping make a relationship special. Younger children tend to be more competitive with friends. Sharing and helping increase with age. Even in early childhood conflicts arise between the child's desire to do what a friend wants in order to maintain the friendship and the desire for independence. Overall, in order to survive, friendships must be sources of gratification for both participants.

Some researchers have been interested in how friendships develop. Studies by Smollar and Youness (1982) and Gottman (1983) shed some light on this area. Smollar and Youness (1982) looked at friendship development as it relates to social development in general. Smoller and Youniss (1982) found that from ages six to ten, children indicated that strangers would become friends if they did something together (such as play or talk) and/or if they shared or helped each other. Not interacting or interacting in a negative fashion means strangers will not become friends. Children over twelve rely more on getting acquainted through talking rather than the action-oriented techniques of the younger children. Maintaining a friendship for younger children is dependent on positive interaction. Cooperation is the means for sustaining a relationship. Not until adolescence do children base friendships on personal qualities.

How conflicts are handled is influenced by the friendship levels of the participants. Hartup, Laursen, Stewart, and Eastenson (1988) compared the handling of conflicts by preschoolers who were either friends or nonfriends. Conflicts between friends tended to be less "heated" than those between nonfriends. In addition, friends were more likely to end the conflict by disengaging (turning away) rather than standing firm or negotiating. Friends neutralized the conflict by avoiding the standing firm alternative which would end in a winner/loser outcome. Friends were also more likely to remain near each other after the conflict.

Siblings

Siblings (brothers and sisters) constitute another important social network for young children. Pepler, Corter, and Abramovitch (1982) analyzed sibling relationships and compared the relationships between siblings with those between peers. Sibling interaction consisted of both positive and negative behaviors. Siblings expressed empathy for each other. There was also frequent helping, cooperation, and affection. On the other hand there were object struggles, verbal insults, and physical aggression. However, twice as many positive as negative behaviors were observed. Older siblings exhibited more prosocial behaviors than younger siblings. The older siblings also exhibited most of the negative behaviors. Older siblings usually retaliated to younger siblings' aggression

whereas younger siblings were more likely to give in to older siblings. Younger siblings engaged in much more frequent imitation than older siblings. This supports the importance of older siblings as models for their younger brothers and sisters. Same-sex sibling pairs exhibited more imitation than mixed-sex pairs. Younger siblings have an important role in maintaining the relationship by responding positively to their older siblings.

In comparing the sibling and peer relationships of young children, Pepler, Corter, and Abramovitch (1982) looked at several factors. Mixed-age peer interaction is similar to sibling interaction in that the older child can direct the social activity and the younger child has an opportunity to imitate a more competent playmate. Sibling interaction provides an opportunity for positive and negative interactions and thus may provide a situation in which more complex social exchanges occur. Sex differences are insignificant in sibling interactions whereas they are not in peer interactions. Siblings may be so close that familiarity overrides sex differences. Pepler et al. concluded that siblings provide a unique social experience that cannot be matched by peers.

Pepler et al. (1982) extended their research by observing and comparing children who had siblings with only children (having no siblings) as they played in preschool classrooms. They found no significant differences in the actions of the two sets of children. If children with siblings have an advantage that carries over to the peer group, it was not identified.

Social Isolation and Unpopularity

As already indicated, when children are in groups, differences in the degrees of popularity are apparent early in the school year. Some unpopular children may be socially isolated who seldom, if ever, interact with peers, while others may be children who attempt to interact but are rejected (Roopnarine & Honig, 1985). An unpopular child may be shy and withdrawn or disruptive and aggressive. The unpopular child is the one that other children choose least

Siblings   socially isolated often as being someone with whom they would like to play. This has become an important area for study since it has been discovered that peer rejection during the elementary school years is predictive of school dropout, antisocial behavior, delinquency, sexual disorder, and psychopathology in adolescence and early adulthood (Rubin, 1982). It may be that if children who are isolated and unpopular can be discovered early, they can be helped to develop social skills. However, while we can probably be assertive in working with those children who are aggressive and/or have difficulty in entering play groups, caution should be taken with children who are shy. It is estimated that approximately 15 percent of all children are born with a predisposition to be shy (Bullock, 1993). It is important to be supportive of these children as they are even more likely to back off from new situations if they are pushed (Bullock, 1993).

In a review of research on unpopularity, Roopnarine and Honig (1985) found that popular children tend to play with other popular children, and unpopular children play with other unpopular children. Thus unpopular children have little, if any, opportunity to observe the behavior of popular children. Unpopular children spend their time differently than popular children. Rejected children spend more time in verbal and physical aggression. When they try to make social contacts, they are rejected. Rejected children wander, look on, and hover on the edge of activities. When they do enter a group, they are often ignored. Popular children give and receive more positive reinforcement than unpopular children.

Research indicates that children with good early family relationships "often are more popular in nursery school, tend to engage frequently in more social contact, and are more effective in offering guidance and suggestions to others. . . . Poor family relationships are also accompanied by dependence on the teacher and poor impulse controls." (Hartup & Moore, 1990, p. 10) Rejected children with their inept modes of interacting meet persistent and recurring social failure and diminish the number of opportunities to attain more positive social skills.

Rubin (1982) targeted preschool isolated children and observed their play behaviors. He found their play was less cognitively mature. They played fewer social games and did less dramatic play. Both of these kinds of play correlate with higher-level cognitive functioning. In this sample of children, in contrast to their more aggressive peers, the isolate children were just as popular as the more sociable children. When placed in a situation with another child, the isolates were more likely to talk to themselves. Their speech was at a more egocentric level. They also talked more to inanimate objects than did more sociable children. The more social group had higher mental ages than the isolate children. The isolates' mental ages could be depressed due to a lack of the social play experiences that we know enhance cognitive development. (This will be discussed in Unit 33.)

Coplan, Rubin, Fox, Calkings, and Stewart (1994) looked in more detail at children who spend most of their time alone. These researchers defined three types of withdrawal behavior:

- Solitary passive play involves playing quietly with objects and/or constructive activity while playing alone. This type of play is reinforced by adults and accepted favorably by peers during early childhood.

- Solitary active play involves repeated motor activity with or without objects and/or solitary dramatizing. This type of play is usually associated by adults with being aggressive and impulsive and immature and is associated with peer rejection.

- Reticent behavior is defined as looking at others without any accompanying play, that is, onlooking and unoccupied. It seems to indicate anxiety about joining a group possibly due to fear of rejection or lack of confidence regarding how to enter.

The Coplan et al. (1994) study involved observations of preschoolers in play groups of four in order to see if the three types of solitary behavior defined actually would occur. The results of the study confirmed that social withdrawal does come in more than one form. The authors concern is that if these children continue to spend most of their time in solitary activity by the time they reach middle childhood they will all be rejected by their peers.

MORAL DEVELOPMENT

Morality does not have a universal definition (Damon, 1988). Morality is constantly evolving and changing. However, Damon (1988, p. 5) lists several facets which are usually included in the conceptualization of morality:

1. An evaluative orientation towards actions and events that distinguishes the good from the bad and prescribes conduct consistent with the good.
2. A sense of obligation toward standards shared by a social collective.
3. A concern for the welfare of others.
4. A sense of responsibility for acting on one's concern for others through acts of caring, benevolence, kindness and mercy.
5. Concern for the rights of others, a concern for justice and fairness.
6. A commitment to honesty as the norm in interpersonal dealings.
7. Awareness that violations may result in emotional responses such as shame, guilt, outrage, fear and contempt.

Moral values are learned from parents, caretakers, peers, teachers, television, etc. Moral reasoning is the cognitive aspect of morality that leads the person to make a moral judgement. That is, the person considers his values relative to a problem situation and then judges what should be done in that situation. For example, one five-year-old child takes a toy away from another five-year-old child. The first child has been taught to value self-control and generosity, but he wants the toy back. He also has been taught to value obedience, so he controls his impulse to grab the toy (self-control). Searching through his values, he comes to honesty. He runs to his mother and tells her that the other child has stolen his toy. Since he has been taught that stealing is wrong, he sees this as a way out of his dilemma. The nature of "stealing" versus "borrowing" is not a distinction he has made yet. Running to mother comes under the third aspect of morality: action. This is the follow-through on the reasoned judgment of this young child.

Moral development also has an emotional element, the **conscience**. This emotional element includes feelings of guilt and anxiety. In the previous example, the child felt some anxiety about grabbing the toy back or attacking the other child due to fear of punishment and loss of approval from his mother. This led him to search further for a way to retrieve his toy. If he had attacked the other child and gotten away with it, he would likely feel guilty. That is, he would feel uncomfortable because he had not done what was consistent with the values he had been taught. The development of conscience, or inner control, is the major objective of moral training during the preschool period (Sears et al., 1957).

Much of the research on moral development focuses on the development of **moral reasoning** and the making of **moral judgments**. The work of Piaget (1965) and the work of Kohlberg (1968) have been looked at most closely. Basically, for Piaget and Kohlberg, as the person becomes less egocentric his moral judgments become more mature. The preschool child is still in the preoperational period and thus is egocentric and perception bound. Three-, four-, and five-year-olds:

- Are relatively hedonistic; that is, they are most interested in their own welfare and pleasure.

- Are controlled by external sanctions; that is, fear of punishment and fear of loss of approval.

- Have values that are situation specific; that is, what is right or wrong in one situation is not necessarily generalized to another situation.

- Are able to verbalize good behavior, but with actions depending on the need for approval and the threat of punishment.

How often the adult says of the young child, "I know he knows better!" And the adult is right; the child does "know better" but is not yet able to reason and act consistently with his knowledge. It is not until the

KEYTERMSKEYTERMSKEYTERMSKEYTERMSKEYTERMSKEYTERMSKEY

Morality	moral reasoning
conscience	moral judgments

child is close to six that he begins to develop standards, to generalize, and to internalize sanctions so that he acts morally not just to avoid punishment but because he *should* act that way.

Piaget constructed a two-stage theory of moral reasoning (Figure 29–4). In the first stage, moral realism (age four to age ten), the child's evaluation centers on the degree of damage and not the intention of the child. The four-year-old in the example reacts in exactly this way. From seven to ten, the child experiences the transition as evidenced by his consideration of each child's intentions. He is able to consider both the amount of damage and the intentions. The preschool child, besides focusing on the consequences, is also characterized by viewing rules as unchangeable and viewing punishment for rule breaking as automatic. The preschool child considers rules as always having been here rather than as something invented by people. Not considering intentions, he feels that any and all transgressions must be punished; forgiveness is not yet in his domain. It is only gradually during Piaget's transition period (coinciding with concrete operations) that the child begins to see that rules are arbitrary and ever changing and that punishment is socially determined and not automatic.

During the early years, the child learns the values of people in his environment but does not yet reason and act in the same ways as an adult. The preschooler needs help to see intentionality. Through cooperative effort and responsibility, the child can be helped to move to the next stage.

In Piaget's view, merely following a morality of obedience will not result in the internalization of autonomous rules of moral judgment (DeVries & Kohlberg, 1990; DeVries & Zan, 1994). As with other concepts, the child needs the freedom to develop moral rules through his own cognitive actions. The child needs autonomy to figure out for himself how to apply rules in different situations.

Kohlberg and Likona (1990) proposed that the creation of a 'just community' in the classroom would promote young children's moral development. In the just community classroom the social-moral curriculum is all-inclusive. "The overarching goal is to create a classroom community in which the ideals of justice and cooperation become lived realities for children" (Kohlberg & Likona, 1990, p. 157). A just community is a developmentally designed school democracy that stimulates moral and social advancement. Some of the approaches used are:

- encouraging student generated rule-making

- providing support structures (such as clear rules, a system for taking turns, etc.)

- promoting group decision-making

- using spontaneous interpersonal conflicts as the basis for discussion

- fostering a moral community

- developing caring relations

- promoting cooperative learning.

Age	Stage	Characteristics
4–7	Moral Realism (Preoperational)	• Centers on consequences of act. • Rules are unchangeable. • Punishment for rule breaking is automatic.
7–10	Transition (Concrete Operational)	Gradually changes to second stage thinking.
11+	Moral Autonomy, Realism, Reciprocity (Formal Operations)	• Considers intentions. • Realizes rules are arbitrary conventions. • Punishment is socially determined, not inevitable.

Figure 29–4 **Piaget's two-stage theory of moral development with transition period.**

To use all these approaches requires a great many teacher skills, a teacher who models understanding and fairness, and a sustained commitment. DeVries and Zan (1994) have described how to develop a classroom community for young children. Research done by DeVries and her colleagues (DeVries, R., Haney, J., and Zan, 1991; DeVries, Halcyon, R., and Morgan, 1991) and by Schmidt (1993) contrasts the behavior of children enrolled in more democratic classrooms where positive guidance strategies are used that support students constructing their own solutions to problems and more authoritarian classrooms where more negative guidance strategies are used that promote obedience through fear. The results from both studies document the more advanced sociomoral behaviors of the children from the more democratic classrooms.

With so many young children spending most of their day in childcare settings, it is important to try to find out what effect, if any, this experience has on their conceptions of moral and social rules. Siegal and Storey (1985) compared the moral judgments of preschoolers who had been in day care for at least eighteen months with the judgments of preschoolers who had recently enrolled. They were interested in whether or not the children with more experience dealing with social rules would be able to discriminate better between moral rules (rules that generalize across situations) and social rules (arbitrary rules that are specific to the situation). Moral rules are rules that apply in every situation such as sharing, not hitting, not shoving, not throwing things at another child, and not taking another child's possessions. Social rules are situation specific, such as having to participate in show and tell, sitting in a certain place at story time, putting toys away in the correct place, and putting personal belongings in the correct place. Both the preschool veterans and the newly enrolled viewed moral transgressions as equally unacceptable. The preschool veterans were much more tolerant of social transgressions. They seemed to feel these transgressions were to be expected and that the children would find solutions without adult intervention. The day-care experience seemed to give the children

a higher level of understanding so they could discriminate between the rules that are standards and those that are arbitrary.

The child's values are reflected in his moral reasoning and in his judgments. Equally important, however, are his actions. He may be able to talk about a positive moral solution and yet when it comes to his behavior, he may not follow through. Two related areas of behavior that are of concern to those who work with young children are prosocial and aggressive behaviors.

Prosocial Behavior

The outward manifestations of positive moral development are seen in **prosocial behaviors** that reflect generosity, nurturance-giving, sympathy, and helping (Figure 29–5). They involve attempts to join another person, collaborate with another, offer suggestions, follow the lead of another, and engage in conversations. Research supports that young children are capable of and do demonstrate the use of prosocial behaviors (Buzzelli, 1992; Moore, 1977) and that parents and teachers can promote prosocial behavior through prosocial curricula (DeVries, R., Haney, J., & Zan, 1991; DeVries, Halcyon, R., and Morgan, 1991; Doescher and Sugawara, 1989; Kim and Stevens, 1987; Schmidt, 1993). For example, Schmidt asked children from positive (PG) and negative guidance (NG) kindergartens, "What would you do if a friend got hurt on the playground?" The PG children answered consistently that they would try to help their friend by getting a Band-Aid, consoling the friend, or staying with the friend until the friend felt better. The NG children all responded that they would go get the teacher. The PG children showed a mature level of sociomoral development; the NG children's responses reflected a lack of knowledge of moral responsibility.

Violence and Aggression

The headlines tell the story: "Teenage homicides become deadly epidemic" (Bayles, 1993). A kindergartner draws a picture of a homicide in her journal—she had witnessed her Aunt shooting her

Figure 29–5   **Young children display both positive and negative feelings.**

mother. Children's Defense Fund (CDF) reported the results of two polls that indicated "nearly three-quarters of the surveyed parents and more than half of the children said their top worry is that a loved one would become a victim of a violent crime" (*State of America's children yearbook*, 1994, p. 63).

The CDF yearbook reports additional frightening information. Guns are the major concern of parents and children. Every two hours a child dies of gunshot wounds. Data from 1991 revealed that 801 children from ages 1 to 14 died of gunshot injuries including homicide, suicide, and accidental shooting. Further, it is estimated that each day 30 to 67 children are wounded. Children exposed to this **violence** are more likely than their classmates to suffer from depression, low self-esteem, excessive crying, and worries about dying or being injured. Many inner-city children who are exposed to this excessive violence develop psychological defense mechanisms that inhibit their ability to learn in school and may cause them to be aggressive. Poverty is the strongest predictor of criminal activity. With 40 percent of African-American children living in poverty, it is no surprise that African-American males are the largest group of both attackers and victims. Children have easy access to weapons and they have experience with violence not only in their neighborhoods but also on television and with video games.

In response to this epidemic of violence NAEYC published a position statement on violence in the lives of children in 1993 (NAEYC Position statement on violence in the lives of children, 1993). "Schools and child care programs can be vitally important support systems by strengthening children's resilience and providing resources for parents so they can serve as psychological buffers to protect their children" (p. 81). In Unit 30 we will look further at some of the steps adults can take to protect young children. Meantime this unit will close with a description of some of the research on aggressive behavior and the effects on young children's current and future social development.

Aggressive behavior is the other side of the coin from prosocial behavior. One of the foremost challenges for adults who work with young children is helping them to handle their hostile feelings in positive ways while developing more prosocial behavior.

For young children *aggressive* behavior is defined as that which "has the capacity to hurt or injure or damage, regardless of intent." (Caldwell, 1977, p. 6) According to Caldwell, there are two types of aggression:

- **Instrumental aggression:** aggression which is designed to unblock a blocked goal, such as getting back an object, territory, or privilege.
- **Hostile aggression:** aggression that is person oriented—the person has done something nega-

tive and the aggressive act is directed toward him personally, such as using criticism, ridicule, tattling, or verbal disapproval (Hetherington & Parke, 1979).

Young children tend to engage in much more instrumental aggression than hostile. Often the most aggressive children are also the most prosocial. It may be that these children are overall the most socially active. Modeling seems to be a primary factor in the learning of aggressive behaviors. It is, therefore, obvious why children exposed to violence in their neighborhoods, on television and through video games are more likely to be dangerously aggressive.

The young child needs to learn to develop positive social skills that will preclude the need to be excessively aggressive. At times, events will cause him to be angry. For young children, these events are most likely someone taking something he has (or not giving him something he wants); not letting him join in an activity; not sharing materials; or hurting his feelings or hurting him physically. The child must gradually learn control and compromise to solve these problems. In Unit 30 we'll look at some of the means being used to help children develop nonviolent procedures for handling problems. The rest of this unit will look at a number of areas that relate to violence and aggression: socioeconomic status and conduct, classroom conflict, rough-and-tumble play, and young children's views of authority.

Socioeconomic Status and Conduct

Dodge, Pettit, and Bates (1994) followed 585 children of whom 51 were from the lowest socioeconomic class (SES) from preschool through third grade. The purpose of the study was to find the process in socialization that might explain the relationship between early SES and later child behavior problems. The results indicated that the lower the children's SES at the preschool level, the more likely they were to be rated by teachers and peers as being aggressive. Poverty-related factors in early childhood that predicted later behavior problems included: harsh discipline, neighborhood and family violence,

more transient peer groups (thus no stable friendships), less cognitive stimulation in the home. Further their mothers tend to be less warm, are experiencing a relatively high level of family stressors, perceive they have less social support and feel relatively isolated, and are likely to approve of aggression as a way to solve problems. It's not that these parents want their children to be aggressive, but they perceive that aggression is the only means of survival in a violent neighborhood. On the other hand, harsh discipline has the strongest relationship to later behavior problems, suggesting that the children learn from the aggressive models. The authors conclude that these factors make the poverty level environment "a breeding ground for aggressive behavior development" (p. 662).

The results of a study by Campbell, Pierce, March, Ewing, and Szumowski (1994) with middle-class and upper-middle-class boys at ages four and six indicated that those children identified by teachers and/or parents as having problems have basic difficulties in control of activity, impulsivity, noncompliance, and aggression that they could not get under control in any situation. The most extreme problem boys were still problems when followed up at age six.

Classroom Conflict

Peer conflict is another area that is a major focus for research. In her review of research on peer conflict in the classroom, Wheeler (1994) found that problems of peer conflict have led to an interest on teaching children how to resolve conflicts independent of adult assistance. Wheeler (1994) notes that peer conflicts have a structure that can be identified (p. 296):

- issues are the arguable event and the initial opposition;
- strategies are the ways children deal with the mutual opposition;
- outcomes are the endings to the conflict.

Most commonly issues involve control of the physical or social environment. The most common disputes for the youngest children center on possessions. As children get older, conflicts center on issues of morality (physical harm, psychological harm, distribution of toys and rights) and social order (rules about how things should be done). Strategies may be physical or verbal and aggressive or nonaggressive. The outcomes may be unresolved, may be the result of an adult imposed solution, submission of one child to another, or a compromise arrived at through mutual discussion.

Some other points of interest emerged from Wheeler's (1994) review. In looking at the contexts of conflict it has been found that children who are engaged in cooperative or associative play use less aggression than children who are engaged in onlooker, solitary or parallel play. Friends have more frequent but less intense conflicts than nonfriends. If left alone by adults children can generate their own conflict solutions. When parents step in they are usually inconsistent and biased. If the first move toward resolution is aggressive, the followup responses are aggressive. If the first move is conciliatory, there is more likelihood a peaceful solution will be reached. It appears that relative to outcomes most conflicts are unresolved, that is, they are just dropped.

Rough-and-Tumble Play

Rough-and-tumble play (R&T) is a type of play that may appear aggressive but actually serves constructive purposes for young children (MacDonald, 1992). R&T involves playful wrestling, chasing, mock attacks and is generally boisterous and lively. It has been most extensively studied at the elementary school level where it is most prevalent (see Unit 31) but it does emerge at the preschool level (McBride-Chang & Jacklin, 1993). McBride-Chang and Jacklin (1993) found a relationship between fathers' amount of R&T with their children and children's amount of R&T. MacDonald's (1993) concern is that with the closer supervision of children's out of school activities that is prevalent today, children don't have the opportunity to engage in the fun and excitement of R&T that they had when they were more on their own in the neighborhood.

Views of Authority

Considering that children are becoming more aggressive and less under control it is important to look at their relationships with authority. Laupa (1994) found that preschoolers consider both adult status and social position of authority in relation to particular situations. That is, they don't view the need to be obedient to just any adult. For example, they give more authority to teachers than to other adults. They are also quite willing to accept peers as authorities in the context of play. While preschoolers still see teachers as major authorities, they are beginning to differentiate among authority figures relative to their position and the context.

As our world becomes more violent, children are exposed to more aggression and they are displaying more aggressive and violent behaviors. No longer can it be assumed that they will learn moral behaviors through being told standards. Teaching children to live in peace has become more complex than in the past. We will look further into the adult role in Unit 30.

SUMMARY

Between toddlerhood and school age, children make great strides in social development. They learn to develop more complex relationships with peers who serve as play companions, reinforcers, models, and friends. Siblings also serve as important sources of social interaction. Children who are not popular may be isolates or may exhibit behaviors unacceptable to others. These children need special adult attention to help with the development of appropriate social skills. Young children begin to acquire moral values, to reason about problems of right and wrong, to develop judgments, and to act in light of these judgments. They learn that positive behaviors are "right" and that aggressive behaviors are "wrong."

With both neighborhood and community environments becoming more violent and family life becoming more stressful, adults who work with young children are being faced with more aggressive behaviors and children who present more serious behavioral and emotional problems. Helping children develop positive behavior patterns is a greater challenge than ever.

FOR FURTHER READING

Asher, S. R., & Cole, J. D. (Eds.) (1990). *Peer rejection in childhood*. New York: Cambridge University Press.

Bennet, M. (Ed.). (1993). *The development of social cognition*. New York: Guilford.

Berndt, T. J., & Ladd, G. W. (Eds.) (1989). *Peer relationships in child development*. New York: John Wiley.

Damon, W. (1988). *The moral child*. New York: The Free Press.

Dunn, J. (1988). *The beginnings of social understanding*. Cambridge, MA: Harvard University Press.

Dunn, J. (1993). *Young children's close relationships: Beyond attachment*. Thousand Oaks, CA: Sage.

Eisenberg, N., & Mussen, P. (1989). *The roots of prosocial behavior in children*. New York: Cambridge University Press.

Eisenberg, N. (1992). *The developing child: The caring child*. Cambridge, MA: Harvard University Press.

Elkind, D. (1993). *Images of the young child*. Washington, DC: National Association for the Education of Young Children.

Foyle, H. C., Lyman, L., & Thies, S. A. (1992). *Cooperative learning in the early childhood classroom*. Westhaven, CT: National Education Association.

Grusec, J. E., & Lyton, H. (1988). *Social development: History, theory, and research*. New York: Springer-Verlag.

Hart, C. H. (Ed.) (1993). *Children on playgrounds: Research perspectives and applications*. Albany, NY: SUNY Press.

Hartup, W. W., & Rubin, Z. (Eds.) (1986). *Relationships and development*. Hillsdale, NJ: Erlbaum.

Hoot, J. L., & Roberson, G. (Eds.). (1994). Creating safer environments for children in the home, school and community [Special issue] *Childhood Education, 70,*.

Kostelnik, M. J., Stein, L. C., Whiren, A. P., & Soderman, A. K. (1993). *Guiding children's social development*. Albany, NY: Delmar.

Parke, R. D., & Ladd, G. W. (Eds.). (1992). *Family-peer relationships: Modes of linkage*. Hillsdale, NJ: Erlbaum.

Pryor, J. B., & Day, J. D. (1985). *The development of social cognition*. New York: Springer-Verlag.

Rubin, K. H., & Asendorpf, J. B. (Eds.). (1993). *Social withdrawal, inhibition, and shyness in childhood*. Hillsdale, NJ: Erlbaum.

Schrader, D. E., & Damon, W. (Eds.) (1990). *The legacy of Lawrence Kohlberg*. San Francisco: Jossey-Bass.

Shantz, C. U., & Hartup, W. W. (Eds.). (1992). *Conflict in child and adolescent development*. New York: Cambridge University Press.

Yawkey, T. D., & Johnson, J. E. (Eds.) (1988). *Integrative processes and socialization: Early and middle childhood*. Hillsdale, NJ: Erlbaum.

SUGGESTED ACTIVITIES

1. Do your own survey to find out who the peers of some young children are. Interview three mothers of children at each of at least three of the following age levels: 3, 4, 5, 6, and/or 7. Do they play more with children in their neighborhood? From their school? Do the mothers arrange playmates for them?

2. Go to a preschool center. Observe five three-year-olds and five four-year-olds using Rubin's adaptation of Parten's social participation and Smilansky's cognitive categories as defined in this unit. During free-play time, observe each child in each group in turn, changing every 3 seconds until each child has been observed a total of 5 minutes (100 three-second intervals).

Set up an observation sheet for each child:

	Cognitive Categories				
	Functional	Constructive	Dramatic	Games With Rules	Not Playing
Name of Child _____ Age _____					
Date _____ Time _____					
Unoccupied					
Onlooker					
Solitary					
Parallel					
Associative					
Cooperative					

a. Draw a table comparing the percentages of each category observed in each group.

b. Which social categories appeared most frequently/least frequently in each group? Which cognitive categories?

c. How do your results compare with Rubin's?

d. Find out the level of each child's social participation by giving points for each social act and adding up the totals:

cooperative	= (+3)	onlooker	= (−1)
associative	= (+2)	solitary	= (−2)
parallel	= (+1)	unoccupied	= (−3)

e. Find out the level of each child's cognitive activity by giving points and totaling:

not playing = (0)
functional = (1)
constructive = (2)
dramatic = (3)
games with rules = (4)

3. Observe four or more three-year-olds and four or more four-year-olds during free play, snack, and/or lunch. Observe each in turn in 3-minute blocks for a total of 30 minutes each. As you observe, write down a de-

scription of each instance of giving positive social reinforcements. After you have finished your observations apply the Hartup-Charlesworth Categories to each incident. See the example in the unit.

Hartup-Charlesworth Categories

I. Giving positive attention and approval.
   a. attending
   b. offering praise and approval
   c. offering help
   d. smiling and laughing
   e. offering guidance and suggestions, giving directions on the use of materials, or verbal help
   f. informing another of a third person's needs
   g. making a request which is carried out with pleasure

II. Giving affection and personal acceptance.
   a. physical affection such as kissing, hugging, patting, hand holding, sitting near
   b. verbal affection, attention, acceptance-giving status

III. Submission
   a. passive acceptance when another child takes a position or possession
   b. imitation
   c. sharing
   d. accepting another's idea, help, or material
   e. letting another play when he or she requests
   f. compromise
   g. following an order or request willingly
   h. cooperation—working together

IV. Giving tokens—gives food, toy, or other object spontaneously.
   a. Figure the percentages of each type of reinforcement given by each total age group and by boys and girls separately:

| Categories | Percentages Given | | | | | |
| | Three-year-olds | | | Four-year-olds | | |
	Boys	Girls	Total	Boys	Girls	Total

   b. Compare boys and girls and total age groups. Do you detect any age and/or sex differences?

4. Discuss with a small group in class: Should we always expect young children to obey their parents? Why or why not? Relate the discussion to the young child's developmental stage.

5. Observe the use of negative reinforcement using the categories developed by Hartup, Glazer, and Charlesworth. Use the same method as for observing positive reinforcement.

Negative Reinforcement Categories

   a. Noncompliance
     (negativism, rejection, ignoring)
   b. Interference
     (snatching, annoying, teasing)
   c. Derogation
     (insults, disapproves, blames, tattles)
   d. Attack
     (hits, pulls, pushes, etc.; threatens, commands)
     (1) Figure the percentages of each type of negative reinforcement given by each total age group and by boys and girls separately:

Category	Percentages Given					
	Three-year-olds			Four-year-olds		
	Boys	Girls	Total	Boys	Girls	Total

     (2) Compare boys, girls, and total age groups. Do you detect any age and/or sex differences?

6. Make an entry in your journal.

REVIEW

A. Describe what a peer is.

B. Categorize each of the following examples of child play behavior. Rate each according to all three category systems—Parten's, Smilansky's, and Hartup and Charlesworth's.

Categories			Incident
Parten	Smilansky	Charlesworth/Hartup	Example
			1
			2
			3
			4
			5
			6

1. Janie comes over to the block area and moves one of the blocks. Aaron sees her and exclaims, "Janie wrecked it!" They argue between themselves until Janie walks away. Aaron goes on building with the blocks. Two other children are building near him.
2. The blocks have fallen down. Aaron sees Andy start to build and he does the same next to Andy. They share the blocks and compare buildings.
3. As Carmen watches the children fish she blurts out, "Get the hook in him, David!"
4. Miguel gives the yellow car to Bill. Bill then follows Miguel.
5. Ronnie suggests that they all pile leaves. "Come on, get in here," he shouts. Six children are piling leaves.
6. Maria and her friends are all riding bikes. She slows herself by dragging her feet. Her friends do, also.

C. In the research by Charlesworth and Hartup and Hartup et al., information was collected on positive and negative reinforcement. Write the number of each correct statement concerning the research results.
   1. Four-year-olds gave more positive reinforcements than three-year-olds.
   2. Younger children gave reinforcement to more children than did older children.
   3. Dramatic play activities brought forth a lot of positive reinforcement.
   4. Popular children usually were the ones who gave the most positive reinforcement.
   5. Almost as much negative reinforcement as positive reinforcement was given.

D. For each of the following examples, write either *0* for friendship stage 0, or *1* for friendship stage 1.
   1. "She is my friend. She gives me popcorn."
   2. "Girls who wear dresses are nice."
   3. "I'm mad at Nora. She always wants to be boss."
   4. "Bob is my friend. He lets me ride his trike."
   5. "Johnny, you are nice. You share toys and play the things I like."

E. The most successful group entry technique is:
   1. Push in and demand attention.
   2. Say politely, "May I play with you?"
   3. Hover around the edge of the group and then move into a role in the group that fits with what is already going on.
   4. Hover around the edge of the group and then move into the group with a new idea.

F. Consider the following two examples. Decide which child, Isabel or Kate, is most likely to develop prosocial behaviors. Explain why.
   1. Isabel and Theresa are playing. Suddenly Isabel yells to Theresa, "Give me my dolly or I'll hit you." Theresa holds on tightly to the dolly. Isabel hits her. Theresa cries. Isabel's mother, Mrs. Sanchez, comes in and asks, "What's going on, girls?" She finds out what happened as she comforts Theresa. She explains to Isabel that hitting is not the way to get her dolly back. She then explains to Theresa that that particular doll is very special to Isabel. She then gets the girls to agree that Theresa will play with the doll for ten minutes and then give it to Isabel.
   2. Kate and Bill are playing. Kate takes Bill's truck. Bill is crying and runs to get his mother. Mrs. Hopkins. Mrs. Hopkins comes in looking angry. She says, "Kate, you are a bad girl. Give that truck back to Bill. You go sit on that chair for ten minutes and then I expect you to come back and play nicely."

G. Decide which of the following examples show instrumental aggression and that show hostile aggression. Mark *I* for instrumental and *H* for hostile.
   1. "Mommy, mommy, Janie took a cookie!"
   2. "Jason, you look ugly."
   3. Jason pushes Rudy off the chair that he wants.

4. Isabel tries to pull Maria off the swing because she feels it is her turn.
5. "You don't know how to do it right."
Which of the examples above are most likely to involve preschool children? Why?

H. Select the correct answer(s) to the following. There may be more than one correct answer or no correct answers.
  1. Parten's play categories can be used to find the level of children's
     a. cognitive play.
     b. dramatic play.
     c. social participation.
     d. functional play.
  2. A child who can accurately process social information will most likely
     a. find a social strategy that works and stick with it in all situations.
     b. use a variety of strategies with choice depending on the situation.
     c. select the most appropriate strategy, positive or negative.
     d. use only positive strategies such as asking or showing.
  3. The results of Ladd's kindergarten study indicated the following regarding early peer relationships:
     a. Children who have high status in the group at the beginning of kindergarten will have high status at the end.
     b. Children who were rejected early in the kindergarten year were likely to remain rejected at the end of the year.
     c. Popular children tend to have a positive attitude toward school.
     d. Less popular children tend to have a positive attitude toward school.
  4. Smilansky's play categories can be used to find the level of children's
     a. cognitive play.
     b. cooperative play.
     c. social participation.
     d. associative play.
  5. A small group of children is playing house. One is the father, one the mother, one the big brother, and one the baby. Each plays his role in relation to the others. This is categorized as
     a. cooperative play by Parten.
     b. functional play by Smilansky.
     c. dramatic play by Smilansky.
     d. associative play by Parten.
  6. A child is playing alone away from the other children. He appears to be making a building out of building toys. His play would be categorized as
     a. parallel by Parten.
     b. functional by Smilansky.
     c. solitary by Parten.
     d. constructive by Smilansky.
  7. Peers serve an important function as models for other children. The children most likely to be imitated are those who
     a. are warm and rewarding.
     b. are powerful.
     c. control resources.
     d. the child perceives as being similar to himself.
  8. The playground has been selected as an excellent place for observation of children's social behavior because
     a. there is more room for the researchers.
     b. it is more natural and less restrictive.
     c. the children tend to go wild.
     d. researchers are no longer allowed in classrooms.

9. Berndt (1983) found that children's views of what is special about friendship are related to age and development in several ways. According to Berndt,
   a. the importance of sharing and helping increases with age.
   b. older children are more competitive with their friends.
   c. a desire for independence is usually subordinated to the desire to maintain a friendship.
   d. children will persevere even when a friendship is not gratifying.

10. Younger children are likely to become friends if
    a. they interact, share, and/or help each other.
    b. the guest child agrees with the host.
    c. the children can agree on a common-ground activity.
    d. they can successfully exchange information.

11. Some factors that research has documented regarding children's friendships are
    a. friendships are special relationships that develop with other people and serve several functions for young children such as being an emotional resource, a cognitive resource, a context in which basic social skills are learned, and is a forerunner of future relationships.
    b. friends resolve conflicts more calmly than nonfriends.
    c. children who enter elementary school with preschool friends are more likely to feel satisfied with school and maintain those friendships.
    d. children who start out aggressive at the beginning of kindergarten usually attain popularity by the end of the year.

12. Sibling relationships are unique in that
    a. due to sibling rivalry there are more negative than positive interactions.
    b. younger siblings rarely imitate older siblings.
    c. sibling relations are usually more positive than peer relations.
    d. children with siblings play better with their peers.

13. Unpopular young children are most likely children who
    a. are withdrawn and isolated.
    b. are aggressive.
    c. spend time observing popular children to learn techniques for making friends.
    d. will drop out of school in adolescence, display antisocial behavior, become delinquents, etc.

14. Coplan et al. discovered
    a. children who spend most of their time alone during preschool usually have many friends by the end of third grade.
    b. there are three types of children who spend most of their time alone: solitary passive, solitary active, and reticent.
    c. solitary active play by preschoolers is usually looked upon favorably by adults.
    d. solitary passive play by preschoolers is usually looked upon favorably by adults.

15. Morality includes
    a. values and actions.
    b. judgments and values.
    c. values, judgments, and actions.
    d. reasoning, thinking, and acting.

16. Research by DeVries and her colleagues and by Schmidt indicates
    a. more democratic approaches to classroom guidance support children's moral development.
    b. children from positive guidance classrooms are more likely than those from negative guidance classrooms to help a friend who is in trouble.
    c. children from more authoritarian classrooms are more obedient and have a better understanding of good behavior.
    d. children from authoritarian classrooms are better at constructing their own solutions to problems.

17. Young children may not always obey even though they know what the rules and expectations for behavior are because
    a. young children are innately bad.
    b. they have not been well disciplined.
    c. their parents are not good models.
    d. developmentally, they have not reached the point at which they are able to act in a way consistent with what they have been taught.

18. The method for promoting children's moral development that is recommended by Kohlberg and Likona includes the following:
    a. The creation of a just community in the classroom.
    b. Discussions of moral dilemma stories are enough to do the job.
    c. A democratic approach which includes such activities as the children making their own rules and engaging in group decision making.
    d. Having discussions of moral problems a daily group activity.

19. The foremost worry for parents and children is
    a. poverty.
    b. the poor quality of public schooling in their neighborhoods.
    c. kidnapping.
    d. a loved one will be the victim of a violent crime.

20. Regarding socioeconomic status (SES) and school behavior problems
    a. family context is a stronger influence than SES on the chances a child will be a behavior problem in school.
    b. the lower a child's SES is when he/she starts school, the more chance he or she will be identified as a behavior problem student.
    c. a multitude of predictive factors (such as harsh discipline in the home, violence in the neighborhood, mothers who feel isolated and stressed) are part of the poverty picture.
    d. SES level is not a good predictor of school problem behavior.

21. Several other factors relative to aggressive acts are
    a. poverty is not the only factor in the development of problem behaviors—middle- and upper-middle-class boys may demonstrate problem behaviors in preschool and at home that continue into the elementary grades.
    b. peer conflict has an identified structure: issues, strategies, and outcomes.
    c. young children nearly always arrive at a satisfactory outcome for their conflicts.
    d. rough and tumble play is dangerous and should never be allowed.
    e. preschool children already discriminate between levels of adult authority.

The Adult Role in Affective Development

OBJECTIVES

After studying this unit, the student should be able to:

■ Recognize the major components of love and affection.

■ Identify examples of various types of guidance techniques.

■ State the advantage of using the inductive method of guidance.

■ Recognize the characteristics of the authoritative, authoritarian, permissive, and harmonious parenting approaches.

■ State which guidance methods can be labeled as positive and list the negative effects of punishment.

■ Identify examples of shaping, modeling, and coaching.

■ Understand the factors that underlie the development of moral autonomy.

■ Explain how crisis-oriented literature can be used.

■ Analyze discrepancies in beliefs and actions regarding teacher affective behavior.

■ Explain how the affective curriculum is implemented.

A s described in Unit 29, young children are faced with increasing violence in their lives. In addition, the emerging variety of lifestyles that exist may place the child in a situation that is less predictable than what is ideal for young children. Adults who work with young children have an ever-greater challenge in fulfilling their responsibility for supporting the affective development of children.

The developmentally appropriate practice guidelines for adult interaction (Bredekamp, 1987, pp. 9–12) include the following:

• Adults respond quickly and directly to children's needs, desires, and messages and adapt their responses to children's differing styles and abilities.

• Adults facilitate a child's successful completion of tasks by providing support, focused attention, physical proximity, and verbal encouragement. Adults recognize that children learn from trial and error and that children's misconceptions reflect their developing thoughts.

- Teachers are alert to signs of undue stress in children's behavior, and are aware of appropriate stress-reducing activities and techniques.
- Adults facilitate the development of self-esteem by respecting, accepting and comforting children, regardless of the child's behavior.
- Adults facilitate the development of self-control in children.

When following these guidelines, adults should also keep in mind the specific experiences and cultural backgrounds of the children. Background factors such as economic hardship (McLoyd, 1990), family ecology (Harrison, Wilson, Pine, Chan, & Buriel, 1990), and racial/ethnic socialization (Lin & Fu, 1990; Thornton, Chatters, Taylor, & Allen, 1990) as previously discussed enter into the affective development of young children. For example, some cultural groups (such as Mexican-Americans) emphasize the affective domain to a greater extent than others with the result that some children enter school with a greater sensitivity to their own and others' feelings. Some cultures (such as Native Americans) may emphasize self-reliance and independence more than others.

LOVE AND AFFECTION

In Lansing, Michigan, an adult education course presented by the public schools has the title "Tickle, Cuddle, Kiss and Hug." The course teaches how to hug, squeeze, and tickle children. A first reaction might be concern that such "natural" behaviors might be taught. However, expressing **love and affection** to young children may be a more complex procedure than we might think at first.

Alan Fogel (1980) points out the complexities of giving affection. He feels that the emotional aspects of affection giving (that is, what each person

feels) are as important, or possibly even more important, than the observed behavior (such as tickling, cuddling, and kissing) Fogel identifies three main aspects of affection-giving. Children need love from a warm and accepting adult. Love helps children feel competent and secure. Adults' past experiences affect their reactions to children's needs for love. One adult may accept a child with warmth that another adult can't tolerate. Some adults feel ambivalent or uncertain about expressing love to children. To be effective, the adult must feel the child needs affection at the same time the child feels the need for affection.

Fogel goes on to point out that while young children need to achieve autonomy and move ahead toward independence, they also need to learn to trust that adults will offer support and help when needed. Children need adults who they can count on for love and respect even when they are out of control. At the same time adults must work through their feelings with other adults as young children are not at a point where they can serve this function for adults.

Adults need to be cautious in relation to the value of love. Love is a spontaneous and natural feeling that cannot be turned on and off at will. Acceptance and respect come first. Love for a particular child or love for a particular adult does not necessarily follow. Rita M. Warren (1977, p. 4) warns, ". . . indiscriminate hugs, back-patting and head-touching may be unrelated to love and may dilute instead of strengthen the child's growing understanding of relationships between people." An adult can have a positive relationship with a child without necessarily feeling or expressing love and affection. Acceptance and respect are the most necessary ingredients for a good relationship (Figure 30–1).

Usually the most effective way to start a relationship with a small child is to stand back, be low-key, and let the child make the first move when he feels comfortable. The overzealous, effusive adult too often scares off and overwhelms the small child. Touching is important in relating to the preschool child but it must be done on the child's terms. Some preschoolers need hugs and cuddling on adult laps.

Figure 30–1 **A supportive adult is there when needed.**

Others gain the same positive feelings from a pat on the shoulder or a minute or two of undivided adult attention to their conversation, and/or their activity.

While research indicates that closeness and physical affection are necessary for healthy affective development, a problem regarding the giving of physical affection has emerged from concerns about child sexual abuse. ". . . publicity about sexual abuse may be creating unwarranted negative attitudes toward normal physical affection." (Hyson, Whitehead, & Prudoe, 1988, p. 55) Hyson et al. (1988) demonstrated, through an experimental study, that knowledge of the prevalence and effects of sexual abuse can lower adults' level of approval for physical affection giving to young children while knowledge of the need for closeness and physical affections can raise the level of approval. Their research indicates the need to clarify for adults the difference between sexual abuse and good touch.

DISCIPLINE AND GUIDANCE

What is discipline? The term **discipline** is often associated with punishment. For some adults, the terms are synonymous. In fact, discipline is a much broader concept of which punishment is only one part.

The term discipline has lost much of its original meaning and become a rather negative term. It had respectable origins in a Latin root that established its connections with learning and education. It still retains its connections with education in the dictionary: "training that develops self-control, character, an orderliness and efficiency," but today is used synonymously with punishment, most particularly corporal punishment (Fraiberg, 1959). In teaching the child to be a disciplined, self-controlled individual, various techniques can be used. Today the term **guidance** is used to distinguish positive techniques from the negative connonation of the term *discipline*. Punishment is only one of those techniques.

The most common disciplinary techniques are outlined in Figure 30–2. These techniques fall into two major categories:

- Child behavior is inhibited.
- Child behavior is directed.

There are two types of inhibiting techniques: power assertive and psychological. Both of these techniques inhibit or stop the child from proceeding with the unacceptable activity in which he is engaged. Power-assertive techniques include physical punishment such as spanking, verbal punishment such as shouting and threats, and physical inhibition such as holding the

Child Behaviors	Practices
Inhibited	1. Power Assertive • physical punishment • shouting • threats • physical inhibition 2. Psychological • love withdrawal and guilt production • induction (reasons, consequences stressed)
Directed	3. Modeling • observational learning • modeling statements 4. Reinforcement

Figure 30–2 **Discipline techniques**

child or restricting his activities. Psychological techniques include love withdrawal and guilt-producing strategies such as shaming or making the child feel he has lost the adult's love and approval. The second psychological technique is the use of induction. Inductions include reasoning and the stressing of consequences (Figure 30–3). That is, the child is told why he cannot be allowed to do what he is doing, and any negative consequences are described.

The directing techniques include the behaviorist approaches of modeling and reinforcement. Modeling includes observational learning and modeling statements. Through observational learning, the child watches what other children do and then does the same to receive positive reinforcement and self-satisfaction. Modeling statements are used by the adult to clarify for children exactly which models are behaving appropriately:

"Good, Jason, you are putting the blocks back on the bottom shelf."

"I can see that Derrick has his coat on and is ready to go outside."

"Isabel and Theresa, you are sharing the dolls."

Figure 30–3   With the inductive method of inhibiting undesirable behavior, reasons are given and consequences explained.

Adult reinforcement can be very powerful not only relevant to the behavior of the child to whom it is directed, but also for the children who observe the reinforcement and use that child as a model. Modeling statements can be a very powerful technique in directing children's behavior.

More than one discipline technique can be used with the same child depending on the child's age and other circumstances. There are several factors that can be considered in making a choice:

- During the preverbal period, power assertion techniques such as physical inhibition and mild punishment (such as gently holding the child along with "no !") used in conjunction with positive reinforcement and plenty of opportunities for observation of positive models probably works best.

- Inductive methods (reasoning and stressing consequences) are strongly related to later positive moral development and the development of inner control. By age two, when the child has some language skills, reasoning and explanation can be given using simple, short sentences.

- Punishment brings about short-term inhibition but is not very effective in the long run.

How do parental discipline techniques affect child behavior? Some of the best-known studies of **parental styles** have been done by Diana Baumrind and her colleagues (1971, 1975). Baumrind identifies four styles of parenting, outlined in Figure 30–4. The three most common types of approaches to parenting are authoritarian, permissive, and authoritative. A few parents use the harmonious style.

The parents who used authoritative control techniques were controlling and warm and communicated clearly with their children. The children were judged to be the most mature. Parents insisted on mature and obedient behavior. The children were independent, responsible, and assertive. The authoritarian parents were less nurturant and sympathetic toward their children. They used less rational methods of control and more threats. The children of these par-

Style	Parent Behavior	Child Outcome
Authoritarian	Low on nurturance and sympathy. Use less rational control methods and more threats than others.	Discontent, withdrawn, distrustful.
Authoritative	Controlling but warm and has good communication.	Mature: independent, responsible and assertive.
Permissive	Disorganized and not in control. Use withdrawal of love or ridicule.	Immature.
Harmonious	Encourage independence and individuality.	Girls: very competent. Boys: Low in competence.

Figure 30–4 **Baumrind's four parenting styles**

ents were more discontent, withdrawn, and distrustful. The children of the permissive parents tended to be the most immature. These parents tended to use withdrawal of love or ridicule as punishment techniques. The permissive parents were not as well organized and controlling as the others.

The harmonious parents were nonconformists. They didn't display control types of behaviors and yet their children seemed to know that was expected and to follow through. These parents were generally very well educated and provided their children with very enriched environments and encouraged independence and individuality. When their children disobeyed they looked on it more as a difference of opinion than as "bad behavior." Baumrind found only eight families of this type. The girls were very highly competent; the boys were very low in competence.

The authoritative approach seemed to have the most positive overall effect on child behavior. Children of authoritative parents tended to be the most mature and well adjusted. These parents had a balance of high expectations for their children with clear communications concerning their expectations and strong, warm relationships with them. They used mainly inductive methods of control. They listened to the child's opinions when they disagreed and always gave clear reasons for their decisions.

There has been increasing interest in looking further at how parental discipline styles, as defined by Baumrind, affect child behavior. Power assertive (authoritarian) mothers of preschool children tend to have children who view hostile methods as being the successful means for solving peer conflict and use more antisocial behaviors in their play (Hart, DeWolf, & Burts, 1992). Inductive mothers (authoritative) tend to have children who believe positive strategies will bring success in resolving conflicts and exhibit more prosocial and positive behaviors during playground play (Hart, DeWolf, & Burts, 1992). Children of inductive mothers were also more popular with their peers (Hart, DeWolf, Wozniak, & Burts, 1992). The results of these two studies support the advantage for children of inductive (authoritative) discipline.

Punishment is an area of discipline that merits attention. The use of corporal (or physical) punishment has been a controversial issue (Richardson and Evans, 1993). Corporal punishment in schools was banned by law in twenty-two states as of 1993 (Richardson & Evans, 1993). Therefore, corporal punishment is still inflicted in many schools and used by a majority of parents although research indicates that is has no long-term positive effects and correlates with a number of negative effects such as delinquency, vandalism, and poor grades (Cran, 1987). Other negative effects of corporal punishment that have been documented are (Corporal punishment, 1981):

- Hitting children makes them more aggressive.

- Corporal punishment does not develop self-control. It lets the child know which kind of behavior is inappropriate but does not let him know what is appropriate.

- Corporal punishment is often applied unfairly.

- The line separating punishment from abuse is a thin one.

Children who received physical punishment at home acted out more in school according to the results of a study with kindergartners and their parents (Michels, Pianta, & Reeve, 1993). Kindergartners who received nonphysical punishment (e.g., time out, attention to the misbehavior from the parent) exhibited relatively little acting out behavior in school. Weiss, Dodge, Bates, and Pettit (1992) found the degree of harsh discipline ("severe, strict, and often physical," p. 1324) used by parents was directly related to the amount of aggressive behaviors exhibited by children in school. That is, the harsher the discipline, the higher the children were rated by their teachers on aggressive behavior in the classroom.

Discipline styles of childcare givers are also of concern. Scott-Little and Holloway (1992) found that caregivers who blamed the misbehavior on factors internal to the child used more power-assertive methods of discipline than caregivers who considered external causes that were out of the child's control. These researchers point out the need for caregivers to be give assistance in looking in more depth at the causes of children's misbehavior.

Nonphysical methods of punishment, such as deprivation of privileges or isolation, are preferable to physical punishment. However, punishment will be most effective if accompanied by an explanation (inductive approach). The preferred and most effective discipline methods are those that are preventive. These are **positive guidance techniques** that teach children what the expected behaviors are and how to solve their conflicts using words rather than physical force. Inductive methods use positive statements that tell the child exactly what he is supposed to do and why. For this reason it is most likely to support long-term generalization as discussed in Unit 29. The following examples show positive statements that clearly explain what the child should not do and what he/she should do (Stone, 1978, pp. 26–27).

- It's hard for Meredith to wait so long for a turn. Let her have the truck in three minutes. I'll time it on my watch.

- It bothers me when you call Kevin stupid. He is not stupid. He's playing his own way and that's fine.

We'll look next at some views of positive guidance applied in the early childhood classroom.

TEACHING FOR DEMOCRACY, NONVIOLENCE, AND MORAL DEVELOPMENT

Teaching for democracy, nonviolence, and moral development begins with positive guidance. Historically, the concept of positive guidance goes back to 1950 and the publication of the first edition of Katherine Read Baker's textbook, *The Nursery School: A Human Relationships Laboratory*. Baker presented her view of the nursery school as a human relationships laboratory where guides or simple rules give support (1992). With this approach, the adult takes a low-keyed, positive, consistent role as a guide rather than a director. The emphasis is on telling the child what he should be doing, not what he should not be doing.

Josh is throwing blocks. The guidance-oriented teacher say, "The blocks are used for building, Josh" rather than "Stop throwing those blocks!"

Isabel is washing dolls in a tub of soapy water. Water is dripping on the floor. The guidance-oriented teacher says, "Keep the water in the tub,. Isabel." rather than "Isabel! Don't be so messy. You are spilling water all over the floor."

What about the adult's and the child's feelings? Both adult and child may at times display strong feelings. These feelings can be difficult to cope with when displayed as anger. While we accept the child's right to be angry, he cannot be allowed to destroy property and hurt other people. He needs to know that adults have feelings, too. Therefore, he needs to know when an adult disapproves of his behavior and feels angry herself. Disapproval has to be open and direct to let the child know he has done something wrong. It is through receiving disapproval from a respected adult that the child develops those guilt feelings which he needs for self-control. The adult does not need to yell and scream and degrade the child but can let him know how she feels in a firm, constructive way:

> Isabel refuses to help clean up the materials she has been using. She says to Mrs. Sanchez, "You're a dummy!" "Isabel," says Mrs. Sanchez firmly, "I don't like being called a dummy. Just do your job and then you can go play with your friends."

In this case Mrs. Sanchez is direct and to the point so Isabel knows that she disapproves, but doesn't reject Isabel as a person.

Teaching for Democracy

Articles by Joanne Hendrick (1992) and Polly Greenberg (1992a and 1992b) remind us that we live in a democratic country. Both Hendrick and Greenberg point out that preparation for democratic participation should begin in early childhood. Hendrick (1992) suggests we begin during the preschool years to transfer some adult power to children by encouraging them to make decisions (the power to choose), by building autonomy (the power to try), and by fostering competence (the power to do) (p. 51). This doesn't mean adults should step back and let the children run wild. It means adults provide realistic choices such as selecting which center to go to, provide encouragement to try new things (in the zone of proximal development), and support children when they tackle difficult problems (provide scaffolding). In this atmosphere, children can learn to value themselves and others, trust adults, and trust their peers.

In the first article, Greenberg describes how developmentally appropriate practice supports democratic living based on the ideas of John Dewey (1992a). Just as with parenting, teaching that is autocratic or too permissive is not supportive of child development. She also supports a democratic approach that develops democratic character in children. Greenberg states, "... democratic character is a cluster of characteristics, interests, and motivations in an individual that add up to a habit of acting in a way that's at once self-fulfilling and of benefit to the group" (p. 59). In Greenberg's second article (1992b), she describes

how to institute some simple democratic practices in the classroom that will develop democratic character. Her suggestions include using preventive discipline, positive guidance, and never shaming or demeaning a child (e.g., making threats, labeling a child "bad," ignoring needs for help) and teaching personal and social responsibility throughout the day.

Teaching for Nonviolence

Adults who work with young children have an opportunity to counteract some of the negative effects on children of the violence in the family and the community. Wallach (1993, p. 7) suggests, "Child care centers, recreation programs, and schools can be resources for children and offer them alternative perceptions of themselves, as well as teaching them skills." Professionals in these settings can offset some of the negative effects of violence. Wallach (1993, pp. 7–8) provides the following guidelines for professionals:

1. Make sure that your program provides opportunities for children to develop meaningful relationships with caring and knowledgeable adults.

2. Organize schedules and time with the children so they provide as much consistency as possible.

3. Provide clear structure and very clear expectations and limits.

4. Offer children many opportunities to express themselves.

Opportunities for involvement in play, art, and storytelling can be therapeutic offering an opportunity to express feelings. Most important is collaboration with the children's families.

Parry (1993) describes "Choosing Nonviolence," the Rainbow House educational program for helping children survive in a violent world. It has been used in Head Start, child care and primary classrooms. It is an approach that teaches children that they have a choice. There are three key concepts in the program (p. 14):

1. Understand what violence is; be able to name it in their lives, their toys, their choices, and so forth.

2. Realize they have the power to choose and control how they will act and how they will be.

3. Learn the power of language so that they can use it to say how they feel, to protect and defend themselves without being violent. They learn to speak out and find alternatives to violence for settling conflicts.

According to Wallach (1993) and Parry (1993), adults who work with young children can provide a therapeutic haven and alternative behaviors for children who live in a violent environment.

Teaching for Moral Development

There is a growing constructivist movement based on Piaget's theory and growing out of Kohlberg's concept of the Just Community (described in Unit 29). Kamii (1984) described the basic constructivist philosophy relative to guidance practices. Kamii believes, from the Piagetian perspective, that reward and punishment have only short-term effects. Punishment leads to finding ways to get away with unacceptable behavior without getting caught, blind conformity, and revolt. Rewards maintain the adult in the power position and never give the children opportunities to think for themselves. The crux of the Piagetian approach is reciprocity or exchange of viewpoints between adult and child and allowing children an opportunity to make their own decisions. These two elements enable the child to develop personal values and achieve moral autonomy. Children can only learn about decision making by making and living with their own decisions. For young children these decisions are simple ones: which clothing to wear today, which activity to choose at school, etc. By 5 years of age children are capable of making many decisions for themselves if they have been give the opportunity for trial and error in previous years. With five-year-olds, the teacher should be able to leave the room for a few minutes without having chaos result: the children can govern themselves. If the teacher has approached

problems with "What do you think we should do?", soon the children will do the same. Self-governance with small decisions will generalize to bigger ones. According to Kamii this approach supports moral development as well as intellectual development in general, as it forces children to think about different points of view.

The constructivist approach has been elaborated in more detail by DeVries and Zan (1994). DeVries and Zan have developed guidelines and a plan for "moral classrooms." They define **moral classrooms** as "classrooms in which the sociomoral atmosphere supports and promotes children's development" (p. 7). These are not classrooms in which children are indoctrinated with values through specific lessons on character; they are classrooms in which there is a feeling of **community in the classroom** and where the teacher is a friendly mentor. The basic atmosphere is one of respect. The teacher respects the children's ideas and consults them when there is a problem in the classroom. The teacher uses positive strategies to engage children in learning so threats and punishments are not needed. In moral classrooms teachers use what DeVries and Zan refer to as "persuasive strategies" such as making suggestions, elaborating on children's ideas, reminding children of the reasons for rules, offering choices, encouraging the generation of ideas, and upholding the value of fairness. In the moral classroom, there are "moral children." Moral children deal with questions of right and wrong and good and bad in relation to their everyday activities. They worry about how people are treated, about aggression, and about questions of fairness. "They construct their morality out of daily life experiences" (p. 28). DeVries and Zan have documented the success of this type of classroom in the research described in Unit 29.

The constructivist approach can be carried from the preschool and kindergarten into the primary grades. Castle and Rogers (1993/94) explain how children can learn through constructing their own classroom rules. Discussions on creating rules provide opportunities for active involvement, reflection, making meaningful connections, developing respect for rules, developing a sense of community, experiencing problem solving through negotiation, experiencing cooperation, having opportunities for inductive thinking, and acquiring a sense of ownership of the rules developed.

Teaching for democracy, nonviolence, and moral classrooms are all positive procedures designed to develop the whole child. There are other methods for helping children in the emotional, personality, and social development areas that focus on more specific behaviors and behavior change and can be adopted as needed.

Other Strategies for Affective Development

Several strategies have been used successfully to teach skills to children (Asher, Oden & Gottman, 1977). These methods include shaping, modeling, and coaching. As previously described, shaping involves giving positive reinforcement each time a child demonstrates any behavior that is close to the desired behavior to increase the probability that the child will behave in the same way again. For the isolate, this involves first observing and finding out how often the child interacts with other children. Then, the teacher must be sure someone is watching the child at all times so that reinforcement can be given immediately every time the child interacts with another child. At first the child may be reinforced for just being next to or near another child. Once there is some contact, he is reinforced for interaction only. General reinforcement has been found to be most effective. For example, four boys are playing in the sandbox. The adult says, "You boys are playing nicely." This approach avoids the possibility of embarrassing the target child by mentioning him specifically.

Once the isolate is playing close to other children, he needs to develop some interaction skills. Modeling and coaching are ways of giving direct instruction. Sometimes from viewing filmed examples children learn long-lasting skills that they had not been able to learn by watching their peers in the classroom. It may be that the film narration which calls their attention to the skills is necessary to make them focus on the most relevant and basic behaviors.

Shaping and modeling and other aspects of the behaviorist approach are described in detail by Eva Essa (1990) in her book *Practical Guide to Solving Preschool Behavior Problems*. Even through this approach usually does not have long-term results, it is the way to get children started on the right track through achieving externally controlled changes in behavior. By gradually accompanying this approach with the inductive approach as the child is able to handle it, the inductive methods can eventually take over. Some children are too extreme in their use of inappropriate behaviors to deal with them inductively in the beginning. For the child who is very aggressive, antisocial, disruptive, destructive, overly emotionally dependent, and/or isolated, the adult can shape more appropriate behavior first, then move gradually to inductive, reciprocal, and discussion approaches.

Children can be taught directly how to interact with others. That is, they can be coached on how to play with other children. Children have been taught various kinds of prosocial behavior such as sharing and taking turns. Much coaching comes through the use of inductive control methods since these spell out social rules quite clearly. Coaching has helped aggressive children to be more prosocial and isolated children to be more popular.

Another method that has become widely used in all areas of social development is using literature as a means for helping children solve problems in appropriate ways. For example, Krogh and Lamme (1983) describe a developmental approach to teaching sharing behavior through literature. As pointed out in Unit 29, sharing is an important aspect of young children's definitions of friendship. Krogh and Lamme view literature as a vehicle for taking the abstract concept of sharing and putting it into a more concrete context. Children can hear about someone else's experiences with sharing, discuss how they themselves would solve the problem, and give their opinions on how the character in the book goes about solving the problem. Krogh and Lamme (1983, p. 191) suggest asking questions such as:

- Do you have a toy (or whatever fits the story) you don't like to share?

- How do you feel about sharing?

- How do you feel the boy in our story felt after he decided to share?

• How do people feel when they share?

Many methods have been developed for helping children learn appropriate and satisfying social skills. Several of the articles and books listed for further reading at the end of the unit contain positive methods for helping children develop social skills.

GIVING SUPPORT IN TIMES OF CRISIS

An important responsibility for adults in the child's affective development is helping the child through crises. In Unit 27 we looked at children's emotional development. Among the areas considered were fear, anxiety, and stress. Whereas moderate amounts of each of these can be motivational, large amounts can be detrimental to the child's functioning. Children's concepts of death and fears regarding war were discussed. In our modern fast-paced culture children also have to cope with many changes that center on the family. Events such as moving, divorce, mothers going out to work, and other immediate social changes can be traumatic for the young child (Sunal & Hatcher, 1985). Young children may have difficulty understanding and discussing these traumatic events. Crisis-oriented books can be used to help young children through these experiences (Sunal & Hatcher, 1985; Jalongo, 1983) just as they can be used as instructional support for social skills. Several resources for crisis-oriented children's books are included in the further reading section at the end of this unit.

LISTENING TO CHILDREN

Crucial to the adult role in affective development is listening closely to the children. Adults need to be observant and attentive. In the book *Listen to the Children* (Zavitkovsky, Baker, Berlfein, & Almy, 1986), a series of anecdotes with accompanying photographs and analyses are presented centering on five areas for listening: (1) when they (the children) trust an adult to understand, (2) developing self-control, (3) figuring things out, (4) interacting with others, and (5) listening to parents. Each anecdote and ac-

companying commentary and questions to consider provides powerful food for thought for the adult who works with young children. For example in "Hit him!" (p. 16) the teacher explains that even though Kevin is angry with Greg, he must use words, not fists, to express his anger. Then she asks Kevin what he would like to do. He responds, "Hit him!" and that is exactly what he does. This story reminds us of how careful we must be in what we do and say. The author of the commentary suggests that the teacher should have gone a step further and had Kevin come up with a solution (other than hitting). She points out that children can be very clever and creative in solving their own problems and are more likely to live with a solution they have developed themselves. In "I just helped her cry" (p. 38) a young boy explains to his mother that when his friend's doll broke he could not fix it but he could help her cry. The incident reflects this boy's developing understanding of another's feelings and how he can help. As reflected in this collection of delightful and touching anecdotes, most of the affective curriculum is based on spontaneous, unplanned events, the adult's sensitivity to what the children mean and what they feel, and ability to respond in a sensitive manner.

Teachers also need to spend more time listening to and reflecting on their own thoughts and behaviors (Bowman, 1989). Young children are easily hurt and embarrassed by sarcastic and insensitive remarks and actions, especially when they are shamed in front of their peers or in the presence of other adults. It is very important for teachers and other adults who work with young children to be reflective practioners.

SUMMARY

The adult has a variety of roles in the child's affective development. Love and affection giving, early experiences, discipline, and teaching social skills and values are all critical areas that enter into affective development. Love is built on a foundation of acceptance and respect. Inner feelings are more important than outward behaviors. Once the inner feelings have been established, the observable expressions of love come spontaneously.

Positive responses from other people are necessary for normal affective development during early childhood. These responses must begin at birth for optimum development to occur. As children develop beyond infancy, they must learn self-control. Self-control comes about through the techniques of discipline used by adults to help children learn the difference between appropriate and inappropriate behavior. An authoritative approach to discipline where demands are high but where there is warmth and reinforcement for independent behavior seems to be most effective. Punishment may have an immediate effect on stopping an unwanted behavior but it has no long-term positive effects. Harsh punishment may even be harmful by presenting an aggressive model for the child to imitate when solving problems.

To combat the increasingly violent nature of our society, it is suggested that preventive teaching be done using positive guidance approaches such as teaching for democracy, teaching nonviolent techniques for solving problems, and creating a moral classroom. These techniques all include discussion, reflection, negotiation strategies, and other positive ways to resolve conflict. Children with good positive social skills are most likely to feel good about themselves. Social skills can also be taught through shaping, modeling, and coaching.

There are affective aspects reflected in all adult/child interaction. Although we may look at cognitive and affective development as separate areas for purposes of study, in reality they are interrelated and need to be recognized as such by adults who work with young children. The affective curriculum comes mostly from day-to-day incidents. Adults need to be

FOR FURTHER READING

Charles, C. M. (1992). *Building classroom discipline: From models to practice* (4th ed.). White Plains, NY: Longman.

Hewlett, B. S. (Ed.). (1992). *Father-child relations: Cultural and biosocial contexts.* New York: Aldine de Gruyter.

Honig, A. S., & Wittmer, D. S. (1991). *Prosocial development: Caring, helping, and cooperating: A resource guide for parents and professionals.* New York: Garland.

Hoot, J. L., & Roberson, G. (Eds.). (1994). Creating safer environments for children in the home, school, and community [Special issue]. *Childhood Education, 70.*

Katz, L. G., & McClelland, D. E. (1991). *The teacher's role in the social development of young children.* Urbana, IL: ERIC/EECE.

Malm, K. (1992). *Behavior management in K-6 classrooms.* Westhaven, CT: National Education Association.

Paley, V. G. (1993). *You can't say, "You can't play".* Cambridge, MA: Harvard University Press.

Phinney, J. S., & Rotheram, M. J. (1987). *Children's ethnic socialization.* Newbury Park, CA: Sage.

Powell, D. R. (Ed.) (1988). *Parent education as early childhood intervention.* Norwood, NJ: Ablex.

Sinclaire, C. (1994). *Looking for home: A phenomenological study of home in the classroom.* Albany, NY: SUNY Press.

Positive Guidance: Books

Baker, K. R., Gardner, P., & Mahler, B. (1987). *Early childhood programs: A laboratory for human relationships* (8th ed.). New York: Holt, Rinehart, and Winston.

Cherry, C. (1981). *Think of something quiet.* Belmont, CA: David S. Lake.

Cherry, C. (1983). *Please don't sit on the kids.* Belmont, CA: David S. Lake.

Clemens, S. G. (1983). *The sun's not broken: A cloud's just in the way.* Mt. Rainier, MD: Gryphon House.

Goffin, S. G., & Vartuli, S. (Eds.) (1987). Teacher as a decision maker [Special edition]. *Dimensions.*

Feeney, S., Christensen, D., & Moravcik, E. (1991) (4th ed.). *Who am I in the lives of children?*. New York: Merrill.

Hildebrand, V. (1990) (4th ed.). *Guiding young children*. New York: Macmillan.

Marion, M. (1995). *Guidance of young children* (4th ed.). New York: Merrill/Prentice-Hall.

Miller, D. F. (1990). *Positive child guidance*. Albany, NY: Delmar.

Positive Guidance: Articles

Bailey, S., & Osborne, S. (1993). Guiding children's behavior: The issue of compliance. *Day Care and Early Education*, *21*(2), 4–8.

Betz, C. (1994). Beyond time-out: Tips from a teacher. *Young Children*, *49*(3), 10–14.

Dinwiddle, S. A. (1994). The saga of Sally, Sammy and the red pen: Facilitating children's social problem solving. *Young Children*, *49*(5), 13–19.

Gottschall, S. M. (1992). Guns, ghosts, and monsters: Menace or meaning in aggressive play? *Day Care and Early Education*, *20*(2), 14–16.

Heath, H. E. (1994). Dealing with difficult behaviors–Teachers play with parents. *Young Children*, *49*(5), 20–27.

Marian, M. (1993). Responsible anger management: The long bumpy road. *Day Care and Early Education*, *20*(3), 4–8.

Stone, J. (1993). Caregiver and teacher language–Responsive or restrictive? *Young Children*, *48*(4), 12–18.

Thinking about aggressive play [Special section]. (1992). *Young Children*, *48*(1).

Wakefield, A. P. (1994). Letting children decide: The benefits of choices. *Dimensions of Early Childhood*, *22*(3), 14–16.

Wittmer, D. S., & Honig, A. S. (1994). Encouraging positive social development in young children. *Young Children*, *49*(5), 4–12.

Helping With Crises, Fears, and Feelings

Carlson-Paige, N. & Levin, D. E. (1986). The Butter-Battle Book: Uses and abuses with young children. *Young Children*, *41*(3), 37–42.

Crase, D. R. (1986). IDEAS! Helping young children deal with death. *Dimensions, 14*(3), 15–18.

Essa, E., & Murray, C. I. (1994). Research in review. Young children's understanding and experience with death. *Young Children*, *49*(4), 74–81.

Fleisher, P. (1985). Teaching children about nuclear war. *Phi Delta Kappan, 67*, 215–217.

Gottschall, S. (1989). Understanding and accepting separation feelings. *Young Children*, *44*(6), 11–16.

Hildebrand, J. M. (1994). Books for children. Books about children and their problems. *Childhood Education, 70*, 305–307.

Jalongo, M. R. (1983). Using crisis-oriented books with young children. *Young Children*, *39*(2), 64–74.

Jalongo, M. R. (1983). When young children move. *Young Children*, *40*(6), 51–74.

Kleckner, K. A., & Engel, R. E. (1988). A child begins school: Relieving anxiety with books. *Young Children*, *43*(5), 14–18.

Lamme, L. L., & McKinley, L. (1992). Creating a caring classroom with children's literature. *Young Children*, *48*(1), 65–71.

MacIsaac, P., & King, S. (1989). What did you do with Sophie, teacher? *Young Children*, *44*(2), 37–38.

Miller, H. L. (1987). Helping kindergartners deal with death: A teacher's response. *Childhood Education, 64*, 31–32.

Riley, S. S. (1989). Pilgrimage to Elmwood Cemetry. *Young Children*, *44*(2), 33–36.

Rogers, F., & Sharapan, H. B. (1991). Helping parents, teachers, and caregivers deal with children's concerns about war. *Young Children*, *46*(3), 12–13.

Skeen, P. (1983). Stepfamilies and relationships. *Dimensions, 11*(2), 23–24.

Skeen, P., Robinson, B. E., & Flake-Hobson, C. (1984). Blended families: Overcoming the Cinderella myth. *Young Children*, *39*(2), 64–74.

Theilheimer, R. (1990). Books for children: Family feelings. *Day care and early education, 18*(2), 47–48.

Van Cleaf, W. W., & Martin, R. J. (1986). Seuss's Butter Battle Book: Is there a hidden harm? *Childhood Education, 62*(3), 191–194.

Wolfle, J. (1987). Children shouldn't die—But mine did: A parent's response. *Childhood Education, 64*, 29–31.

SUGGESTED ACTIVITIES

1. Think back to your childhood. What can you remember about your need for love and affection? Do you feel you were loved and respected? Did you receive love and affection through outward demonstrations such as hugging, kissing, tickling, and holding? Would you characterize your family as very warm, moderately warm, or on the cool side when it comes to expressing affection? How do you express love and affection? Is it easy and spontaneous for you? Do you feel your needs are being fulfilled? How would you react if you were a teacher and one of the children clung to you and demanded constant attention? How would you feel if a child you really liked seemed to freeze every time you came near him? Write a short essay (two or three pages) on your feelings about love. Share your ideas with a small group in class.

2. Read an article or book on early emotional or social experience. Write a short review and reaction to the article including:
   a. title and author
   b. publisher and title of journal or book
   c. date of publication and pages
   d. a statement of the author(s) main message
   e. List the subpoints the authors presented to support the main message.
   f. What did you learn from reading this article (or book)? How does the information relate to your own experience and other things you have read? Was the article of value to you? Why?
   g. Develop three discussion questions. Use the questions as a guide as you lead a small group discussion in class.

3. Observe a preschool, kindergarten, or first grade teacher for 60 minutes. Write down everything she does. Write a running description of what you observe. Find all the teacher actions that you could categorize as disciplinary approaches as defined in the unit. Categorize each approach by using the categories outlined in Figure 30–2. Which kinds of techniques did this teacher use most often? How would you evaluate the skill of this teacher in the area of discipline? Do you feel the children were learning right from wrong? Self-control? Get together with other students in class who have done the same activity. Compile your data. Make an outline of the categories on chart paper (or on the chalkboard) and hang it on the wall. See if the same trends hold true when all the frequencies are added together. What does the chart tell you about disciplinary techniques used by the teachers?

4. Interview four sets of parents of young children. Ask them how they define discipline. Ask them what kinds of methods they use. Compare your results with those obtained by the students described in the unit. What conclusions can you draw regarding parents' views and techniques of discipline? Compare your results with those of other students who may have done the same activity.

5. Have you ever heard the expression, "Practice what you preach"? Observe a teacher for two or three 60-minute periods. Fill out a form like the following one with information on what you observed the teacher doing. Then have the teacher fill out the form. Compare your responses with the teacher's. Were there any discrepancies? Would you say this teacher follows the expression above? If not, what are the differences between what the teacher says and actually does?

WHAT DO YOU VALUE IN THE AFFECTIVE AREA: A SELF-CHECKLIST

Mark each item as it applies to you and your teaching.

A = Always   F = Frequently   S = Sometimes   O = Occasionally   N = Never

	A	F	S	O	N
(1) I accept children's feelings, both positive and negative.					
(2) I reinforce physical independence; that is, I give children opportunities to do things for themselves.					
(3) I reinforce emotional dependence by giving children all the affection and attention they need.					
(4) When a child is afraid, I try to comfort him and help him find a way to cope with his fear.					
(5) When a child is angry, I try to help him find a way to handle his angry feelings without making him feel that it is wrong to be angry.					
(6) I consciously try to make my classroom and my actions not be those which encourage sex-role stereotypes.					
(7) When children ask about the parts of the body or about reproduction, I give them honest but simple answers based on their level of understanding.					
(8) I try to help the children develop self-esteem and a positive self-concept.					
(9) I respect the children's cultures: their customs and their behaviors.					
(10) I encourage good peer relationships and opportunities for peer interaction.					
(11) I provide settings for dramatic play and give the children help in developing more mature levels of play interaction.					
(12) I discuss rules and expectations with the children, providing the reasons for all limits and restrictions.					

6. Obtain an early childhood storybook that deals with a potential crisis or social problem situation that young children might face such as moving, starting school, sharing, death, sibling rivalry, or joining a blended family. See the resource list under Further Reading.

The children's librarian can also help you. Most libraries have lists of crisis-oriented children's books. Read the book to a small group of preschool or kindergarten students. Discuss the book with them, asking questions regarding what they think about the characters, their feelings and their actions. Find out if any of them have had experiences like those in the story. How did they solve their problem? Discuss the children's responses in class.

7. Make an entry in your journal.

REVIEW

A. Write the number of each correct statement.

1. Outward expressions of love such as tickling, hugging, and squeezing are the most important of the components of the adult/child affectional relationship.

2. The emotional aspects of affection (what the person feels) may be more important than the outward expression of affection.
3. The child's need for love is a feeling of emptiness he has which needs to be filled in order for him to feel competent and complete.
4. Usually an adult will be able to emphathize and feel the same feelings the child feels.
5. It is uncommon for an adult to feel ambivalent about expressing his feelings to a child.
6. The adult who achieves success in working in the affective area with young children is one who works through his personal feelings outside of the school setting with other adults.
7. Love cannot be turned on and off whenever one feels like it: it is spontaneous and natural.
8. Love and affection are not essential to a positive adult/child relationship; acceptance and respect are equally, if not more, important.

B. Decide whether the disciplinary technique(s) used in each of the following examples are power assertive (physical punishment, shouting, threats, or physical inhibition); psychological (love withdrawal or induction); modeling (observational learning or modeling statements); or reinforcement.
1. "I can't stand it when you do that. I'm going in the other room until you can behave yourself."
2. "Mary and Janie, you are picking up the toys and putting them away in the right places. You're good workers."
3. "The children at Johnny's table are sitting up nicely and look like they are ready to eat."
4. "Larry! How could you make such a mess! Now you get a spanking and if you ever do this again you'll get an even harder spanking."
5. "I just can't let you pick up that hot kettle. It's too big and heavy and you may burn yourself. If you would like to cook, we have plenty of other pans your size."
6. Jack watches as Isabel is praised by the teacher for washing out paintbrushes. Jack then proceeds to do the same.
7. "You didn't clean up your room. No TV for you tonight."

C. What is the advantage of using the inductive method for discipline?

D. Describe the negative effects of corporal/harsh punishment.

E. According to the Piagetian view of discipline, what is the advantage of adult and child exchanging viewpoints and allowing children to make their own decisions?

F. Match the characteristics in Column I to the parenting approaches listed in Column II.

Column I	Column II
1. This type of technique produces the most mature children.	a. authoritative
2. The children whose parents use this type of technique tend to be the most immature.	b. authoritarian
3. The children whose parents used this technique always seem to know what their parents expect without being told.	c. permissive
4. Boys reared under this type of parenting approach tend to be low on competence while girls are very high on competence.	d. harmonious
5. Children of these parents are independent, competent, and assertive.	
6. These parents are not very nurturant or sympathetic and use threats.	
7. The children of this type of parent are likely to be discontented, withdrawn, and distrustful.	
8. These parents use withdrawal of love or ridicule as punishment techniques.	
9. These parents tend to be very well educated.	
10. This method seems to be the most positive overall according to Baumrind.	

G. Which disciplinary methods are considered positive approaches according to the text?

H. Select the correct answer to the following. There is only one correct answer for each.
1. "If you want to play in the sandbox with the other children, you have to take turns and share the trucks and cars." This is an example of
    a. shaping.   b. modeling.   c. coaching.
2. Rudy is an isolate. He never plays with any other children. Mrs. Chen takes some movies of the other children playing. One day she takes Rudy to another room and shows him the film. She points out some of the social skills used by the other children. This is an example of
    a. shaping.   b. modeling.   c. coaching.
3. "Let's think about what cowboys do. Anyone have any ideas?" Yes, they ride horses and herd cows." "Now" let's pretend we are cowboys." This is an example of
    a. shaping.   b. modeling.   c. coaching.
4. Bill has been engaged in solitary play only. One day he moves close to a group and looks on as they play. Mr. Brown smiles at him and pats him on the shoulder. Bill begins to spend more time near other children observing. This is an example of
    a. shaping.   b. modeling.   c. coaching.

I. Mrs. Ramirez learns that Kate is going to have her appendix out. She finds a book about a little girl name Madeleine who also has her appendix removed. She plans to read it to Kate and discuss it with her. Is this a good idea? Why?

J. Mrs. Harper goes through the values self-checklist included in the suggested activities section of this unit. She rates herself either *always* or *frequently* on each item. You observe her as she works with the children in her family day-care home. The following describes what you observe. Decide if Mrs. Harper's beliefs are consistent with her practices. Tell the reasons for your answers.

   The children are engaged in play activities. Two children are playing house and dressing up in grown-up clothes. They are the mother and father and have a baby doll who they refer to as "Baby Mindy." Both children are girls. "Mrs. Harper, Mrs. Harper," says the girl playing Mother, "How do the babies get in the mothers' tummies?" Mrs. Harper looks embarrassed and says, "That's something you should ask your Mommy." Sally wants to go to the bathroom. She starts in the door but stops and runs to Mrs. Harper. "Please turn the light on in the bathroom for me; it's dark and scary." "Okay," says Mrs. Harper, "but let me show you, you can reach around from outside like this and turn it on yourself." Mrs. Harper notices that Pete is trying to feed the bird. Birdseed is falling on the floor. Mrs. Harper says, "Pete, I know it's your turn today, but I can't let you do it when you are so messy."

K. Think about the following statement: "The affective curriculum can be planned in a developmental sequence just like the psychomotor and the cognitive." Is this true? Explain your response.

L. Explain what is meant by preventive discipline/guidance approaches.

Section

VIII

The Primary Child: Making the Transition from Preschool to Primary

Making the connection from preschool to primary is the focus of much concern. A major element in this concern is the concept of **READINESS**. In 1989 President Bush and the members of the National Governors' Conference adopted the goal "by the year 2000, all children will start school ready to learn." This statement has generated a great deal of response. To clarify the implications of the stated national goal and define **READINESS**, the National Association for the Education of Young Children issued a position statement on school readiness that is included as the introduction to this section. [NAEYC Position Statement on School Readiness (1990). *Young Children, 46*(1), 21–23. Used with permission.]

NAEYC POSITION STATEMENT ON SCHOOL READINESS
Adopted July 1990

PREAMBLE

State and local efforts for educational reform and improved accountability have prompted considerable concern regarding children's "readiness" to enter kindergarten and first grade. The issue gained national prominence when the President and the nation's governors adopted it as a national education goal, vowing that "by the year 2000, all children will start school ready to learn." The construct of school readiness is based on the assumption that there is a predetermined set of capabilities that all *children need before entering school. Therefore, any discussions of school readiness must consider at least three critical factors:*

1. *the diversity and inequity of children's early life experiences;*
2. *the wide range of variation in young children's development and learning; and*
3. *the degree to which school expectations of children entering kindergarten are reasonable, appropriate, and supportive of individual differences.*

POSITION

The National Association for the Education of Young Children (NAEYC) believes that those who are committed to promoting universal school readiness must also be committed to

1. addressing the inequities in early life experience so that all children have access to the opportunities which promote school success;
2. recognizing and supporting individual differences among children; and
3. establishing reasonable and appropriate expectations of children's capabilities upon school entry.

The current construct of readiness unduly places the burden of proof on the child. Until the inequities of life experience are addressed, the use of readiness criteria for determining school entry or placement blames children for their lack of opportunity. Furthermore, many of the criteria now used as readiness measures are based on inappropriate expectations of children's abilities and fail to recognize normal individual variation in the rate and nature of development and learning. NAEYC believes it is the responsibility of schools *to meet the needs of children as they enter* and to provide whatever services are needed *in the least restrictive environment* to help each child reach his or her fullest potential.

Every child, except in the most severe instances of abuse, neglect, or disability, enters school ready to learn. However, all children do not succeed in school.

A lack of basic health care and economic security places many children at risk for academic failure before they enter school. Families who lack emotional resources and support are likewise not always capable of preparing their children to meet school expectations.

It is a public responsibility to ensure that all families have access to the services and support needed to provide the strong relationships and rich experiences that prepare children to succeed in school. At a minimum such services include basic health care, including prenatal care and childhood immunizations; economic security; basic nutrition; adequate housing; family support services; and high-quality early childhood programs.

Supporting families' childrearing efforts is critically important for ensuring that more young children enter school ready to succeed. But, such efforts address only half of the problem. Attention must also be given to ensuring that the expectations used to determine readiness are legitimate and reasonable.

Expectations of the skills and abilities that young children will bring to school must be based on knowledge of child development and how children learn. A basic principle of child development is that there is tremendous normal variability both among children of the same chronological age and within an individual child. Children's social skills, physical development, intellectual abilities, and emotional adjustment are equally important areas of development, and each contributes to how well a child does in school. Within any group of children, it is likely that one child will possess exceptional language and social skills, but be average in physical development and emotionally less mature than is typical of the age group. Another child may have excellent skills in large and small muscle control but be less advanced in language abilities. Other children will present still different configurations of development. When readiness expectations are based on a narrow checklist focusing on only one or two dimensions of development, the complexity of growth is ignored and completely normal children may be judged inadequate.

Wide variability also exists in the rate of children's growth. The precise timing of when a child will achieve a certain level of development or acquire a specific skill cannot be predicted, nor does development and learning occur in a uniform, incremental fashion. Raising the legal entry age or holding an individual child out of school a year are misdirected efforts to impose a rigid schedule on children's growth in spite of normal differences.

A prevalent, fundamental misconception is that children's learning occurs in a sequential, hierarchical process and that certain basic skills must exist before later learning can occur. This misconception is the basis for requiring acquisition of such isolated skills as recognizing upper and lower case letters, counting to 20, or coloring within the lines prior to school entry. In fact, children's acquisition of higher order thinking processes and problem-solving abilities occurs in tandem with and may outpace acquisition of basic skills. For example, children are able to comprehend and compose far more complex stories than they can read or write. To focus only on sounding out letters or forming letters properly on the lines ignores children's complex language capabilities and often squelches their burgeoning interest in reading and writing. This does not mean that the acquisition of basic skills is unimportant; rather, focusing solely on isolated skills deprives children of the meaningful context that promotes effective learning.

Because learning does not occur in a rigid sequence of skill acquisition and because wide variability is perfectly normal, it is inappropriate to determine school entry on the basis of the acquisition of certain skills and abilities. Schools may reasonably expect that children entering kindergarten will be active, curious, and eager to learn. They will know about themselves and will be interested in making new friends and sharing experiences with them. Although gaining in self-control, kindergarten children's enthusiasm will sometimes overwhelm them, as, for example, they call out an answer before the teacher calls on them. First graders, unless they have had extremely negative experiences in kindergarten, will also bring enthusiasm and curiosity to their work. Typical six-year-olds are gaining fine motor control, but for many, writing within narrow lines can still be difficult. Likewise, six-year-olds are gaining in their ability to move beyond their firsthand experiences to more abstract thought, but the here and now remains the most meaningful.

It is often assumed that tests exist to reliably determine which children are "ready" to enter school. Because of the nature of child development

and how children learn, it is extremely difficult to develop reliable and valid measures of young children's abilities. When tests are used to make decisions which have such considerable impact on children's lives as denial of entry or assignment to a special class, they must offer the highest assurance of reliability and validity. No existing readiness measure meets these criteria. *Therefore, the only legally and ethically defensible criterion for determining school entry is whether the child has reached the legal chronological age of school entry.* While arbitrary, this criterion is also fair.

The nature of children's development and learning also dictates two important school responsibilities. Schools must be able to respond to a diverse range of abilities within any group of children, and the curriculum in the early grades must provide meaningful contexts for children's learning rather than focusing primarily on isolated skill acquisition.

Today not only do many kindergartens and primary grades focus on skill acquisition in the absence of meaningful context, but the expectations that are placed on children are often not age-appropriate. Whether the result of parental pressures or the push to improve student performance on standardized tests, the curriculum has shifted. Children entering kindergarten are now typically expected to be ready for what previously constituted the first grade curriculum. As a result, more children are struggling and failing.

Even those children who have received every advantage prior to school entry find the inappropriate demands difficult to meet, often experiencing great stress and having their confidence as successful learners undermined. The potentially greatest danger lies in the lowered expectations of parents who see their children struggle or fail, since parental expectations are the most powerful predictor of children's later school success.

STRATEGIES FOR SCHOOLS TO SUCCEED WITH EVERY CHILD
Providing a Foundation for Later Learning

Children who come to school with a history of rich experiences—being read to frequently, going to the store with their own grocery list, dictating or writing letters to grandma, taking trips to the park or the zoo, and so on—have a rich background of firsthand experience upon which later learning can be based. These experiences depend on families having the time, energy, financial, and emotional resources. Given the growing numbers of young children who spend major portions of their day outside their home in early care and education settings, it is equally critical that all early childhood programs offer these types of rich experiences as well.

Early intervention services have been successfully devised to provide families with an array of comprehensive support services to help them provide the rich environment so critical for early learning. The federally funded Head Start program is the best-known example of this type of program; a number of states and communities offer variations on the theme with considerable success. Successful intervention efforts have several key elements:

1. they provide comprehensive services to ensure that a wide range of individual needs are met;

2. they strengthen parents' roles as first teachers;

3. they provide a wide array of firsthand experiences and learning activities either directly to children or through parent education.

Intervention efforts which include these critical elements are most likely to result in lasting improvements in children's achievement. Less successful are the too frequent remedial efforts in which children are drilled on isolated skills. Often, emphasis on drill and practice only causes these children to lag further behind their counterparts, because learning devoid of context is much more difficult to attain and to apply to new situations. Decontextualized learning activities lack any real meaning or challenge for the learner. Moreover, children whose background and experiences are not congruent with school expectations cannot call upon their own experiences to provide the needed context.

Making Schools Responsive to Individual Needs

Providing comprehensive services and family support to children prior to school entry will better prepare many children to succeed in school. Because of individual differences in development, however, there will always be variation in the skills and abilities of any group of children entering school. Schools and teachers must be able to respond to such variation by individualizing their curriculum and teaching practices.

Making schools more responsive to the needs of individual learners will require ensuring that teachers and administrators understand child development and how children learn. They must know how to plan and implement a developmentally appropriate curriculum that emphasizes child-initiated learning experiences as opposed to teacher lectures, small group as opposed to whole-group activities, integrated lessons as opposed to strict demarcations between subject areas, and active hands-on learning with a variety of materials and activities as opposed to drill and practice of repetitive seatwork. Rather than imposing rigid, lock-step distinctions between grades, schools must be able to offer continuous progress for children through the primary grades, recognizing that children's development timetables do not conform to the yearly calendar.

Making the necessary changes will require new resources and understanding. In addition to ensuring that teachers of young children have specialized training in child development and early education, class size should be reduced and additional adults available to ensure individualized instruction. Investments in classroom equipment and materials are also needed so that children have access to a wide array of materials and activities for hands-on learning.

The investment and commitment needed to ensure that every child enters school ready to succeed and that schools are ready to ensure their success will not be small. But, it is necessary. As we enter the 21st century, our human resources are our most precious commodity. For too long we have reserved educational achievement for the very few. We have used labeling and sorting mechanisms as a sieve and allowed too many children to fail. This nation can no longer afford such costly errors of omission. We must provide every child with the firm foundation so critical to school success and we must ensure that schools are prepared to meet the needs of individual children as they arrive at the school door. Only then will our nation be ready to enter the 21st century.

SOURCES FOR ADDITIONAL INFORMATION

Bredekamp, S. & Shepard, L. (1989) How best to protect children from inappropriate school expectations, practices, and policies. *Young Children, 44*(3), 14–24.

Bredekamp, S. (Ed.). (1987) *Developmentally appropriate practice in early childhood programs serving young children from birth through age 8 (expanded ed.).* Washington, DC: NAEYC.

Kamii, C. (Ed.) (1990). *Achievement testing in the early grades: The games grown-ups play.* Washington, DC: NAEYC.

National Association of Elementary School Principals. (1990). *Early childhood education and the elementary school principal: Standards for quality programs for young children.* Alexandria, VA: Author.

National Association of State Boards of Education (1988). *Right from the start: The report of the NASBE Task Force on Early Childhood Education.* Alexandria, VA: Author.

Shepard, L. A. & Smith, M. E. (1989). *Flunking grades: Research and policies on retention.* Lewes, England: Falmer Press.

Willer, B. & Bredekamp, S. (1990). Public Policy report. Redefining readiness: An essential requisite for educational reform. *Young Children, 45*(5), 22–24.

Unit 31

The Primary Child

OBJECTIVES

After studying this unit, the student should be able to:

- List the characteristics of a classroom setting that is developmentally appropriate for primary-level children.

- Analyze and evaluate the extent to which a primary classroom supports the development of young children.

- Identify the typical cognitive characteristics of six- through eight-year-old children.

- Explain how primary children move from the concrete to the symbolic.

- Explain the function and value of private speech.

- Recognize strategies commonly used by beginning readers.

- Explain the functions of writing and drawing in promoting self-esteem.

- Recognize the affective characteristics of primary-level children.

- Give an example of how social interaction can benefit children in primary classrooms.

- State how primary-level children might experience stress.

- Understand the important factors relevant to the development of self-esteem and moral development in primary years.

- Describe the adult role with primary children.

- List the important factors that affect level of achievement for primary-level children.

- Develop a vision of the ideal primary classroom setting.

In this unit we will look at some of the characteristics of the five- through eight-year-old children who are students in primary classrooms (grades one through three). Factors concerning the preschool-to-primary connection will be considered later in Unit 32. Let's look in on two primary-grade classrooms:

In Mr. Marcos' class we observe children in various learning centers. There is the soft buzz of conversation as they concentrate on their activities and projects. The class appears to include children of an unusually broad range of sizes. Mr. Marcos explains that at the primary level in this school children are randomly assigned to classes across the conventional grade levels. Only about one third of his students were new to him this year, the rest have been with him one or two years. As we look around the room we note some children are using dry lima beans to develop their own math problems. Another group is measuring the growth of their bean plants and recording the results on graphs. Still others are building unit block structures to house a variety of miniature farm animals and farm equipment. Mr. Marcos is working with a group that is drawing pictures and writing and/or dictating their own versions of *Jack and the Beanstalk* for a class book. Still others are in the library area looking at various fiction and nonfiction books about plants. We also notice that in all the centers children are helping each other.

Next, we go to another school in the same district. As we enter Ms. Brown's class, we are immediately struck by the difference in atmosphere. First, we note the silence as the children sit working at their individual desks. One group is filling in workbook pages, another has several ditto worksheets to complete, and a third sits with Ms. Brown taking turns reading from a basal. We note that some of the workbook and worksheet children do not seem to know what they are supposed to do but appear to be trying hard to look busy. The children with Ms. Brown who are waiting for a turn to read seem restless and bored. Ms. Brown explains that in this school, children are given a readiness test when they enter kindergarten and then are grouped homogeneously according to their test scores. This year she has the "lowest" group.

Which classroom is an example of developmentally appropriate practice? Which is an example of developmentally inappropriate practice? Relate these classroom practices to the developmental characteristics of primary-level children described in this and other units.

In the **primary grades** (one through three) we find children from ages five through eight. It is a period when development in the physical, cognitive, social, and emotional areas becomes integrated and all areas begin to work together in a coordinated manner (Allen & Marotz, 1994; Bredekamp, 1987). Gross motor skills are well developed and integrated with newly developed concrete operational cognitive skills enabling children to begin to play games that have rules and games that require complex combinations of motor skills. (See Unit 16.) Fine motor skills are also integrated with cognitive skills, as writing skills are refined and used to express inner thoughts. Perceptual development and cognitive development reach the point at which children can be expected to attain some expertise in conventional reading and connect concrete experiences in arithmetic with abstract symbols. Primary children usually have attained almost adultlike use of speech. Play is still an important activity for children. Both cognitive and social development continue to be supported through play. Children are into Erikson's stage of Industry versus Inferiority. (See Units 1 and 26.) Being productive is very important to primary children and they are deeply affected by experiences that make them feel inferior and unproductive.

School is a major aspect of the primary child's life. As the NAEYC guidelines suggest, instruction for primary children should fit their developmental characteristics (Bredekamp, 1987). For example, primary children are physically active. They find long periods of sitting still hard to handle. They still need to engage in active learning rather than passive kinds of activities. Cognitively, primary children are in the process of moving into concrete operations. They begin to be able to mentally manipulate objects but still need concrete experiences through which they can make the connections to symbols. Peers are of increasing importance and provide conversation and

primary grades

work partners. Primary children work well in small cooperative groups (Figure 31–1). In this period of industry versus inferiority, successful accomplishment of tasks provides feelings of self-esteem and self-worth as a basis for further development. Prior to this period children have learned the rules of appropriate and inappropriate behavior. Now adults must offer them support in achieving self-control through providing opportunities for independence and responsibility while providing necessary adult guidance. Inappropriate practices can destroy children's self esteem and their motivation to learn (Nuttals, 1993).

In this unit we will examine some of the cognitive and affective characteristics of primary children, the adult role with primary children, some sociocultural factors, and the place of schooling in their lives.

COGNITIVE CHARACTERISTICS

As already described, during the primary years young children pass through the transition period and enter the concrete operations period. As a result they begin to be able to handle more complex cognitive problems and to connect symbols with concrete experiences. In this part of the unit, examples of re-

Figure 31–1 **Primary children enjoy working together independent of adults.**

search on the primary level child's cognitive development will be described (Figures 31–2a and 31–2b).

Stipek and MacIver (1989) reviewed studies which looked at how children view their own intellectual competence. Preschool through first grade age children tend to focus on social behavior rather than academic achievement as the criteria for 'smartness.' That is, sharing is smart and hurting another child is not smart. Social relationships are more important than knowing the alphabet, or being able to count, read, or write. By second grade, children perceive work habits such as being neat and putting forth effort as indications of intelligence. Being good and following rules may also be seen as indicators of intellectual ability. By seven, children seem to understand the concept of effort and how it can affect success but do not perceive differences in ability as affecting success. By second grade, children begin to understand the concept of task difficulty, that is, a hard task is one that most children cannot do. However, the perception that ability is a stable trait does not seem to really take hold until the fifth or sixth grade when repeated failure causes task persistence to decrease.

According to Stipek and MacIver (1989) most younger children feel pretty good about their intellectual competence no matter how they actually perform. Young children seem to view their competence in terms of their successes rather than their failures. They appear to believe that with effort they will eventually succeed. Younger children are also very responsive to positive social reinforcement. That is, praise makes them feel more successful than stickers or other concrete rewards. Apparently praise is more salient to preoperational children who can process only one idea at a time. It seems children need to be well into concrete operations to be able to consider both praise and other forms of reward simultaneously. Younger children also tend to receive praise at face value whereas older children weigh it relative to the task they have accomplished. When symbols are used to denote success, younger children can relate to symbols such as stars and happy faces but not to letter grades. Letter grades do not seem to affect children's perception of ability until the third or fourth grade. This is probably because to really understand letter grades one has to be able to understand an ordinal scale.

(a) (b)

Figure 31–2 Now that this second grader is into concrete operations, he can accomplish multistep tasks. First, he weighs himself alone (a). Then he weighs himself with a bag of cans collected by the class as a recycling project (b). Finally, he will subtract his weight from his weight plus the weight of the cans to determine the weight of the cans alone.

For younger children, effort is a primary indicator of intellectual competence. Being a hard worker and practicing a lot is also being "smart." Comparisons with peers take on increasing importance during the primary grades. Preschoolers through second graders are inconsistent in the way they use information regarding how well others are doing. At some point in the period between third and fifth grade, comparison with peers takes on great importance. In summary, primary level students still respond to adult approval and to task success (whether easy or difficult) as criteria for their intellectual competence. Consequently, it is relatively easy to promote an atmosphere that enables them to feel good about themselves as learners.

Stipek and MacIver (1989) suggest several factors within the classroom setting that may account for the change in children's views of intellectual competence as children progress from preschool to primary to upper elementary. In a preschool usually any product is accepted if the child has demonstrated reasonable effort in working on it. As children proceed through the grades, they are give more tasks to complete that have either right or wrong answers. Their accomplishments with these tasks provide specific, concrete feedback. However, during the primary grades teachers emphasize good work habits and appropriate conduct so these aspects may appear more salient to the primary level child than actual academic performance. Stipek and MacIvers (1989, p. 535) conclude that educators should consider the way children evaluate intellectual competence at different ages and design "instructional practices that maximize self-confidence and positive motivation for children" for each age group. An important consideration is that cognitively, primary-level children are more similar to preschool and kindergarten children than to upper-elementary students. They still respond best and feel more confident in doing tasks that are open-ended and emphasize process rather than product. Their confidence can be eroded quickly by adult responses that indicate they are not making progress.

Primary children are gradually moving into connecting the concrete with the symbolic. The development of the concept of time provides a good example of how young children move from the concrete to the symbolic. As young children move from preschool to kindergarten and through the primary grades, they are expected to develop an understanding of clocks and time sequence. Studies by Friedman and Laycock (1989) and Friedman (1990) examined the development of children's concept of time and time sequence. The clock system is complex. It involves not only reading what the clock face has to tell us, but also developing a sense of time relationships (i.e. 2:00 PM or 10 minutes). In addition, the child must understand the meaning of time; such as, what usually happens at 5:00 and where does 5:00 fall in the course of the day? Further, children experience both analog clocks (traditional mechanical clocks) and digital clocks (electronic clocks). Friedman and Laycock (1989) found that digital time could be read with high accuracy by first graders and perfectly by second graders. On the other hand, the ability to read and understand analog clocks varied greatly. Whole hours could be read by first graders and half hours by second graders. Ordering activities into time sequence developed before being able to order clock times. By third grade children usually have some skill in reading analog time to the minute but even fifth graders may have some difficulty.

Friedman (1990) looked further into children's development of an understanding of the temporal patterns of daily activities. He found that from age four on, children have the ability to arrange daily activities in logical order. They were able to select which activities should come next after a target activity (such as, if it were breakfast time, they knew lunchtime would occur before bedtime). Placing events in reverse order was a more difficult task but could be done by six- and seven-year-olds. Friedman also examined children's understanding of the relative duration of activities (i.e., time needed for drinking a glass of milk compared with going to the grocery store); he studied their understanding of the duration of time between events, such as time between dinner and going to bed

or between waking up and eating breakfast. Again, by age four and five children demonstrate a knowledge of relative time duration. Friedman compares these results with research that has demonstrated that although young children can memorize the order of the days of the week and the months of the year they have difficulty in applying this knowledge. Friedman suggests that the frequent drilling on these name sequences may actually interfere with real understanding. These abstract concepts should be learned in the meaningful context of everyday experiences.

Bivens and Berk (1989) have done a longitudinal study of this development from first through third grade. Their observations support Vygotsky's theory that overt private speech gradually becomes internalized private speech during this period. Along with this internalization there also develops an increasing degree of physical self-control and an increase in on-task behavior. The interaction of private speech and increased physical control seem to facilitate each other's development and result in more appropriate school learning behavior. By third grade the cumulative effect of private speech use and increased self-control appears to be related to higher levels of achievement.

By fourth grade, children are usually expected to be able to read conventionally and apply their reading skills to the learning of content material such as social studies, science, English language arts, and mathematics. Developing literacy skills is a major focus of the primary educational program. A study by McIntyre (1990) provides a picture of how this development took place in a whole-language first-grade classroom where storybook reading by the teacher, with child involvement and interaction encouraged, took place on a daily basis. McIntyre observed these first graders during their independent reading time in the classroom reading center. The reading center contained over 1200 books from which the children could make independent selections. Children could read independently and/or with other students during a daily 60- to 90-minute reading and writing period. She found several strategies children used:

1. Reading the pictures with oral-like language. That is, as the children 'read' they used language that was more like conversation than like written storybook language.

2. Reading pictures with textlike language. The children used textlike language although the text is not exactly memorized.

3. Saving the text from memory. The children use the text language they remember and read in a chantlike rhythm. Their eyes are focused on the pictures rather than the print.

4. Reading the text from memory. The reader's eyes focus on the print as they read a familiar book from memory.

5. Reading the text, skipping words. Children read the words but skip so many words and pages that the story doesn't make any sense. The reader is looking for the familiar rather than reading for meaning.

6. Reading the text. The children actually read the text with minimal or no help.

7. Repeated reading. Children may repeat what another child has read or try to read along with the reader.

8. Browsing. No reading is going on but there is interaction with books such as flipping through them, carrying them around, fighting over a book, grabbing a book, or passing a book on to someone else.

Strategies 1 through 6 just described tend to be developmental but may be intermixed. The last two strategies were used by all the children observed throughout the course of reading development. These observations demonstrate how, under the right classroom conditions, first graders can become conventional readers following their natural developmental capabilities and strategies.

Besides exhibiting a natural readiness in learning to read, primary children are also eager authors. Anne Haas Dyson (1989) has documented in detail the worlds of child writers in her three-year study in a multicultural primary (kindergarten through grade three) Language Arts classroom. In this classroom writing was observed to grow out of the children's drawing and talking. Talking and drawing were the tools the children used initially to organize the world. Writing gradually became a part of their symbolic tool box. Dyson (1989) and Salyer (1994) emphasize the importance of the classroom as a community

where social interaction supports literacy development. Daily journal writing was an especially significant activity that afforded the children opportunities to express themselves freely. Experiences from home and school could be recorded. Children repeated themes that were the most salient to them. Their drawings and writings became more elaborate with each repetition. Unlike the often-observed rote repetition type of drill and practice that stifles children's initiative, this child-controlled repetition reflected increasing initiative and growing cognitive abilities. The children's writings reflected their increasing mastery of written language and the use of symbols. Writing also provided a vehicle for building self-esteem. This open-ended approach provided success for everyone at their own developmental level.

AFFECTIVE CHARACTERISTICS

The primary period is the gateway to increasing self-consciousness and sensitivity that reaches its peak in adolescence. Alan Shapiro (n.d.) in writing about the meaning of the daily sharing period (show and tell, bring and brag, or news time) when individual children have their time in the limelight in front of the whole class, presents examples of this sensitivity:

> It feels embarrassing when you go up front. You have to talk and you feel scared and frightened. (a female third grader) (p. 31)

> It feels crazy when you stand in front of the room . . . everybody looks at you. (female third grader) (p. 32)

While these children find getting up in front of the class a risky business, others find it an exciting and worthwhile experience:

> Oh, I like it because I like to tell about me and what I do, and what I have and what my cousins do. (male first grader) (p. 35)

> When they say things, I like to know what they say . . . and I say something and they know what I say. (female third grader) (p. 35)

It can be seen from these examples that the same type of activity results in different feelings for each child. We will look at the highlights of development during the primary grades in the areas of peer relationships, social interaction, self-esteem, and moral development.

Peer Relationships

Peer relationships become increasingly important during the primary years. Hart, McGee, and Hernandez (1993) review some of these factors. Peer popularity in grade school continues to be related to friendly approaches, nurturance giving, cooperation, conversation, and giving positive reinforcement just as it was during the preschool period. Both aggressive and withdrawn children are rejected by peers. Popular grade-school children engage in more cooperative play and less onlooker behavior when observed on the playground. As with younger children, group entry is accomplished most successfully by approaching the group silently, hovering, and then imitating the behavior of the group members.

Grade-school children (especially boys) enjoy rough-and-tumble play (R&T) and use it as a means to develop games with rules (Hart et al., 1993). R&T play also affords opportunities to improve social problem-solving skills. This appears to be an especially important factor for boys. Because R&T play serves an essential educational function, Pellegrini and Perlmutter (1988) suggest it is extremely important for elementary children to play outdoors or in large indoor spaces every day. The research indicates the longer the time periods are during which children are confined to sedentary activity, the longer recess time they need. Adequate recess time is especially important for aggressive children who need adult modeling and coaching to assist them in learning the difference between R&T play and aggression. Pellegrini and Smith (1993) have reviewed research that provides support for the cognitive and social values of recess.

Popular children seem to have a better grasp on the goals and strategies that are appropriate to peer situations (Hart et al., 1993). Unpopular children may actually believe that unfriendly strategies will result in social success. Further, unpopular children tend to misread cues from others and believe an attack is called for when actually the other child intended no harm (Hart et al., 1993). Popular children tend to generate more than one solution to a social

problem and make their selection after consideration of these alternatives.

Special attention has been paid to school-yard bullies (Olweus, D., 1991; Olweus, 1993; Roberts, 1988). The bully is a type of aggressive child who seems to gain satisfaction from doing physical and/or psychological harm to others. Most bullies are boys and use physical means to bully. Girl bullies tend to be verbal—taunting or excluding children from play groups. Bullies usually have a history of parental rejection and harsh discipline. They do what their parents have done to them. Television also provides aggressive models who win out. Bullies tend to always be on the defensive, believing that others are out to get them. Chances are good they will grow up to be abusive parents, abusive spouses, and have a 1 in 4 chance of having a criminal record by age 30. Roberts reports that experts agree that ignoring or punishing bullies will not solve the problem. They must be taught socially acceptable alternative actions and reactions to responding to their anger.

Loneliness is a problem for some primary-grade students (Hart et al., 1993). As early as first grade rejected children have been identified as feeling lonely. Loneliness may be related to behaviors such as aggression, disruptiveness, or shyness. Less accepted children tend to attribute their social failure to their own incompetence (rather than to traits of the rejector). Nonbehavioral factors such as physical attractiveness, social class, name, and handicapping conditions appear to affect popularity.

For grade school children, proximity is the major factor in friendship choice. Most of their closest friends live in their neighborhood. They usually have mixed-age friendships with skill levels, mutual interests, and social status being more important than age. Cooperation is the major factor in developing and maintaining friendships. When conflict does occur, friends are able to arrive at an agreement. Friends serve multiple functions for children: play, teaching, nurturance, intimacy, protection, and caregiving. They also support feelings of self-worth, provide companionship, pass on social norms, and serve as models of social skills (Hart et al., 1993).

In our multicultural society, the peer relationships of children from different ethnic groups placed in the same school setting are of interest. Howes and Wu

(1990) point out that school integration is based on the idea that everyday contacts between children from different ethnic groups will decrease stereotyped views.

Social Interaction: Benefits in the Classroom

As described in Unit 28, before entering the primary grades, children are developing a view of culturally acceptable sex-type roles. Further development takes place during middle childhood (ages 5 to 12 years). Serbin, Powlishta, and Gulko (1993) found evidence of both cognitive and affective development aspects of children's views of sex roles as they progress through middle childhood. General level of cognitive development was related to children's flexibility of views and knowledge about sex-role stereotypes. Affective aspects in terms of preferred roles, professions, and activities related to sex typing in the home. Affective and cognitive aspects were related in that children with flexible views about sex-typed roles were less sex typed in their stated preferences. During middle childhood, children tend to see their own sex group as having the most positive characteristics.

Children's natural interest in and attachment to peers can be a valuable factor in planning and organizing the primary classroom. It is apparent that opportunities for social interaction are necessary for normal social development (Figure 31–3). Currently, there is a rebirth of interest in using cooperative learning strategies in school (Ajose & Joyner, 1990). **Cooperative learning** can be defined as "the process whereby small, heterogeneous groups of students work together to achieve mutual learning goals." (Ajose & Joyner, 1990, p. 198) Students, usually in groups of two to four, are provided with a problem to solve. They are required to work together to arrive at a solution. Through cooperative learning, children gain in both cognitive and social skills and thus benefit more than in competitive or individualistic learning settings. Cooperative learning also provides a way to integrate children from different ethnic

groups and to integrate special needs children.

Figure 31–3 Primary children benefit from the social interaction that takes place as they do their daily activities.

Children like to invent board games. Castle (1990) describes the variety of games children invent. Game inventing puts children in a position of power as they decide on the game to invent, select needed materials, and set up the rules. This process provides a valuable educational experience as they use skills they have learned in school: writing (rules, game labels, etc.), arithmetic (scoring), and incorporation of theme or unit topics as the focus of the game. Working together on game development provides opportunities for cooperation, negotiation, and problem solving. Children learn how to resolve conflicts without relying on the teacher. Children enjoy working on and playing the games because they can talk and play with friends and do something interesting.

Stress

Stress continues to be a problem beyond the kindergarten level. The results of a study by Gonzali and Crase (1991) with upper-elementary grade children and adolescents indicated that academic stress and low self-concept were correlated. Children with moderate amounts of academic stress received better grades than those with the lowest or highest amounts of academic stress.

Hoffner (1991) looked at how children ages 6 to 11 years of age said they would react to six different stressful events: 1) having a cavity filled by the dentist; 2) being lost in the woods overnight; 3) flying in an airplane that might crash; 4) being locked in a dark basement; 5) having a cut stitched by a doctor; 6) believing that you failed an important test. Younger children and girls reported the most fear. The most-frequently mentioned coping strategies were reinterpretation (focusing mentally on the threat and using information to reevaluate it in a more positive way) and distraction (cognitive, think about something else, or behavioral, read, watch TV, etc.). Younger children tended to select behavioral and older children cognitive coping techniques.

Self-Esteem

During the primary-grade period as children enter concrete operations, they also enter the stage of industry versus inferiority. Primary children venture out into new social worlds (i.e., sports, lessons, hobbies) that contribute to their identities and their feelings of competence. However, school is the place where they spend the most out of home time. In school they meet the challenge of many new standards against which they evaluate themselves. Entering first grade they are expected to act with more autonomy and responsibility, be more mature, task-directed, and self-controlled (Curry & Johnson, 1990). Children become capable of comparing themselves with others and thus new possibilities open up for developing feelings of inferiority. Curry and Johnson (1990, p. 69) categorize four components of self-esteem: competence, power, acceptance, and virtuousness.

Looking at competence, young children, as noted by Stipek and McGiver (1989) earlier in the unit, are quite flexible in their beliefs about academic success. They begin school feeling smart and that hard work will pay off in success. Curry and Johnson (1990) point out that sometimes this extreme optimism can mask feelings of inferiority. Social-emotional maturity probably contributes to school success to a greater degree than self-expectations. The trend to try to fit children to the curriculum rather than the curriculum to the children impedes developing

feelings of competence. A number of means (such as changing the age of school entrance, keeping children out of school for an extra year, placing children in transition classes, and retaining children in kindergarten or first grade) have been employed to give children time to get ready. None of these means has shown overall success, especially when children are placed in classrooms that are boring and/or stressful. Adjusting the child's pace through the system does not compensate for inappropriate instructional practices (Curry & Johnson, 1990). Parents tend to have high expectations for their children's school success but may not have the skills to support their children's learning. Many teachers are aware of child development but tend to place too much weight on age and view immature children as learning disabled. Early educational experiences have been criticized for being "too demanding, too lax, or too insensitive" (Curry & Johnson, 1990, p. 76). By "too demanding" is meant the pushing down of academics to lower and lower levels so children are asked to perform in ways that are not developmentally appropriate. "Too lax" refers to a lack of challenge: spending a whole year on boring worksheets lacks intellectual excitement. "Insensitivity" refers to the lack of recognition of children's developmental needs: learning is presented as an isolated, passive activity rather than something that is intellectually and socially active.

According to Johnson and Curry (1990) power assessment is a critical component of self-esteem during middle childhood. Power is assessed relative to others and relative to an inner sense of power and control. When success is based on competitive comparisons, it can be hard on the ego. When success is based on hard work and doing your best through interest, effort, and collaboration, learners can develop feelings of power over their own accomplishments.

Peer rejection is one of the best predictors of later maladjustment. Children do not have to be extremely popular to feel accepted, but they do have to feel good about themselves.

Everyone needs a social place in the classroom but Curry and Johnson (1990) caution that shyness should not be confused with rejection. Shyness appears to be an inherited characteristic to some extent but also seems to be triggered by stressors in the environment (Cowley, 1991). Some children are just slower to warm up and if nurtured and allowed to move at their own pace, they will eventually enter social situations (Cowley, 1991).

Finally, virtue or moral worth is an important component of self-esteem (Curry & Johnson, 1990). School-age children evaluate themselves according to new standards of moral worth. Being good or bad in the classroom and being a nice friend are newly defined. Fairness is of primary concern. Moral development is discussed further in the next section of this unit.

Moral Development

According to Damon (1988) sharing is a very significant moral behavior that underlies children's understanding of distributive justice. The division of the world's goods is understood through the basic understanding of the concept of sharing that develops from the child's earliest naturally occurring interactions with others. By the elementary years children begin to have an objective idea about fairness. The first aspect of fairness that elementary children use regularly is equality. Their major concern is the concept of equal shares. Concerns with merit and benevolence as the basis of justice enter their thoughts during middle or late elementary school.

Damon (1988) explains that the most important aspect of moral development that the family contributes is respect for authority. A close affectionate attachment to parents is the strongest element in building respect for authority. Moral rules and values are introduced in the family in many different ways. Preschoolers obey because they have to, "I clean my room because my mother says I have to." As children get into middle childhood, obedience becomes a sign of respect for adults, "I clean my room because my mother wants me to and she is the person who cares for me."

According to Damon (1988) the peer group is the ideal setting for moral development. This is the only place where children interact with equals. Cooperative play in the peer group is necessary for the development of moral standards. It is in this setting that children try out the moral rules they have learned in the family. With friends fairness is natural. Children only realize the value of norms of fairness and honesty when they discover them in their social play.

Reciprocity, or give and take, is the primary norm of childhood. The standards learned through interaction with peers are the basis for lifelong moral standards. Truth and honesty are especially important components of children's friendships. As children become more skilled in perspective taking (seeing another's point of view), they become better able to act on their moral knowledge.

THE ADULT ROLE WITH THE PRIMARY-AGE CHILD

The overall role of adults with children of any age is to promote self-esteem and moral worth. Curry and Johnson (1990) describe six principles that underlie the development of children's self-esteem (pp. 91–95):

1. Adult feedback must be authentic. Praise must be given for real accomplishments. Too much empty praise can actually lower self-esteem. Too many stickers and/or comments such as "Good job" or "Well done" may cause children to rely on outside judgments rather than on their internal judgment of the quality of their accomplishments. Children need to learn to recognize and deal with their own errors and develop an acceptance that things do not always turn out as expected. When praise is given it should be specific, i.e., "The story you wrote is very interesting."

2. Adults and children need goodness of fit. Adults should work with children at a developmental level that they find interesting and challenging. Primary children are reaching for independence and for abstract ideas and need adults who can support these efforts.

3. Scaffolding supports autonomy. Adults must gauge the amount of support and challenge necessary for children's optimal growth.

4. Individuals are different. Adults must consider temperamental and cultural differences when working with children.

5. Self-esteem is multifaceted. Acceptance, power and control, competence and moral virtue must all be considered.

6. Children are resilient. Adults make mistakes and

children normally run into problems. Part of good mental health is learning how to deal with conflict and frustration through discovering solutions to the problems that life presents.

Damon (1988) suggests the following principles for fostering moral growth (pp. 117–119):

1. Moral awareness is built from within by children through natural encounters with their peers, not by imposition from outside.

2. Moral awareness is shaped by the natural encounters with others and the natural emotional reactions to these encounters. For example empathy supports moral compassion and prosocial behavior; shame, guilt and fear support obedience and rule following; and love for and attachment to adults supports respect for authority.

3. Through their relationships with adults children learn the social standards, rules, and conventions. "*Authoritative* adult-child relations, in which firm demands are made of the child while at the same time there is clear communication between adult and child about the nature and justification of these demands, yield the most positive results for the child's moral judgment and conduct."

4. It is through peer relations that children are introduced to norms of direct reciprocity and to standards of sharing, cooperation, and fairness. It is with peers that children can experiment and discover new ways of interacting with others.

5. Social influence shapes children's morality. This influence varies from culture to culture. However, every culture has some kinds of standards for values such as truth, human rights, human welfare, and justice.

6. "Moral growth in school settings is governed by the same developmental processes that apply to moral growth everywhere." That is, moral values are acquired through interaction with adults and peers, not through listening passively to lectures or lessons. Children learn democratic values by par-

ticipating in a democratic setting.

The context for children's full participation and moral learning is created by adults who "practice a **respectful engagement** with the child" (p. 119). Moral education is based on a cooperative relationship between adult and child. The adult must respect the children's initiatives and their reactions. The situation is not one of extreme permissiveness or strict authoritarian indoctrination. Adults should serve as models by openly discussing their feelings about moral issues that come up in their lives and discussing with children their reactions and feelings to the moral issues they face. Young children can gain experience in introspection and self-monitoring. They can also gain experience in recognizing and discussing the feelings of others. Finally, and most important, children must be given real and appropriate responsibilities through which they can learn what it means to be a responsible member of society (Figure 31–4).

Research on Parental Factors

Hart, Ladd, & Burleson (1990) looked at the relationships between maternal disciplinary styles, children's expectations of the outcomes of social

Figure 31–4 **Primary children develop moral development that is supported by opportunities to have real and appropriate responsibilities in the classroom.**

strategies, and children's peer status. The subjects were mothers of first and fourth graders and their children. Children of mothers who were more power assertive (authoritarian) were found to be less well accepted by their peers. They expected that aggressive assertive methods (such as threatening to hit another child) would solve social conflicts.

Cohen (1990) found that for first-grade boys maternal attachment was related to peer acceptance and teacher ratings of behavior. Boys who had less secure attachment relationships with their mothers were viewed by teachers and by peers as less socially competent. The results of both of these studies are consistent with the recommendations that parental love and an authoritative approach to discipline support positive social adjustment out of the home.

Some adults believe that yelling, speaking in a stern voice, and/or spanking will make children well behaved even though these methods do not have long-term positive effects on behavior. A study reported by Zambarano (1991) sheds some light on why shouting and physical punishment do not curb behavior effectively. Dramatized incidents were created with a parent and child involved in various situations in which child behavior needed to be changed. The incidents varied as to the tone of the adult voice (loud or soft) and as to whether the child was spanked or not spanked. The voice messages and to some extent the spanking behavior made it clear to adult and twelve-year-old viewers what the parent's message was. However, for the four- to eight-year-olds, the messages were not clear. While yelling and spanking may seem like clear messages to adults, this research indicates that for young children, speaking in a clear and careful manner gets the message over best. As described in Unit 30, inductive methods work best.

SOCIO-CULTURAL INFLUENCES ON CHILD DEVELOPMENT AND BEHAVIOR

Phinney and Rotheram (1987) express concern with the problems of ethnic socialization of children,

that is, the process of acquiring ethnic identity. Ethnic identity refers to the acquisition of ethnic group patterns. According to research described by Aboud (1987), children gradually learn to recognize members of other ethnic groups. By age seven, children begin to recognize that ethnicity is unchangeable but this doesn't seem to be stable knowledge until about age ten. Primary children are still in the process of attaining an understanding of their own ethnic identity and those of other groups.

Phinney and Rotheram (1987) describe several themes in ethnic socialization. First, different ethnic groups are distinguished not just by easily observed characteristics such as skin color, hair texture, food preferences, etc., but also by attitudes, values and behaviors. They believe it is important to help young children develop positive attitudes about these differences through positive interaction. Although biculturalism can be stressful, children can be helped to feel proud of being able to function well in two cultures. Second, young children perceive ethnicity in concrete ways. It is not until adolescence that children can consider the choices they have in terms of selecting an identity. Thirdly, when children are in the minority they are made very aware of this fact by their fewer numbers in a group and by the need to follow majority customs and rules. Majority children may be shielded from ethnic differences or see them in a stereotyped fashion. Finally, the environmental and sociocultural contexts influence children's ethnic socialization. Family and community factors are important influences. With an ever-increasing emphasis on pluralism, children from diverse cultures are more aware of their cultural heritage and hopefully majority children are becoming more aware of how diverse our society is.

McCracken (1993) points out several reasons we value the diversity that exists in our culture: because it is the right thing to do; because appreciation of each other will lead to a more harmonious world; and because it is illegal to discriminate. As primary children delve into content in more depth, it is essential to celebrate diversity making it a part of the total curriculum as suggested in the **anti-bias approach** (McCracken, 1993).

Phinney and Rotheram (1987) point out several implications of ethnicity for education. Multicultural education is very important. Learning about ethnic diversity and the promotion of interethnic relations must be expanded. Such programs need to fit the developmental levels and interests of children. Because young children learn by experience and think concretely, firsthand experience with members of other groups is essential. McCracken (1993) describes how the diverse primary curriculum should look.

Phinney and Rotheram (1987) point out that each cultural group needs to learn about its own culture to build personal self-esteem. In integrated settings interaction between ethnic groups will not necessarily just happen. Designing work groups that force children of different ethnic backgrounds to work together cooperatively has proven to be successful in promoting cross-ethnic interaction. Younger children select friends according to interests and are therefore the most open to cross-ethnic interaction.

Nelson-LeGall and Jones (1990) observed average achieving African-American third- and fifth-grade children as they worked on a multitrial verbal task. These researchers were interested in learning more about which factors influence African-American children to seek help when needed. When children thought they were responding correctly they did not seek help. When they believed their responses were incorrect, they tended to seek help. However, there was a difference in the kind of help sought. Academically confident children sought hints that would help them figure out the solutions on their own. Children who were not academically confident sometimes asked for hints and other times tried to get answers. Younger children were much less consistent about seeking help. This study provides normative information on average-achieving African-American children and their courses of action under conditions of perceived failure and perceived success. It shows that the African-American children studied did not give up under conditions in which they thought they were failing and sought help when needed.

Rotheram-Baron and Phinney (1990) compared patterns of social expectations among African-American and Mexican-American third- and sixth-grade children. These children were asked to respond to eight videotaped scenes of everyday social situations with same ethnic, unfamiliar peers in a school setting. Mexican-American children more frequently than African-American children, say Rotheram-Baron and Phinney, reported an expectation for sharing and for relying on adults when solving social problems. African-American children relied more on apologizing, getting angry, and initiating action than did their Mexican-American counterparts. For both groups, socially desirable responses increased and emotional responses decreased with age. The groups were more alike at the third-grade level than at the sixth. Girls tended to use apology more frequently than boys. Children with the highest self-esteem were the most similar to their own ethnic group. The authors suggest these differences in social expectations may account for a decrease in cross-ethnic friendships and increase in self-segregation as children move into higher grades. They recommend that these differences in reactions should be openly discussed as a part of the multicultural education program.

SCHOOL ACHIEVEMENT AND ADJUSTMENT

Of great concern to educators at all levels are the variable degrees of achievement of children from different ethnic groups and socioeconomic levels. Slaughter-Defoe, Nakagawa, Takanishi, and Johnson (1990) express concern that research promotes stereotypes of Asian-American students being more likely to fail and African-American students being more likely to be high achievers in school. They believe the research is at fault for not differentiating among subgroups with different cultural, language, immigration, and economic backgrounds. This point should be carefully considered when looking at the results of cross-cultural research on school achievement.

Cross-cultural comparison of school achievement has been of increasing interest to child development researchers. A few studies in this area will be briefly described. Patterson, Kupersmidt, and Vaden (1990) report the results of a study which looked at income level, gender, ethnicity, and household composition as predictors of children's competence in school. Their subjects were African-American and European-American elementary students enrolled in second through fourth grades. Household income level and gender were the best predictors of competence in conduct and peer relations. That is, boys and children from low-income homes were likely to be the least competent. Income level and ethnicity were the best overall predictors of academic achievement. Since African-American children were more likely to live in lower-income families they were also more likely to be among those with lower competence in school. A caution in looking at these results is a consideration of whether poverty, per se, causes lower achievement and more conduct problems or whether those who teach low-income children have a preconceived picture of these children as poor achievers and as lacking in appropriate school social skills.

Luster and McAdoo (1991) looked at a sample of six- to nine-year-old African-American children included in the National Longitudinal Survey of Young. More than half of these children would be considered to live in conditions that would put them 'at risk': born to mothers who are under 20 years old, live below the poverty line, and often have less than a twelfth grade education. Consistent with other studies, children who did well on the achievement tests had mothers who were relatively intelligent and well educated, lived in financially secure families with relatively small numbers of children, and had relatively supportive home environments. The likelihood of children having behavior problems in school was associated with a mother with low self-esteem and relatively low intelligence, low income level, large family size, low quality home environment, and absence of a male partner in the home. The results of this study show clearly that being African-American does not doom a child to school failure. It demonstrates the diversity among African-American children and documents that African-American children who live under conditions of low risk do well academically and have few behavior problems.

Another large-scale study on early school achievement and school adjustment is being done in the Baltimore (MD) City Public Schools (Entwisle & Alexander, 1990; Alexander & Entwisle, 1988). Alexander and Entwisle (1988) reported on a diverse sample of children who were studied during their first- and second-grade experience. African-American and European-American students began first grade with similar scores on the *California Achievement Test (CAT)* but the African-American students' score began to lag behind by the end of the first year. African-Americans also received lower grades on their report cards than European-Americans received. African-American children appeared to have more difficulty making the adjustment to grade school than did European-American children. Parents held beliefs about their children's achievement that were above what the children actually accomplished. European-American parents made better use of the information (test scores and report cards) that they received from the school in evaluating how well their children were progressing and could progress. In their 1990 report Entwisle and Alexander looked closely at the math competence of the students in their sample as measured by the *CAT* when the children entered first grade as compared with when they reached the end of first grade. At first grade entrance both the minority and the majority children tested about the same on verbal performance and math computation skills and were close on reasoning. By the end of first grade the majority students had moved ahead. The authors suggest that the effects of parents' psychological and material resources had a greater effect on school performance than did racial differences. Kindergarten attendance had a positive effect on entering-first-grade math skills and on first-grade attendance. These authors also suggest the possibility that something happens in the school setting that causes European-Americans to pull ahead and African-Americans to achieve at a slower rate during first grade.

The results of the LSU studies (Charlesworth, Hart, Burts & DeWolf, 1993) shed some light on a possible reason for the trend found by Entwisle and Alexander (1990). Charlesworth et al. (1993) found that African-American children who attended more developmentally appropriate kindergartens (DAP) did better than African-American children who attended less developmentally appropriate kindergartens (DIP). Twice as many stress behaviors were observed in the DIP kindergartens as in the DAP (Burts, Hart, Charlesworth, & Kirk, 1990; Burts, Hart, Charlesworth, Fleege, Mosley, & Thommason, 1992). A portion of the children observed in kindergarten were followed up in first grade to determine their academic status (Burts, Hart, Charlesworth, De-Wolf, Ray, Manuel, & Fleege, 1993). The results indicated the first graders who had attended the more developmentally appropriate kindergartens had higher reading grades on their report cards than students who had attended the less developmentally appropriate kindergartens. There were no significant differences in report card grades between the high and low SES children who had attended developmentally appropriate kindergartens whereas higher SES students had an advantage over the lower SES students if they had attended the more developmentally inappropriate kindergartens. Similar results were obtained for achievement test scores. Further, first-grade students who had attended the more developmentally inappropriate kindergartens were rated by their first-grade teachers as being more hostile and aggressive, more anxious and fearful, and more hyperactive and distractible than the children who attended the more developmentally appropriate kindergartens (Charlesworth et al., 1993). The results of these studies suggest that a DAP kindergarten experience can have positive effects on academic achievement and social behavior in the primary grades.

Fears centering on achievement are common from ages 6 to 11 (King and Ollendick, 1989). Estimates of text anxiety range from 10 to 30 percent of the school-age population. School phobia, depression, and other anxiety disorders are not uncommon among school-age children (King & Ollendick, 1989). Unfortunately, teachers often perceive behaviors that reflect anxiety as noncompliance. King and Ollendick (1989) suggest teachers can use teaching practices that are conducive to fear reduction. If the climate of the classroom is low-anxiety producing, students will be able to face fear-provoking situations with minimal anxiety. For example, some students (as shown in the unit introductory examples) fear speaking in front of others. These children should have other options for demonstrating their communication skills.

Fincham, Hokoda, and Sanders (1989) did a longitudinal analysis of learned helplessness, test anxiety and achievement. Children were studied in the third grade and then again in the fifth grade. Children who exhibit **learned helplessness** attribute failure to external factors rather than effect. They tend to do worse after each failure experience. Test-anxious children are those who experience unpleasant emotional feelings in the test situation and perform more poorly than children who do not have these unpleasant feelings. In their study Fincham et al. (1989) found that learned helplessness and achievement were positively related over time and that teacher ratings were accurate indicators of children's degrees of learned helplessness. Unlike previous investigations, they did not find that test anxiety was directly related to achievement test scores. They concluded that the measure of test anxiety they used was not a reliable one. The significant factor for those who work with primary children to be aware of is that learned helplessness is well established by third grade. This factor makes it even more important that primary teachers build on the young child's eagerness to learn and provide as many success experiences as possible through developmentally appropriate individualized instructional practices.

SCHOOLING

Looking back at the beginning of the unit note that Mr. Marcos' class with its active child involvement, individual and small group activities, and communication between students is appropriate for primary children (Figure 31–5). Ms. Brown's classroom, on the other hand, is developmentally inappropriate as children work individually and silently on abstract assignments. Charlesworth (1989) recommends multiage grouping and continuous progress for young children in kindergarten through the primary grades. Connell (1987) provides a delightful description of her ungraded primary classroom, which combined kindergarten and first and second grades and for which she designed a curriculum that fit the needs and developmental levels of the students.

A number of models have been designed for the

Figure 31–5 **In the developmentally appropriate primary classroom, students have time to explore activities at their own pace.**

primary level that can provide a developmentally appropriate educational experience. These include the can-do primary classroom (Wasserman, 1990), the whole-language primary curriculum (Raines, 1995), the moral classroom (DeVries & Zan, 1994), success for all, accelerated schools, and the school development program (King, 1994).

In her book *Schooling* (1990) Sylvia Farnham-Diggory presents an overview of the way our schools today are built on old theories of learning that do not incorporate our current knowledge about how children grow and develop and how they learn. She points out how the school reforms of the eighties were bureaucratic: tougher standards, more testing, homogeneous grouping, and a more fractionated skill and drill curriculum. Only in a few instances was attention paid to child development and to practices that better fit the curriculum to the students. Classrooms have become places in which children are forced to fit into a nonchildlike mold. Farnham-Diggory suggests a plan where schools become a place for a cognitive apprenticeship, "a place where people go to develop skills in learning to learn, problem solving, and the creative application of ideas" (p. 56). The apprenticeship model operates on several principles:

1. Human minds are designed for complex, situated learning. Human minds are designed to deal with rich environments which provide many concrete experiences that the mind can investigate and organize.

2. Education must begin where the student is.

3. Human learning is a social enterprise.

The teacher uses a variety of instructional techniques: modeling, coaching, scaffolding, articulation (summaries, critiques, or dialogues), reflection, and exploration. These are facilitative techniques; not didactic or 'pour in the knowledge' techniques. They open up the classroom to the students constructing their own knowledge. Here and there you will find individual teachers, small groups of teachers, and occasionally whole schools that have adopted developmentally appropriate practices and made them work.

SUMMARY

Developmentally, primary-grade children are in many ways more like kindergartners than they are like upper elementary students. They are still in the process of integrating the physical and motor, affective, and cognitive skills and concepts that developed during the preoperational periods and are just entering concrete operations. They still learn best through concrete experience which they are just beginning to associate with abstract symbols such as letters and numbers.

School is the center of existence for primary children. They are still at a level in which they believe they can learn no matter what their native ability, socioeconomic status, and ethnic group. They respond best to open-ended tasks and activities. One right-answer kind of task to which they may not respond correctly can quickly bring upon feelings of failure. Learning reading, writing, and arithmetic naturally provides the success that will support them in later schooling.

Primary-level children are entering a period of self-consciousness that peaks in adolescence. Peer relationships are very important to them; more important than academics. Opportunities to interact in the classroom can enhance learning and build social skills that can only be learned through the give-and-take of interaction with peers.

Self-esteem continues to develop as children enter

the period of industry versus inferiority. They meet new standards for maturity when they enter first grade. As they measure themselves against these standards, new avenues open for developing higher or lower levels of self-esteem depending upon how they perceive themselves relative to their peers. Children need to feel competent, powerful, socially accepted, and morally worthy. Moral worth is an extremely important part of self-esteem. Moral worth is measured according to such attributes as good and bad, meeting social standards, degree of concern for others, caring, benevolence, kindness, mercy, justice and fairness, honesty, and reactions to moral violations such as shame, guilt, outrage, fear, and contempt. Adults have the responsibility of providing an environment that promotes self-esteem and moral worth. Adults need to be appropriate models who show respect for the children.

A growing body of research supports the value for child development of an authoritative parental discipline style. Physical punishment and yelling do not send clear messages to young children and have no lasting positive effects on their behavior.

Socio-cultural influences continue to be vital considerations relative to child development. Primary children are still in the process of attaining an understanding of their own ethnic identity and those of other groups. Multicultural education continues to be a necessary component of the school environment and curriculum. Current research is breaking down many of the ethnic group stereotypes relative to school achievement. Risk factors such as low socioeconomic status are damaging to children from any ethnic group.

Our approach to schooling for primary children is in need of reform. Developmentally appropriate instructional practices are gradually taking hold but the

FOR FURTHER READING

Alexander, K. L., Entwisle, D. R., & Dauber, S. L. (1993). First-Grade classroom behavior: Short- and Longterm consequences for school performance. *Child Development, 64*, 801–814.

Anglin, J. M. (1993). Vocabulary development: a Morphological analysis. *Monogr. of the Society for Research in Child Development, 58* (No. 10, Serial No. 238).

Foyle, H. C., Lyman, L., & Thies, S. A. (1992). *Cooperative learning in the early childhood classroom*. Westhaven, CT: National Education Association.

Fuller, B., & Clarke, P. (1994). Raising school effects while ignoring culture? Conditions and the influence of classroom tools, rules, and pedagogy. *Review of Educational Research, 64*, 119–158.

Gullo, D. (1992). *Developmentally appropriate teaching in early childhood: Curriculum, implementation, evaluation*. Westhaven, CT: National Education Association.

Kasten, W. C., & Clarke, B. (1993). *The multi-age classroom: A family of learners*. Katonah, NY: Owen.

Katz, L. G., & Chard, S. C. (1989). *Engaging children's minds: The project approach*. Norwood, NJ: Ablex.

Krogh, S. (1995). *The integrated early childhood curriculum* (2nd ed.). New York: McGraw-Hill.

Lee, V., & Das Gupta, P. (Eds.). (1995). *Children's cognitive and language development*. Cambridge, MA: Blackwell.

Manning, M. M., Manning, G. L., Long, R., & Wolfson, B. J. (1992). *Reading and writing in the primary grades: A whole language view*. West Haven, CT: National Education Association.

Multicultural education: A bibliography, 1976–94. (1994, Summer). *Kappa Delta Pi Record, 30*, 168–169.

Olweus, D. (1994). *Bullying at school: What we know and what we can do*. Cambridge, MA: Blackwell.

Pellegrini, A. D. (1995). *School recess and playground behavior*. Albany, NY: SUNY Press.

Perry, T., & Fraser, J. W. (Eds.). (1993). *Freedom's plow: Teaching in the multicultural classroom*. New York: Routledge.

Putnam, J. W. (Ed.). (1993). *Cooperative learning and strategies for inclusion: Celebrating diversity in the classroom*. Baltimore, MD: Brooks.

Richardson, V., Casanova, U., Placier, P., & Guilfoyle, K. (1989). *School children at risk*. New York: Falmer.

Rogers, C., & Kutnick, P. (Eds.). (1991). *The social psychology of the primary school*. New York: Routledge.

Shantz, C. U., & Hartup, W. W. (1992). *Conflict in child and adolescent development*. New York: Cambridge University Press.

Thorne, B. (1993). *Gender-play: Girls and boys in school*. New Brunswick, NJ: Rutgers University Press.

Troyna, B., & Hatcher, R. (1992). *Racism in children's lives: A study of mainly-white primary schools*. New York: Routledge.

SUGGESTED ACTIVITIES

1. Using the information in this unit, develop a checklist of factors you would look for in a developmentally appropriate primary classroom. Divide the list into sections such as Classroom Organization and Materials, Teacher Behavior, and Activities for Students. Bring your checklist to class and compare it with checklists prepared by other students or give copies to the whole class for their responses and comments. Discuss the checklist with the rest of the students, make any suggested changes. Provide copies of the modified checklist for everyone in the class.

2. Arrange to visit two or more primary classrooms. Observe for one hour or more in each class. Take notes on what you see. After you leave, take a copy of your checklist of developmentally appropriate practices. Put a (+) for items observed and a (–) for items not observed. Evaluate the degree of developmental appropriateness of each classroom. Explain where you found positives and on which items improvements could be made. Share your findings with the class.

3. In the library look through recent issues of journals such as *Young Children, Dimensions, Childhood Education, Science and Children, Teaching Children Mathematics,* and *Language Arts.* Select five articles that describe developmentally appropriate instructional practices for primary classrooms. Write a summary of each article. Share what you find out with the class.

4. Interview several primary teachers. Find out what they are doing to incorporate multicultural education in their classrooms. Also, ask them what methods they use to promote positive self-esteem and moral worth in their students.

5. Make an entry in your journal.

REVIEW

A. Look back at the beginning of the unit. Write an analysis of Mr. Marcos' and of Ms. Brown's classrooms relative to how well what is described does or does not fit the developmental characteristics of primary level students. Compare the two classrooms.

B. Select the items below that describe cognitive characteristics that are typical for six through eight-year-old children.
   1. During the primary period, children begin to see good work habits as indications of intelligence.
   2. Being good and following rules are viewed as evidence of being smart.
   3. Primary-level children can usually understand that no matter how hard you work you are limited by your innate ability.
   4. Young children perform better with constructive criticism than with praise.
   5. Primary children do not weigh praise against task difficulty.
   6. Primary children should receive letter grades because they are meaningful to them.
   7. Comparisons with peers do not take on great importance until between the third and fifth grade.

8. It is relatively easy to make primary level children feel good about themselves because they are very responsive to adult approval.
9. During the primary period children move into being able to use abstract symbols without connecting them to the concrete.

C. Using time as an example, explain how primary-level children move from the concrete to the symbolic.

D. Visiting a first-grade classroom you notice that many of the children talk to themselves as they work. Is this expected behavior? Is this activity of any value?

E. Match the descriptions below with the reading strategies described by McIntyre (1990).
   1. Bill sits on a pillow in the reading center. He holds the book *The Little Engine That Could* on his lap. His eyes focus on the pictures as he reads in a chant-like voice, "I think I can — I think I can — I think I can. Up, up, up. Faster and faster the little engine is climbing. At last they reach the top of the mountain." His teacher notices that he uses words very close to the book's exact language.
   2. Mr. Marcos hands Lai a book she has never seen before. "I think you will like *Fish is Fish*." Lai opens the book, she looks at the pictures and then her eyes focus on the print and she reads aloud as follows, "At the end of the woods there was a pond, and there a minnow and a tadpole swam among the weeds. They were in-sep-ar-able friends." Mr. Marcos notes that she reads exactly what the book says.
   3. Kate selects *Fish is Fish*. Her eyes focus on the pictures and she reads, "A minnow and a tadpole are in the pond in the woods. They were friends and swam in the weeds."

F. Explain why and how writing and drawing promote literacy and self-esteem.

G. Select the statements that describe affective characteristics of primary level children.
   1. Primary level children are not especially sensitive about specific situations such as talking in front of the rest of the class.
   2. Peers become less important to children as they proceed from first to third grade.
   3. Aggressive but not withdrawn children are usually rejected by peers.
   4. If a child hovers silently and then enters a play group by imitating what the group members are doing, the group entry is most likely to be successful.
   5. Rough-and-tumble play includes running, jumping, laughing, chasing, and other physically active acts.
   6. Rough-and-tumble play is dangerous and should never be allowed as it has no value for young children.
   7. Recess is not necessary for primary children. It is a waste of time.
   8. Children who master appropriate social strategies are most likely to be popular with their peers.
   9. Bullies need to be taught appropriate methods for reacting to anger.
   10. Friends serve many functions for young children. Besides being playmates, they support feelings of self-worth and provide nurturance and intimacy.
   11. In ethnically diverse groups children tend to stick with friends from their own group.

H. Give an example of a way social interaction can benefit children in the primary classroom.

I. Describe a situation in which a young child might feel stressed.

J. Select the correct answer for each of the following questions.
   1. Self-esteem includes the way children feel about themselves in the following areas.
      a. physical
      b. social and moral
      c. emotional
      d. cognitive
      e. all of the above

2. According to Erikson, during the primary grades children enter
   a. the preoperational period.
   b. the period of initiative versus guilt.
   c. the period of industry versus inferiority.
   d. concrete operations.
3. According to Piaget, during the primary-grades children enter
   a. the preoperational period.
   b. the period of initiative versus guilt.
   c. the period of industry versus inferiority.
   d. concrete operations.
4. Self-esteem, according to Curry and Johnson, consists of four components.
   a. power, happiness, acceptance, and love
   b. competence, power, acceptance, and virtuousness
   c. competence, power, love, and virtuousness
   d. acceptance, competence, power, and dominance
5. The best way to ensure that children will feel competent in school is to
   a. fit the curriculum to the child.
   b. fit the child to the curriculum.
   c. change the age of school entrance.
   d. place children in transition classes.
6. One of the following will *not* help children feel powerful and in control.
   a. Success is based on hard work.
   b. Success is based on doing your best.
   c. Success is based on beating out the competition.
   d. Success is based on collaborative learning.
7. Moral worth is an important component of self-esteem. Some of the facets of moral worth are
   a. not having a positive feeling about being a good person.
   b. kindness, mercy, justice and fairness, honesty.
   c. meanness, carelessness, cheating and lying.
   d. trying to win by competing with others.
8. Sharing is a significant moral behavior that is learned
   a. from the time of the child's first naturally occurring interactions.
   b. from direct instruction provided by significant adults.
   c. from being forced to divide groups of toys equally with peers.
   d. during interactions which begin during the primary period.
9. "I take out the trash because Dad wants me to and he is one of the people who cares for me." This is an example of
   a. obeying because one has to.
   b. obeying as a sign of respect for adults.
   c. obeying as it occurs in adolescence.
   d. obeying as it occurs during the preoperational period.
10. One of the following is not true.
    a. The peer group is the ideal setting for moral development.
    b. In the peer group children have the opportunity to try out moral rules with equals.
    c. Children gain an understanding of norms of fairness as they discover them during their play.
    d. Truth and honesty are not important components in the friendships of young children.

K. Describe in your own words and in no more than one page the components of the adult's role with the primary child that you believe to be most important.

L. Explain "ethnic identity" and why it is important.

M. List the factors that you believe have the greatest effect on school achievement. Explain why each of these factors is important.

N. Describe what you envision as the ideal primary school setting that would strongly support child development.

Unit 32

Preschool to Primary: Bridging the Gap

OBJECTIVES

After studying this unit, the student should be able to:

■ Explain why continuity is needed in educational programs from prekindergarten to primary.

■ Assess whether or not a classroom has the characteristics of developmental appropriateness.

■ Identify the basic factors in the concept of readiness.

■ List the major factors to consider in the assessment of readiness.

■ List the skills a child probably will need to deal with the world of the future.

On January 20, 1990, in his second State of the Union message, President Bush formally announced the national education goals (Boyer, 1993). During the first years of Bill Clinton's presidency, the national education goals were modified somewhat and labeled "Goals 2000 Program." Each state is developing standards to meet the goals. This statement builds on the traditional concept of readiness, which, as you will see later in the unit, is now outmoded (Kagan, 1990; NAEYC Position Statement on School Readiness, 1990; Willer & Bredekamp, 1990). This concept of readiness, among other faults, tends to promote the view that preschool, kindergarten, and primary are separate entities with their only relationship being that each exists to ready children for the next level. This factor has tended to promote the belief that there is an imaginary gap between each level. In this unit we will examine the case for bridging that imaginary gap by looking at early childhood as a continuum of growth and development rather than as separate stages related only by a vague concept referred to as readiness.

From the cognitive developmental or constructivist point of view early childhood is a unique period in child development that merits consideration beyond the conventional readiness point of view. Early childhood educators are becoming increasingly concerned with the movement to include more prekindergarten children in public education and at the increase in inappropriate academic pressures being placed on young children (Kagan, 1990; NAEYC Position Statement on School Readiness, 1990; Willer & Bredekamp, 1990).

CONTINUITY

In the early years of schooling (kindergarten and primary) young children are passing through the second transition period. Symbolic play serves as a vehicle that supports children's development from purely concrete activity to connecting the concrete with the abstract (Figures 32–1a and 32–1b). Unfortunately, play is not a part of many of today's kindergarten programs and is seldom included in the primary grades (Wasserman, 1990). This lack of play opportunities represents one of the major factors that creates the gap between preschool, kindergarten, and primary education. (The specific values of play will be described in Unit 33.)

The question of **continuity** is by no means a new one. For example, Dorothy H. Cohen (1972) expressed a concern regarding preschool to kindergarten continuity and Betty Caldwell (1973) a concern about the chasm between kindergarten and primary. Cohen's conclusion that "Children of four, five, six, and seven are continuations of themselves" is as relevant today as it was in 1972. As an example, consider the reactions of Kate at different ages and stages to a trip to the zoo.

At age three Kate goes to the zoo. Back at the Child Development Center she shows her response to the trip by painting a yellow and black blob, which she tells us is a tiger. She also shows an interest in leafing through an assortment of animal books, which are available and pointing out some of her favorites. In addition she is observed in a wooden packing crate growling and begging for food just as she had seen the tigers do at the zoo during the feeding time. When asked to dictate a story about the trip to the zoo, she responds, "I like the tiger at the zoo. He eats meat. He growls. That's all."

At age four Kate visits the zoo again. At preschool the next day she paints a cagelike design with a yellow and black animallike figure. She tells us to write on her picture that this is a hungry tiger. She requests that several animal stories be read to her. She is observed playing zoo animals with two other children; one child is the keeper and the other two are being fed. Later they build some square structures with the unit blocks and put all the small rubber animals in the enclosure. When asked to dictate a story about the zoo Kate responds, "We went on the little yellow bus to the zoo. First we saw the wild animals. I liked the tigers best. Then we went to the petting zoo. I liked the horses and the rabbits. Then we ate a picnic lunch. We came home on the bus."

At age five Kate again visits the zoo. Back at school she paints a picture of a tiger in a cage that is fairly recognizable to the adult eye. She also asks for a large piece of drawing paper and with markers and crayons draws a larger overview of the zoo with several cages each containing one of her favorite animals. On each cage she draws a rectangle and asks the teacher how to spell the names of each of the animals so she can label each cage. With some help from her teacher she makes a zoo book with captions such as, "This is a tiger" and "The rabbit wiggles his nose." She leafs through all the zoo storybooks and soon has her favorite stories memorized. She is observed pretending to read a story to one of her classmates. Kate and three other children build a rather elaborate zoo with the unit blocks. They each take responsibility for different roles, such as the zoo keeper who feeds the animals, the zoo keeper who cleans, the zoo doctor, and the snack stand salesperson. Kate also displays curiosity with follow-up questions regarding the animals.

At age six Kate visits the zoo again. In her first-grade class she enjoys again reliving the experience. She writes and illustrates her own zoo storybook. She reads some books about the zoo and zoo animals. She asks her teacher to read the class some informational books. From these books they learn how much each animal eats in a day and proceed to figure out their intake per week. The books also tell them statistics such as the weight and height of each animal so they can compare the sizes. She and the other children work together to build a miniature zoo using boxes to make cages and clay to make the animals. In her developmental classroom there is a dramatic play center. The class members relive their zoo experience using large boxes for cages. They make signs for each cage. Each sign has the name of the animal and a brief description of its habits and life-style.

The examples of Kate's behavior demonstrate that as Kate grows and matures, her responses to the

Figure 32–1a   Symbolic activity supports the shift to the use of abstract symbols, such as those representing numbers.

Figure 32–1b   Young children engage in symbolic activity in their representational dramatic play. This young girl is pretending to be a dog and eating imaginary food off the plates.

same experience and the same raw materials also grow and mature. Her growth in curiosity, in perceptual-motor ability (drawing, painting, and building), in language, and in sociodramatic play capacity is reflected in her response at each level.

Cohen warned that cutting up children's early years into small, unrelated pieces could only damage them. Today, we see her warning becoming a reality. Children approach learning as their developmental levels lead them supported by adult scaffolding at the right moments. Unfortunately, some of the concerns of the seventies regarding the moving down of the first-grade curriculum into the kindergarten and the kindergarten curriculum into the prekindergarten curriculum blossomed into reality in the eighties. Efforts are being made to increase continuity (Barber & Seefeldt, 1992; Edson, 1994; Kohler, Chapman, & Smith, 1994; Mitchell, 1993; Vail & Scott, 1994) and overcome the barriers to smooth transitions. In previous units some of the barriers to smooth transitions and continuity have been described. **Barriers** include instructional strategies that are not consistent with the principles of child development (sit still workbook/worksheet and large group instruction); inappropriate placement procedures (extra-year readiness classes before kindergarten and transitional classes

after kindergarten) (Bredekamp, 1990; Brewer, 1990; Patton & Wortham, 1993; Uphoff, 1990); current evaluation procedures (Charlesworth, Fleege, & Weitman, 1994; Kamii, 1990); retention and other practices that doom children to failure (McGill-Franzen & Allington, 1993; Smith & Shepard, 1988); and lack of teachers and school administrators qualified and/or certified in child development and early childhood education (Burts, Campbell, Hart, & Charlesworth, 1991).

Efforts Aimed at Achieving Continuity

Programs that attempt to sustain continuity from prekindergarten through the primary educational years have been developed. One example was the major national effort called Follow Through. Follow Through attempted to extend the types of programs developed for preschool children attending Head Start through to compulsory kindergarten and primary education (Hodges & Sheehan, 1978; Maccoby & Zellner, 1970). A number of program models that could be used as the basis for continuity grew out of these efforts (Goffin, 1994; Roopnarine and Johnson,

1993). Although some of the national evaluation results interpret the success of the program as being only moderate, the individual sponsors believe that much has been learned. They believe that the evaluation studies were of such poor quality that they are of questionable value (Hodges & Sheehan, 1978). Since those early days Follow Through has continued and since 1988 has directed its efforts toward establishing sites around the country that can demonstrate proven successful appropriate practices in grades K–3. Follow Through's objective is to disseminate its models to school systems where there is high risk of children failing (Walgren, 1990).

Since the publication of the NAEYC guidelines (Bredekamp, 1987), there has been increased interest in developing programs that provide continuity. The NAEYC guidelines for developmentally appropriate practice and those for developmentally appropriate curriculum and assessment (NAEYC, 1991) have provided a nationally recognized justification that ties education from birth through age eight together in one continuous developmental sequence. The NAEYC documents have provided support for those who wish to attempt reform of early education practices.

The Developmentally Appropriate Classroom

Developmentally appropriate classrooms have some common elements that ensure that instruction fits the students' developmental levels. Constance Kamii (1984) reminds us that the stage concept is not the core of Piaget's contribution to a developmental view of education. For Piaget the aims of education were intellectual and moral autonomy. Autonomy is the ability to govern oneself. Moral autonomy is achieved through exchanging points of view regarding moral issues rather than through externally determined rewards and punishments (as discussed in Unit 30). Intellectual autonomy comes through constructing knowledge from within rather than internalizing it directly from outside. (See Section VI.) Children are not pressured to arrive at "correct" answers but are encouraged to think autonomously and discover relationships on their own. Kamii points out that most of our education is not based on developing autonomous learning but on the belief that all knowl-

Figure 32–2   Six-year-olds are ready to play games on their own. They can now integrate information to keep track of the rules of the game, take turns, and see another's point of view regarding the play of the game.

edge comes out of the teacher's head. Social interaction is an invaluable process in the development of intellectual autonomy. Comparing answers, judgments, and hypotheses forces children to question, to evaluate, and to think about what they are doing. They also remember their conclusions and learn about the process of problem solving. Play is an important component in young children's learning and should not be cut off after kindergarten. As children move into concrete operations, they naturally become interested in games with rules (Figure 32–2). These games can be very effective for teaching (Kamii, 1985) and a much more natural and developmentally appropriate method than worksheets. For example, Kamii has found that first-grade arithmetic can be taught successfully with group games using cards or dice. In fact she has found that "worksheets are harmful for first graders' development of arithmetic while play is highly beneficial" (Kamii, 1985, p. 6). Needless to say, this statement applies to pre-first grade also.

Teachers in developmentally appropriate classrooms understand and apply child development to their practice as described in earlier units. Teachers consider individual and age appropriateness relative to development and culture (New, 1994; Powell,

1994; Williams, 1994). For example, they are warm and affectionate toward the children, they use positive discipline strategies, encourage exploration and independence, are sensitive to the needs of families, and take time to observe and record observations while children are working independently. The physical environment is arranged in interest centers that provide for individual and group learning experiences, there are concrete materials, an area for messy play, furniture is a size the fits the children and is movable. Centers might include writing, library, mathematics, manipulatives and games, art, dramatic play, blocks, music, science, social studies, and gross motor. Block centers and sand play are a part of the primary classroom as well as the preprimary (Ewing & Eddowes, 1994; Harris, 1994). Centers can be combined and integrated to support project work.

Developmentally appropriate practice is supported by constructivist theoretical views. Some of the models that particularly fit the DAP criteria are the moral classroom (DeVries & Zan, 1994), the cognitively oriented curriculum, and the Bank Street model. (For descriptions see Goffin, 1994; and Roopnarine & Johnson, 1993.)

THE CONCEPT OF READINESS

The term readiness is commonly used to describe some end point that is reached during a certain age or stage that then enables the child to move on to the next level. In the eighties the use of this term became extremely questionable (Charlesworth, 1985). The meaning of the term changed from letting children get ready through the normal course of development with appropriate adult support and guidance to making them ready. For example, Graue (1992) believes the popular conceptions of readiness as biologically determined and/or the result of environmental stimulation and as a fixed sequence of developments is not accurate. Further, the current views of readiness have European-American middle-class roots, which means they may not be applicable to all cultures. In addition, readiness can't be accurately mea-

sured and when such measures are made and used for making ready/not-ready decisions, the result may be the misplacement of children in the wrong grades and/or in the wrong special programs. Graue's point of view is that readiness is a culturally defined term. Every community of adults has a personal view of readiness that determines when children are "ready" to enter school and/or move on to the next grade in that community. From this view, readiness is a socially constructed concept rather than a characteristic of children. That is, each community of adults defines readiness in its own way. Graue does not believe we can throw away the idea of readiness—it's too deeply ingrained in our culture. Somehow all those concerned, academic, policy, and parent communities, must come to a consensus.

The popular definition of readiness as academic capability has brought about a focus in classrooms on pressure for academic achievement that has forced the primary curriculum to be pushed down into kindergarten and the kindergarten curriculum into prekindergarten. David Elkind (1986) expressed a concern that in the push to hurry young children's learning they are being miseducated by being taught using methods and materials more appropriate for older children. Elkind believes children need time for reflective abstraction. Elkind is concerned that this focus on right and wrong makes children dependent on adults for all the answers and precludes them developing independent thought and action.

A major problem for early educators is parental pressure for more and more formal academics for their young children (Webster, 1985). The results of a survey by Loraine Webster demonstrated that parents want a heavy academic program for their kindergartners. Early childhood teachers commonly have difficulty coming up with a defense for the developmentally appropriate program. Barbara Simmons and JoAnn Brewer (1985) developed answers to questions frequently asked by parents who do not understand how children learn through a developmentally appropriate program.

Willer and Bredekamp (1990) proposed that a redefinition of readiness was an essential requisite to educational reform. They express concern that readi-

readiness

ness is being used as an exclusionary device. That is, by setting up certain prerequisites for school entry, readiness becomes a gatekeeping concept. The blame for not being ready is placed on the children rather than on the possibility that expectations placed on the children may not be appropriate. Willer and Bredekamp suggest it is important that the schools need to be ready to help children succeed at learning. They describe a number of assumptions (Figure 32–3), which underlie the gatekeeping point of view and explain why these assumptions are not accurate and how they hinder reform efforts (pp. 22–24). Willer and Bredekamp (1990) suggest four reform strategies for ensuring that children are ready to succeed (p. 24):

1. Lay the foundation for school success by eradicating childhood poverty.

2. Prepare schools and teachers to respond to individual needs rather than trying to mold every child to be the same as they move down the assembly line of education.

3. Make schools places where developmentally appropriate practice predominates.

4. Invest the resources needed to accomplish these goals.

As Sharon L. Kagan (1991, p. 276) states, "instead of individualizing entry and homogenizing services, we should homogenize entry and individualize services." Readiness needs to be redefined with a broad definition that includes every aspect of children's development and children's lives, both inside and outside of school.

Because a clear understanding of the term *readiness* is essential to working constructively with young children, the *NAEYC Position Statement on School Readiness* was included in the Introduction to this section. This statement summarizes the essential aspects of the term *readiness* as it applies to schooling and should be read and re-read by those who work with young children. Whether child readiness is defined from inside the child and/or from the social

Inaccurate Assumptions	Rationale for Inaccuracy
Learning only occurs in school.	Learning occurs before children enter school, both at home and in various early childhood settings outside the home. Many conditions such as poverty, drugs, and poor health care work against children's natural desire to learn.
Readiness is a special inherent condition within the child.	Environmental factors and the inherent variations interact to produce a variety of developmental patterns in children.
Readiness is a condition that is easily measured.	Readiness for school is not easily measured due to a variety of factors such as the lack of valid and reliable assessment instruments and the nature of the assessment situation.
Readiness is mostly a function of time; some children need more time than others.	Adults cannot just wait for children to blossom but need to facilitate development by providing an environment in which children can construct knowledge.
Children are ready to learn when they can sit quietly at a desk and listen to the teacher.	Children are active learners who construct knowledge through concrete activities and interaction with peers and adults.
Children who aren't ready don't belong in school.	It is those children who are most likely labeled as unready who most need the advantages of developmentally appropriate schooling. This assumption leads to the homogenizing of classrooms so that only those who fit a specific readiness mold are let in and are then put under pressure as they are taught inappropriate curricula using inappropriate practices.

Figure 32–3 **Countering the gatekeeping point of view**

context of the community, it is important to keep in mind that children are both learning; they need to be in a setting that is ready to nurture their learning (Children are born learning, 1993).

ASSESSMENT PRACTICES

Much that takes place in current practice in the area of early childhood assessment is dangerous to child growth and development (Kamii, 1990). The administration of inappropriate group paper and pencil standardized achievement tests to young children has been escalating until it is almost universal. Administration of these tests to young children is stressful, is not a valid and reliable measure of the children's achievement, and encourages teaching to the test which narrows down the scope of the curriculum. Further, preparation for the tests, time spent taking the tests, and recovery from the test-taking experience uses up valuable instructional time. In addition, the results are frequently used to make a variety of decisions about children and their educational futures:

- making decisions regarding grade placement, instructional level and/or need for special help or eligibility for an enrichment program.
- evaluating effectiveness of instruction
- evaluating teacher effectiveness
- comparing schools and districts
- satisfying public and administrative demands for accountability

Another current practice, already mentioned, involves the misuse of the results from group paper-and-pencil achievement and readiness tests and from individually administered achievement, readiness, and screening instruments as the sole criteria for making important decisions about the placement of children. Decisions might include placement in regular or so-called "developmental" kindergarten, placement in transition classes or special education, retention in a grade, or providing Chapter 1 or other special services.

Several points need to be considered regarding the misuse of tests and test scores. First, take a paper-and-pencil test is very stressful for young children. Children demonstrate increased frequencies of stress behaviors, respond with wrong answers to questions they could answer correctly under other circumstances, and copy answers from other students' test booklets (Charlesworth et al., 1994; Fleege, Charlesworth, Burts, & Hart, 1993; Fleege & Charlesworth, 1993).

The pressure to perform well in the tests forces teaching to the test. This practice "dummies down" instruction by narrowing the instruction to fit the specific skills included on the test. Drill and practice, workbooks/worksheets, flashcards, and large group instruction take over as methodology. Reading and math skills are emphasized leaving little, if any, time for science, social studies, art, music, and play (Charlesworth et al., 1994; Madaus, 1988). Results of a study by Burts, Charlesworth, and Fleege (1991) indicated that students from teach-to-the-test classrooms did not obtain significantly higher scores on the *California Achievement Test (CAT)* than children from more developmentally appropriate classrooms.

Readiness and screening instruments have been used increasingly to implement the homogenizing of classes by determining placement of students in classes with other students of similar apparent capabilities. Screening and readiness instruments are not designed to be used to make placement decisions. The purpose of screening instruments is to identify children who may need indepth diagnosis. The purpose of readiness instruments is to provide information that will assist in planning instruction. (NAEYC and NAECS/SDE, 1991; NASBE, 1990) Readiness instruments are not reliable and valid predictors of school success (see studies by Graue and Shepard, 1989; Lichtenstein, 1990).

Developmentally Appropriate Assessment

There is a growing nationwide movement to eliminate the use of **inappropriate assessment procedures** with young children, especially misuse of readiness test results and the elimination of paper-and-pencil whole-group achievement testing through third grade. Simultaneously, alternative **appropriate assessment procedures** are being developed. (Bergan & Feld, 1993; Meisels, 1993, 1994; Schweinhart, 1993) This type of assessment is referred to as authentic evaluation. "Authentic evaluation of educational achievement directly measures actual performance in the subject area. Standardized multiple-choice tests, on the other hand, measure test-taking skills directly, and everything else either indirectly or not at all" (Pett 1990, p. 8). Authentic evaluation is also referred to as performance, appropriate, alternative, or direct evaluation. A wide variety of techniques may be used such as teacher observations recorded as anecdotes or on checklists, portfolios of student work (Grace and Shores, 1991; *Portfolio News*; Vavrus, 1990), performances while investigating a problem in science or math (Shavelson, Carey & Webb, 1990), products such as written compositions and reports, drawings and paintings, and structures, and audio and video tapes. Skills can be observed as children engage in normal developmentally appropriate activities and through direct interviews using concrete materials rather than paper and pencil tests. As documented in the Fleege et al. (1991) study, children may be able to apply concepts in concrete situations that they cannot deal with on a group-administered, paper-and-pencil, multiple-choice test. These various forms of authentic evaluation can be placed on a scale or summarized numerically in some way for assembling data on performance to report to administrators.

A developmentally appropriate readiness instrument can be helpful aid in providing directions for curriculum and instruction. Such as instrument should be selected with care, using the following criteria:

1. The instrument should be designed to be individually administered. A test that has been designed and normed for group administration is not appropriate.

2. Required child responses should be mainly motoric (e.g. pointing, constructing, sorting), verbal (e.g. naming an object or a pictured object, answering a question) or require responses to auditory stimuli (e.g. following directions, sound discrimination). Paper and pencil should be used only as a check of perceptual-motor functioning (e.g. copy a shape, write his/her name, draw a person). Concrete materials and pictures should be the main media for obtaining responses.

3. The instrument should be broad in scope, sampling a variety of developmental areas: expressive and receptive language, reasoning, auditory reception, gross and fine motor development, perceptual development and general behavior.

4. The instrument should be relatively short, taking no more than thirty minutes to administer.

5. The instrument should provide information that will be useful for further diagnosis and curriculum planning.

6. The instrument should be normed on a large representative sample of children.

7. Information on validity and reliability should be in the instrument's manual.

8. Instruction for administration should be clear and specific so that a teacher, parent or teacher aide can easily do the administration.

9. The availability of a follow-up curriculum guide would be a valuable feature.

10. Other valuable features would be provision of a parent questionnaire and reasonable cost.

Much of the assessment can be done through observation of students during their regular activities, while some must be done through individual interviews. Appropriate tasks for use with young children have been included throughout this text.

PREPARING FOR THE FUTURE

In 1977 Karen Hartman, then a teacher of four-year-olds, asked herself the following question:

[Considering what she and those before her had been doing with four-year-olds] How relevant was this routine, this philosophical regime, initiated by Caroline

Figure 32–4 Hopefully, some of the skills children learn during their early years will help them cope with an increasingly stimulating world of sights, sounds, and technology.

Pratt in 1914, for children who would ultimately cope with future shock, both externally and internally? (Hartman, 1977, p. 32)

She then proceeded to do a self-evaluation relative to what she was doing in teaching preschool children and whether it might be teaching them the skills they would need in the future. She found that she was teaching the following skills, which should be helpful to children who will deal with a world of increasing complexity as they develop toward adulthood.

- By teaching them to focus on a task with few materials at a time, she was helping them develop the focusing skill necessary to deal with the highly stimulating world outside.

- By offering a carefully selected limited supply of materials in the classroom, she was helping the

children develop decision-making ability before being faced with the many choices of the future.

- By coping effectively with the environment provided for them, they were learning independence.

- Through offering firsthand (rather than vicarious) experiences, she was keeping their curiosity and their inner resources alive.

Hopefully, learning to focus on a task, make independent decisions, and maintain curiosity and creativity will enable today's young children to deal with our increasingly complex technological environment in the future (Figure 32–4).

SUMMARY

The concept of readiness as preparation for the next level tends to underlie the belief that prekindergarten, kindergarten, and primary levels of education are totally separate periods. This concept was reflected in the goal set forth by former President Bush and the Nation's governors that, by the year 2000, all children in America will enter school ready to learn. Actually preschool through primary should be treated as a continuous period of development. From this view, the transitions from preschool to kindergarten to primary education programs can be made smooth using familiar materials and activities as children progress from one level to another. Developmentally appropriate classrooms should be available for all young children.

It is time to redefine readiness, not as a gatekeeping concept used to keep so-called "not ready" children out of programs, but as the concept that we must help children to be ready to succeed in schools that are ready to accept them as they are. As a part of this redefinition, readiness assessment should function as a means of finding out where to begin instruction, not as a gatekeeper for deciding who is let in and who is kept out of classrooms.

Besides reforming readiness assessment, the whole area of assessment of young children is in need of change. Paper-and-pencil, multiple-choice, group-administered, standardized achievement tests should not be used with young children. They increase the levels of stress, use up valuable instructional time with preparation, and are too abstract to provide reliable or valid measures of young children's academic achievement. In addition, they overlook areas such as social development, motor development, problem solving, and thinking. Authentic evaluation procedures that provide information from natural occurring learning experiences are the wave of the future. Preparation for the future in a technological world demands a workforce of creative thinkers and problem solvers.

FOR FURTHER READING

Assessment: The winter of our discontent. (1993). [Special issue]. *Educational Horizons, 72*(1).

Barbour, N. H. & Seefeldt, C. (1993). *Developmental continuity: Across preschool and primary grades.* Wheaton, MD: Association for Childhood Education International.

Beaty, J. J. (1990). *Observing development of the young child.* Columbus, OH: Merrill.

Beaty, J. (1992). *Preschool appropriate practices.* Fort Worth, TX: Harcourt Brace.

Crnic, K. A. (1994). School readiness: Scientific perspectives [Special Issue]. *Early Education and Development, 5*(2).

FairTest. (1990). *Standardized tests and our children: A guide to testing reform.* Cambridge, MA: Author.

Glascoe, F. P., & Byrne, K. E. (1993). The accuracy of three developmental screening tests. *Journal of Early Intervention, 17*, 368–379.

Graue, E. M. (1993). *Ready for what? Constructing meanings of readiness for kindergarten.* Albany, NY: SUNY Press.

Haney, W. M., Madaus, G. F., & Lyons, R. (1993). *The fractured marketplace for standardized testing.* Hingham, MA: Kluwer.

Lee, F. Y. (1992). Issues in education: Alternative assessments. *Childhood Education, 69*, 72–73.

Mitchell, R. (1991). *Testing for learning: How new approaches to evaluation can improve American schools.* New York: The Free Press.

Morison, P. (1992). Testing in American schools: Issues for research and policy. *SRCD Social Policy Report, 6*(2).

Moxley, R. A., Kenny, K. A., & Hunt, M. K. (1990). Improving the instruction of young children with self-recording and discussion. *Early Childhood Research Quarterly, 5*, 233–249.

Neil, M., & Medina, N. J. (1989). Standardized testing: Harmful to educational health. *Phi Delta Kappan, 70*(9), 688–697.

Performance-based assessment. (1994). [Special Issue]. *ERIC Review, 3*(1).

Phi Delta Kappan [Special section on assessment]. (1993). *74*(6).

Pierson, C. A., & Beck, S. S. (1993). Performance assessment: The realities that will influence the rewards. *Childhood Education, 70*, 29–32.

Raver, C. C., & Zigler, E. F. (1991). Three steps forward, two steps back: Head Start and the measurement of social competence. *Young Children, 46*(4), 3–8.

Reifel, S. (Ed.). (1993). Perspectives on developmentally appropriate practice. *Advances in early education and day care* (Vol. 5). Greenwich, CT: JAI Press.

Robinson, S. L., & Lyon, C. (1994). Early childhood offerings in 1992: Will we be ready for 2000? *Phi Delta Kappan, 75*, 775–778.

Shepard, L. A., & Smith, M. L. (1989). *Flunking grades: Research and policies on retention*. New York: Falmer.

Shores, E. F. (1992). *Explorers' Classrooms*. Little Rock, AR: Southern Early Childhood Association.

Simmons, B. & Brewer, J. (1985). When parents of kindergartners ask, "Why?" *Childhood Education, 61*, 177–184. (Available as a pamphlet from ACEI, Dept. CE, 11141 Georgia Ave., Suite 200, Wheaton, MD 20902. Single copies, $1.20 for nonmembers, $1.00 for members.)

Smith, F. (1986). *Insult to intelligence: The bureaucratic invasion of our classrooms*. Portsmouth, NH: Heinemann.

SUGGESTED ACTIVITIES

1. Within small groups in class discuss the following questions:
   a. What knowledge must be obtained and which skills must be mastered by the young child in order to be ready for the first grade?
   b. What knowledge and which skills can be developed during early childhood that will help the child as an adult deal with a world of increasing complexity?
   c. What are the kinds of visual and auditory overstimulation the group foresees in the future?

2. Review Units 16–31. Make a list of skills that should be developed by young children by the end of the preoperational period. Compare your list with the lists developed by other class members. Fill in any skills you missed.

3. Obtain some copies of readiness, screening, and/or achievement assessment instruments commonly used with young children. Your instructor can provide a list of assessment, readiness, and screening instruments that are frequently used. Using the list of criteria in this unit, individually or in small groups, analyze each test. Also, compare the items included with the class-devised list of skills.
   a. Note which skills each test has that the class did not include and which skills the class listed that are not included in each test examined.
   b. Compare the strengths and weaknesses of each test relative to content and to the selection criteria from this unit. Rank the tests from the one you feel is best and would be most useful to the one you feel would be least useful. State the reasons for your decisions.

4. Try some of the assessment tasks suggested in the text (see especially Units 16, 21, 22, 23, 24, and 25) or use one or more of the readiness, screening, and/or assessment instruments reviewed for Activity 3 with one or more five-year-old prekindergarten or kindergarten children. If possible, videotape the assessment session. Play the videotape for the class and have the class members evaluate the child(ren)'s performance and your interviewing technique. Prepare a report including the name, age, and sex of the child interviewed, a description of what you did, the results, and your analysis and evaluation.

5. Read about some of the Follow Through model programs. Information on resources can be obtained in your library through the reference librarian. Some of the more highly publicized models are:

Bank Street Model
Bank Street College of Education
610 W. 112th Street
New York, NY 10025

Behavior Analysis Model
Support and Development Center for Follow-
    Through
Department of Human Development
University of Kansas
Lawrence, KS 66044

Cognitively Oriented Curriculum
High/Scope Educational Research Foundation
600 N. River
Ypsilanti, MI 48197

Direct Instruction Model
University of Oregon
Department of Special Education
College of Education
Eugene, OR 97403

Language Development Approach (SEDL)
Southwest Educational Development Labora-
    tory
Follow-Through Division
211 E. Seventh Street
Austin, TX 78701

Compare the objectives and instructional approaches of each program reviewed. Evaluate each relative to what you have learned about child development from this text. Do you feel that each program follows through at a level and in a way that works with the child as he leaves the preschool period and enters the shift to middle childhood? Share what you discover with a small group in class.

6. Visit a prekindergarten, a kindergarten, and a primary classroom. Using the checklist provided in this unit determine how closely each classroom fits the criteria for developmental appropriateness. Discuss your findings in class.

7. Make an entry in your journal.

REVIEW

A. How would you explain to a kindergarten teacher that continuity is needed between your program for prekindergartners and her program? Or to a first-grade teacher that continuity is needed between your kindergarten program and his first-grade curriculum?

B. Select the correct answer to the following. There is only one correct answer for each.
  1. According to David Elkind the hurried child syndrome means that
    a. children tend to run too fast and don't watch where they are going.
    b. children want to do more and move ahead faster than we allow them to do.
    c. today, we put emphasis on making the child grow up as fast as possible.
  2. The core of Piaget's contribution to education is that
    a. intellectual and moral autonomy are the aims of education.
    b. education should follow a developmental pattern.
    c. children develop according to the stage concept.
  3. Constance Kamii believes that
    a. worksheets are useful if young children are mature enough to use a pencil.
    b. worksheets with good, clear art work can supplement concrete activities.
    c. worksheets are harmful, even in the primary grades.

4. The traditional definition of the term *readiness* is based on the concept that
    a. each level of early childhood is designed to ready the child for the next stage.
    b. learning of a particular type may be done whenever the teacher is ready.
    c. schools should be ready to teach the variety of children they receive.
5. Willer and Bredekamp (1990) propose a redefinition of readiness that emphasizes
    a. children develop at individual rates; readiness is mostly a function of time.
    b. readiness is a special inherent condition within the child.
    c. we need to ensure that children enter school ready to succeed and that schools are ready to help all children succeed.
6. Homogenizing the classroom refers to
    a. making sure each classroom has a wide variety of children at different levels of development.
    b. using readiness test scores to group children so that those of similar abilities who are ready are in the same classes.
    c. using readiness test scores as the basis for being sure all teachers get a fair share of students at every level of ability.
7. Using readiness as a gatekeeper refers to
    a. keeping those evaluated as unready out of the grade level for which they are eligible according to their age.
    b. making sure all children who are ready have a class to enter.
    c. making sure all children are ready to learn when they enter school.
8. If we push a child too hard to learn new things,
    a. it motivates him that much more to master the task.
    b. the child develops a stronger will to achieve and gain our approval.
    c. the child may become turned off to learning and not want to try new things.
9. An important factor regarding learning is that it
    a. only takes place in school.
    b. takes place not only in school but also at home and in various other settings out of the home.
    c. is not a natural desire for children to want to learn.
10. By offering the child tasks that he can master through self-instruction,
    a. we make learning too easy and the child loses motivation.
    b. the child develops self-reinforcement as he learns through his own activity.
    c. the child may make a lot of mistakes that we might miss, meaning that he does not really learn the task.

C. Write the number of each correct statement.
1. Standardized achievement tests offer the most accurate and valid means for assessing the achievement of young children.
2. Through the use of authentic assessment methods teachers can document children's real progress more accurately than the information obtained from group standardized tests.
3. During the administration of a group paper and pencil standardized test young children show increased frequencies of stress behaviors.
4. Selecting a readiness test is an easy task since there are many that fit all the selection criteria.
5. It is all right to individually administer a test designed for group administration.
6. By age five a child should have no problems dealing with a group-administered, standardized, paper and pencil test.
7. Child test responses should be motoric, verbal, or require a response to auditory stimuli.
8. Paper and pencil tasks have no place in a test used with young children.

9. A test used with young children should be broad in scope.
10. A test used with young children should be completed in 30 minutes or less.

D. List the four skills Karen Hartman feels should be developed by preschool children so they will be able to deal with the future-shocked world.

Section IX

Special Areas of Development

In this section we'll examines some areas of development that deserve special attention: play, technology, and special needs and disabilities. These areas stand on their own as "special," and they also relate to each other. Play is often refered to as a lost art due to the inroads of technology, i.e., television and video games. Technology is also viewed as the key to future success in school and in the work place. Characters from television and movies are the focus of the play of many young children. Play and technology are viewed as having value for children with special needs and disabilities. Play is the major vehicle of young children's learning. As an introduction to these topics we'll look at a smorgasbord of play, technology, and special needs and disabilities.

Stories that appeared in the Baton Rouge *LA Morning Advocate* exemplify the public interests in these three areas:

Children learn best by playing. (May 4, 1990, p. 1C & 2C) This article is directed at parents and focuses on the importance of play as the heart of developmentally appropriate practice. It was written by a freelance writer who was also a graduate student in early childhood education. Unit 33 supplies more support for the importance of play to child development.

Regulating TV for children. (October 7, 1990, p. 8B) This was a column by Richard Reeves out of Washington, DC, reporting on efforts to get Congress to put regulations on children's TV. In Unit 34 you'll find out the results of these efforts to obtain regulatory legislation.

Ninja Turtles unplugged by K. C. day-care centers. (May 6, 1991, p. 30) Datelined Kansas City, MO this article reports that children in several Kansas City day-care centers are no longer allowed to play out the actions of their "Shredder-stomping heroes in half-shells". Although the turtles are good guys in terms of fighting crime, their methods were deemed too violent. In this the right thing to do? See what you think after reading Unit 34.

Myoelectric limb allows girl to grasp life with both hands. (October 25, 1989, p. ID) A color photograph above the headline depicts smiling 7 month old Angel who was born missing her left arm below the elbow. Thanks to the wonders of technology Angel has a battery operated arm and hand that she can use to help her learn about the world through normal sensorimotor grasping activities. In Unit 35 you'll find out about the current focus on handicapped infants and toddlers.

Many adults who don't understand play is essential support for normal child development believe it is a waste of time. For this reason, adults who work with young children need to know as much about play and its role in children's learning as possible. Says Catherine Garvey (1990, p. ix):

> Research on the growth of social competence, readiness for formal schooling, and the ability to cope with intrapersonal and interpersonal affect; on family relationships and processes; and on the problems of handicapped, disturbed, or developmentally delayed children have frequently involved studies of play activities or identified play as a positive influence in other areas of development.

This introduction concludes with a brief description of the content of children's dramatic play as recorded by a kindergarten teacher and the experience of integrating a handicapped child into a classroom as described by a first-grade teacher. Vivian Paley (1984) describes how male and female sex-typed behavior is worked through during kindergarten as the boys become superheroes. While three and four-year-old girls and boys play similarly in the doll corner at five and six there is a change. While girls tend to stick with conventional housekeeping activities, the boys become rougher as they introduce their favorite superhero characters into their dramatic play. The impact of television and films can be seen in the boys' play as the popular characters of the early 1980's appear (such as Woody Woodpecker, Dracula, Frankenstein, Superman, Mighty Mouse, Luke, Han Solo, and Darth Vader). The girls' play is inspired by the popular dolls of the time: Barbie and Strawberry Shortcake.

Two weeks before school starts Mrs. B, a first-grade teacher, was informed she would be teaching a mainstreamed child. The child was born with spina bifida:

> He has paralysis of the lower extremities and is confined to a wheelchair, except for the use of a walker at home and when he is with the physical therapist. I had never dealt with a physically handicapped child (or adult) and was very nervous about this situation. However, this child's physical therapist and nurse came to speak with me about accommodating him. This gave me confidence to work with him. They provided me with information that I was not aware of, or had never thought of, not only in dealing with him, but also they provided knowledge about physical characteristics that is helpful in knowing how to work with him.

Mrs. B learned about his catheterization process, about watching that his shunt didn't become blocked and back up, and that due to a lack of sensitivity in his limbs he could be hurt and not know it. A special desk was installed in her classroom for him. The desk has a special angle because he can't bend from the waist. Ramps were installed so he could get in and out of the room in his wheelchair. A teacher's bathroom was made into a catheterization room.

> Upon meeting J, I found him to be a very inquisitive and active (yes, active!) child. He moved in his wheelchair with great agility and seemed to be at ease with me and other adults.

Mrs. B had a week to prepare the children in her class for J's arrival. After his arrival some changes took place in the classroom routine. For example, they now traveled at a slower pace. He needed help when he dropped things on the floor and because the classroom was small and crowded the furniture had to be moved frequently to provide space for J to move. Fortunately, the other children were very helpful. Mrs. B found this experience to be a challenge but also very rewarding.

With this background move on now to Units 33, 34, and 35: Play, Technology, and Special Needs and Disabilities.

Garvey, C. (1990). *Play*, Enlarged edition. Cambridge, MA: Harvard University Press.
Paley, V. G. (1984). *Boys and girls: Superheroes in the doll corner*. Chicago, IL: University of Chicago Press.
And thanks to Deneé Babin for sharing her experience with J.

Unit 33

The Young Child at Play

OBJECTIVES

After studying this unit, the student should be able to:

- Define play and provide examples.

- Identify the theories of play.

- Categorize play according to the resources used.

- Recognize the normal play of three-, four-, five-, six-, and seven-year-olds.

- List the functions of play.

- Evaluate the adult's role in play.

- Identify the role of the teacher in providing materials, equipment, and space for play.

- Recognize how television can enhance the child's imaginative play.

- Recognize the role of superhero play in child development.

Much of children's time is spent engaged in an activity called play. In spite of the fact that play is what children spend a lot of time doing, it is a rather vague concept that is not easy to define. The point where activity is no longer play and becomes something else (and vice versa) is rather vague. "Rather than a category, property, or stage of behavior, play is a *relative* activity" (Fromberg, 1987, p. 35).

King (1992) also points out another problem in coming up with a definition of play. King asked kindergartners to categorize their daily activities as either work or play. Kindergartners labeled activities specifically assigned by the teacher as work and ac-

KEYTERMSKEYTERMSKEYTERMSKEYTERMSKEYTERMSKEY

play

tivities that were student selected as play. Activities the teacher intended to be play were viewed by the children as work. King concludes, "Children who seem to be playing in kindergarten may, in fact, be children who are enjoying their work" (p. 45). Definitions are socially constructed in the context of the activity. As you observe children at work and play remember your definitions of work and play relative to specific child activities may be different.

Garvey (1990) list five characteristics that are essential to the definition of play (pp. 4–5):

1. Play is pleasurable and enjoyable. Whether or not the enjoyment is visible externally, internally it is positively valued by the player.

2. Play has no extrinsic goals. It is motivated intrinsically. The means are enjoyed without their necessarily being any end objective. Pure play is essentially unproductive.

3. Play is spontaneous and voluntary. The player is not forced to play but makes a voluntary choice.

4. Play involves some active engagement on the part of the player. It is not a passive way of functioning.

5. Play has certain systematic relations to what is not play. That is it is linked with non-play areas, such as creativity, problem solving, language learning, the development of social roles, and a number of other cognitive and social phenomena (Figure 33–1).

These links with nonplay phenomena are the attributes of play many researchers are looking for and curriculum proposers such as Wasserman (1990) link to school instruction. Finally, play is not a literal activity. That is, it is not what it appears to be. Children may run, not because of any real threat but just for the fun of it. Play is related to everything that children do: cognitive, affective, and psychomotor.

THEORIES OF PLAY

Over the years, many individuals have speculated on the reasons for play. In the late 1800s, some

Figure 33–1 **Play is an activity that is pleasurable and enjoyable, has intrinsic value, is spontaneous and voluntary, involves active engagement, and is systematically related to nonplay.**

rather simplistic **theories of play** were developed, referred to as the classical theories. More recent, broader theories of play are referred to as the contemporary theories.

The classical theories include four major types. The surplus energy theory views play as a means for getting rid of extra energy. After being under adult control and held down for a period of time, the child must let go and be active. The relaxation theory sees play as a way to gain new energy. Thus, it is a view opposite to the surplus energy theory. Play relaxes the child and prepares him for work. A third theory is that of preexercise or practice, in which play is thought to be a means for practicing skills needed in adulthood. It is felt that this activity is instinctive. In the fourth classical theory, recapitualization theory, play is viewed as a vehicle through which children live through the evolutionary activities of their ancestors from prehistoric times to the present.

Contemporary theories are much broader than the classical theories. Further, they are much more dynamic. The three major theories are the psychoanalytic theories of Freud and Erikson, and Piaget's cognitive-developmental theory of play. Freud's theory of play emphasizes the expression of emotions and the mastery of difficulties the child might meet.

theories of play

Through fantasy the child experiences both pleasant and unpleasant feelings in a safe way. He takes care of his baby doll just as his parents took care of him. He fights feared monsters and kills them without fear of reprisal or punishment. From Freud's point of view, the child is free to express himself while the adult stays out of the way.

Erikson emphasizes the importance of play as a vehicle for children to find their identity. Play is a means for facing reality and mastering the skills needed for living. Toddlers use play to master skills. Preschoolers who have attained a sense of autonomy use their initiative to attack problems creatively through play. From Erikson's view the adult can take a more active role in play. The adult must provide real experiences, such as really washing dishes, wiping the table, setting the table, dusting, folding laundry, and sweeping. These real experiences enrich the child's spontaneous play.

Piaget views play as it relates to mental development. Play serves the functions of assimilation and accommodation. There are three stages in the development of play that are defined by the type of assimilative acts the child uses:

1. **Practice play:** The child repeats the same activities over and over. This is typical of the toddler.

2. **Symbolic play:** The child makes himself be something that he is not (such as a superhero or a parent) or uses a material as something for which it normally is not (such as sand for food or a block for a car). This is typical of the preschool preoperational child (Figure 33–2).

3. **Games with rules:** This type of play is typical of the school-aged child.

For Piaget, the child must have some degree of control over his own activity to develop properly through play.

Play probably includes something of each of these theories. Freud addresses the emotional aspect of play, Erikson the social, and Piaget the intellectual.

Figure 33–2   One of the most important aspects of play is the use of symbolic representation.

THE DEVELOPMENT OF PLAY

Vehicles for Play

Catherine Garvey (1990) describes the development and nature of the various vehicles children use for play. Young children mainly use four sets of resources: play with motion and interaction, objects, language, and social materials.

Play with Motion and Interaction

This is described by Garvey (1990, p. 25):

The kind of play that most clearly reflects exuberance and high spirits is based on the resource of motion. The running, jumping, skipping, shrieking, and laughing of children at recess or after school is joyous, free, and almost contagious in its expression of well-being.

An interest in interaction with other children is evident in infants and toddlers, but it is during the preschool period that social interaction begins to develop and mature at a rapid rate (Figure 33–3).

Eventually play with motion becomes integrated with games with rules. From about six or seven on we see activities such as jump-rope with accompanying rhymes, chasing games such as Cops-and-Robbers, and other games with rules like Red Rover Come Over, Hopscotch, and Hide-and-Seek.

Figure 33–3 Play with motion involves high spirits and gross motor activity.

Figure 33–4 Space, materials, and equipment support children's play activities.

Play with Objects

Children use objects as links between themselves and their environment (Figure 33–4). They do this in several ways (Garvey, 1990, p. 41):

- They provide a means by which a child represents or expresses his feelings, concerns, or preoccupying interests.
- They provide a channel for social interaction with adults or other children.
- An unfamiliar object tends to set up a chain of exploration, familiarization, and eventual understanding: an often-repeated sequence that eventually leads to more mature conceptions of the properties (shapes, texture, size) of the physical world.

Interaction with objects begins in infancy. The nine-month-old infant grasps an object and puts it in his mouth. He waves the object and bangs it. By 12 months of age, the child usually looks at the object, turns it over, touches it, and then puts it in his mouth, waves it and/or bangs it. By 15 months, the child visually inspects an object before he does other activities with it. By the time he reaches 3 years of age, he is acting out themes with objects, such as feeding a doll using a toy cup and saucer or having a doll drive a toy truck. By the time the child is three, Garvey indicates the child interacts with objects in the following ways (1990, p. 44):

1. He uses objects in the way they are intended. He no longer, for example, puts every toy in his mouth when he plays but only those that are supposed to go in the mouth such as a spoon or fork.

2. He organizes his objects so that things that belong together are used together (such as horse and rider, cup and saucer, doll and doll clothes).

3. He performs sequences of actions such as cooking a meal, eating the meal and washing the dishes.

4. He uses objects appropriately for himself (such as brushing his teeth with a real toothbrush), on others (such as a doll), or has others use objects (such as a doll brushing her teeth).

5. Where he doesn't have a needed object he can pretend it is there (such as eating pretend soup with a toy spoon).

6. He uses objects for things that he may need but doesn't have (he stirs his coffee with a stick when he doesn't have a spoon).

The three-year-old is well into the period of symbolic representation. Garvey has found that younger children need very realistic types of toys to get started in the world of pretend. As the child gains skill at pretending and imagining, he then makes use of abstract items such as big cardboard cartons (used as a house, a cave, or a castle).

When a child meets a new object, he usually goes through a sequence of four activities: exploration, manipulation, practice, and repetition. Garvey presents the following example. A three-year-old boy approaches a large wooden car he has never seen before. Garvey indicates that the child goes through the following sequence (1990, pp. 46–47):

1. **Exploration:** He paused, inspected it and touched it.

2. **Manipulation:** He then tried to find out what it could do. He turned the steering wheel, felt the license plate, looked for a horn and tried to get on the car.

3. **Practice:** Having figured out what the object was and what it could do, he got to work on what *he* could do with *it*. He put telephones on it, took them off, next put cups and dishes on it. Now he knew what could be done with the car.

4. **Repetition:** He then climbed on it and drove furiously back and forth with suitable motor and horn noises.

The first three activities are not clearly playful as is the last. The first three are more experimentation than play.

The young child gains in several ways from playing with objects. As Garvey shows, highly imaginative players are also excellent at solving problems involving the use of objects. Much of the young child's social life centers on objects. Toddlers' social activity centers on exchanging objects. Three-year-olds spend time deciding who things belong to, as in "This is yours and this is mine." Things are passed out: "One for you and one for me."

Emotional attachments to toys can be very strong. How often we see a young child who goes everywhere carrying a scruffy stuffed animal or find a child treasuring a set of toy cars. Children also express emotion through objects. A doll may become the child's own little brother or sister.

For older children play with objects becomes very complex. Complex structures are built with building materials. "All through these changes, however, objects continue to arouse curiosity and the de-sire to learn. They provide enjoyment in mastering their use or in understanding the properties of things, and they also continue to facilitate social contacts and to assist in the expression of ideas and feelings" (Garvey, 1990, p. 57).

Play with Language

Play with language includes play with noises and sounds, playful use of the linguistic system, and social play with language. Play with noises begins with the babbling stage. Older children also play with sounds and syllables in a rhythmic way. A child 2 years and 2 months of age says as she builds with her toys:

> go, bib bib bib, bib bib bib
> go, bib bib bib

She finds her "sleepy time" book and chants:

> sleepy time a sleepy time
> sleepy sleepy time
> sleepy time

Between two and three, children begin to use noise words when playing with objects or pretending to be an animal such as "bow-wow" for a dog, "ding-a-ling" for a phone or "pow-pow" for a gun. Children also begin to change their voices to fit different characters, such as using a deep voice for a father and a high squeaky voice for a child. Sound play is found most often when the child is playing alone. This child talks as she plays alone in the bathtub with an assortment of objects:

> Water is in this water is in this water is in this water is in this water is clear.
> Water in the cup. Water in the cup there . . . put some shampoo in water.
> I put shampoo on it.
> I put shampoo on it.
> I put shampoo on it.

She repeats phrases and sentences in a rhythmical way, as if experimenting with the language.

During social play, language play falls into three categories: spontaneous rhyming and word play, play with fantasy and nonsense, and play with conversation.

Play with Social Materials

Play with social materials is play that centers on the social world and according to Garvey provides the principal resource of make-believe or pretending. When this type of play includes characters, dramatic themes, and story lines, it is called **dramatic play**. This is a very complex type of play that integrates all the child's resources into one whole. This type of play seldom is seen before the age of three.

There are certain themes used by young children. Two popular ones are treating/healing (someone is hurt and is helped to get well) and averting threat (some danger such as a monster is posed and the play consists of the children saving themselves). Other popular plans are packing for and taking a trip; shopping, cooking, dining; repairing; and telephoning. Objects often influence the choice of themes. That is, the kinds of dramatic play props available may provide inspiration. Dress-up clothes, kitchen equipment, or vehicles may inspire a theme or plan (Figure 33–5).

The play of younger children usually follows some kind of rules. This is not in the sense of a formal game, but in the sense that the children involved put some specific limitations on what can be done during the play activity. Some teasing may be allowed, for example, but it can't get mean or the play breaks up.

Young children's play also contains ritual; that is, some kind of controlled repetition. A ritual usually includes some kind of turn taking, with each person's contribution being a turn. Two turns, one by each participant, is a round. Look at this example from Garvey:

	First Child	Second Child
Round 1	You're a girl.	No I'm not.
Round 2	You're a girl.	No I'm not.

These rarely occur in the busy preschool room but occur frequently when a pair of children play together in privacy.

Figure 33–5 **Dressing up in adult clothing is a favorite part of symbolic dramatic play.**

Dramatic Play

The dramatic play of preschoolers at ages three, four, and five has some distinct characteristics. Three-year-olds usually have no preconceptualized theme or plot (Brown, Curry, and Tittnich, 1971). Much of their play involves a display of fear due to the appearance of some threatening aggressive character who may be imaginary or one of the other children pretending. When a three-year-old becomes a character he *is* that character. His is not the conscious pretending of the older child. For three-year-olds, roles are fluid and constantly changing. They do a lot of collecting and gathering and carrying things around in purses and suitcases. These containers must be searched daily for clothes, kitchen equipment, and manipulative toys which have been packed and carried about. Play is very repetitious. The child may do the same thing in the same way every day for long periods.

Four-year-old dramatic play involves the management of aggressive impulses (Brown, Curry, & Tittnich, 1971). There are usually aggressive heroes who attack and rescue. There may be a monster or a

dramatic play

ghost who attacks—the rest of the children respond by running. There is usually a safe or cozy place where those attacked can hide and be protected. For some, the open aggression is too threatening and they vent their hostile feelings by being silly or using bad language. Masculine and feminine traits are exaggerated and props such as cowboy outfits, fire fighter, police and medical equipment, dresses, veils, coats, ties, and grown-up shoes are needed. There is usually a lot of gross motor activity, especially running and jumping. More roles are used and groups are set up according to some criteria. For example, the author had a group of four-year-old boys (before sneakers were as popular as they are now) who had a leather sole club; only the children with leather soles on their shoes could belong. Fantasy and reality are now more clearly separated and the four can role play and consciously pretend. Hiding is often a part of the action.

The five-year-old uses complex dramatization (Brown, Curry, & Tittnich, 1971). He works through his fears and hostilities in his play (Figure 33–6). Roles are not only real-life types, but also cultural folk heroes such as "superheroes" and characters from fairy tales.

In the primary grades, children continue to enjoy dramatizing (Wasserman, 1990). "Opportunities to dramatize—either purely inventive scenarios or those stories read and loved in class—should be part of the daily life in a primary classroom" (Wasserman, 1990, p. 175). An accessible supply of props (such as dressup clothes, hats, shoes, crowns, scarves, tools, flashlights, etc.) are essential materials for the primary classroom. Spontaneous dramatic play should be encouraged. It is not unusual for the dramatizing of a favorite story to evolve into a whole new plot. Puppets and a puppet stage should also be available.

THE FUNCTIONS OF PLAY

Over the years, an increasing amount of research and experimentation has been done to try to document the functions served by play. The following are examples of the functions identified by some of this research. Play enhances cognitive development, especially divergent thinking and problem

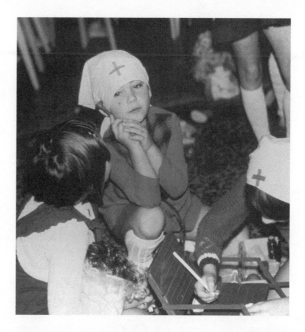

Figure 33–6   Dramatic play can have a therapeutic function. These children work through their feelings about medical happenings.

solving (Christie & Johnson, 1983). Further, through play children can learn the planning skills that are needed to be efficient problem solvers (Casey, 1990; Casey & Lippman, 1991; Rosen, 1974). Imaginative play experience relates positively to better attention span, self-control, and ability to interact and communicate with other children (Freyberg, 1975). Playing with materials aids children in using materials to solve later problems. Children who had an opportunity to play freely with sticks and clamps were able later to figure out how to use these materials to obtain a prize that was out of reach (Bruner, 1975). Rubin (1982) found that playing alone has some values, depending on whether it's constructive or functional. Time spent in parallel constructive play (e.g., art, puzzles, blocks) is positively related to high social and cognitive competence. Time spent in parallel functional play was associated with low social and cognitive competence.

Through dramatic play, children gradually develop the distinction between fantasy and reality (Scarlett, 1981). Children who have imaginary playmates tend to be bright and healthy, imaginative, and creative (Jalongo, 1984; Pines, 1978). Dramatic play can also function in a therapeutic way for both normal children and children with emotional and behavior problems (Brown, Curry, & Tittnich, 1971) and for children who are hospitalized (Farnum, 1974) or who have fears and anxiety regarding normal medical care (Henkens-Matzke & Abbott, 1990; Klein, 1979).

Development in language and literacy is supported by play activities of many kinds. Symbolic play and literate behavior are closely related. Story reenactments facilitate comprehension and retention (Pellegrini, 1985). The first stages of reading and writing are enhanced by teacher extension of children's literacy-related symbolic play through supplying literacy props in centers (e.g., paper and writing implement, maps, magazines, *TV Guides*, menus, as mentioned in Unit 24) and encouraging children's attempts to write (such as writing a shopping list in the housekeeping center) (Campbell & Foster, 1993; Morrow, 1990; Neuman & Roskos, 1993; Perlmutter & Laminack, 1993; Schrader, 1990). Play facilitates language and social development (Monaghan, 1985). The social interaction during play facilitates social development by helping children become less self-centered and more able to see the points of view of others. It supports language development through the opportunities to apply language to real-life situations.

Young children's role playing provides a window into their view of other people's social roles (McLloyd, Ray, & Etter-Lewis, 1985). Role playing also provides a view of children's language development (Sachs, Goldman, & Chaille, 1985). Social play promotes maturity: children act more mature when engaged in pretend play than when engaged in nonpretend play (Berliner, 1990). By elementary school, children usually select playmates of the same sex. They also may have contests with the boys against the girls, have pollution rituals (one sex is contaminated if touched by the other), or invasion rituals such as when one sex teases or interrupts the other sex's games. Overall, boys engage in more play with motion and include more conflict in their play. Girls tend to solve their problems in more low-key ways (Garvey, 1990).

Play is a medium of expression and learning for all children, including those with disabilities (Wishon, 1986). Most important, play activities are done for fun (Kramer & Schaefer-Hernan, 1991).

ADULT ROLES IN CHILD PLAY

As with other areas of child activity, adults can intervene, join in, and/or be directive in play. They also can step back, stay out, and serve as a guide when needed. Research has indicated that adults can enhance child play directly. There are two basic types of sociodramatic play training: **outside intervention** and **inside intervention** (Christie, 1982). During outside intervention, the adult stays outside the play but offers questions, suggestions, directions, and clarifications that will help the children enhance their dramatic play roles. For example, "What else can doctors do?" or "Fire fighters use hoses to get the water to the fire." Inside intervention involves the adult in the play activity. The adult actually takes on a role. The adult can then demonstrate various types of play behaviors such as imitation, using objects for make-believe, doing make-believe actions, showing how to enter already established play situations, using appropriate verbal communication, and extending the story line. For example, as a patient the adult might say, "Oh doctor, I have a headache and a stomach ache. Please help me." As the children pick up the play techniques, the adult can gradually phase out. The adult needs to be cautious about not dominating the play (Traywick-Smith, 1985). The following are examples of some of the research that supports the value of using play-training techniques.

The studies by Morrow (1990), Neuman and Roskos (1993), and Schrader (1990) all involved enhancing literacy knowledge and concepts through providing both literacy props and adult support during play activities. Morrow (1990) found that including reading and writing materials in dramatic play centers increased the frequency of observed literacy play. Morrow compared the frequency of literacy behaviors observed with and without teacher guidance.

outside intervention   inside intervention

With teacher guidance the frequency of literacy play behaviors was higher than without teacher guidance. All experimental classrooms were supplied with a special container filled with literacy materials: book-making materials, different sizes and types of paper, ready-made blank booklets, magazines and books, and pencils, felt-tip pens, crayons, and colored pencils. In two sets of experimental classrooms (with teacher guidance and without teacher guidance) a thematic center was set up as a veterinarian's office. In the no guidance classrooms, with literacy materials only and with the veterinarian centers, the teachers introduced the materials the first day, discussed how they might be used, and did not refer to them again. In the teacher guidance condition the teachers discussed potential uses of the materials at the beginning of each play period. In addition, the children were told that they could pretend to read and write. Addition of the literacy materials increased the frequency of literacy dramatic play compared to control groups where there was no intervention. Where teacher guidance was used there was a greater increase in literacy behaviors than under the no guidance conditions (Figure 33–7).

In the study by Schrader (1990), four prekindergarten teachers participated in a workshop designed to acquaint them with how to determine children's intentions in their play activities and particularly as their intentions related to literacy. Schrader was interested in whether the teachers would be able to follow the children's literacy interests rather than impose their own ideas. Each classroom had three centers designed for symbolic play: the post office, the office, and the house. Each was stocked with a supply of literacy materials. The teachers were observed to determine if they used their knowledge regarding the determination of children's intentions to extend and expand the children's play or if they ignored the children's intentions and redirected them in some other directions. Examples of an extending style would be, "Did you write the address on the envelope? You could buy a stamp. You could write a check for it. You could fill out the order form. Why don't you look it up in the phone book?" (pp. 87, 89). A redirecting style would be one like the following in which the teacher ignores what the children are doing and redirects their attention to a writing activity that she selects, "I'd like

you to write me a story. Ok? Write me a story." Schrader found that literacy play based on extending the children's natural activities was much richer than that which came from teacher suggestions and preconceived ideas. Teaching from the children's natural inclinations requires spontaneity and creativity on the part of the teacher. "This requires teachers to focus not on teaching per se but on the process of learning that belongs to the child. Consequently, teachers must exercise self-control when participating in children's symbolic play. They must refrain from pressuring children to cooperate with the teacher's own preconceived priorities" (p. 99).

Neuman and Roskos (1993) focused on children of poverty enrolled in Head Start classes. They found that classrooms in which not only materials were provided but a parent-teacher was actively involved in assisting the children, resulted in the children increasing in their ability to read environmental print (e.g., office signs such as EXIT, COME IN, OPEN, and CLOSED) and label functional print items (e.g., telephone book, calendar). "These findings suggest that adult interaction in literacy-enriched play settings may represent an important opportunity for assisting minority children who live in poverty to think, speak, and behave in literate ways" (p. 95).

Adults have a responsibility to be active facilitators (Ford, 1993) of children's play both through providing active support and space and materials.

PLAY MATERIALS AND SETTINGS

Adequate play materials and play space are necessary for promoting play activities (Frost, 1992; Hart, 1993). Materials that fit both small and large budgets can be found. Detailed descriptions of what might be done with particular materials and ideas for arranging materials and equipment are also available. The major factor is for the adult to provide materials and equipment that fit the developmental levels of the children; arrange and rearrange as needed; provide new things as they are needed; and be sure she is involved in all the roles previously listed in this unit.

The placing of materials and equipment can have a noticeable effect on what children do. For example, in one study by Kinsman and Berk (1979), a change

The following dialog took place one week before a presidential election. Kate is 3 years and 10 months of age. She has cut out pictures of the candidates from the cover of a magazine and she and mother are using them for paper dolls.

Mother	Kate
What do they say to each other?	Nothing. You're not gonna vote for me. I want to vote to your no.
You're not gonna vote for me?	Yeah.
Who are you gonna vote for?	May I have this one Mom? I want this.
I'll have this one. Okay. I've got C. Who have you got?	President F.
Okay. What does President F. say to C.?	No, I'm not gonna kiss you. I'm gonna kiss myself. 'kay. I'm not gonna kiss you, I'm gonna kiss myself.
You are, huh. Well I'm not gonna kiss you either.	Oh, beans!
Ah! Ooh! He hit me. Ouch!	(Take) that!
Ouch! Why did you hit me President F.?	Because I think you are mean.
You, oh, I'm not mean. What makes you think I'm mean, President F.?	Because you are icky.
Ah, but I just want to move into your White House.	Okay, come on.
Can I come and move in with you? Where can I stay in your White House?	In my bed.

Again, mother asks questions and goes along with her assigned roles. The play theme is much more sustained and complex than in the first example.

Figure 33–7 **Example of adult involvement in child play**

made in the arrangement of the block and the housekeeping areas altered the play and social behaviors of groups of preschool and kindergarten children.

Whether settings are **thematic** or **nonthematic** can have an effect on dramatic play (Figure 33–8). Dodge and Frost (1986) explored ways to set up dramatic play areas that would encourage role play but not dictate the roles to be taken (such as would be the case with a home center, a medical center, a firefighter center, etc.). They and others had noted that as children neared age five and their thinking extended outside their immediate experience the usual housekeeping area became less enticing as a setting for role playing. They found five-year-olds were inspired by more open-ended props such as empty cardboard cartons, spools, planks, and crates. Along with these open-ended materials, various types of realistic props were available to use in whatever roles the children chose. In this type of nonthematic setting the children engaged in more dramatic role play using many different themes. When structured play centers were available, the play was richer in content if more than

Figure 33–8   Nonthematic play equipment inspires a variety of dramatic play roles.

one center was available (such as a home, a grocery store, and an office) and if there were things in each center that interested both males and females.

McLoyd (1983) compared three-and-one-half and five-year-olds' play with high-structure and low-structure objects. High-structure objects are realistic items such as a tea set, ironing board, tool kit, and a telephone. Low-structure objects are open-ended items that do not have any predetermined use relative to a specific role, such as pipe cleaners, cardboard boxes, metal cans, foam cups, and blocks. High-structure objects increased the frequency of parallel and solitary pretend play for the three-and-a-half-year-olds. Overall the quality of the play with the two types of toys was about the same at each level. McLoyd concluded that we cannot recommend one type of toy as better than the other at this point.

Thomas (1984) found that the toy preferences of early readers (children who read at age four) were different from those of four-year-old nonreaders. Early readers preferred reading readiness toys such as books and alphabet cards whereas those who did

not read early preferred gross motor, construction, and fantasy toys.

Rogers and Sawyers (1988) reviewed research on the effects of toys and materials on play. When too few or no toys are available for children, the number of aggressive acts is much greater. There are more negative interactions when children are playing with small toys than when they are playing on large pieces of equipment such as slides and climbers. Art materials, manipulatives, clay, sand, and water inspire less social pretend play than dress-up outfits and other dramatic play props or small cars and blocks. Obviously, the kinds of materials adults provide can determine the type of play in which children will engage. Children's interest is enticed by novelty, variety, and complexity. Toys should be rotated so that the same things are not available everyday. Open-ended toys like blocks and Legos® grow in complexity with children's cognitive growth and ability to use them in more complex ways.

Rogers and Sawyer (1988) also examined research on the effects of space on children's play. Space needs to be adequate and equipment and materials placed for maximum stimulation of the most complex, advanced forms of play. The smaller the space, the more social interaction takes place. Aggression also increases. However, in a larger space there is more rough-and-tumble play and more running. Small groups are more conducive to friendships and imaginative play. The younger the children, the smaller the group should be. Outdoor play is also important every day. The more mobile the outdoor equipment is, the more frequent will be imaginative play activities.

PLAY AND TELEVISION

Some critics believe that since the introduction of television, children have lost much of their playtime by spending time watching television. It also is felt that children may learn socially unacceptable behaviors from television. Dorothy and Jerome Singer (1978) investigated the possibilities for children gaining ideas and skills for spontaneous imaginative play from watching television. Singer and Singer found that children picked up more ideas from a live model than from TV. However, if they watched TV with an adult who interpreted what was going on in the program (as opposed to watching the program with just other children or alone), there was a measurable increase in their imaginative play during free-play time in their day-care center. They also found that the parents of the children who showed the most imagination were the parents who did more monitoring of their children's TV viewing and who allowed less viewing of adult-oriented aggressive programs. In looking at program content, they found that make-believe animals and puppets seemed to have the most positive effect on the play of the children. Singer and Singer held meetings with the parents to assist them in seeing the importance of program selection on the behavior of their children. They found the parents most eager to help.

These authors see that the right kind of television programs can make a positive contribution to the play behavior of young children.

Adults who work with young children can educate parents regarding the appropriate uses of television, but otherwise they have no control over what children view at home. They frequently must handle role play that centers on the type of superheroes seen on TV. Kostelnik, Whiren, and Stein (1986) point out that these characters are attractive to young children because they are always good, they have powers children would like to have, they always win, they are in control, they never make mistakes, and they receive lots of positive recognition. Children gain some psychological benefits from taking on the superhero role. They become powerful, gain prestige, and become characters that they cannot be in real life. The clearcut good vs. bad fits with their level of moral development. However, the rough-and-tumble nature of this play is often too disruptive for the classroom. Kostelnik et al. suggest several things adults can do to make this play constructive and within realistic boundaries:

- Help children recognize the positive characteristics of their favorite superheroes.
- Introduce real-life heroes and heroines.
- Explain that when TV shows are filmed, the actors and actresses do not really do all those dangerous feats.
- Limit the times and the places where superhero play can take place (such as only outdoors).

- Use the superheroes as a way to lead into the study of related concepts (such as Spiderman could be the lead-in to the study of spiders).
- Help children decide on a goal for their hero (rather than using the role as an excuse to run around and be wild).
- Do not let rough-and-tumble play get out of hand.
- Help children to learn how to get out of the play when it gets too wild or they are tired of it.
- When the play gets too rough explain why it is out of bounds.
- Limit the area in which superhero play can take place.
- Be clear that aggression is not allowed.
- Offer other challenges for children so they do not need to fall back on superhero play.
- Build children's confidence in other areas.

As an example of an incident that was handled constructively, several four- and five-year-old boys were pretend shooting in their classroom while playing with the unit blocks. Their teacher had a meeting with them and explained they could role play shooting at home where they had plenty of space and not so many other children around but that it was not allowed at school. She then went on to tell them they would have to think of another way to use the blocks. She also suggested some possibilities. The boys decided they would build a hideout. They followed through, still able to be heroes, but heroes engaged in an activity that was safe and had an acceptable indoor noise level.

SUMMARY

Play is what young children are involved in most of their waking hours. Through play they integrate all their knowledge and skills. Play promotes cognitive, affective, and psychomotor development. A child uses a number of kinds of resources in play: motion and interaction, objects, language, and social materials. During the preschool period the child's dramatic characters and themes become more complicated, and the number of children who play together increases. By the primary grades boys and girls usually play separately. Their play becomes much more complex and has more rules. For example, their play with motion becomes more structured activities like Jump-Rope with rhymes and Hide-and-Seek. Around age seven they begin to be interested in competitive games.

Play serves a number of functions for the young child: it aids in developing problem-solving skills; promotes social and cognitive competence; aids in the development of the distinction between fantasy and reality; promotes curiosity and playfulness; helps communication, attention span, self-control, social, language, and literacy skills; provides a vehicle for the adult to learn how children view the world; and can be therapeutic. Adults can help children develop higher-level play through outside and/or inside intervention and by the amount of space, number of children in the space, and the amount and types of play materials provided.

Adequate materials and space promote good play. Both thematic and nonthematic settings for dramatic play seem to promote different but valuable kinds of role play. Both realistic and ambiguous props should be available. Although television has been highly criticized for lowering the quantity and quality of play, the right kinds of shows can promote imagination and creativity. Children enjoy playing the superheroes they view on TV, and this type of play can have some positive values if done under controlled conditions.

FOR FURTHER READING

Bergen, D. (Ed.). (1988). *Play as a medium for learning and development*. Portsmouth, NH: Erlbaum.

Block, M. N., & Pellegrini, A. D. (Eds.). (1990). *The ecological context of children's play*. Norwood, NJ: Ablex.

Carlsson-Paige, N., & Levin, D. E. (1987). *The war play dilemma*, New York: Teachers College Press.

Cohen, D., & MacKeith, S. (1990). *The development of imagination*. New York: Routledge.

Dimidjian, V. J., (Ed.). (1992). *Play's place in public education for young children*. Westhaven, CT: National Educational Association.

Goelman, H., and Jacobs, E. V. (Eds.). (1993). *Children's play in child care settings*. Albany, NY: SUNY Press.

Goldstein, J. H. (Ed.). (1994). *Toys, play, and child development*. New York: Cambridge University Press.

Haight, W. L., and Miller, P. J. (1993). *Pretending at home: Early development in a sociocultural context*. Albany, NY: SUNY Press.

Hekkendoorn, J., van der Kooij, R., & Sutton-Smith, B. (1994). *Play and intervention*. Albany, NY: SUNY Press.

Isenberg, J. P., & Jalongo, M. R. (1993). *Creative expression and play in the early childhood curriculum*. New York: Merrill/Macmillan.

Jones, E., & Reynolds, G. (1992). *The play's the thing: Teacher's roles in children's play*. New York: Teachers College Press.

Klugman, E., & Smilansky, S. (Eds.). (1990). *Children's play and learning*. New York: Teachers College Press.

Paley, V. G. (1986). *Mollie is three: Growing up in school*. Chicago: University of Chicago Press.

Paley, V. G. (1988). *Bad guys don't have birthdays: Fantasy play at four*. Chicago, IL: University of Chicago Press.

Pellegrini, A. D. (1985). The relations between symbolic play and literate behavior: A review and critique of the empirical literature. *Review of Educational Research, 55*, 107–121.

Reifel, S., & Yeatman, J. (1993). From category to context: Reconsidering classroom play. *Early Childhood Research Quarterly, 8*, 347–367.

Scales, B., Almy, M., Nicolopoulou, A., & Ervin-Tripp, S. (Eds.). (1991). *Play and the social context of development in early care and education*. New York: Teachers College Press.

Smilansky, S., & Shefatya, L. (1990). *Facilitating play*. Gaithersburg, MD: Psychosocial and Educational Publications.

Stambak, M., & Sinclair, H. (Eds.). (1993). *Pretend play among 3-year-olds*. Hillsdale, NJ: Erlbaum.

Tegano, D. W., & Burdette, M. P. (1991). Length of activity periods and play behaviors of preschool children. *Journal of Research in Childhood Education, 5*, 93–99.

Traywick-Smith, J. (1994). *Interactions in the classroom: Facilitating play in the early years*. New York: Merrill/Macmillan.

SUGGESTED ACTIVITIES

1. With a small group of students in class, discuss the question, "What is play?" Compare your answers with the definition from the text. See if the group can agree on one definition. Write the definition on a piece of chart paper or on the chalkboard. Ask for reactions from the rest of the class.

2. You are teaching in a child development center, a kindergarten, or a primary classroom. A parent comes to you and says, "Why do the children spend so much time playing? They can play at home. Why should I have to pay money for my child to play?" How would you respond?

3. In your neighborhood, at a childcare center, or in an elementary school question six children ages three, four, five, six, seven and eight regarding their play activities and preferences. You might ask:
   a. What do you do when you play?
   b. What do you like to do the most when you play? At home? At school?
   c. When you are not playing, what are you doing?

   Compare the children's responses by age and whether their answers pertain to home or school. Report on your results in class.

4. Question four parents and/or teachers about how they feel about play. Do they value play? In what ways? Some questions to ask are:
   a. Describe play in your own words.
   b. Does play have value for children? If so, what is the value (are the values)?
   c. What kinds of things support children's play? What kinds of things discourage children's play?
   d. What is the role of play at home? At school? (If interviewing a parent, ask specifically what she does to promote play at home; if interviewing a teacher, ask what she does to promote play at school.)

5. Following are some cards with play samples. Make enough photocopies so each student in the class can work with one card at a time. Divide into small groups, each with a set of cards. Pass the cards from person to person. For each card categorize the behavior described using the work sheet in Figure 33–9. After everyone has categorized each example, compare your results. Discuss any discrepancies and see if you can arrive at an agreement. State a reason for each categorization.

Theresa: I'm high in the sky. (She's swinging.) Jason: I'm high in the sky. I can fly. (He's on a swing next to Theresa's.) Theresa: I'm high in the sky. I can fly, fly, fly. Jason: I can fly, I can fly and eat pie up so high.	Bill and Rudy come running across the playground laughing and shouting. Bill grabs Rudy around the waist and they fall to the ground laughing. Bill growls and roars like a wild beast as the two boys roll over and over on the grass.
In the playroom there is a big block with a steering wheel on it. Another block serves as a seat for the pretend vehicle. Isabel: Let's take a trip on this airplane, Kate. Kate: Okay, let's get in. They drive along. Isabel: This engine sounds bad. We'll have to land and fix it.	Mrs. Chen has placed a new piece of equipment on the playground. Phong comes up to it and looks it over. It is a large boxlike structure with a ladder on one side, bars on another, and a hole in the top. Phong climbs the ladder, peers down the hole and then drops inside the box. Next he calls out, "Rudy! Come and get in my boat!"

Play Sample	Play: How well does the behavior fit Garvey's five criteria?					Resource/Vehicles			
	1. Enjoyable	2. Intrinsic motivation	3. Spontaneous	4. Active engagement	5. Related to non-play	Motion/ Interaction	Objects	Language	Social Materials
Theresa and Jason									
Bill and Rudy									
Isabel and Kate									
Phong									

Figure 33–9 **Play category worksheet**

6. Visit a day-care center, preschool, kindergarten, or primary classroom. During free-time play, observe four different children (or groups of children) for fifteen minutes each. Take detailed notes on everything you observe. Categorize the children's activities using the play category worksheet. Compare how closely each child's play activity fits the who, why, and what criteria. Compare the vehicles or resources for play used by each child or group of children. Give a report in class describing what you found out about the quality of children's play.

7. Visit a pediatrics department in a hospital. Find out what kinds of play materials, activities, and space are available for children and who is responsible for the play program. Observe the play therapist at work. Find out if the hospital offers any preparatory play activities program for children before they enter the hospital to help them work through any fears or do away with any misconceptions they may have. Evaluate the program. Write a report on your findings and your evaluation.

8. Visit a child development, day-care, preschool center, kindergarten or primary classroom. Observe one or more teachers for a total of 60 minutes during play time. Write down everything the teacher(s) does (do). Evaluate each teacher's behavior by answering the following questions:
   a. Did the teacher get involved in the play in a directing way ("Now we will do this")?
   b. Did the teacher get involved by offering guidance (suggest a toy or prop; suggest an idea)?
   c. Did the teacher get involved by becoming a part of the activity (as a model or as a participant)?
   d. Did the teacher spend time observing the children's play?
   e. Was there any evidence that the teacher had planned in some way to support spontaneous play (supply special materials or props, read a story, show a film, or take the children on a trip which might expand their role playing)?
   f. How effective was each teacher in any or all the roles observed? Do you feel the teacher was more supportive or directive?

9. Visit a well-equipped child development center or a curriculum materials center, or look through some current materials and equipment catalogues. Decide which materials you would buy to furnish a center for 12 four-year-olds if you had $3000 to spend. Be sure to have something for each play category. State a reason for buying each piece of material or equipment you decide to purchase.

10. Watch *Mr. Rogers' Neighborhood*. Describe what kinds of things in the program you think might inspire interesting fantasy and imaginative play in young children. Tell how you might watch this program with a small group of children, interpret the program for them, and follow up on what was viewed in a way that would support and enhance the children's play. Do the same activity watching *Sesame Street* and *Barney*. Compare the results.

11. Make an entry in your journal.

REVIEW

A. Define play. Give at least three examples.

B. Match the theories in Column I to their descriptions/definitions in Column II.

Column I	Column II
1. surplus energy theory	a. Through play the child gains his identity.
2. relaxation theory	b. The child relives the activities of his ancestors.
3. preexercise theory	c. Through play the child expresses his emotions and masters his problems, especially his fears.
4. recapitulation	d. Play is a means for getting rid of excess energy.
5. Freud's theory	e. During play the child practices skills he will need in adulthood.
6. Erikson's theory	f. Play develops through three stages: practice, symbolic, and games with rules.
7. Piaget's theory	g. Play serves as a means for the child to gain new energy.

C. Categorize each of the following examples as play with motion and interaction (*MI*), play with objects (*O*), play with language (*L*) and/or play with social materials (*SM*).
   1. Dot is playing with clay, "Gooky, gooky, cooky. Cooky, cooky, gooky."
   2. Lee Kwan says to Isabel, "Let's cook dinner."
   3. The children come running out to the playground laughing and shrieking as they race toward their favorite piece of play equipment.
   4. Kate laughingly says to Bill, "You are a super-duper-pooper."
   5. Bill says, "This is my truck and that is your truck."
   6. Theresa says, "Derrick, you be sick and I'll be the doctor."

D. Read each of the following play descriptions carefully. Decide if each child is probably five, four, or three years of age.
   1. Derrick pretends to be a ghost and "attacks" the other children who run off screaming.
   2. "Let's get dressed up like grown-ups and then hide in our house so the bad guys can't get us."
   3. As assortment of empty food containers is set up on the shelves of the grocery store by the teacher. The children spend the morning packing the containers into bags and carrying them to the housekeeping area.
   4. "Don't let any boys touch you—they are poison!" shouts Shelly to the other girls as they all run screaming across the playground.
   5. "Come on. I'll be the police and you guys be the robbers."

E. List ten functions of play.

F. Select the correct answer to the following. There is only one correct answer for each.
   1. When children are playing, adults sometimes suggest how a toy can be used more imaginatively or how a new role or scene might make the play more interesting.
      a. An adult should definitely not take that role.
      b. Sometimes an adult might take that role.
      c. It is appropriate for an adult to take that role often.
   2. Mrs. Goodbird and Jason are sitting at the kitchen table. Jason is playing with his clay and some toy trucks. He fills the trucks and moves them around the table. His mother unloads the trucks for him and then he drives them back and fills them up again. They talk about what they are doing as if they were really a truck driver and a truck unloader.
      a. This is a good example of how a parent can teach her child about how to pretend.
      b. To help Jason his mother should be more directive and have him play her way.
      c. Getting involved in a child's play like this is undignified for the adult and of no help to the child.
   3. Mrs. Tanaka brings in some new props for the children: dress-up clothes, fire hats, construction worker hats, and medical kits. When the children don't seem to know what to do, she gets out a medical kit and says, "I feel sick. Who will check me." Isabel says, "I will. I will be the doctor. Theresa, you be the nurse."
      a. This teacher is being too directive.
      b. This teacher has done a good job of bringing in materials and presenting an idea, while leaving it up to the children to elaborate on it.
      c. The teacher should be more directive. She should tell the children what to do. She should assign roles and make them play with the props so they will all know what to do with them.
   4. Mr. Brown sits near where the children are playing with blocks. He observes closely but does not intervene in any way.
      a. Observing is one of the roles an adult may take in the child's play.
      b. Observing is not a role that the adult should take in child's play.
      c. Mr. Brown must be tired today or he would be more involved.

5. Mrs. Kirk has set up a medical center. Among the many dramatic play props are pads and pencils to write prescriptions, a book to record appointments, a clipboard with paper to record the patient's progress, telephones, telephone book, Post-it® notes for messages, and magazines in the waiting area. In order to get the highest rate of literacy behaviors from her class:

   a. Mrs. Kirk should sit back and let them use their imaginations.

   b. Mrs. Kirk should explain everything the first day and then let the children use them in their natural way.

   c. Mrs. Kirk should discuss the possibilities and materials in the center each day to provide guidance for their activities.

6. Schrader found in her research that one style of teacher interaction produced much richer literacy play in the classroom:

   a. Extending the play by building on the children's natural intentions.

   b. Redirecting the play so the children were sure to do what she believed they should do.

   c. Keeping out of the play so the children could engage in their natural ways of learning to be literate.

7. If Joan, a teacher, provides appropriate and adequate play materials, equipment, and space for play,

   a. she has done her job. The children can take it from there.

   b. that is only the beginning. She will have to follow up with rearranging and bringing in new things when needed, and play a number of roles such as observer, reflector, or elaborator.

   c. children really don't need many raw materials. She could have saved herself a lot of trouble.

8. Singer and Singer feel

   a. television is all bad and children should never watch it.

   b. some TV programs are not too bad, but they still take valuable time away from play.

   c. certain types of TV programs enhance the fantasy and imaginative play of young children.

9. Mrs. Garcia sits down with a small group of children to watch an educational program that features puppets and fantasy characters. She sits quietly, not saying anything. Singer and Singer would say

   a. this is a good procedure.

   b. the type of program is good but she should interpret the action for the children and follow up on it if she wants the children to benefit fully from the experience.

   c. she really doesn't need to sit with the children. They can benefit from viewing a good program on their own.

10. Young children like to take on the roles of the superheroes they see on television.

   a. This is an unhealthy type of play; children should be discouraged from playing these roles.

   b. Playing these kinds of characters makes children feel big and important and should be encouraged without any adult interference.

   c. Playing superhero roles may have some value for children as long as adults make sure the play doesn't get out of hand and that there are limits on when, where, and how.

Unit 34

The Impact of Technology

OBJECTIVES

After studying this unit, the student should be able to:

- Identify the important factors regarding young children and television.

- List the criticisms and the positive aspects of television viewing for children.

- Describe how both parents and teachers can help young children get the most value from television.

- Evaluate and handle situations in which teacher, parent, and/or child has a problem regarding television viewing.

- Describe how learning from computer instruction relates to the constructivist and the behaviorist points of view.

- Identify basic factors in the use of computers with young children.

- Realize the importance of video games in the lives of young children.

Tremendous technological advances are being made each day as we move toward the twenty-first century. In this unit we look at several questions regarding technology and our young children. What effect do technological advances have on our children? When, where, and how should young children be introduced to modern technology? How should our technological wonders be used with young children? Is technology providing solutions to some of our educational problems or making them more complicated?

Technology presents a multitude of challenges for adults who work with young children in school and home settings. Advances in video and computer technology are available to provide new vehicles for learning for children in school. Unfortunately few

KEYTERMSKEYTERMSKEYTERMSKEYTERMSKEYTERMSKEY

technology

schools are equipped to make the best use of the vast array of available video and computer materials (Meade, 1991). Some teachers have scrounged funds and equipment wherever they could and even spent some of their own money to provide students with up-to-date technology to support their learning. Technology also provides challenges to families (Swick & Robinson, 1988). Families are challenged to explore new technologies and how they might affect their lives. Families need to learn how to take the best advantage of new and old technologies such as telecommunications, television, electronic toys, and computers. In homes at all socioeconomic levels, children spend several hours each day watching television (both regular programming and videotapes) and/or playing video games. In many affluent homes children also have daily exposure and experience with personal computers. Technology in the workplace is far ahead of technology in the school and the home. The challenge for the future is to have our children enter the workplace ready to handle the technological requirements of their jobs.

SOURCES AND CRITICISMS OF TELEVISION

Programs are provided by the commercial networks and by the public network (PBS). Commercial programs are paid for by advertising (commercials). Public programs are paid for by funds collected through taxes and funds donated by business and industry and the viewing public. There is no advertising on **public television**. The widespread use of cable TV has added greater variety to available programming, both good and bad.

Numerous criticisms have been leveled at television, some regarding television in general, some directed at public television, and many at **commercial television**. Some of these criticisms include the following:

- Commercial television presents too many aggressive, violent models, both live and in cartoons (Cantor, 1977; Rubinstein, 1978; Honig, 1983; Notar, 1989; Charren, 1990; NAEYC Position Statement, 1990; NAEYC Position Statement on Violence, 1993).

- Commercial television presents too much advertising, with content that promotes products such as snacks, candy, sugared cereals, and soft drinks which are unhealthy for children and toys which children pressure their parents to purchase. Many programs are actually half-hour commercials (Larrick, 1977; Honig, 1983; Notar, 1989; Charren, 1990; NAEYC Position Statement, 1990; Schatzky with Verrucci, 1994).

- Some of the content is frightening and increases fears and nightmares (Cantor, 1977).

- Television promotes sexism through depicting stereotyped male and female roles (Sternglanz, 1974; Honig, 1983; Schatzky with Verrucci, 1994).

- Television may tend to desensitize feelings and emotions regarding violence (Sex and violence, 1975; Honig, 1983; Schatzky with Verrucci, 1994).

- Television viewing makes children passive and expectant of being entertained (Cantor 1977; Honig, 1983; NAEYC Position Statement on Violence, 1993).

- Commercial television has a lot of poor quality cartoons and not enough educational programming (Current Evaluation, 1979; Notar, 1989; Charren, 1990).

- Some of the first PBS shows were criticized for being too academic (Cohen, 1974) but presently there are a large number of educational and some entertainment programs for young children (Current Evaluation, 1979; Schatzky with Verrucci, 1994).

- Television offers children only sight and sound and does not respond to them; children learn best through multisensory experiences with a

KEYTERMSKEYTERMSKEYTERMSKEYTERMSKEYTERMSKEY

public television   commercial television

responsive environment (Skutch, 1977; Schatzky with Verrucci, 1994).

- Television's emphasis on the visual may dull the child's auditory sensitivity, which makes learning to use phonics in reading more difficult (Sawyer & Sawyer, 1980).

- Beyond the preschool years, prolonged television viewing may have a number of negative effects on behavior: making children more tense, anxious, restless, and suspicious; promoting shorter attention spans; producing children who thrive on noise, strife and confusion, get too little sleep, lack respect for adults, feel school is irrelevant and feel that problems should be settled with violence (Larrick, 1977; Pena, French, & Doerman, 1990; NAEYC Position Statement, 1990; Schatzky with Verrucci, 1994).

LEARNING FROM TELEVISION

Although there has been much criticism of television, researchers and critics have also looked at the positive factors, such as shown in the work of Singer and Singer. Television offers numerous models encouraging observational learning for children. For this reason, adults who work with young children need to be aware of the models children are viewing in terms of the kinds of behaviors available for imitation.

Meltzhoff (1988) found that children as young as 14 and 24 months old imitate televised action, not only immediately, but also a day after the viewing of a TV presentation. Research studies by Coates, Pusser, and Goodman (1976) and Friedrick and Stein (1978) show children imitate what they see on film. What could this mean in real life? Suppose four-year-old Tracy's favorite television heroine is Wonder Woman. Tracy watches as her dad backs his car out of the garage. Suddenly she darts behind the car and extends her arms. Her mother picks her up before she is hurt, and asks, "What are you doing, Tracy!" Says Tracy, "I'm Wonder Woman." Fortunately, the car was moving at a slow speed and Tracy's mother was alert. After seeing a cartoon character hit another cartoon character on the head with a golf club followed by a quick recovery of the victim, Tim gets angry at his little brother and hits him on the head with a golf club. Tim's little brother is rushed to the hospital emergency room. Tim cannot understand why his brother didn't just bounce up, unhurt like the television character.

Television presents fantasy actions for the child to copy in his play. These actions are usually simple and repetitive. Often they require the child just to move fast from place to place or speak short, simple bits of dialogue. Mukerji (1977) points out that this kind of play cuts down on the need for the child to devise his own pretend play and thus cuts down on his need to think and use his own creative play ideas.

When a child becomes very involved in these television roles, he may not be able to distinguish the line between fantasy and reality. Tracy may be confused and not understand why she will never be as strong as Wonder Woman. The normal young child may have enough fantasy ideas without getting more from television.

Potts and Henderson (1991) reported on the number of physical injuries observed in several popular children's commercial television programs observed during a week early in 1990. On the average there were 25.6 injuries per hour of viewing. The rate varied from relatively few in educational programming and situation comedies to 45 injuries per hour in cartoons. Injuries are viewed as purposely caused, result in little if any pain or damage, and the victims are usually males who receive little if any sympathy, thus providing a distorted view of physical injury and its consequences (Figure 34–1).

The adult who works with young children needs to consider the number and kind of aggressive acts a child might see in a program in light of the fact that children do learn from models through observation. By age three, children imitate televised models as readily as live models (McCall, Parke, & Kavanaugh, 1977). Most of the cartoon aggressors on television are animals. It may be that children would not be as prone to imitate animals as they would be cartoons of real people or equally aggressive acts by real actors.

Children who are already prone to be aggressive appear to be the ones who are most likely to be even more aggressive after viewing violent behaviors on

Figure 34–1 **Young children may imitate aggressive and violent behaviors they see on television.**

television (Honig, 1983). There seems to be a sensitive period before age eight when children receive long-lasting effects from viewing violent TV. Viewing of television violence has been found to have the following effects (Honig, 1983):

- It is associated with higher levels of aggression for both boys and girls.
- Over time, aggressive children watch more and more violent programs.
- For boys there is an association between low reading achievement and watching violent programs.
- The lower children's intellectual level, the more likely they are to believe that TV violence is real.

Aggressive children are usually disliked by their peers, watch more violent television, and become even more aggressive. These factors underscore the importance of adults with work with young children, including the development of prosocial behavior in the curriculum (as described in Units 29 and 30).

Reviews of research (Honig, 1983; Quisenberry, 1982) on the effects and characteristics of commercials have identified the following factors:

- There is no evidence that commercials improve language skills although they could be used to do so by knowledgeable adults.
- The females shown are mostly female stereotype housewives.

- Younger children believe commercials more than do older children.
- Upper middle-class children have a better understanding of the content of commercials than lower-class children.
- African-American children found commercials more believable than European-American children.
- Parents feel that the commercials foster a materialistic orientation in children.
- Younger (three- to seven-year-old) children gain less information from commercials than older children and become more frustrated by the interruptions.
- To counteract commercials reasoning works better than a direct order but if the product is desirable counter-influence is ineffective.
- Commercials are successful in selling products. Children do everything possible to get parents to buy products which catch their interest.

Levin, Petros, and Petrella (1982) found three- to five-year-old children could discriminate the commercials from the programs. They suggest that training on discriminating and understanding advertising can begin as young as age three. Greer, Potts, Wright, and Huston (1982) reported a study that compared various forms and placements of commercials. Commercials were chosen that were high or low on formal features: action, pace, and visual change. Commercials were either clustered at the beginning or end of the program or dispersed throughout. Children were observed in a play situation before and after viewing the program and commercials. Those children who observed the commercials that were high on action, fast paced, and included frequent visual changes were more aggressive in the play sessions following the TV viewing (although the commercials contained no aggression). These very active, fast-changing commercials seemed to excite the children and resulted in more aggressive acts during play. The highest number of aggressive acts appeared after viewing the clustered commercials. Viewing attention was highest for the commercials high on formal features. Overall, commercials are effective in accomplishing their sales purpose but provide some negative side effects. For parents probably the most annoying aspect of commercials are their children's demands for the advertised products. This problem escalates during the pre-Christmas season. Some parents have dealt successfully with this problem by keeping a list with the child of everything the child wants. A deadline is set and at that time the child picks one or more items he/she wants the most, the number depending on the family's budget. At that point discussion is closed. The child has had an opportunity to make a choice and learned something about economics, and parents will invest their money in something the child really wants.

Commercials are also useful for educational purposes as public service announcements (PSAs). Rosenkoetter and Rosenkoetter (1991) had third, sixth, and ninth graders assess the effectiveness of four different drug abuse PSAs. Most of the younger children (75 percent) believed that the PSAs were effective while the percentage decreased for the sixth graders (52 percent) and the ninth graders (34 percent). The younger children felt that more straightforward commercials such as one featuring the death of a drug-addicted rat were the most effective. Sheibe and Barber (1991) looked at the salience and comprehensibility of three types of anti-drug appeals: fear, celebrity endorsement, and peer approval. Third, fourth, and fifth graders viewed the PSAs. The PSA appeals became more salient with age. The celebrity appeal was most salient and most understandable. Fear was the least comprehensible overall.

Pezdek and Hartman (1983) were interested in how young children attend to television when distractions are present. They found that five-year-olds have the ability to operate at a complex cognitive level. They are able to play with toys or listen to a record and attend visually and/or auditorially to a TV show. Although they are less attentive when they have distractors present, they comprehend as much as children who have no distractors. These results suggest that young viewers are not the passive recipients of television that they are often characterized to be.

The child may also learn something about male and female sex roles from television. Sternglanz (1974) rated ten popular television shows to find out what kind of male and female behavior was pre-

sented. Of 147 characters, 33 percent were female and 67 percent male—not quite fair to females. There were more good males than bad (67 as compared to 25) but females were almost always good rather than bad (43 as compared to 2). Males were more aggressive, more constructive, and more active. Females were shown as quiet and unaggressive and were often punished for high activity. Male activity effected change; female activity was neutral. Four out of five female stars were witches. The child learns that men are strong and powerful and women meek and quiet. He learns that the only females with power are witches. Since this study was done, an effort was made on some shows to show less stereotyped sex-role behavior. More strong, active females, female professionals, and males who take a protective role with children and animals were included. However, a 1981 study (Honig, 1983) reported that three times as many men as women appeared on TV and that these males were most often in traditional male areas such as the law, medicine, and policework.

Children view parenting styles on television as they watch shows that focus on families. Scheibe and Grossman (1993) did a content analysis of parenting styles on prime-time TV programs for the years 1983, 1987, and 1991. Two-thirds of the parents depicted were authoritative. However, there was an increase in authoritarian parenting depicted with time. Sons were treated in a more authoritarian manner than were daughters, and older children were treated in a more authoritarian style than were younger. Fathers were depicted increasingly in nontraditional roles.

Television serves an important function as it can show the child both feelings and values through the themes it presents. Feelings surrounding life and death can be shown. The child then has a chance to voice questions about how and why things happen as they do.

Children can learn positive values and prosocial behavior from television. They can learn ideas about what is good and what is bad. Research shows that children learn positive social behavior from shows like *Mr. Rogers' Neighborhood* and *Sesame Street* (Figure 34–2). *Mr. Rogers* is a model who shows the child how to be honest, to share, to love, and to be kind. Research such as that by Friedrich and Stein (1978) and Coates and associates (1976) shows children increase their prosocial and decrease their antisocial behavior in nursery school play after viewing these positive kinds of television programs. As Moore (1977) suggests television could be of great help in showing the child how to get along well with others.

Television shows can have even broader social value. Both Mukerji (1977) and Moore (1977) point out that the child can learn positive things about children from other cultures and communities as they see them depicted on television as they really are rather than in stereotyped ways. *Sesame Street* and *Mr. Rogers' Neighborhood* regularly include people of many cultures, people with handicaps, people of a wide age range, and non-stereotyped males and females.

Family situation comedies (sitcoms) are very popular with children and provide some examples of prosocial behavior (Rosenkoetter, 1993). Rosenkoetter analyzed two fifties sitcoms (*Leave it to Beaver* and *I Love Lucy*) and two eighties sitcoms (*The Cosby Show* and *Growing Pains*). He found that the most common moral theme was resisting temptation such as taking something that belongs to another person, and the next most frequent was general responsibility. Rosenkoetter looked specifically at first and third graders' family sitcom viewing and mothers' reported frequency of prosocial behaviors displayed by their children. There was a positive relationship for first graders' frequency of sitcom viewing and frequency of reported prosocial behaviors.

Children can also learn facts about nature, social life, numbers, letters, and other concepts. Some pro-

Figure 34–2 **Positive behaviors, such as giving help to a younger child, can be learned from television.**

grams take the child to parts of this country and to other lands that she probably would never see otherwise. Television may teach a child to count, recognize numbers, play games, sing, dance, and read. Besides social and emotional development, intellectual development can also be affected through viewing quality television.

The Harvard preschool study (White & Watts, 1973) found that well-developed children are more likely to watch high-quality programs such as those on public television or the better commercial shows that have some educational values. The less well-developed child is more likely to view cartoons, quiz shows, soap operas, and other adult programs.

Although a great deal of research has been done regarding the effects of television on young children's behavior, the picture is not clear. For example, Singer and Singer (1979) feel that the rapid-paced format of *Sesame Street* shortens the child's attention span and has a negative effect on learning. On the other hand, the producers of *Sesame Street* feel the rapid pace is needed to hold the young child's attention. According to Singer and Singer (1979, p. 56):

> Yet it seems possible that they are actually creating a psychological orientation in children that leads to a shortened attention span, a lack of reflectiveness, and an expectation of rapid change in the broader environment. The pacing of television itself may be stimulating an appetite for novelty and lively action, as well as expectation that problems can be resolved in a very short space of time.

They found the slower, reflective pace of *Mr. Rogers' Neighborhood* to be much more conducive to child learning than the fast pace of *Sesame Street*. Singer and Singer (1979) also found that after watching Mr. Rogers over a period of 2 weeks on a daily basis at school, children "increased their level of imaginative play and showed more positive emotional reactions to the other children than did children who watched *Sesame Street* or a group of control films." The Singers strongly believe that more slow-paced, reflective children's programming is needed.

Gerald S. Lesser (1979) takes an opposing view. Lesser believes there is not one best style of television for children, but that there should be a variety of styles provided to fit the individual differences we find in children. He cites research he believes shows no observable negative effects on the play behavior of young children who watch fast-paced as opposed to slow-paced segments of *Sesame Street*.

Research by Joel Cooper and Diane Ruble (1980) brings to our attention some further ramifications. They compared the play behavior of children who watched television with children who did not watch television. They found that both groups played in an equally aggressive manner. They also found that:

- Up until the age of eight, more girls than boys imitated television violence.

- Four- and five-year-old boys and second-grade boys were less aggressive in their play after viewing a violent program than boys who had seen a nonviolent program. Boys seemed to be able to burn off some of their hostility through watching violent activity.

- Ten-year-old boys and girls were more aggressive after seeing an aggressive show but were no more aggressive than children who hadn't seen the show. Children who saw a nonviolent show played less aggressively than those in the other two groups.

Cooper and Ruble (1980) recommend putting more effort into looking into the beneficial effects of nonviolent programs.

TELEVISION AT HOME

Children are watching 3 to 5 hours of television per day. Even children as young as 9 months old are watching up to 90 minutes of television per day (Cohen, 1993/94). Public TV and educational commercial television offer many excellent programs. However, these are not necessarily the programs our children are watching. They spend a lot of time watching violence, commercials, and even "steamy sex" (Notar, 1989). In the 1980s the time networks spent showing commercials increased from what it was in the seventies to 12 to 14 minutes per hour. Moreover, during commercials the sound level is increased to attract the attention of the viewer. Many children are at home unsupervised after school with access to adult programming available on cable.

Pinon, Huston, and Wright (1989) looked at how sociological variables such as program access, family attributes, and child characteristics influenced the viewing of *Sesame Street*, a well-established educational program. Two groups of children were followed from ages three to five and ages five to seven. Viewing of *Sesame Street* reached a peak around ages three-and-a-half to four and decreased as the children reached age seven. Peak viewing was about four hours per week. Children who attended daycare watched less educational television than those at home. Children with older siblings spent less time with *Sesame Street* and those with younger siblings spent more.

There are a number of things parents can do at home to make television of value to their children:

- Find out which programs are high quality. See publications such as those distributed through Action for Children's Television (ACT), 20 University Rd., Cambridge, MA 02138 and the National Coalition On TV Violence, P.O. Box 2157, Champaign, IL 61820.

- Do your own program evaluation using the rating sheet for Suggested Activity 2 at the end of this unit.

- Find which channel is the Public Broadcasting Casting outlet.

- The first time a child watches a program, watch with her. Note the child's reaction. Explain content that upsets or confuses her (Figure 34–3).

- Decide which shows are all right for the child to watch alone and which are not. Some shows may need an adult there to talk about frightening or puzzling incidents. Some themes center on death, greed, jealousy, love, and other areas which should be explained to the child while the show is on. The adult has to be ready, also, to answer questions that may arise later.

- Regulate what the child sees:
  1. Limit the number of hours per day television can be viewed.
  2. Allow only quality programs to be seen.
  3. Be sure the older child does his chores before he looks at television.
  4. Turn off the TV when necessary.

Figure 34–3 **Adults can monitor what children view on television. They can also watch with the children to interpret the action and elaborate on the things children might learn from the program.**

- Talk about the advertising. Adults should learn about nutrition so they can explain why sugar-coated cereals and candy bars are not healthy. It should be made clear that not every toy advertised will be bought for the child.
- Spend time doing other things with the child; read stories and play games.
- Encourage the child to play alone, with friends, or with brothers and sisters.

Cohen (1993/94) suggests some other steps parents can take relative to television viewing:

- Before subscribing to cable TV, consider carefully if the money might be better spent in other ways.
- Have the family members make a list of other activities you all enjoy. Each week have family members take turns selecting one of the activities to do.
- Parents should be good role models, limiting their own viewing to quality programs and limiting their viewing time.

The young child will value, enjoy, and learn from quality programs if an interested adult watches with him. For example, Gavriel Salomon (1977) found lower-class children whose mothers co-observed

Sesame Street watched longer, enjoyed it more, and learned more. Co-viewing and discussion are very important parts of home TV viewing according to Abelman (1984). Negative influences can be minimized if parents discuss which events are real and which are not, which behaviors are rewarded and which are not, which motives are good and which are not, give their personal opinions of programs, and clearly specify behaviors that may or may not be imitated.

TELEVISION AT SCHOOL

Today television is usually available in child development centers, daycare centers, daycare homes, and elementary schools. Teachers and day-care providers need to follow guidelines suggested for parents to provide quality experiences with television for their children. In addition, adults who work with young children should find out what the children watch at home. Larrick (1977) suggests several questions the teacher can ask:

- What programs does the child see regularly?
- How many hours of television does he watch each day at home?
- Why does the child watch television instead of doing something else?
- Does the child watch alone or with others in the family?
- Given a choice of free-time activities, what is the child's favorite?

Teachers also should spend time viewing children's programs. They can then communicate knowledgeably with child and parent regarding the content. Larrick suggests that teachers point out quality programs to parents during conferences and in newsletters.

Keeping in mind the cautions in picking materials that are not sexist, racist, or in other ways damaging, teachers can use television-related materials just as suggested for home play. Introducing an activity with a Muppet® puppet, for example, is an excellent way to get the attention of children. Public television stations sometimes provide a guide to their daily educational programs. There are some excellent programs for young children on during the day that are not advertised in the newspapers. Television-related materials can be used as motivators and as a bridge between home and school (Figure 34–4). Abelman (1984) believes that in-school intervention is necessary to interpret television for children whose parents are not taking on this responsibility and that we can make better use of TV as a motivator for children's learning.

Video technology is growing rapidly in its applications in education. Johnson (1990) describes how computer-controlled videodisc technology can create settings for learning. Videodisc technology opens up opportunities that help children "problem-solve, hypothesize, critique, comprehend and transfer knowledge to other settings and situations" (p. 169). Johnson warns that the technology does not stand on its own. An adult must be there to mediate and structure the situation in order for the children to get the most out of the learning opportunity.

Portable video-recorders offer many exciting opportunities in the classroom. For example, students and teachers can record activities. The videotapes can serve as a source of data for teachers to include in portfolios of work to be shared with parents, as vehicles for students and teachers to evaluate experiences, and as records of student activities to be enjoyed again. Students can even write scripts for programs, record the programs, and show them to other classes and at parent meetings.

A recent innovation is using *Mr. Rogers' Neighborhood* for affective staff development (Marazon, 1994). Mr. Rogers provides a model that respects young children and focuses on affective development. Included in the Mr. Rogers' programs are behaviors that exemplify virtue, values, moral, and self-concept themes. Some examples are "kindness, sharing, compassion, caring, joy, peace, love, confidence building, success, forgiveness, understanding, trust, autonomy, uniqueness, patience, honesty and goodness" (Marazon, p. 35). After only one month of Mr. Rogers viewing, the teachers had begun to reflect and modify their behaviors so they were calmer, slower paced, and more patient. As the inservice sessions progressed over the year, they became more self-aware.

Figure 34–4   Television follow-up materials catch the interest of the young child in school.

ACTION FOR TELEVISION REFORM

To improve the quality of children's television shows, a group of parents, teachers, and television professionals in Massachusetts formed a group they named **Action for Children's Television (ACT)**. There are now groups all over the country. ACT works hard to inform the public about television, pressure the networks to upgrade show quality, and encourage stricter regulations of program and commercial content. ACT has waged a long, hard fight with commercial television to obtain quality programming for children. ACT, along with other child advocate organizations such as the Children's Defense Fund and the National Association for the Education of Young Children, was instrumental in persuading Congress to pass The Children's Television Act of 1990, which reinstates guidelines that were in effect before the television industry, was deregulated in the early 1980s (Washington Update, 1990). The major regulations in this act include:

1. Commercials are limited to 12 minutes per hour during weekdays and 10.5 minutes per hour on weekends.

KEYTERMSKEYTERMSKEYTERMSKEYTERMSKEYTERMSKEY

Action for Children's Television (ACT)

2. Stations must document their attention to children's programming when applying for or renewing licenses.

3. The National Endowment for Children's Educational Television was created to stimulate the development of good programming for children.

In 1990 the National Association for the Education of Young Children published a position statement on media violence in the lives of children (NAEYC, 1990):

> NAEYC CONDEMNS VIOLENT TELEVISION PROGRAMMING, MOVIES, VIDEOTAPES, COMPUTER GAMES, AND OTHER FORMS OF MEDIA DIRECTED TO CHILDREN. NAEYC supports efforts to use media constructively to expand children's knowledge and promote the development of positive social values. NAEYC also supports measures that can be taken by responsible adults to limit children's exposure to violence throughout the media. (p. 18)

NAEYC suggests that policy makers put stronger limitations on broadcasts, and that teachers help children learn prosocial behaviors and limit violent play activities. NAEYC also suggests that parents censor their children's television viewing and watch TV with their children so that they can explain what is good and bad. Parents are encouraged to write sponsors about advertisements for poor quality products and the abundance of violence.

In 1993 NAEYC published a position statement on the overall violence situation in our society (NAEYC Position Paper on Violence, 1993). Included was the following recommendation for action (p. 82):

> Regulate children's television programming to limit media exposure to violence and restrict practices that market violence through the linkup of media, toys and licensed products.

NAEYC also joined a national task force on media violence (NAEYC joins, 1993). The task force's purpose is to continue and increase government regulation of TV violence.

Levin and Carlsson-Paige (1994) outline the need for developmentally appropriate television that puts children first. Action must be taken to educate parents, teachers, and legislators. Levin and Carlson-Paige describe several ways children are being damaged by spending too much time viewing developmentally inappropriate media content. Children need to develop a sense of trust and safety that is undermined by violent and scary content. They need to develop a sense of autonomy and connection while the media depicts that independence and dependence can't work together. (See Unit 27.) Children need to develop a sense of empowerment and efficacy while TV does not provide models that use peaceful means for gaining these characteristics. TV still gives a distorted picture of sex-roles and doesn't support the acquisition of gender identity. TV doesn't support the development of an understanding and appreciation of how people are alike and different but continues to promote stereotypes. Children need to develop a sense of morality and social responsibility. (See Unit 29.) TV undermines healthy development in this area also by showing violence as a justifiable way of solving problems and not showing enough positive models. Levin and Carlson-Paige describe the need for action to support reform of children's television and television-viewing habits.

COMPUTERS: ISSUES AND CAUTIONS

Questions have surfaced as to the age at which children should be introduced to computers, how they should be introduced, and for what kinds of activities young children should use them. Silvern and McCary (1986) discuss three issues:

1. Can computers change the way children think?

2. Is it worth the effort to include computers in the early childhood curriculum?

3. How does the computer fit into the constructivist view of child development?

Silvern and McCary believe computer software will not enable them to learn anymore than they would through some other instructional method. Children are limited in what they can learn through drill and practice. Working in a small group with a teacher may be as effective as working individually with a computer. However, thought can be changed qualitatively; that is, children may learn to think differently. There is some evidence that experience with LOGO helps children think more divergently and reflectively.

In considering whether computers in the early childhood classroom are worth the trouble, Silvern and McCary consider the most frequent criticisms. First, computers limit the child to working with two dimensions. Silvern and McCary accept this limitation but feel that even three-dimensional materials have limitations and that the experiences offered from color graphics, touch screens, a mouse, a joy stick, etc. offset the two-dimensional limitation. A second criticism is that computers are at a level that is too abstract for preoperational children. Silvern and McCary feel this is the fault of the software available, not the computer. They believe that software appropriate to the preoperational child's level of development can and will be developed. A third criticism is that working with a computer limits mobility to simple eye-hand coordination. Silvern and McCary point out that this is not true at the beginning levels of LOGO, where the children actually imitate the turtle and go through the motions with their own bodies that they will later use in manipulating the turtle on their computer screen. However, Silvern and McCary also remind us that there are many valuable activities such as drawing and painting that require limited body movement.

Next, critics find that working with a computer limits social activity. This is only true if adults make it so. Children have been observed to socialize by sharing responses and working together to solve problems. Computer programs have been criticized for being in a format in which there is only one right answer. Again, Silvern and McCary say this is the fault of the software. Adults have to be careful in their choice of software. Computer time is criticized because there is no linguistic response, thus depriving children of time for language development and providing frustration for nonreaders. This problem can be solved initially by having older children who are readers help the nonreaders. Voice synthesizers have become less expensive and are available at a reasonable price. Critics also feel that computers restrict freedom and creativity. However, there is software that facilitates creativity, exploration, and even dramatic play. Finally, critics question the value of drawing or typing on a computer screen when these tasks can be accomplished with less expensive equipment. Silvern and McCary believe the computer offers a new media for these activities that provides a different and rich experience.

Silvern and McCary suggest the following guidelines to facilitate overcoming the criticisms described above:

1. Do not use the computer as a means for accelerating achievement.

2. Consider the computer as an additional piece of media material that can enrich, not replace, experience with other media.

3. Be sure the experience with the computer relates to children's real-life experiences.

4. Provide opportunities that enable children to construct knowledge.

5. Allow free access, not forced access, to the computer. Children who are developmentally ready and interested can use the computer while other children choose other activities.

The third problem dealt with by Silvern and McCary centers on how constructivist theory relates to computer use. The question regarding computers is whether they are real or representations. Silvern and McCary believe that computers can be considered to be real and thus concrete if the software provides for the child to learn and build on experiences (vs. the right and wrong point of view) and if the activities are matched to the child's ability. Concreteness is then dependent on the adult choosing appropriate software and the ability match of the children who choose to use the computer. A caution here: beware that when there is limited access in terms of the ratio of computers to children, sometimes timid children will avoid the computers and let the more aggressive ones dominate the equipment. One way to ensure everyone has equal access is by having the children sign up for turns and learn to use a timer to limit the amount of time they can use the computer. Silvern and McCary conclude that use of computers can be compatible with constructivism if handled correctly by adults. However, we do need to be careful not to think computers can replace concrete materials and experiences for exploration which are the core of knowledge construction. There are limitations set by the nature of computer programs that are not present in the natural environment. Haugland and Shade (1990) define the computer component of early childhood education as follows:

> Computers are an essential tool for young children. Like crayons, paints, blocks and/or any other learning resource we provide young children, computers are neither good nor bad. The potential benefits and the dangers of computers in the hands of young children depends on how they are utilized. The potential of computers depends upon the wisdom of adults to make wise choices regarding appropriate experiences for young children. (p. vii)

COMPUTERS IN THE EARLY CHILDHOOD CLASSROOM

Computers are being widely used in early childhood classrooms. Hoot (1986) identifies four major uses for computers in early childhood educational settings. **Computer drill and practice** activities provide practice and reinforcement for concepts, such as shape, numeral, letter, and color recognition, after they have been introduced by the teacher. Critics usually refer to these types of activities as "workbooks on a screen" or "computerized flash cards" (Hoot, 1986, p. 2). Since it is questionable as to whether workbook-type activities are appropriate for young children in the first place, drill and practice is often criticized as an inappropriate activity for the early childhood classroom. Most programs for young children fall into this category. Other computer programs are tutorials that teach new concepts and skills. Simulations are a third type of computer activity. Simulations try to offer reality-based, problem-solving activities. Finally, computers can be used as tools, such as for word processing or programming. Hoot (1986, p. 5) warns:

> What computers are or are not capable of doing and what we, as professionals, allow them to do are very different issues. It is our responsibility to make decisions

concerning computer use on the basis of rational justification, rather than the exuberant claims of the computer industry, or pressures from parents or administrators.

Calfee (1985) reminds us that the teacher is the key in the educational process. Even with computerized instruction, someone has to show the students how to interact with the machines, has to provide the programs, and has to help students when they cannot understand or misunderstand the instructions. Schetz and Stremmel (1994) have developed a model for teacher-assisted computer implementation that is based on a Vygotskian view. Teachers and students collaborate in solving problems using the computer. Computers are an exciting educational tool (Figure 34–5). Teachers should not be fearful nor should they jump in without careful investigation.

Wells and Burts (1990) describe the introduction of computers into a class of four-year-olds. The computers were placed in specially made work stations that could be closed and locked for security. The teacher began with an introduction using concrete activities in which the children acted out some of the things that a computer does. These activities were set up in a "Computer Corner." Before using the computers a few simple rules were explained and a pictorial reminder list was put up in the computer area. By the time the computers were put into use, the children were well prepared and eager to start.

Figure 34–5 **Two or more children can work cooperatively at the computer center.**

Computer drill and practice

Selecting good software is a critical part of preparing to use computers in the classroom. Spencer and Baskin (in Hoot, 1986) and Haugland and Shade (1990) provide guidelines for software selection. An abbreviated version of Spencer and Baskin's guidelines can be found in the Suggested Activities section of this unit. Haugland and Shade (1990) suggest the following criteria:

1. Age appropriateness. The concepts and the method of presentation should be appropriate for young children.

2. The child should be in control of the pace and direction of the activity.

3. The instructions should be clear.

4. The program should provide for increasingly complex activities.

5. Children should be able to operate the program independently.

6. The activities should be process rather than product oriented, thereby encouraging exploration and discovery.

7. The software should be a simple model of some aspect of the world. Graphics should be realistic and proportional to the real world objects.

8. Technical qualities should be good: bright colors, clear pictures, animation, and sound.

9. Unlimited opportunities for trial-and-error problem solving.

10. There should be opportunities for children to make transformations of the world that they cannot make in real life such as changing a scene from city to country or the weather from sunny to cloudy.

11. Software should "reflect the diverse backgrounds, cultures, and experiences of young children" and maintain the anti-bias point of view. (Haugland, 1992, p. 44)

The variety of computer-related materials and activities available is changing rapidly. Upgraded and new software is continuously coming on the market (Haugland, 1993, 1994; Shade, 1993, 1994). The new CD ROM technology can provide more exciting and versatile programs. New vistas have opened with the availability of networks and information services (Brett, 1994). Masses of information are available through these online services.

Computers can be valuable tools for the classroom if they are set up as a center where children can choose to go when their interests take them. Too frequently they are set up in a laboratory where everyone has to go for a certain prescribed period of time and where the activities are not necessarily integrated with those in the classroom. Hopefully in the school of the future there will be two or three computers in every classroom with every student having equal opportunity for access.

COMPUTERS AT HOME

More children will enter prekindergarten and kindergarten classes with home computer experience. More often early childhood teachers will be asked by parents to provide advice regarding purchase and use of a home computer. Teachers can share their personal experiences and invite parents to visit the classroom and observe how the children interact with the computers. They can also share books and articles that may be helpful to parents. In addition it can be suggested that parents go to the library and look through some computing magazines, especially *Family Computing*, before they start shopping. Most young children who learn to use computers at home do so because they see their parents use them. For example, as a parent is word processing, his two-year-old climbs in his lap. He lets the child try the keys. The child is delighted with the response and is soon experimenting. Two college professor parents (Reed, 1983) report that their four-year-old uses several simple drill and practice programs, likes to practice writing alphabet letters, and writes his own books using phonetic spelling. From two years of age on a child may be ready to start through exploring the keyboard and using drawing programs. Such young children need careful supervision when using this expensive piece of equipment. On the other hand,

KEYTERMSKEYTERMSKEYTERMSKEYTERMSKEYTERMSKEY

software   CD ROM

young children should not be pushed if they are not interested. Parents should consider carefully before buying a computer just for their child unless the child shows an interest.

Video Games

Video games, a combination of video and computer technology, came into their own in the 1980s. They now have a firm foundation in almost every home where there are children. Children may be spending more time with video games than with television programs. Video games offer opportunities for problem solving and eye-hand coordination experience, but they also usually include rather violent objectives (Rogers 1990).

In 1992 it was estimated that one in three homes owned a video game system (Veciana-Suarez, 1992). In his book *Video Kids: Making sense of Nintendo*, Eugene Provenzo is quoted as stating that too many of the video games are crude and violent. Even through there are some nonviolent games available, still children spend too many hours playing with them when they should be involved in more large-muscle motor activity, preferably outdoors, or reading a good book. Veciana-Suarez reports that Jason Rich, author of *A parent's guide to video games*, suggests that parents play the games with their children both to monitor the content and spend some interactive time with the children. Further, a limit should be set on playing time. Parents should preview games and read reviews before making a purchase. Provenzo warns parents to stay away from games that are described on the box using terms such as *shoots*, *destroys*, or *kills*. Rich says to look for descriptors, such as "dozens of hidden places to explore," which indicate challenging multilevels, nonviolence, and color.

TECHNOLOGY IN THE FUTURE

As we look to the future, how will technology affect people? According to Salomon, Perkins, and Globerson (1991) technology will enhance human intellectual functioning. They take the view that a person working in partnership with technology could be far more "intelligent" than the person working alone. If the activities done with the technological tool are open-ended and the learner is willing to explore the possibilities, more will be gained from the experience. For example, learning LOGO computer programming as a subject matter versus using LOGO programming as something to play around with. Casually playing with the software provides more indepth understanding and longer lasting learning. Essentially they are saying that if we take a constructivist approach with technology we will gain something from the interaction that will affect our next interaction, while a behaviorist approach can enhance performance but not basic intellectual functioning.

Looking ahead to the twenty-first century, Kaha (1990) believes technology will create new learning environments that will result in a different kind of knowledge. Children will enter the classroom having had experiences with television, video games, and computers. The printed page may be unfamiliar. Children will have experienced a lot of fast-moving action so school may seem pretty slow, dull, and unexciting. Children may appear dulled by all this outside stimulation.

Kaha (1990) foresees that in the twenty-first century books will not be the norm. Audio and visual aids will be more common. Technology will not replace the teacher, it will provide more participatory, interactive textbooks. The texts will be able to change to fit the students and students will be able to change the text as their knowledge increases. Knowledge will not be gained through memorization of facts but will be an interactive process.

SUMMARY

Technology, properly used, has the potential to support child development. Television and computing can be especially valuable. Although television has been with us for a relatively long time, we still have not put its potential to full use. Computing is just becoming widespread, and interactive videodisc is in its infancy. Only time will tell if technology will become an everyday learning tool for all young children.

Television is broadcast into nearly every North American home and an increasing number of schools. Viewing can be a negative and possibly damaging experience, or a rich and positive experience for the young child. The content and format of television have been highly criticized. Children imitate what they see in films. There is some evidence to indicate that they are just as apt to imitate the good as the bad. Adults should monitor the content of programs and consider limiting the time (if any) the child can spend watching programs that present hostile models engaging in antisocial activities. There are many programs that offer prosocial models for children to copy.

Children should be encouraged to do other things besides watch television. This can be done by a responsible adult who provides other activities and interesting play materials for the child. Teachers in all-day programs for young children may allow children to watch appropriate TV programs in small groups with an adult providing comments on the program as long as other activity options are available. Teachers can also use television-related books, puppets, and games as motivators for learning activities. They can also join and support community action groups.

Computers are gradually finding a place in early childhood education. If used properly, they can help children think more divergently and reflectively and provide valuable learning experiences both individu-ally and/or cooperatively. Computers should be viewed as an additional teaching tool that will add versatility to classroom instruction. As with other tools and activities in the early childhood classroom, the computer will be useful for some children and not for others. More and better software (programs) is coming on the market daily and enabling teachers to use computers without having to learn to program themselves. However, the teacher who is willing to learn programming can open up new avenues for individualizing instruction. The computer can provide instruction with feedback that can free the teacher to do other kinds of teaching. In the long run it will be each teacher and the way that teacher uses the computer that will determine its value to children and their development.

Like computer software, video games have great potential but must be selected with care. Too many of them include excessively violent content but there are some available that provide nonviolent challenges for young children.

Looking to the twenty-first century the possibilities for enhancement of education through technology are vast. We will look forward in the future to more software that offers avenues for exploring and for textbooks that interact with the students.

FOR FURTHER READING

Beaty, J., & Tucker, W. H. (1987). *The computer as a paintbrush: Creative uses for the personal computer in the preschool classroom.* Columbus, OH: Merrill.

Bryant, J. (Ed.). (1990). *Television and the American family.* Hillsdale, NJ: Erlbaum.

Clements, D. H. (1993). Computer technology and early childhood education. In J. L. Roopnarine & J. E. Christie (Eds.), *Approaches to early childhood education* (pp. 295–316). New York: Merrill/Macmillan.

Cuban, L. (1986). *Teachers and machines: The classroom use of technology since 1920.* New York: Teachers College Press.

Davidson, J. I. (1989). *Children and computers together in the early childhood classroom.* Albany, NY: Delmar.

Guidelines for family television viewing. (1990). *ERIC EECE Newsletter, 2*(2), 1.

Gunter, B., & McAleer, J. L. (1990). *Children and television: The one-eyed monster.* New York: Routledge.

Haugland, S. (1993). Computers and young children: Are computers an important learning resource? *Day Care and Early Education, 20*(3), 30–31.

Hohmann, C. (1990). *Young children and computers.* Ypsilanti, MI: High/Scope.

Liebert, R. M., & Sprafkin, J. (1988). *The early window: Effects of television on children & youth*, 3rd ed. New York: Pergamon.

Nickerson, R. S., & Zodhiates, P. P. (Eds.) (1988). *Technology and education in the year 2020.* Hillsdale, NJ: Erlbaum.

Papert, S. (1994). *The children's machine.* New York: Basic Books.

Postman, N. (1992). *Technopoly: The surrender of culture to technology.* New York: Knopf.

Sprafkin, J., Gadow, K. D., & Abelman, R. (1992). *Television and the exceptional child: A forgotten audience.* Hillsdale, NJ: Erlbaum.

Young, B. M. (1991). *Television advertising and children.* New York: Oxford University Press.

SUGGESTED ACTIVITIES

1. Consider the following list of recommendations. Decide as a teacher of young children which of these ways of regulating television viewing you would recommend to parents. Discuss your preferences with a small group in class. List the group's conclusions on chart paper or on the chalkboard for the reactions of the whole class.

   a. Unlimited viewing: Children may watch whatever they wish whenever they want to.

   b. Some limitations: They may watch as much as they want as long as chores (such as keeping room clean and toys picked up) are done and meals are eaten.

   c. Budgeted time: Parents and child work out a certain number of hours per week that the child may watch television. Within that time the child may watch whatever he wishes.

   d. Limited viewing: Children may watch television at specific times of the day such as in the evening, week-end mornings, in bad weather, or when they are ill. In good weather during the day they may not watch television.

   e. Parent decides which shows the child may watch: For example, educational programs only; no cartoons, scary movies, or programs that include violence.

   f. Children do not watch television. Only adults are allowed to watch.

   g. The family doesn't own a television. If something special is on television, they rent a set.

   h. No one in the family watches television under any circumstances.

2. Do a survey of programs on television that are designed for young children. View one show on public television (such as *Sesame Street, Mr. Rogers' Neighborhood, Barney, Where in the World is Carmen San Diego?, Square One Television,* or other children's programs that are on public television). View one on a commercial network or cable and one hour of Saturday morning or weekday afternoon cartoons. When viewing each program, list how many of each of the following kinds of behaviors are depicted:

   a. violence, aggression, or other antisocial behavior (see lists in this unit and see Unit 29)

   b. positive social acts or moral lessons (see Unit 29)

   c. cognitive concepts (see Units 21–25)

   d. number of commercials and length of commercials and types of products advertised.

   e. sex-role stereotypes (see this unit and Unit 29)

   Rate each program using the Television Program Rating Sheet (Figure 34–6). Which programs would you recommend to parents? Which would you not recommend? Which, if any, would you use if you were working in an all-day day-care program? Report to class the data you collected regarding each program and your recommendations.

3. Decide what you would do in each of the following situations. Discuss your decisions with a small group in class.

   a. It is nap time at the day-care center. Rudy begins to moan in his sleep. Suddenly he sits up crying. He tells you that a giant monster is after him. He saw it at home last night.

   b. You are watching cartoons with a small group of children. During one of the cartoons, one of the character falls off two cliffs, is hit on the head with a boulder three times, is run over by a bulldozer, and is blown up with dynamite. Each time he makes an immediate recovery.

TELEVISION PROGRAM RATING SHEET

Check children's TV programs viewed against the following positive and negative characteristics to help you decide whether or not you would recommend the program be viewed by preschool children.

Characteristic	Not Applicable	Positive	Negative
1. Fits the interests of the intended audience.		Content relates to children's interests, holds their attention.	Not relevant, children lose interest quickly.
2. If an entertainment show, the content is appropriate.		Wholesome, exciting and/or humorous.	Gruesome, violent, and/or antisocial behavior.
3. It aids the child in self-understanding and/or understanding of others.		Deals with problems relevant to young children. Supports positive relationships with others.	Problems are not relevant to young children. Promotes incorrect ideas about people and their characteristics.
4. It promotes positive values.		Fair play, kindness, honesty, empathy, sharing.	Crime, cheating, lying, hurting.
5. It promotes and encourages constructive play and activities.		Promotes and encourages behavior such as constructive fantasy play, working with others, an interest in appropriate play materials (such as books or paint), or further inquiry and problem solving.	Shows details of criminal activities, inappropriate materials being used, or extremely competitive, or very aggressive behavior.
6. The program production is high quality.		Production has high-quality script, music, artwork, sets, sound effects, photography, and acting.	Production is sloppy, artwork or sets are poorly done, cartoons are oversimplified and unattractive, acting and/or voice dubbing is poor, action is hard to follow, too fast, or too slow.
7. Program is free of prejudice.		Nonsexist and nonracist. Equality and understanding are promoted. All races, religions, handicapping conditions, and sexes are presented fairly and honestly.	Unfair to any race, sex, religion, or handicapping condition. Presents unrealistic stereotypes.
8. If program presents academic content such as math, science, social studies, or reading, the concepts are age appropriate and well presented.		Concepts presented clearly, repeated in a variety of formats, and illustrated concretely.	Concepts/skills beyond the young child's level; presentation misleading and confusing.
9. If it is a commercial program, the commercials are acceptable.		Advertise worthwhile products such as wholesome, nutritious food or quality toys. Done in a low-key manner. Brief and not too frequent.	Advertise unhealthy foods, shoddy toys, or other poorly made or unsound products. Use hard sell, are too frequent, and are presented louder than the rest of the program.

Figure 34–6   **Television program rating sheet**

    c. You are watching an educational program with a small group of children. The characters on the show have a puppet show with the theme of sharing and not being selfish.

    d. You find the children in your class are especially fond of one of the puppet characters on a daily television program. The same type of puppet can be purchased in your local toy store.

4. Find three articles in current periodicals that discuss children's television shows or using computers with young children. Look through periodicals such as *Young Children, Early Learning, Day Care and Early Education, Childhood Education, Dimensions, Instructor*, and *Pre-K Today*. Also check current issues of magazines designed specifically for parents. Write a summary and short reaction to the articles you read. Include:

    a. the name of each article, the author, and the name of the periodical.

    b. the date and the page numbers.

    c. a summary (less than a page) of the major points you learned from the article.

    d. a reaction to the article. Did you feel you learned something worthwhile? Do you feel the author was correct? What alternatives would you suggest?

Share what you learned with the rest of the class.

5. Design a television parent information pamphlet that could be distributed to parents in your community. Have two parents of young children read the pamphlet and give you their reactions. Distribute copies to members of the class for their reactions and discussion. Revise the pamphlet. Share it with some adults who work with young children in your community (such as the Head Start Director, a day-care center director, and a kindergarten or primary teacher). Ask if they might be interested in using it with their parents. Offer to help them design a parent meeting with the subject "Young Children and Television."

6. Watch one or more children's television shows with a young child(ren). Note each child's interest level, the kinds of questions he asks, and the responses he gives. After the program, ask the child questions about the content of the program. What was it about? What did he like? What did he learn? Why did the characters do what they did (if there was some kind of story or plot included)? Report the results to the class.

7. Go to a large toy store or department store. List, describe, and note the price of television follow-up materials available. Try to find at least ten items. Share your list with the class.

8. Go to local bookstores and to the library. Find and list, with prices and publishers, at least five television follow-up books. Write a short description and opinion of each book. Share your list with the class.

9. Contact six families with at least one child between the ages of three and eight. Provide the parents with a chart set up as shown below. Have the parents keep a one-week record of the child's television viewing on the chart.

ONE WEEK TV RECORD

Child's name _____ Sex _____

Birthdate _____

Date	Program	Length

Evaluate each child's viewing habits. Are there any improvements you feel could be made?

10. Visit two or more preschool, kindergarten, and/or primary classrooms where computers are being used. Through observation and teacher interviews obtain the following information:

   a. How is computer use managed relative to room placement, time scheduling, turn-taking, number of children working at the same time, etc.?

   b. What types of programs are being used (tutorial, drill and practice, simulation, or as a tool; commercial and/or teacher made)?

   c. How are the students responding? Do they seem motivated? Are they anxious to get a turn? Do they have choices? (Observe at least two students, closely following them through the whole process.)

   d. Write a report including all the information you obtained and an evaluation of the effectiveness of the computer as it is used in these classrooms.

11. Review at least five computer programs. Obtain software from centers or classrooms or a curriculum materials center, or obtain review copies from software manufacturers or your local computer store. Use the following procedure as adapted from suggestions in Spencer, M. & Baskin, (1986). Guidelines for selecting software for children. In J. Hoot (Ed.), *Computers in early childhood education: Issues and practices.* Englewood Cliffs, NJ: Prentice-Hall.

   a. Read the instructions that come with the program. Then try it out. The first time through take note of your first impressions: Did you find the program interesting? Easy to use?

   b. Go through the program two more times. Now note specifics about the program. Are the prompts, questions, and responses logical and clear? Are the graphics, sound, and/or animation of good quality?

   c. Try out each program with children. Note if the children like the program, if they can use it independently once you have gone through it with them, if they want to use it again, and if they feel in control.

   d. Obtain the opinions of teachers and/or parents who have used the program with children.

   e. Write an evaluation of each program including the following information:

      1) Program name, manufacturer, and price.

      2) Type: drill and practice, tutorial, simulation, tool

      3) Concept or skill taught

      4) Brief description

      5) Your evaluation of the program based on the information obtained.

   For detailed evaluation checklists see the Spencer and Baskin article.

12. Make an entry in your journal.

REVIEW

A. Match the terms and phrases in Column I with their definitions and/or examples in Column II.

Column I

a. commercial network
b. PBS
c. ACT
d. imitation
e. values
f. co-observe
g. fantasy
h. males as depicted on television
i. females as depicted on television
j. shows that depict positive social behavior
k. shows that depict negative social behavior
l. shows that present a variety of people and cultures in a positive way
m. television viewing habits of well-developed children
n. viewing habits of less well-developed children
o. Singer and Singer's views of the fast-paced *Sesame Street* show
p. Gerald Lesser's view of the fast pace of *Sesame Street*
q. a way for adults to use the child's fascination with television to advantage

Column II

1. national group that works to improve television for children
2. doing what one has seen someone else do
3. behaviors and ideas that are thought to be good or bad
4. a television network supported by public funds and private donations
5. watch television with a child
6. a television network supported by money from advertising
7. cartoons, adult soap operas, and detective shows
8. watch high-quality PBS and commercial programs
9. pretend ideas or actions
10. may make a child want constant novelty and lively action; may support a short attention span
11. use television follow-up materials; puppets, books, and games
12. cartoons, quiz shows, and soap operas
13. strong and powerful
14. *Sesame Street* and *Mr. Rogers' Neighborhood*
15. meek and quiet
16. There are a variety of learning styles, so a fast pace may be better for some children or for teaching some concepts; a slow pace better for others.
17. *Mr. Rogers' Neighborhood* and *Sesame Street*

B. List ten criticisms of television.

C. Discuss the positive values of television for young children.

D. Describe how parents can help children get the most value from television.

E. Describe how teachers can help parents and children get the most value from television.

F. How should a parent or a teacher handle the following problem situations?
1. You are a teacher of young children. The parents of one of the young children in your class tells you that they feel television is harmful but they don't know how to go about regulating their child's viewing. How would you help them?
2. One of the children in your preschool class comes in every day with a cape made out of a towel pinned around his shoulders. He says he is Superman and runs wildly around the room "flying," climbs on anything available, and jumps off. He "saves" other children who don't want to be "saved" and the children become very angry with him. What could you do?
3. Mrs. Nguyen finds that all her young children want to do is watch television. She feels they should go out to play. What can she do?

4. Mr. Miller finds that the children in his day-care center love the Muppets®. What can he do to capitalize on their interests?

5. Mrs. Ramirez usually has the children in her day-care home watch television in the afternoon just before they leave while she cleans. She limits their viewing to the local public television channel. Evaluate her procedure.

6. Seven-year-old Raymond, one of your second-grade students comes in bleary-eyed every morning. He tells that his favorite television show is a late-night program. What, if anything, should you do?

G. Compare how well the constructivist and behaviorist points of view fit the use of computers in the classroom.

H. Select *all* the statements that are correct.

1. Computers can never be expected to change the qualitative aspects of young children's thinking.

2. Although computers are two dimensional, they provide worthwhile and unique experiences that cannot be obtained through other media.

3. It is possible to develop software that is not too abstract for young children to use.

4. Computers inhibit social development because they can be used by only one child at a time.

5. Software is available that promotes creativity, exploration, and even dramatic play.

6. Computers should be treated as just another type of classroom media that can assist in individualizing and motivating learning.

7. Computers should be used primarily to try to accelerate achievement.

8. Computer programs are teacher-proof. That is, the teacher has no effect on how well they work.

9. A teacher who dives in and becomes knowledgeable can find a multitude of uses for computers in his classroom.

10. Children as young as 2 years of age can become interested in exploring the computer, especially if they see their parents using one.

11. Video game technology is about to expand into more powerful and creative formats.

12. In the twenty-first century we may see printed textbooks replaced by participatory, interactive textbooks.

35

Children with Special Needs and Disabilities

OBJECTIVES

After studying this unit, the student should be able to:

■ Explain what is meant by special needs and at-risk.

■ List at least ten types of special needs conditions.

■ Recognize and label descriptions of special needs conditions.

■ Explain the importance of legislative amendments PL 94–142, PL 99–457 and PL 101–476 and of the Americans with Disabilities Act.

■ Define the major steps involved in identification and placement of special needs children.

■ Recognize the major aspects of inclusion.

■ Know the concepts of the Individualized Education Plan and the Individual Family Services Plan.

■ Know the concept of the least restrictive environment.

■ Recognize factors associated with the special need conditions of attention deficit disorder, culture, giftedness, child abuse, and homelessness.

The text has dealt so far with **typical development**—the way most children grow and learn. Some children, however, need special help because of conditions that make their developmental patterns different from those of most other children. These conditions may delay normal growth and development, distort normal growth and development, or have a severe negative effect on normal growth and development and/or adjustment to life (Allen, 1992). There is some disagreement over what is typical development and what is **atypical development**. There has also been a

KEYTERMSKEYTERMSKEYTERMSKEYTERMSKEYTERMSKEY

typical development   atypical development

great deal of change in philosophy, governmental mandates, and accepted terminology over the years. Generally, today children with special needs or disabilities are referred to as **children first** and having a disability second (i.e., children who are physically, intellectually, visually, etc. challenged).

Special needs include children with mental retardation, visual impairment, hearing impairment, emotional disturbance, learning disability, neurological impairment (such as cerebral palsy or epilepsy), attention deficit disorder (ADD), maternal substance abuse during pregnancy, maternal HIV positive passed on to the fetus, orthopedic or other physical handicaps, giftedness, cultural differences, and environmentally induced disabilities (Figure 35–1). A child may have one or more special need conditions at the same time.

Children such as those just described are frequently referred to as **at-risk.** Hrncir and Eisenhart (1991) concede that this term is convenient and descriptive but warn that it should always be used with caution. It is too often used indiscriminantly for making placement decisions. The criteria for labeling a child at risk should be carefully delineated. Further Hrncir and Eisenhart (1991) describe three limitations on the use of the term:

1. Risk is not static. Rate of development varies and so do environmental characteristics, causing the degree of risk to vary also.

2. Test scores are not effective predictors of risk. As described in Unit 32, test scores obtained during early childhood are not good predictors of later functioning and may not be valid and reliable measures of current functioning.

3. Children are not isolated entities, but develop within an ecological context. The situation both at home and at school affects child behavior. Children may operate well in a developmentally appropriate setting but appear at-risk in a developmentally inappropriate setting.

These authors conclude that the term at-risk must be used with care and not just applied indiscriminantly.

AN OVERVIEW

The Education of All Handicapped Children Act of 1975 (**PL 94–142**, now revised as **PL 101–476**) was a landmark in legislation for children with special needs ages 5 to 21 years. Its purpose is to ensure all children with special needs equal educational opportunity. The act was implemented in the fall of 1978. Unfortunately for children ages three, four, and five, the federal law was not made as strong for them as for the school-aged child (Cohen, Semmes, & Guralnick, 1979).

This weakness was rectified in 1986 when Congress passed **PL 99–457**, the Education of the Handicapped Act Amendments. PL 99–457 amended PL 91–230, the Education of the Handicapped Act, which was passed in 1970. Two new programs were authorized by PL 99–457. Title I, Programs for Infants and Toddlers with Handicaps, gave states five years to institute a program for serving children ages three to five with disabilities. Incentive monies were provided for children birth to age three. Title II, the Preschool Grants Program directed at children 3 through 5 years of age, extends the rights that PL 94–142 gave to older children down to younger children. Since the fall of 1991, states applying for funds under PL 94–142 must show that they provide free and appropriate education to all handicapped children ages three through five as well as for older children. Thus, services for three- through five-year-olds are no longer optional. (See *Journal of Early Intervention, 15*(1), Winter 1991 for a thorough discussion of the law and its implications and implementation.)

In 1992, the **Americans with Disabilities Act (ADA)** went into effect. This law "states that people with disabilities are entitled to equal rights in employment, state and local public services, and public accommodations such as child care and early childhood education programs" (Chandler, 1994). Thus, preschool programs were not just encouraged to include children with disabilities but were required to do so.

KEYTERMSKEYTERMSKEYTERMSKEYTERMSKEYTERMSKEYTERMSKEY

children first	PL 101–476	**Americans with Disabilities Act**
at-risk	PL 99–457	(ADA)
PL 94–142		

Condition	Description
Mental Retardation	Intellectual challenge based on multiple criteria, including IQ test score, level of functional adaptive behavior (i.e., dressing, toileting, feeding) and level of social adaptive behavior.
Polydrug Exposed	Cognitive, motor, and perceptual deficits. Possible behavior problems. Central nervous system damage.
Visual Impairment	Ranges from total lack of vision to correctable vision.
Hearing Impairment	Ranges from total hearing loss to correctable hearing.
Learning Disability	Average or above intellectually but has difficulty learning. Characterized by attentional, memory, and perceptual problems.
Neurological Impairment	Neuromuscular disorder such as cerebral palsy or neurological disorder such as epilepsy.
Attention Deficit Disorder	Inattentive, disorganized, off-task, may be overly active and lacking in self control.
HIV Positive	May lack immune system that will fight diseases.
Orthopedic Handicap	May have one or more missing limbs or limb(s) that do not function properly.
Physical Weakness	Child has to conserve strength: heart condition, bronchial problem, blood condition.
Speech and Language Disorders	Speech difficulty may be an articulation (motor) problem. Language problems include slow or delayed speech development, lack of comprehension, etc.
Emotional and Behavioral Disturbance	Unable to adjust, unhappy, behavior problems.
Giftedness	High intelligence and/or creativity and special talents.
Cultural Differences	Child's culture is not the mainstream model.
Environmentally Induced Disabilities	Abusive treatment, malnutrition, cultural differences.

Figure 35–1   Special needs conditions

Eligibility and Identification

The first steps in providing services for young children with special needs is to define who is eligible and develop a procedure for identifying those children who fit the definition. As is evident in the directions taken by legislation, it is believed that the earlier the children are identified and the sooner services begin, the better. However, as Hrncir and Eisenhart (1991) advise, this process must be carried out with care.

A content analysis of policy documents developed by the states to comply with Part H of PL 99–557 (infant and toddler programs) was done by Harbin, Gallagher, and Terry (1991). The results indicated that there was little agreement among the states as to the specific criteria to be used in defining developmental delay relative to infants and toddlers. Most states relied on standardized tests despite their known lack of reliability and validity for infants and toddlers. Harbin et al. (1991) suggest that other criteria such as documentation through clinical observation during normal activity, standardized assessment and non-standardized assessment activities should also be used. Other factors such as birth weight, maternal age, income level, need for special assistance at birth, etc. should be considered. At least three criteria should be met to determine the need for services.

Shonkoff and Meisels (1991) also advise the use of multiple risk models for developing eligibility criteria. Further, those identified as the target population for early intervention "must be thought of in terms of eligibility for assessment and ongoing formulation of an appropriate service plan—not in terms of eligibility for a fixed set of comprehensive services." (Shonkoff & Meisels, 1991, p. 24)

Meisels (1991) elaborates further on the many dimensions of early identification and prevention. First, through public awareness campaigns identification is linked to prevention. That is, it offers an opportunity to inform the public regarding primary prevention—preventing the disability before it happens. The first step in assessment is through public awareness or Child Find programs. This step is followed by developmental and health screening. "Screening tests that are used for screening large numbers of children should be brief, efficient, inexpensive, objectively scored, reliable, valid, culture-fair, and broadly developmental." (Meisels, 1991, pp. 27–28) Initial more indepth assessment is then carried out with identified children using standardized instruments. If the results indicate the need for early intervention, further assessment is done as a part of putting together an individual program plan for the child. At every point the screening and assessment must be sensitive to the needs of young children and their families. Developmental screening should be done regularly. Other sources of risk, such as poor environment, health problems, and family problems, should be considered as well as screening results. Families should be involved in all phases of screening and assessment. Those who do the screening and assessing should be thoroughly trained.

Taylor, Willits, and Lieberman (1990) provide a description for identification of preschool children with mild disabilities. Identifying preschool children with mild disabilities such as minor speech/language, cognitive/learning or emotional/behavioral problems as required by PL 99–457 is difficult. A cooperative, coordinated effort will be needed by public school personnel, childcare and preschool teachers, and parents. Much of the initial screening information and initial referrals will come from childcare and preschool teachers and parents. Taylor et al. (1990) recommend over-referring from an initial screening so as not to miss anyone who needs services. At the evaluation stage, the evaluation should take place during more than one occasion and besides formal testing, should include observation and informal evaluations. As with infants and toddlers, there is a lack of standardized evaluation instruments available for evaluating three- through five-year-olds. Furthermore, preschoolers can be difficult to test. Procedures may have to be modified in order to get a response. Taylor et al. (1990) believe that because of the limitations of formal testing with young children, informal procedures should be given more weight. Information from parents and other caretakers is extremely valuable and should be obtained through informal interviews. Evaluation should be done by a transdisciplinary team through a carefully planned and integrated approach. Be sure parents are involved at every step, that everything is thoroughly explained, and that they are encouraged to ask questions. Written reports should be organized in a manner that relates to specific objectives for preschool children (rather than in the form of test results). Assessment of young children involves different skills than assessment of older children. Parents and educators must work together in order to discover the developmental strengths and weaknesses of young children. Susan Culpepper (1992, 1993) and Sarah DeHaas-Warner (1994) provide some guidelines that can assist adults in making decisions regarding referrals.

Once young children have been identified, the practice of assigning labels such as mentally retarded, emotionally disturbed, or learning disabled has been seriously questioned. Children may be permanently stigmatized and placed in inferior educational programs because of labels. Many minority group children, for example, have been misclassified as retarded (Hobbs, Egerton, & Matheny, 1975). Further, the definitions of these categories are often unclear and vague. Currently three- through five-year-olds are labeled as noncategorical in an effort to avert the label stigma. Of course, noncategorical can be considered as a label also. Diane Bricker (1993) maintains that the labels used to identify not only children but also the professional field that works with these children, and what the professionals are called must support the "goal of delivering a broad range of quality services to children and their families" and should not interfere with this goal (p. 95).

INTEGRATION

A critical and controversial provision of PL 94–142 is the requirement that children should be placed in the **least restrictive environment**. The least restrictive environment is one in which the child can make the most of his/her potential for learning (Figure 35–2). A major problem arises when trying to assess just what this means. As with class placement for any child, the classroom environment and the teacher will determine which setting is most comfortable or least restrictive for any particular child.

Integrating Through Mainstreaming

From the passage of PL 94–142 until the 1990s, **mainstreaming** was the major means for providing an education that would be as normal as possible for young children with disabilities. Through mainstreaming, it was believed that the child with special needs would have the opportunity to participate in the same kinds of programs and activities as every other young child through **integration** into regular classrooms. Mainstreaming could range from a part-time placement in a regular class but with the self-contained special education class as the child's home base, to full-time placement in a regular class. Mainstream placement was earned "through the ability to 'keep up' with the work assigned by the teacher to the other students in the class" (Rogers, 1993).

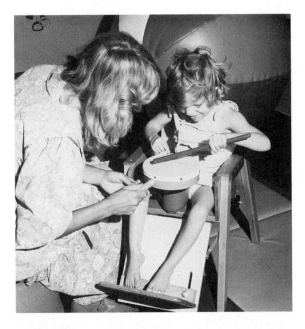

Figure 35–2 **The least-restrictive environment offers the special needs child the same opportunities as the nonspecial needs child.**

Through mainstreaming, the young child with special needs was supposed to have the opportunity to participate in regular preschool activities and receive any special help he may need relative to his special needs. In its early stages there were many misunderstandings about the definition and implementation of mainstreaming. To combat this problem, the Council for Exceptional Children developed a set of guidelines (What is mainstreaming?, 1978). These guidelines clearly stated that mainstreaming was not wholesale return of all exceptional children in special classes to regular classes, not placing children with special needs in regular classrooms without needed support services, and not assuming that placing children in the mainstream would be less costly than placement in a self-contained special education classroom. Unfortunately, mainstreaming did not always work in compliance with the guidelines.

A report of research on mainstreaming by Wol-

KEYTERMSKEYTERMSKEYTERMSKEYTERMSKEYTERMSKEY

| least restrictive environment | mainstreaming | integration |

ery et al. (1993) revealed a number of barriers to success. The most frequently cited barriers to successful preschool mainstreaming were (p. 80):

1. untrained staff and lack of consultation;
2. inadequate staff/child ratios;
3. objections of parents, teachers, and administrators;
4. lack of funds, space, equipment, and transportation;
5. architectural or structural restrictions

An additional barrier surfaced relative to attitudes held by placement team members, teachers, administrators, and parents regarding mainstreaming (Rose & Smith, 1993). Results of a national survey indicated that major attitudinal concerns centered on questions of turf; teacher preparedness; awareness; the belief that typically developing children would lose in the mainstreaming process; and problems in communication, collaboration, and respect.

A study done by Pam Fleege (1990) in kindergartens where children were mainstreamed for part of the day from their self-contained noncategorical preschool class documents an unsuccessful attempt at mainstreaming that provides information on the impediments to avoid. In this particular situation communication between the special education teacher and the kindergarten teachers was not satisfactory and the guidance counselor had been left out of the whole process. A major objective of mainstreaming is the social integration of the special needs students with the regular students. In this case there was very little integration. Since the kindergarten classrooms were developmentally inappropriate, there were very few occasions for social interaction. The mainstreamed children were either seated separately or at tables where no talking was allowed. This was not a successful situation. In spite of some of the barriers as reported by Wolery et al. (1993) and poor implementation as reported by Fleege (1990), mainstreaming did experience some success and did provide some benefits for young children, particularly at the preschool level.

Integrating Through Inclusion

Mainstreaming has disappeared from the special education vocabulary and the concept of **inclusion** has replaced it. Inclusion carries a different meaning than mainstreaming. Rogers (1993, p. 1) provides the following definition:

> Inclusion: The term is used to refer to the commitment to educate each child, to the maximum extent appropriate, in the school and classroom he or she would otherwise attend. It involves bringing the support services to the child (rather than moving the child to the services) and requires only that the child will benefit from being in the class (rather than having to keep up with the other students).

The term **full inclusion** is also widely used. This term means that all the services and support needed by the children are present and available in the schools the children would normally attend. Those who support full inclusion tend to believe support services should be delivered as training and technical assistance to the regular classroom teachers (Rogers, 1993).

According to Rogers (1993), there are two major arguments for inclusion: the civil rights argument and the fact that the conventional special-education approaches have not been successful nor cost effective. With inclusion, the bureaucracy can be trimmed from one to two and budgets can be merged. This does not mean the educational program will be cheaper. It does mean that service delivery will be more efficient and hopefully more effective. Successful inclusion is invisible. There are no longer separate rooms for each disability. The special education teachers team teach with the regular teachers and provide consultation. Inclusion works best in schools that have adopted practices that are designed to meet the needs of individual students such as peer tutoring, multi-age grouping, and cooperative learning. In this type of setting it is a natural procedure to meet each of the students where they are.

According to Diamond, Hestenes, and O'Connor (1994, p. 71), "Successful integrated programs must

KEYTERMSKEYTERMSKEYTERMSKEYTERMSKEYTERMSKEYTERMSKEY
inclusion   full inclusion

meet children's educational needs while addressing parents', teachers', and administrators' concerns that the program be developmentally appropriate for all children." This can be accomplished if all those involved (parents, regular and special education teachers, and administrators) work together. In their review of research, Diamond et al. (1994) report there is strong evidence that children with disabilities who are enrolled in regular classrooms demonstrate higher levels of social interaction than their peers than in self-contained classes. Children with disabilities make gains in language, cognitive, and motor-skill development that are as great as their peers who are enrolled in self-contained special education classrooms. Further, they do better in classrooms in which there are child-directed activities (versus teacher-directed). Having the special child in the class full-time resulted in the regular students viewing them as integral parts of the class (not just visitors from another class, which is how they viewed part-time mainstreamed students). Further, through having children with special needs in the class the typical children learned about disabilities as a natural part of daily life.

It is extremely important that both the regular and special needs students be prepared to deal openly and honestly with whatever handicapping conditions they meet. Baum and Wells (1985) suggest ways to promote young children's awareness of special needs through stories, art, science, dramatic play, language, and snack time activities. For example, ask children how they would eat or paint without hands or if they could not see. Professionally or teacher-made puppets can be used to dramatize various types of special needs. *The Kids on the Block* is such a set of puppets: some of the puppets have various exceptionalities such as blindness, deafness, cerebral palsy, epilepsy, and mental retardation, and others are nonhandicapped. Scripts for short skits are included. The skits follow a format where the nonhandicapped child displays a lack of knowledge about the exceptionality and is put straight by the exceptional child. Both children and adults get very involved in these skits. These puppets are available from Kids on the Block, Inc., Suite 510, Washington Building, Washington, DC 20005.

Research on integration indicates that successful implementation does not just happen but requires planning and preparation. When left to their own devices, special needs children play with other special needs children and nonspecial needs with other nonspecial needs children. Consequently, planned social situations must be set up that promote social interaction between the two groups (Raver, 1979; Spiegel-McGill, 1989; Kohler, Strain, Maretsky, & DeCesare, 1990; Cooper, 1990; Odom & McConnell, 1991; Bergen, 1993; Brown, Althouse, & Anfin, 1993; Huyett, 1994; Knight & Wadsworth, 1993; Leister, Koonce, & Nisbert, 1993; Venn et al., 1993). The results of a study by Burstein (1986) indicate that structured situations arranged during center time are probably best for facilitating peer interaction and on-task behavior for the young special needs student.

Classroom Survival Skills

The rapid growth of inclusion has brought a focus in the prekindergarten program, not only on the development of social skills with peers, but also on the development of classroom survival skills for kindergarten and in the kindergarten for survival skills for first grade (Carta, Atwater, & Schwartz, 1991). Researchers have gathered data on kindergarten teachers' expectations for success (e.g., Rule, Innocenti, Coor, Bonem, & Stowitschek, 1989; Beckoff & Bender, 1989). Carta, Atwater, & Schwartz (1991) designed a survival skills intervention strategy for two groups of special needs students, one group attending a special education preschool and one attending a regular kindergarten. The intervention strategy focuses on three sets of skills found previously to be essential for moving early childhood students from special education programs to typical elementary classrooms. These skills included:

1. participating appropriately during group instruction
2. completing individual work with a minimum of teacher direction
3. managing in-class transitions independently.

Teachers and students were observed during the intervention period to assess how well teachers were implementing the intervention and to assess any immediate effects on the students. The first year results showed positive changes in all three skill areas. There were also gains in achievement measures and decrease in the frequencies of problem behaviors. The intervention effects carried over into the students' regular kindergarten and first-grade placements.

Family Involvement

With the advent of PL 94–142 the family became an integral part of the planning for the education and placement of handicapped children through participation in the development and evaluation of the **individualized education program (IEP)**. This involvement has been included in the regulations for PL 99–457, Part H through parent involvement in the **individualized family service plan (IFSP)**.

It is mandated that every special needs child have an Individual Education Program (IEP). This plan is designed to ensure that the child receives the education to which he is entitled. It is developed cooperatively through a committee made up of school personnel and the child's parents. No child can be placed in any kind of special education program unless the IEP has been written. To receive federal funds, the school must follow through on the services stated in the IEP.

The development of an IEP and the placement of the special needs child are achieved through a specifically defined process. The process can only be undertaken with the parent's signed permission. With the parent's permission, the assessment team proceeds with the assessment task. The assessment team is made up of the teacher and other professionals such as a nurse, physician, social worker, speech and language therapist, psychologist, and special educator. Test and observational data are collected, evaluated, and discussed by the team with the parent who then becomes a member of the planning team. The parent has final authority regarding placement.

Whereas PL 94–142 focuses on the child, PL 99–457 focuses on the family. This focus is operational-ized through the IFSP (McGonigel, Kaufman, & Johnson, 1991; Widerstrom, Mowder, & Sandall, 1991).

> The IFSP venture involves family and early intervention professionals working together to develop a plan that includes services and supports that will enhance the development of the child and the capacity of the family to meet the special needs of the child. (Widerstrom et al., 1991)

The IFSP must contain information on the child's current level of functioning, a statement of the family's strengths and weaknesses, the expected outcomes for the child and the family, the intervention services that will be needed, the number of days and sessions for which the service will be provided, the length of time of each session, and whether the service is individual or group. The location for service (i.e., home, early intervention center, hospital, etc.) must be designated. Any services needed that are not specified under the law will be described with steps to be implemented to acquire the services. Anticipated dates of service initiation and duration must be specified. If the child is nearing age three, a plan for transition out of infant/toddler services must be included. Meetings with the family, case manager, and interdisciplinary team members should be planned with the family and take place in a situation that is comfortable for the family. The IFSP must be reviewed every 6 months. "The message of PL 99–457 is that early intervention for children with special needs must respect the family" (Widerstrom et al., 1991).

With the focus on the whole family through development of the IFSP, researchers became interested in looking at **family-centered practice**. McBride, Brotherson, Joanning, Whiddon, and Demmitt (1993) identified three major principles of family-centered practice that reflect the beliefs and values that serve as a framework for practice (p. 415):

1. establishing the family as the focus of services;

2. supporting and respecting family decision-making;

KEYTERMSKEYTERMSKEYTERMSKEYTERMSKEYTERMSKEY

| individualized education program (IEP) | individualized family service plan (IFSP) | family-centered practice |

3. providing intervention services designed to strengthen family functioning.

McBride et al. (1993) interviewed professionals and families regarding their experiences with family-centered practice using the three principles above as criteria for evaluation of practice. The results indicated that while the families felt satisfied with the services received, the professionals varied in their degrees of family centeredness. The professionals also varied in the degree to which they had switched their focus from the child to the whole family. The authors conclude that both preservice and inservice education programs need to focus more strongly on family-centered delivery of services.

Teachers for the Integrated Classroom

Like all teachers, teachers who teach in an integrated classroom need an indepth knowledge of the normal growth and development of young children and knowledge of the various exceptionalities with which she must work (Aldridge, 1990; Parsons, 1988; Peters & Skrtic, 1988).

New curriculum and teaching skills must be learned to aid those teaching an integrated class. For example, Rosalind Engel (1980) developed a procedure for choosing and using books about exceptionalities to help children understand themselves and others. Teachers of special needs children must also have excellent skills for working with parents and identifying family needs (Garshelis & McConnell, 1993; McBride et al., 1993; Levitt & Cohen, 1976).

The role of the teacher in the placement of and successful educational programming for the young special needs child is critical. She spends several hours each day with the child in contrast to the specialists who spend a limited time and the parent who may have difficulty maintaining objectivity. The teacher must be objective and factual. She must be able to document classroom behavior in accurate, objective language. Her records should withstand the test of careful scrutiny by other professionals. Keep-

ing up with these heavy demands can be very stressful for teachers. White and Phair (1986) describe a wide range of negative emotions that are experienced in the integrated classroom: denial, sadness, anger, guilt, fear, overprotection, defensiveness, jealousy/competition, frustration, exhaustion, and fatalism. These feelings must be faced and discussed to alleviate the effects of stress. Eventually, as the future progress of former students is observed, teachers will feel more secure and the job will be less stressful.

ATTENTION DEFICIT DISORDER (ADD)

Some special attention is focused on the so-called hyperactive child because this type of child can easily achieve success in the developmentally appropriate environment but is usually doomed to failure in the developmentally inappropriate classroom (Landau & McAninch, 1993).

All teachers at some point have had one or more students who had difficulty sitting down and sticking with a task. These students get up and roam around during large-group activities, are disorganized, seem to have difficulty interpreting messages, and frequently do not seem to be paying attention. These children might tend to act on impulse (hyperactive) or withdraw and daydream (hypoactive). Impulsive children may speak out of turn, generally talk excessively, have difficulty establishing relationships with others, and are often viewed as behavior problems. Previously these symptoms were referred to as **hyperactivity**. However, the disorder was renamed **attention deficit disorder (ADD)** when it became recognized that most of the symptoms could be present with or without hyperactivity (Buchoff, 1990; Divoky, 1989).

There is a major controversy surrounding the proper treatment of the hyperactive ADD child (Divoky, 1989). The major bone of contention centers on whether the treatment of choice for the children should be behavioral or medical. Behavioral treatment could center on a behavior modification plan within the current classroom setting and/or a change of setting. A medical treatment plan involves the pre-

hyperactivity   attention deficit disorder (ADD) scribing of medication (usually Ritalin) to treat the disorder and calm the children down. Divoky (1989) describes the evidence for and against drug therapy. Some people believe that the drugs are dangerous and will result in later addiction. Others are concerned that school personnel often coerce parents into obtaining medication and that the medication is prescribed without proper diagnosis and followup. Other people are convinced that the drug therapy really works well in spite of rather nebulous scientific evidence that it does. Landau and McAninch (1993) recommend a combination of both approaches.

There is a suspicion that these children would not show up as problems in a developmentally appropriate classroom setting. For example, Divoky (1989, p. 600) describes an IEP for a third grader that includes the following statements:

- "Casey is able to learn in a regular classroom situation only when he is heavily invested in the activity."
- "For most academic instruction he needs one-to-one or small-group instruction with realistic expectations, clear behavioral limits, and frequent change of activities."
- "He also needs to be able to move around during the day to help burn off excess energy."

Look carefully at these statements. Essentially, they describe the kinds of conditions we refer to as developmentally appropriate practice. The school personnel had written drug therapy into Casey's IEP. Casey's parents refused to sign. The case (along with others around the country) went into litigation.

Buchoff (1990) suggests several steps teachers can take in working with ADD students. Teachers can help these students be more organized by seating them near the teacher, away from distracting sounds, and near students who are good models. Organization can also be helped by eliminating extraneous materials from the work area, help the children design charts that will help them keep track of time sequence and transitions, and other aids that help them keep track of what they are supposed to be doing. Help them understand directions by giving the directions carefully and by not giving them more than one at a time. In managing the classroom have the chil-

dren help develop the rules, use nonverbal cues to remind them about acceptable behavior, and do not ridicule the children when they break a rule or show excessive anger. Above all, try to develop the children's pride and self-esteem.

If teachers believe a child has a serious problem that is more than can be coped with in the classroom, they should be supportive and neutral while suggesting that parents get a professional diagnosis. Above all they should not make the parents feel guilty. Teachers should be careful about discriminating between a hyperactive child and a very active child. Very active normal children differ from hyperactive children in that they are more likely to be engaged in some socially acceptable constructive activity rather than engaging in "disturbing behaviors that are highly visible, unpredictable, unprovoked, and not easily controlled by the presence or even intervention of teachers" (Buchan, Swap, & Swap, 1977, pp. 314–315).

CULTURE AND SPECIAL NEEDS

As discussed earlier in this text, children who speak a language other than English as their first language and/or come from homes with different customs and life-styles from the mainstream Anglo middle-class model face a number of problems when they enter school. Culture may serve as a direct handicap for the child in two ways:

- Lack of knowledge of the culture of the school may handicap the child in his learning.
- Lack of knowledge of the culture of the school may lead to misplacement and mislabeling of the child as retarded (Figure 35–3).

It may also serve as a handicap in reverse:

- Lack of knowledge of the child's culture on the part of the educator may handicap the child in her learning.
- Lack of knowledge of the child and her culture by the educator may result in mislabeling and misplacement in classrooms for the retarded.

Figure 35–3 **Children from diverse cultures have special educational needs. They are the most likely to be mislabeled and misplaced in classes for the retarded, learning disabled, or behaviorally disturbed.**

The special needs of these children from nonmainstream cultures have been the impetus to the development of many types of early intervention programs as mentioned in Unit 25. Underlying the problems these children face may be racism, which forces the child to act as if he were handicapped. In discussing the mental health of black children, Hector F. Meyers (1979, p. 27) points out that the staff in schools that serve ethnic minorities are ". . . almost morbidly preoccupied with the early identification of deficits and handicaps rather than the identification of individual patterns of skills." That is, the staff seeks and works with apparent weaknesses rather than seeking the child's strengths and working with those. They may also subordinate the child's cultural differences rather than making the most of them. These practices and attitudes then manufacture incompetence and poor mental health. Asa Hilliard III (1980, p. 587) concludes:

> It should be clear that cultural diversity requires no unusual special education. What is required is that normal valid professional practice be provided.

Hilliard believes that children from any cultural group have a right to communication in their own language, sensitivity to their cultural patterns, and diagnosis that reflects their cultural uniqueness.

THE GIFTED AND TALENTED

Does your child use the word "because" or "cause" even though the child may confuse the meaning of the word? (Parent answers): Yes, she has been doing this since age three years. For instance, she recently said, "It is fall, a season of the year, because it is getting ready for winter, because it gets so cold and I wear my heavy coat, because I need to keep warm because I might catch cold . . ." She frequently talks in paragraphs with all the thoughts connected by "because." (Girl, aged 3 years, 5 months at time of report) (Gallagher & Ramsbotham, 1977, p. 44)

This sample of a parent's description of her daughter's language behavior is just one example of how a gifted young child might behave.

Although prekindergarten reading capability may be a sign of giftedness, research by Vukelich and Cassiday (Majority of Intellectually Gifted, 1980) indicates that most gifted children are not readers at the time of kindergarten entrance. Further, when gifted preschool nonreaders were given formal reading instruction, most of them still did not learn to read. Readiness and interest probably are as important factors as IQ score in determining when a child learns to read.

There is evidence to support that children who perform in a gifted way have both genetic superiority and a superior environment. Looking back at the childhood behaviors of such eminent people as Albert Einstein and Mozart, it was evident during early childhood that they were unusually bright and they were encouraged to pursue their interests. The gifted child can be identified through a combination of observations by parents, teachers, and other adults, and the diagnostic use of intelligence tests and tests of creativity. Recently, it was found that a standardized achievement test designed for kindergarten aged and above is useful in gathering information on gifted preschoolers. Another sign of giftedness may be an unusually high frequency of the use of the prosocial behaviors when engaged in activities with peers.

For some children, giftedness may be a unitary trait. For most it is probably present in one or more specific areas such as general intelligence, spatial reasoning, memory, reading, and/or mathematics

(Roedell, Jackson, and Robinson, 1980). Identifying young gifted children has been a problem because appropriate assessment instruments have not been available. Usually tests designed for older children are used. A number of checklists have been designed that can be used by teachers and parents to aid in identification (see Kitano, 1982). A group of preschool teachers who received special training in using the checklists were able to make fairly accurate judgments. Roedell, Jackson, and Robinson feel that teachers can learn to identify gifted children with greater accuracy when trained in what to look for.

Special school-based programs for the gifted are widespread. Over half the states even have programs for four-year-olds (Wolfle, 1989). If a child is socially, intellectually, and physically advanced, early school entrance might be considered. However, since most gifted children are not gifted in every area, it is probably best to place them in an enriched regular early childhood classroom where they have the advantage of maintaining social contact with their peers. Instruction is suggested that will enhance their special aptitudes and characteristics (Kitano, 1982; Wolfle, 1989). This enrichment will benefit both the gifted and nongifted students. Kitano (1982) suggests the following:

- Provide activities that enhance creativity.
- Provide activities that enhance higher cognitive processes (analysis, synthesis, and evaluation).
- Provide activities that enhance executive operations (forecasting, planning, decision making, communication).
- Provide activities that promote inquiry and problem solving (observing, hypothesizing, experimenting, evaluating).
- Provide activities that provide for affective development.
- Incorporate process and content objectives into units (that is, the student will apply creativity, higher-level cognitive processes, executive operations, inquiry, and problem solving and use positive affective behaviors during the process of reaching content objectives).

Most important, always keep in mind that these children are still only three- or four-years-old; do not put excessive pressure on them. They love to do everything other children their age enjoy but can carry activities further with more depth (Wolfle, 1989).

Kindergarten and primary teachers also have a special role in recognizing and supporting young gifted children (Kitano, 1989). As already described young gifted children have many positive traits that reflect their intellectual capacities and talents. They also may tend to have some negative traits:

- impatience with regular curriculum and repetitious activities
- inability to develop social relationships with children of lower ability
- difficulty in conforming to group tasks
- unusual vulnerability to criticism
- sensitivity to others' perceptions of them as "show offs."

They may become disruptive or withdraw and thus be identified as a behavior problem. These problems are least likely to surface in a developmentally appropriate classroom in which the curriculum is age appropriate and geared to the individual and children are encouraged to explore and create. As Kitano (1989) suggests consider all children as potentially gifted and provide opportunities for all children to express their abilities. Teachers must be alert for the gifted and talented in every classroom regardless of socioeconomic level (Karnes & Johnson, 1989). Karnes and Johnson (1989) report dramatic results from the BOHST (Bringing Out Head Start Talents) project which provided stimulating and challenging activities that were designed to bring out the hidden talents of Head Start students.

A question may arise concerning why gifted young children are considered in the special needs category. The active minds and bodies of these children often overwhelm adults who do not realize or recognize giftedness in a young child. The result may be that the child is stifled, loses motivation, and does not pursue the potential of his talents. Gifted children need the same degree of careful guidance as any other child, whether average or developmentally handicapped. For example, June Yennie-Donmoyer (1993, p. 137) describes Andrew, an eighth grader.

A quintessentially [i.e., classic, model, representative] gifted student, Andrew was also, without doubt, one of the most at-risk students I had ever met. He was extremely unhappy, unable to make friends, and, it seemed to me, self-destructive.

Andrew was an active and exhausting infant. At three he went to nursery school where his teacher complained that he ran wild during large-group activities. Kindergarten went well because the students had choices and Andrew was able to find activities that interested him and he was fortunate to have excellent teachers through elementary school and junior high. Very early, Andrew showed signs of extraordinary intelligence and inventiveness. However, socially he was a failure, rejected by his peers. He was soon known as a troublemaker and a loner. Fortunately, in high school he found his place with other gifted and talented students. Unfortunately, many gifted students fall through the cracks because they don't have the family and teacher support Andrew had.

ABUSE AND NEGLECT

According to the Children's Defense Fund (*State of America's children year book*, 1994) during 1992 more than 2.9 million children were reported abused or neglected. This was close to triple the number reported in 1980. Approximately half were neglected and half abused. Increased family stress due to drugs and violence is believed to be related to the increase in **abuse and neglect**. Increasing numbers of children are in foster care or are living with relatives other than immediate family members. The loss of parents to AIDS is increasingly becoming a cause of parentless children. Approximately 3,000,000 children have serious emotional disturbances and only about one-third are receiving adequate care. Advocates for emotionally disturbed children are trying to move toward more family-focused, community-based approaches with more money to put into keeping early identified disturbances from intensifying. These children who are abused and neglected are handicapped in reaching their developmental potential.

In every state, there are laws mandating that suspected cases of abuse be reported by professionals, such as teachers (Gootman, 1993).

According to Sedlak (1989), in 1986 1,025,200 children nationwide experienced countable maltreatment under the harm standard, a significant 64% increase above 1980. Under the more inclusive endangerment standard, 1,584,700 children experienced maltreatment. The increase from 1980 was accounted for primarily by increases in the numbers of physically and sexually abused children and increases in the rate of reporting rather than increases in the actual number of incidents of maltreatment alone. This indicates an increase in professional awareness besides the increase in maltreatment due to the new definition. Three levels of severity were categorized relative to the degree of injury/impairment.

1. Serious injury/impairment was defined as a life-threatening condition or a long-term impairment of physical, mental, or emotional capacities, or required professional treatment aimed at preventing such long-term impairment. Examples would be loss of consciousness, broken bones, loss of schooling requiring special education services, chronic and debilitating drug/alcohol abuse, emotional/psychological symptoms requiring professional treatment, suicide attempts, diagnosed cases of failure to thrive, third degree burns or extensive second degree burns, etc. Fifteen percent of maltreated children fell into this category.

2. Moderate injuries/impairments were those where observable symptoms persisted for at least 48 hours. These would include bruises, depression or emotional distress, etc. About 72 percent of maltreated children fell into this group.

3. Inferred injury included children who did not fit in either of the first two categories but where the situation predicted that a not-yet-detectable injury/impairment had probably oc-

curred. Examples would be sexual abuse involving intrusion or genital molestation, abandonment, close confinement involving tying and binding.

Sedlak (1989) reports several interesting findings relevant to demographic factors. Girls experienced more abuse than boys. In particular, girls had four times the chance of being sexually abused. Maltreatment according to the harm standard increased significantly with age. Moderate injury frequencies increased with age, while fatalities were most prevalent among younger children, especially infants and toddlers. The income effect was very significant. Children in families with incomes under $15,000 per year were five times more likely to have experienced countable maltreatment than those in families with incomes over $15,000 per year. There were no racial or ethnic differences or urban as compared with rural differences. Over all Child Protection Services officially came in contact with only a portion of the known maltreated children: 62 percent of the sexually abused, 49 percent of the physically injured, 37 percent of the emotionally injured, and 17 percent of the educationally neglected.

Two studies done by researchers at the University of Minnesota provide valuable information concerning the factors that lead to child maltreatment (Erikson, 1990). The first study looked at indicators of risk. This study, done by Drs. Byron Egeland and Alan Stroufe, followed 267 low-income women and their first-born children beginning during pregnancy. In the first six years 60 children were identified as receiving maltreatment, including physical abuse, neglect, verbal abuse, sexual abuse, or emotional neglect. Now these children are teenagers and they have all experienced problems in social relationships with both peers and adults. A number of risk factors were identified that predict which parents are most likely to be abusers: failure to prepare for arrival of the baby; lack of understanding of the parent/child relationship; insensitivity to the infant's messages; a high degree of parental stress, especially relationship difficulties; lack of social support from the parent; and the parent having experienced abuse as a child.

Breaking the abuse cycle is an important problem. These researchers looked more closely at the 30 percent of abused parents who did not abuse their child. The factors which appeared to enable them to break the pattern were:

1. nurturance and support during childhood from some adult other than the abuser
2. a supportive relationship with their current partner
3. involvement in therapy for at least 6 months.

The second study reported by Erikson (1990) is one designed to put the research findings described above to work. STEEP (Steps Toward Effective Enjoyable Parenting) is a preventive intervention program for new parents and their infants. This experimental project was done with 75 first-time mothers beginning in their second trimester. All mothers were low income, at least 17-years-old, and had no more than a high school education. Home visits and counseling sessions designed to help parents understand parenting and to be more effective were used for the intervention procedure. Each parent is attached to a facilitator/counselor. The objective is to give the parents enough support so that they are empowered to find solutions to their problems. All the results are not in as yet, but the researchers have seen a number of individual successes that make them believe they have found a procedure that works.

Some signs of abuse and neglect that can be easily spotted are:

• Poor physical care: child comes to school dirty and dressed in dirty clothing; child is weak and ill and not taken to the doctor; child is hungry and shows signs of undernutrition; child is tired and cranky.

• Battering: child has bruises; broken bones, etc.

Other types of abuse, such as sexual abuse and emotional abuse (name calling, cursing, ignoring, and rejecting) may be more difficult to spot. However, watch for signs such as reluctance to leave school, sophisticated sexual knowledge or play, radical behavior changes or regressive behavior, withdrawal or standing back and watching adults, or events that are revealed through discussion, stories, or drawings (Meddin & Rosen, 1986).

Unfortunately, children with special needs are most likely to be victims of abuse and neglect (Disabled children, 1994; Goldman, 1993). Their vulnerability is sometimes masked by their disabilities. For example, they may have limited communication abilities. Children with orthopedic problems are likely to fall and injure themselves and this can be used as an excuse for injury that was actually due to physical abuse. Parents may expect too much from the disabled child and abuse him out of frustration or expect too little and neglect his needs. Young special needs children are especially vulnerable to sexual abuse because they may be much more dependent on caretakers than other children. Goldman (1993) suggests that childcare personnel can be an important line of defense for these children.

The reporting of child abuse can be done anonymously. In most cities, there is now a child abuse hot line. Parents Anonymous groups, growing in numbers, help parents to face their problems and find ways to handle them.

HOMELESSNESS

Children's Defense Fund reports that families with children are the fastest-growing group within the homeless population (*State of America's children yearbook*, 1994). According to a 1993 survey, they constitute 43 percent of the homeless, up from 32 percent in 1992. These figures indicate that an increasing number of America's children are likely to face the risks associated with unstable, inadequate housing or actual **homelessness**. These children "typically develop more severe health, developmental and nutritional problems than other poor children and are more likely to suffer lead poisoning, educational disruption, emotional stress, and family separation" (p. 37). It is estimated that 100,000 children are homeless every night. Within this group, minorities, especially African-Americans, are disproportionately represented. The shortage of low-rent housing has reached the crisis stage.

Overall, homeless families reflect great diversity: unemployed couples who cannot afford hous-

ing, mothers leaving relationships (often abusive ones), Aid to Families with Dependent Children (AFDC) mothers who cannot manage on the amount they receive, and mothers with a history of homelessness and poverty. The conditions they live in, in shelters and homeless hotels, are usually squalid and dismal. The children are at high risk for eventually being placed in foster care. The families are under stress and this may increase the chances for child abuse and neglect. Of course many homeless families are not in shelters or homeless hotels; they live in vacant buildings, in cars, or are temporarily sharing the housing of friends or relatives.

The homeless suffer from both poor mental and physical health. Solarz (1988) reports that a Boston study found that children had serious developmental and emotional problems. For example, half of the homeless preschoolers had at least one serious developmental lag compared to 16 percent living in subsidized housing. Other researchers observed two-and-a-half to five-year-old homeless children in daycare centers and found they had many problem behaviors: short attention span, weak impulse control, withdrawal, aggression, speech delays, and regressive behaviors. Affective relationships with mothers were likely to be detached with stronger bonds to siblings.

It is estimated that 40 percent of school-aged homeless children do not attend school. A large portion of those who do attend school are very likely to have repeated grades. They may have to stay out of school to care for younger siblings while their parents are job hunting. When they move, which they do frequently, they may have to change schools and thus break the continuity of their schooling. Often they cannot be enrolled because they do not have necessary documents such as birth certificates. Therefore they are at-risk educationally.

Eddowes (1994) suggests schools can provide a safe haven for homeless children for the part of the day they attend. The school can provide support services and outreach programs. Some school systems have opened schools in shelters. Other school systems have special classrooms just for homeless children. Still others provide special services within regular classrooms. Eddowes suggests no matter where the program is located special services can be provided, such as bathing facilities, clean clothes, tooth brushes, and nutritious meals. Like other programs, the educational component should be individualized.

In this unit, a variety of factors have been described that presents risks to young children. As a final area, we'll look briefly at efforts to provide for success for all children.

EDUCATIONAL MODELS FOR AT-RISK CHILDREN

Donmoyer and Kos (1993) describe three models that emerge as the most successful at attempting to do whole-school restructuring. These three models are Comer's School Development Model, Levin's Accelerated Schools Model, and Slavin's Success for All approach. Comer's model stresses school-community linkages, Levin's an enriched curriculum for all (not just the gifted), and Slavin's a very precise method of instruction. Their commonality is that in each model the whole school becomes focused on a common philosophy that forms a basis for the program for children and provides a belief that *all* children can succeed.

SUMMARY

Many young children have special needs due to conditions that inhibit them from developing in typical patterns. Some of these special needs conditions are mental retardation, visual impairment, hearing impairment, emotional disturbance, learning disabilities, neurological impairment, attention deficit disorder, maternal substance abuse during pregnancy,

maternal HIV positive passed on to the fetus, orthopedic or other physical disabilities, and giftedness. Other risk factors include being a member of a cultural/ethnic minority, being abused and/or neglected, and being a member of a homeless family.

The 1970s saw landmark legislation mandating the education of all handicapped children of school age. Legislation in the 1980s has mandated appropriate educational programs for all three- to five-year-old handicapped children and family services for infants and toddlers. Now all young children in need of services must be identified, screened, evaluated, and a treatment plan developed. An IEP (Individualized Education Plan) must be written for all handicapped children three years of age and older and an IFSP (Individualized Family Service Plan) for infants and toddlers and their families.

Inclusion in the least restrictive environment is a crucial aspect of the education of young special needs children. Inclusion is placing special needs children is a setting in which they have the same opportunities as their typically developing peers.

Well trained and certified early childhood special education teachers are sorely needed. In addition regular early childhood classroom teachers need skills for identifying potential students with special needs and for working with children with special needs and disabilities in their classrooms. With thousands of children newly eligible for special education services, both already developed and new service delivery models must be documented and disseminated.

We also face additional challenges in providing services to meet the needs of young children who are minority group members, maltreated, or are homeless. In Unit 37 we will examine some of the ways you can work to provide the needed services for all young children.

FOR FURTHER READING

From the Parent, Teacher and Child's View

(also see Donmoyer & Kos below)

Axline, V. A. (1964). *Dibs: In search of self.* Boston: Houghton-Mifflin.

Bricker, D. (1986). *Early education of at-risk and handicapped infants, toddlers and preschool children.* Glenview, IL: Scott, Foresman.

Clarke, L. (1973). *Can't read, can't write, can't talk too good either*. New York: Walker.

Fawcett, G. (1994). Beth starts like Bear! *Phi Delta Kappan, 75*, (721–722).

Long, K. (1978). *Johnny's such a bright boy, what a shame he's retarded*. Boston: Houghton, Mifflin.

General Resources

Bailey, D. B., & Wolery, M. (1992). *Teaching infants and preschoolers with disabilities* (2nd ed.). New York: Macmillan.

Barnett, D. W., & Carey, K. T. (1992). *Designing interventions for preschool learning and behavior problems*. San Francisco: Jossey-Bass.

Bryant, D. M., & Graham, M. A. (Eds.). (1993). *Implementing early intervention: From research to effective practice*. New York: Guilford.

Donmoyer, R., & Kos, R. (Eds.). (1993). *At-risk students: Portraits, policies, programs and practices*. Albany, NY: SUNY Press.

Ferguson, P. M., Ferguson, D. L., & Taylor, S. J. (Eds.). (1992). *Interpreting disability: A qualitative reader*. New York: Teachers College Press.

Franklin, B. M. (1994). *From "backwardness" to "at-risk": Childhood learning difficulties and contradictions of school reform*. Albany, NY: SUNY Press.

Harry, B. (1992). *Cultural diversity, families, and the special education system: Communication and empowerment*. New York: Teachers College Press.

Hellendoorn, J., van der Kooij, R., & Sutton-Smith, B. (Eds.). (1994). *Play and intervention*. Albany, NY: SUNY Press.

Meisels, S. J., & Shonkoff, J. P. (Eds.). (1990). *Handbook of early childhood intervention*. New York: Cambridge University Press.

Norris, J., & Hoffman, P. (1993). *Whole language intervention for school-age children*. San Diego, CA: Singular.

Odom, S. L., & Karnes, M. B. (Eds.). (1989). *Early intervention for infants and children with handicaps*. Baltimore, MD: Brookes.

Slavin, R. E., Karweit, N. L., & Wasik, B. A. (1994). *Preventing early school failure: Research, policy, and practice*. Des Moines, IA: Longwood Division, Allyn and Bacon.

Thompson, T., & Hupp, S. C. (Eds.). (1991). *Saving children at risk: Poverty and disabilities*. Newbury Park, CA: Sage.

Zeanah, C. H. (Ed.). (1993). *Handbook of infant mental health*. New York: Guilford.

Assessment

Bagnato, S. J., Neisworth, J. T., & Munson, S. M. (1989). *Linking developmental assessment and early intervention: Curriculum-based prescriptions*, 2nd Ed. Rockville, MD: Aspen.

Bailey, D. B., & Wolery, M. (1989). *Assessing infants and toddlers with handicaps*. New York: Merrill/Macmillan.

Benner, S. M. (1992). *Assessing young children with special needs: An ecological perspective*. White Plains, NY: Longman.

Bricker, D., & Cripe, J. J. W. (1992). *An Activity-based approach to early intervention*. Baltimore, MD: Brookes.

Specific Disabilities

Barkley, R. A. (1990). *Attention deficit hyperactivity disorder*. 2nd ed. New York: Guilford.

Cicchetti, D., & Beeghly, M. (Eds.). (1990). *Children with Down syndrome: A developmental perspective*. New York: Cambridge University Press.

Dykens, E. M., Hodapp, R. M., & Leckman, J. F. (1993). *Behavior and development in fragile X syndrome.* Thousand Oaks, CA: Sage.

Gadow, K. D. (Volumes appear regularly). *Advances in learning and behavioral disabilities.* Vol 1–6. Greenwich, CT: JAI.

Hinshaw, S. P. (1994). *Attention deficits and hyperactivity in children.* Thousand Oaks, CA: Sage.

Hodapp, R. M., Burack, J. A., & Zigler, E. (Eds.). (1990). *Issues in the developmental approach to mental retardation.* New York: Cambridge University Press.

Nannis, E. D., & Cowan, P. A. (Eds.). (1988). *Developmental psychopathology and its treatment.* San Francisco: Jossey-Bass.

Pepler, D., & Rubin, K. H. (Eds.). (1990). *The development and treatment of childhood aggression.* Hillsdale, NJ: Erlbaum.

Rowitz, L. (Ed.). (1991). *Mental retardation in the year 2000.* New York: Springer-Verlag.

Schloper, E., van Bourgondien, M. E., & Briston, M. M. (Eds.). (1994). *Preschool issues in autism.* New York: Plenum.

Spekman, N. J., & Herman, K. L. (1993). Risk and resilience in individuals with learning disabilities. [Special Issue]. *Learning disabilities: Research and Practice, 8*(1).

Thompson, T., & Gray, D. B. (Eds.). (1994). *Destructive behavior in developmental disabilities: Diagnosis and treatment.* Thousand Oaks, CA: Sage.

Wodrich, D. L. (1994). *Attention deficit hyperactivity disorder: What every parent wants to know.* Baltimore, MD: Brookes.

The Gifted and Talented

Borland, J. H. (1989). *Planning and implementing programs for the gifted.* New York: Teachers College Press.

Sapon-Shevin, M. (1994). *Playing favorites: Gifted education and the disruption of community.* Albany, NY: SUNY Press.

Schneider, B. H. (1987). *The gifted child in peer group perspective.* New York: Springer-Verlag.

VanTassel-Baska, J. L., & Olszewski-Kubilius, P. (Eds.). (1989). *Patterns of influence on gifted learners: The home, the self, and the school.* New York: Teachers College Press.

Inclusion/Integration

Gaylord-Ross, R. (Ed.). (1989). *Integration strategies for students with handicaps.* Baltimore, MD: Brookes.

Giangreco, M. F., Cloninger, C. J., & Iverson, V. S. (1993). *Choosing options and accommodations for children (COACH): A guide to planning inclusive education.* Baltimore, MD: Brookes.

Lipsky, D. K., & Gartner, A. (Eds.). (1989). *Beyond separate education.* Baltimore, MD: Brookes.

Peck, C. A., Odom, S. L., & Bricker, D. (1993). *Integrating young children with disabilities into community programs: Ecological perspectives on research and implementation.* Baltimore, MD: Brookes.

Putnam, J. W. (Ed.). (1993). *Cooperative learning and strategies for inclusion.* Baltimore, MD: Brookes.

Stainbeck, S., & Stainbeck, W. (Eds.). (1992). *Curriculum considerations in inclusive classrooms.* Baltimore, MD: Brookes.

Wolery, M., & Wilbers, J. S. (Eds.). (1994). Including children with special needs in early childhood programs. *Research Mongr., Volume 6.* Washington, DC: National Association for the Education of Young Children.

Abuse and Neglect

Besharov, D. J. (1990). *Recognizing child abuse: A guide for the concerned.* New York: The Free Press.

Cicchetti, D., & Carlson, V. K. (Eds.). (1989). *Child maltreatment: Theory and research on the causes and consequences of child abuse and neglect.* New York: Cambridge University Press.

Hoorwitz, A. N. (1992). *The clinical detective: Techniques in evaluation of sexual abuse*. New York: W. W. Norton.

Jaffe, P. G., Wolfe, D. A., & Wilson, S. K. (1990). *Children of battered women*. Newbury Park, CA: Sage.

Janko, S. (1994). *Vulnerable children, vulnerable families: The social construction of child abuse*. New York: Teachers College Press.

National Research Council. (1993). *Understanding child abuse and neglect*. Washington, DC: National Academy Press.

Willis, D. J., Holden, E. W., & Rosenberg, M. (Eds.). (1992). *Prevention of child maltreatment: Developmental and ecological perspectives*. New York: Wiley.

SUGGESTED ACTIVITIES

1. Form a discussion group with a few fellow students. Discuss your feelings about and experiences with young children with special needs. Ask the group:
    a. Has anyone ever had any experiences with special needs young children? At home? In a school setting?
    b. What happened? How did you feel about the child(ren)? Did they enjoy the experience? Did they have any difficulties?
    c. How would they feel about teaching in an integrated class? A class for special needs children only?

2. Visit a curriculum materials center and/or look through some materials catalogs that specialize in materials for young handicapped children. Categorize the kinds of materials available for various kinds of special needs children. Compare these materials with the kinds you would use with non-special needs children. What are some differences you find between materials for special needs and non-special needs children? Do you find any similarities? If possible, bring some materials to class to share with the other students. Give a report on your findings and use the materials as examples to illustrate what you found out.

3. Visit a child developmental center or an elementary school with integrated/inclusive classes for special needs students within the age span birth through age eight. Interview the director/principal and one or more teachers. Ask about the following or other questions you might devise:
    a. the objectives of the program
    b. the screening and placement procedures
    c. the criteria for admitting a child to the program
    d. the staffing of the program and the training required for the staff
    e. the types of activities and services offered

    Visit at least one classroom in each center/school and record what you observe. Write down your observation of the children, the teachers, and their relationships and your feelings about what you observed. Compare and contrast the two classrooms.

4. Speak with an officer or a member of a local organization that specializes in looking out for the interests of special needs children (such as chapters of the Council for Exceptional Children or the National Association for Retarded Citizens). Find out what the group does and who the members are. If possible, attend one or more meetings. Write a short report describing what you learned and what you did. Give your opinion about the group and its activities.

5. Do a survey in your community. Find out what kinds of services are available for young special needs children. Who is eligible for each program? Do all children who need services seem to be receiving them? Do you feel your community is doing a good job for its young special needs population? If not, what more is needed?

6. From the list in Figure 35–1, pick out one type of special needs condition. Try to learn as much as you can about the condition through:
   a. reading books and articles.
   b. talking to professionals who work with that type of child.
   c. visiting programs that deal with that type of condition.

7. Teachers of young children should be familiar with children's rights as they have been developed under PL 94–142, PL 99–457, and the ADA and under your state and local implementation guidelines. Through the library and your state and local education agencies, do some research regarding the rights of the young special needs child in your state. Share what you find out with the class.

8. The area of special education for the young special needs child is one that is complex and constantly changing. If you feel that this is an area about which you would like to know more, write a report on one or more books or articles dealing with that area. Include in your report:
   a. the title and author of the book or article
   b. the periodical in which the article appeared; the publisher of the book and pages read
   c. a short summary of what you learned from the book or article
   d. your reaction to the book or article:
      1) How does it relate to your personal experiences, future plans, and vocational interests?
      2) What did you learn that you feel was especially important and/or interesting?
      3) Did you feel it was interesting and worthwhile? If not, what are your criticisms?

9. Make an entry in your journal.

REVIEW

A. Explain the terms *special needs* and *at-risk* as they apply to young children.

B. List at least ten special need conditions.

C. Read each of the examples below. Decide which type of special need condition is being described.
   1. Hai-Ba-Trung is very bright and is rapidly learning English. However, she seems to have some problem in remembering, paying attention, and perceiving details.
   2. Aretha suffers from a heart condition. She cannot engage in some of the strenuous physical activities in which the other children are involved.
   3. Lisa just turned five. She draws beautifully, with animation and life. She can read picture books and is just beginning to be interested in writing stories.
   4. Tony wears a hearing aid and an amplifier. With these aids he is able to participate successfully in all the preschool activities.
   5. Five-year-old Denise operates at a three-year-old level. She is learning but at a much slower rate than the other children.
   6. Carlos is bright and bubbly at home. At school he is quiet and alert. He watches everything closely but does not participate. When given a battery of tests for placement, he is shy and answers in a whisper. Because he is still learning English, he is not always sure what all the test questions mean. He receives low scores and is placed in a class for the retarded.
   7. Mary Jane is unusually aggressive toward other children and defiant in her relationships with her teachers.
   8. Bobby has a brace on his left leg. Despite this handicap, he is exceptionally agile. He pulls the brace along as he makes his way rapidly around the room and the playground. He climbs the ladder to the playhouse as well as anyone. He does most of the physical activities except things like hanging on upside down by his knees on the parallel bars.

9. Lisa is 20 months old and is enrolled in a childcare center. The teacher notices that, unlike the other children, she has not begun to put on dress-up clothes and play grownup roles. Instead she goes to the dramatic play center and scatters the clothes around on the floor.

10. Billy has difficulty controlling his behavior. His attention span is short; he interrupts during group discussions and gets up and roams around the room during group storytime; he is short-tempered, and very disorganized relative to time and space.

D. Why are amendments PL 94–142 and PL 99–457 and the ADA so important?

E. Match each of the lettered terms in Column I with their numbered definitions or descriptions in Column II.

Column I	**Column II**
a. identification	1. Potential special needs children are found at an early age so that the risk of problems developing is kept to a minimum.
b. screening	
c. labeling or classifying	2. Developmental and health screening assist in this process.
d. placement	3. This practice must be used with caution so as not to stigmatize children for life.
e. prevention	
f. eligibility criteria	4. This practice involves deciding on the best type of educational setting for the child.
	5. These define who may be considered for participation.
	6. This is an initial step which provides information for deciding whether an indepth diagnosis is called for.

F. Give your opinion regarding the concept of inclusion. Consider the definitions given in the text and the skills required for teaching an integrated class.

G. Select the correct answer to each of the following. There is only one correct answer for each.
1. The IEP is
   a. a plan the teacher devises in order to provide an educational program for the young handicapped child.
   b. an individualized education plan that is developed cooperatively by teachers, support personnel, and parents.
   c. an individualized education plan that is prepared by diagnosticians.
   d. not required but recommended by federal and state laws.
2. The IFSP is
   a. an Individualized Family Service Plan that is prepared by a transdisciplinary team and the parents.
   b. an Individualized Family Service Plan that gives direction for finding families in need.
   c. an Individualized Family Service Plan that is prepared by an interdisciplinary team and approved by the parents.
3. The least restrictive environment means
   a. the special needs child in the regular classroom should be allowed to do anything he wants to do with no limits.
   b. the special needs child should be given minimal limits with more leeway than the non-special needs child.
   c. an environment in which the special needs child can make the most of his potential for learning.
   d. the child should have minimal structure and order.
4. Survival skills training in the prekindergarten and/or kindergarten should focus primarily on
   a. appropriate lunchroom, bathroom, hall, and playground behavior.
   b. learning all of the alphabet, recognizing numerals 1 to 10, and doing worksheets carefully.

    c. participating appropriately in groups, completing individual work with minimal teacher assistance, and managing in-class transitions independently.

    d. raising hands and taking turns during group activities, completing workbooks independently, and remembering how to make in-class transitions without being reminded.

5. Mr. Santos notes that one of the children in his three-year-old group is very destructive of materials, has a short attention span, has no friends, and seems anxious and fearful. He decides this child has a problem and should be referred for in-depth diagnosis. This example illustrates a

    a. teacher who does a good job of identifying a high-risk learner.

    b. child who is a normal three-year-old and will outgrow this behavior.

    c. teacher who does not understand his responsibilities for identifying high-risk learners.

    d. teacher who is misusing diagnostic guidelines.

6. A special needs condition that is both baffling as to its origins and difficult to deal with is

    a. hypoactivity.   c. high activity level.

    b. hypertension.   d. attention deficit disorder.

7. Niki learned to read on her own at age four. Her language development has been very advanced since she first began to speak at age twelve months. Her parents have supported her intellectual development in every way possible. Now they feel she should be considered for early entrance to first grade.

    a. If she is as socially mature as she is intellectually mature, this avenue should be explored.

    b. They should not consider early entrance—it never works out well.

    c. It is better to enroll her in one of the many available programs for the young gifted child.

    d. There are really no diagnostic methods available to help identify young gifted children.

8. Abused children come from

    a. only the lowest income families.

    b. all kinds of families at all economic levels.

    c. families that lack religious conviction.

    d. mostly families with a history of mental illness or alcohol or drug addiction.

9. When it comes to being responsible for reporting cases of child abuse

    a. teachers should mind their own business and keep their suspicions to themselves.

    b. teachers should report cases if they feel no one will find out that they were the ones who told.

    c. teachers should be careful not to get involved in lawsuits.

    d. teachers should know that laws in at least forty-three of the fifty states require that they report any suspected cases of abuse.

10. Relative to levels of severity most maltreated children fall in the category of

    a. serious injury or impairment.

    b. moderate injury or impairment.

    c. inferred injury.

    d. unknown injury or impairment.

The Whole Child

To have a complete understanding of child development we need to look at the whole child, that is, the child in the context of home, school, and community. Almost daily the popular press has stories about the problems facing today's children and families. If this information is newsworthy, then there must be some concern and interest in the population in general about the well-being of children and families in the United States. As an introduction to this section we'll look at children and families in the context of the community as they appear in the daily newspaper. Regularly we find stories about the economic status of families, the changing appearance of families, and the problems of educating young children. The following are a selection of such stories that appeared in daily newspapers.

nic groups; they include more working poor (two and single parent families with parents earning wages below the poverty level) than welfare families; and most of these families have only one or two children.

EDUCATION, FAMILY STABILITY, AND INCOME. (*The Advocate*, Baton Rouge, LA, October 30, 1992) The gap between the rich and poor is widening. Education and family stability are the keys to financial success. The trend away from married-couple families has brought an increase in low-income, unskilled workers, mainly single mothers with children.

NEWS ABOUT CHANGING FAMILIES, SCHOOLS, AND COMMUNITIES

NEWS ABOUT THE ECONOMIC STATUS OF FAMILIES

STUDY DISPELS MYTHS ABOUT THE CHILD OF POVERTY, (*Morning Advocate*, Baton Rouge, LA, June 3, 1991) A study by the Children's Defense Fund documents that ineffective government programs and low wages had pushed 2.2 million American children into poverty during the 1980's. Contrary to the mythology of poverty more poor children live outside of cities than in them; they are members of many racial and eth-

TRADITIONAL SUPPORT INSTITUTIONS SAID FAILING CHILDREN. (*The Advocate*, Baton Rouge, LA, June 23, 1993) American society is making some changes that are costly for the welfare of children. A 3-year study by the National Academy of Sciences indicates that problems such as increasing school failure, drug abuse, and violence are happening in part due to deterioration in our society. The increase in single-parent families with low income, lack of available health care, and schools that are not meeting student's needs all contribute to lessening chances for success for our children.

TIME HAS COME FOR THREE-PARENT FAMILY. (*Standard-Examiner*, Ogden, UT, May 3, 1994) Ellen Goodman (tongue-in-cheek) suggests that the time has come for the three-parent family. With two incomes needed to keep up a middle-class life style, two parents could work and one could stay home and take care of the house and act as primary caregiver to the children. This would be cheaper than hiring a nanny and have the advantage that if one parent lost his or her job, the home parent might be able to get one.

AMERICAN FAMILY NO LONGER SIMILAR TO JUNE CLEAVER'S. (*Standard-Examiner*, Ogden, UT, August 10, 1994) A new Census Bureau study indicates that families constitute 71 percent of households, down from 81 percent in 1970. The majority do not have children under eighteen living at home. Among those that have children, single-parent families are increasing in number. This study found 10.9 million single parents raising children compared to 3.8 million in 1970. The Census Bureau can no longer identify the so-called "typical American family." There are too many variations.

CHILD CARE AND SCHOOLING

NEIGHBOR DEFENDS WOMAN WHO CARED FOR 54 CHILDREN. (May 27, 1990) Ignoring the state limit of 6 children in home child care, a Maryland woman, with the assistance of one teenager, cared for 54 children, from infants through age 10, in her home. Most of the infants stayed in car seats while the older children sat on benches in the basement. A neighbor was quoted as saying, "(She gave) a lot of help to people who couldn't afford licensed care."

PUSHY PARENT'S NURSERY SCHOOL. (June 2, 1989) Ellen Goodman comments on the problems and anxieties attached to getting children into the most elite nursery school. She finds it appalling that children as young as two and three years old could have their whole future determined by being accepted or rejected by a preschool and thus tracked into their future educational experiences at such an early age.

CAN WE SAVE OUR BLACK CHILDREN? (Series of articles by Edward Pratt, *The Advocate*, Baton Rouge, LA, June, 1992) Reporter Edward Pratt spend about 10 weeks interviewing about 150 people in the Baton Rouge community investigating what was happening with African-American children and what was being done to improve the quality of their lives. He came across many heart-breaking stories. He also met many people in business, industry, government, churches, schools, and community organizations who were trying to help.

DISADVANTAGED AND AT-RISK CHILDREN

This introduction closes with some food for thought provided to us by Janice E. Hale in a keynote address, *Educational excellence for children in diverse cultures*, delivered at the March 1991 meeting of the Southern Association on Children Under Six in Atlanta, GA. Dr. Hale's premise is that African-American and other children at-risk don't enter schools disadvantaged—they leave disadvantaged. Schools, she believes, reproduce generations of failure. High-risk must be conceptualized individually within each culture. For example, the African-American child cannot be compared with the Anglo child. There is a difference in how language is used. European-American children bring the kind of language to school that teachers associate with intelligence because it is like teacher language. It is rich with vocabulary and concepts. African-Americans bring another kind of language. For them, it's not what you say, but how you say it. Oratory is deeply rooted in African-American culture through the speech of black preachers. African-American male language evolved into rapping, a skill which demands high level cognitive activity that doesn't show up on a standardized paper and pencil test. Churches provide a contrast in cultural uses of printed and oral language. European-American churches have everything written down (hymns, prayers, etc.) thus exposing children to the concept of print even in church. In African-American churches much of the service is spontaneous with spontaneous and dramatic prayer shouted out by the congregation members. The African-American culture is strong in the area of oral expression. School therefore assumes a literacy and oral language background that is not part of African-American culture. Hale believes that African-Americans need to attend early childhood programs that stress the literacy and oral skills such as concepts about print, problem solving, reasoning, prediction, etc. that white children learn incidently. Hale says we must not continue to predict children's success in school on the basis of culturally learned behaviors but instead recognize and build on those behaviors. Anglo children tend to be more quiet and fit in the school student stereotype, whereas African-American children, especially boys, tend to be more outgoing and expressive. Hale believes that low SES African-Americans, coming from crowded, noisy households where people are talking, music is playing and the phone is ringing constantly need a dynamic, active approach

to education, whereas whites have a higher tolerance for monotony. Hale characterizes low SES education as "concentration camp education" where children are trained to be inmates: to get in line and walk down the hall, to work with ditto sheets and workbooks, and do boring homework. When the children get bored, they move, and are then punished. Boredom leads to drugs and a nonproductive and often destructive adulthood. She suggests that programs be developed on models such as Stanford University's Henry Levin's Accelerated School that emphasizes acceleration for lower socioeconomic level students rather than remediation.

In Unit 36 we will look in more detail at the whole child in context. In Unit 37 we'll examine the ways you, as an individual concerned with young children and their development, can promote public policy action that will make life better for children and their families.

36

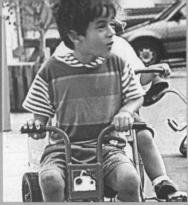

A Look at the Whole Child

After studying this unit, the student should be able to:

- List the factors that make up the whole child.

- Explain his or her view of the status of American children.

- Describe the American family of today.

- Evaluate the quality of day care, kindergarten, and primary programs.

- Identify important factors we have learned from research on the quality of child care.

- Identify important factors which support the need for concern regarding elementary level schooling.

- Understand the need for parent involvement in the education of young children.

- Know why social class, economic status, and racism are relevant to the development of young children.

We have now looked at the young children's development from conception through age eight. We have seen that young children are complex and at times puzzling persons identified as infants, toddlers, three-, four-, five-, six-, seven-, and eight-year-olds. We have looked at young children as they strike out on their own, developing more initiative and relying less on constant adult supervision.

Adults who work with young children must keep in mind the children's histories, their present status, and their probable future needs. Throughout the text the readers have been encouraged to view children, not as isolated individuals, but as persons acting and reacting within a context of family, community, and a larger society. Child development includes these factors as they interact with affective, cognitive, and psychomotor development to obtain a picture of **the whole child**.

KEYTERMSKEYTERMSKEYTERMSKEYTERMSKEYTERMSKEY

the whole child

THE STATUS OF AMERICA'S CHILDREN

From interviews with adults and children in his community Edward Pratt, an African-American newspaper reporter, writes about some of the emotional moments that particularly stuck with him (Pratt, 1992).

- There was a little eight-year-old boy, whose busted sneakers barely touched the floor when he sat, who coolly told a schoolmate how to commit murder and get away with it.

- I watched a nine-year-old boy ignore several requests from a school teacher to sit down. The boy just folded his arms and stared at her. He finally sat down after she grabbed his shoulders and tried to force him into his chair. I can't imagine doing that when I was that age.

Pratt was very disturbed by the attitudes of three teen-age boys incarcerated in the local juvenile facility. They said that they felt no qualms about shooting people. "Their attitude was, 'get them before they get you'" (p. 7). Pratt found that it was not just European-Americans but also most of the African-American middle-class that was ignoring these African-American children living in poverty and violence. There were some bright spots: e.g., teachers and counselors that really cared, industries that donated their employees as tutors on company time, community groups working on substance-abuse problems.

As referred to in previous units, the Children's Defense Fund Yearbook for 1994 (*State of America's children*, 1994) is full of facts and figures substantiating the fact that the status of America's children is getting worse. The 1994 yearbook contains a chart entitled "Moments in America for Children." Some of the moments included in a list of sixteen are:

- Every 5 seconds of the school day a student drops out of public school.

- Every 10 seconds a teenager becomes sexually active for the first time.

- Every 26 seconds a baby is born to an unmarried mother.

- Every 30 seconds a baby is born in poverty.

- Every 5 seconds a child is arrested for a violent crime.

- Every 2 hours a child is murdered.

There is no doubt that children and families are in crisis. However, according to the CDF 1994 yearbook (*State of America's children*, 1994) we may be reaching a turning point as Congress has passed some legislation for a new child protection and family support program and has increased funding for preventive community-based mental health services for children.

What effects are these crisis conditions having on our schools? According to Reed and Sautter (1990) teachers are alarmed at the rise in health and social problems they see reflected in their classrooms. They report that surveys of teachers indicate:

> ...teachers worry about constant pupil turnover, about students' health problems, and about students' preoccupation with health problems.... Such concerns are more common among teachers of children from low-income families. Guidance counselors report that, even at the elementary level, they find themselves "dealing with one crisis after another" in a child's life. (p. K7)

Teachers are also seeing more children with learning disabilities, with low self-esteem and with a belief that they cannot learn (Figure 36–1).

What can be done to alleviate these problems? At the federal level, programs like Head Start have documented a positive impact on the later lives of young children. For example, in one study nearly 60 percent of Head Start graduates were employed at age 19 as compared with 32 percent for a control group. Federal Chapter 1 funds are being steered more and more in the direction of working with younger children. However, these programs serve less than half of the eligible children. Programs for four-year-olds are increasing in number through funding by states and by local school districts to identify and alleviate problems before they have gone too far.

School systems across the country are trying to attack the problems brought on by increasing poverty in two ways: by mobilizing parents and by integrating community health resources into the schools

Figure 36–1   Young children need time to grow and develop with minimal stress in a healthy and developmentally appropriate environment.

(Reed and Sautter, 1990). Parent involvement will be discussed later in this unit.

Reed and Sautter (1990) provide some examples of the methods being used to integrate community services with the public schools. In several states, efforts are being made to make schools also function as community centers. They serve children and families and provide links to available family support services that can offer help for social, psychological, and health problems. Schools are also linking up with other service providers to work with the conventional population of children with disabilities and special needs and some of the new ones such as the homeless and the crack children who are now entering the system.

In the summer of 1994 the Southern Early Childhood Association (SECA) published a report from the SECA Public Policy Institute calling for linkage between health and human services and schools (We can do it!, 1994). At the higher-education level, the Dewitt Wallace-*Reader's Digest* Fund sponsored a study of collaboration between schools of education and schools of social science directed at developing collaboration between the two areas (Quaranta, Weiner, Robison, & Tainsh, 1992).

TODAY'S FAMILY

As we look at today's **family** and the forecast for the future in the twenty-first century, we see that the so-called traditional family as depicted by a kindergartner in his family drawing in Figure 36–2 is becoming more and more only one of many types of American families (Footlick, 1990). Families continue to split and sometimes recombine, the rate of births to single mothers has continued to increase, there is an increasing number of homeless families, and homosexual households. An increasing variety of family types is becoming common:

- the traditional working father and nonworking mother
- families blended from two families after remarriage by both parents
- homosexual couples heading families
- extended families made up of relatives and/or nonrelatives in the same household
- two-parent families with both parents working
- two-parent families with father at home and mother working
- homeless families
- single parent families, parents divorced
- single parent families, mothers unmarried
- single parent families, child(ren) adopted
- foster care families
- children with no family

More mothers of young children are working outside the home, more and more parents are separated or divorced, there is an increasing number of stepfamilies, of families where the parents are not married, and families that include grandmother, teenage mother, and child(ren) (grandchildren). The number of families where mothers are raising children and grandchildren is increasing rapidly in the poverty areas of our big cities. Teenage mothers are not mature enough to fulfill the needs of a young child. The risks of child abuse and neglect are very

Figure 36–2   What happened to the traditional family?

high. The factor that keeps a great many of these children thriving is that there is often a strong extended family network of older siblings, aunts, mother, and grandmothers to give support. The constant element that is missing is a father.

Hoffman (1984) summarized the results of research on maternal employment. As already mentioned, the increase in employed mothers has resulted in more young children in child care. Quality child care seems to be beneficial for young children. Research (Hoffman, 1984) has also centered on the quantity and quality of mother-child and father-child interaction. The more educated a mother is, the less difference there is in the amount of time employed mothers spend with their young children as compared with nonemployed mothers. When the mother is employed, the fathers appear to spend less time with the child(ren). What seems to happen is that when the couple arrives home, the husband attends to household chores while the wife is involved in an intensive period of interaction with the child. No significant differences in quality of interaction have been identified. Mother's satisfaction with her state of employment or nonemployment seems to go along with quality interaction. Quality of attachment also seems to be about the same for employed mothers and children as nonemployed mothers and children. Mother employ-

ment seems to have no effect one way or the other on father-daughter attachment, but father-son attachments have been found to be less secure.

McBride and Mills (1994) reported an updated study comparing father and mother involvement with their preschool children. Out of the 100 families studied, 70 of the mothers and 100 of the fathers were employed outside the home. McBride and Mills (1994) found patterns of paternal involvement in childrearing were much the same as found in previous studies in spite of apparent changes in societal contexts for fatherhood. On both workdays and nonworkdays, mothers spent more time in interaction with and accessibility to their children than fathers. More of mothers' time with children was spent in parallel (i.e. cooking, picking up toys) and functional (i.e. bathing, dressing, feeding) activities while most of fathers' time with children was spent in play. Even in dual-earner families, mothers were the childrearing leaders. On the other hand, in dual-earner families the fathers spent more time involved with children than the fathers in the single-earner families. This indicates that while employed mothers still carry more of the childrearing load than their husbands, when wives work fathers are taking more responsibility. The higher families rated on a measure of positive family functioning, the closer were mothers' and fathers' estimates of the spouses' amount of interaction with the children. McBride and Mills (1994) believe their results indicate a need for more parent education for fathers. Such a program has been designed by McBride and McBride (1993).

In the introduction to his edited book on nontraditional families, Michael Lamb (1982) reminds us that the traditional family as we once knew it was of fairly recent origin. Shared economic and childcare responsibilities have been known in cultures throughout history. Up until the industrial revolution we were an agrarian society. Everyone shared in the economic life of the family. Prior to the 1830s children were the father's property and went to him if the marriage was dissolved. The only long-lasting traditional belief is that mothers should have the predominant responsibility for child rearing. Lamb concludes that overall we have been very flexible about learning to manage as family styles have come and gone. Although divorce, single parenting, and step-parenting are all difficult for adults and children to deal with, so is an unhappy traditional marriage. As we look toward the next century, it is apparent that the variety of families of today is now the norm and will likely continue to be so. Adults who work with young children need to be aware of family structure and tailor parent contacts and parent education and involvement to fit that structure. Footlick (1990) points out that there is still some difficulty for many people in defining family. There are still those who want to retain the family of the fifties: mother, father, children, mother stays home and cares for the children; then reject all other groups living together as being eligible for the family label. However, those who are in daily contact with young children realize this is no longer a viable and realistic definition. Other aspects that are changing relative to family demographics are the relative numbers of ethnic groups within our society. According to Zill (reported in U.S. Children and Their Families, 1991) by 2010 the percentage of African-American and Hispanic youth will increase from 27 percent to 33 percent of the child population and a disproportionate number of these children live in families at the lowest socioeconomic levels.

Issues of the family must be faced and dealt with for the social and economic future of the country (Footlick, 1990). We can no longer ignore the growing underclass that lives in poverty. Some sectors believe that a national family policy must be developed that includes the following kinds of things (Footlick, 1990, p. 20):

- Child and family allowances with payments scaled to the number of children in each family
- Guarantees to mothers of full job protection, seniority and benefits upon their return to work after maternity leave
- Pay equity for working women
- Cash payments to mothers for wages lost during maternity leave
- Full health-care programs for all children
- National standards for day care.

All Americans do not support these suggestions, mainly due to the increased burden they would bring to taxpayers. American business will need to employ even more women to fill the needs for workers in the future while many mothers will continue to work due to personal choice and others due to financial need. The family will continue to take on new aspects that we cannot even foresee at this point. Meantime, we need a national policy that will support families and child development.

EXTENDING THE FAMILY

Now we will look at the two locations where young children today spend a large portion of their time out of the home: in child care and in school. Further we will examine factors in parent involvement in both of these out of home institutions.

In 1988 Valora Washington (1988a and 1988b) described the trends in demographics and in instruction in early childhood. We have already examined some of these factors such as the changing family configurations, the increasing number of young children living in poverty, the increase in the percentage of minorities in the ranks of young children, and the problems relevant to developmentally appropriate versus inappropriate instructional practices. Washington also calls attention to the need to deal with the problems of licensing requirements and staff qualifications. Rust and Williams (1989) point out how the field of early childhood has expanded from a concern with the development and education of three-, four-, and five-year-olds to encompass infants and toddlers and primary age children also. This expansion of focus has taken early educators into many new settings where children can be found. "These settings now range from the infants' own homes or homes of other caregivers to informal and formal public and private school classrooms, as well as a variety of nonschool situations, such as work place or employer-provided facilities, and hospital and hospice programs" (pp. 334–335). Education has become an essential part of care whatever the location.

Child Care

In days past when supplemental care was needed for young children, the nuclear family was extended by hiring a helper who came in by the day or actually lived in the home. Now this "Mary Poppins" figure is a fantasy of the past except for those families at the upper income levels. Today supplemental care is usually in an out-of-home location. According to a survey done in the spring of 1991 (West and Hausken, 1993) about 5.7 million (68%) preschool children in the United States were receiving care or education outside the home. More four- and five-year-olds than three-year-olds participated. Three-fourths of employed and half of nonemployed mothers' children received some type of outside care or education. On the average, preschoolers spent 19 hours per week in programs where African-American children spent more time than any other group. Twice as many children are enrolled in center-based as in home-based programs. Programs for after-school care for school-age children are also growing in number. Fifty percent of kindergarten and primary children are left on their own for part of the day (Click, 1994). It is estimated that in the future 34 million school-age children will need child care.

Today, as indicated in previous units, the search for the factors that define quality child care is the focus of a great deal of research. Phillips and Howes (1987) summarized the results of this work. The pioneering study in this area was the National Day Care Study (Ruopp, 1979). The major finding regarding quality indicated that two factors were present in high-quality programs for preschool children: there were relatively small groups of children and the caregivers had child-specific education/training. Well-trained teachers with a small ratio of children per teacher brought the most positive outcome relative to positive classroom behaviors and higher test scores for the children. This leads to higher salaries for teachers and a higher cost for the consumer. According to Phillips and Howes (1987) research conducted since the National Day Care Study has confirmed some of the results, contradicted others, and looked into new areas. Quality is not an easy concept to define but researchers continue to try to pin it down.

Studies which have looked at child care in a global fashion, that is, high quality compared with low quality, have confirmed that better child care has more positive effects on children's cognitive and social development. Other studies have looked at specifics such as adult-child ratio, group size, and caregiver training and experiences. The results have supported that lower child/staff ratios have positive effects on verbal interaction, opportunities for play, and nurturant, nonrestrictive caregiver behavior. Group size is also a significant factor with smaller group size appearing "to facilitate constructive caregiver behavior and positive developmental outcomes for children" (Phillips & Howes, 1987, p. 6). The more recent research indicates that both the amount of specialized child development/early childhood education training and years of experience teaching tend to relate to more positive teacher behavior and better outcomes for children. However, this is a complex area that warrants a great deal more study. Research on stability of the caregiver has provided a mixed picture. When the child remains in the same setting, having a stable caregiver does appear to be a plus for development. On the other hand, studies that examined the number of changes in settings children experienced, showed no association with child outcomes. A more recent area of research has been an examination of the joint effects of family and the childcare setting. For example, families that select low-quality care tend to have more stressful lives and to be less involved and invested in what is happening with their children. Mothers' attitudes toward the use of child care (whether comfortable with the idea or not) also appear to be of importance in influencing child behavior. The effects that child care may have, appears to be the result of the interaction of a number of variables within home and childcare settings that are still in need of much more study. Clarke-Stewart, after examining five major childcare studies, concludes that "the best predictors of advanced child development, and hence our best clues as to indexes of quality child care, are (Clarke-Stewart, 1987, p. 118) a licensed program (usually in a center)" in which:

- the child's interaction with the caregiver is frequent, verbal, and educational, rather than custodial and controlling

- children are not left to spend their time in aimless play together

- there is an adequate adult-child ratio (for older preschoolers probably not lower than 1:12) and a reasonable group size (probably not larger than 25)

• the caregiver has a balanced training in child development, some degree of professional experience in child care, and has been in the program for some period of time.

A critical element in childcare quality is the regulation of homes and centers through standards which are usually provided by licensing agencies in each state. Phillips, Lande, and Goldberg (1990) compared licensing regulations among the states. There is great variability in stringency among states and within states. That is, even within states, regulations may be stringent on one item such as the number of children allowed in a child care home and lax on another such as staff/child ratio. Some states, overall, have very low standards which do not even meet the minimums suggested by national organizations or by federal departments. If federal standards, such as those developed by the Department of Health, Education and Welfare (HEWDCR) were imposed, many states would have to make drastic changes in upgrading their licensing requirements with resulting increases in the cost of care. Phillips et al (1990) found that the median level of standards was about at the same level as the Accreditation Guidelines of NAEYC's National Academy of Early Childhood Programs and the Accreditation Profile of the National Association for Family Day Care (NAFDC) that are less stringent than the federal guidelines. Phillips et. al. (1990) recommend a gradual upgrading of regulations to meet at least the NAEYC and NAFDC standards through a cooperative federal and state effort. Enforcement procedures would also need to be improved along with opportunities for staff training to upgrade instructional practices. Of course, with more training, salaries and costs would increase. Specific information on the cost of quality care is the content of an NAEYC publication edited by Barbara Willer (1990). At present the average childcare worker earns an amount below the poverty line. Providing quality care and eliminating harmful care is an enormous and important challenge for the future.

Within communities parents need guidance in finding the best care for their young children. Bradbard and Endsley (1980) found that parents were usually at a loss as to how to go about finding a good childcare setting for their child and that professionals offer little help. Bradbard and Endsley developed and field-tested a guide that can be used by parents to rate childcare facilities. Checklists and guides to use in selecting quality child care are available from many sources such as the Southern Early Childhood Association (SECA) and the National Association for the Education of Young Children (NAEYC) and their affiliate groups and from state licensing agencies and local service and action groups. See Units 10 and 13 for infant and toddler care checklists.

Schooling

Teachers have reported informally that one of the strongest impediments to developmentally appropriate practice is the principal's point of view. The results of a study by Burts, Campbell, Hart, Charlesworth, DeWolfe, and Fleege (1991) that looked at the relationship between kindergarten teachers' beliefs and practices and principals' beliefs support this view. The results found that there were about equal numbers of principals in the samples with appropriate as with inappropriate beliefs. The majority of principals did not believe that active exploration and adjusting instruction for individual interests and abilities were important. There was little relationship between principals' beliefs and teachers' beliefs. Older principals, who most likely had studied their teacher education courses when socialization was the objective of kindergarten, had more appropriate beliefs than younger principals, who had probably been educated with an emphasis on academic achievement and skills training. Principals certified in kindergarten or who had inservice training in early childhood education had more appropriate beliefs overall than those who were not knowledgeable about the field. The results of this study support the need for principals to have early childhood education training if developmentally appropriate practices are to become widespread.

Efforts are being made to improve the quality of education for young children. For example, at the preschool level there is a great deal of interest in the programs developed in Reggio Emilia, Italy (Gandini, 1993; Malaguzzi, 1993; Bredekamp, 1993). The **Reggio Emilia** is an all-day program that combines care, education, and social services. A unique factor is that the public schools of Reggio Emilia were literally built from the ground up by parents after World War II. In Italy free programs are open to all three to six-year-olds. Parents pay a fee for infants and toddlers. The Reggio philosophy is based on theories, such as those of Dewey, Piaget, and Vygotsky. There is a set of basic principles that include, for example, that children have the preparedness, curiosity, and interest to construct their own knowledge; parent participation is essential; the layout of the school encourages communication and peer interaction; time is not set by the clock; teachers work in partnerships; teachers view themselves as researchers collecting information on each child; the curriculum is emergent; project work is promoted; and art is a central focus.

Bredekamp (1993) found the experience very thought provoking and particularly picked up on the core of the Reggio philosophy: *the image of a competent child who has rights.* She believes the challenge for American educators is to reclaim this image. She would like to see more of the Reggio philosophy reflected in the future revision of the DAP guidelines. She hopes that standards can be devised in a way that leaves room for questioning. She also hopes we can somehow incorporate some of the approaches to instruction that provide teacher assistance as needed while children move toward their self-selected goals.

The state of Missouri, in consultation with Rheta DeVries, has developed Project Construct, a process-oriented curriculum and assessment framework designed for working with children ages three through seven. It is a program based on principles derived from constructivist theory. Thus, children are viewed as competent to take the lead in constructing their own knowledge through meaningful activities provided by the teacher (*Understanding the possibilities,* 1992).

Parent Involvement

As mentioned earlier in this unit, parents are the child's first and most significant teachers. However, in today's society from infancy on, children may spend more time with other adults than with their parents. Therefore, getting parents involved through a partnership with care givers or teachers is one of the prime goals in our nation (Reed & Sautter, 1990; Epstein, 1991). Unfortunately those children most in need of **parent involvement** are least likely to benefit from it. Parents in poverty may not feel comfortable or capable of becoming fully involved in their children's school. (Reed & Sautter, 1990) Head Start has been the model for successful parent involvement (Zigler and Styko, 1993).

Epstein (1991) describes more recently instituted national, state, district and individual school initiatives promoting parent involvement. At the national level Chapter 1 includes an emphasis on parent involvement. FIRST (Fund for the Improvement of Schools and Teaching) grants fund local programs designed to create, develop and, implement new school/family/community partnerships. Even Start links the education of young children with the education of their underachieving parents. A new 5-year Center on Families, Communities, Schools, and Children's Learning is being funded. States are also working on parent involvement. California has developed a state-wide policy on parent involvement. Other states, such as Illinois, provide competitive grants which school systems can win to fund development of solutions to the parent-involvement problem. Missouri's Parents as Teachers program has worked to have all parents involved in the education of their children from birth to three. Success is Homemade will extend family involvement from kindergarten through grade 12. Individual districts and school within districts have also initiated parent-involvement programs. From all these experiences, we have learned that parent involvement must continue all through the educational program; it is not something that can end after early childhood. All families must be involved, not just those at the lower socioeconomic levels. Parent involvement makes the teacher's job easier. It takes several years to develop a fully operational program. There must be family/school coordinators to guide the program.

KEYTERMSKEYTERMSKEYTERMSKEYTERMSKEYTERMSKEYTERMSKEY

parent involvement

There should be room in the schools set aside for parents ("Parent Clubs," "Parent Centers") where they can talk with each other and obtain resource materials. Parents may also be directly involved in school policy decision making as members of a school site council in a school that has site-based management (David, 1994). Parental involvement does not require parents to come to school. Those parents who can may volunteer. Those who cannot can become involved at home by learning how to help their children do better in school. Parent involvement can be accomplished on a modest budget of about $25 per pupil per school year.

SOCIOLOGICAL FACTORS

A number of factors regarding the relationship between sociocultural status and child development have been discussed. Some of these factors include the following:

- The current focus is on celebrating diversity, multicultural education, and anti-bias curriculum.

- Adults who work with young children and families from a culture different from their own should learn about the children's and families' cultures and respect and incorporate the customs and language.

- Caution is needed in applying developmental theories to culturally diverse children.

- Lower socioeconomic level parents may not recognize the infant's need for motor activity and sensory stimulation and may not be able to provide proper nutrition, with the child then possibly showing signs of neurological impairment.

- Adults who feel powerless have fewer resources, less time, and less energy to give their infant.

- The child's behavior and development in language are affected by factors such as dialect, mother tongue, and the parental use and reinforcement of the child's use of language.

- Discrimination based on faulty use and interpretation of intelligence test results has resulted in mislabeling and misplacement of children in special education classes.

- Lower-class families usually have less access to needed health care facilities and often lack the means for supplying their children with adequate nutrition.

Children often arrive at school with a learning style that does not fit the school's instructional approaches. As discussed previously the importance of learning styles cannot be overemphasized.

Fantini and Russo (1982) conclude that economic status and social class are the most important factors in support of strong families and strong child development. Underlying this support must be nondiscriminatory attitudes and actions toward minorities and women. The pluralistic nature of our society must be recognized and cultural differences respected. Fantini and Russo feel educational policies must go from the point of view of institutional reform rather than learner change. That is, the institutions must change to fit the learners, rather than the learners changing to fit the institutions. Fantini and Russo present the following guidelines:

I. Economic support of children should be implemented through the economic support of their families, including a vigorous policy of antidiscrimination toward minorities and toward women who are increasingly the partial or sole sources of family support.

II. Research should be promoted which works toward a comprehensive understanding of both universals—material and psychological—in parenting in the further delineation of the specific sociocultural factors which affect the process.

III. Any social policy recommendations, whether concerned with research or intervention, must be respectful of a new pluralistic concept of the family and of the diverse cultural models of parenting.

IV. Schools must be considered central to parenting: First, pedagogically, since parenting is, in very essential ways, a teaching process; and second, institutionally, since the educational

Figure 36–3a–e Today's family may be any one of a variety of configurations. (Photo a from Marotz, *Health, Safety, and Nutrition for the Young Child*, by Delmar Publishers. Photo b from Gordon & Browne, *Beginnings and Beyond, 3E*, by Delmar Publishers. Photo c from Wilson, *Infants and Toddlers*, by Delmar Publishers)

Figure 36–3e (Continued)

system is closely identified with community participation and offers the personnel, facilities and capabilities to provide choices in support services and access to information.

Fantini and Russo recommend further that a presidential advisory board evaluate government policy on family-related issues. This board would act as an advocate for American children and their families. Since public policy is such a strong force in child development, this area warrants a further look in the final unit which follows.

We have a long way to go in providing the best educational opportunities for all our young children. Racism and classism still underlie many of our educational policies and practices (Comer, 1989; Pine & Hilliard, 1990; Banks, 1993; Bowman & Stott, 1994; Kessler, 1992). For the adult who works with young children, a time comes when these questions must be faced and important educational decisions made. Whatever the outcome, if teachers, parents, and allied workers cooperate and develop policies that fit the values identified by the group the program serves, the program stands a better chance of enhancing the development of the whole child.

SUMMARY

The whole child is more than the sum of his or her parts: personal history, present status, and affective, cognitive, and psychomotor components determine what the child is today, but the child has the potential for becoming more. Children also are affected by, and affect, their family and society. As the twenty-first century nears, our children are in a perilous situation. An ever-increasing proportion live in poverty and thus are likely to face early mortality due to poor prenatal care, poor nutrition, and lack of proper medical attention.

Today the family is a different and more diverse entity than it was in the past (Figure 36–3). The number of families made up of working father, nonworking mother, and one or more children is rapidly shrinking. Adults need to be prepared to work with these different types of families. With more working mothers, the family has extended out of the home to the child care provider. Federal, state, and local government agencies are focusing increasingly on early development and education programs. Quality child care and developmentally appropriate practices in preschool and elementary school instruction are goals for the twenty-first century. A further objective is to get families more involved in the education of their children and to make the school a community center where education, family, and community work together for the benefit of children. Increasing numbers of minority- and female-headed households trying to survive below the poverty level makes the job of adults who work with young children more and more challenging. Sociocultural status has an immense impact on the child and the family.

FOR FURTHER READING

Beardsley, L. (1990). *Good day/Bad day: The child's experience of child care*. New York: Teachers College Press.

Bretherton, I., & Watson, M. (Eds.). (1990). *Children's perspectives on the family*. San Francisco: Jossey-Bass.

Burns, A., & Scott, C. (1994). *Mother-headed families and why they have increased*. Hillsdale, NJ: Erlbaum.

Cath, S. H., Gurwitt, A., & Gunsberg, L. (Eds.). (1989). *Fathers and their families*. Hillsdale, NJ: Analytic Press.

A Children's Defense Fund Budget. (published yearly). Washington, DC: Children's Defense Fund.

Coner-Edwards, A. F., & Spurlock, J. (Eds.). (1988). *Black families in crisis: The middle class*. New York: Bruner/Mazel.

Cromwell, E. S. (1994). *Quality child care: A comprehensive guide for administrators and teachers*. Des Moines, IA: Longwood Division, Allyn and Bacon.

Edwards, C., Gandini, L., & Forman, G. (Eds.). (1993). *The hundred languages of children*. Norwood, NJ: Ablex. (Reggio Emilia)

Gottfried, A. E., & Gottfried, A. W. (Eds.). (1994). *Redefining families: Implications for children's development*. New York: Plenum.

Gouke, M., & Rollins, A. M. (1990). *One-parent children: A research guide*. New York: Garland.

Huston, A. C. (Ed.). (1992). *Children in poverty: Child development and public policy*. New York: Cambridge University Press.

Kontos, S. (1992). Family day care: Out of the shadows and into the limelight. *Research Monograph and of the National Association for the Education of Young Children, Volume 5*. Washington, DC: NAEYC.

Koralek, D. G., Colker, L. J., Dodge, D. T. (1993). *The What, Why, and How of high-quality early childhood education: A guide for on-site supervision*. Washington, DC: National Association for the Education of Young Children.

Lamb, M. E., Sternberg, K., Hwang, C., & Broberg, A. G. (Eds.) (1991). *Nonparental childcare*. Hillsdale, NJ: Erlbaum.

Lerner, J. V., & Galambos, N. L. (1991). *Employed mothers and their children*. New York: Garland.

McAdoo, H. P., & McAdoo, J. L. (1985). *Black children: Social, educational and parental environments*. Newbury Park, CA: Sage.

McAdoo, H. P. (1988). *Black families*, (2nd Ed.). Newbury Park, CA: Sage.

McCartney, K. (Ed.) (1990). *Child care and maternal employment: A social ecology approach*. San Francisco: Jossey-Bass.

Parke, R. D., & Kellam, S. G. (Eds.). (1994). *Exploring family relationships with other social contexts*. Hillsdale, NJ: Erlbaum.

Peters, D. L., & Pence, A. R. (Eds.). (1992). *Family day care: Current research for informed public policy*. New York: Teachers College Press.

Powell, D. R. (1989). *Children and their families*. Washington, DC: National Association of Young Children.

Slaughter, D. T. (Ed.) (1988). *Poverty: A developmental perspective*. San Francisco: Jossey-Bass.

Swick, K. J. (1992). *Teacher-parent partnerships to enhance school success in early childhood education*. Westhaven, CT: National Education Association.

Wang, M. C., & Gordon, E. W. (Eds.). (1994). *Educational resilience in inner-city America*. Hillsdale, NJ: Erlbaum.

Zigler, E. F., & Lang, M. E. (1990). *Child care choices: Balancing the needs of children, families, and society*. New York: Free Press.

Zigler, E., & Styfco, S. J. (Eds.). (1993). *Head Start and beyond: A national plan for extended childhood intervention*. New Haven: Yale University Press.

SUGGESTED ACTIVITIES

1. To find out how well acquainted typical American citizens are with the realities of family life today, look back through the units and select 10 facts about today's families. List them numbered 1–10 in a true/false format such as:

TODAY'S FAMILIES QUIZ

Decide if each of the following is true or false. Circle your response to each statement.
true/false 1. (list your statements)

Make ten or more copies and administer the quiz to ten friends or relatives. Bring your results to class for discussion.

2. Visit two or more childcare centers that enroll infants and toddlers. Use the checklist in Unit 10 (infant caregiver) and the checklist in Unit 13 (toddler caregiver) to evaluate each facility and its staff. Compare the centers. Which seemed best? Why? Did you find the checklists were helpful?
Why or Why not? Report your findings in class.

3. Looking through the text, make a list of factors that would indicate a program for preschoolers, kindergartners, and primary students was developmentally appropriate. Visit two preschool, kindergarten, and/or primary classrooms that enroll children who live in poverty. Use your list of factors to evaluate the programs. Find out if there is a parent-involvement program. Report your findings in class.

4. Make an entry in your journal

REVIEW

A. List the factors that make up the whole child.

B. Explain your view of the status of America's children today using the information in the unit as the basis for your opinion.

C. Describe "Today's American Family."

D. Evaluate the following description of a day-care center using what you have learned about the factors that indicate quality child care for young children.

The First Avenue Child Development Center is located in a working-class neighborhood of a mid-sized city. The director, Mrs. Tanaka, has a bachelor's degree in child development. The two teachers, Ms. Miller and Mr. Santos, have associate degrees in early education. All three are actively involved with the children and it is noted that they smile, pat, and hug children and give verbal approval frequently. The children smile and laugh and there is a feeling of relaxed business in the center.

A flexible approach to grouping is used with the 35 children, ages $2\frac{1}{2}$ to $5\frac{1}{2}$, who are enrolled. Sometimes each teacher and the director takes a group and sometimes the children are divided into two groups, depending on the objectives and activities for the day. During the afternoon nap and the play period following, two high school students who have taken the child development course offered at their high school work at the center, allowing each of the regular staff a chance for a break and filling in when the teacher who has opened up in the morning leaves in mid-afternoon.

There are lots of materials such as toys, games, and art materials available on low shelves where the children can easily reach them. Indoor equipment includes dolls, dress-up clothes, records and record player, blocks, and books. The room arrangements are such that there are not clearly defined areas for the use of each type of materials. The outdoor play area is small and includes a sandbox, a slide, and a small jungle gym. Inside, the children play well and there is almost no bickering over materials as there is plenty for everyone. Outside there is not quite enough room (although only half the group usually uses the playground at one time). The equipment is crowded. Teachers must intervene often to stop pushing and shoving, and to make sure everyone gets his turn.

The program seems to include both free-play and structured small group activities. Sometimes the whole groups gets together for a film or a special visitor. The schedule indicates that the children will take a trip to the farm next week and will begin the next day on a gardening project on a small plot in the play yard.

The center is very clean. The walls are yellow and sunlight streams in the large windows. Bulletin boards contain teacher information and interesting, colorful pictures and displays for the children. Many of the children's paintings are used to decorate the room. Near the entrance is a small office with a room off to the side, which is used both as a teacher's lounge and a place to isolate sick children. In case of the need for emergency medical care, all parents have signed a release allowing their child(ren) to be treated by the staff at the clinic down the street. Menus for the week follow government guidelines for nutrition. Observing the lunch period, we find the food is served family style. Several children have helped bake cookies which are served for dessert.

When the parents arrive to pick up their children, one of the teachers makes a point of talking with each one and passing along some information regarding the parent's child. Today Mrs. Tanaka is trying to arrange times for parent visits and conferences.

E. Select the statements below that are true.
   1. The field of early childhood education has expanded from its concern with mainly three-, four- and five-year-olds to a concern with the whole period from birth through eight.
   2. Most child care for young children takes place in the child's own home.
   3. It really is not at all clear whether high versus low quality care makes any difference in the development of children.
   4. When selecting child care it should be kept in mind that both the amount of specialized child development/early childhood education training and years of experience the staff have are critical factors related to quality.
   5. Child care licensing standards in most states are above the minimum recommended by NAEYC and other professional organizations.
   6. We should be just as concerned about the quality of later more formal schooling as we are about early child care.
   7. The principal's point of view is critical in determining whether or not classroom instruction is developmentally appropriate or not.
   8. Schools need to develop programs that focus on community and parent involvement in children's education.
   9. The best parent involvement programs require that every parent volunteers some time to participate in the school program.
   10. Racism and classism have been eliminated from educational programs.

Action for Children

OBJECTIVES

After studying this unit, the student should be able to:

■ List and describe some of the current policy issues relevant to the young children and their families.

■ Know how to obtain materials for planning an advocacy action.

■ Understand why young children need advocates.

■ Identify the conditions that describe the area of public policy for children and families.

■ Explain what the One hundred first Congress accomplished for young children and their families.

■ Describe what advocates for children might do in taking action for them.

dults who work with young children may feel helpless in the face of what appear to be insurmountable national problems. In fact, during the 1970s we lost many battles in the fight for our children and families because we did not have the skills, knowledge, and experience to mount strong advocacy campaigns. Whereas adult special interest groups (e.g., gun ownership advocates, farmers, industrialists, etc.) can campaign firsthand for their interests, children cannot. Consequently, it is left up to caring adults to protect their interests and welfare. Child advocates are adults who work to see that children's rights are protected. They work through the political system for child-centered public policy. They also work for public awareness so parents and other adults are informed about policy issues and can join the advocate ranks. During the 1980s adults who work with young children realized that they would have to pull some of their energies away from their immediate daily work with children to seek changes in social policies and services.

In the 1990s various stake holders are getting together to form coalitions on issues effecting children. For example, "in September 1993, nearly 300 early childhood professionals, business leaders, researchers, parents, community planners, health and human service professionals, clergy, funders, and local, state, and federal policy makers gathered in Washington, DC for the first Forum on State and Community Planning in Early Childhood Education" (Galinsky, Shubilla, Willer, Levine, and Daniel, 1994). A cross-section of stake holders in promoting sound early childhood development and education came together to share ideas and strategies. Their purpose was to go beyond coming up with a list of recommendations to actually collaborating to create new systems for high-quality early childhood service delivery. They identified eight components that need to be addressed to achieve systemic reform: creating linkages, using data in planning, improving the quality of programs, developing a coordinated professional development system, financing the system, creating new systems of governance, building public awareness, and developing a public policy agenda. To achieve these goals, a planning group must have a clear mission and convince a cross-section of influential players to buy into the mission. The Forum will continue meeting each year to work on long-term goals and actions for reform.

THE GRASS-ROOTS LEVEL

Advocacy at its worst is a time consuming, exhausting, and often disappointing effort. Advocacy at its best is made up of both large and small victories: a large victory being one that changes or develops new policy at the federal, state, or local levels. Small victories occur when one parent, one teacher, or one other person who is concerned with young children perceives the need for change and joins in the advocacy struggle. The author, after being involved at the local level in a national childcare awareness campaign, realized that the general public in her city probably did not perceive there was a problem and for the most part ignored the campaign. It was evident that a successful public awareness campaign in an area with a population of over 400,000 would re-

quire grass-roots support and a great deal of labor by enthusiastic and persistent community volunteers.

Laura Smith (fictitious name) is a mother and a teacher. She held a position as a special education home-based teacher working with preschoolers with disabilities. She worked with the children individually in their homes or in their child care centers. Some of the things she saw going on in the name of early education and child care she found appalling. Laura, feeling ill-equipped to address the problem, took a leave of absence and returned to school to obtain her masters degree. During the course of her studies she found herself in a seminar with a focus on issues of public policy. The following, in Laura's own words, is the story of how she instituted action for children in her community.

Laura's Story: A Grassroots Effort

In the beginning there was a discussion in class about the lack of knowledge that persists in the general public about what constitutes high quality in an early childhood program. I immediately envisioned that educating the community was going to take longer than seven days! However, I decided I would take on the responsibility of looking at the problem.

The initial approach was to enlist the help of organizations that would disseminate information on quality early childhood programs. As I began gathering information prior to approaching interested organizations and persons, it became apparent that most of the information in the community dealt only with surface issues such as cleanliness, staffing, and furnishings. It did not address the fundamentals and content knowledge of child development and the way it is applied to early childhood programs and practices. At this point I realized that a full understanding of development as it relates to early childhood education could not be accomplished solely through the distribution of flyers and pamphlets.

I wanted to raise the community's awareness of the need for high quality, developmentally appropriate, early childhood programs. Also, I felt that organizations and individuals should be surveyed to determine the level of interest and support within the community. Therefore, I developed a short interest survey (Figure 37–1) which could be used to survey those persons or organizations interested in educating the community by becoming volunteers, providing financial support, or participating on a planning committee. I surveyed a community cross-section including representatives from organizations such as the YWCA, the Junior League, a hospital, the local public school system, local private schools, a local industry, a pediatrician, media personnel, university professors, and parents of young children. Each person was contacted first by phone and an appointment was made to discuss the survey and answer any questions.

Every person contacted, with one exception, was very interested. However, each had a specific focal point. For example, the industry wanted to educate its employees, the YWCA had specific groups such as teen parents that it wanted to target, and a church-affiliated preschool wanted to inform other church preschools and network among them.

With such a positive response and the support of my classmates I decided to move ahead. I foresaw a long-term project with the initial step being the formation of an Executive Committee to develop a Mission Statement (Figure 37–2) form a Planning Committee, create by-laws, obtain non-profit status, and establish goals and objectives. Realistically, I knew it would take at least two years to become operational.

Looking back, what have we accomplished? We have become a viable, active, and recognized group in the community. Probably our most difficult task was obtaining non-profit status. This required the services of an accountant and a lawyer and took two years to accomplish. Fortunately, the lawyer volunteered his services and the accountant kindly agree to work for a small portion of her normal fee. With the aid of many volunteers, a Membership Action Grant from the National Association for the Education of Young Children, and support services for design, typesetting, and printing from a local hospital's publication department, we developed an initial one-page flyer (Figure 37–3). Later we created a professional quality brochure defining developmentally appropriate practices for children, infancy through age eight. We also developed a checklist for selecting an early childhood program and a one-page flyer warning parents about the dangers of inappropriate assessment practices. We disseminated these city-wide. QEEC members gave

presentations on developmentally appropriate practice to many groups of parents and professionals, worked with individual schools to make changes, instituted a fall all workshop for teachers and a spring information session for parents looking for criteria for kindergarten selection, answered a multitude of requests for information, participated in community activities for children (Figure 37–4) and collaborated with other organizations in child advocacy activities. Our long-term goal is to serve as a model that other communities can use in developing advocacy and public information campaigns.

PUBLIC POLICY

In 1979 Kenneth Keniston, commenting on the conclusions from a study of public policy by the Carnegie Council on Children, stated that public policy was letting the family down. He believed that we were not very protective of children and their families. He stated that we needed to use more preventive policies rather than the usual after-the-fact policies. According to Keniston family policy must put "greater" emphasis on changing the social and economic factors that contribute so massively to family problems...": The council recommended that parents be stronger advocates for children and more powerful in making child-rearing choices. The Council recommended that seven changes be made in national family policy

1. Parents need jobs. Something needs to be done to ensure that all parents have work.

2. The benefits of working should be distributed fairly by doing away with discrimination recruiting and unfair job qualifications.

3. Parents need assurance of a minimally decent income from their jobs.

4. Parents need jobs to be more flexible with more flexible work schedules and maternity and paternity leave.

5. Parents need access to and some control over decent medical, dental, social, and psychological services.

6. The health care system needs to be altered to stress preventative measures.

INTEREST SURVEY

Volunteer Organization: _____

Contact person and phone number: _____

Address: _____

Interest level: interested _____   moderately interested _____   need more information _____

Present Involvement in Education issues:

_____

_____

_____

_____

As an interested organization the possible allocation of our resources are:

    1. manpower, volunteers _____

    2. financial support _____

    3. participation in planning committee _____

Comments:

FACTS.....

- Nearly 80 percent of the mothers with preschool age children will be in the workforce by 1990.
- A typical American family will pay 3,000 to 5,000 dollars per child for Daycare a year.
- Presently in Baton Rouge the average consumer has very little information on how to determine **quality** in Early Childhood Programs.

What should the consumer look for in order to determine **quality** in an Early Childhood Program?

The **National Association for the Education of Young Children** (NAEYC) believes that a high quality Early Childhood Program provides a safe and nurturing environment that promotes the physical, social, emotional and cognitive development of young children while responding to the needs of families. A major determinant of program quality is the extent to which knowledge of child development is applied in program practices — the degree to which the program is **developmentally appropriate**. NAEYC believes that high quality, **developmentally appropriate programs** should be available to all children and their families.

The purpose of the attached interest survey is to determine the interest level of community organizations or persons, interested in educating the Baton Rouge community on the current knowledge of child development and how it relates to quality Early Childhood Programs.

Figure 37–1 **This interest survey, with accompanying fact sheet, served as a vehicle for encouraging dialog with potential advocates. (Used with permission of the Quality Early Education Coalition, 910 Marquette, Baton Rouge, LA 70806)**

MISSION STATEMENT
of
THE QUALITY EARLY EDUCATION COALITION

The Quality Early Education Coalition is a non-profit organization composed of citizens concerned with:

1. creating an awareness within the Baton Rouge community about high quality, developmentally appropriate, early childhood programs;

2. initiating and supporting change within the existing structure of early childhood education;

3. developing a model for community action.

The Coalition was formed in response to the recent prevalence of inappropriate academic instruction for children birth to age 8 in the Baton Rouge community. We believe this trend has developed as a result of a lack of information regarding appropriate practice. Thus, the Coalition seeks to inform the community as to the nature and importance of developmentally appropriate practice (DAP).

The Quality Early Education Coalition is committed to the expansion of developmentally appropriate practice and program quality in the Baton Rouge community according to the definitions that follow. The National Association for the Education of Young Children (NAEYC) has defined "developmentally appropriate practice" as a safe and nurturing environment that promotes the physical, social, emotional and cognitive development of children birth to 8 while responding to the needs of families.

The chart below contrasts appropriate practice with inappropriate practice.

Appropriate Practice	Inappropriate Practice
Infants are held and carried frequently. The adults talk to the infant before, during and after moving the infant around.	Infants are wordlessly moved about at the adult's convenience. Nothing is explained to the infant.
Diapering, sleeping, feeding and play areas are separate to ensure sanitation and provide quiet, restful areas.	Areas are combined and are noisy and distracting.
Children are expected to be physically and mentally active. They choose from among activities the teacher has set up or the children spontaneously initiate.	Children are expected to sit down, watch, be quiet, and listen, or do paper-and-pencil tasks for long periods of time. A major portion of time is spent passively sitting, listening, and waiting.
Objects children can manipulate and experiment with such as blocks, cards, games, woodworking tools, arts and crafts materials, including paint and clay are readily accessible. Tables are used for children to work alone or in small groups. A variety of work places and spaces is provided and flexibly used.	Available materials are limited primarily to books, workbooks, and pencils. Children are assigned permanent desks and desks are rarely moved. Children work in a large group most of the time and no one can participate in a playful activity until all work is finished.

Program quality is the extent to which knowledge of child development is applied in program practices — the degree to which the program is developmentally appropriate.

Once awareness throughout the Baton Rouge community has been established, the Coalition will seek to initiate and support change in early education through organizing volunteers, soliciting financial support, and providing consultation.

Through our efforts, The Quality Early Education Coalition will develop a model for community action which will be disseminated to other interested communities not only in our state, but also nationwide.

The goal of The Quality Early Education Coalition is to develop and implement a plan of action to accomplish the above mission.

Figure 37–2 Quality Early Education Coalition Mission Statement (Used with permission of the Quality Early Education Coalition, 910 Marquette, Baton Rouge, LA 70806)

THE QUALITY EARLY EDUCATION COALITION

PURPOSE

The Quality Early Education Coalition is a non-profit organization composed of citizens concerned about high quality, developmentally appropriate, early childhood programs. Our work initiates and supports change within the existing structure of early childhood education.

DEVELOPMENTALLY APPROPRIATE PRACTICE

The National Association for the Education of Young Children (NAEYC) has defined "developmentally appropriate practice" as a safe and nurturing environment that promotes the physical, social, emotional and cognitive development of children birth to eight while responding to the needs of families. Appropriate environments provide children challenges, support and success based on individual needs, interests and learning abilities.

HOW CHILDREN LEARN

Children learn through activities that:

- Are interesting
- Yield success and satisfaction
- Encourage independence
- Require hearing, seeing, tasting, smelling and feeling things
- Are child-initiated
- Foster creativity
- Are supported by adults
- Require active exploration of real things

CHILDREN LEARN BY DOING

- Dancing, singing, playing music
- Painting, cutting, pasting, squeezing and pounding clay
- Scribbling, drawing, writing
- Counting objects, sorting and classifying
- Exploring sand and water, planting seeds, caring for pets
- Talking, listening, role playing
- Hearing stories and looking at books
- Puzzles, stringing beads, building with blocks
- Pretending to be adults, fantasy persons or animals

WHAT PARENTS CAN DO

- Provide appropriate activities for learning
- Provide opportunities for children to learn by doing
- Look for and support developmentally appropriate practices in schools

CHILDREN AT THEIR BEST

Adults who understand normal child development can provide personal and academic support through developmentally appropriate practices. The result is children who are happy, confident and successful.

FOR INFORMATION: Write, QEEC, 910 Marquette Ave., B.R., LA 70806

Production of this flyer funded by a Membership Action Grant from the National Association for the Education of Young Children and by Woman's Hospital.

The contents and views presented reflect the work of this Membership Action Group and do not necessarily represent the position of the National Association for the Education of Young Children or Woman's Hospital.

Figure 37–3   **This brief handout provides basic information about QEEC and child development. (Used with permission of the Quality Early Education Coalition, 910 Marquette, Baton Rouge, LA 70806)**

Figure 37–4 QEEC collaborates with the district LACUS (Louisiana Association on Children Under Six) affiliate as co-sponsors of a developmentally appropriate children's activity center during a community event.

7. Parents and children need changes in the laws and legal practices that affect families. More effort needs to be put into noninstitutional placement of children and support for keeping families together.

Keniston suggests that government maintain a more protective role and enlarge people's freedom of choice. Parents, he believes, should be given more resources so they can do a better job. Looking at the statistics accumulated during the next decade it is apparent that our country has continued with the same policies that Keniston and the Carnegie Council saw as outdated in the 1970s. Families are in more danger than ever as we proceed through the last decade of the twentieth century.

In 1994 (15 years later), a report was released from another Carnegie-funded group: the task force on Meeting the Needs of Young Children (Starting points, 1994). The task force focused particularly on the needs of our youngest children, three-years-old and under, and their families. The task force identified four key areas that need to be addressed immediately as a step toward improving life for young children and their families: promote responsible parenthood, guarantee quality childcare choices, ensure good health and protection, and mobilize communities to support young children and their families. They called on all

segments of the nation and its communities to take action to achieve the identified goals.

As already mentioned, minority families, and particularly African-American families are at-risk at the highest degree. Valora Washington (1985; 1988; 1989) has written extensively on our public policy for children, and African-American children in particular. Overall, she supports Keniston's view that while we have talked a lot about valuing children and families our policies do not reflect such values. Politically we have tended to take a noninterventionist position based on a belief that parental rights take precedence over children's needs. On the other hand, Washington (1985) points out that in emergencies, such as the 1930s depression when federally supported day-care centers were opened, we have intervened. There have also been a number of programs provided for poor children and their families in the areas of income support, health care, protection from abuse, nutritional assistance, and child care. Historically most of these programs have only served a small fraction of those needing their services. Some programs such as free and partial school lunch subsidies and Chapter 1 educational benefits are available on a fairly broad basis. By the mid-1980s the enthusiasm of the war-on-poverty years of the 1970s died out, and with harder times, politicians became less supportive of governmental assistance to children and families. Washington (1985) suggests that our best strategy, because we have a basic belief of noninterference in the family, is to help parents to do more for their children rather than offering only direct services to children.

When considering support for minority families, the problems presented by race and racism must also be recognized (Washington, 1988, 1989). Prejudiced points of view and lack of attention to ethnic differences in family life styles affect policy decisions. For example, African-Americans more than European-Americans are more likely to be looked upon as the undeserving poor who are poor through their own fault and thus not deserving of assistance. In setting up assistance guidelines the fact that African-Americans are more likely than European-Americans to live in an extended family group is not considered. Washington (1988) concludes that with the projected increases in our populations' African-Americans and other minority ethnic groups, these groups will be more essential resources in our economy and our political arena. More opportunities must be made available for these children so they can grow up to be productive citizens.

Of course, children not only need to be fed, clothed, and kept safe and healthy, but they also need to be provided with educational opportunities (Washington, 1989). African-American parents in general have high educational aspirations for their children but their children are at great risk for educational failure. Washington believes that studies of African-American children can shed light on the link between education and public policy. For example, so-called compensatory education programs have not considered the African-American child's family configuration or learning style. The color-blind approach to policy development assumes that problems of African-American learners can be solved in the same way as problems of white learners. "This approach has led to educational policy solutions indifferent to the fact that both poverty and educational failure among blacks often result from political, instructional, and economic systems that condone and foster institutional racism" (Washington, 1989, p. 287). Washington points out equal educational opportunity programs have "focused on changing individual children who were expected to accommodate to the schools, rather than adapting to the needs of the children and their communities" (p. 289). As described earlier in the text, each cultural group has a distinct learning style which needs to be considered in planning educational programs.

Washington (1989) believes that the risk to African-American learners can be reduced by linking research, policy, and practice. That is, policy and practice should be based on what has been found from studies of African-American child development. The deficit view of African-American (as well as other minority group) students must be dropped and a view that emphasizes instruction based on cultural and learning style and family involvement must replace it. Washington (1989) recommends the need for policy to be based on a multicultural perspective.

As we move toward the twenty-first century, it is apparent that public policy has not been created with consideration of the development of children in the context of their families, their cultures, and their true educational needs. The next part of the unit will provide an overview of recent and future policy issues.

Issues

A patchwork of public policy issues in many areas has appeared in this and other units. As already mentioned, it has been a recent phenomena for those who work with young children to become actively engaged in public policy activities. A massive, well-organized grass-roots effort finally achieved success in 1990 (Mann, 1991). The payoff for all this time and effort came through with the One hundred and first Congress in 1990 (Willer, 1991). In the January 1991 Public Policy Report in *Young Children* Barbara Willer reported on "The Children's Congress" that enacted historic legislation in child care, Head Start, and children's television. In 1971, former President Nixon vetoed the first effort at comprehensive Child Care legislation. Twenty years later a freestanding federal child care program finally was at last a reality. Head Start was reauthorized with a larger budget and provision for full funding to serve all eligible three- through five-year-olds by 1994. The Earned Income Tax Credit was increased providing income support to low-income working families with children. Two additional new tax credits were enacted. One provides credit for children's health insurance expenses and the other for families with children under one year of age.

Issues frequently resurface as authorizations are for a limited time period. When reauthorization becomes due (such as for Head Start and for federally supported childcare programs), advocates have to be ready to deal with the issues again. Other issues involve lengthy battles, discussion, and debate with little or no benefit to children and families resulting. The following are brief descriptions of some issues of the 1990s.

Goals 2000: Educate America Act (Goals, 1994). The first goal of this act, the "readiness" goal, was described in Unit 32. This bill was passed in 1993. A major issue relative to this legislation is whether we have enough kindergartens, staffed with qualified early childhood teachers to provide a developmentally appropriate environment in which children can learn (Robinson and Lyon, 1944).

Violence is a major issue of concern as a public health issue for children (Elders, 1994). Prevention is the focus of the legislative effort with a focus on family violence, youth violence, sexual assault, media violence, and firearms.

Infant mortality continues to be a major policy issue (*State of America's children*, 1994; Wilson & Neidich, 1991). Prenatal care could alleviate much of the problem.

Federal child care programs, such as the Child Care Development Block Grant, At-risk, and AFDC-related childcare, are proposing regulations changes (Public Policy Alert!, May 1994). Proposed rule changes could provide greater coordination and consistency across these federal childcare programs and give states greater flexibility in the promotion of quality services.

In a 1991 talk, Joan Lombardi warned us that all the success we have had in promoting advances in early education and care do not mean we can become complacent. For example, we know what developmentally appropriate practice is, but now we need policies that support it. Lombardi recommended a number of actions that child advocates need to take:

Federal

- Be sure that Congress authorizes full funding for Child Care and Head Start.
- Be sure that training monies are readily available.
- Work for parental maternity/paternity leave legislation such as that available in other countries.
- Be sure Congress authorizes full funding for WIC and for maternal and child health services.
- Invite your legislators to visit quality programs.

State

- Develop coalitions of groups and organizations (for example in one state fourteen organizations have organized the Coalition for Families and Children with the mission to ensure practical and creative use of that state's share of the Child Care Block Grant)
- Speak at hearings on child and family issues.

- Reach out to the business community as partners.
- Have press conferences to address issues.
- Keep in touch with other states.

Community

- College and university personnel should document the plight of our children.
- Speak up and have the courage of your convictions.
- Within organizations provide training for new leaders.
- Teach teachers how to speak with parents and empower them to stand up for their convictions.
- Reach out to doctors. They are our natural allies but they are not well informed.
- Get more involved politically. Run for local office.
- Gain influence with parents by showing them that you care.
- Be model professionals, support each other, work together, show that we love and respect children (Figure 37–5).

Now we know that organization and hard work can affect the content of social policy legislation. In the final section of the unit some of the "hows" of advocacy are presented.

CHILD ADVOCACY

With advocacy an accepted activity for those who work with young children, there are a wealth of advocacy materials available. All the major early childhood education organizations publish policy reports that keep members up-to-date on policy issues and developments. They publish inexpensive informational pamphlets that can be used to support advocacy activities. They also have developed materials that provide step-by-step procedures for advocacy.

In the eighties, organizations concerned with the development and education of young children were forced to become deeply and actively involved in the politics of child advocacy. For example, journals such as *Young Children* (the National Association for the Education of Young Children) and *Dimensions* (the Southern Early Childhood Association) have

Figure 37–5   Professionals work together to plan activities for young children and their families.

regular public policy reports. They also send out special policy alerts to members, alerting them to contact their legislators regarding laws that may be pending. Organizations such as the Children's Defense Fund and the National Black Child Development Institute monitor events in Washington, DC and elsewhere and publish informational material. The Society for Research in Child Development is now publishing *Washington Report*, which relates research in child development to policy issues pending in Congress.

Joan Lombardi and Stacie Goffin (1986) suggest a number of strategies for child advocacy at the state level. They list five steps to success:

1. Get acquainted with state decision makers.
2. Know your facts.
3. Share your expertise by writing letters, visiting policy makers, testifying and suggesting legislation.

4. Maintain contact.
5. Join with others.

Lombardi and Goffin state the importance of being proactive rather than reactive. That is, be on the offensive rather than the defensive. Do not wait until a problem, such as potential budget cuts that may result in program cuts, is at hand but study the issues and begin working for improvements. Ask groups of legislators to sponsor legislation dealing with early childhood issues such as funding more programs, providing health care for needy children, or launching a parent awareness campaign on choosing quality child care.

Goffin and Lombardi (1988) have written a handbook for NAEYC that offers detailed suggestions for early childhood advocacy and other helpful information such as an outline of the structure of the Congress, a list of advocacy resources and a list of national organizations. Black and Puckett (1987) outline ways to tell parents, administrators, and other teachers about developmentally appropriate practice.

Lizabeth Schorr (1989) has organized and analyzed the results of research that documents the successful outcomes of a number of intervention programs for young children and their families. Schorr has identified several factors that are common to successful programs:

- They are comprehensive and intensive.
- Staff have the time, training, and skills necessary to build relationships of trust and respect with children and families.
- Children are dealt with as part of a family, and the family as part of a neighborhood and community.
- Programs cross long-standing professional and bureaucratic boundaries by providing services in non-traditional settings and without a lot of time-consuming screening within the high-risk population.

In addition, Schorr suggests that current policies which tend to fragment services be revised and streamlined for better coordination. The challenge now is to be sure legislators have this information and use it as the basis for designing legislation.

SUMMARY

Advocacy for children and families has become a normal part of the activities of adults who work with young children. During the 1980s we realized that we could not just sit back and wait for the government to develop family-centered/child-centered policies. Public policy changes through legislation do not just happen. Many hours of organized volunteer work is needed to get things done. Advocacy begins at the grass-roots level with community groups and coalitions, builds at the state level, and becomes a force to be reckoned with at the national level. All the major early childhood development and education organizations can provide assistance for helping advocates plan action for children and families.

FOR FURTHER READING

Burchby, M.M. (1992). A kindergarten teacher speaks to the governors—A story of effective advocacy. *Young Children, 47*(6), 40–43.

CDF Reports. Newsletter of the Children's Defense Fund, CDF, P.O. Box 7584, Washington, DC 20077-1245.

Children's Defense Fund. (1990). *An advocates guide to the media.* Washington, DC: Author.

Children's Defense Fund. (1986). *Mounting a prenatal campaign in your community.* Washington, DC: Author.

Cochran, D. C. (1993). Public policies as they affect programs for young children. In J. L. Roopnarine & J. E. Johnson, Eds., *Approaches to early childhood education* (2nd ed.) (pp. 337–354). New York: Merrill/Macmillan.

Dimidjian, V. J. (1992). *Early childhood at risk: Actions and advocacy for young children.* Westhaven, CT: National Education Association.

Fennimore, B. S. (1989). *Child advocacy for early childhood educators.* New York: Teachers College Press.

Ferber, M. A., & O'Farrell, M. B. (Eds.). (1991). *Work and family: Policies for a changing workforce.* Washington, DC: National Academy Press.

Goffin, S. G., & Stegelin, D. A. (Eds.). (1992). *Changing kindergartens.* Washington, DC: National Association for the Education of Young Children.

McCartney, K., & Phillips, D. (Eds.). (1993). *An insiders' guide to providing expert testimony before Congress.* Chicago, IL: Society for Research in Child Development.

National Black Child Development Institute. (1990). *African-American family reading list.* Washington, DC: Author.

National Black Child Development Institute. (1990). *The status of African-American children: Twentieth anniversary report, 1970–1990.* Washington, DC: Author.

Patton, C. (1993). Food for thought. What can we do to increase public knowledge about child development and quality child care? *Young Children, 49*(1), 30–31.

Peck, J. T., McCaig, G., & Sapp, M. L. (1988). *Kindergarten policies: What is best for children?* Washington, DC: National Association for the Education of Young Children.

Pizzo, P. (1993). Empowering parents with child care regulation. *Young Children, 48*(6), 13–15.

Public policy report. A primer on welfare reform, young children, and early childhood services. (1994). *Young Children, 49* (4), 67–68.

Sugarman, J. M. (1991). *Building early childhood systems: A resource handbook.* Edison, NJ: Child Welfare League of America.

Washington, V., & LaPoint, V. (1989). *Black children and American institutions: An ecological review and re-source guide.* New York: Garland.

Willer, B. (1989). *A comparison of early childhood/child care bills introduced in the 101st. Congress.* Washington, DC: National Association for the Education of Young Children.

SUGGESTED ACTIVITIES

1. Read some recent policy reports such as the Public Policy Report in *Young Children*, *The Black Child Advocate* (National Black Child Development Institute), or *Social Policy Report* (Society for Research in Child Development). Report to the class on what you find are the important current issues in public policy for young children and their families.

2. Using guidelines from materials referred to in the unit, plan an advocacy action activity designed to change a policy or to inform the public. (See Jensen & Chevalier, 1990; Goffin & Lombardi, 1988; or Lombardi & Goffin, 1986.) Discuss the proposed activity with a group of students in class. Obtain their opinions and suggestions. Consider actually following through on your plan. Possibly some of the other students will join you.

3. Obtain an appointment with one of your local policy makers such as a school board member, a city council member, the mayor, a state legislator, or a U.S. Congressperson. Interview him or her regarding opinions on child and family issues you have read about in this book or elsewhere, that you believe are relevant to your city, state, and the nation.

4. Find out which groups in your community are active child advocates. Check with the local affiliates of the following: NAEYC, SECA (if you are in the South), Council for Exceptional Children, League of Women Voters, Junior League, Kiwanis International, Head Start Association, Parent and Teachers Association, YMCA and the YWCA. Make appointments to interview the presidents/directors of at least three of these groups. Find out what kinds of policy issues they are working on. Report back to class on the results.

5. Look back through your journal. Note any comments you made that may provide a lead to some policy issue(s) that should be acted upon in your community, state, and/or in the nation. Research the issue so you are thoroughly familiar with the pros and cons of the problem. Consider joining or building a coalition to work on the issue.

REVIEW

A. Explain the role of the child advocate. Why is it necessary for children to have advocates?

B. How would you feel about starting a local grass-roots organization like QEEC in your community? Why do you feel it might or might not work? Explain how you might apply some of Laura's ideas.

C. Select the statements that describe the conditions of public policy for children and families:
   1. Historically public policy in the United States has supported the child and the family.
   2. Our policies are usually developed after-the-fact rather than as a preventive measure.
   3. Family policy should help parents to provide a better life for their children and help them feel more empowered.
   4. During the 1980s, policy-makers tried diligently to overcome the faults described by the Carnegie report.
   5. African-American and other minority children and their families have been the victims of public policy guided by race and racism.

6. So-called compensatory education programs have not considered the racial and cultural factors in the lives of children and families.

7. There has been a national effort to reduce institutional racism as it influences policy for children and families.

8. Child development research probably will not offer much help in the development of educational policies for African-American children.

D. Explain why the one hundred and first Congress is referred to as "The Children's Congress." What did they accomplish for young children and their families?

E. Describe some of the actions that adults who work with young children can take to advocate for young children.

Glossary

abortion—the termination of the life of an unborn child.

abuse and neglect—children with identifiable poor physical care, battering, sexual, and/or emotional abuse signs.

accommodation—the means for changing the old concepts to fit a new piece of learning.

acquired immune deficiency syndrome (AIDS)—a communicable disease caused by a virus that attacks the immune system.

Action for Children's Television (ACT)—a group of parents, teachers, and television professionals that informs the public about television, pressures the networks to upgrade show quality, and encourages stricter regulations of program and commercial content.

adult-to-child language (ACL)—a special form of speech that adults use when speaking with children that tends to be slower and more deliberate and contain shorter sentences than adult-to-adult language.

affective growth—centers on the self-concept and the development of social, emotional, and personality characteristics.

affective development—the area of development that includes emotions, personality, and social behaviors.

affective—the area that centers on the development of social, emotional, and personality characteristics and the self-concept.

aggressive—opposite of prosocial behavior; "has the capacity to hurt or injure or damage, regardless of intent" (Caldwell, 1977, p. 6).

Americans with Disabilities Act (ADA)—"states that people with disabilities are entitled to equal rights in employment, state and local public services, and public accommodations such as child care and early childhood education programs" (Chandler, 1994).

amniocentesis—a method of providing prenatal information by sampling the amniotic fluid.

amnion—a sac lining the uterus.

amniotic fluid—the liquid that fills the amnion.

anal stage—Freud's second stage (congruent with the toddler period) when independent toileting is a major concern and goal.

animism—giving human characteristics to nonhuman things such as cars, trees, wind, or the sun.

anoxia—the state in which the oxygen supply in the blood dips below the safe level.

anti-bias approach—celebrating diversity making it part of the total curriculum.

Apgar Scale—the usual means for monitoring the vital signs of a newborn.

appropriate assessment procedures—authentic evaluation of educational achievement that directly measures actual performance in the subject area.

artificialism—the young child's feeling that everything in the world is made for people.

assertiveness—to attain one's goals with perseverance but not aggression.

assimilation—an incorporation process when new ideas and concepts are fit into old ideas or concepts.

at-risk—special needs children.

attachment—the relationship of belonging between infant and caregiver.

attention deficit disorder (ADD)—a condition in which most of the hyperactivity symptoms are present with or without hyperactivity.

attention—a critical aspect of perception involving ignoring irrelevant information and finding relevant information.

atypical—children that need special help because of conditions that make their developmental patterns different from those of most other children.

autonomy versus shame and doubt—Erikson's second stage in which the toddler must deal with crisis.

autonomy—children will be able to explore and think through problem solutions and construct knowledge independently through their own actions.

autonomy—growth toward independence.

baby biographies—diary records of interesting things a particular child does each day.

baby tender—Skinner's environment for optimal conditions for the child.

baby talk (BT)—a simplified form of speech with short, simple sentences and simple vocabulary that is within the child's realm of experience.

barriers—instructional strategies that are not consistent with the principles of child development; inappropriate placement procedures.

behavior modification—B. F. Skinner's theory of using a combination of verbal and nonverbal actions to help the toddler learn desired behavior and give up undesirable behaviors.

behavioral geneticist—one who is concerned with heredity and environment as a two-way interaction and influence.

behaviorist theories—ideas emphasizing change that originates in the environment through learning.

biculturalism—practicing the language and customs of two different social groups.

bidialectic—speaking two dialects.

bilingual—speaking two languages.

bonding—the process whereby parents and child determine they are special to each other.

brain lateralization—development of both left and right brain functions and the communication between the two.

causality—why things happen as they do in the world; "why" questions.

categorization—sorting and grouping items according to similar attributes.

CD ROM—compact disc software that contains great varieties of information and activities in an easy-to-store format.

centering—in cognitive functioning, Piaget refers to the process of being overwhelmed by one aspect.

cephalocaudal—growth from head to toe.

Cesarian section—removing the baby from the uterus using a surgical method.

child care—an arrangement in a home or center for caring for children while their adult family members are at work, school, etc.

child science—the child's gradual acquisition of the knowledge that some constants exist in the world and that there are reasons for these constants.

child advocates—adults who work to see that children's rights are protected.

child-initiated structure (CS)—in writing, children make their own decision about what to write.

children first—children with special needs and/or disabilities should be thought of primarily as children.

chorionic villus sampling (CVS)—a method of providing prenatal information by cutting cells from the chorionic villi.

chromosomes—the major units that control heredity.

classical conditioning—learning takes place through the association of a stimulus and a response.

classification—the ability to classify and categorize items in the environment.

cognitive growth—centers on the mind and how the mind works as the child grows and learns.

cognitive development—the acquisition of knowledge and the way the knowledge is used.

cognitive structure—includes all the parts of the cognitive system; the content of the child's mind and how it is organized.

cognitive functioning—describes how the cognitive system works.

cognitive development—changes in cognitive structure and functioning that may take place over time.

cognitive developmental approach—stresses stages in the development of logical thinking, reasoning, and problem solving as the indicators of the growth of intelligence.

cognitive—pertains to the mind and how it works.

commercial television—paid for by advertisers.

communicative phase—when children begin to name and label their drawings.

community in the classroom—a sense of group belongingness.

competent six-year-old—one who can manage well in the school situation both socially and cognitively.

compliance—immediate and appropriate response by the child to an adult's request (Honig, 1985a).

computer drill and practice—uses the computer to provide practice and reinforcement for concepts, such as shape, numeral, letter, and color recognition, after they have been introduced by the teacher.

conception—the moment when fertilization takes place.

concepts—"the cognitive categories that allow people to group together perceptually distinct information, events or items" (Wellman, 1982).

concrete operational period—when a child uses language to direct his own activities and the activities of others; the child is able to see another's point of view and consider it along with his own; the child is no longer as easily fooled by the way things look as he was before.

conscience—inner control; an emotional element that includes feelings of guilt and anxiety.

conservation—the ability to understand the transformation of materials without being fooled by appearances.

constructivism—a belief that learning takes place based on the process of stage change brought about as the child constructs knowledge.

constructivist—a believer in the idea that children construct their own knowledge through interaction with the environment.

context of play—interaction with peers that takes place within a play context.

continuity—development is a continuous process that needs to be recognized as programs are planned for children as they move from grade to grade.

control techniques—methods used by an adult to modify children's behavior and get them to comply.

cooperative learning—"the process whereby small, heterogeneous groups of students work together to achieve mutual learning goals" (Ajose & Joyner, 1990, p. 198).

coordinated play—play that involves both children doing something together.

creativity—an aspect of behavior that reflects originality, experimentation, imagination, and a spirit of exploration.

Crisis III: Initiative versus Guilt—a stage in Erikson's theory of development through which children pass between ages 3 and 6; children deal with the crisis that results from a desire to make their own choices but meet the demands of their developing consciences.

Crisis IV: Industry versus Inferiority—a stage in Erikson's theory of development through which children pass during middle childhood and cope with the need to be productive and successful and not be overwhelmed by failure and inferiority.

critical periods—the idea that growth in certain areas may be more important at particular times.

cultural diversity—refers to differences relevant to membership in a variety of culture groups.

cultural groups—that social community to which an individual belongs and whose customs the individual practices.

cultural style—the personality of a group.

D'Nealian alphabet—a slanted manuscript alphabet.

declaratives—meaningful verbalizations.

developmental theories—ideas that explain changes in the child due to interaction between growth and learning.

developmental biodynamics—research designed to consider in detail the processes that relate the sensory and motor development.

developmentally appropriate practices (DAPs)—instructional practices that are both age and individually appropriate as defined by NAEYC (Bredekamp, 1987).

dialect—a variation of the standard speech of a language.

differentiation—the process the child goes through as he gains control of specific parts of his body.

digestive fallacy—children believes a baby is swallowed, develops in the mother's stomach, and then is eliminated.

discipline—instruction that teaches the child internal control.

discipline—the original meaning is "to teach"; today, it means to teach techniques of socially appropriate behavior.

discrimination—perceiving differences.

dizygotic (DZ) siblings—twins that develop from separate eggs fertilized at the same time.

DNA—a complex molecule that contains genetic information.

dramatic play—play that centers on the social world and includes characters, dramatic themes, and story line.

ecological research model—viewing children in all their roles in all the areas of their environment.

ego—to Freud, this is characterized by reason and common sense and operates on the reality principle.

egocentric—centers perception on the most obvious and is bound by what is seen.

embryo—the second stage of the gestation period; usually lasts from about 3 to 8 weeks.

emergence of autonomy—infants begin to take the lead in the interactions with adults.

emerging competencies—newly developing skills or abilities.

emotional dependency—the need for affiliation with others that develops from early bonding and attachment.

encouragement—the types of social rewards that are motivating and promote autonomy by making specific statements.

environmental—factors that begin to play a role as soon as conception occurs.

equilibration—brought about through the balance between assimilation and accommodation.

ESL—English as a Second Language.

ethnic socialization—the developmental processes by which children acquire the behaviors, perceptions, values, and attitudes of an ethnic group, and come to see themselves and others as members of such groups (Rotheram & Phinney, 1986).

ethological approach—an observer evaluates the child in her natural environment and stays in the background taking notes of the child's behavior.

examining—when the child fingers and turns an object while looking at it with an intent expression.

Exosurf®—a drug that helps babies form surfactant to coat the inner lining of the lungs and keep the airspaces from collapsing.

exosystem—a child's interactions and relationships with local government, parents' work place, mass media, and local industry.

expressive language delay (ELD)—when a child by age four exhibits delay in language development and is still speaking in one-word phrases with very limited vocabularies.

expressive speakers—use a diverse speech that includes a large number of combinations such as "stop it" and "I want it."

extinction—unlearning; if a behavior is not rewarded, it gradually is no longer used.

extrinsic rewards—concrete and social rewards.

family ecology—"important family functionings that are a reflection of the interactions between the family as a social system and other societal institutions and systems" (Harrison et al., 1990, p. 348).

family—those persons who inhabit the same living area.

family-centered practice—educational plans and practices developed from the family's point of view (versus the professionals').

fantasy—"a particularly vivid use of the imagination to create mental images or concepts that have little similarity to the real world" (Isenberg and Jalongo, 1993, p. 7).

fear—develops most likely through a combination of genetic and learned factors and are acquired through conditioning and observational learning.

fertilization—the joining of sperm and egg.

fetal alcohol syndrome (FAS)—a group of child behaviors associated with maternal alcohol intake during the fetal period.

fetus—the third stage of the gestation period; usually lasts from 9 weeks until birth.

five *P's*—factors common to the roles of parent and teacher as reflected in our knowledge of child development: 1. provides the learning environment, 2. predictability, 3. ping-pong, 4. persistence, and 5. professor.

follicle—fluid-filled sac that houses the ovum.

formal operations period—Piaget's fourth period; appears in early adolescence, around 11 or 12 years of age.

four *R's*—factors common to the roles of parent and teacher as reflected in our knowledge of child development: 1. responsiveness, 2. reasoning, 3. rationality, and 4. reading.

friendship—special relationships that develop with other people.

full inclusion—all the services and support needed by the children are present and available in the schools the children would normally attend.

function—a means by which a child achieves some purpose through the use of language.

fundamental motor skills—the foundation for more specialized motor skills that will be learned when the child is older.

fussing—female interchanges.

gene—the biological unit of heredity.

generalization—the process of finding similarities among things.

genetic counseling—assessment of maternal and paternal genetic makeup and its possible effects on off-spring.

genetics—the study of the factors involved in the transmission of hereditary characteristics in living organisms.

genotype—the set of genes an individual receives at conception that makes him unique.

gestational period—the period of pregnancy; usually lasts about 9 1/2 calendar months.

giftedness—"children who show evidence of advanced skill attainment relative to their peers" (Karnes and Schwedel, 1983, p. 475).

growth—a series of steps or stages the child goes through on the way to becoming an adult.

guidance—techniques used by adults to teach children socially appropriate behavior.

guided participation—a vehicle through which the child learns what needs to be learned to function in a particular culture.

habituation—a feature of getting used to something.

handedness—determining right-hand dominance, left-hand dominance, or no preference.

happiness—the expression of positive emotions such as pleasure, joy, and delight.

hereditary—factors determined at conception.

hierarchy of needs—to Maslow, a series of levels a person must fulfill to achieve self-actualization.

high-risk—children who are at risk for school failure and possibly even for survival due to various environmental, mental, physical, and/or emotional problems.

holophrases—one-word sentences.

holophrastic stage—a stage in language development when the child speaks one-word sentences.

Home Observation for Measurement of the Environment (HOME)—a scale used to rate a home environment.

homelessness—having no stable place to call home.

hostility and anger—the emotions that underlie aggressive behavior.

humor—understanding (jokes, riddles, etc.) that requires a higher level of cognitive development than that required as a response to tickling and peek-a-boo games that provoke laughter in infants.

hyperactivity—symptoms to include impulsive children who may speak out of turn, generally talk excessively, have difficulty establishing relationship with others, and are often viewed as behavior problems.

id—to Freud, this is present at birth and contains the person's unconscious motives and desires and operates on the pleasure principle.

identify—a girl sees herself as being like her mother and the boy sees himself as being like his father.

imagination—"the ability to form rich and varied mental images or concepts of people, places, things and situations not present. . ." (Isenberg and Jalongo, 1993, p. 7).

imitation—doing actions one has observed another doing.

inappropriate assessment procedures—addresses misuse of readiness test results and the elimination of paper-and-pencil, whole-group achievement testing through third grade.

inclusion—the commitment to educate each child, to the maximum extent appropriate, in the school and classroom he or she would otherwise attend; involves bringing the support services to the child and requires only that the child will benefit from being in the class.

Individualized Education Program (IEP)—a set of objectives that must be written for every special education student.

Individualized Family Service Plan (IFSP)—a plan with specific objectives that must be developed for all families enrolled in birth to three-year-old special education programs.

information-processing approach—emphasizes the process the individual uses to try to solve problems.

input—in cognitive functioning, this is the stimulus.

inside intervention—sociodramatic play in which the adult is involved in the play activity.

integrated movements—combining specific movements in order to perform more complex activities such as walking, climbing, building a block tower, or drawing a picture.

integration—allowing the special needs child to socialize with the typical students.

intelligence quotient (IQ)—a score assigned to a person's responses on an intelligence test.

intelligence—the ability to benefit from experience, that is, the extent to which a person is able to make use of his or her capacities and opportunities for advancement in life.

interactionist theory of language development—states that the sequence and timing of speech development is biologically determined, while the specific language the child learns is determined by the environment in which he lives.

interactionist—one who views the child as entering the environment with a variety of potential behaviors that may or may not develop depending on the process of development and the opportunities presented in the environment.

intrinsic rewards—used in the development of a desire within the child to learn through internal motivation.

kindergartners—children enrolled in kindergarten classrooms; usually between the ages of $4^1/_2$ and 6 years old.

language—a well-ordered system of rules that each adult member of the language community tacitly comprehends in speaking, listening, and writing.

learned helplessness—when failure is attributed to external factors rather than lack of effort.

learning styles—the method in which a child acquires knowledge.

learning theory—view of language acquisition; explains language acquisition through the mechanisms of classical conditioning, operant conditioning, and imitation.

learning—behavior change that results from experience.

learning—behavioral changes that come about due to influences from the environment.

least restrictive enviroment—one in which the child can make the most of his or her potential for learning.

limit testing—infant and adult test their abilities to communicate and affect the other's behavior.

love and affection—fondness or caring for another.

macrosystem—a child's interactions and relationships with the dominant beliefs and ideologies of the culture.

mainstreaming—placing the child with special needs in regular classrooms, which would allow the opportunity to participate in the same kinds of programs and activities as every other young child.

malnutrition—a state of being underfed.

maturationist—one who feels growth patterns are fixed.

memory—the retention of what is learned over a period of time.

mesosystem—the interactions and relationships between and among the child's home, school, church, peer group, and neighborhood.

metacognition—refers to knowledge and thinking about cognition.

microsystem—a child's relationship to home, school, neighborhood, peer group, and church.

monozygotic (MZ) siblings—twins that develop from one egg that has divided into two or more parts after fertilization so the same hereditary characteristics are present in each.

moral classrooms—"classrooms in which the sociomoral atmosphere supports and promotes children's development" (DeVries & Zan, 1994).

moral reasoning—standards; to generalize and internalize sanctions so a person acts morally not just to avoid punishment but because he should act that way.

moral judgments—decisions made regarding solutions to moral dilemmas.

morality—ethical behavior; the development of an understanding of right and wrong.

moral reasoning—when a person considers his values relative to a problem situation and then judges what should be done in that situation.

morphemes—the smallest meaningful units in a language and strings of sounds that have meaning.

motor development—the development of skill in the use of the body and its parts.

multicultural education—teaching with respect to the diversity within our culture.

NAEYC—National Association for the Education of Young Children.

natural childbirth—birth without the aid of drugs for pain reduction.

nature versus nurture—the relative influence of heredity and environment in a child's development.

neonatal period—the first 2 weeks of newborn life.

Neonatal Behavior Assessment Scale (NBAS)—a dynamic assessment of interactive behavior used to indicate the degree of control the newborn has over his sensory capacities.

neonate—a child from birth to 2 weeks of age.

newborn—a child who has just been born.

nonthematic—the use of open-ended materials and various types of realistic props.

normal—typical.

normative/maturational view—a way of looking at development that stresses certain norms.

norms—what most children do at a certain age.

nutrition—"the science of food and how it is used by the body" (Endres and Rockwell, 1994, p. 1).

object permanence—the knowledge that objects continue to exist even when one is not perceiving them (Ault, 1983).

object recognition—the features the infant uses to identify objects.

object manipulation—fingering the surface of, looking at, and transferring the object from hand to hand to explore it.

one-to-one correspondence—the basis of understanding equality.

operant conditioning—behavior is shaped by careful use of reinforcements (rewards) for appropriate behavior and at the same time, inappropriate behavior is ignored so it is not rewarded with attention.

operations—actions that take place internally as part of the organized cognitive structure.

output—in cognitive functioning, this is the response.

outside intervention—sociodramatic play in which the adult stays outside of the play but offers questions, suggestions, directions, and clarifications that will help the children enhance their dramatic play roles.

overdiscriminations—when a child cannot seem to find a place for certain things that do not look the way they are expected to.

overgeneralizations—when a child encounters a new thing and places it in his mind where there is something like it.

ovum—female egg cell.

parent education—providing information and materials to the parents of children.

parent involvement—various means through which parents collaborate in and support their children's education.

parental styles—parental discipline techniques identifying four styles of parenting: authoritarian, permissive, authoritative, harmonious.

pediatrician—a physician who specializes in the care of children from birth to age 21.

peer reinforcement—a critical role in children's behavior is determined by positive or negative reinforcement given by peers.

peer popularity—children who gave the most positive reinforcement were likely to be very well liked by their peers.

peers—those who are the same age and/or developmental level.

perception—the ways we know about what goes on outside our bodies.

perinatologist—a physician who specializes in the care of women who are at high risk during pregnancy.

personality traits—develop from initial genetic temperament characteristics as children experience their environment.

Phallic Stage—Freud stated children ages three to six are in this stage, in which the child concentrates on sex-role identification and conscience development.

phenotype—the individual's external, measurable characteristics that reflect the genotype.

phonemes—the smallest units of language; the speech sounds in language.

physical growth—development of the body and its parts.

physical dependency—relying on others to care for one's basic needs, such as nourishment, comfort, and elimination.

PL 94–142—the Education of All Handicapped Children Act of 1975, which ensures all children with special needs ages 5 to 21 years have equal educational opportunity.

PL 101–476—revision of PL 94–142.

PL 99–457—the Education of the Handicapped Act Amendments; Title I, Programs for Infants and Toddlers with Handicaps; gave states 5 years to institute a program for serving children ages three through five with disabilities.

placenta—the covering that protects the developing infant and serves as a medium of exchange for food and oxygen.

planning—an important human higher-level cognitive ability that enables us to consider ways to solve problems prior to actually embarking on a solution and thus cuts down on time lost with trial-and-error approaches.

play—related to everything that children do: cognitive, affective, and psychomotor.

play—the actions and activities children do to amuse and entertain themselves that enable them to construct knowledge.

portfolio—an ongoing record of a child that includes information collected by the teacher and the student.

positive guidance techniques—teach children what the expected behaviors are and how to solve their conflicts using words rather than physical force.

post-traumatic stress disorder—"re-experiencing" a violent or stressful event through play.

poverty—a low economic level at which people are poor and lack money needed for basic living.

pragmatics—the rules for using language appropriately and to advantage.

preconcepts—partial, immature concepts.

premature infant—the child born prior to the completion of the 40-week gestation period.

preoperational period—Piaget's second stage of cognitive development (ages two to seven).

preoperational period—may last from about the age of two until about seven when the focus of development is language and speech.

preschoolers—three-, four-, and some five-year-olds who have not yet entered elementary school.

prevention—involves making the environment healthy and safe for the child and minimizing the need for excessive restraint.

primary period—children ages six through eight or grades first through third.

primary grades—grades one through three.

processing—in cognitive functioning, this is the internal activity.

prolonging attention—maintaining communication and interaction.

proprioception—the sense that tells us where the parts of our body are in relation to the whole.

prosocial behavior—outward manifestations of positive moral development that reflect generosity, nurturance-giving, sympathy, and helping.

protolanguage—meaningful sound combinations that are not words.

proximodistal—from the center out.

psychometric approach—stresses the measurement of individual differences, that is, the comparing of one person to others. It also stresses acquired knowledge and language skills as those behaviors to be measured in arriving at an estimate of the individual's intelligence.

public television—paid for by funds collected through taxes and funds donated by business, industry, and the viewing public.

random scribble—the first stage in the development of art when young children enjoy exploring the movement of their arms and shoulders and the resulting patterns on the paper.

readiness—an end point that is reached during a certain age or stage that enables the child to move on to the next level.

reciprocity—communication exchange in an equal give-and-take manner.

Recommended Daily Dietary Allowances (RDA)—minimum amounts of nutrients obtained from the four basic food sources that our bodies need each day.

referential speakers—use mainly nouns with some verbs, proper names, and adjectives.

reflective learning—learning that takes place from the inside out.

Reggio Emilia—an all-day program in an Italian city that combines care, education, and social services free to all three to six-year-olds, with parents paying a fee for infants and toddlers.

reinforcements—positive consequences that are likely to increase positive behavior; rewards.

representational thinking—Piaget's sixth stage when a child begins to think before acting.

respectful engagement—moral education based on a cooperative relationship between adult and child. The adult must respect the child's initiatives and reactions.

rewards—positive consequences that are likely to increase positive behavior; reinforcements.

Rh factor—a substance found in 85 percent of humans; when present, it is referred to as RH positive; when absent, Rh negative.

rhythm—being in a mutual exchange mode that promotes communication between adult and child.

rough-and-tumble play—happy activity; not aggressive or hostile; includes play fighting, smiling, jumping.

routines—formal games, instructional games, and joint book-reading.

Rowe v. Wade—the court case that legalized abortion.

running record—a naturalistic observation done by an outside person that describes what the child did in a factual way and in great detail; also referred to as a specimen record.

scaffolding—a process through which an adult supports the child's learning, providing support as the child moves from the current developmental level to a higher level.

schema—partial pictures of what an infant actually sees and experiences to include the highlights of what the infant perceives.

self-concept—a person's idea about who they are.

self-concept—the way a person feels about himself.

self-control—the child's ability to manage her own behaviors.

self-esteem—how the person evaluates his self-concept; how much respect the person has for himself.

semantics—the study of meaning that refers to words used in the correct context and attached to the appropriate referent.

semen—liquid ejaculated from the male's reproductive organs.

sensorimotor period—Piaget's first stage of cognitive development that lasts from birth to age two in which children learn to use their senses as a means to find out new things.

sensory involvement—using all the senses as a bridge from the concrete to the abstract.

sequential growth—the set order in which growth proceeds.

seriation—ordering; putting things in order according to some criteria such as size, age, or color.

sex-role standards—behaviors society regards as appropriate for males and females.

sex-stereotyped—treating boys and girls differently based on their sex.

sexuality—"includes the biological nature of the person, the physical aspects of sex relations, and many other aspects of sex-linked behavior" (Lively & Lively, 1991, p. 21).

shame—a feeling of embarrassment that may occur when children feel they have not lived up to certain behavioral standards.

shaping—gradual acquisition of a learned behavior.

shows—calling attention to something by pointing.

siblings—brothers and sisters.

social referencing—infants gain information from others in order to understand and evaluate events and behave in the appropriate manner in a situation.

socially isolated—persons who seldom, if ever, interact with peers, or may be attempt to interact but are rejected.

software—the individual programs installed for use on the computer.

sonography—*see ultrasound.*

spatial concepts—concepts that include: in, on, over, under, into, together, beside, between, on top, inside, outside and below.

specialized movements—individual skills developed relative to each person's particular needs and interests.

specimen record—*see running record.*

sperm—male reproductive cell.

stereotypes—a belief that all members of certain groups have identical beliefs and behaviors.

strange situation—a setting in which the infant is placed in an unfamiliar room and is allowed to explore some toys either with the mother or a stranger present.

stranger anxiety—fear of strangers.

stress—"nonspecific response of the body to any demand that exceeds the person's ability to cope, a person-environment relationship that threatens or taxes personal resources, and a mental state in response to strains or daily hassles" (Honig, 1986, p. 51).

strong nominals—those nouns that refer consistently to at least two referents.

strong relationals—words that are used consistently for potentially reversible relationships.

structural-innatist theory—explains language acquisition as a human being born with a biological need to develop rule systems for language, while reinforcement and imitation give feedback and build vocabulary.

successive approximation—gradual learning in discrete steps.

superego—to Freud, this begins to develop around the age of four; the conscience or the part of the personality that holds on to the moral values of society.

syntax—set of rules that has to do with the way words are placed in sequence to make an acceptable sentence or phrase.

talk—the oral aspect of language.

teacher researcher—a classroom teacher who does a carefully planned and documented study of action designed to solve a classroom instructional problem or introduce a new teaching practice; often done in collaboration with university personnel.

teacher-imposed structure (TS)—in writing, teachers tell children what to write and remind children to be careful with capitalization and punctuation.

technology—equipment developed through use of scientific knowledge, i.e., computers, videos, audio, etc.

telegraphic sentences—children between 18 months and 2^1/2 years begin to put two or three words together in sentences, which, by adult standards, are incomplete.

temperament—distinctive personal characteristics a child is born with that seem to stay with her as she grows.

terrible twos—a time period when the child's active exploration and striving for independence put heavy demands on adult guidance.

thalidomide—a drug taken by pregnant women in the early 1960s for the relief of morning sickness that caused retarded limb development when taken during the embryonic period.

thematic—the use of set play centers that suggest specific roles to be taken such as: home center, medical center, a fire fighter center.

theories of play—referred to as the classical theories: surplus energy theory, relaxation theory, preexercise or practice theory, and recapitualization theory. Most recently, contemporary theories have been developed that are much broader.

theories—ideas designed to show one plan or set of rules that explains, describes, or predicts what happens and what will happen when children grow and learn.

theory of multiple intelligences—developed by Gardner, views intelligence as being potentially divided into seven types.

TLC—tender loving care.

transition period—from five to seven when the way the child thinks changes from preoperational to concrete operational.

triarchic approach—developed by Sternberg, focuses on coping; pinpoints more specifically certain areas to be evaluated using the information-processing approach to evaluation.

trust—confidence that develops relative to other humans' behavior.

typical—the way most children grow and learn.

Abelman, R. (1984). Children and TV: The ABC's of TV literacy. *Childhood Education, 60*, 200–205.

Aboud, F. E. (1987). The development of ethnic self-identification and attitudes. In J. S. Phinney & M. J. Rotheram (Eds.), *Children's ethnic socialization*, (pp. 32–55). Newbury Park, CA: Sage.

Ackerman, D. (1990, March 25). The power of touch. *Parade*, 4–5.

Agras, W. S. (1985). The relation between neonatal and later activity and temperament. *Child Development, 56*, 38–42.

Ajose, S. A., & Joyner, V. G. (1990). Cooperative learning: The birth of an effective teaching strategy. *Educational Horizons, 68*, 197–207.

Aldridge, J. (1990). Early education of the handicapped. Staff development ideas. *Day Care and Early Education, 17*(3), 26.

Alejandro-Wright, M. N. (1985). The child's conception of racial identification: A socio-cognitive developmental model. In M. B. Spencer, G. K. Brookins, & W. R. Allen (Eds.), *Beginnings: The social and affective development of black children* (pp. 185–200). Hillsdale, NJ: Erlbaum.

Alexander, J. G. & Vincent, J. L. (1989). Staff member's ability to recognize and prevent common health problems of children in day care centers. *Dimensions, 18* (1), 22, 24.

Alexander, G. M., & Hines, M. (1994). Gender labels and play styles: Their relative contribution to children's selection of playmates. *Child Development, 65*, 869–879.

Alexander, K. L., & Entwisle, D. R. (1988). Achievement in the first 2 years of school: Patterns and processes. *Monographs of the Society for Research in Child Development, 53* (2, Serial No. 218).

Allen, K. E., & Marotz, L. (1994). *Developmental profiles: Birth to six* (2nd ed.). Albany, NY: Delmar.

Allen, K. E. (1992). *Mainstreaming in early childhood education* (2nd ed.). Albany, NY: Delmar.

Ambron, S. R. (1978). *Child development,* (2nd Ed.). New York: Holt, Rinehart, & Winston.

Ames, L. B. (1989). *Arnold Gesell: Themes of his work.* New York: Human Sciences Press.

Anderson, B. E. (1989). Effects of public day care: A longitudinal study. *Child Development, 60*, 857–866.

Annis, L. (1978). *The child before birth.* Ithaca, NY: Cornell University Press.

Apgar, V. A. (1953). A proposal for a new method of evaluation of the newborn infant. *Current Researches in Anesthesia and Analgesia, 32*, 260–267.

Apgar, V. A. & Beck, J. (1978). A perfect baby. In *Readings in Human Development 78/79*. Guilford, CT: Dushkin. Reprinted from V. A. Apgar & J. Beck (1972). *Is my baby alright?* New York: Simon & Schuster.

Apgar, V. A. & Beck J. (1973). *Is my baby alright?* New York: Trident Press.

Aronson, S. S. (1983). Injuries in child care. *Young Children, 38* (6), 19–20.

Asher, S. R., Oden, S. L., & Gottman, J. M. (1977). Children's friendships in school settings. In L. G. Katz (Ed.), *Current topics in early childhood education* (Vol. 1, pp. 33–61). Norwood, NJ: Ablex.

Asquith, P. & French, L. (1989, April). *Talking while playing: Fantasy in the kitchen.* Paper presented at the meeting of the American Educational Research Association, Kansas City, MO.

Ault, R. (1983). *Children's cognitive development, 2nd ed.* New York: Oxford University Press.

Ayman-Nolley, S. (1988). Piaget and Vygotsky on creativity. *The Quarterly Newsletter of the Laboratory of Comparative Human Cognition, 10*, 107–111.

Babies abandoned by crack cocaine addicts crowding hospitals. (1989, July 2) *Baton Rouge Sunday Advocate*, p. 6A.

Baecher, R. E. (1977). Goals and directions of bilingual programs in the early childhood years. In D. Persky & L. Golubchick (Eds.), *Early Childhood* (pp. 278–284). Wayne, NJ: Avery.

Baldwin, D. A. & Markman, E. M. (1989). Establishing word-object relations: A first step. *Child Development, 60,* 381–398.

Banks, J. A. (1993). Multicultural education: Development, dimensions, and challenges. *Phi Delta Kappan, 75,* 22–28.

Barbour, N. H. (1988). Can we prepackage thinking? *Childhood Education, 65* (2), 67–68.

Barglow, P., Vaughn, B. E., Molitor, N. (1987). Effects of maternal absence due to employment on the quality of infant-mother attachment in a low-risk sample. *Child Development, 58,* 945–954.

Bartlett, E. J. (1981). Selecting an early childhood language curriculum. In C. B. Cazden (Ed.), *Language in early childhood education (Revised edition)* (pp. 83–96). Washington, DC: National Association for the Education of Young Children.

Baum, D., & Wells, C. (1985). Promoting handicap awareness in preschool children. *Teaching Exceptional Children, 17*(4), 282–287.

Baumrind, D. (1993). The average expectable environment is not good enough: A response to Scarr. *Child Development, 64,* 1299–1317.

Baumrind, D. (1975). *Early socialization and the discipline controversy.* Morristown, NJ: Programs Modular Series.

Baumrind, D. (1978). Note: Harmonious parents and their preschool children. In J. K. Gardner (Ed.), *Readings in developmental psychology* (pp. 140–144). Boston: Little, Brown. Originally published in *Developmental Psychology*, 1971, *4,* 99–102.

Bayles, F. (1993, August 1). Teen-age homicides become deadly epidemic. *Baton Rouge Morning Advocate,* 1A, 8A.

Beal, C. R. & Belgrad, S. L. (1990). The development of message evaluation skills in young children. *Child Development, 61,* 705–712.

Beardslee, W. R., & Mack, J. E. (1986, Winter). Youth and children and the nuclear threat. *Newsletter of the Society for Research in Child Development,* 1–2.

Beckoff, A. G., & Bender, W. N. (1989). Programming for mainstream kindergarten success in preschool: Teachers' perceptions of necessary prerequisite skills. *Journal of Early Intervention, 13,* 269–280.

Behrend, D. A., Rosengran, K. S., & Perlmutter, M. (1989, April). *Parental scaffolding and private speech: Relations between two sources of regulation.* Paper presented at the meeting of the Society for Research in Child Development, Kansas City, MO.

Belsky, J. (1990). Infant day care: A cause for concern? In M. A. Jensen and Z. W. Chevalier (Eds.) *Issues and advocacy in early education* (pp. 182–189). Boston: Allyn & Bacon.

Belsky, J. (1988). The "effects" of day care reconsidered. *Early Childhood Research Quarterly, 3,* 235–272.

Belsky, J. & Braungart, J. M. (1991). Are insecure-violent infants with extensive day-care experience less stressed by and more independent in the strange situation? *Child Development, 62,* 567–571.

Belsky, J. & Rovine, M. J. (1988). Nonmaternal care in the first year of life and the security of infant-parent attachment. *Child Development, 59,* 157–167.

Benedict, J. (1994). *A comparative study of the oral language of students in basal-based and whole language kindergartens.* Unpublished doctoral dissertation, Louisiana State University, Baton Rouge, LA.

Bentzen, W. R. (1993). *Seeing young children: A guide to observing and recording behavior, 2nd ed.* Albany, NY: Delmar Publishers.

Bergen, D. (1993). Teaching strategies: Facilitating friendship development in inclusion classrooms. *Childhood Education, 69,* 234, 236.

Berk, L. E. (1994). *Child development, 3rd ed.* Boston: Allyn & Bacon.

Berk, L. E. (1985). Why children talk to themselves. *Young Children, 40* (5), 46–52.

Berliner, D. (1990). Helping kids learn how to learn: Berliner on research. *Instructor, 99* (5), 16–17.

Berliner, D. (1990). Play is the work of childhood. *Instructor*, March 22–23.

Bernat, V. (1993). Teaching peace. *Young Children, 48*(3), 36–39.

Berndt, T. J. (1983). Social cognition, social behavior, and children's friendships. In E. T. Higgins, D. N. Ruble, & W. W. Hartup (Eds.), *Social cognition and social development* (pp. 158–189). New York: Cambridge University Press.

Bernstein, B. (1972). A critique of the concept of compensatory education. In C. B. Cazden, V. P. John, & D. Hymes (Eds.), *Functions of language in the classroom* (pp. 135–151). New York: Teachers College Press.

Bernstein, A. C. (1976). How children learn about sex and birth. *Psychology today, 9,* 31–35+.

Bigler, R. S., & Liben, L. S. (1993). A cognitive-developmental approach to racial stereotyping and reconstructive memory in Euro-American children. *Child Development, 64,* 1507–1518.

Billman, J. (1992). The Native American curriculum: Attempting alternatives to tepees and headbands. *Young Children, 47* (6), 22–25.

Birch, L. L., Marlin, D. W., & Rotter, J. (1984). Eating as the "means" activity in a contingency: Effects on young children's food preferences. *Child Development, 55,* 431–439.

Bissex, G. L. (1985). Watching young writers. In A. Jaggar & M. T. Smith-Burke (Eds.), *Observing the language learner* (pp. 99–114). Newark, DE: International Reading Association.

Bivens, J. A., & Berk, L. E. (1989, April). *A longitudinal study of the development of elementary school children's private speech*. Paper presented at the meeting of the Society for Research in Child Development, Kansas City, MO.

Black, J. K. (1981). Are young children really egocentric? *Young Children, 36* (6), 51–55.

Black, B. (1989, March). *Negotiation in social pretend play: Strategy use as a function of social status*. Presentation at the meeting of the American Educational Research Association, San Francisco, CA.

Black, J. K., & Puckett, M. B. (1987). Informing others about developmentally appropriate practice. In S. Bredekamp (Ed.), *Developmentally appropriate practice in early childhood programs serving children from birth through age eight* (pp. 83–87). Washington, DC: National Association for the Education of Young Children.

Bloch, M. N., Tabachnick, B. R., & Espinosa-Dulanto, M. (1994). Teacher perspectives on the strengths and achievements of young children: Relationship to ethnicity, language, gender, and class. In B. L. Mallory & R. S. New (Eds.), *Diversity and developmentally appropriate practices* (223–249). New York: Teachers College Press.

Bloom, L., Lightbown, P., & Hood, L. (1975). Structure and variation in child language. Monographs of the Society for Research in *Child Development, 40* (2, Serial No. 160).

Bomba, A. K. & Knight, K. B. (1993). Family style dining in the child care center: Yes, it can work! *Day Care and Early Education, 21* (1), 4–5.

Borensweig, J. & Wilmshurst, A. (1981). Learning kits for young Native Americans. *Young Children, 36* (4), 18–23.

Bornstein, M. H., Tamis-LeMonde, C. S., Tal, J., Ludemann, L., Toda, S., Rahn, C. W., Pecheux, M., Azuma, H., & Vardi, D. (1992). Maternal responsiveness to infants in three societies: The United States, France, and Japan. *Child Development, 63*, 808–821.

Bower, T. G. R. (1977). *The perceptual world of the child*. Cambridge, MA: Harvard University Press.

Bowman, B. T., & Stott, F. M. (1994). Understanding development in a cultural context: The challenge for teachers. In B. L. Mallory & R. S. New (Eds.), *Diversity and developmentally appropriate practices* (pp. 119–133). New York: Teachers College Press.

Bowman, B. T., & Stott (1989). Self-reflection as an element of professionalism. *Teachers College Record, 90*(3), 444–451.

Boyer, E. L. (1993). Ready to learn: A mandate for the nation. *Young Children, 48*(3), 54–57.

Bracey, G. W. (1994). Research: More on the importance of preschool. *Phi Delta Kappan, 75*, 416–417.

Bradbard, M., & Endsley, R. (1980). Educating parents to be discriminating day care consumers. In S. J. Kilmer

(Ed.), *Advances in early education and day care*, vol. 1 (pp. 187–201). Greenwich, CT: JAI Press.

Braine, M. D. S. (1976). Children's first word combinations. Monographs of the Society for Research in *Child Development, 41* (1, Serial No. 164).

Brazelton, T. B. (1992). *Touchpoints: The essential reference*. Reading, MA: Addison-Wesley.

Brazelton, T. B. (1990). Saving the bathwater. *Child Development*, 61, 1661–1671.

Brazelton, T. B. (1982). Behavioral competence of the newborn infant. In J. K. Gardner (Ed.), *Readings in developmental psychology, 2nd ed*. (pp. 79–90). Boston: Little-Brown.

Brazelton, T. B. (1978). Early parent-infant reciprocity. In J. K. Gardner (Ed.) Readings in developmental psychology (pp. 71–78). Boston: Little-Brown. Reprinted from V. C. Vaughn & T. B. Brazelton (Eds.), *The family–Can it be saved?* Chicago: Year Book Medical Publishers, 1976.

Brazelton, T. B. (1977). From dependence to independence: The toddler comes of age. In *Readings in Early Childhood Education 77/78*. Guilford, CT: Dushkin.

Brazelton, T. B. (1977, November). *Why must we think about a passive model for infancy?* Keynote address presented at the annual meeting of the National Association for the Education of Young Children.

Brazelton, T. B. & Cramer, B. G. (1990). *The earliest relationship: Parents, infants, and the drama of early attachment*. Reading, MA: Addison-Wesley. *BR second city in state to have full-time perinatologist*. (1990, August 16). Baton Rouge Morning Advocate, p. 6F.

Brazelton, T. B. (1991, February 25). What parents need to say. *Newsweek, 117*(8), 52.

Bredekamp, S. (Ed.) (1987). *Developmentally appropriate practice in early childhood programs serving children from birth through age eight*. Washington, DC: National Association for the Education of Young Children.

Bredekamp, S. (1990). Extra-year programs: A response to Brewer and Uphoff. *Young Children, 45*(6), 20–21.

Bredekamp, S. (1993). Reflections on Reggio Emilia. *Young Children, 49*(1), 13–17.

Bretherton, I. & Waters, E. (Eds.) (1985). *Growing points of attachment theory and research*. Monographs of the Society for Research in Child Development, 50, (1–2).

Brett, A. (1994). Online for new learning opportunities. *Dimensions of Early Childhood Education, 22*(3), 10–13.

Brewer, J. (1990). Transitional programs: Boom or bane? *Young Children, 45*(6), 15–18.

Bricker, D. (1993). A rose by any other name, or is it? *Journal of Early Intervention, 17*, 89–96.

Brinker, R. P., Baxer, A., & Butler, L. S. (1994). An ordinal pattern analysis of four hypotheses describing the interactions between drug-addicted, chronically disadvantaged, and middle-class mother-infant dyads.

Child Development, 65, 361–372.

Brofenbrenner, U. (1992). Ecological systems theory. In R. Vasta (Ed.), *Six theories of child development* (pp. 187–250). London and Philadelphia: Jessica Kingsley.

Brofenbrenner, U. (1989, April). *The developing ecology of human development: Paradigm lost or paradigm regained.* Presentation at the biennial meeting of the Society for Research in Child Development, Kansas City, MO.

Brofenbrenner, U. (1979). *The ecology of human development.* Cambridge, MA: Harvard University Press.

Brookins, G. K. (1985). Black children's sex-role ideologies and occupational choices in families of employed mothers. In M. B. Spencer, G. K. Brookins, & W. R. Allen (Eds.), *Beginnings: The social and affective development of black children* (pp. 257–272). Hillsdale, NJ: Erlbaum.

Brooks, P. H. & Roberts, M. C. (1990). *Social science and the prevention of children's injuries.* Social policy report, the Society for Research in Child Development, 4 (1).

Brooks, R. L. & Obrzut, J. T. (1981). Brain lateralization: Implications for infant stimulation and development. *Young Children, 36*(3), 9–16.

Brown, L. J. (1988). Helping children learn to solve problems. *Day Care and Early Education, 16* (2), 26–30.

Brown, T. (1988). Why Vygotsky? The role of social interaction in constructing knowledge. *The Quarterly Newsletter of the Laboratory of Comparative Human Cognition, 10,* 111–117.

Brown, N. S., Curry, N. E., & Tittnich, E. (1971). How groups of children deal with common stress through play. In *Play: The child strives toward self-realization* (pp. 26–28). Washington, DC: National Association for the Education of Young Children.

Brown, M. H., Althouse, R., & Anfin, C. (1993). Guided dramatization: Fostering social development in children with disabilities. *Young Children, 48*(2), 68–71.

Brownell, C. A. (1990). Peer social skills in toddlers: Competencies and constraints illustrated by same-age and mixed-age interaction. *Child Development, 61,* 838–848.

Brownell, C. A. & Carriger, M. S. (1990). Changes in cooperation and self-other differentiation during the second year. *Child Development, 61,* 1164–1174.

Bruner, J. S. (1975). Play is serious business. *Psychology Today, 8,* 82–83.

Buchan, B., Swap, S., & Swap, W. (1977). Teacher identification of hyperactive children in school settings. *Exceptional Children, 43,* 314–315.

Buchoff, R. (1990). Attention deficit disorder: Help for the classroom teacher. *Childhood Education, 67,* 86–90.

Bullock, J. R. (1990). Child-initiated activity: It's importance to early childhood education. *Day Care and Early Education, 18* (2), 14–16.

Bullock, M. & Lutkenhaus, P. (1988). The development of volitional behavior in the toddler years. *Child Devel-*

opment, 59, 664–674.

Bullock, J. (1993). Supporting the development of shy children. *Day Care and Early Education, 20*(4), 8–10.

Burchinal, M., Lee, M., & Ramey, C. (1989). Type of daycare and preschool intellectual development in disadvantaged children. *Child Development, 60,* 128–137.

Burg, K. (1984). The microcomputer in the kindergarten: A magical, useful, expensive toy. *Young Children, 39*(3), 28–33.

Burgess, B. J. (1978). Native American learning styles. In L. Morris (Ed.), *Extracting learning styles from social/cultural diversity* (pp. 41–53). Southwest Teacher Corps Network.

Burstein, N. D. (1986). The effects of classroom organization on mainstreamed preschool children. *Exceptional Children, 52,* 425–434.

Burton, A. W. (1992). The development of motor skills. *Early Report, 19* (2), 3–4.

Burts, D. C., Hart, C. H., Charlesworth, R., & Kirk, L. (1990). A comparison of the frequencies of stress behaviors observed in kindergarten children in classrooms with developmentally appropriate vs. developmentally inappropriate instructional practices. *Early Childhood Research Quarterly, 5* (3), 407–423.

Burts, D. C., Hart, C. H., Charlesworth, R., Fleege, P. O., Mosley, J., & Thomasson, R. H. (1992). Observed activities and stress behaviors of children in developmentally appropriate and inappropriate kindergarten classrooms. *Early Childhood Research Quarterly, 7,* 297–318.

Burts, D. C., Hart, C. H., Charlesworth, R., DeWolf, D. M., Ray, J., Manuel, K., & Fleege, P. O. (1993, Fall/Winter). Developmentally appropriateness of kindergarten programs and academic outcomes in first grade. *Journal of Research in Childhood Education, 8*(1), 23–31.

Burts, D. C., Campbell, J., Hart, C. H., & Charlesworth, R. (1991, April). *Comparison of principals' beliefs and kindergarten teachers' beliefs and practices.* Paper presented at the American Educational Research Association, Chicago, IL.

Burts, D. C., Charlesworth, R., & Fleege, P. O. (1991, April). *Achievement of kindergartners in developmentally appropriate and developmentally inappropriate classrooms.* Presentation at the Society for Research in Child Development, Seattle, WA.

Bushell, D., Jr. (1982). The behavior analysis model for early education. In B. Spodek (Ed.) *Handbook of research in early childhood education* (pp. 156–184). New York: The Free Press.

Bushnell, E. W. & Boudreau, J. P. (1993). Motor development and the mind: The potential role of motor abilities as a determinant of aspects of perceptual development. *Child Development, 64,* 1005–1021.

Buzzelli, C. A. (1992). Research in review. Young children's moral understanding: Learning about right and wrong. *Young Children, 47*(6), 47–53.

Cadiz, S. M. (1994). Food for thought: Striving for mental health in the early childhood center setting. *Young Children, 49*(3), 84–86.

Caldwell, B. M. (1977). Aggression and hostility in young children. *Young Children, 32*(2), 4–13.

Caldwell, B. M. (1978). Bridging the chasm between kindergarten and primary. In *Readings in early childhood education, 77/78*. Guilford, CT: Dushkin Publishing Group.

Calfee, R. (1985). Computer literacy and book literacy: Parallels and contrasts. *Educational Researcher, 14*(5), 8–13.

Campbell, K. C. & Arnold, F. D. (1988). Stimulating thinking and communicating skills. *Dimensions, 16* (2), 11–13.

Campbell, F. A., & Ramey, C. T. (1994). Effects of early intervention on intellectual and academic achievement: A follow-up study of children from low-income families. *Child Development, 65*, 684–698.

Campbell, S. B., Pierce, E. W., March, C. L., Ewing, L. J., & Szumowski, E. K. (1994). Hard-to-manage preschool boys: Symptomatic behavior across contexts and time. *Child Development, 65*, 836–851.

Campbell, E. N., & Foster, J. E. (1993). Play centers that encourage literacy development. *Day Care and Early Education, 21*(2), 22–26.

Cannella, G. S. (1993). Learning through social interaction: Shared cognitive experience, negotiation strategies, and joint concept construction for young children. *Early Childhood Research Quarterly, 8*, 427–444.

Cannella, G. S. (1986). Praise and concrete rewards: Concerns for childhood education. *Childhood Education, 62*, 297–301.

Cannella, G. S. (1988). The effects of environmental structure on writing produced by young children. *Child Study Journal, 18* (3), 207–221.

Cantor, P. (1977). *Understanding a child's world*. New York: McGraw-Hill.

Capute, A. J., Palmer, F. B., Shapiro, B. K., Wachtel, R. C., & Accardo, P. J. (1980). Clinical applications of the language and auditory milestone scale. In A. P. Reilly (Ed.), *The communications game* (pp. 81–89). Piscataway, NJ: Johnson and Johnson.

Cardinal, D. N. & Shum, K. (1993). A descriptive analysis of family-related services in the neonatal intensive care unit. *Journal of Early Intervention, 17*, 270–282.

Carew, J. V., Chan, I., & Halfar, C. (1976). *Observing intelligence in young children*. Englewood Cliffs, NJ: Prentice-Hall.

Carl, B. & Richard, N. (no date). *One piece of the puzzle: A practical guide for schools interested in implementing a school readiness program*. Lumberville, PA: Modern Learning Press.

Carlson, K. & Cunningham, J. L. (1990). Effect of pencil diameter on the graphomotor skill of preschoolers. *Early Childhood Research Quarterly, 5*, 279–293.

Caron, A. J., Caron, R. F., & MacLean, D. J. (1988). Infant discrimination of naturalistic emotional expressions: The role of face and voice. *Child Development, 59*, 604–616.

Carr, K. S. (1988). How can we teach critical thinking? *Childhood Education, 65* (2), 69–73.

Carroll, J. J., & Steward, M. S. (1984). The role of cognitive development in children's understandings of their own feelings. *Child Development, 55*, 1426–1492.

Carta, J. J., Atwater, J. B., & Schwartz, I. S. (1991, April). *The effects of classroom survival skills intervention on young children with disabilities: Results of a two year follow-up*. Presented at the meeting of the Society for Research in Child Development, Seattle, WA.

Caruso, D. A. (1989). Attachment and exploration in infancy: Research and applied issues. *Early Childhood Research Quarterly, 4*, 117–132.

Caruso, D. A. (1988). Play and learning in infancy: Research and implications. *Young Children, 43* (6), 63–70.

Caruso, D. A. (1984). Infant exploratory play: Implications for child care. *Young Children, 40* (1), 27–30.

Casanova, U. (1990). Helping kids learn how to learn: Casanova on practice. *Instructor, 99* (5), 16–17.

Casey, M. B. (1990). A planning and problem-solving preschool model. *Early Childhood Research Quarterly, 5*, 53–67.

Casey, M. B., & Lippman, M. (1991). Learning to plan through play. *Young Children, 46*(4), 52–58.

Cassidy, D. J. (1989). Questioning the young child: Process and functioning. *Childhood Education, 65*, 146–149.

Castenada, A. M. (1987). Early mathematics education. In C. Seefeldt (Ed.), *The early childhood curriculum: A review of current research* (pp. 165–182). New York: Teachers College Press.

Castillo, M. S. & Cruz, J., Jr. (1974). Special competencies for teachers of preschool Chicano children: Rationale, content, and assessment process. *Young Children, 29* (6), 341–347.

Castle, K., & Rogers, K. (1993/94). Rule-creating in a constructivist classroom community. *Childhood Education, 70*, 77–80.

Castle, K. (1990). Children's invented games. *Childhood Education, 67*, 82–85.

Catherwood, D. (1993). The robustness of infant haptic memory: Testing its capacity to withstand delay and haptic interference. *Child Development, 64*, 702–710.

Caughy, M. O., DiPietro, J. A., & Strobino, D. M. (1994). Day-care participation as a protective factor in the cognitive development of low-income children. *Child Development, 65*, 457–471.

Caulfield, R. (1994). Infants' sensory abilities: Caregiving implications and recommendations. *Day Care and Early Education, 21* (4), 31–35.

Cawfield, M. E. (1992). Velcro time: The language connection. *Young Children, 47* (4), 26–30.

Cazden, C. B. (1990, November). *Cultural capital in the preschool: Teacher education for language and liter-*

acy. Presentation at the annual meeting of the National Association of Early Childhood Teacher Educators, Washington, DC.

Cazden, C. B. (1981). On evaluation. In C. B. Cazden (Ed.), *Language in early childhood education (Revised edition)* (pp. 153–158). Washington, DC: National Association for the Education of Young Children.

Cazden, C. B., Baratz, J. C., Labov, W., & Palmer, F. H. (1981). Language development in day care programs. In C. B. Cazden (Ed.), *Language development in early childhood education (Revised edition)* (pp. 107–125). Washington, DC: National Association for the Education of Young Children.

Cazden, C. B., Bryant, B. H., & Tillman, M. A. (1981). Making it and going home: The attitudes of black people toward language acquisition. In C. B. Cazden (Ed.), *Language in early childhood education (Revised edition)* (pp. 107–125). Washington, DC: National Association for the Education of Young Children.

Celebrating Head Start's 25th Anniversary. (1990). Special section. *Young Children, 45* (6).

Chandler, P. A. (1994). *A place for me: Including children with special needs in early care and education settings*. Washington, DC: National Association for the Education of Young Children.

Charles, C. M. (1974). *The teacher's petit Piaget*. Belmont, CA: Fearon.

Charlesworth, R. & Lind, K. K. (1995). *Math and science for young children, 2nd ed*. Albany, NY: Delmar Publishers.

Charlesworth, R. & Miller, N. (1985). Social studies and basic skills in the kindergarten. *The Social Studies, 76*, 34–37.

Charlesworth, W. R. (1978). Ethology: Understanding the other half of intelligence. *Social Science Information, 17*, 231–277.

Charlesworth, R., & Hartup, W. W. (1967). Positive social reinforcement in the nursery school peer group. *Child Development, 38*, 993–1002.

Charlesworth, R. (1989). Behind before they start? Dealing with the problems of kindergarten failure. *Young Children, 44*(3), 5–13.

Charlesworth, R., Hart, C. H., Burts, C. C., & DeWolf, M. (1993). The LSU Studies: Building a research base for developmentally appropriate practice. In S. Reifel (Ed.), Perspectives on developmentally appropriate practice, *Advances in Early Education and Day Care, 5*, 3–28.

Charlesworth, R., & Lind, K. K. (1995a). Whole language and primary grades mathematics and science: Keeping in step with national standards. In S. Raines (Ed.), *Whole language across the curriculum: Grades 1, 2, and 3* (pp. 156–178). New York: Teachers College Press.

Charlesworth, R., & Lind, K. K. (1995b). *Math and science*

for young children, 2nd ed. Albany, NY: Delmar.

Charlesworth, R. (1985). Readiness: Should we make them ready or let them bloom? *Day Care and Early Education, 12*(3), 25–27.

Charlesworth, R., Fleege, P. O., & Weitman, C. J. (1994). Research on the effects of group standardized testing on instruction, pupils and teachers: New directions for policy. *Early Education and Development, 5*, 195–212.

Charren, P. (1990). What's missing in children's TV. *World Monitor*, December, 28–30, 32–34. [Reprinted in K. M. Paciorek & J. H. Munro (Eds.), *Early Childhood Education 91/92* (pp. 109–112). Guilford, CT: Dushkin].

Cherry, C., Godwin, D., & Staples, J. (1989). *Is the left brain always right?* Belmont, CA: David S. Lake.

Chess, S. (1990). Comments: "Infant day care: A cause for concern." In M. A. Jensen & Z. W. Chevalier (Eds.), *Issues and advocacy in early education* (pp. 196–197). Boston: Allyn & Bacon.

Children are born learning. (1993). *Dimensions of Early Childhood, 22*(1), 5–8.

Children's nuclear fears: What parents can do about them. *Today's Child, 32*(4), 6.

Chira, S. (1994). How boys and girls learn differently. In K. M. Paciorek & J. H. Munro (Eds.), *Early Childhood Education 94/94* (pp. 78–80). Guilford, CT: Dushkin. (Originally published in *Redbook*, September 1992, 191–192, 194–195.

Christie, J. F. (1982). Sociodramatic play training. *Young Children, 37*(4), 25–32.

Christie, J. F., & Johnson, E. P. (1983). The role of play in social-intellectual development. *Review of Educational Research, 53*, 93–115.

Church, M. (1979). Nutrition: A vital part of the curriculum. *Young Children, 35* (1), 61–65.

Clabaugh, G. K. (1993). The cutting edge: The limits and possibilities of multiculturalism. *Educational Horizons, 71*, 117–119.

Clark, P. (1985). Curiosity in the classroom. *Early Report, 12*(3), 3–4.

Clarke-Stewart, A. (1984). Day care: A new context for research and development. In M. Perlmutter (Ed.), *Parent-child interaction and parent-child relations in child development* (pp. 61–100). Hillsdale, NJ: Erlbaum.

Clarke-Stewart, A. (1987). In search of consistencies in child care research. In D. Phillips (Ed.), *Quality in child care: What does research tell us?* (pp. 105–120). Washington, DC: National Association for the Education of Young Children.

Clay, M. (1972). *Sand—the concepts about print test*. London: Heinemann. Goodman, Y., & Alwerger, B. (1981). *A study of the development of literacy in preschool children*. Program in Language and Literacy Occasional Paper No. 4. Tucson, AZ: University of Arizona.

Click, P. (1994). *Caring for school-age children*. Albany,

NY: Delmar.

Coates, B., Pusser, H. E., & Goodman, I. (1976). The influence of "Sesame Street" and "Mr. Rogers' Neighborhood" on children's social behavior in the preschool. *Child Development, 47*, 138–144.

Cohen, D. H. (1972). Continuity from prekindergarten to kindergarten. In K. R. Baker (Ed.), *Ideas that work with young children*. Washington, DC: National Association for the Education of Young Children.

Cohen, S. (1993/94). For parents particularly: Television in the lives of children and their families. *Childhood Education, 70*, 103–104.

Cohen, S., Semmes, M., & Guralnick, M. J. (1979). Public Law 94–142 and the education of preschool handicapped children. *Exceptional Children, 45*, 279–290.

Cole, M. & Cole, S. R. (1989). *The development of children*. New York: W. H. Freeman.

Cole, O. J., & Washington, V. (1986). A critical analysis of the assessment of the effects of Head Start on minority children. *Journal of Negro Education, 55*(1), 91–106.

Coll, C. T. G. (1990). Developmental outcome of minority infants: A process oriented look at our beginnings. *Child Development, 61*, 270–289.

Comer, J. P. (1989). Racism and the education of young children. *Teachers College Record, 90*, 352–361.

Condon, W. S. (1979). Neonatal entrainment and enculturation. In M. Bullowa (Ed.), *Before speech: The beginnings of interpersonal communication* (pp. 131–148). Cambridge, England: Cambridge University Press.

Condon, W. S. & Sander, S. W. (1974). Synchrony demonstrated between movements on the neonate and adult speech. *Child Development, 45*, 256–262.

Connell, D. R. (1987). The first 30 years were the fairest: Notes from the kindergarten and ungraded primary (K-1-2). *Young Children, 42*(5), 30–39.

Cooper, J., & Ruble, D. (1980). Don't underestimate the power of nonviolent television programs, psychologist advises. *Today's Child News Magazine*, May 5.

Coplan, R. J., Rubin, K. H., Fox, N. A., Calkins, S. D., & Stewart, S. L. (1994). Being alone, playing alone, acting alone: Distinguishing among reticence and passive and active solitude in young children. *Child Development, 65*, 129–137.

Copple, C., DeLisi, R., & Sigel, I. E. (1982). Cognitive development. In B. Spodek (Ed.), *Handbook of research in early childhood education* (pp. 27–46). New York: The Free Press.

Cornell, C. E. (1993). Language and culture monsters that lurk in our traditional rhymes and folktales. *Young Children, 48*(6), 40–46.

Corporal punishment: Effects on children. (1981). *ERIC/EECE Newsletter, 13*(6), 1, 3.

Cortes, C. E. (1978). Chicano culture, experience and learning. In L. Morris (Ed.), *Extracting learning styles from social/cultural diversity* (pp. 29–40). Southwest Teachers Corps Network.

Cowley, G. (1991). The bold and the bashful. *Newsweek, 117*(26), 24–27.

Cross, W. E. (1985). Black identity: Rediscovering the distinction between personal identity and reference group orientation. In M. B. Spencer, G. K. Brookins, & W. R. Allen (Eds.), *Beginnings: The social and affective development of black children* (pp. 155–172). Hillsdale, NJ: Erlbaum.

Crowley, G. (1991). Children in peril. *Newsweek*, special edition.

Cryan, J. R. (1987). The banning of corporal punishment: In child care, school and other educative settings in the U.S. *Childhood Education, 63*, 146–153.

Culpepper, S. (1992). Early childhood special education: How to recognize handicaps in preschoolers. Part I: Hearing, vision, motor, and language impairments. *Day Care and Early Education, 20*(2), 41–43.

Culpepper, S. (1993). Early childhood special education: How to recognize handicaps in preschoolers. Part II: Cognitive and emotional exceptionalities. *Day Care and Early Education, 20*(2), 39–40.

Current evaluations of children's television programs. (1977). *Today's Child News Magazine*, June-September, 4–7.

Curry, N. E., & Johnson, C. N. (1991). *Beyond self esteem: Developing a genuine sense of human value*. Washington, DC: National Association for the Education of Young Children.

Damon, W. (1988). *The moral child: Nurturing children's natural moral growth*. New York: The Free Press.

Daniels, D., Plomin, R., & Greenhalgh, J. (1984). Correlates of difficult temperament in infancy. *Child Development, 55*, 1184–1194.

David, J. L. (1994). School-based decision making: Kentucky's test of decentralization. *Phi Delta Kappan, 75*, 706–712.

Davis, J. (1993). Why Sally *can* draw. *Educational Horizons, 71*, 86–93.

DeHaas-Warner, S. (1994). The role of child care professionals in placement and programming decisions for preschoolers with special needs in community-based settings. *Young Children, 49*(5), 76–78.

DeHoogh, E. (1978). *Poniendo la campana al gato (Belling the cat) (Vol. 1)*. Skokie, IL: National Textbook Company (Spanish and English versions).

DeLoache, J. S., Cassidy, D. J., & Brown, A. L. (1985). Precursors of mnemonic strategies in very young children's memory. *Child Development, 56*, 125–137.

DeLoache, J. S., Sugarman, S., & Brown, A. L. (1985). The development of error correction strategies in young children's manipulative play. *Child Development, 56*, 928–939.

Derman-Sparks, L. (1993/94). Empowering children to create a caring culture in a world of difference. *Childhood Education, 70*, 66–71.

Derman-Sparks, L. (1993). Revisiting multicultural education. *Dimensions of Early Childhood, 21* (2), 6–10.

Derman-Sparks, L. & the ABC Task Force. (1989). *Antibias curriculum: Tools for empowering young children*. Washington, DC: National Association for the Education of Young Children.

DeVries, E. & Kohlberg, L. (1990). *Constructivist early education: Overview and comparison with other programs*. Washington, DC: National Association for the Education of Young Children. (Original work published in 1987).

DeVries, R., Halcyon, R., & Morgan, P. (1991). A study of children's enacted interpersonal understanding. *Early Childhood Research Quarterly, 6*, 473–517.

DeVries, R., Haney, J., & Zan, B. (1991). Socio-moral atmosphere in direct-instruction, eclectic, and constructivist kindergartens: A study of teachers' enacted interpersonal understanding. *Early Childhood Research Quarterly, 6*, 449–471.

DeVries, R., & Zan, B. (1994). *Moral classrooms, Moral children: Creating a constructivist atmosphere in early education*. New York: Teachers College Press.

Diamond, K. E., Hestenes, L. L., & O'Connor, C. E. (1994). Research in review. Integrating young children with disabilities in preschool: Problems and promise. *Young Children, 49*(2), 68–73.

Dickinson, D. K., & Tabors, P. O. (1991). Early literacy: Linkages between home, school and literacy achievement at age five. *Journal of Research in Childhood Education, 6*(1), 30–46.

Disabled children: A population vulnerable to maltreatment. (1994, March). *Developments, 8*(1), 10.

Divoky, D. (1989). Ritalin: Education's fix-it drug. *Phi Delta Kappan, 70*, 599–605.

Dixon, G. H. (1980). Child development in the family health care center. *Young Children, 35* (3), 49–56.

Dodge, K. A., Pettit, G. S., & Bates, J. E. (1994). Socialization mediators of the relation between socioeconomic status and child conduct problems. *Child Development, 65*, 649–665.

Dodge, M. K., & Frost, J. L. (1986). Children's dramatic play: Influence of thematic and non-thematic settings. *Childhood Education, 62*, 166–170.

Doescher, S., & Sugawara, A. I. (1989). Encouraging prosocial behavior in young children. *Childhood Education, 65*, 213–216.

Dokecki, P. R., Baumeister, A. A., & Kupstas, F. D. (1989). Biomedical and social aspects of pediatric AIDS. *Journal of Early Intervention, 13*, 99–113.

Donmoyer, R., & Kos, R. (1993). At-risk students: Insights from/about research. In R. Donmoyer and R. Kos (Eds.), *At-risk students* (pp. 7–36). Albany, NY: SUNY Press.

Duffy, F. H., Als, H., & McAnulty, G. B. (1990). Behavioral and electrophysiological evidence for gestational age effects in healthy preterm and fullterm infants studied two weeks after expected due date. *Child Develop-*

ment, 61, 1271–1286.

Dunn, J. & Kendrick, C. (1980). The arrival of a sibling: Changes in patterns of interaction between mother and first-born child. *Journal of Child Psychology and Psychiatry, 21*, 119–132.

Dunn, J. & Munn, P. (1985). Becoming a family member: Family conflict and the development of social understanding in the second year. *Child Development, 56*, 480–492.

Dunn, J. & Shatz, M. (1989). Becoming a conversationalist despite (or because of) having an older sibling. *Child Development, 61*, 399–410.

Dunst, C. J. & Lingerfeldt, B. (1985). Maternal ratings of temperament and operant learning in two- to three-month-old infants. *Child Development, 56*, 555–563.

Dwyer, J. (1993, October 10). The quirky genius who is changing our world. *Parade Magazine, 8*, 10.

Dyrli, O. E. (1971). Assessing intellectual development stages of children. In J. E. Weigand (Ed.), *Developing teacher competencies* (pp. 1–42). Englewood Cliffs, NJ: Prentice-Hall.

Dyson, A. H. (1993). From invention to social action in early childhood literacy: A reconceptualization through dialogue about difference. *Early Childhood Research Quarterly, 8*, 409–426.

Dyson, A. H. (1989). *Multiple worlds of child writers: Friends learning to write*. New York: Teachers College Press.

Easterbrooks, M. A. & Goldbert, W. A. (1984). Toddler development in the family: Impact of father involvement and parenting characteristics. *Child Development, 60*, 90–95.

Eckerman, C. O., Whatley, J. L., & Kutz, L. S. (1975). Growth of social play with peers during the second year of life. Developmental Psychology II (pp. 42–49). Reprinted in R. C. Smart (Ed.) (1977). *Readings in child development and relationships, 2nd ed.* (pp. 81–92). New York: Macmillan.

Eddowes, E. A. (1994). *Childhood Education, 70*, 271–273.

Edelmann, M. W. (1992). *Measure of our success: A letter to my children and yours*. Boston, MA: Beacon Press.

Edson, A. (1994). Crossing the great divide: The nursery school child goes to kindergarten. *Young Children, 49*(5), 69–75.

Edwards, L. C., & Nabors, M. L. (1993). The creative arts process: What it is and what it is not. *Young Children, 48*(3), 77–81.

Egg diagnosis. (1990, August 4). *Baton Rouge Morning Advocate*, p. 3A.

Eimas, P. D. & Quinn, P. C. (1994). Studies on the formation of perceptually based basic-level categories in young infants. *Child Development, 65*, 903–917.

Eisenberg, N., Wolchik, S. A., Hernandez, R., & Pasternack, J. F. (1985). Parental socialization of young children's play. A short-term longitudinal study. *Child Development, 56*, 1506–1513.

Eisenberg, N., Fabes, R. A., Nyman, M., Bernzweig, J., &

Pinuelas, A. (1994). The relations of emotionality and regulation to children's anger-related reactions. *Child Development, 65,* 109–128.

Elders, J. (1994). Violence as a public health issue for children. *Childhood Education, 70,* 260–262.

Elkind, D. (1981). *Children and Adolescents: Interpretive essays on Jean Piaget.* New York: Oxford University Press.

Elkind, D. (1993). *Images of the young child.* Washington, DC: National Association for the Education of Young Children.

Elkind, D. (1986). Formal education and early childhood education: An essential difference. *Phi Delta Kappan, 67,* 631–636.

Endres, J. B. & Rockwell, R. E. (1994). *Food, nutrition, and the young child.* New York: Merrill/Macmillan.

Endsley, R., & Bradbard, M. (1981). *Quality day care: A handbook for parents and caregivers.* Englewood Cliffs, NJ: Prentice-Hall.

Engel, R. (1980). Understanding the handicapped through literature. *Young Children, 35*(3), 27–32.

Entwisel, D. R., & Alexander, K. L. (1990). Beginning school math competence: Minority and majority comparisons. *Child Development, 61,* 454–471.

Epstein, J. L. & Evans, J. (1979). Parent-child interaction and children's learning. *The High/Scope Report, 4,* 39–43.

Epstein, J. L. (1991). Paths to partnership: What we can learn from federal, state, district and school initiatives. *Phi Delta Kappan, 72,* 344–349.

Erickson, M. F. (1991). The importance of attachment in children's development. *Early Report, 18*(2), 5–6.

Erickson, M. F. (1990). Using research in preventive intervention. *Early Report, 17*(3), 2–3.

Essa, E. L., & Murray, C. I. (1994). Research in review: Young children's understanding and experience with death. *Young Children, 49*(4), 74–81.

Essa, E. (1990). *Practical guide to preschool behavior problems* (2nd ed.). Albany, NY: Delmar.

Evans, M. A. (1985). Play beyond play: Its role in formal informative speech. In L. Galda & A. D. Pellegrini (Eds.), *Play, language and stories* (pp. 129–146). Norwood, NJ: Ablex.

Ewing, J., & Eddowes, E. A. (1994). Sand play in the primary classroom. *Dimensions of Early Childhood, 22*(4), 24–25.

Fabricus, W. V. & Cavalier, L. (1989). The role of causal theories about memory in young children's memory strategy choices. *Child Development, 60,* 298–308.

Faggella, K. & Horowitz, J. (1990). Different child, different style. *Instructor, 100,* 49–54.

Fagot, B. I., Hagan, R., Leinbach, M. D., & Kronsberg, S., (1985). Differential reactions to assertive and communicative acts of toddler boys and girls. *Child Development, 56,* 1499–1505.

Fantini, M. D., & Russo, J. B. (1980). Parenting in a pluralistic society: Toward a policy of options and choices. In M. D. Fantini & R. Cardenas (Eds.), *Parenting in a multicultural society* (pp. 271–280). New York: Longman.

Farnham-Diggory, S. (1990). *Schooling.* Cambridge, MA: Harvard University Press.

Farnsworth, M., Schweinhart, L. J., & Berrueta-Clement, J. R. (1985). Preschool intervention, school success and delinquency in a high-risk sample of youth. *American Educational Research Journal, 22,* 445–464.

Farver, J. A. M. (1992). Communicating shared meaning in social pretend play. *Early Childhood Research Quarterly, 7,* 501–516.

Fathers' role in child care undergoing 'modest but meaningful' changes. (1984). *Growing Child Research Review, 3* (3), 1.

Fenson, L., Cameron, M. S., & Kennedy, M. (1988). Role of perceptual and conceptual similarity in category matching at age two years. *Child Development, 59,* 897–907.

Ferguson, C. A. (1977). Baby talk as a simplified register. In C. E. Snow & C. E. Ferguson (Eds.), *Talking to children* (pp. 209–235). Cambridge, England: Cambridge University Press.

Fernald, A. (1993). Approval and disapproval: Infant responsiveness to vocal affect in familiar and unfamiliar languages. *Child Development, 64,* 657–674.

Fernald, A. (1989). Intonation and communicative intent in mothers' speech to infants: Is the melody the message? *Child Development, 60,* 1497–1510.

Field, T., Gewirtz, J. L., Cohen, D., Garcia, R., Greenberg, R., & Collins, K. (1984). Leave-takings and reunions of infants, toddlers, preschoolers, and their parents. *Child Development, 55,* 628–635.

Fincham, F. D., Hokoda, A., & Sanders, R., Jr. (1989). Learned helplessness, test anxiety, and academic achievement: A longitudinal analysis. *Child Development, 60,* 138–145.

Fitzgerald, L. M. & Goncu, A. (1993). Parent involvement in urban early childhood education: A Vygotskian approach. In S. Reifel (Ed.), *Advances in early education and day care: Perspectives on developmentally appropriate practice* (pp. 197–212). Greenwich, CT: JAI Press.

Flaste, R. (1976). Temperament's role: Infants she studied are grown now. In S. White (Ed.) *Human development in today's world* (pp. 80–81). Boston: Little-Brown. Reprinted from the New York Times Magazine, 1975.

Flavell, J. H., Green, F. L., & Flavell, E. R. (1993). Children's understanding of the stream of consciousness. *Child Development, 64,* 387–398.

Flavell, J. H., Speer, J. R., Green, F. L., & August, D. L. (1981). *The development of comprehension monitoring and knowledge about communication.* Monographs of the Society for Research in Child Development, 46, (5, Serial No. 192).

Fleege, P. O., Charlesworth, R., Burts, D. C., & Hart, C. H. (1992). Stress begins in kindergarten: A look at behavior during standardized testing. *Journal of Research in Childhood Education, 7*(1), 20–26.

Fleege, P. O., & Charlesworth, R. (1993). "Teacher, Why am I failing? I know the answers": The effects of developmentally inappropriate assessment. In R. Donmoyer & K. Kos (Eds.), *At-risk students: Portraits, policies, programs, and practices* (219–228). Albany, NY: SUNY Press.

Fleege, P. O. (1990). Factors that impede successful mainstreaming: An ethnographic study. Unpublished manuscript.

Flinchum, B. M. (1975). *Motor development in early childhood*. St. Louis, MO: Mosby.

Foerster, L. M. & Little Soldier, D. (1978). Learning centers for young Native American. *Young Children, 33* (3), 53–57.

Fogel, A. (1980). Expressing affection and love to young children. *Dimensions, 8*(2), 39–44.

Footlick, J. K. (1990). What happened to the family? *Newsweek*, special edition.

Ford, S. A. (1993). The facilitator's role in children's play. *Young Children, 48*(6), 66–73.

Forman, G. & Kaden, M. (1987). Research on science education for young children. In C. Seefeldt (Ed.), *The early childhood curriculum: A review of current research* (pp. 141–164). New York: Teachers College Press.

Fraiberg, S. (1977). How a baby learns to love. In P. Cantor (Ed.), *Understanding a child's world*. New York: McGraw-Hill. (Reprinted from Redbook, May 1971, pp. 123–133).

Fraiberg, S. (1959). *The magic years*. New York: Charles Scribner's Sons.

Frede, E., & Barnett, W. S. (1992). Developmentally appropriate public school preschool: A study of implementation of the High/Scope curriculum and its effects on disadvantaged children's skills in first grade. *Early Childhood Research Quarterly, 7*, 483–500.

Freedle, R. & Lewis, M. (1977). Prelinguistic conversations. In M. Lewis & L. A. Rosenblum (Eds.), *Interaction, conversation and the development of language* (pp. 157–185). New York: John Wiley.

Freedman, D. G. (1982). Ethnic differences in babies. In J. K. Gardner (Ed.), *Readings in developmental psychology* (pp. 110–118). Boston: Little, Brown.

French, L. A., Lucariello, J., Seidman, S., & Nelson, K. (1985). The influence of discourse content and context on preschoolers' use of language. In L. Galda & A. D. Pellegrini (Eds.), *Play, language and stories* (pp. 1–28). Norwood, NJ: Ablex.

Freyberg, J. T. (1975). Hold high the cardboard sword. *Psychology Today, 8*, 63–64.

Friedman, W. J., & Laycock, F. (1989). Children's analog and digital clock knowledge. *Child Development, 60*, 357–371.

Friedman, W. J. (1990). Children's representations of the patterns of daily activities. *Child Development, 61*, 1399–1412.

Friedrich, L. K., & Stein, A. H. (1973). Aggressive and prosocial behavior of preschool children. *Monographs of the Society for Research in Child Development, 38* (4, Serial No. 151).

Frodi, A., Bridges, L., & Grolnick, W. (1985). Correlates of mastery-related behavior: A short-term longitudinal study of infants in their second year. *Child Development, 56*, 1291–1298.

Fromberg, D. P. (1987). Play. In C. Seefeldt (Ed.), *The early childhood curriculum: Reviews of current research* (pp. 35–74). New York: Teachers College Press.

Frost, J. L. (1992). *Play and playscapes*. Albany, NY: Delmar.

Furrow, D. (1984). Social and private speech at two years. *Child Development, 55*, 355–362.

Galda, L. (1984). Narrative competence: Play, story telling, and story comprehension. In A. Pellegrini & T. Yawkey (Eds.), *The development of oral and written language in social context* (pp. 105–118). Norwood, NJ: Ablex.

Galinsky, E., Shubilla, L., Willer, B., Levine, J. & Daniel, J. (1994). National Institute. State and community planning for early childhood systems. *Young Children, 49*(2), 54–57.

Gall, S. N. & Jones, E. (1990). Cognitive-motivational influences on the task-related help-seeking behavior of black children. *Child Development, 61*, 581–589.

Gallagher, J. J., & Ramsbotham, A. (1977). Early childhood programs for the gifted. *Educational Horizons, 56*, 44.

Gallas, K. (1994). *The languages of learning: How children talk, write, dance, draw, and sing their understanding of the world*. New York: Teachers College Press.

Gandini, L. (1993). Fundamentals of the Reggio Emilia approach to early childhood education. *Young Children, 49*(1), 4–8.

Garber, H. L. & Slater, M. (1983). Assessment of the culturally different preschooler. In K. D. Paget & B. A. Bracken (Eds.) *The psychoeducational assessment of preschool children* (pp. 443–471). New York: Grune & Stratton.

Garcia, E. E. (1986). Bilingual development and the education of bilingual children during early childhood. In B. Spodek (Eds.), *Today's kindergarten* (pp. 15–31). New York: Teachers College Press.

Gardner, H. & Winner, E. (1979). The child is father of the metaphor. *Psychology Today, 12*, 81–91.

Gardner, H. (1983). *Frames of mind: Theory of multiple intelligences*. New York: Basic Books.

Gardner, H. (1984). Assessing intelligences: A comment on 'Testing intelligence without IQ tests'. *Phi Delta Kappan, 65*, 699–700.

Gardner, H. (1982). *Developmental psychology: An introduction*. Boston: Little, Brown.

Gardner, H., & Hatch, T. (1989). Multiple intelligences go to school: Educational implications of the theory of multiple intelligences. *Educational Researcher, 18*(8), 4–9.

Gardner, H. (1993). *Multiple intelligences: The theory in practice*. New York: Basic Books.

Gardner, H. (1992). *The unschooled mind*. New York: Basic Books.

Garshelis, J. A., & McConnell, S. R. (1993). Comparison of family needs assessed by mothers, individual professionals, and interdisciplinary teams. *Journal of Early Intervention, 16*, 36–49.

Garvey, C. (1990). *Play*, Enlarged edition. Cambridge, MA: Harvard University Press.

Gelfer, J. I., & Perkins, P. G. (1992). Constructing student portfolios: A process and product that fosters communication with families. *Day Care and Early Education, 20* (2), 9–13.

Gelman, D. (1990). A is for apple, P is for shrink. *Newsweek, 116* (26), 64–66.

Gelman, D. (1982). Preschool thought. In J. K. Gardner (Ed.), *Readings in developmental psychology* (pp. 188–195). Boston, Little, Brown.

Genishi, C. (1987). Acquiring oral language and communicative competence. In C. Seefeldt (Ed.), *The early childhood curriculum: A review of current research* (pp. 75–106).

Genishi, C. & Dyson, A. H. (1984). *Language assessment in the early years*. Norwood, NJ: Ablex.

Genishi, C., Dyson, A. H., & Fassler, R. (1994). Language and diversity in early childhood: Whose voices are appropriate? In B. L. Mallory & R. S. New (Eds.), *Diversity and developmentally appropriate practices* (pp. 250–268). New York: Teachers College Press.

Gesell, A., Ilg, F., Ames, L. B., & Rodell, J. (1974). *Infant and child in the culture of today* (rev. ed.). New York: Harper and Row.

Gestwicki, C. (1992). *Home, school, and community relations: A guide to working with parents*. Albany, NY: Delmar.

Ginsburg, H. P. (1980). Children's surprising knowledge of arithmetic. *Arithmetic Teacher*, September, 42–44.

Ginsburg, H. P., Lopez, L., Chung, Y. E., Netley, R., Chao-Yuan, C., McCarthy, C., Cordero, M., Blake, I., Song, M., Baroody, A., & Jaegers, R. (1989, April). *Early mathematical thinking: Role of social class, racial, and cultural influences*. Presentation at the biennial meeting of the Society for Research in Child Development, Kansas City, MO.

Ginsburg, H. P. & Opper, S. (1979). *Piaget's theory of intellectual development, 2nd ed*. Englewood Cliffs, NJ: Prentice-Hall.

Glascott, K. (1994). A problem of theory for early childhood professionals. *Childhood Education, 70*, 131–132.

Goals 2000: Educate America Act. (1994). *Phi Delta Kappa Legislative Newsletter, 3*(3), 1.

Godwin, L. J., Groves, M. M., & Horm-Wingerd, D. M. (1993). "Don't leave me": Separation distress in infants, toddlers, and parents. *Day Care and Early Education, 20* (3), 13–17.

Goffin, S. G. (1994). *Curriculum models and early childhood education*. New York: Merrill/Macmillan.

Goffin, S. G., & Lombardi, J. (1988). Speaking out: Early childhood advocacy. Washington, DC: National Association for the Education of Young Children.

Goldberg, S. (1983). Parent-infant bonding: Another look. *Child Development, 54*, 1355–1382.

Goldhaber, J. & Smith, D. (1993). Infants and toddlers at play: Looking for meaning. *Day Care and Early Education, 20* (3), 9–12.

Goldman, R. L. (1993). Early education special education: Sexual abuse of young children with special needs—Are they safe in day care? *Day Care and Early Education, 20*(4), 37–38.

Gonzales-Mena, J. (1993). *The child in the family and the community*. New York: Merrill/Macmillan.

Gonzales-Mena, J. (1992). Taking a culturally sensitive approach in infant-toddler programs. *Young Children, 47* (2), 4–9.

Goodman, E. (1991, January 11). Let's treat people as well as banks. *Baton Rouge, LA, Morning Advocate*, 8B.

Goodman, Y. M. (1985). Kidwatching: Observing children in the classroom. In A. Jaggar & M. T. Smith-Burke (Eds.), *Observing the language learner* (pp. 9–18). Newark, DE: International Reading Association and Urbana, IL: National Council of Teachers of English.

Goossens, F. A. & Van IJzendoorn, M. H. (1990). Quality of infants' attachments to professional caregivers: Relation to infant-parent attachment and day-care characteristics. *Child Development, 61*, 832–837.

Gootman, M. E. (1993). Reaching and teaching abused children. *Childhood Education, 70*, 15–19.

Gopnik, A. & Meltzoff, A. N. (1992). Categorizing and naming: Basic-level sorting in eighteen-month-olds and its relation to language. *Child Development, 63*, 1091–1103.

Gordon, I. J. (1976). Parenting, teaching, and child development. *Young Children, 31* (3), 173–183.

Gottman, J. M. (1983). How children become friends. *Monographs of the Society for Research in Child Development, 48*(3, Serial No. 201).

Gould, S. J. (1982). Racist arguments and IQ. In J. K. Gardner (Ed.), *Readings in developmental psychology* (2nd. Ed.) (pp. 233–235). Boston: Little-Brown.

Gozali, E., & Crase, S. J. (1991, April). *Academic stress among school age children and early adolescents in the United States and Indonesia*. Paper presented at the meeting of the Society for Research in Child Development, Seattle, WA.

Grace, C., & Shores, E. F. (1992). *The portfolio and its use*. Little Rock, AR: Southern Early Childhood Association.

Graham, S. (1994). Motivation in African-Americans. *Re-

view of Educational Research, 64, 55–118.

Graham, S. (1993/94). Reviews of research: Are slanted manuscript alphabets superior to the traditional manuscript alphabet? *Childhood Education, 70,* 91–95.

Granger, R. C. (1976). The nonstandard speaking child: Myths past and present. *Young Children, 31* (6), 478–485.

Grantham-McGregor, S., Powell, C., Walker, S., Chang, S., & Fletcher, P. (1994). The long-term follow-up of severely malnourished children who participated in an intervention program. *Child Development, 65,* 428–439.

Gratz, R. & Boulton, P. (1993). Taking care of kids: A director's concerns about environmental hazards. *Day Care and Early Education, 21* (2), 29–31.

Graue, M. E., & Shepard, L. A. (1989). Predictive validity of the Gesell School Readiness Tests. *Early Childhood Research Quarterly, 4,* 303–315.

Guidelines for appropriate curriculum content and assessment in programs serving children ages 3 through 8. (1991). *Young Children, 46*(3), 21–38.

Graue, M. E. (1992). Meanings of readiness and the kindergarten experience. In S. Kessler & B. B. Swadener (Eds.), *Reconceptualizing the early childhood curriculum* (pp. 62–92). New York: Teachers College Press.

Greenberg, P. (1992a). Why not academic preschool? Part 2. Autocracy of democracy in the classroom? *Young Children, 47*(3), 54–64.

Greenberg, P. (1992b). Ideas that work with young children. How to institute some simple democratic practices pertaining to respect, rights, responsibilities, and roots in any classroom (Without losing your leadership position). *Young Children, 47*(5), 10–17.

Greer, D., & Potts, R. (1982). The effects of television commercial form and commercial placement on children's social behavior and attention. *Child Development, 53,* 611–619.

Grieve, R., Tumner, W. E., & Pratt, C. (1983). Language awareness in children. In M. Donaldson, R. Grieve, & C. Pratt (Eds.), *Early childhood development and education.* Oxford, England: Blackwell.

Growing Child (1973). 22 North Second Street, Lafayette, IN 47902.

Gully, B. (1988). The role of peers in the social development of infants. *Dimensions, 16* (4), 20, 26.

Gully, S. B. (1982). The relationship of infant stimulation to cognitive development. *Childhood Education, 58,* 247–252.

Gutierrez, J. & Sameroff, A. (1990). Determinants of complexity in Mexican-American and Anglo-American mothers' conceptions of child development. *Child Development, 61,* 384–394.

Gutierrez, J., Sameroff, A., & Karrer, B. M. (1988). Acculturation and SES effects on Mexican-American parents' concepts of development. *Child Development,* 59, 250–255.

Guttman, M. & Frederiksend, C. H. (1985). Preschool children's narratives: Linking story comprehension, production and play discourse. In L. Galda & A. D. Pellegrini (eds.), *Play, language and stories.* (pp. 99–128). Norwood, NJ: Ablex.

Gylys, B. A. (1971). *A comparison of cultural influences upon medical behavior: Low income group vs. middle income group.* Unpublished masters project, University of Toledo.

Hale, J. (1981). Black children: Their roots, culture, and learning styles. *Young Children, 36* (2), 37–50.

Hale, J. (1978). Cultural influences on learning styles of Afro-American children. In L. Morris (Ed.), *Extracting learning styles from social/cultural diversity* (pp. 7–28). Southwest Teacher Corps Network.

Hale-Benson, J. (1990). Visions for Children: African-American early childhood education program. *Early Childhood Research Quarterly, 5,* 199–213.

Haley, G. L. (1982, March). *Creative response styles: The effects of socioeconomic status and problem solving training.* Paper presented at the American Educational Research Association, New York City.

Halliday, M. A. K. (1979). One child's protolanguage. In M. Bullowa (Ed.), *Before speech: The beginnings of interpersonal communication* (pp. 171–190). Cambridge, England: Cambridge University Press.

Halliday, M. A. K. (1975). *Learning how to mean: Explorations in the development of language.* London, England: Edward Arnold.

Halverson, L. E. (1971). The significance of motor development. In G. Engstrom (Ed.), *The significance of the young child's motor development* (pp. 17–33). Washington, DC: National Association for the Education of Young Children.

Harbin, G. L., Gallagher, J. J., & Terry, D. V. (1991). Defining the eligible population: policy issues and challenges. *Journal of Early Intervention, 15,* 13–20.

Harris, T. (1994). The snack shop: Block play in a primary classroom. *Dimensions of Early Childhood, 22*(4), 22–23.

Harrison, A. O., Wilson, M. N., Pine, C. J., Chan, S. Q., & Buriel, R. (1990). Family ecologies of minority children. *Child Development, 61,* 347–362.

Harste, J. C., Woodward, V. A., & Burke, C. L. (1984). *Language stories and literacy lessons.* Portsmouth, NH: Heinemann.

Hart, C. H., DeWolf, D. M., & Burts, D. C. (1992). Linkages among preschoolers' playground behavior, outcome expectations, and parental disciplinary strategies. *Early Education and Development, 3,* 265–283.

Hart, C. H., DeWolf, D. M., Wozniak, P., & Burts, D. C. (1992). Maternal and paternal disciplinary styles: Relations with preschoolers' playground behavioral orientations and peer status. *Child Development, 63,* 879–892.

Hart, C. H., Ladd, G. W., & Burleson, B. R. (1990). Children's expectations of the outcomes of social strategies: Relations with sociometric status and maternal discipline styles. *Child Development, 61*, 127–137.

Hart, C. H., McGee, L. M., & Hernandez, S. (1993). Themes in the peer relations literature: Correspondence to outdoor peer interactions portrayed in children's storybooks. In C. H. Hart (Ed.), *Children on playgrounds: Research perspectives and applications*, 371–416. Albany, NY: SUNY Press.

Hart, C. H. (Ed.). (1993). *Children on playgrounds: Research perspectives and applications*. Albany, NY: SUNY Press.

Hartman, K. (1977). How do I teach in a future shocked world? *Young Children, 32*(3), 32–36.

Hartup, W. W. (1978). Peer interaction and the behavioral development of the individual child. In J. K. Gardner (Ed.), *Readings in developmental psychology*. New York: Little-Brown.

Hartup, W. W., Glazer, J. A., & Charlesworth, R. (1967). Peer reinforcement and sociometric status. *Child Development, 38*, 10017–10024.

Hartup, W. W., Laursen, B., & Stewart, M. I. (1988). Conflict and friendship relations of young children. *Child Development, 59*, 1590–1600.

Hartup, W. W., & Moore, S. G. (1990). Early peer relations: Developmental significance and prognostic implications. *Early Childhood Research Quarterly, 5*, 1–17.

Hartup, W. W. (1991). Having friends, making friends, and keeping friends: Relationships in educational contexts. *Early Report, 19*(1), 1–2.

Harvey, J. (1977). Special program needs of the culturally diverse child. *Exceptional Children, 43*, 158–179.

Harwood, R. L. & Miller, J. G. (1989, April). *Perceptions of attachment: A comparison of Anglo and Puerto Rican mothers*. Presented at the biennial meeting of the Society for Research in Child Development, Kansas City, MO.

Hatch, T. C., & Gardner, H. (1986). From testing intelligence to assessing competencies: A pluralistic view of intellect. *Roeper Review, 8*(3), 147–150.

Hatch, J. A. (1990, April). *Unsuccessful social adjustment patterns in young children*. Presentation at the meeting of the American Educational Research Association, Boston, MA.

Haugland, S. W., & Shade, D. D. (1990). *Developmental evaluations of software for young children*. Albany, NY: Delmar.

Haugland, S. (1992). Computers and young children: Maintaining an anti-bias curriculum. *Day Care and Early Education, 20*(2).

Haugland, S. (1993). Computers and young children: The outstanding developmental software. *Day Care and Early Education, 21*(2).

Haugland, S. (1994). Computers and young children: Selecting software that facilitates developmental gains. *Day Care and Early Education, 21*(4).

Hay, D. F., Murray, P., Cecire, S., & Nash, A. (1985). Social learning of social behavior in early life. *Child Development, 56*, 43–57.

Health clinics in schools. (1990, Winter). *Child Health Talk*, pp. 6–7.

Heath, S. B. (1985). Narrative play in second language learning. In L. Galda & A. D. Pellegrini (Eds.), *Play, language and stories* (pp. 147–166). Norwood, NJ: Ablex.

Heath, S. B. (1982). Questioning at home and at school: A comparative study. In G. Spindler (Ed.), *Doing the ethnography of schooling* (pp. 102–131). New York: Holt, Rinehart, & Winston.

Heath, S. B. (1980). The function and uses of literacy. *Journal of Communication, 30*, 123–133.

Heath, S. B. (1983). *Ways with words*. New York: Cambridge University Press.

Heineke, C. M., Diskin, S. D., Ramsey-Klee, D. M., & Given, K. (1983). Pre-birth parent characteristics and family development in the first year of life. *Child Development, 54*, 194–208.

Hellmich, N. (1993, March 24). Arnold asks kids to shape up. *USA Today*, 5D.

Hendrick, J. (1992). Where does it all begin? Teaching the principles of democracy in the early years. *Young Children, 47*(3), 51–53.

Henkens-Matzke, A., & Abbott, D. A. (1990). Game playing: A method for reducing young children's fear of medical procedures. *Early Childhood Research Quarterly, 5*, 19–26.

Henninger, M. L. (1994). Planning for outdoor play. *Young Children, 49*(4), 10–15.

Henninger, M. L. (1993/94). Enriching the outdoor play experience. *Childhood Education, 70*, 87–90.

Henry, T. (1990, September 2). Schools unprepared for 'crack' babies. *Baton Rouge, LA, Morning Advocate*, 1D.

Herman, J. F., Kolker, R. G., & Shaw, M. L. (1982). Effects of motor activity on children's intentional and incidental memory for spatial locations. *Child Development, 53*, 239–244.

Hess, R. D., Holloway, S. D., Dickson, W. P., & Price, G. G. (1984). Maternal variables as predictors of children's school readiness and later achievement in vocabulary and mathematics in sixth grade. *Child Development, 55*, 1902–1912.

Hess, R. D. & McDivett, T. M. (1984). Some cognitive consequences of maternal intervention techniques: A longitudinal study. *Child Development, 55*, 2017–2030.

Hestenes, L. L., Kontos, S., and Bryan, Y. (1993). Children's emotional expression in child care centers varying in quality. *Early Childhood Research Quarterly, 8*, 295–308.

Hignett, W. F. (1988). Food for thought. Infant/toddler day care, yes; BUT we'd better make it good. *Young Chil-*

dren, 44 (1), 32–33.

Hildreth, G. (1936). Developmental sequences in name writing. *Child Development, 7,* 291–302.

Hilliard, A. G., III. (1994). How diversity matters. *Kappa Delta Pi Record, 30,* 114.

Hilliard, A. G., III. (1989). Teachers and cultural styles in a pluralistic society. *NEA Today, 7* (6), 65–69.

Hilliard, A. G. & Vaughn-Scott, M. (1982). The quest for the "minority" child. In S. G. Moore & C. R. Cooper (Eds.), *The young child: Reviews of research* (Vol. 3, pp. 175–189). Washington, DC: National Association for the Education of Young Children.

Hilliard, A. G., III (1980). Cultural diversity and special education. *Exceptional Children, 46,* 587.

Hinitz, B. F. (1987). Social studies in early childhood education. In C. Seefeldt (Ed.), *The early childhood curriculum: A review of current research* (pp. 237–256). New York: Teachers College Press.

Hirshberg, L. M. & Svejda, M. (1990). When infants look to their parents: I. Infants' social referencing of mothers compared to fathers. *Child Development, 61,* 1175–1186.

Hitz, R. & Driscoll, A. (1988). Praise or encouragement? New insights into praise: Implications for early childhood teachers. *Young Children, 43* (5), 6–13.

Hodges, W. L., & Sheehan, R. (1978). Follow Through as ten years of experimentation: What have we learned? *Young Children, 34*(1), 4–14.

Hoffman, S. J. (1985). Play and acquisition of literacy. *Quarterly Newsletter of the Laboratory of Comparative Human Cognition, 7,* 89–95.

Hoffman, L. W. (1984). Maternal employment and the young child. In M. Perlmutter (Ed.), *Parent-child interactions and parent-child relation in child development* (pp. 101–127). Hillsdale, NJ: Erlbaum.

Hoffner, C. (1991, April). *Children's strategies for coping with upsetting events.* Paper presented at the meeting of the Society for Research in Child Development, Seattle, WA.

Hoge, R. D. (1988). Issues in the definition and measurement of the giftedness construct. *Educational Researcher, 17*(7), 12–16.

Holden, G. W. & West, M. J. (1989). Proximate regulation by mothers: A demonstration of how differing styles affect young children's behavior. *Child Development, 60,* 64–69.

Holliday, B. G. (1985). Towards a model of teacher-child transactional processes affecting black children's academic achievement. In M. B. Spencer, G. K. Brookings, & W. R. Allen (Eds.), *Beginnings: The social and affective development of black children* (pp. 117–130). Hillsdale, NJ: Erlbaum.

Holloway, S. D. (1988). Concepts of ability and effort in Japan and the United States. *Review of Educational Research, 58* (3), 327–345.

Holmes, J. G. (1993). Teachers, parents, and children as writing role models. *Dimensions of Early Childhood, 21*(3), 12–14.

Honig, A. S. (1993). Mental health for babies: What do theory and research tell us? *Young Children, 48* (3), 69–76.

Honig, A. S. (1993). Toilet learning. *Day Care and Early Education, 21* (1), 6–9.

Honig, A. S. (1989). Quality infant/toddler caregiving: Are there magic recipes? *Young Children, 44* (4), 4–10.

Honig, A. S. (1986). Emerging issues in early childhood education, Part I. *Day Care and Early Education, 13* (3), 6–11.

Honig, A. S. (1985a). Compliance, control, and discipline (Part 1). *Young Children, 40* (2), 50–58.

Honig, A. S. (1985b). Compliance, control, and discipline (Part 2). *Young Children, 40* (3), 47–52.

Honig, A. S. (1984). Developmental effects on children of pregnant adolescents. *Day Care and Early Education, 12* (1), 36–42.

Honig, A. S. (1982). Infant-mother communication. *Young Children, 37* (3), 52–62.

Honig, A. S. (1981). Recent infancy research. In B. Weissbourd & J. S. Musick (Eds.) *Infants: Their social environments* (pp. 5–46). Washington, DC: National Association for the Education of Young Children.

Honig, A. S. & DiPerna, C. (1985). Peer relations of infants and toddlers. *Day Care and Early Education, 10* (3), 36–39.

Honig, A. S. & Lansburgh, T. W. (1990). The tasks of early childhood—Part I: The will to try. *Day Care and Early Education, 18* (2), 4–10.

Honig, A. S. (1986). Stress and coping in children, Part I. *Young Children, 41*(4), 50–63.

Honig, A. S. (1988). Humor development in young children. *Young Children, 43*(4), 60–73.

Honig, A. S. (1983). Sex role socialization in early childhood. *Young Children, 38*(6), 57–70.

Honig, A. S. (1983). Television and young children. *Young Children, 38*(4), 63–76.

Hoot, J. (1986). Computers in early childhood education. In J. Hoot (Ed.), *Computers in early childhood education* (pp. 1–5). Englewood Cliffs, NJ: Prentice-Hall.

Horner, T. M. (1980). Two methods of studying stranger reactivity in infants: A review. *Journal of Child Psychology & Psychiatry, 21,* 203–219.

Hornik, R. & Gunnar, M. R. (1988). A descriptive analysis of infant social referencing. *Child Development, 59,* 626–634.

Horowitz, F. D. (1989). Nature-nurture. In M. R. Gunnar & E. Thelen (Eds.) *Systems and development: The Minnesota symposium on child psychology,* (Vol. 22) (pp. 211–218). Hillsdale, NJ: Erlbaum.

Horowitz, F. D. (1984). The psycho-biology of parent-offspring relations in high-risk situations. In L. P. Lipsitt & C. Rovee-Collier (Eds.) *Advances in infancy research* (Vol. 3) (pp. 1–22). Norwood, NJ: Ablex.

Horowitz, F. D. (1982). The first two years of life: Factors related to thriving. In S. G. Moore & C. R. Cooper (Eds.) *The young child: Reviews of research* (Vol. 3) (pp. 15–34). Washington, DC: National Association for the Education of Young Children.

Howard, G. R. (1993). Whites in multicultural education: Rethinking our role. *Phi Delta Kappan, 75*, 36–41.

Howes, C. (1989). Research in review: Infant child care. *Young Children, 44* (6), 24–28.

Howes, C. (1985). Sharing fantasy: Social pretend play in toddlers. *Child Development, 56*, 1253–1258.

Howes, C., Hamilton, C. E., & Matheson, C. C. (1994). Children's relationships with peers: Differential associations with aspects of the teacher-child relationship. *Child Development, 65*, 253–263.

Howes, C. & Olenich, M. (1986). Family and child care influences on toddlers' compliance. *Child Development, 57*, 202–216.

Howes, C., Unger, O., Seidner, L. B. (1989). Social pretend play in toddlers: Parallels with social play and with solitary pretend. *Child Development, 60*, 77–84.

Howes, C., & Wu, F. (1990). Peer interactions and friendships in an ethnically diverse school setting. *Child Development, 61*, 537–541.

Hrncir, E. J., & Eisenhart, C. E. (1991). Use with caution: The "At-risk" label. *Young Children, 46*(2), 23–27.

Hurlock, E. B. (1978). *Child Development, 6th ed.* New York: McGraw-Hill.

Huyett, B. (1994). Early childhood special education. Involving the special needs child in learning centers. *Day Care and Early Education, 21*(4), 43–44.

Hyland, C. R. (1989). What we know about the fastest growing minority population: Hispanic Americans. *Educational Horizons, 67*, 131–135.

Hymes, J. L., Jr. (1990). *The year in review: A look at 1989.* Washington, DC: National Association for the Education of Young Children.

Hyson, M. C., Hirsh-Pasek, K., Rescorla, L., Cone, J., & Martell-Boinske, L. (1989). *Building the scaffold: Parents' involvement in young children's learning.* Unpublished manuscript, University of Delaware.

Hyson, M. C. (1979). Lobster on the sidewalk. In L. Adams & B. Garlick (Eds.), *Ideas that work with young children* (Vol. 2, pp. 183–185). Washington, DC: National Association for the Education of Young Children.

Hyson, M. C., Whitehead, L. C., & Prudoe, C. M. (1988). Influences on attitudes towards physical affection between adults and children. *Early Childhood Research Quarterly, 3*, 55–75.

Inagaki, K. (1992). Piagetian and post-Piagetian conceptions of development and their implications for science education in early childhood. *Early Childhood Research Quarterly, 7*, 115–133.

Infants and children at risk: A symposium report. (1992). *Early Report, 20* (2).

Irvine, J. J. (1990). Transforming teaching for the twenty-first century. *Educational Horizons, 69* (1), 16–21.

Isbell, R. T. & Raines, S. C. (1991). Young children's oral language production in three types of play centers. *Journal of Research in Childhood Education, 5*, 140–146.

Isenberg, J. P., & Jalongo, M. R. (1993). *Creative expression and play in the early childhood curriculum.* New York: Merrill/Macmillan.

Jackson, J. F. (1993). Human behavioral genetics, Scarr's theory, and her views on interventions: A critical review and commentary on their implications for African-American children. *Child Development, 64*, 1318–1332.

Jackson, C. L., & Sacks, A. (1994, April/May). Minority gifted: Not so minor. *Pi Lambda Theta Newsletter, 38*(6), 8.

Jacobs, J. H. (1990). Child mental health: Service system and policy issues. *Social Policy Report*, Society for Research in Child Development, 4 (2).

Jacobson, S. W., Fein, G., Jacobson, J. L., Schwartz, P. M., & Dowler, J. K. (1985). The effect of intrauterine PCB exposure on visual recognition memory. *Child Development, 56*, 853–860.

Jalongo, M. R. (1990). The child's right to expressive arts: Nurturing the imagination as well as the intellect. *Childhood Education, 66*, 195–201.

Jalongo, M. R. (1989). Career education. *Childhood Education, 66*, 108–115.

Jalongo, M. R. (1983). Using crisis-oriented books with young children. *Young Children, 39*(2), 64–74.

Jalongo, M. R. (1984). Imaginary companions in children's life and literature. *Childhood Education, 60*, 166–171.

Javernick, E. (1988). Johnny's not jumping: Can we help obese children? *Young Children, 43* (2), 18–23.

Jennings, C. & Terry, G. (1990). Children's stories: A natural path to teaching thinking. *Dimensions, 18* (2), 5–8.

Jensen, A. R. (1985). Compensatory education and the theory of intelligence. *Phi Delta Kappan, 66*, 554–558.

Jensen, M. A., & Chevalier, Z. W. (1990). *Issues and advocacy in early childhood education.* Boston: Allyn & Bacon.

Johnson, R. T. (1990). Reviews of research: The videobased setting as a context for learning story information. *Childhood Education, 66*, 168–171.

Jones, E. & Derman-Sparks, L. (1992). Meeting the challenge of diversity. *Young Children, 47* (2), 12–17.

Jones, J. (1990, July 3). Low-tech birthing centers gaining acceptance in high-tech medical world. *Baton Rouge, LA, Morning Advocate*, 11A. Reprinted from the Los Angeles Times.

Joos, S. K., Pollitt, E., Mueller, W. H., & Albright, D. L. (1983). The Bacon Chow study: Maternal nutritional supplementation and infant behavioral development. *Child Development, 54*, 669–676.

Julius, A. K. (1978). Focus on movement: Practice and theory. *Young Children, 34* (1), 19–26.

Kagan, S. L. (1990). Readiness 2000: Rethinking rhetoric

and responsibility. *Phi Delta Kappan, 72,* 272–279.

Kaha, C. W. (1990). Learning environments for the twenty-first century. *Educational Horizons, 69*(1), 45–49.

Kamii, C. (1986). Cognitive learning and development. In B. Spodek (Ed.) *Today's kindergarten* (pp. 67–90). New York: Teachers College Press.

Kamii, C. (Ed.) (1990). *Achievement testing in the early grades: The games grown-ups play.* Washington, DC: National Association for the Education of Young Children.

Kamii, C. (1984). Obedience is not enough. *Young Children, 39*(4), 11–14.

Kamii, C. (1984). Autonomy: The aim of education envisioned by Piaget. *Phi Delta Kappan, 65,* 410–415.

Kamii, C. (1985). Leading primary education towards excellence—Beyond worksheets and drill. *Young Children, 40*(6), 3–9.

Kantor, R., Elgas, P. M., & Fernie, D. (1993). Cultural knowledge and social competence within a preschool peer-culture group. *Early Childhood Research Quarterly, 8,* 125–148.

Kantrowitz, B. (1990, special issue). High school homeroom. *Newsweek,* 50–54.

Kantrowitz, B. with Crandall, R. (1990, August 20). A vital aid for preemies. *Newsweek,* 70.

Kappa Delta Pi Record. (1992). *Celebrating diversity.* (Special issue), 29 (1).

Karnes, M. B., & Schwedel, A. M. (1983). Assessment of preschool giftedness. In Paget, K. D., & Bracken, B. A. (Eds.), *The psychoeducational assessment of preschool children* (pp. 473–507). New York: Grune & Stratton.

Karnes, M. B., & Johnson, L. J. (1989). Training for staff, parents, and volunteers working with gifted young children, especially those with disabilities and from low-income homes. *Young Children, 44*(3), 49–56.

Katz, L. G. (1994). From our president: Misguided intentions in drug-abuse prevention. *Young Children, 49* (3), 2–3.

Katz, L. G. (1993). Student motivation and dispositions. *ERIC/EECE Newsletter, 5* (1), 1–2.

Katz, L. G. (1993). Self-esteem in early childhood programs. *ERIC/EECE Newsletter, 5*(2), 1–2. Adapted from Lillian G. Katz, *Distinctions between self-esteem and narcissism: Implications for practice.* Urbana, IL: ERIC/EECE.

Kendall, E. D. (1983). Child care and disease: What is the link? *Young Children, 38* (5), 68–77.

Keniston, K. (1979). Children and politics? *Forum,* Spring/Summer, 10–11.

Kermoian, R. & Campos, J. J. (1988). Locomotor experience: A facilitator of spatial cognitive development. *Child Development, 59,* 908–917.

Kessler, S. (1989). Boys' girls' effect on the kindergarten curriculum. *Early Childhood Research Quarterly, 4,* 479–503.

Kessler, S. (1992). The social context of early childhood curriculum. In S. Kessler & B. B. Swadener, Eds., *Reconceptualizing the early childhood curriculum: Beginning the dialogue* (pp. 21–42).

Kilgo, J., Holder-Brown, L., Johnson, L. J., & Cook, M. J. (1988). An examination of the effect of tactile-kinesthetic stimulation on the development of preterm infants. *Journal of the Division of Early Childhood, 12,* 320–327.

Kim, Y., & Stevens, J. H., Jr. (1987). The socialization of prosocial behavior in children. *Childhood Education, 63,* 200–206.

King, M. L. (1985). Language and language learning for child watchers. In A. Jaggar & M. T. Smith-Burke (Eds.), *Observing the language learner* (pp. 19–38). Newark, DE: International Reading Association and Urbana, IL: National Council of Teachers of English.

King, N. J., & Ollendick, T. H. (1989). Children's anxiety and phobic disorders in school settings: Classification, assessment, and intervention issues. *Review of Educational Research, 59,* 431–470.

King, J. A. (1994). Meeting the needs of at-risk students: A cost analysis of three models. *Educational evaluation and policy analysis, 16,* 1–20.

King, N. R. (1992). The impact of context on the play of young children. In S. Kessler & B. B. Swadener, Eds., *Reconceptualizing the early childhood curriculum.* New York: Teachers College Press.

Kinsman, C. A., & Berk, L. E. (1979). Joining the block and housekeeping areas: Changes in play and social behavior. *Young Children, 34*(1), 66–75.

Kirp, D. L. & Epstein, S. (1989). *AIDS in America's school houses: Learning the hard lessons.* Phi Delta Kappan, 70, 584–593.

Kitano, M. K. (1983). Early education for Asian-American children. In O. N. Saracho & B. Spodek (Eds.), *Understanding the multicultural experience in early childhood education* (pp. 45–66). Washington, DC: National Association for the Education of Young Children.

Kitano, M. K. (1980). Early education for Asian-American children. *Young Children, 35*(2), 17–26.

Kitano, M. (1982). Young gifted children: Strategies for preschool teachers. *Young Children, 37*(4), 14–24.

Kitano, M. K. (1989). The K-3 teacher's role in recognizing and supporting young gifted children. *Young Children, 44*(3), 57–63.

Klahr, D. (1989, April). Information processing approaches to cognitive development. Presented at the biennial meeting of the Society for Research in Child Development, Kansas City, MO. Condensation of a paper in R. Vast (Ed.) (1989). *Annals of child development* (Vol. 6). Greenwich, CT: JAI Press.

Klein, D. (1979). Rx for pediatric patients. *Young Children, 34*(1), 13–19.

Knight, D., & Wadsworth, D. (1993). Physically challenged students: Inclusion classrooms. *Childhood Education,*

69, 211–215.

Knutson, J. (1993). Comment: Diversity in American schools—Past and present. *Educational Horizons, 72*, 114.

Koenig, G. (1986). *Observation drawing*. Unpublished manuscript, Louisiana State University, College of Education.

Kohlberg, L. (1968). The child as a moral philosopher. *Psychology Today, 2*, 25–30.

Kohlberg, L., & Lickona, T. (1990). Moral discussion and the class meeting. In R. DeVries & L. Kohlberg, *Constructivist early education: Overview and comparison with other programs* (pp. 143–181). Washington, DC: National Association for the Education of Young Children. (Original work published in 1987).

Kohlberg, L., & Selman, R. (1972). *First things: Values: A strategy for teaching values* [Filmstrip kit]. Guidance associates.

Kohler, P., Chapman, S., & Smith, G. (1994). Transition procedures for preschool children. *Dimensions of Early Childhood, 22*(3), 26–27.

Kohler, F. W., Strain, P. S., Maretsky, S., & DeCesare, L. (1990). Promoting positive and supportive interactions between preschoolers: An analysis of group-oriented contingencies. *Journal of Early Intervention, 14* 327–341.

Koralek, D. G., Colker, L. J., & Dodge, D. T. (1993). *What, why, and how of high quality early childhood education: A guide for on-site supervision*. Washington, DC: National Association for the Education of Young Children.

Korner, A. F., Zeanah, C. H., Linden, J., Berkowitz, R. I., Kraemer, H. C., & Kostelnik, M. J., Stein, L. C., Whiren, A. P., & Soderman, A. K. (1993). *Guiding children's social development* (2nd ed.). Albany, NY: Delmar.

Kostelnik, M. J., & Whiren, A. P. (1986). Living with he-man: Managing superhero fantasy play. *Young Children, 41*(4), 3–9.

Kramer, L., & Schaefer-Hernan, P. (1991, April). *What's real in children's fantasy play?* Presented at the meeting of the Society for Research in Child Development, Seattle, WA.

Krauss, M. W., Upshur, C. C., Shonkoff, J. P., & Hauser-Cram, P. (1993). The impact of parent groups on mothers of infants with disabilities. *Journal of Early Intervention, 16* (4), 8–20.

Krechevsky, M. (1991). Project Spectrum: An innovative assessment alternative. *Educational Leadership, 48*(5), 43–48.

Krogh, S. L., & Lamme, L. L. (1983). Learning to share: How literature can help. *Childhood Education, 59*, 188–192.

Kuebli, J. (1994). Research in review: Young children's understanding of everyday emotions. *Young Children, 49*(3), 36–47.

Ladd, G. W. (1990). Having friends, keeping friends, mak-ing friends, and being liked by peers in the classroom: Predictions of children's early school adjustment? *Child Development, 61*, 1081–1100.

Ladd, G. W., & Price, J. (1993). Playstyles of peer-accepted and peer-rejected children on the playground. In C. H. Hart (Ed.), *Children on playgrounds: Research perspectives and applications* (pp. 130–161). Albany, NY: SUNY Press.

LaFreniere, P., Strayer, F. F., & Gauthier, R. (1984). The emergence of same-sex affiliative preferences among preschool peers: A developmental/ethological perspective. *Child Development, 55*, 1958–1965.

Lally, J. R., Provence, S., Szanton, E., & Weissbourd, B. (1987). Developmentally appropriate care for children from birth to age 3. In S. Bredekamp (Ed.), *Developmentally appropriate practice in early childhood programs serving children from birth through age 8* (pp. 17–46). Washington, DC: National Association for the Education of Young Children.

Lamb, M. E., & Sagi, A. (Eds.) (1983). *Fatherhood and family policy*. Hillsdale, NJ: Erlbaum.

Lamme, L. L. (1979). Handwriting in early childhood curriculum. *Young Children, 35* (1), 20–27.

Landau, S., & McAninch, C. (1993). Research in review. Young children with attention deficits. *Young Children, 48*(4), 49–58.

Lane, S. & Bergan, J. R. (1988). *Effects of instructional variables on language ability of preschool children*. American Educational Research Journal, 25, 271–283.

Languis, M., Sanders, T., & Tipps, S. (1980). *Brain and learning*. Washington, DC: National Association for the Education of Young Children.

Laosa, L. M. (1977). Socialization, education, and continuity: The importance of sociocultural context. *Young Children, 32* (5), 21–27.

LaPoint, S. A., Boutte, G. S., Swick, K. J., & Brown, M. H. (1993). Cultural sensitivity: How important is it for effective home visits? *Day Care and Early Education, 20* (4), 11–14.

Larkin, J. M. (1993). Rethinking basic skills instruction with urban students. *The Educational Forum, 57*, 413–419.

Larrick, N. (1977). Children of television. In *Readings in early childhood education 77/78* (pp. 43–46). Guilford, CT: Dushkin. [Reprinted from *Teacher Magazine*, September 1975]

Laupa, M. (1994). Who's in charge? Preschool children's concept of authority. *Early Childhood Research Quarterly, 9*, 1–18.

Lauritzen, P. (1992). Facilitating integrated teaching and learning in the preschool setting: A process approach. *Early Childhood Research Quarterly, 7*, 531–550.

Lawton, J. T. & Fowell, N. (1989). A description of teacher and child language in two preschool programs. *Early Childhood Research Quarterly, 4*, 407–432.

Lazar, I., Darlington, R. B., Murray, H., Royce, J., & Snipper, A. (1982). Lasting effects of early education: A report from the consortium for longitudinal studies. *Monographs of the Society for Research in Child Development, 47*(2–3, Serial No. 195).

Leboyer, F. (1976). *Birth without violence.* New York: Knopf.

Lee, P. C. (1989). Is the young child egocentric or sociocentric? *Teacher's College Record, 90*, 375–391.

Lee, C. (1977). *The growth and development of children, 2nd ed.*, New York: Longman.

Lee, C. L. & Bates, J. E. (1985). Mother-child interaction at age two years and perceived difficult temperament. *Child Development, 56*, 1314–1325.

Lefrancois, G. R. (1992). *Of children: An introduction to child development, 7th ed.* Belmont, CA: Wadsworth.

Legerstee, M., Corter, C., & Kienapple, K. (1990). Hand, arm, and facial actions of young infants to a social and nonsocial stimulus. *Child Development, 61*, 774–784.

Leister, C., Koonce, D., & Nisbet, S. (1993). Best practices for preschool programs: An update on inclusive settings. *Day Care and Early Education, 21*(2), 9–12.

Lesser, G. S. (1979). Stop picking on Big Bird. *Psychology Today, 12*, 57–60.

Lester, B. M., Hoffman, J., & Brazelton, T. B. (1985). The rhythmic structure of mother-infant interaction in term and preterm infants. *Child Development, 56*, 15–27.

Levin, S. R. (1982). Preschooler's awareness of television advertising. *Child Development, 53*, 933–937.

Levin, D. E., & Carlsson-Paige, N. (1994). Developmentally appropriate television: Putting children first. *Young Children, 49*(5), 38–44.

Levitt, E., & Cohen, S. (1976). Educating parents of children with special needs—Approaches and issues. *Young Children, 31*(4), 263–272.

Lewis, M. (1977). The busy, purposeful world of a baby. *Psychology Today, 10*, 53–56.

Lewis, M. & Feiring, C. (1989). Infant, mother, mother-infant interaction behavior and subsequent attachment. *Child Development, 60*, 831–837.

Lewis, M., Sullivan, M. W., Stanger, C., & Weiss, M. (1989). Self development and self-conscience emotions. *Child Development, 60*, 146–156.

Lewis, M., & Michalson, L. (1983). *Children's emotions and moods.* New York: Plenum.

Lichenstein, R. (1990). Psychometric characteristics and appropriate use of the Gesell School Readiness Screening Rest: *Early Childhood Research Quarterly, 5*, 359–378.

Lillard, A. S. (1993a). Pretend play skills and the child's theory of mind. *Child Development, 64*, 348–371.

Lillard, A. S. (1993b). Young children's conceptualization of pretense: Action or mental representational state? *Child Development, 64*, 372–386.

Lin, C. C., & Fu, V. R. (1990). A comparison of child-rearing practices among Chinese, Immigrant Chinese, and Caucasian-American parents. *Child Development, 61*, 429–433.

Little Soldier, L. (1992). Working with Native American children. *Young Children, 47* (6), 15–21.

Lively, V., & Lively, E. (1991). *Sexual development of young children.* Albany, NY: Delmar.

Lockman, J. J. & Thelen, E. (1993). Developmental biodynamics: Brain, body, behavior connections. *Child Development, 64*, 953–959.

Lomax, E. M. R. (1978). *Science and patterns of childrearing.* San Francisco, Freeman.

Lomax, R., & McGee, L. M. (1987). Young children's concepts about print and reading: Toward a model of word reading acquisition. *Reading Research Quarterly, 22*, 237–256.

Lombardi, J. (1991, March). *New directions for early childhood advocacy.* Presentation of the meeting of the Southern Association On Children Under Six. Atlanta, GA.

Lombardi, J., & Goffin, S. G. (1986). IDEAS! Child advocacy at the state level: Strategies for success. *Dimensions, 14*(2), 15–18.

Louv, R. (1994). The crisis of the absent father. In K. M. Paciorek & J. H. Munro (Eds.), *Early Childhood Education 94/95* (pp. 49–51). Guilford, CT: Dushkin. Originally published in R. Louv. (1993). *Father love.* Pocket Books.

Lovinger, S. L. (1972). Sociodramatic play and language development. *Psychology in the Schools, 11*, 313–320.

Lucy, J. A. (1988). The role of language in the development of representation: A comparison of the views of Piaget and Vygotsky. *The Quarterly Newsletter of the Laboratory of Human Cognition, 10*, 99–103.

Luster, T., & McAdoo, H. P. (1991, April). *Factors related to the achievement and adjustment of young black children.* Paper presented at the meeting of the Society for Research in Child Development, Seattle, WA.

Lyle, J., & Hoffman, H. (1971). Explorations in patterns of television viewing by preschool age children. In J. P. Murray, et al. (Eds.), *Television and social behavior (vol. 4), Television in day-to-day life: Patterns of use.* Washington, DC: U.S. Government Printing Office.

Lyon, T. D. & Flavell, J. H. (1993). Young children's understanding of forgetting over time. *Child Development, 64*, 789–800.

Lyons-Ruth, K., Alpern, L., & Repacholi, B. (1993). Disorganized infant attachment classification and maternal psychosocial problems as predictors of hostile-aggressive behavior in the preschool classroom. *Child Development, 64*, 572–585.

Maccoby, E. E., & Jacklin, C. N. (1985, April). *Gender segregation in nursery school: Predictors and outcomes.* Presentation at the Society for Research in Child Development, Toronto, Ontario, Canada.

Maccoby, E. E., & Zellner, M. (1970). *Experiments in pri-*

mary education: Aspects of project Follow-Through. New York: Harcourt Brace Jovanovich. NAEYC Position Statement School on School Readiness. (1990). *Young Children, 46*(1), 21–23.

MacDonald, K. (1992). A time and place for everything: A discrete systems perspective on the role of children's rough-and-tumble play in educational settings. *Early Education and Development, 3,* 334–335.

Madaus, G. F. (1988). The influence of testing on the curriculum. In L. N. Tanner (Ed.), *Critical issues in curriculum* (pp. 83–121). Chicago, IL: National Society for the Study of Education distributed by the University of Chicago Press.

Maguire, J. (1990). *Hopscotch, hangman, hot potato, & hahaha: A rulebook of children's games.* New York: Prentice-Hall.

Maier, H. W. (1978). *Three theories of child development* (3rd. ed.). New York: Harper & Row.

Majority of intellectually gifted not reading before kindergarten (1980). *Today's Child, 28,* 7.

Malaguzzi, L. (1993). For an education based on relationships. *Young Children, 49*(1), 9–12.

Malatesta, C. Z., Culver, C., Tesman, J. R., & Shepard, B. (1989). *The development of emotion expression during the first two years of life.* Monographs of the Society for Research in Child Development, 54 (1-2, Serial No. 219).

Malina, R. M. (1982). Motor development in the early years. In S. G. Moore & K. Cooper (Eds.) *The young child: Reviews of Research* (Vol. 3, pp. 211–229). Washington, DC: National Association for the Education of Young Children.

Mallory, B. L., & New, R. S. (Eds.) (1994). *Diversity & developmentally appropriate practices.* New York: Teachers College Press.

Mangelsdorf, S., Gunnar, M., Kestenbaum, R., Lang, S., & Andreas, D. (1990). Infant-proneness-to distress temperament, maternal personality, and mother-infant attachment: Associations and goodness of fit. *Child Development, 61,* 820–831.

Mann, J. (1991). Public policy report. Congress remembers the children—finally. *Young Children, 46*(2), 81.

Many parents say they'd stay at home. (1990, August 13). *Baton Rouge, LA Morning Advocate,* 2D.

Marazon, R. E. (1994). *Mr. Rogers' Neighborhood*—As affective staff development for teachers of young children: A story of conflict, conversion, conviction, and celebration. *Young Children, 49*(5), 34–37.

Marotz, L. R., Cross, M. Z., & Rush, J. M. (1993). *Health, safety, and nutrition for the young child, 3rd edition.* Albany, NY: Delmar Publishers.

Martinez, M. A. (1987). Dialogues among children and between children and their mothers. *Child Development, 58,* 1035–1043.

Marvin, C., & Mirenda, P. (1993). Home literacy experiences of preschoolers enrolled in Head Start and special education programs. *Journal of Early Interven-*

tion, *17*, 351–367.

Matheny, A. P., Jr., Wilson, R. S., & Nuss, S. M. (1984). Toddler temperament: Stability across settings and over ages. *Child Development, 55,* 1200–1211.

Maxim, G. W. (1980). *The very young: Guiding children from infancy through the early years.* Belmont, CA: Wadsworth.

McAdoo, J. L. (1979). Father-child interaction patterns and self-esteem in black preschool children. *Young Children, 34*(1), 46–53.

McBride B. A., & Mills, G. (1993). A comparison of mother and father involvement with their preschool age children. *Early Childhood Research Quarterly, 8,* 457–478.

McBride, B. A. (1989). Interaction, accessibility, and responsibility: A view of father involvement and how to encourage it. *Young Children, 44* (5), 13–19.

McBride, S. L., Brotherson, M. J., Joanning, H., Whiddon, D., & Demmitt, A. (1993). Implementation of family centered services: Perceptions of families and professionals. *Journal of Early Intervention, 17,* 414–430.

McBride, B. A., & McBride, R. J. (1993). Parent education and support programs for fathers. *Childhood Education, 70,* 4–9.

McBride-Chang, C., & Jacklin, C. N. (1993). Early play arousal, sex-typed play, and activity level as precursors to later rough-and-tumble play. *Early Education and Development, 4,* 99–108.

McCall, R. B., Parke, R. D., & Kavanaugh, R. D. (1977). Imitation of live and televised models by children one to three years of age. *Monographs of the Society for Research in Child Development, 42,* (5, Serial No. 173).

McConnell, A., & Hardman, M. (1988). A synthesis of "Best Practice" guidelines for early childhood services. *Journal of the Division of Early Childhood, 12,* 328–341.

McCormick, P. (1994). How kids survive trauma. In K. M. Paciorek & J. H. Munro (Eds.), *Early Childhood Education 94/95* (pp. 183–185). Guilford, CT: Dushkin.

McCoy, C. L., & Masters, J. C. (1985). The development of children's strategies for the social control of emotions. *Child Development, 56,* 1214–1222.

McCracken, J. B. (1993). *Valuing diversity: The primary years.* Washington, DC: National Association for the Education of Young Children.

McCune, L. (1989, April). *Toward an integrative theory of early language acquisition: Evidence from longitudinal trends in vocal behavior.* Presented at the biennial meeting of the Society for Research in Child Development, Kansas City, MO.

McGee, L. M., Charlesworth, R., Cheek, M., & Cheek, E. (1982). Metalinguistic knowledge: Another look at beginning reading. *Childhood Education, 59,* 123–127.

McGee, L. M. (1985). *Evaluation of East Baton Rouge, Louisiana, Preschool Program.* (Report to the State Department of Education). Louisiana State University.

McGee, L. M., & Richgels, D. J. (1990). *Literacy's beginnings: Supporting young readers and writers.* Boston: Allyn & Bacon.

McGee, L. M., Richgels, D., & Charlesworth, R. (1986). Emerging knowledge of written language: Learning to read and write. In S. J. Kilmer (Ed.), *Advances in early education and day care (Vol. IV)* (pp. 67–121). Greenwich, CT: JAI Press.

McGill-Franzen, A., & Allington, R. L. (1993). Flunk'em or get them classified: The contamination of primary grade accountability data. *Educational Researcher, 22*(1), 19–22.

McGlaughlin, B. N. & Morgan, N. L. (1981). Fine motor development. In M. Tudor (Ed.), *Child Development* (pp. 427–430). New York: McGraw-Hill.

McGonigel, M. J., Kaufman, R. K., & Johnson, B. H. (1991). A family-oriented process for the individualized family service plan. *Journal of Early Intervention, 15*, 46–56.

McGowan, R. J., & Johnson, D. L. (1984). The mother-child relationship and other antecedents of childhood intelligence: A causal analysis. *Child Development, 55*, 810–820.

McIntyre, E. (1990). Young children's reading strategies as they read self-selected books in school. *Early Childhood Research Quarterly, 5*, 265–277.

McLean, S. V. (1993). Learning from teachers' stories. *Childhood Education, 69*, 265–268.

McLoyd, V. (1990). The impact of economic hardship on black families and children: Psychological distress, parenting, and socioemotional development. *Child Development, 61*, 311–346.

McLoyd, V. C. (1983). The effects of the structure of play objects on the pretend play of low-income preschool children. *Child Development, 54*, 626–635.

McLoyd, V. C., Ray, S. A., & Etter-Lewis, G. (1985). Being and becoming: The interface of language and family role knowledge in the pretend play of young African girls. In L. Galda & A. D. Pellegrini (Eds.), *Play, language, and stories* (pp. 29–44). Norwood, NJ: Ablex.

McMackin, M. D. (1993). The parent's role in literacy development: Fostering reading strategies at home. *Childhood Education, 69*, 142–145.

McQueen, A. B. & Washington, V. (1988). Effect of intervention on the language facility of poor, black adolescent mothers and their preschool children. *Early Child Development and Care, 33*, 137–152.

Mead, D. E. (1976). *Six approaches to child rearing.* Provo, UT: Brigham Young University Press.

Meade, J. (1991). Tuning in, logging on. *Teacher Magazine, 2*(4), 29–31.

Meddin, B. J., & Rosen, A. (1986). Child abuse and neglect: Prevention and reporting. *Young Children, 41*(4), 26–30.

Meisels, S. J. (1987). Uses and abuses of developmental screening and school readiness testing. *Young Children, 42* (2), 4–6, 68–73.

Meisels, S. J. (1993). Remaking classroom assessment with the work sampling system. *Young Children, 48*(5), 34–40.

Meisels, S. J. (1994). Designing meaningful measurements for early childhood. In B. L. Mallory & R. S. New (Eds.), *Diversity and developmentally appropriate practices* (pp. 202–222). New York: Teachers College Press.

Meisels, S. J. (1991). Dimensions of early identification. *Journal of Early Intervention, 15*, 26–35.

Meltzoff, A. N. (1988). Infant imitation and memory: Nine-month-olds in immediate and deferred tests. *Child Development, 59*, 217–225.

Meltzoff, A. N. (1985). Immediate and deferred imitation in fourteen and twenty-four-month-old infants. *Child Development, 56*, 62–72.

Meltzoff, A. N. & Moore, M. K. (1983). Newborn infants imitate adult facial gestures. *Child Development, 54*, 702–709.

Meltzoff, A. N. (1988). Imitation of televised models by infants. *Child Development, 59*, 1221–1229.

Meyer, C. A., Klein, E. L., & Genishi, C. (1994). Peer relationships among four preschool second language learners in "Small Group Time." *Early Childhood Research Quarterly, 9*, 61–86.

Micheli, L. J. (1990, October 29). Children and sports. *Newsweek*, 12.

Michels, S., Pianta, R. C., & Reeve, R. E. (1993). Parent self-reports of discipline practices and child acting-out behaviors in kindergarten. *Early Education and Development, 4*, 139–144.

Miller, D. F. (1990). *Positive child guidance.* Albany, NY: Delmar Publishers.

Miller, L. B., & Bizzell, R. B. (1983). Long-term effects of four preschool programs: Sixth, seventh, and eighth grades. *Child Development, 54*, 727–741.

Miller, L. B. (1984). Long-term effects of four preschool programs: Ninth- and tenth-grade results. *Child Development, 55*, 1570–1589.

Miller, P. H. (1989). *Theories of developmental psychology* (2nd. ed.). New York: Freeman.

Mills, B. C., & Spooner, L. (1988). Preschool stress and the three R's. *Dimensions, 16*(2), 8–10.

Minoura, Y. (1993). Culture and personality reconsidered: Theory building from cases of Japanese children returning from the United States. *The Quarterly Newsletter of the Laboratory of Comparative Human Cognition, 15*, 63–71.

Mizokawa, D. T. & Ryckman, D. B. (1988, April). *Attributions of academic success and failure to effort or ability: A comparison of six Asian-American ethnic groups.* Presented at the annual meeting of the American Educational Research Association, New Orleans, LA.

Moll, L. C. (1990). Introduction. In L. C. Moll (Ed.), *Vygotsky and education: Instructional implications of sociohistorical psychology* (pp. 1–27). New York:

Basic Books.

Moll, L. C. (1990). *Vygotsky and education*. New York: Cambridge University Press.

Molnar, J., & Klein, T. (1991, April). *The developmental status of homeless preschoolers living in emergency shelters in New York City*. Paper presented at the meeting of the Society for Research in Child Development, Seattle, WA.

Monaghan, P. (1985, April). *The development of symbolic expression in preschool play and language*. Paper presented at the meeting of the American Educational Research Association, Chicago, IL.

Moore, S. G. (1978). Research in review: Child-child interactions of infants and toddlers. *Young Children, 33* (7), 64–69.

Moore, E. G. J. (1982). Language behavior in the test situation and the intelligence test achievement of transracially and traditionally adopted black children. In L. Feagans & D. C. Farran (Eds.), *The language of children reared in poverty* (pp. 141–162). New York: Academic Press.

Moore, E. G. J. (1985). Ethnicity as a variable in child development. In M. B. Spencer, G. K. Brookins, & W. R. Allen (Eds.), *Beginnings: The social and affective development of black children* (pp. 101–116). Hillsdale, NJ: Erlbaum.

Moore, S. G. (1985). Social effects of peers on curiosity. *Early Report, 12*(3), 1–2.

Moore, S. G. (1979). Social cognition: Knowing about others. *Young Children, 34*(3), 54–61.

Moore, S. G. (1977). The effects of television on the prosocial behavior of young children. *Young Children, 32*(5), 60–65.

Morrison, G. S. (1991). *Early childhood education today, 5th ed*. Columbus, OH: Merrill.

Morrow, R. D. (1989). What's in a name? In particular, a Southeast Asian name? *Young Children, 44* (6), 20–23.

Morrow, L. M. (1990). Preparing the classroom environment to promote literacy during play. *Early Childhood Research Quarterly, 5*, 537–554.

Mosley, J. G. (1992). *A comparison of language and graphic products of students from kindergarten classrooms differing in developmental appropriateness of instruction*. Unpublished doctoral dissertation, Louisiana State University, Baton Rouge.

Mothers raising mothers. (1986). *U.S. News and World Report*, March 17, 24–25.

Moyer, J. (1990). Who's creation is it anyway? *Childhood Education, 66*(3), 130–131.

Mukerji, R. (1977). Television and early childhood: Default or design? In B. Spodek (Ed.), *Teaching practices: Reexamining assumptions*. Washington, DC: National Association for the Education of Young Children.

Munroe, R. L. & Munroe, R. H. (1975). *Cross-cultural human development*. Monterey, CA: Brooks/Cole

Publishing.

Musatti, T. (1986). Early peer relations: The perspectives of Piaget and Vygotsky. In E. Mueller & C. Cooper (Eds.), *Process and outcome in peer relations* (pp. 25–53). New York: Academic Press.

Myers, H. F. (1975). Mental health and the black child. *Young Children, 34*, 25–31.

NAEYC (National Association for the Education of Young Children) & NAECS/SDE (National Association of Early Childhood Specialists in State Departments of Education). (1991). Guidelines for appropriate curriculum content and assessment in programs serving children ages 3 through 8. *Young Children, 46*(3), 21–38.

NAEYC position statement on violence in the lives of children. (1993). *Young Children, 48*(6), 80–84.

NAEYC Position Statement on Media Violence in Children's Lives. (1990). *Young Children, 45*(5), 18–21.

National Association of State Boards of Education. (1990). *Right from the start: The report of the NASBE task force on Early Childhood Education*. Alexandria, VA: Author.

National Association of Early Childhood Specialists in State Departments of Education. (1987). *Unacceptable trends in kindergarten entry and placement*. Unpublished paper.

National Association of Elementary School Principals. (1990). *Early Childhood Education and the Elementary School Principal*. Alexandria, VA: Author.

Necochea, J. & Cline, Z. (1993). Building capacity in the education of language minority students. *The Educational Forum, 57*, 402–412.

Nelson, C. A. & Horowitz, F. D. (1983). The perceptions of facial expressions and stimulus motion by two- and five-month-old infants using holographic stimuli. *Child Development, 54*, 868–877.

Nelson, K. (1982). Individual differences in language development: Implications for development and language. In J. K. Gardner (Ed.), *Readings in developmental psychology, 2nd ed*. Boston: Little, Brown.

Nelson, K. (1973). *Structure and strategy in learning to talk*. Monographs of the Society for Research in Child Development, 38 (1–2, Serial No. 38).

Nelson, K. E., Denninger, M. M., Bonvillian, J. D., Kaplan, B. J., & Baker, N. (1984). Maternal input adjustments and non-adjustments as related to children's linguistic advances and to language acquisition theories. In A. Pellegrini & T. Yawkey (Eds.), *The development of oral and written language in social contexts* (pp. 31–56). Norwood, NJ: Ablex.

Nelson, C. (1991). The capabilities of the human newborn. *Early Report, 18*(2), 1–2.

Nelson-Le Gall, S., & Jones, E. (1990). Cognitive-motivational influences on the task-related help-seeking behavior of black children. *Child Development, 61*, 581–589.

Neuman, S. B., & Roskos, K. (1993). Access to print for children of poverty: Differential effects of adult mediation and literacy-enriched play settings on environmental and functional print tasks. *American Educational Research Journal, 30*, 95–122.

New, R. S., & Mallory, B. L. (1994). Introduction: The ethics of inclusion. In B. L. Mallory & R. S. New (Eds.), *Diversity & developmentally appropriate practices* (pp. 1–13). New York: Teachers College Press.

New, R. S. (1994). Culture, child development, and developmentally appropriate practices: Teachers as collaborative researchers. In B. L. Mallory & R. S. New (Eds.), *Diversity and developmentally appropriate practices* (pp. 65–83). New York: Teachers College Press.

Newport, E. L., Gleitman, H., & Gleitman, L. R. (1977). Mother, I'd rather do it myself: Some effects and noneffects of maternal speech style. In C. E. Snow & C. A. Ferguson (Eds.), *Talking to children* (pp. 109–149). Cambridge, England: Cambridge University Press.

Newton, N. (1975). Putting the child back in childbirth. *Psychology Today, 9*, 24–25.

Nicolich, L. M. (1977). Beyond sensorimotor intelligence: Assessment of symbolic maturity through analysis of pretend play. *The Merrill-Palmer Quarterly, 23*, 89–99.

Nicolson, S., & Shipstead, S. G. (1994). *Through the looking glass: Observations in the early childhood classroom.* New York: Merrill/Macmillan. Ninio, A. & Rinott, N. (1988). Fathers' involvement in the care of their infants and their attributions of cognitive competence to infants. *Child Development, 59*, 652–663.

Nobels, W. W. (1977). Extended self: Rethinking the so-called Negro self-concept. In M. Coleman (Ed.), *Black children just keep on growing* (pp. 159–165). Washington, DC: National Black Child Development Institute.

Notar, E. (1989). Children and commercials. *Childhood Education, 66*, 66–67.

Nuru, N. H. (1980). Black English: Who be a winner? *Black Child Journal, 1*, 14–20.

Nuttall, D. (1993). Letters I never sent to my daughter's third grade teacher. *Young Children, 48*(6), 6–7.

O'Brien, M. & Dale, D. (1994). Family-centered services in the neonatal intensive care unit: A review of research. *Journal of Early Intervention, 18*, 78–90.

O'Neil, D. K. & Astington, J. (1990, April). *Young children's understanding of the role sensory experiences play in knowledge acquisition.* Presented at the annual meeting of the American Educational Research Association, Boston, MA.

Odom, S. L., & McConnell, S. R. (1991, April). *Comparison of interventions for promoting social competence of young children with disabilities.* Presented at the meeting of the Society for Research in Child Development, Seattle, WA.

Okagaki, L. & Sternberg, R. J. (1993). Parental beliefs and children's school performance. *Child Development, 64*, 36–56.

Oller, D. K. (1977). *Infant vocalization and the development of speech.* Paper presented at the University of Wisconsin Conference on Early Intervention with Infants and Young Children, Madison, WI.

Olweus, D. (1991). Bully/Victim problems among school children: Basic facts and effects of a school based intervention program. In D. J. Pepler & K. H. Rubin (Eds.) (1991). *The development and treatment of childhood aggression* (411–448). Hillsdale, NJ: Erlbaum.

Olweus, D. (1993). Bullies on the playground: The role of victimization. In C. H. Hart (Ed.), *Children on playgrounds* (85–128). Albany, NY: SUNY Press.

Ornstein, R. E. (1973). Right and left thinking. *Psychology Today, 6,* 87–92.

Osofsky, J. (1989, April). *Affective relationships in adolescent mothers and their infants.* Invited address at the biennial meeting of the Society for Research in Child Development, Kansas City, MO.

Oviatt, S. L. (1982). Inferring what words mean: Early development in infants' comprehension of common object names. *Child Development, 53*, 274–277.

Paguio, L. P. & Resurreccion, A. V. A. (1987). Children's food preferences: Development and influences. *Childhood Education, 62*, 296–300.

Palkovitz, R. (1985). Fathers' birth attendance, early contact, and extended contact with their newborns: A critical review. *Child Development, 56*, 392–406.

Pang, V. O. (1990). Asian-American children: A diverse population. *The Educational Forum, 55* (1), 49–66.

Parmelee, A. H., Jr. (1986). Children's illnesses: Their beneficial effect on behavioral development. *Child Development, 57*, 1–10.

Parry, A. (1993). Children surviving in a violent world—"Choosing non-violence". *Young Children, 48*(6), 13–15.

Parsons, A. S. (1988). IDEAS! Integrating special children into day care programs. *Dimensions, 16*(3), 15–18.

Parten, M. B. (1932). Social participation among preschool children. *Journal of Abnormal and Social Psychology, 27*, 243–269.

Passow, A. H. (1977). Fostering creativity in the gifted child. *Exceptional Children, 43*, 362.

Patterson, C. J., Kupersmidt, J. B., & Vaden, N. A. (1990). Income level, gender, ethnicity, and household composition as predictors of children's school-based competence. *Child Development, 61*, 485–494.

Patton, M. M., & Wortham, S. C. (1993). Transition classes, A growing concern. *Journal of Research in Childhood Education, 8*, 32–42.

Paul, R. (1989, April). *Profiles of toddlers with delayed ex-*

pressive language development. Presented at the biennial meeting of the Society for Research in Child Development, Kansas City, MO.

Pellegrini, A. D. (1991). *Applied child study*. Hillsdale, NJ: Erlbaum.

Pellegrini, A. D. (1984). The effects of classroom ecology on preschoolers' functional use of language. In A. Pellegrini & T. Yawkey (Eds.), *The development of oral and written language in social contexts* (pp. 129–144). Norwood, NJ: Ablex.

Pellegrini, A. D. & Perlmutter, J. C. (1988). Rough-and-tumble play on the elementary school playground. *Young Children, 43* (2), 14–17.

Pellegrini, A. D., Perlmutter, J. C., Galda, L., & Brody, G. H. (1990). Joint reading between black Head Start children and their mothers. *Child Development, 61*, 413–453.

Pellegrini, A. D. (1989). Elementary school children's rough-and-tumble-play. *Early Childhood Research Quarterly, 4*, 245–260.

Pellegrini, A. D., & Smith, P. K. (1993). School recess: Implications for education and development. *Review of Educational Research, 63*, 51–68.

Pellegrini, A. D. (1985). The relations between symbolic play and literate behavior: A review and critique of the empirical literature. *Review of Educational Research, 55*, 107–121.

Pena, S., French, J., & Doerann, J. (1990). Heroic fantasies: A cross-generational comparison of two children's television heroes. *Early Childhood Research Quarterly, 5*, 393–406.

Pepler, D., Corter, C., & Abramovitch, R. (1982). Social relations among children: Comparison of sibling and peer interaction. In K. H. Rubin & H. S. Ross (Eds.), *Peer relationships and social skills in childhood* (pp. 209–227). New York: Springer-Verlag.

Perez, S. A. (1994). Responding differently to diversity. *Childhood Education, 70*, 151–153.

Perlmutter, J. C., & Laminack, L. L. (1993). Sociodramatic play: A stage for practicing literacy. *Dimensions of Early Childhood, 21*(4), 13–16.

Perry, D. G. (1989, April). *Social learning theory*. Presentation at the biennial meeting of the Society for Research in Child Development, Kansas City, MO.

Persson-Blennow, I. & McNeil, T. F. (1980). Questionnaires for measurement of temperament in one- and two-year-old children: Development and standardization. *Journal of Child Psychology and Psychiatry, 21*, 37–46.

Peters, S., & Skrtic, T. (1988). Special Ed urges, "Look to us and what we've learned." *Holmes Group Forum, 2*(3), 5–6.

Peterson, C. C. (1974). *A child grows up*. Port Washington, NY: Alfred Publishing.

Pett, J. (1990). What is authentic evaluation? Common questions and answers. *FairTest Examiner, 4*, (1), 8–9.

Pezdek, K., & Hartman, E. F. (1983). Children's television viewing: Attention and comprehension of auditory versus visual information. *Child Development, 54*, 1015–1023.

Pflaum, S. W. (1986). *The development of language and reading in the young child, 3rd ed*. Columbus, OH: Merrill.

Phillips, C. B. (1994). The movement of African-American children through sociocultural contexts: A case of conflict resolution. In B. L. Mallory & R. S. New (Eds.), *Diversity and developmentally appropriate practices* (pp. 137–154).

Phillips, D., McCartney, K., Scarr, S., & Howes, C. (1990). Selective review of infant day care research: A cause for concern! In M. A. Jensen & Z. W. Chevalier (Eds.), *Issues and advocacy in early education* (pp. 190–195). Boston: Allyn & Bacon.

Phillips, D. A., Voran, M., Kisker, E., Howes, C., & Whitebook, M. (1994). Child care for children in poverty: Opportunity or inequity. *Child Development, 65*, 472–492.

Phillips, D., Lande, J., & Goldberg, M. (1990). The state of child care regulation: A comparative analysis. *Early Childhood Research Quarterly, 5*, 151–179.

Phillips, D. A., & Howes, C. (1987). Indicators of quality in child care: Review of research. In D. A. Phillips (Ed.), *Quality in child care: What does research tell us?* (pp. 1–20). Washington, DC: National Association for the Education of Young Children.

Phinney, J. S., & Rotheram, M. J. (Eds.) (1987). *Children's ethnic socialization*. Newbury Park, CA: Sage.

Physical fitness facts. (1988). *Young Children, 43* (2), 23.

Piaget, J. (1971). *Science of education and the psychology of the child*. New York: Viking Press.

Piaget, J. (1966). *The child's conception of physical causality*. Totowa, NJ: Littlefield-Adams.

Piaget, J. (1965). *The moral judgement of the child*. New York: The Free Press.

Pianta, R. C., Stroufe, L. A., & Egeland, B. (1989). Continuity and discontinuity in maternal sensitivity at 6, 24, and 42 months in a high-risk sample. *Child Development, 60*, 481–487.

Pine, G. J., & Hilliard, A. G., III. (1990). RX for racism: Imperatives for America's schools. *Phi Delta Kappan, 71*, 593–600.

Pines, M. (1979). Good smaritians at age two? *Psychology Today, 13*, 64–70.

Pinon, M. F., Huston, A. C., & Wright, J. C. (1989). Family ecology and child characteristics that predict young children's educational television viewing. *Child Development, 60*, 846–856.

Plomin, R. (1983). Developmental behavioral genetics. *Child Development, 54*, 253–259.

Plomin, R., DeFries, J. C., & Fulker, D. W. (1988). *Nature and nurture during infancy and early childhood*. New York: Cambridge University Press.

Plunkett, J. W., Cross, D. R., & Meisels, S. J. (1989). Temperament ratings by parents of preterm and full-term infants. *Early Childhood Research Quarterly, 4*, 317–330.

Poest, C. A., Williams, J. R., Witt, D. D., & Atwood, M. L. (1990). Challenge me to move: Large muscle development in young children. *Young Children, 45* (5), 4–10.

Poest, C. A., Williams, J. R., Witt, D. D., & Atwood, M. L. (1989). Physical activity patterns of preschool children. *Early Childhood Research Quarterly, 4*, 367–376.

Policy regarding nondiscriminatory evaluation. (1977). *Exceptional Children, 43*, 403.

Pollitt, E., Gorman, K. S., Engle, P. L., Martorell, R., & Rivera, J. *Early supplementary feeding and cognition.* Monograph of the Society for Research in Child Development, 58 (No. 7, Serial No. 235).

Pollitt, E., Mueller, W., & Leibel, R. L. (1982). The relation of growth to cognition in a well-nourished preschool population. *Child Development, 53*, 1157–1163.

Pontecorvo, C. & Orsolini, M. (1989). *Discussing and explaining a story in preschool.* Manuscript submitted for publication. *Preemies' IQ.* (1990, June). Stanford Observer, 23 (6), 23.

Portfolio News, Portfolio Assessment Clearinghouse, University of California, San Diego, Teacher Education Program, 9500 Gilman Drive–0700, LaJolla, CA 92093-0070.

Potts, R., & Henderson, J. (1991, April). *A content analysis of physical injuries in children's television programming.* Paper presented at the meeting of the Society for Research in Child Development, Seattle, WA.

Pratt, E. (1992, June 3). Can we save our black children? *The Advocate*, Baton Rouge, LA.

Price, D. W. W. & Goodman, G. S. (1990). Visiting the wizard: Children's memory for a recurring event. *Child Development, 61*, 664–680.

Price, G. (1982). Cognitive learning in early childhood: Mathematics, science, and social studies. In B. Spodek (Ed.), *Handbook of research in early childhood education* (pp. 264–294). New York: The Free Press.

Public policy alert. (1994, May 31). Changes proposed for Child Care Development Block Grant, At-risk, and AFDC-related child care program regulations.

Quaranta, M. A., Weiner, M., Robison, E., & Tainsh, P. (1992, May). *Collaboration for social support of children and families in public schools: Final report.* New York: Fordham University Graduate School of Education and Graduate School of Social Service.

Quisenberry, J. (1982). Television commercials' effects on young children. *Childhood Education, 58*, 316–322.

Radin, N. (1982). Primary care-giving and role sharing fathers. In M. E. Lamb (Ed.), *Non-traditional families: Parenting and child development* (pp. 173–204). Hillsdale, NJ: Erlbaum.

Radin, N., Oyserman, D., & Benn, R. (1989, April). *The influence of grandfathers on the young children of teen moth-*

ers. Presented at the biennial meeting of the Society for Research in Child Development, Kansas City, MO.

Raikes, H. (1993). Relationship duration in infant care: Time with a high ability teacher and infant-teacher attachment. *Early Childhood Research Quarterly, 8*, 309–325.

Raines, S. C. (1990). Representational competence: (Re)presenting experiences through words, actions, and images. *Childhood Education, 66*, 139–144.

Raines, S. C. (Ed.). (1995). *Whole language across the curriculum: Grades 1, 2, and 3.* New York: Teachers College Press.

Ramirez, J. D. (1989, April). *The role of extralinguistic context in egocentric speech production.* Paper presented at the meeting of the Society for Research in Child Development, Kansas City, MO.

Ramsey, P. G. (1982). Multicultural education in early childhood. *Young Children, 37* (2), 13–24.

Raspberry, W. (1989, October 19). U.S. infant-mortality rate shameful. *Baton Rouge Morning Advocate*, p. 17B.

Raspberry, W. (1989, October 20). Universal access prenatal care proposed. *Baton Rouge Morning Advocate.*

Raspberry, W. (1985, July 15). Too little 'lap time'. *Morning Advocate, Baton Rouge, LA.*

Raver, S. A. (1979). Preschool integration: Experiences from the classroom. *Teaching Exceptional Children, 12*, 22–26.

Recommendations for certification of early childhood special educators. (1989). *Journal of Early Intervention, 13*, 195–211.

Reed, S. (1983). Preschool computing. What's too young. *Family Computing, 1*(3), 55–68.

Reed, S., & Sautter, R. C. (1990). Children of poverty: The status of 12 million young Americans. *Phi Delta Kappan, 71*, K1–K12.

Reifel, S. (1984). Block construction: Children's developmental landmarks in representation of space. *Young Children, 40* (1), 61–67.

Rescorla, L. & Schwartz, E. (1989, April). *Outcome of toddlers with specific expressive language delay.* Presented at the biennial meeting of the Society for Research in Child Development, Kansas City, MO.

Restak, R. (1975). The danger of knowing too much. *Psychology Today, 9*, 21+.

Reutzel, D. R., & Hollingsworth, P. M. (1988). Whole language and the practitioner. *Academic Therapy, 23*, 405–416.

Rice, M., & Woodsmall, L. (1988). Lessons from television: Children's word learning when viewing. *Child Development, 59*, 420–429.

Richardson, R. C., & Evans, E. D. (1993). Empowering teachers to halt corporal punishment. *Kappa Delta Pi Record, 29*, 39–42.

Richgels, D. (1986a). Beginning first graders' "invented spelling" ability and their performance in functional classroom writing activities. *Early Childhood Re-*

search Quarterly, 1, 85–97.

Richgels, D. J. (1986b). An investigation of preschool and kindergarten children's spelling and reading abilities. *Journal of Research and Development in Education.*

Ricks, D. (1979). Making sense of experience to make sensible sounds. In M. Bullowa (Ed.), *Before speech: The beginnings of interpersonal communication* (pp. 245–268). Cambridge, England: Cambridge University Press.

Rieser, J. J. & Heiman, M. L. (1982). Spatial self-reference systems and shortest-route behavior in toddlers. *Child Development, 53*, 524–533.

Rinkel, P. (1992). Myths and stereotypes about long-term effects of prenatal alcohol and other drug exposure. *Early Report*, 20 (1), 2–3.

Rist, M. C. (1990, July). The shadow children: Preparing for the arrival of crack babies in school. *Phi Delta Kappa Research Bulletin*, (No. 9).

Roberts, M. (1988). School yard menace. *Psychology Today, 22*(2), 52–56.

Robinson, E. J. & Robinson, W. P. (1983). Ways of reacting to communication failure in relation to the development of the child's understanding about verbal communication. In M. Donaldson, R. Grieve, & C. Pratt (Eds.), *Early childhood development and education* (pp. 83–103). Oxford, England: Blackwell.

Robinson, S. L., & Gladstone, D. H. (1993). *Dimensions of early childhood, 22*(1), 23–25.

Roche, A. F. (Ed.) (1979). *Secular trends in human growth, maturation, and development.* Monographs of the Society for Research in Child Development, 44 (Nos. 3 & 4).

Rodning, C., Beckwith, L., & Howard, J. (1989). *Characteristics of attachment organization and play organization in prenatally drug exposed toddlers.* Manuscript submitted for publication.

Rodriguez, R. (1976). On becoming a Chicano. In S. White (Ed.), *Human development in today's world* (pp. 103–105). Boston: Little-Brown. (Originally published in *Saturday Review Magazine*, February 8, 1975).

Roe, K. (1990). Vocal interchange with mother and stranger as a function of infant age, sex, and parental education. *Early Childhood Research Quarterly, 5* (1), 135–145.

Roedel, W. C., Jackson, N. E., & Robinson, H. B. (1980). *Gifted young children.* New York: Teachers College Press.

Rogers, F., & Sharapan, H. B. (1991). Helping parents, teachers, and caregivers deal with children's concerns about war. *Young Children, 46*(3), 12–13.

Rogers, C. S., & Sawyers, J. K. (1988). *Play in the lives of children.* Washington, DC: National Association for the Education of Young Children.

Rogers, M. (1990). Nintendo and beyond. *Newsweek, 115*(25), 62–63.

Rogers, J. (1993). The inclusion revolution. *Phi Delta Kappa Research Report*, No. 11.

Rogoff, B. & Mosier, C. (1993). IV. Guided participation in San Pedro and Salt Lake. In B. Rogoff, J. Mistry, A. Goncu, & C. Mosier. *Guided participation in cultural activity by toddlers and caregivers.* Monograph of the Society for Research in Child Development (pp. 59–101), 58 (No. 8, Serial No. 236).

Roopnarine, J. L. & Johnson, J. E. (1993). *Approaches to early childhood education.* New York: Merrill/Macmillan.

Roopnarine, J. L., & Honig, A. S. (1985). The unpopular child. *Young Children, 40*(6), 59–64.

Rose, S. A. (1994). Relation between physical growth and information processing in infants born in India. *Child Development, 65*, 889–902.

Rose, S. A. (1983). Differential rates of visual information processing in full-term and preterm infants. *Child Development, 54*, 1189–1198.

Rose, S. A., Feldman, J. F., McCarton, C. M., & Wolfson, J. (1988). Information processing in seven-month-old infants as a function of risk status. *Child Development, 59*, 589–603.

Rose, D. F., & Smith, B. J. (1993). Public policy report. Preschool mainstreaming: Attitude barriers and strategies for addressing them. *Young Children, 48*(4), 59–62.

Rosen, C. E. (1974). The effects of sociodramatic play on problem-solving behavior among culturally disadvantaged preschool children. *Child Development, 45*, 920–927.

Rosenkoeter, L. I., & Rosenkoeter, S. E. (1991, April). *The child's appraisal of drug abuse and anti-drug TV spots.* Paper presented at the meeting of the Society for Research in Child Development, Seattle, WA.

Rosenkoetter, L. I. (1993, March). *Children's values and the television sitcom.* Paper presented at the biennial meeting of the Society for Research in Child Development, New Orleans, LA.

Rosow, L. V. (1994/95). How schools perpetuate illiteracy. In K. M. Paciorek & J. H. Munro (Eds.), *Early Childhood Education 94/95* (pp. 101–103). Guilford, CT: Dushkin. (Originally printed in *Educational Leadership, 49*(1), 41–44, 1991.)

Ross, H. S., Lollis, S. P., & Elliott, C. (1982). Toddler-peer communication. In K. H. Rubin & H. S. Ross (Eds.) *Peer relations and social skills in childhood* (pp. 73–98). New York: Springer-Verlag.

Rosser, P. L. (1977). Child development theory: Physiological development. In M. Coleman (Ed.), *Black children just keep on growing* (pp. 169–178). Washington, DC: Black Child Development Institute.

Rotherham-Baron, M. J., & Phinney, J. S. (1990). Patterns of social expectations among Black and Mexican-American children. *Child Development, 61*, 542–556.

Rovet, J. & Netley, C. (1983). The triple X chromosome syndrome in childhood: Recent empirical findings.

Child Development, 54 831–845.

Rozycki, E. G. (1993). From the trenches. Immigrants in the New America: Is it time to heat up the melting pot? *Educational Horizons, 71* 126–127.

Rubin, K. H. (1977). Play behaviors of young children. *Young Children, 32*(6), 16–24.

Rubin, K. H. (1982). Social and social-cognitive developmental characteristics of young isolate, normal, and sociable children. In K. H. Rubin & H. S. Ross (Eds.), *Peer relationships and social skills in childhood* (pp. 353–374). New York: Springer-Verlag.

Rubin, K. H. (1982). Nonsocial play in preschoolers: Necessary evil? *Child Development, 53*, 651–657.

Rubinstein, E. A. (1978). Television and the young viewer. *American Scientist, 66*, 685–693.

Ruble, D. N., Higgins, E. T., & Hartup, W. W. (1983). What's social about social-cognitive development? In E. T. Higgins, D. N. Ruble, & W. W. Hartup (Eds.), *Social cognition and social development* (pp. 3–12). New York: Cambridge University Press.

Ruff, H. A. (1986). Components of attention during infants' manipulative exploration. *Child Development, 57* 105–114.

Ruff, H. A., McCarton, C., Kurtzberg, D., & Vaughn, H. G., Jr. (1984). Preterm infants' manipulative exploration of objects. *Child Development, 55*, 1166–1173.

Rule, S., Innocenti, M. S., Coor, K. J., Bonem, M. K., & Stowitschek, J. J. (1989). Kindergartners' preacademic skills and mainstream teachers' knowledge: Implications for special educators. *Journal of Early Intervention, 13*, 212–220.

Ruopp, R. R. (1979). *Children at the center.* Cambridge, MA: Abt Books

Rust, F. C., & Williams, L. R. (1989). The care and education of young children: Expanding contexts, sharpening focus. *Teachers College Record, 90*, 334–336.

Ryan, F. J. (1993). The perils of multiculturalism: Schooling for the group. *Educational Horizons, 71*, 134–138.

Sachs, J., Goldman, J., Chaille, C. (1985). Narratives in preschoolers' sociodramatic play: The role of knowledge and communicative competence. In L. Galda & A. D. Pellegrini (Eds.), *Play, language and stories* (pp. 45–62). Norwood, NJ: Ablex.

Sachs, J., Goldman, J., & Chaille, C. (1984). Planning in pretend play: Using language to coordinate narrative development. In A. Pellegrini & T. Yawkey (Eds.), *The development of oral and written language in social contexts* (pp. 119–128). Norwood, NJ: Ablex.

Sagan, C., & Druyan, A. (1990, April 22). Is it possible to be pro-life and pro-choice? *Parade Magazine,* 4–8.

Saloman, G. (1977). Effects of encouraging mothers to co-observe "Sesame Street" with their five-year-olds. *Child Development, 48*, 1146–1151.

Saloman, G., Perkins, D. N., Globerson, T. (1991). Partners in cognition: Extending human intelligence with intelligent technologies. *Educational Researcher, 20*(3),

2–9.

Salyer, D. M. (1994). Noise or communication? Talking, writing and togetherness in one first grade class. *Young Children, 49*(4), 42–47.

Sameroff, A. J. & Seifer, R. (1983). Familial risk and child competency. *Child Development, 54*, 1254–1268.

Samuels, S. C. (1977). *Enhancing self concept in early childhood.* New York: Human Sciences Press.

Saracho, O. N. & Hancock, F. M. (1983). Mexican-American culture. In O. N. Saracho & B. Spodek (Eds.), *Understanding the multicultural experience in early childhood education* (pp. 3–16). Washington, DC: National Association for the Education of Young Children.

Sautter, R. C. (1994). An arts education school reform strategy. *Phi Delta Kappan, 75*, 432–437.

Sawin, D. B. (1981). Fathers' interactions with infants. In B. Weissbourd & J. S. Musick (Eds.), *Infants: Their social environments* (pp. 169–184). Washington, DC: National Association for the Education of Young Children.

Sawyer, W. E., & Sawyer, J. C. (1980). Preschool experiences and reading readiness skills: Predicting the most efficient reading instruction. *Educational Researcher, 9*(May).

Saxe, G. B., Guberman, S. R., & Gearhart, M. (1987). Social processes in early number development. Monographs of the Society for Research in *Child Development, 52,* (2, Serial No. 216).

Scarlett, W. G. (1981). On the development of make-believe. *Day Care and Early Education, 9*(2), 23–26.

Scarr, S. (1993). Biological and cultural diversity: The legacy of Darwin for development. *Child Development, 64*, 1333–1353.

Schacter, F. F., Kirshner, K., Klips, B., Friedricks, M., & Sanders, K. (1974). *Everyday preschool interpersonal speech usage: Methodological, developmental, and sociolinguistic studies.* Monographs of the Society for Research in Child Development, 39 (3, Serial No. 156).

Schacter, F. F. & Strage, A. A. (1982). Adults' talk and children's language development. In S. G. Moore & C. R. Cooper (Eds.), *The young child: Reviews of Research* (Vol. 3) (pp. 79–94). Washington, DC: National Association for the Education of Young Children.

Schaffer, R. (1977). *Mothering.* Cambridge, MA: Harvard University Press.

Schatzky, D., with Verrucci, L. (1994). Television, kids, and the real Danny Kaye. In K. M. Paciorek, & J. H. Munro (Eds.), *Early Childhood Education 94/94* (pp. 40–48). Guilford, CT: Dushkin. Originally published in *The World and I,* June 1992, 499–517, a publication of the Washington Times Corporation.

Scheibe, C. L., & Barber, T. (1991). Children's comprehension of anti-drug public service announcements on television. Paper presented at the biennial meeting of the Society for Research in Child Development, Seattle, WA.

Scheibe, C. L., & Grossman, S. (1993, March). *Parenting styles in prime-time television (1963–1991).* Paper presented at the biennial meeting of the Society for Research in Child Development, New Orleans, LA.

Schenck, L. Y. (1990). *Pregnant teens = GRADS.* Kappa Delta Pi Record, 26, 35–37.

Schetz, K. F., & Stremmel, A. J. (1994). Teacher-assisted computer implementation: A Vygotskian perspective. *Early Education and Development, 5,* 18–26.

Schickendanz, J. A. (1986). *More than ABC's: The early stages of reading and writing.* Washington, DC: National Association for the Education of Young Children.

Schmidt, D. (1985). Adult influences on curiosity in children. *Early Report, 12*(3), 2–3.

Schmidt, H. M. (1993). *Impact of teacher guidance strategies on children's interpersonal relations.* Unpublished masters thesis Louisiana State University, Baton Rouge, LA.

Schneider-Rosen, K. & Wenz-Gross, M. (1990). Patterns of compliance from eighteen to thirty months of age. *Child Development, 61,* 104–112. *Scholar questions conventional analyses of Chicano childrearing practices.* (1994, April). Stanford School of Education, 3.

Schorr, E. (1989). Early interventions aimed at reducing intergenerational disadvantage: The new social policy. *Teachers College Record, 90,* 362–374.

Schrader, C. T. (1990). Symbolic play as a curricular tool for early literacy development. *Early Childhood Research Quarterly, 5,* 79–103.

Schweinhart, L. J., & Weikart, D. P. (1985). Evidence that good early childhood programs work. *Phi Delta Kappan, 66,* 545–551.

Schweinhart, L. J. (1986). What do we know so far? A review of the Head Start synthesis project. *Young Children, 41*(2), 49–55.

Schweinhart, L. J., Weikart, D. P., & Larner, M. B. (1986). Consequences of three preschool curriculum models through age 15. *Early Childhood Research Quarterly, 1,* 15–46.

Schweinhart, L. J., Barnes, H. V., & Weikart, D. P. (1993). *Significant benefits: The High/Scope Perry Preschool study through age 27.* Ypsilanti, MI: High/Scope.

Schweinhart, L. J. (1993). Observing young children in action: The key to early childhood assessment. *Young Children, 48*(5), 29–33.

Scientists track down sex-determining gene. (1990, July 19). *Baton Rouge Morning Advocate,* p. 3A.

Scott-Little, M. C., & Holloway, S. D. (1992). Child care providers' reasoning about misbehaviors: Relation to classroom control strategies and professional training. *Early Childhood Research Quarterly, 7,* 595–606.

Sears, R. R., Maccoby, E., & Levin, H. (1957). *Patterns of child rearing.* Evanston, IL: Row, Peterson.

Sedlak, A. J. (1989, April). *National incidence of child abuse and neglect.* Paper presented at the meeting of the Society for Research in Child Development, Kansas City, MO.

Seefeldt, C. (1983). The new arrivals. *Childhood Education, 60,* 75–76.

Seefeldt, C. (1987). The visual arts. In C. Seefeldt (Ed.), *The early childhood curriculum: A review of current research* (pp. 183–210). New York: Teachers College Press.

Segal, M. & Adcock, D. (1976). *From one to two years.* Rolling Hills Estates, CA: B. L. Winch.

Semaj, L. T. (1985). Afrikanity, cognition and extended self-identity. In M. B. Spencer, G. K. Brookins, & W. R. Allen (Eds.), *Beginnings: The social and affective development of black children* (pp. 173–184). Hillsdale, NJ: Erlbaum.

Sera, M. D., Troyer, D., & Smith, L. B. (1988). What do two-year-olds know about the sizes of things? *Child Development, 59,* 1489–1496.

Serbin, L. A., Powlishta, K. K., & Gulko, J. (1993). The development of sex typing in middle childhood. *Monogr. of the Society for Research in Child Development, 58* (No. 2, Serial No. 232).

Serpell, R. (1994). Negotiating a fusion of horizons: A process view of cultural validation in developmental psychology. *Mind, Culture, and Activity, 1* (1 & 2), 43–68.

Sevigny, M. J. (1979, March). A look at the art of young children. In A. B. Johnson, D. J. Radeloff, J. Dermer, & E. Roemer (Eds.), *Young children internationally.* Proceedings of the Second Annual Early Childhood Conference, Bowling Green State University, Bowling Green, OH.

Sexton, D., Snyder, P., Sharpton, W. R., & Stricklin, S. (1993). Infants and toddlers with special needs and their families. *Childhood Education, 69,* 278–286.

Shade, D. D. (1993). Computers and young children: Peace of mind for teachers and parents—Fun for kids? *Day Care and Early Education, 20*(4).

Shade, D. D. (1994). Computers and young children: New frontiers in computer hardware and software *or* what computer should I buy? *Day Care and Early Education, 21*(3).

Shaffer, D. D. (1993). Making Native American lessons meaningful. *Childhood Education, 69,* 201–203.

Shapiro, L. (1990, May 28). Guns and dolls. *Newsweek,* 56–65.

Shapiro, A. (n.d.). Show'n tell—It's a window on their lives. In M. van Manen (Ed.), *Texts of teaching* (pp. 31–36), Human Sciences Research Project, 441 Education South, Faculty of Education, University of Alberta, Edmonton, Canada, T6G 2G5.

Shatz, M. & Gelman, R. (1973). *The development of communication skills: Modifications of the speech of young children as the function of listener.* Monographs of the Society for Research in Child Development, 38 (5, Serial No. 152).

Shavelson, R. J., Carey, N. B., & Webb, N. M. (1990). Indicators of science achievement: Options for a powerful policy instrument. *Phi Delta Kappan, 71,* 692–697.

Sheppard, W. G., Shank, S. B., & Wilson, D. (1973). *Teaching social behavior to young children.* Champaign, IL: Research Press.

Sherman, T. (1985). Categorization skills in infants. *Child Development, 56,* 1156–1573.

Shonkoff, J. P., & Meisels, S. J. (1991). Defining eligibility for services under PL 99–457. *Journal of Early Intervention, 1521–25.*

Siegal, M., & Storey, R. M. (1985). Day care and children's conceptions of moral and social rules. *Child Development, 56,* 1001–1008.

Siegal, M., & Cowen, J. (1984). Appraisal of intervention: The mother's versus the culprit's behavior as determinants of children's evaluations of discipline techniques. *Child Development, 55,* 1760–1766.

Siegler, R. S., & Richards, D. D. (1982). The development of intelligence. In R. J. Sternberg (Ed.), *Handbook of human intelligence* (pp. 901–974). New York: Cambridge University Press.

Signs of high-risk in the preschool child. (n.d.) Mimeographed from the Washburn Child Guidance Clinic, Minneapolis, MN.

Silvern, S. B., & McCary, J. C. (1986). Computers in the educational lives of children: Developmental issues. In J. Hoot (Ed.), *Computers in early childhood education* (pp. 6–21). Englewood Cliffs, NJ: Prentice-Hall.

Simmons, B., & Brewer, J. (1985). When parents of kindergartners ask, "Why?". *Childhood Education, 61,* 177–184.

Simon, S. B., & Olds, S. W. (1977). *Helping your child learn right from wrong.* New York: McGraw-Hill.

Singer, J. S., & Singer, D. G. (1979). Come back, Mr. Rogers, come back. *Psychology Today, 12,* 56–60.

Singer, J. S., & Singer, D. G. (1978). Family television viewing habits and spontaneous play of preschool children. In M. S. Smart & R. C. Smart (Eds.), *Preschool children* (pp. 279–287). New York: Macmillan.

Skeen, P. & Hodson, D. (1987). AIDS: What adults should know about AIDS (And shouldn't discuss with very young children). *Young Children, 42 (4),* 65–71.

Skinner, B. F. (1979). My experiences with the baby-tender. *Psychology Today, 12,* 28–40.

Skutch, M. (1977, November). *I watched TV today and it paid attention to me.* Presentation at the meeting of the National Association for the Education of Young Children, Chicago, IL.

Slaughter-Defoe, D. T., Nakagawa, K., Takanishi, R., & Johnson, D. J. (1990). Toward cultural/ecological perspectives on schooling and achievement in African- and Asian-American children. *Child Development,* 61, 363–383.

Slobin, D. I. (1972). Children and language: They learn the same way all around the world. *Psychology Today, 6,* 71–74+.

Smetana, J. G. (1984). Toddlers' social interactions regarding moral and conventional transgressions. *Child Development, 55,* 1767–1776.

Smilansky, S. (1968). *The effects of sociodramatic play on disadvantaged children: Preschool children.* New York: John Wiley.

Smith, D. G. (no date). *Living with children.* Texts of childhood. Edmonton, Canada: University of Alberta Human Science Research Project.

Smith, J. (1991, January 23). Words from kindergartners. *Baton Rouge, LA, Morning Advocate,* 9B.

Smith, N. R. (1982). The visual arts in early childhood education. In B. Spodek (Ed.), *Handbook of research in early childhood education* (pp. 295–317). New York: The Free Press.

Smith, N. R. (1983). *Experience and art: Teaching children to paint.* New York: Teachers College Press.

Smith, D. J., Allen, J., & White, P. (1990). Helping preschool children cope with typical fears. *Dimensions, 19*(1), 20–21.

Smith, T. (1991). A look at recent research on attachment. *Early Report, 18*(2), 7.

Smith, P. K. (1989, April). *Rough-and-tumble play and its relationship to serious fighting.* Paper presented at the meeting of the Society for Research in Child Development, Kansas City, MO.

Smith, M. L., & Shepard, L. A. (1988). Kindergarten readiness and retention: A qualitative study of teachers' beliefs and practices. *American Educational Research Journal, 25,* 307–333.

Smolak, L. (1986). *Infancy.* Englewood Cliffs, NJ: Prentice-Hall.

Smollar, J., & Youness, J. (1982). Social development through friendship. In K. H. Rubin & H. S. Ross (Eds.), *Peer relationships and social skills in childhood* (pp. 279–298). New York: Springer-Verlag.

Snow, C. E., Dubber, C., & DeBlauw, A. (1982). Routines in mother-child interaction. In L. Feagans & D. C. Farran (Eds.), *The language of children reared in poverty* (pp. 53–74). New York: Academic Press.

Snow, M. E., Jacklin, C. N., & Maccoby, E. E. (1983). Sex-of-child differences in father-child interaction at one year of age. *Child Development, 54,* 227–232.

Sodian, B. & Schneider, W. (1990). Children's understanding of cognitive cuing: How to manipulate cues to fool a competitor. *Child Development, 61,* 697–704.

Solarz, A. L. (1988). Homelessness: Implications for children and youth. *SRCD Social Policy Report, 3*(4).

Solorzano, L. (1986, March 31). Educating the melting pot. *U.S. News and World Report,* 20–21.

Sonnenschein, S., Baker, L., & Freund, L. (1993). Mother-child interaction on a spatial concept task as mediated by maternal notions about the task and the child.

Early Education and Development, 4 (1), 32–44.

Sophian, C. & Huber, A. (1984). Early development in children's causal judgments. *Child Development, 55,* 512–526.

Soto, L. D. (1992). The politics of early bilingual education. In S. Kessler & B. B. Swadener (Eds.), *Reconceptualizing the early childhood curriculum: Beginning the dialogue* (pp. 189–204). New York: Teachers College Press.

Soto, L. D. (1991). Research in review: Understanding bilingual/bicultural young children. *Young Children, 46* (2), 30–36.

Southern Association On Children Under Six (SACUS). (1990). *Continuity of learning for four- to seven-year-old children.* Little Rock, AR: Author.

Special report: Infants and toddlers exposed to violence. (1994). *Developments, 8* (2), 5–8.

Spencer, M. B. (1985). Cultural cognition and social cognition as identity correlates of black children's personal-social development. In M. B. Spencer, G. K. Brookins, & W. R. Allen (Eds.), *Beginnings: The social and affective development of black children* (pp. 215–230). Hillsdale, NJ: Erlbaum.

Spencer, M. B., & Mardstrom-Adams, C. (1990). Identity processes among racial and ethnic minority children in America. *Child Development, 61,* 290–310.

Spezzano, C. & Waterman, J. (1977). The first day of life. *Psychology Today, 11,* 110–116.

Spiegel-McGill, P., Zippiroli, S. M., & Mistrett, S. G. (1989). Microcomputers as social facilitators in integrated preschools. *Journal of Early Intervention, 13,* 249–260.

Sprung, B. (1983). Beginning equal: The project on nonsexist childrearing. *Day Care and Early Education, 11*(2), 6–7.

Sprunger, L. W., Boyce, W. T., & Gaines, J. A. (1985). Family-infant congruence: Routines and rhythmicity in family adaptations to a young infant. *Child Development, 56,* 564–572.

Stark, R. E., Rose, S. N., & McLagen, M. (1975). Features of infant sounds: The first eight weeks of life. *Journal of Child Language, 3,* 205–211. *The state of America's children yearbook, 1994.* (1994). Washington, DC: Children's Defense Fund.

Starting points: Executive summary of the report of the Carnegie Corporation of New York Task Force on Meeting the Needs of Young Children. (1994). *Young Children, 49*(5), 58–61.

State of America's children yearbook: 1994. (1994). Washington, DC: Children's Defense Fund.

Steinberg, L. (1989, March). *Parenting academic achievers: When families make a difference (and when they don't).* Presented at the annual conference of the American Educational Research Association, San Francisco.

Steinman, C. (1979, February 25). Caesarean births: A new perspective. *Toledo Blade,* E1, E6.

Stephan, C. W. & Langlois, J. H. (1984). Baby beautiful: Adult attributes of infant competence as a function of infant attractiveness. *Child Development, 55,* 576–585.

Sternberg, R. J. (1985). *Beyond IQ: A triarchic theory of human intelligence.* New York: Cambridge University Press.

Sternglanz, S. H. (1974). Sex role stereotyping in children's television programs. *Developmental Psychology, 10,* 710–715.

Stevens, J. H. & Baxter, D. H. (1981). Malnutrition and children's development. *Young Children, 36* (4), 60–71.

Stevens, J. H., Jr. (1988). Social support, locus of control, and parenting in three low-income groups of mothers: Black teenagers, black adults, and white adults. *Child Development, 59,* 635–642.

Stevenson, H. W., & Lee, S. (1990). Contexts of achievement. *Monographs of the Society for Research in Child Development, 55* (1–2, Serial No. 221).

Stevenson, H. W., Chen, C., & Uttal, D. H. (1990). Beliefs and achievement: A study of black, white, and Hispanic children. *Child Development, 61,* 508–523.

Stile, S. W., Kitano, M., Kelley, P., & Lecrone, J. (1993). Early intervention with gifted children: A national survey. *Journal of Early Intervention, 16*(4), 30–35.

Stipek, D., Recchia, S., & McClinitic. (1992). Self-evaluation in young children. *Monogr. of the Society for Research in Child Development, 57,* (No. 1, Serial No. 226).

Stipek, D., & MacIver, D. (1989). Developmental change in children's assessment of intellectual competence. *Child Development, 60,* 521–538.

Stone, J. G. (1978). *A guide to discipline* (rev. ed.). Washington, DC: National Association for the Education of Young Children.

Stroufe, L. A. (1991). Sorting it out: Attachment and bonding. *Early Report, 18*(2), 3–4.

Study says first three years perilous for many children. (1994, April 12). *Ogden, Utah Standard-Examiner,* 1A, 2A.

Sunal, C. S., & Hatcher, B. (1985). A changing world: Books can help children adapt. *Day Care and Early Education, 13*(2), 16–19.

Super, C. M., Herrera, M. G., & Mora, J. O. (1990). Long-term effects of food supplementation and psychosocial intervention on the physical growth of Colombian infants at risk of malnutrition. *Child Development, 61,* 29–49.

Swick, K. J. & Manning, M. L. (1983). Father involvement in home and school settings. *Childhood Education, 60,* 128–134.

Swick, K. J. (1987). Managing classroom stress. *Dimensions, 15*(4), 9–11.

Swick, K. J., & Robinson, S. L. (1988). Technology, children, & families: Confronting the challenge. *SACUS Public Policy Institute Report.* Washington update. (1990). *Young Children, 46*(1), 61.

Szabo, J. A. (1990). Fairy tales, first graders and problem

solving? *Instructor, 20* (6), 45–46.

Tafoya, T. (1983). Coyote in the classroom: The use of American Indian oral tradition with young children. In O. N. Saracho & B. Spodek (Eds.), *Understanding the multicultural experience in early childhood education* (pp. 35–44). Washington, DC: National Association for the Education of Young Children.

Tan, L. E. (1985). Laterality and motor skills in four-year-olds. *Child Development, 56*, 119–124.

Task Force on Media Violence. (1993). *Young Children, 48*(5), 48–49.

Taunton, M., & Colbert, C. (1984). Artistic and aesthetic development: Considerations for early childhood educators. *Childhood Education, 61*, 55–63.

Taylor, R. L., Wilts, P., & Lieberman, N. (1990). Identification of preschool children with handicaps. The importance of cooperative effort. *Childhood Education, 67*, 26–31.

The AmFAR Report. (1993). Special Edition, January 1993. New York: American Foundation for Aids Research.

'Test-tube' triplets mark birthday. (1986, July 26). *Baton Rouge LA Morning Advocate*, 4B.

The child's defender. (1993). Teaching Tolerance, 2 (1), 8–12.

The genetic counselor. (1977, April). *The Exceptional Parent*, M14–M17.

The telltale gene. (1990). *Consumer Reports, 55 (7)*, 483–488.

The Hartup-Charlesworth System. (1973). In E. G. Boyer, A. Simon, & G. R. Karafin (Eds.), *Measures of maturation* (Vol. II, pp. 1009–1045).

Thelen, E. (1984). Learning to walk: Ecological demands and phylogenetic constraints. In L. P. Lipsitt & C. Rovee-Collier (Eds.), *Advances in infancy research* (Vol. 3). Norwood, NJ: Ablex.

Theriot, R. & Bruce, B. (1988). Teenage pregnancy: A family curriculum. *Childhood Education, 64*, 276–279.

Thomas, B. (1984). Early toy preferences of four-year-old readers and nonreaders. *Child Development, 55*, 424–430.

Thompson, C. M. (1988). "I make a mark": The significance of talk in young children's artistic development. *Early Childhood Research Quarterly, 5*, 215–132.

Thornburg, K. R., Pearl, P., Crompton, D., & Ispa, J. M. (1990). Development of kindergarten children based on child care arrangements. *Early Childhood Research Quarterly, 5*, 27–42.

Thornton, M. C., Chatters, L. M., Taylor, R. J., & Allen, W. R. (1990). Sociodemographic and environmental correlates of racial socialization by black parents. *Child Development, 61*, 401–409.

Tittle, B. & St. Claire, N. (1989). Promoting the health and development of drug-exposed infants through a comprehensive clinic model. *Zero to Three, 9 (5)*, 18–20.

Toddler's curiousity flattens pop's wallet. (1982, July 30). *Baton Rouge, LA, Morning Advocate*, 2A.

Tong, B. R. (1978). Warriors and victims: Chinese American sensibility and learning styles. In L. Morris (Ed.), *Extracting learning styles from social/culture diversity*. Southwest Teacher Corps Network.

Torrance, E. P. (1983). Preschool creativity. In K. D. Paget & B. A. Bracken (Eds.), *The psychoeducational assessment of preschool children* (pp. 509–519). New York: Grune & Stratton.

Tots' normal development is rough on families. (1984). *Growing Child Research Review, 3* (2), 3.

Tough, J. (1982a). Language, poverty and disadvantage in school. In L. Feagans & D. C. Ferran (Eds.), *The language of children reared in poverty* (pp. 3–18). New York: Academic Press.

Tough, J. (1982b). Teachers can create enabling environments for children and then children will learn. In L. Feagans & D. C. Ferran (Eds.), *The language of children reared in poverty* (pp. 265–268). New York: Academic Press.

Tough, J. (1977). *The development of meaning*. London: Allen & Unwin.

Tough, J. (1973). *Focus on meaning: Talking with some purpose to young children*. London, England: Allen & Unwin.

Traywick-Smith, J. (1994). Authentic dialogue with children: A sociolinguistic perspective on language learning. *Dimensions of Early Childhood, 22* (4), 9–16.

Traywick-Smith, J. (1985). Developing the dramatic play enrichment program. *Dimensions, 13*(4), 7–10.

Trevarthen, C. (1989, Autumn). Origins and directions for the concept of infant intersubjectivity. *SRCD Newsletter*, 1–4.

Trevarthen, C. (1979). Communication and cooperation in early infancy: A description of primary intersubjectivity. In M. Bullowa (Ed.), *Before speech: The beginnings of interpersonal communication* (pp. 321–347). Cambridge, England: Cambridge University Press.

Tudge, J. (1990). Vygotsky, the zone of proximal development, and peer collaboration: Implications for classroom practice. In L. C. Moll (Ed.), *Vygotsky and education: Instructional implications and applications of sociohistorical psychology*. New York: Cambridge University Press.

Tudge, J. & Caruso, D. (1988). Cooperative problem solving in the classroom: Enhancing young children's cognitive development. *Young Children, 44* (1), 46–52.

U.S. children and their families: Current conditions and recent trends. (1991, Winter). *SRCD Newsletter*, 1–3.

Ubell, E. (1993, February 7). Are births as safe as they could be? *Parade Magazine*, 9–11.

Understanding the possibilities: A curriculum guide for project construct. (1992). Columbia, MO: Project Construct National Center.

Unwed mothers had quarter of births in U.S. in 1988. (1990, August 16). *Baton Rouge Morning Advocate*, p. 10A.

Uphoff, J. K. (1990). Extra-Year programs: An argument for

transitional programs during transitional times. *Young Children, 45*(6), 19–20.

Uzgiris, I. C. (1984). Imitation in infancy: Its interpersonal aspects. In M. Perlmutter (Ed.), *Parent-child interaction and parent-child relations in child development* (pp. 1–32). Hillsdale, NJ: Erlbaum.

Vail, C. O., & Scott, K. S. (1994). Transition from preschool to kindergarten for children with special needs; Issues for early childhood educators. *Dimensions of Early Childhood Education, 22*(3), 21–25.

Van Der Veer, R. (1986). Vygotsky's developmental psychology. *Psychological Reports, 59*, 527–536.

Vance, M. B. & Boals, B. (1985). The role of parents and caregivers in nurturing infants. *Dimensions, 13* (2), 19–21.

Vandell, D. L. & Wilson, K. S. (1987). Infants' interactions with mother, sibling, and peer: Contrasts and relations between interaction systems. *Child Development, 58*, 176–186.

'Vanishing twins' possible cause of some birth defects. (1993, October 8). Ogden, UT Standard Examiner, p. 3A.

Vann, K. R. & Kunjufu, J. (1993). The importance of an Afrocentric multicultural curriculum. *Phi Delta Kappan, 74*, 490–491.

Vartuli, S. & Rogers, P. (1985). Parent-child learning centers. *Dimensions, 14* (1), 11–14.

Vavrus, L. (1990). Put portfolios to the test. *Instructor*, August, 48–53.

Veach, D. M. (1979). Choice with responsibility. In L. Adams and B. Garlick (Eds.), *Ideas that work with young children* (Vol. 2, pp. 45–48). Washington, DC: National Association for the Education of Young Children.

Veciana-Suarez, A. (1992, October 23). Parents urged to monitor use of video games. *The Advocate*, Baton Rouge, LA, p. 2C.

Venn, M. L., Wolery, M., Werts, M. G., Morris, A., DeCesare, L. D., & Cuffs, M. S. (1993). Embedding instruction in art activities to teach preschoolers with disabilities to imitate their peers. *Early Childhood Research Quarterly, 8*, 277–294.

Vernon, P. E. (1979). *Intelligence: Heredity and environment*. San Francisco: Freeman.

Vibbert, M. & Bornstein, M. H. (1989). Specific associations between domains of mother-child interaction and toddler referential language and pretense play. *Infant Behavior and Development, 12*, 163–184.

Wade, M. G. (1992). Motor skills, play, and child development: An introduction. *Early Report, 19* (2), 1–2.

Wadsworth, B. G. (1984). *Piaget's theory of cognitive and affective development* (3rd. ed.). New York: Longman.

Wagner, R. K., & Sternberg, R. J. (1984). Alternative conceptions of intelligence and their implications for education. *Review of Educational Research, 54*, 179–223.

Walgren, C. (1990). Introducing a developmentally appro-

priate curriculum in the primary grades. *High/Scope Resource, 9*(2), 4–10.

Walker, D., Greenwood, C., Hart, B., & Carta, J. (1994). Prediction of school outcomes based on early language production and socioeconomic factors. *Child Development, 65*, 606–621.

Wallach, L. B. (1993). Helping children cope with violence. *Young Children, 48*(4), 4–11.

Wardle, F. (1987). Are you sensitive to interracial children's special identity needs? *Young Children, 42 (2)*, 53–59.

Warren, R. M. (1977). *Caring*. Washington, DC: National Association for the Education of Young Children.

Washington, V. (1988). The black mother in the United States: History, theory, research, and issues. In B. Birns & D. F. Hay (Eds.), *The different faces of motherhood* (pp. 185–213). New York: Plenum.

Washington, V. (1988a). Trends in Early Childhood Education. Part I: Demographics. *Dimensions, 16*(2), 4–7.

Washington, V. (1988b). Trends in Early Childhood Education. Part II: Instruction. *Dimensions, 16*(3), 4–7.

Washington, V. (1985). Social and personal ecology influencing public policy for young children. In C. S. McLoughlin & D. F. Gullo (Eds.), *Young children in context: Impact of self, family and society on development* (pp. 254–274). Springfield, IL: Charles C. Thomas.

Washington, V. (1988). Historical and contemporary linkages between black child development and social policy. In D. T. Slaughter (Ed.), *Black children and poverty: A developmental perspective* (pp. 93–105). San Francisco: Jossey-Bass.

Washington, V. (1989). Reducing the risks to young black learners: An examination of race and educational policy. In J. B. Allen & J. M. Mason (Eds.), *Risk makers, risk takers, risk breakers: Reducing the risks for young literacy learners* (pp. 281–294). Portsmouth, NH: Heineman.

Wasserman, S. (1990). *Serious players in the primary classroom: Empowering children through active learning experiences*. New York: Teachers College Press.

Watson, J. (1976). Smiling, cooing, and 'The Game'. In J. Bruner, A. Jolly, & K. Sylva (Eds.), *Play: Its role in child development and evolution* (pp. 268–276). New York: Basic Books.

Watt, M. R., Roberts, J. E., & Zeisel, S. A. (1993). Ear infections in young children: The role of the early childhood educator. *Young Children, 49* (1), 65–72.

Waxman, S. R. & Kosowski, T. D. (1990). Nouns mark category relations: Toddlers' and preschoolers' word-learning biases. *Child Development, 61*, 1461–1473.

We can do it! Linking health and human services to schools. A SECA public policy report. *Dimensions of Early Childhood, (4)*, 5–8.

Weintraub, M. (1978). Fatherhood: The myth of the second-class parent. In J. H. Stevens, Jr. & M. Mathews (Eds.), *Mother-child, father-child relationships* (p. 118). Washington, DC: National Association for the Education of Young Children.

Weintraub, M., Jaeger, E., & Hoffman, L. (1988). Predicting infant outcome in families of employed and nonemployed mothers. *Early Childhood Research Quarterly, 3*, 361–378.

Weiss, B., Dodge, K. A., Bates, J. E., & Pettit, G. S. (1992). Some consequences of early harsh discipline: Child aggression and a maladaptive social information processing style. *Child Development, 63*, 1321–1335.

Weitzman, N., Birns, B., & Friend, R. (1985). Traditional and non-traditional mothers' communications with their daughters and sons. *Child Development, 56*, 894–898.

Wellman, H. M. (1982). The foundations of knowledge: Concept development in the young child. In S. G. Moore & C. Cooper (Eds.), *The young child: Reviews of research (Vol. 3)* (pp. 115–134). Washington, DC: National Association for the Education of Young Children.

Wells, J. R., & Burts, D. C. (1990). On-line in the classroom. *Dimensions, 18*(4), 10–12.

Wertsch, J. V. (1985). *Vygotsky and the social formation of mind*. Cambridge, MA: Harvard University Press.

West, B. (1986). Culture before ethnicity. *Childhood Education, 62*, 175–181.

West, B. (1983). The new arrivals from Southeast Asia: Getting to know them. *Childhood Education, 60*, 84–89.

West, J., & Hausken, E. G. (1993). *Profile of preschool children's child care and early education program participation*. Washington, DC: National Association for the Education of Young Children.

Weston, C. R., Ivins, B., Zuckerman, B., Jones, C., & Lopez, R. (1989). Drug exposed babies: Research and clinical issues. *Zero to three, 9*(5), 1–7.

Whaley, K. & Swadener, E. B. (1990). Multicultural education in infant and toddler settings. *Childhood Education, 66*, 238–242.

What is mainstreaming? (1975). *Exceptional Children*, p. 174.

Wheeler, D. L. (1993, March 10). Psychologist deflates the modern craze of 'Baby Bonding'. *Chronicle of Higher Education, A6-A7, A13.*

Wheeler, E. J. (1994). Reviews of research: Peer conflicts in the classroom—Drawing implications from research. *Childhood Education, 70*, 296–299.

White, B. L. (1975). *The first three years of life*. Englewood Cliffs, NJ: Prentice-Hall.

White, B. L., & Watts, J. C. (1973). *Experience and environment*. (Vol. 1). Englewood Cliffs, NJ: Prentice-Hall.

White, B. P., & Phair, M. A. (1986). "It'll be a challenge!" Managing emotional stress in teaching disabled children. *Young Children, 41*(2), 44–48.

Whitehurst, G. J., Fischel, J. E., & Arnold, D. (1989, April). *Correlates and discriminants of development expressive language disorder*. Presented at the biennial meeting of the Society for Research in Child Development, Kansas City, MO.

Widerstrom, A. H., Mowder, B. A., & Sandall, S. R. (1991). *At-risk and handicapped newborns and infants: Development, assessment, and intervention*. Englewood Cliffs, NJ: Prentice-Hall.

Widmayer, S. M., Peterson, L. M., Larner, M., Carnaham, S., Calderon, A., Wingerd, J., & Marshall, R. (1990). Predictors of Haitian-American infant development at twelve months. *Child Development, 61*, 410–415.

Willatts, P. (1989, April). *Development of planning in infants*. Paper presented at the annual conference of the British Psychological Society, St. Andrews, Scotland.

Willatts, P., Domminney, C., & Rosie, K. (1989, April). *How two-year-olds use forward search strategy to solve problems*. Presented at the biennial meeting of the Society for Research in Child Development, Kansas City, MO.

Willatts, P. & Rosie, K. (1989, April). *Planning by 12-month-old infants*. Paper presented at the biennial meeting of the Society for Research in Child Development, Kansas City, MO.

Willer, B., & Bredekamp, S. (1990). Public policy report. Redefining readiness: An essential requisite for educational reform. *Young Children, 45*(5), 22–24.

Willer, B. (Ed.) (1990). *Reaching the full cost of quality*. Washington, DC: National Association for the Education of Young Children.

Willer, B. (1991). Public policy report. 101st Congress: The children's Congress. *Young Children, 46*(2), 78–80.

Williams, C. K. & Kamii, C. (1986). How do children learn by handling objects? *Young Children, 42* (1), 23–26.

Williams, H. G. (1983). Assessment of gross motor functioning. In K. D. Paget & B. A. Bracken (Eds.), *The psychoeducational assessment of preschool children* (pp. 225–260). New York: Grune & Stratton.

Williams, L. R. (1994). Developmentally appropriate practices and cultural values: A case in point. In B. L. Mallory & R. S. New (Eds.), *Diversity and developmentally appropriate practices* (pp. 155–165). New York: Teachers College Press.

Williamson, P. A. (1993). Encouraging social competence and story comprehension through thematic fantasy play. *Dimensions of Early Childhood Education, 21*(4), 17–20.

Wilson, L. C. (1990). *Infants and toddlers: Curriculum and teaching*. Albany, NY: Delmar Publishers.

Wilson, A. L., & Neidich, G. (1991). Infant mortality and public policy. *SRCD Public Policy Report, 5*(2).

Winton, P. J., Turnbull, A. P., & Blacher, J. (1985). Expectations for and satisfaction with public school kindergarten: Perspectives of parents of handicapped and nonhandicapped children. *Journal of the Division for Early Childhood, 9*(2), 116–124.

Wishart, J. G. & Bower, T. G. R. (1984). Spatial relations and the object concept: A normative study. In L. P. Lipsitt & C. Rovee-Collier (Eds.), *Advances in in-*

fancy research (Vol. 3, pp. 57–123). Norwood, NJ: Ablex.

Wishon, P. (1986). Play and the physically handicapped child: Review of research. *Dimensions, 14*(2), 23–24.

Wodtke, K. H., Harper, F., Schommer, M., & Brunelli, P. (1989). How standardized is school testing? An exploratory observational study of standardized group testing in kindergarten. *Education Evaluation and Policy Analysis, 2*(3), 223–235.

Wolery, M., Holcombe, A., Venn, M. L., Brookfield, J., Huffman, K., Schroeder, C., Martin, C. G., & Fleming, L. A. (1993). Research report. Mainstreaming in early childhood programs: Current status and relevant issues. *Young Children, 49*(1), 78–84.

Wolf, D. (1989, Spring). Novelty, creativity, and child development. *SRCD Newsletter,* 1–2.

Wolfe, P. (1977). Heredity or environment. Excerpt from Pregnancy, birth, and the newborn baby. (1972). Delacorte Press. Reprinted in P. Cantor (Ed.) *Understanding a child's world* (pp. 15–25). New York: McGraw-Hill.

Wolfle, J. (1989). The gifted preschooler: Developmentally different, but still 3 or 4 years old. *Young Children, 44*(3), 41–48.

Wortham, S. C. & Wortham, M. R. (1989). Infant/toddler development and play: Designing creative play environments. *Childhood Education, 65,* 295–299.

Yamamoto, K. (1972). The child and his image. Boston: Houghton-Mifflin.

Yarro, B. (1977, June). *The changing world of child birth.* Detroit Free Press, 1C, 3C.

Yawkey, T. D. & Miller, T. J. (1984). The language of social play in young children. In A. Pellegrini & T. Yawkey (Eds.), *The development of oral and written language in social contexts* (pp. 95–104). Norwood, NJ: Ablex.

Yennie-Donmoyer, J. (1993). Andrew: The story of a gifted at-risk student. In R. Donmoyer and R. Kos (Eds.), *At-risk students* (pp. 135–152). Albany, NY: SUNY Press.

Yonas, A., Pettersen, L., & Granrad, C. E., (1982). Infants' sensitivity to familiar size as information for distance. *Child Development, 53,* 1285–1290.

Young, V. M. L. (1981). Human genetics: Blueprint for development. In M. Tudor (Ed.). *Child Development* (pp. 47–61). New York: McGraw-Hill.

Younger, B. A. (1993). Understanding category members as "the same sort of thing": Explicit categorization in ten-month infants. *Child Development, 64,* 309–320.

Younger, B. A. (1990). Infants' detection of correlations among feature categories, *Child Development, 61,* 614–620.

Younger, B. A. (1985). The segregation of items into categories by ten-month-old infants. *Child Development, 56,* 1574–1583.

Youth indicators 1993: Trends in the well-being of American youth. Washington, DC: U.S. Department of Education, Office of Educational Research and Improvement.

Yussen, S. R. & Santrock, J. W. (1978). *Child development.* Dubuque, IA: Brown.

Zambarano, R. J. (1991, April). *Effects of tone-of-voice and physical punishment on children's and adults' interpretation of a brief disciplinary prohibition.* Paper presented at the meeting of the Society for Research in Child Development, Seattle, WA.

Zaslow, M. J., Pedersen, F. A., Suwalsky, J. T. D., & Rabinovich, B. A. (1989). Maternal employment and parent-infant interaction at one year. *Early Childhood Research Quarterly, 4,* 459–478.

Zavitkovsky, D., Baker, K. R., Berlfein, J. R., & Almy, M. (1986). *Listen to the children.* Washington, DC: Na-